HOUGHTON MIFFLIN SOCIAL STUDIES

Across the Centuries

*W*e have not journeyed all this way

across the centuries,

across the oceans,

across the mountains,

across the prairies, because

we are made of sugar candy.

Winston Churchill

Jacqueline M. Córdova
J. Jorge Klor de Alva
Gary B. Nash
Franklin Ng
Christopher L. Salter
Louis E. Wilson
Karen K. Wixson

Across the
Centuries

Houghton Mifflin Company • Boston

Atlanta • Dallas • Geneva, Illinois • Princeton, New Jersey • Palo Alto

Consultants

Sandra Alfonsi
Academic Advisory Board
Hadassah
Queens, New York

Charmarie Blaisdell
Department of History
Northeastern University
Boston, Massachusetts

Richard Griswold del Castillo
Department of Mexican American Studies
San Diego State University
San Diego, California

Ross Dunn
Department of History
San Diego State University
San Diego, California

Benjamin Elman
Director, Center for Chinese Studies
University of California, Los Angeles
Los Angeles, California

Stephen Fugita
Department of Psychology
Santa Clara University
Santa Clara, California

Erich Gruen
Department of Classics and History
University of California, Berkeley
Berkeley, California

Charles Haynes
Senior Scholar for Religious Freedom
Freedom Forum First Amendment Center
Arlington, Virginia

Lidwien Kapteijns
Department of History
Wellesley College
Wellesley, Massachusetts

Shabbir Mansuri
Founding Director
Council on Islamic Education
Fountain Valley, California

Michelle Maskiell
Department of History
University of Montana
Missoula, Montana

Doug Monroy
Department of Southwest Studies
The Colorado College
Colorado Springs, Colorado

Forrest Turpin
Christian Educators Association
  International
Pasadena, California

Skirball Institute
Los Angeles, California

Rabbi Alfred Wolf
Founding Director
Skirball Institute
Los Angeles, California

Elliot N. Dorff
Rector
University of Judaism
Los Angeles, California

Robert Ellwood
School of Religion
University of Southern California
Los Angeles, California

B. Srinivasa Murthy
Department of Religious Studies (retired)
California State University, Long Beach
Long Beach, California

Ven. Dr. Havanpola Ratanasara
Buddhist Sangha Council of Southern
  California
Los Angeles, California

Rev. Thomas P. Rausch, S.J.
Rector, Jesuit Community
Loyola Marymount University
Los Angeles, California

ISBN: 0-395-93066-9
23 24 25 26   VH   08 07 06 05

Developed by Ligature, Inc.

Acknowledgments

Grateful acknowledgment is made
for the use of the material listed below.
The material in the Minipedia is
reprinted from *The World Book* *Encyclopedia* with the expressed permission of the publisher. © 1998 by World
Book, Inc.

–Continued on page 557.

From Your Authors

*W*omen gad about in the market place. . . . They go out visiting, to see their relatives, and proceed there by starlight or carrying torches, night after night; they take a large suite with them, setting the street ablaze . . . maids, messengers, clerks, and footmen."

So begins an account of real events in China's history. The ladies were having too much fun for the writer of this account. He was more worried about the nomadic horsemen who were attacking the northern frontier. In Chapter 8 of this book, you will read more about Chinese life and the problems of keeping such a large empire together.

Most of the people you will meet in this book lived long ago in places that may seem very far away from home. But they all had feelings just like yours and faced many of the same challenges you will face in your life. And whether they were great leaders or ordinary people, their decisions and actions helped shape the world you live in.

As you read about these people, places, and events, we hope you will ask many questions. Some questions may be about history: "What caused these people to make the decisions they did?" or "How do we know about these events?" Other questions may be about geography: "What are the land and weather like in that place?" or "Why did people choose to settle there?" Still other questions may be about economics: "How did people meet their needs for food and shelter?" or "How did people work out ways for using scarce resources?"

Most of all, we hope you catch the excitement of thinking, questioning, and discovering answers about your world—now and in the 21st century.

Beverly J. Armento
Professor of Social Studies
Education
Department of Middle/
Secondary Education and
Instructional Technology
Georgia State University

Jacqueline M.K. Córdova
Professor of Spanish
and TESOL
Department of Foreign
Languages and Literatures
California State University,
Fullerton

J. Jorge Klor de Alva
President
University of Phoenix

Gary B. Nash
Professor of History
University of California,
Los Angeles

Franklin Ng
Professor of Anthropology
California State University,
Fresno

Christopher L. Salter
Professor and Chair
Department of Geography
University of Missouri

Louis E. Wilson
Associate Professor and Chair
Department of
African American Studies
Smith College

Karen K. Wixson
Professor of Education
University of Michigan

Contents

About Your Book xii
Map and Globe
Handbook G1

Unit 1   1
Links to the Ancient World

Chapter 1   2
A Changing World View

Lesson 1   *Connections in the Roman Empire*   4
Lesson 2   *The Expanding Horizon*   10
Lesson 3   *Traveling Through the Past*   16

Chapter 2   24
Empires of the Ancient World

Lesson 1   *The Fall of the Roman Empire*   26
Lesson 2   *Acquainted Cultures*   32
Lesson 3   *The Rise of the Byzantine Empire*   42

Unit 2   48
The Growth of Islam

Chapter 3   50
The Roots of Islam

Lesson 1   *Desert Bloom—Caravan Cities*   52
Lesson 2   *Muhammad and Islam*   58
Lesson 3   *Early Islam*   65

Chapter 4   72
The Empire of Islam

Lesson 1   *A Century of Expansion*   78
Lesson 2   *The Golden Age*   85
Lesson 3   *Islamic Spain*   95

Unit 3   104
Sub-Saharan Africa

Chapter 5   106
West Africa

Lesson 1   *The Roots of Mighty Empires*   108
Lesson 2   *The Empire of Ghana*   112
Lesson 3   *The Empires of Mali and Songhai*   118
Lesson 4   *Village Society in West Africa*   124

Chapter 6   134
Central and Southern Africa

Lesson 1   *The Spread of Bantu*   136
Lesson 2   *The Rise of Coastal Trading States*   141
Lesson 3   *The Rise of the Zimbabwe State*   145
Lesson 4   *The Kongo Kingdom*   149

Unit 4   158
Asian Civilizations

Chapter 7   160
Three Empires

Lesson 1   *The Mongols*   162
Lesson 2   *The Ottoman Empire*   170
Lesson 3   *The Mughal Empire*   178

Chapter 8   190
China

Lesson 1   *An Emerging Empire*   192
Lesson 2   *The Flowering of Chinese Culture*   202
Lesson 3   *China and the Larger World*   209

Chapter 9   220
Japan

Lesson 1   *Land of the Rising Sun*   222
Lesson 2   *A Developing National Culture*   227
Lesson 3   *The Power of the Shoguns*   231
Lesson 4   *Japan: Unified Yet Isolated*   237

Unit 5   246
Medieval Societies

Chapter 10   248
Feudal Europe and Japan

Lesson 1   *Europe After the Roman Empire*   256
Lesson 2   *Daily Life in Feudal Europe*   262
Lesson 3   *Two Feudal Societies*   271

Chapter 11   280
Europe: Rule, Religion, and Conflict

Lesson 1   *The Power of the Church*   282
Lesson 2   *The Byzantine Empire*   289
Lesson 3   *The Crusades*   295

Unit 6 Europe: 1300–1600	306	Chapter 12 *The Renaissance*	308	Lesson 1 *Europe at the End of the Middle Ages*	310
				Lesson 2 *The Italian Renaissance*	316
				Lesson 3 *Renaissance Life*	325
				Lesson 4 *Renaissance in Northern Europe*	329

		Chapter 13 *Reformation and the Scientific Revolution*	336	Lesson 1 *The Decline of Church Authority*	338
				Lesson 2 *Martin Luther and the Reformation*	342
				Lesson 3 *Era of Reformation*	349
				Lesson 4 *Scientific Revolution*	353

		Chapter 14 *The Age of Exploration*	362	Lesson 1 *Travel, Trade, and Exploration*	364
				Lesson 2 *Adventure and Profit*	371
				Lesson 3 *Exploring the Americas*	377

Unit 7 Civilizations of the Americas	392	Chapter 15 *Early American Civilizations*	394	Lesson 1 *Origins*	396
				Lesson 2 *The Olmec*	400
				Lesson 3 *The Maya*	404
				Lesson 4 *The Tiwanakans and the Moche*	412

		Chapter 16 *Two American Empires*	420	Lesson 1 *The Aztec*	422
				Lesson 2 *The Inca*	429
				Lesson 3 *The Arrival of the Spanish*	437

Unit 8 Europe: 1600–1789	448	Chapter 17 *European Rule and Expansion*	450	Lesson 1 *The French Monarchy*	452
				Lesson 2 *The English Monarchy*	458
				Lesson 3 *European Expansion*	464

		Chapter 18 *The Enlightenment*	474	Lesson 1 *A New Order of Ideals*	476
				Lesson 2 *Ideas in Action*	480
				Lesson 3 *Economic Changes*	490
				Lesson 4 *After the American Revolution*	497

Time/Space Databank	503	Primary Sources	504
		Minipedia	513
		Atlas	518
		Glossary of Geographic Terms	534
		Gazetteer	536
		Biographical Dictionary	539
		Glossary	543
		Index	549
		Acknowledgments	557

Understanding Skills

Each "Understanding Skills" feature gives you the opportunity to learn and practice a skill related to the topic you are studying.

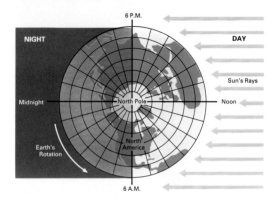

Location: Using Time Zones — 8
Sequence: Making Parallel Timelines — 69
What You Read: Identifying Main Ideas — 94
Reference Sources: Using the Readers' Guide — 101
Critical Thinking: Interpreting Proverbs — 123
Relief Maps: Making a Vertical Profile — 140
Art: Reading Mughal Paintings — 186
Location Decisions: Comparing Two Maps of China — 216
Critical Thinking: Recognizing Assumptions — 243
Group Decisions: How a Guild Works — 275
Historical Maps: Drawing Conclusions — 303
Technical Drawings: Reading a da Vinci Sketch — 324
Text Organization: Identifying Patterns — 348
Critical Thinking: Making Hypotheses — 357
Map Symbols: Reading a Wind and Current Map — 382
Note Taking: Recording Information — 416
Topography: Analyzing Elevation — 436
Critical Thinking: Identifying Values — 443
Critical Thinking: Predicting Consequences — 457
Relationships: Identifying Stereotypes — 471
Reports: Presenting Primary Sources — 496

Understanding Concepts

Each "Understanding Concepts" feature gives you more information about a concept that is important to the lesson you are reading.

History — 18
Civilization — 35
Empire — 86
Kinship — 126
Conquest — 167
Isolation — 239
Hierarchy — 264
Religious Persecution — 315
Reform — 351
Epidemics — 441
Colonialism — 469
Progress — 499

Exploring

The story of the past is hidden all around you in a world of the present. "Exploring" pages tell you the secrets of how to find it.

Archaeology: Clues and Connections — 20
Origins of Sports and Games — 93
Japanese and American Schools — 276
Nonverbal Communication — 410

Making Decisions

Much of history is made of people's decisions. These pages take you step-by-step through fascinating problems from history and today. What will you decide?

Trade Between the Kongo and Portugal   154
The Great Wall   198
Scientific Discoveries   358
Industrial Growth   494

Literature

Throughout history people have expressed their deepest feelings and beliefs through literature. Reading these stories, legends, poems, and shorter passages that appear in the lessons will help you experience what life was like for people of other times and places.

"A King's Adviser" from *Kalilah and Dimnah*,   38
     by Hassan Techranchian
Medieval Muslim Literature   74
"The Cow-Tail Switch" retold by   128
     Harold Courlander and George Herzog
"Heaven My Blanket, Earth My Pillow"   200
     by Yang Wan-Li
"The Story of Roland" from *Charlemagne   250
     and His Knights* by Katharine Pyle
"The Audience" by C. Walter Hodges   384
"The Legend of the Lake" retold by   444
     Douglas Gifford
"To the Assembly for Protection" from   486
     The Journal of Madame Royale, by
     Elizabeth Powers

Primary Sources

Reading the exact words of the people who made and lived history is the best way to get a sense of how they saw themselves and the times in which they lived. You will find more than 50 primary sources throughout this book including the following:

Bernal Díaz, from *Cortés and the Conquest of Mexico   16
     by the Spaniards in 1521*
Description of fall of Roman Empire   26
Qur'an, 3:142   65
Abu Jafar al Mansur, 752   85
al-Bakri, from *Book of the Roads   115
     and Kingdoms,* 1068
Description, from *The Periplus of the Erythraean Sea*   141
Description of Suleiman, from inscription on   176
     Romanian fortress
Marco Polo, from *Travels*   209
Lady Murasaki, from *The Diary of Murasaki Shikibu*   229
William Langland, from *Piers the Plowman*   266
Nicetas Choniates, 1204   301
Giovanni della Casa, from *The Book of Manners*   316
From *The Book of Margery Kempe,* c. 1432   341
Christopher Columbus, from his journal   379
John Lloyd Stephens, from historical bulletin, 1869   404
"In the midst of the plain . . .," from Aztec codex   428
Louis XIV, from letter to his son   454
Jean-Jacques Rousseau, from *The Social Contract*   479
The *Magna Carta* (excerpts)   504
The English Bill of Rights (excerpts)   505
The Declaration of the Rights of Man and   506
     the Citizen (excerpts)
The Declaration of Independence   509

A Closer Look

Take a closer look at the objects and pictures spread out on these special pages. With the clues you see, you'll become a historical detective.

Conserving Mosaics	44
Irrigation Technology	54
The Great Mosque at Cordoba	97
Trading Gold and Salt	114
The Taj Mahal	184
The Voyages of Zheng He	213
Medieval Farming	267
da Vinci's Notebooks	320
The Spice Trade	367
The Mayan Calendar	408
Machu Picchu	434
Morning at Versailles	455

A Moment in Time

Someone or something from the past is frozen at an exciting moment. You'll get to know these people or things by reading about where they are and the objects around them.

A Mapmaker	14
An Abbasid Scholar	91
A Kongo King	151
A Samurai	233
A Crusader	298
A Printer	346
A Parisian Market Woman	484

Making a Hypothesis

1. Define the question.	→	2. Gather evidence.	→	3. Examine the clues.

Charts, Diagrams, and Timelines

These visual presentations of information help give you a clearer picture of the people, places, and events you are studying.

The Caravan Camel	11
Barbarian Takeovers in the Roman Empire	30
Timelines showing contact between Rome, Persia, India, and China	33
Religious Populations of the World Today	68
Parallel Timelines, Muslim and Other Empires	69
Umayyad Tax Revenues, A.D. 727 and 738	84
Population Comparison of Major Cities, c. 1000	98
Migrations of Bantu Speakers	138
Bantu Languages	139
Kongo Slave Trade	153
Peoples of Central and Southern Africa	156
Social Bonds Among the Mongol	163
Population Change in South China, 500–1500	205
Inventions in China and Europe	206
Writing Styles of Japan	229
Political Struggles in Feudal Japan	238
Becoming a Medieval Knight	265
Major Christian Churches During the Reformation	350
Costs of Spices, c. 1350 and Today	368
Silver and Gold Exported from the Americas, 1520–1650	379
Life in the Americas	399
The Mayan Number System	409
Aztec and Inca Population Decline After 1520	441
English Monarchy During the Reign of Louis XIV	462
African People Brought into the New World, 1500–1800	466
Specialization of Labor	492
World Civilizations, A.D. 500–1700, Maps and Timelines	532

Maps

The events of history have been shaped by the places in which they occurred. Each map tells its own story.

Ancient Inca Roads	G1
Modern Australia	G2
The Eastern Mediterranean in the 600s B.C.	G3
The Four Hemispheres	G4
The Netherlands, 1995	G5
World: Mercator and Peter Projections	G6
World: Goode and Robinson Projections	G7
Where Slaves Were Sent in the New World	G8
Western Indonesia: Relief and Physical Profile	G9
Battle of Yorktown	G10
Population and Economic Resources of South Africa	G11
Early Empires, Akkad, Assyria, Babylonia	G12
World: Gross National Product	G14
Cantino, Portuguese Navigational Map, 1502	1
De La Salle's Map of the World, c. 1450	3
The World the Romans Knew, A.D. 150	5
World Time Zones	8
Parthian Stations of Isidore of Charax	10
Journey of Xuanzang, A.D. 629–645	13
Medieval T-O Map	15
Time Zone Map of North America	23
Breakup of the Western Roman Empire	27
Invasions at the Fall of Rome	36
Arabian Peninsula Trade Routes, A.D. 570	53
Expansion of Islam, 622–661	67
Further Expansion of Islam	80
Baghdad: An Ideal Location	85
The City of Baghdad	87
Islamic Spain	96
Africa: Climate Regions	109
Ancient Jenne-jeno	111
Ancient African Empires: 700–1600	121
Bantu-speakers' Migration in Africa	137
Africa: Physical Regions	140
Africa: Trade Routes	142
The Zimbabwe Kingdom	146
The Kongo Kingdom	150
Portolan Map of West Africa	155
Elevation of Southeast Africa	157
Mongol Empire, c. 1200–1294	166
The Expansion of the Ottoman Empire	171
India's Physical Regions and Kingdoms	179
The Expansion of the Mughal Empire	183
Division of the Han Empire, A.D. 220–264	193
Tang and Song: Trade Routes and Canals	205
People's Republic of China: Physical Regions	216
People's Republic of China: Land Use and Resources	217
China: Great Wall and Grand Canal	219
Japan: Physical Regions	224
Warrior Clans of Japan, 940–1150	230
Barbarian Kingdoms	257
Division of Charlemagne's Kingdom	260
Christian T-O Map	280
Trade Routes to Constantinople	290
Four Major Crusades	296
The Holy Land During the Crusades	299
The Great Plague, 1346–1353	311
Italian City-States, 1454	317
Trade Routes, c. 1500	330
Lutheranism in Central Europe	347
Christian Churches in Europe, 1600	352
Map Based on Marco Polo's Account	362
Portolan Map of West Africa	365
Eurasian Trade Routes Before the Age of Exploration	366
Portuguese Exploration Around Africa	374
European Exploration	378
Prevailing Winds and Ocean Currents	382
The Bering Strait	397
The Americans, 18,000–500 B.C.	398
Olmec Territories	401
Mayan Civilization, A.D. 300–900	405
Andes Elevations	412
Expansion of the Aztec Empire	423
Expansion of the Inca Empire	430
The Inca Road in Central Peru	436
Portuguese Slave Trade, 1500–1800	465
European Colonies in the New World	470
Russia, Prussia, and Austria in 1780	481
World Empires, 500–1500	515
World Empires, 1500–1900	516
World Empires, 1900	517
World: Political	518
Mexico, Central America, and the Caribbean: Political	518
Europe: Political	519
World: Physical	520
Northern Polar Region: Physical	520
Southern Polar Region: Physical	521
Eurasia: Political/Physical	522
The Middle East: Political/Physical	524
Africa: Political/Physical	525
North America: Political/Physical	526
South America: Political/Physical	527
Pacific Rim: Political/Physical	528
World: Religions and Languages	529
World: Vegetation and Climate	530
World: Population, Land Use, and Resources	531
The World in 750	532
The World in 1492	533

Starting Out

What makes this textbook so much more interesting than others you've used? In this book, the people of the past speak directly to you, through their actual words and the objects they used. You'll walk inside their houses and look inside their cooking pots. You'll follow them as they go to school, build cities, fight wars, work out settlements for peace.

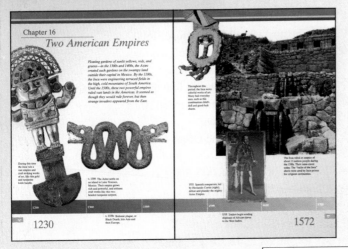

The titles outline the lesson. The red titles tell you the main topics discussed in the lesson on the Maya.

When and where? The timeline at the beginning of each lesson tells you when these events took place. The lesson title tells you what the lesson is about.

From unit to chapter to lesson— each step lets you see history in closer detail. The photos show you where events happened. The art introduces you to the people.

Right from the beginning the lesson opener pulls you into the sights, sounds, and the smells of historical investigation.

Like a road sign, the question that always appears here tells you what to think about while you read the lesson.

Look for these key terms. They are listed here so you can watch for them. The first time they appear in the lesson they are shown in heavy black print and defined. Key terms are also defined in the Glossary.

LESSON 3

The Maya

THINKING FOCUS

In what ways were the Maya an advanced civilization?

Key Terms

* stele
* codex

▶ *The seven-inch-tall ceramic ballplayer at top right is part of the religious art of the Maya. Real players on the losing side sometimes became sacrifices to the gods. The large Mayan temple, on the right, was built between A.D. 600 and 800. Artist Frederick Catherwood, who accompanied explorer Stephens, painted this view of the Mayan temple.*

I t is impossible to describe the interest with which I explored these ruins. The ground was entirely new. . . . We could not see ten yards before us, and never knew what we should stumble upon next. The beauty of the sculpture, the solemn stillness of the woods, disturbed only by the scrambling of monkeys and the chattering of parrots, the desolation of the city, and the mystery that hung over it, all created an interest higher, if possible, than I had ever felt among the ruins of the Old World.

With these words, John Lloyd Stephens described his discovery in 1839 of a ruined city in the jungles of Central America. Among the ruins and tangled vines, he found a temple with a broad stairway that was inscribed with thousands of strange symbols. He also found a

ball court watched over by six enormous stone parrots. And he found heavy stone columns carved with images of jaguars, birds, serpents, and men in fabulous feathered headdresses. Stephens had no idea who the builders of this city were, but he was sure he had found evidence of a magnificent civilization.

A Growing Civilization

Stephens had discovered the ruins of Copan, an ancient Mayan city. Like the Olmec, the Maya settled in a fertile region. Notice on the map on page 405 that this region stretched south along an extended finger of land that is surrounded by water.

The 125,000 square miles that the Maya occupied contained both highlands and lowlands. The highlands in the south ran along a mountain range that included active volcanoes. A long rainy season and deep, fertile soil made this area good for farming.

The lowlands were located in the central and northern part of the region. Some lowlands were covered with dense tropical forest with fertile soil. Others had only rough, dry grass or cactus and were not good for farming. But they were rich in the limestone the Maya needed for building and in the flint they used in stonework.

Archaeologists think the Maya may have begun farming the fertile areas of the lowlands as early as 1800 B.C. Between 1800 and 500 B.C., the Maya established small farming villages. They gathered food from the forests and also raised crops. Between 100 B.C. and A.D. 200, some of the villages grew into cities with impressive palaces and pyramids. Mayan artisans carved huge stone figures and pillars to adorn their cities.

During the height of Mayan civilization, between A.D. 250 and 900, about three million people lived in Mayan cities scattered through the region. Look at the map at the above right to find the major cities.

Mayan cities were built around religious centers. At the heart of

Take a closer look, in this case at the Mayan calendar. Look at the diagram to see how it works.

Charts and graphs help you understand difficult information—in this case the Mayan number system.

Every map tells a story. The maps in this book tell the story of the rise and fall of cities, states, and trade routes.

Frozen at a moment in time, the European mapmaker extends your knowledge of the world. You learn all about him through his equipment, his clothes, and the place he's working.

A CLOSER LOOK

The Mayan Calendar

Why do people have good days and bad days? Why do crops grow well one year and poorly the next? The Maya believed it was because different gods ruled each day. By consulting their two calendars and using the right mathematics, Mayan priests knew which gods ruled which days. Then the priests had to figure out what influence the gods would have.

On the 260-day religious calendar, each day was given a name and a number. The name *Imix* meant "water lily," and represented the ocean. *Ik* was named for the wind, and *Akbal* was named for the darkness of night.

Historians use the diagram above to explain the 260-day religious calendar. Each name and each number was a divine being—two gods for every day. When you turn the wheels, you discover that the same name and the same number only fall together once every 260 days. Then the cycle starts all over again.

1 Imix—the New Year's day of the Mayan 260-day year

Dates were skillfully carved in Mayan hieroglyphs like these

The other Mayan calendar was based on the earth's orbit around the sun and had 365 days like ours. Each of these days had a god, too. This calendar had 18 months of 20 days each, plus 5 extra days. It was considered bad luck to do anything on those 5 days, so people did very little. They didn't even eat!

---

to record information about astronomical events. The detailed astronomical charts and tables that they made using this system are quite accurate. Their system was based on the number 20 instead of 10, which is the basis for our decimal system. As you can see at the top of this page, they used dots and dashes to represent numbers and even had a symbol for zero.

To record important dates and events in the lives of their rulers, the Maya developed hieroglyphs. Each hieroglyph represents a sound. When the pictures are put together, they can make up part of a word or a whole word. Some hieroglyphs represent ideas, such as "life" or "happiness." Others represent objects like "corn" or "water."

The Mayan priest-kings used hieroglyphs to write record books, each of which was known as a **codex.** Archaeologists have studied the three existing codices and deciphered part of them to learn about religious ceremonies, astronomy, and Mayan calendars.

The codices reveal that the Maya had two calendars. They used them to determine the best time to plant crops, hunt, and perform religious ceremonies. The Mayan priest-kings developed the calendars from their close observations of the movements of the sun, moon, and stars.

Mayan cultural achievements also included the magnificent architecture of their cities and beautiful works of decorative art. For example, Mayan artisans made jewelry out of jade, gold, and shells. King Pacal, in his tomb at Palenque, was found wearing a life-size mosaic mask made from jade. He also wore jewelry of jade and mother-of-pearl. The Maya were also accomplished weavers, and they communicated nonverbally through their weaving designs. (See Exploring Nonverbal Communication on pages 410–411.)

These are only some of the achievements of the ancient Mayan civilization. The Mayan culture has survived, however, unlike many other early American cultures. Today, Mayan people live in Guatemala, Belize, and parts of Mexico.

The Mayan Number System

	0	1	4	5	11	19	20	126	1092	Positional Values
x 400										
x 20										
x 1										

In the Mayan number system, symbols represented basic numerical values. Find the bar above that equals 5. Vertical positions also indicated that the basic value was multiplied by a certain number (1, 20, 400, and so on). Thus, the representation above for 1,092 translates into this equation: $12 + (14 \times 20) + (2 \times 400) = 1{,}092$. Translate the representation for 126 into a numerical equation.

Describe the Mayan writing and number systems.

REVIEW

1. **FOCUS** In what ways were the Maya an advanced civilization?
2. **CONNECT** What agricultural techniques made Mayan farming more efficient than Olmec farming?
3. **BELIEF SYSTEMS** What did the Maya worship? What important role did the priest-kings play in the Mayan religion?
4. **CULTURE** How have archaeologists learned so much about King Pacal?
5. **CRITICAL THINKING** Why was the invention of a number system important in Mayan society?
6. **WRITING ACTIVITY** Write a message for a classmate using your own hieroglyphs. First, write out the message you want to send. Then create simple pictures for each sound, word, or idea you want to get across. Remember, when someone looks at your picture, they will need to be able to guess the sound, word, or idea it represents. Trade messages, and decipher them.

409

Early American Civilizations

...yan Civilization, A.D. 300–900

Early city A.D. 400–500
Late city A.D. 500–900
Marsh

Gulf of Mexico
Uxmal
NORTHERN AREA
YUCATAN PENINSULA
Palenque
Yaxchilán
CENTRAL AREA
Tikal
Caribbean Sea
SOUTHERN AREA
Izapa
Kaminaljuyú
Copán

...ty, the Maya usually built tall ...tone pyramids that were sur-...ded by large, open plazas. At ...op of the pyramids they built ...es. The Mayan priest-kings ...ed the steps of the pyramids ...rform religious ceremonies at ...temples.

Find Copan on the map. Look at the Copan ball court below. Guess the size of the buildings by comparing them with the car in the background.

What were Mayan cities like?

A MOMENT IN TIME

A Mapmaker

8:47 A.M. August 27, 1500
In the mapmaker's house,
Santofa, Spain.

xiii

Continuing On

As you get to know the people of the past, you'll want ways of understanding and remembering them better. This book gives you some tools to use in learning about people and places and remembering what you've learned.

Giving you the inside story is the purpose of two special paragraphs. Across Time & Space connects what you're reading to things that happened centuries ago or continents away. Its companion, How Do We Know?, tells you where information about the past comes from. (See page 414 for an example.)

Across Time & Space

The Inca built many rope bridges that spanned steep-cliffed canyons and crossed over fast-flowing rivers. Today, many Inca descendants still rely on rope bridges. They often spin as much as 20,000 to 30,000 feet of rope from grass to build or repair their bridges.

■ *What methods did the Inca use to control their empire?*

▼ *The llama was very important to the Inca. Its wool, shown here, was spun into thread, which was used to make beautiful fabrics like the weaving below. These fabrics were used by all levels of society.*

length of the empire. Roads were built in the highlands and along the coast. When necessary, the roads included tunnels, causeways, and stone or even rope bridges. Built to quickly move the Inca army, the highways also helped transport crops and other goods throughout the empire. Scholars estimate that the Inca built nearly 10,000 miles of roads.

Under Inca rule, the commoners had few individual freedoms. They weren't allowed to travel without government approval. The government also decided when and whom they married. Marriage was encouraged, because only married couples were assigned plots of land

from which goods for tribute could be raised. ■

Working the Land

Though they enjoyed little freedom, Inca subjects rarely went hungry. The Inca's clever farming techniques allowed them to make full use of their varied lands. In addition, their strong organizational skills made them efficient producers and distributors of food.

Once the Inca conquered a region, they took total control of the land. They sent administrators, who were members of the nobility, to evaluate the geographic resources of the region. Then they divided the region's farmland into three parts. The commoners harvested one part of the farmland for government workers, one part to support Inca religious leaders, and one part for themselves.

The farmland varied greatly from region to region because the Inca Empire lay in and around the Andes. Some valleys lie as high as 8,000 feet above sea level. Others are only a few hundred feet above sea level. Because soil, temperature, and other conditions change as altitude increases, only certain crops could be grown in

certain areas. In the low valleys, farmers grew maize (corn), beans, and squash. In the mountains, they raised llamas and alpacas for wool and meat. This growing of crops according to the height of the land is called a **vertical economy.**

The Inca were able to grow surplus amounts of food by using very productive farming techniques. One of these techniques was **terrace farming.** The soil on the mountain slopes in the highlands was thin and didn't receive enough rainfall. The Inca carried topsoil and gravel from the more fertile lowlands to the hillsides. There, they packed it into narrow farming terraces like the ones pictured above. To protect against drought, the Inca constructed elaborate canal systems for irrigation.

The government built huge warehouses to store surplus food in case of emergencies such as crop failure or war. The quipu recorded how much food was stored and where it was stored. Because the government distributed food and goods to the people, free trade and huge markets like those the Aztec enjoyed did not exist in the Inca Empire. ■

⋀ *Inca terraces were such an effective farming technique that they are still used in modern-day Peru.*

■ *Why was Inca agriculture so productive?*

Praying to the Ancestors

Not all of the commoners worked to produce food for the empire. Some commoners helped to build massive cities. To learn more about an Inca city, see A Closer Look on page 434.

Other commoners paid their tribute by making pieces of art and

433

Two American Empires

You're in charge of your reading. See the red square at the end of the text? Now find the red square over in the margin. If you can answer the question there, then you probably understand what you just read. If you can't, perhaps you'd better go back and read that part of the lesson again.

A picture is worth a thousand words. But just a few words in a caption can help you understand a picture, a photograph, a map, or in this case, how past and present are related.

Every age has its great storytellers. Many chapters include short examples of fine writing from or about the period. The literature is printed on a tan background with a blue initial letter and a multicolored bar.

A special kind of Understanding page looks at concepts—the big ideas that help put all the pieces together. This section helps you understand ideas like Civilization, Conquest, or Reform.

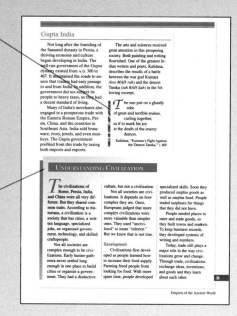

Gupta India

Not long after the founding of the Sassanid dynasty in Persia, a thriving economy and culture began developing in India. The well-run government of the Gupta dynasty existed from A.D. 300 to 467. It maintained the roads to ensure that traders had easy passage to and from India. In addition, the government did not subject its people to heavy taxes, so they had a decent standard of living.

Many of India's merchants also engaged in a prosperous trade with the Eastern Roman Empire, Persia, China, and the countries in Southeast Asia. India sold brassware, ivory, jewels, and even monkeys. The Gupta government profited from this trade by taxing both imports and exports.

The arts and sciences received great attention in this prospering society. Both painting and writing flourished. One of the greatest Indian writers and poets, Kalidasa, describes the results of a battle between the war god Kumara (koo MAH rah) and the demon Taraka (tah RAH kah) in the following excerpt.

*T*he sun put on a ghastly robe
of great and terrible snakes,
curling together,
as if to mark his joy
at the death of the enemy
demon.

Kalidasa, "Kumara's Fight Against the Demon Taraka," c. 400

UNDERSTANDING CIVILIZATION

*T*he civilizations of Rome, Persia, India, and China were all very different. But they shared common traits. According to historians, a civilization is a society that has cities, a written language, specialized jobs, an organized government, technology, and skilled craftspeople.

Not all societies are complex enough to be civilizations. Early hunter-gatherers never settled long enough in one place to build cities or organize a government. They had a distinctive culture, but not a civilization.

Not all societies are civilizations. It depends on how complex they are. Once, Europeans judged that more complex civilizations were more valuable than simpler ones. They used "uncivilized" to mean "inferior." But we know that is not true.

Development
Civilizations first developed as people learned how to increase their food supply. Farming freed people from looking for food. With more spare time, people developed specialized skills. Soon they produced surplus goods as well as surplus food. People traded surpluses for things that they did not have.

People needed places to meet and trade goods, so they built towns and markets. To keep business records, they developed systems of writing and numbers.

Today, trade still plays a major role in the way civilizations grow and change. Through trade, civilizations exchange ideas, inventions, and goods and they learn about each other.

26

Empires of the Ancient World

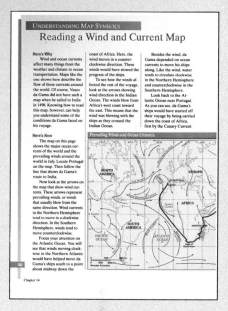

UNDERSTANDING MAP SYMBOLS
Reading a Wind and Current Map

Here's Why
Wind and ocean currents affect many things from the weather and climate to ocean transportation. Maps like the one shown here describe the flow of those currents around the world. Of course, Vasco da Gama did not have such a map when he sailed to India in 1498. Knowing how to read this map, however, can help you understand some of the conditions da Gama faced on his voyage.

Here's How
The map on this page shows the major ocean currents of the world and the prevailing winds around the world in July. Locate Portugal on the map. Then follow the line that shows da Gama's route to India.

Now look at the arrows on the map that show wind currents. These arrows represent prevailing winds, or winds that usually blow from the same direction. Wind currents in the Northern Hemisphere tend to move in a clockwise direction. In the Southern Hemisphere, winds tend to move counterclockwise.

Focus your attention on the Atlantic Ocean. You will see that winds moving clockwise in the Northern Atlantic would have helped move da Gama's ships south to a point about midway down the coast of Africa. Here, the wind moves in a counterclockwise direction. These winds would have slowed the progress of the ships.

To see how the winds affected the rest of the voyage, look at the arrows showing wind direction in the Indian Ocean. The winds blow from Africa's west coast toward the east. This means that the wind was blowing with the ships as they crossed the Indian Ocean.

Besides the wind, da Gama depended on ocean currents to move his ships along. Like the wind, water tends to circulate clockwise in the Northern Hemisphere and counterclockwise in the Southern Hemisphere.

Look back to the Atlantic Ocean near Portugal. As you can see, da Gama's ships would have started off their voyage by being carried down the coast of Africa. first by the Canary Current

Prevailing Winds and Ocean Currents

Chapter 14

Some tools you'll always use. The Understanding pages walk you through skills that you will use again and again, as a student and later on in life.

Those who lived in and around Tiwanaku resettled in small groups on the mountainsides.

Archaeologists disagree about why people deserted the city. Some think a drought destroyed the city's fragile agricultural system. Others speculate that Lake Titicaca may have flooded and made the nearby fields unusable. Still others believe that outsiders invaded the city. Whatever the reason, by 1400, all that was left of Tiwanakan culture were ruins high in the Andes.

Moche Lifestyle
The ancient city of Moche was the civic and religious hub of the Moche civilization. It was located on Peru's Pacific coast in the midst of irrigated farmlands.

Much like the Tiwanakans, the Moche probably used great numbers of laborers from the lower class to do their work. These workers dug and maintained aqueducts and built great pyramids and temples. To build temples, the Moche mixed river mud and straw to form bricks called **adobe** (uh DOH bee).

Most commoners farmed or fished and hunted for food. Priests, artisans, warriors, and engineers were members of the elite. The 1987 discovery of the tombs of the "Lords of Sipan," the richest tomb found in the Americas, has added to our knowledge of Moche crafts.

◄ The figure at left is a Tiwanakan condor god made of a beaten sheet of gold. The one-foot tall Moche pot below is decorated with the ruler's head at the top of the vessel. Examine each artifact carefully. What does each imply about that civilization, its people and their beliefs?

The Moche did not have a system of writing, but Moche pottery recovered from tombs reveals much about their culture. Clay figures and painted pottery jars show people farming, cooking, weaving, and giving birth. These ceramics tell of war and sacrifice, of glorious rulers and many gods.

Some experts think that the Moche culture was absorbed by other Andean cultures. Others believe the Moche were conquered by outsiders. But the truth remains unknown. In about 600, the Moche abandoned their city and moved to nearby areas. Six hundred years later, the Tiwanakans would do the same. ■

■ Compare and contrast Tiwanakan and Moche lifestyles.

REVIEW

1. **FOCUS** In what ways did the Tiwanakans and the Moche adapt to the land?
2. **CONNECT** What did the Tiwanakan lifestyle have in common with other early civilizations in the Americas?
3. **CULTURE** What does Moche pottery tell us about Moche culture?
4. **CRITICAL THINKING** In what ways were the Moche and the Tiwanakans similar?
5. **ACTIVITY** The condor was an emblem of a Tiwanakan god. What symbols do we use in our society to represent important things? Make a list of modern symbols such as the American eagle and the American flag. Tell what each symbol represents.

415

Early American Civilizations

The things people make and use tells a great deal about them. In this book you'll find lots of photographs of the paintings people made, the tools and weapons they used, and the gold they wore.

Letters, diaries, books—short passages from these primary sources let people from the past speak to you. When you see a tan background, a red initial letter, and a gray bar, you know that the quotation is a primary source.

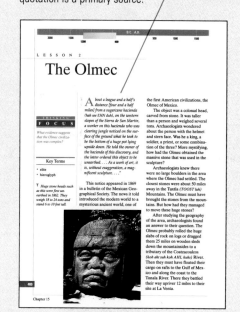

LESSON 2

The Olmec

*A*bout a league and a half's distance [four and a half miles] from a sugarcane hacienda (hah see EHN dah), on the western slopes of the Sierra de San Martin, a worker on this hacienda who was clearing jungle noticed on the surface of the ground what he took to be the bottom of a huge pot lying upside down. He told the owner of the hacienda of this discovery, and the latter ordered this object to be unearthed. . . . As a work of art, it is, without exaggeration, a magnificent sculpture. . . ."

This notice appeared in 1869 in a bulletin of the Mexican Geographical Society. The news it told introduced the modern world to a mysterious ancient world, one of

the first American civilizations, the Olmec of Mexico.

The object was a colossal head, carved from stone. It was taller than a person and weighed several tons. Archaeologists wondered about the person with the helmet and stern face. Was he a king, a soldier, a priest, or some combination of the three? More mystifying, how had the Olmec obtained the massive stone that was used in the sculpture?

Archaeologists knew there were no large boulders in the area where the Olmec had settled. The closest stones were about 50 miles away in the Tuxtla (TOOST lah) Mountains. The Olmec must have brought the stones from the mountains. But how had they managed to move these huge stones?

After studying the geography of the area, archaeologists found an answer to their question. The Olmec probably rolled the huge slabs of rock on logs or dragged them 25 miles on wooden sleds down the mountainsides to a tributary of the Coatzacoalcos (koh aht suh koh AHL kuhs) River. Then they must have floated their cargo on rafts to the Gulf of Mexico and along the coast to the Tonala River. There they battled their way upriver 12 miles to their site at La Venta.

THINKING FOCUS
What evidence suggests that the Olmec civilization was complex?

Key Terms
• elite
• hieroglyph

▼ Huge stone heads such as this were first unearthed in 1862. They weigh 18 to 24 tons and stand 6 to 10 feet tall.

400

Chapter 15

After you read the lesson, stop and review what you've read. The first question is the same one you started out with. The second question connects the lesson to what you've studied earlier. Other questions and an activity help you think about the lesson you've read. Chapter Review questions help you tie the lesson together. (See pages 418 and 419 for an example.)

Also Featuring

Some special pages show up only once in every unit, not in every lesson in the book. These features continue the story by letting you explore an idea or activity, or read a story about another time and place. The Time/Space Databank in the back of the book brings together resources you will use again and again.

School isn't the only place where you can learn social studies. This feature gives you a chance to explore history and geography outside the classroom—at home or in your own neighborhood.

EXPLORING

Nonverbal Communication

Or do people need special knowledge in order to understand them, as they would for the signals of the basketball referee?

Move Ahead

Display your sketches of nonverbal messages on the bulletin board. Try to "read" the messages your classmates drew. Can they "read" yours?
Did you find any nonverbal

➤ *Its beacon flashing in the night, this lighthouse transmits information to incoming sailors about conditions close to shore.*

MAKING DECISIONS

The Great Wall

Had the Great Wall not already existed, Yangdi [the second Sui emperor] would certainly have conceived it. As it was, he had to be content with rebuilding it.

Robert Silverberg,
20th-century historian

➤ *The Great Wall still snakes for thousands of miles across modern China. However, the wall that is still standing is not Shihuangdi's wall, but a later version, built during the Ming Dynasty.*

Background

Records show that Yangdi's rebuilding of the Great Wall in 607 required more than a million workers. Over half of them died of overwork or fled the harsh conditions.

The original building of the Great Wall, begun in 221 B.C., also involved a huge work force. Shihuangdi, the Chinese emperor who conceived of this project, connected shorter walls that had been built along China's northern border centuries before. He also extended the wall for hundreds of miles. The resulting fortified wall was and still is the longest structure on earth.

Before embarking on any massive work, such as the building of the Great Wall of China, a wise decision maker will try to weigh the benefits and the costs of the project. We can look at historical events to try to compare the benefits and the costs of building the Great Wall of China.

Benefits and Costs of the Great Wall

The most obvious benefit of building the Great Wall was protection. The wall helped prevent nomadic horsemen from invading China's farms

along the northern border. Also, it kept farmers living along the border from joining the nomads.

Building the Great Wall enabled Shihuangdi to get rid of his

enemies. He ordered them to work on distant parts of the wall. He also sent soldiers to work on the wall. As a result, the soldiers could not band together and rise up against the emperor.

However, building Shihuangdi's wall is estimated to have required more than 300,000 workers, most of whom were drafted against their will. Thousands of farmers and merchants were required to supply the workers with food, clothing, tools, and shelter. Most of these supplies never made it

to the work sites; bandits roaming the countryside robbed the supply caravans.

The work of constructing the wall was so difficult and living conditions were so harsh that thousands of workers died. Often they were buried in the wall itself. Thus, the Great Wall of China gained the gruesome title of "the world's longest cemetery."

➤ *Sturdy horses, like the one at the left, carried nomads who raided China's northern border. In response, the Great Wall was built, using labor-intensive construction methods as shown. Study the chart for a comparison of the Great Wall's long-range benefits and short-term costs.*

Decision
Build Great Wall

Outcomes

- People are safer
- More farmers stay on farms
- Fewer threats to emperor arise
- Many laborers die
- People become poorer
- Supply caravans often attacked

Decision Point

1. What were the benefits of constructing the Great Wall of China? What were the costs?
2. Do you think these were the only benefits and costs of the Great Wall? Where would you look to find more information about the role of the Great Wall in Chinese history?
3. Based on the information on these pages and any other information you have found,

do you think the benefits and costs of building the Great Wall balanced out? Explain.
4. Collect information from newspapers and magazines about upcoming plans for large government projects in the United States. Discuss the projected benefits and costs of each project. Decide which projects you would support and which you would oppose.

China

➤ *Using a traditional back-strap loom, this Mayan woman weaves patterns used in her village for generations. For the Mayan weaver, snakes symbolize the earth, toads symbolize saints, and eagles symbolize life and death.*

➤ *These coins, which were issued by Shihuangdi, were the standard currency throughout the empire at the time when the Great Wall was being built.*

Chapter 15

Chapter 8

What would you do? The Making Decisions pages show you an important decision from the past. Then you practice the steps that will help you to make a good choice.

Stories have always been important parts of people's lives. Each unit in the book has at least one story about the time and place you're studying. In this case, it's a re-creation of Columbus's audience with King Ferdinand and Queen Isabella.

In Lesson 3 you learned about Columbus's appeal to Ferdinand and Isabella. Here is an imaginative recreation of his second appearance before that King and Queen.

LITERATURE

The Audience

C. Walter Hodges

As you have learned in this chapter, the dream of wealth and the lure of riches drew Columbus and other explorers like him. They undertook journeys of unknown dangers and uncertain outcomes to pursue that dream. But they needed financial support. As you read this story, play the role of the audience—the King or Queen. Would you support Columbus? Why or why not?

The town was taken, the Moors were driven out, the wars were at an end. Now, now at last there must be time to hear Columbus. Now at last the victorious Sovereigns would give him ships to sail in quest of his new horizon.

He went to his friend Alonzo de Quintanilla and implored him to obtain audience for him soon. The Accountant-General promised to do so, and on the following day Columbus was summoned into the presence of Their Majesties.

Father Juan Perez, Luiz de Santangel and I went with him to the audience. The antechamber was full of people, little groups talking in low voices, Court official

The Time/Space Databank is like a reference section of a library at your fingertips. It's the place to go for more information about the places, people, and key terms you meet in this book.

What's a minipedia? It's a small version of an encyclopedia, one that you don't have to go to your library to use. It's bound right into the back of your book so you can quickly look up its articles, charts, and graphs.

The Atlas maps out the world. Special maps tell you about the languages, religions, climates, and resources of the world. Historical maps let you compare what was going on at the same time in different places.

Then the King spoke:
"Señor Columbus is well known to us, I think; but if I remember rightly his proposals were examined by a Special Commission some years ago. Was it not so?"
"At Salamanca, sire."
"And the Commissioners rejected them," continued the King, "on the grounds that you could not bring forward sufficient evidence in support of your theory. Again, was it not so? And was not the Archbishop of Granada here in charge of that Commission?"
Columbus looked across at Talavera, and said nothing. The King continued:
"But since you bring your case again before us, señor, we must presume that you have fresh evidence in support of it. Or that you have fault to find with the method by which it was previously examined."
"Sire, it is not with the method but with the verdict that I have fault to find," said Columbus. "I believe that the members of the commission were all men of great renown for learning and scientific knowledge. But the greater their learning the greater was their error. They were wrong in their conclusions, and I dispute their verdict."
"And what says the Archbishop to that?" asked the King.
Talavera shrugged.
"What can I say, sire, more than Señor C ..
The men whom !

Map and Globe Handbook

*Y*ou are about to begin an exciting journey across the centuries. In this handbook, you'll explore roads built by the Inca almost 500 years ago, learn how people built dikes and dams to reclaim land in the Netherlands, and travel to a mountaintop in Indonesia. In addition, you'll visit empires that existed almost 4,000 years ago, and learn about the battle that ended the American Revolution.

Since all journeys require maps, your adventure starts right here. This handbook will help you unlock the secrets of maps and globes. Turn to page G1, and let your journey begin.

Contents

Understanding Our Planet	**G1**
Understanding a Map	**G2**
Using the Legend and Grid	**G3**
Understanding Hemispheres, Latitude, and Longitude	**G4**
Drawing Inferences from Maps	**G5**
Understanding Projections	**G6**
Interpreting Flow Lines	**G8**
Reading Different Kinds of Maps	**G9**
A Relief Map with a Vertical Profile	**G9**
A Battle Map	**G10**
Comparing Maps	**G11**
A Historical Map and a Timeline	**G12**
A Cartogram	**G14**
Using Geographic References	**G15**

Understanding Our Planet

A map is a representation of a part of the earth drawn on a flat surface. Study the satellite image and the map below. The image shows what South America looks like from miles above the earth. Mapmakers sometimes use these images to help draw maps. Now look at the map of roads that the Inca built almost 500 years ago in the Andes of South America. Notice how the shape of the coastline in the image matches the shape of the map. The locator map in the top right-hand corner helps you find where this region is located on earth.

▲ Satellites collect information in space and send it back to earth. The information can then be turned into images that look like photographs. The colors on this satellite image show different geographical features of South America.

▶ This map shows the roads that the Inca built almost 500 years ago. Look at the size of the empire. How do you think having a systems of roads helped strengthen the Inca Empire?

Ancient Inca Roads

Pasto

Tumbes

Cajamarca

ANDES

Machu Picchu

Pachacamac

Cuzco

Isla del Sol

Arequipa

PACIFIC OCEAN

ANDES

Copiapó

Tucumán

Talca

Legend

Inca Empire A.D. 1525

Inca road system

Inca town

km 0   250   500
mi 0   250   500

Understanding a Map

Take a few minutes to look quickly at the maps in this handbook. You'll notice that there are maps of different sizes, featuring different places. Most of the maps show a portion of the world, and a few represent the entire world. Depending on the type of map, you can find out about a place's climate, population density, migration patterns, elevation, time zones, or people.

All maps share certain characteristics. Every part of a map contains important information. To understand the whole map, you need to know how to read each part of it. Look at the map below. It shows the continent of Australia.

The **compass rose** points out directions. The tips of this compass rose point to north **(N)**, south **(S)**, east **(E)**, and west **(W)**, as well as intermediate, or in-between, directions.

An **inset** is related to the larger map. This inset map is a **locator inset,** which helps you to find what part of the earth is shown on the larger map.

Latitude and **longitude** are imaginary lines that form a **grid** over the earth. A grid is a pattern of lines that cross one another. You can use the grid to locate places on the map.

Modern Australia

The **scale line** shows how much smaller the map is than the actual area it represents.

The **legend,** or **key,** explains what the symbols on the map mean. This legend identifies state, territorial, and national capitals.

Using the Legend and Grid

Maps can help you make connections between different events and cultures. The map below shows four different civilizations that settled in or near the eastern Mediterranean in the 600s B.C. By seeing how close some of these cultures were to each other, you can begin to think about the influences they may have had on each other.

A grid helps you to locate places on the map. Look up Corsica in the map's index, and read the letter and number beside the name, *A1*. Find the letter A on the map, and then find the number 1. Is Corsica located within the square formed by the grid lines?

The Eastern Mediterranean in the 600s B.C.

Index

Athens	**B3**
Carales	**B1**
Corsica	**A1**
Crete	**C3**
Citrium	**C5**
Damascus	**C5**
Jerusalem	**C5**
Massilia	**A1**
Memphis	**D4**
Motya	**B1**
Rome	**B1**
Thapsus	**C1**

Legend:
- Greek settlements
- Assyrian Empire
- Phoenician colonies
- Etruscan settlements

0   150   300 mi.
0   150 300 km
Azimuthal Equidistant Projection

The legend uses different colors to indicate where people were settled in the eastern Mediterranean during the 600s B.C. In Corsica, Etruscan settlements surrounded Greek settlements.

MAP SKILLS

1. **REVIEW** In which grid square is the island of Crete located? Who lived in Crete in the 600s B.C.?

2. **REVIEW** Name at least two cities in grid C5.

3. **THINK ABOUT IT** What appears to be the significance of major rivers and coastlines on the map?

4. **TRY IT** Add four more cities to the map index.

Understanding Hemispheres, Latitude, and Longitude

Northern Hemisphere

Southern Hemisphere

Western Hemisphere

Eastern Hemisphere

When you study a map or a globe, you'll see a grid of lines composed of latitude and longitude. These imaginary lines are used to locate places on a map or globe. This imaginary grid of lines also helps to divide the earth into four hemispheres—northern, southern, western, and eastern. The word hemisphere is from Greek and translates as "half a sphere."

Longitude is the number of degrees east or west of the prime meridian. Lines of longitude meet at the North and the South Poles.

The **Equator** is 0° latitude. It separates the Northern and Southern Hemispheres.

The **prime meridian** is 0° longitude and goes through Greenwich, England. The prime meridian and the longitude line opposite it at 180° separate the earth into the Eastern and Western Hemispheres.

Lines of **latitude** run east and west across the globe. Latitude is the number of degrees north or south of the equator. Lines of latitude never meet.

MAP SKILLS

1. **REVIEW** In which two hemispheres would you find the United States?

2. **REVIEW** What is the approximate latitude and longitude for Cairo, Egypt and Rio De Janeiro, Brazil?

3. **THINK ABOUT IT** Why do you need both the latitude and longitude to locate a place on a map? What would happen if you only had one of the measurements?

4. **TRY IT** Look at the map of China on page 193. At what latitude and longitude is Chengdu located?

Drawing Inferences from Maps

You know from reading that authors don't always spell out every detail. As a reader, you have to rely on your own experience and clues in the text to figure out information about a plot. When you do this, you're making inferences.

You can also make inferences from maps. A map's scale, legend, and details will give you clues. This map shows the canals, dams, and waterways of the Netherlands today. How do you think these natural and human-made features have affected people's lives?

The Netherlands, 1995

Look at the location of Amsterdam, the capital of the Netherlands. From the map, what can you infer about how this city's location affects its residents?

These yellow areas were once under water, but have been reclaimed. That means that people pumped the water out of this part of the bay and now use the land for farms, homes, or other uses.

Legend
- Dam
- Canal
- Fresh water
- Area reclaimed since 1927

The legend shows the many dams and canals in this small country. Look at the location of the dams and canals on the map.

MAP SKILLS

1. **REVIEW** Look at the location of Rotterdam. What can you infer about the kinds of jobs that people in Rotterdam might have?

2. **THINK ABOUT IT** What natural disasters do you think people in the Netherlands worry about? Why?

3. **TRY IT** Look at northern South America on the map of world climates on page 530. Based on its climate pattern, what can you infer about land use there? Now look at the world land use map on page 531 to see if you were correct. Try this for other regions of the world.

Understanding Projections

Suppose you have a map of the world and a sphere. You want to cover the sphere with the map to make a globe. Since the map is flat and the sphere is round, you won't ever have a perfect fit. Cartographers still wrestle with the problem of representing the round earth on a flat map. They use projections, or ways of transferring the curved surface of the earth onto a flat map. All projections have some distortion of distance, direction, size, or shape.

In 1569 the German cartographer (mapmaker) Gerhardus Mercator first published this projection. A Mercator Projection maintains the shapes of the continents but distorts their sizes, especially near the poles. Look at the size of Greenland on this projection. In reality, it's about the same size as Mexico!

WORLD: Mercator Projection

In 1974, Arno Peters, a West German cartographer, created the Peters Projection. The sizes of the continents in relation to each other are accurate, but their shapes are distorted. Look at South America on the Peters Projection map. How does its size and shape compare to that of South America on the Mercator Projection?

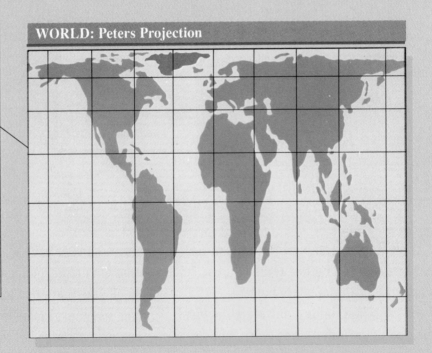

WORLD: Peters Projection

WORLD: Goode Projection

Paul Goode, a cartographer from the University of Chicago, combined elements of two other projections to create the Goode Projection in 1923. Notice how the projection divides the world into sections. These divisions help make the projection of continents more accurate in terms of size and shape, but distances are difficult to measure.

WORLD: Robinson Projection

In 1963, American cartographer Arthur Robinson created this projection. The Robinson Projection shows the sizes, shapes, and distances between the continents fairly accurately. Most of the world maps in this book use the Robinson Projection as their base.

MAP SKILLS

1. **REVIEW** On which projection does Africa look the largest? On which projection does it look the smallest?

2. **REVIEW** Which projection would you use to find out the correct size of Greenland? the shortest route between South America and Australia? the shape of Antarctica? the shape of Africa?

3. **THINK ABOUT IT** Look at South America on the Goode and on the Mercator Projections. Why do they look similar while Greenland and other areas near the poles look so different? Use a globe to answer the question.

4. **TRY IT** Choose a map in this book. Which projection does it use? Explain the advantages of using that particular projection.

Interpreting Flow Lines

Maps can show the movements of people, ideas, and goods by using flow lines. Flow lines are arrows on maps that show where something came from and where it went. Because they vary in thickness, graduated flow lines also show the quantity of what has moved. The map below shows the number of Africans who were enslaved and sent to the Americas.

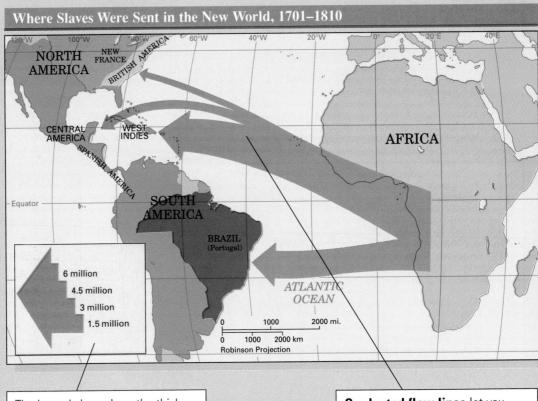

Where Slaves Were Sent in the New World, 1701–1810

The legend shows how the thickness of the arrows relates to the number of Africans who were sent to the Americas.

Graduated flow lines let you compare amounts quickly. Based on the map, were more Africans sent to Central America or the West Indies?

MAP SKILLS

1. **REVIEW** About how many Africans were sent to Brazil as slaves?

2. **REVIEW** Name the four places on the map where Africans were sent. Rank them from where the most Africans went to where the fewest went.

3. **THINK ABOUT IT** What else might you show with flow lines on a map?

4. **TRY IT** Make or obtain a map of your community. Use arrows to mark the flow of your class members as you travel from school to home.

Reading Different Kinds of Maps

As you've already seen, maps can show more than the shape of land. They can show details about historical places; how people have changed their land; and the flow of people, goods, or ideas. In this section, you'll learn to use several different kinds of maps.

A Relief Map with a Vertical Profile

A relief map shows the topography, which means the natural surface features of the land. It does this by showing the land's elevation, or height above sea level. A vertical profile is a diagram on a physical map that presents a side view of an elevation line (also called a profile line) drawn across the map. This map shows the topography of the island of Sumatra, in Indonesia, along an elevation line.

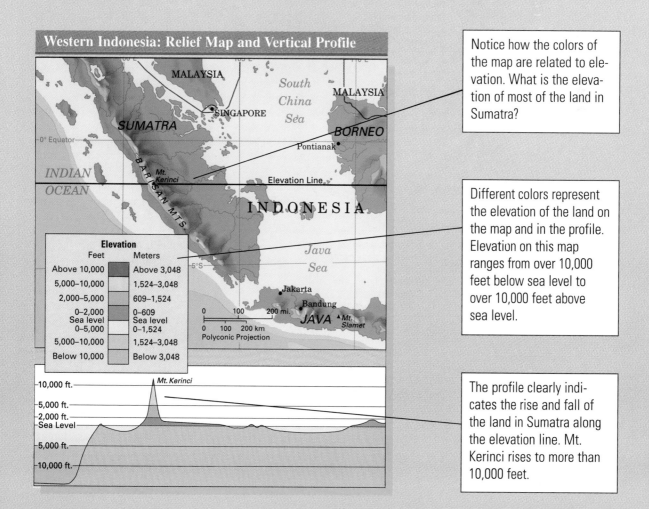

Western Indonesia: Relief Map and Vertical Profile

Notice how the colors of the map are related to elevation. What is the elevation of most of the land in Sumatra?

Different colors represent the elevation of the land on the map and in the profile. Elevation on this map ranges from over 10,000 feet below sea level to over 10,000 feet above sea level.

The profile clearly indicates the rise and fall of the land in Sumatra along the elevation line. Mt. Kerinci rises to more than 10,000 feet.

A Battle Map

A battle map illustrates the events of a particular battle or series of battles. Since the outcome of a battle is often affected by the land on which it occurs, maps are a good way to show battles. The map below uses symbols to show the positions and movements of troops during the Battle of Yorktown that took place during the American Revolution.

The green arrows stand for American troops, the red arrow and shapes stand for British troops, and the blue arrows stand for French forces. The direction of the arrows shows the movement of the forces.

The map shows that Cornwallis's British troops became trapped at Yorktown, because it was on a peninsula. Once Washington's American troops and Rochambeau's French troops moved in, the British troops had nowhere to go to escape. Cornwallis was forced to surrender.

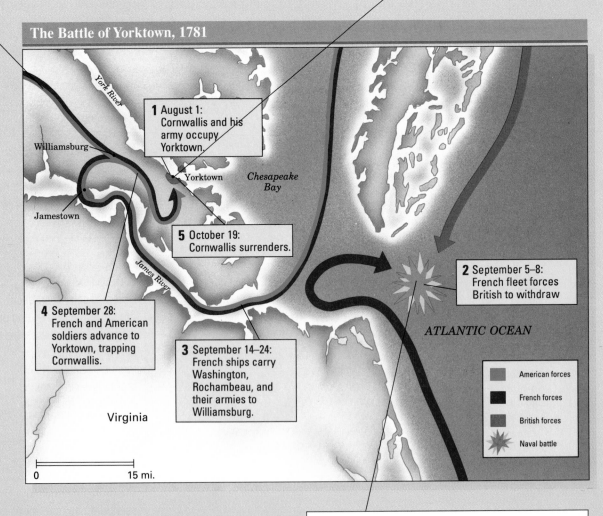

The Battle of Yorktown, 1781

York River

Williamsburg

Jamestown

James River

1 August 1: Cornwallis and his army occupy Yorktown.

Yorktown

Chesapeake Bay

5 October 19: Cornwallis surrenders.

4 September 28: French and American soldiers advance to Yorktown, trapping Cornwallis.

3 September 14–24: French ships carry Washington, Rochambeau, and their armies to Williamsburg.

2 September 5–8: French fleet forces British to withdraw

ATLANTIC OCEAN

Virginia

0   15 mi.

American forces
French forces
British forces
Naval battle

The British navy tried to rescue Cornwallis's troops, but it was stopped by French naval forces.

Comparing Maps

Maps can contain many different kinds of information. Look at the two maps of South Africa below. The top map shows the economic resources of the country and the bottom map shows its population. By comparing the two maps, you can learn how economic use and population are related in South Africa.

South Africa: Economic Resources

There are fewer economic resources along the coast of South Africa between Cape Town and Port Elizabeth. What are they?

According to the legend, manufacturing, gold, and diamonds are all located near Pretoria. The land near Pretoria is also good for farming.

Legend
- Grazing land
- Farm land
- Forest
- Desert
- Citrus fruit
- Sugar cane
- Grapes
- Diamonds
- Gold
- Manufacturing
- Fishing

South Africa: Population

What is the population of the coast between Cape Town and Port Elizabeth? Based on these two maps, what conclusions can you draw about a region's economic resources and its population?

The many red dots near Pretoria show that the city and the region around it are densely populated.

Legend
- Each dot represents 10,000 people

A Historical Map and a Timeline

Many of the maps in this handbook are historical maps. Cartographers today can draw historical maps based on historical records and writings and archaeological discoveries. This historical map shows three empires that existed in the part of the world known as Mesopotamia between 2350 and 1750 B.C. The two rivers in this region, the Tigris River and the Euphrates River, were important for some of the earth's earliest known civilizations.

The red line marks the approximate boundaries of the early empire of Assyria. How did its size compare with the size of Babylonia?

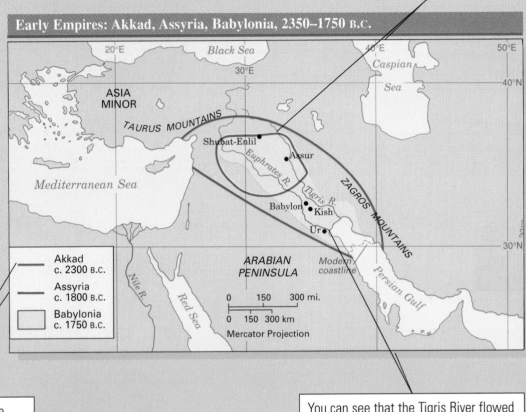

Early Empires: Akkad, Assyria, Babylonia, 2350–1750 B.C.

Akkad
c. 2300 B.C.

Assyria
c. 1800 B.C.

Babylonia
c. 1750 B.C.

The legend shows the colors that represent each empire as well as the time period in which the empires existed.

You can see that the Tigris River flowed through all three empires. Why do you think empires developed near rivers?

Timelines record events that occurred in the past. They present the events in order so you can see and understand the sequence of different events. This timeline gives a sequence of some events that occurred in the Akkadian, Assyrian, and Babylonian empires shown on the map on page G12. It also shows some other events that occurred in this region.

The timeline is broken into intervals of 500 years. The numbers on this timeline decrease as you move to the right, because the dates are B.C., which stands for Before Christ. This means the dates refer to the number of years before Jesus was born, so the numbers decrease as you move closer to Jesus' birth. After Jesus' birth the numbers increase.

The timeline identifies two rulers whose empires were not shown on the map. Based on the information here, can you add those empires to the map? Why or why not?

Mesopotamian Rulers

c. 1813–1781 B.C., Shamshi-Adad rules the Assyrian Empire.

745–727 B.C., Tiglath-Pilaser III rules the New Assyrian Empire.

2500   2000   1500   1000   500

2334–2279 B.C., Sargon rules the Akkadian Empire.

1792–1750 B.C., Hammurabi rules the Babylonian Empire.

605–562 B.C., Nebuchadnezzar rules the New Babylonian Empire.

This area of the timeline shows the reign of Sargon, who created the world's first empire, Akkad. How long did Sargon rule Akkad?

How is the information that you learn from the map on the left page similar to the information on this timeline? How is the information different?

A Cartogram

You already know that maps can show physical features, like land and water. But they can also show statistics, almost like a graph. These kinds of maps are called cartograms. Cartograms look very different from physical maps. The cartogram below shows the gross national product (GNP) for all countries of the world. The GNP is the total value of all the goods and services produced by a country in a single year.

On a physical map, Canada would appear larger than the United States. On this cartogram, it is much smaller. That means that Canada's GNP is considerably smaller than that of the United States. Cartograms often distort the size and shapes of countries.

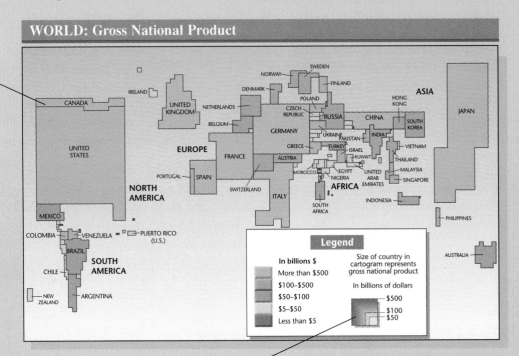

WORLD: Gross National Product

Legend

In billions $
More than $500
$100–$500
$50–$100
$5–$50
Less than $5

Size of country in cartogram represents gross national product

In billions of dollars
$500
$100
$50

Like physical or political maps, cartograms have scales or legends. Scales on cartograms, however, don't measure distance. This scale explains that the size of each country reflects the size of its gross national product.

MAP SKILLS

1. **REVIEW** How did the geography of the land help defeat the British in the Battle of Yorktown?

2. **REVIEW** Which ruler in Mesopotamia controlled the city of Ur and ruled until 1750 B.C.?

3. **REVIEW** Name three countries whose GNPs are equal to or larger than France's.

4. **THINK ABOUT IT** How would changing the elevation line on the map on page G9 change the profile you see?

5. **TRY IT** Compare two different types of maps of your state. Make a table to compare what the maps tell you about your state.

Using Geographic References

What is a cataract? Where is Flanders located? Which languages are spoken in Africa? The Time/Space Databank on pages 503–548 will help you answer these and other geography questions.

The **Atlas,** pages 518–533, includes many types of maps, such as physical, political, historical, climate, land use, and resources. The map on page 529 shows where specific languages are spoken. This portion of the map shows Africa. African, Semitic, Malayo-Polynesian, and Indo-European languages are all spoken in Africa.

The **Glossary of Geographic Terms,** pages 534–535, illustrates and defines key geographic terms, such as cataract. From the description, you can tell that Niagara Falls is a major cataract.

cataract
a large, powerful waterfall

F			
Fernando Póo (island off W. Africa)	4°N	9°E	**465**
Flanders (region noted for woolen trade; France, Belgium)	51 N	3°E	**330**
Florence (cultural center of Renaissance Italy)	44°N	11°E	**317**
Fustat (Cairo; capital of Fatamid caliphate; Egypt)	30°N	31°E	**80**

The **Gazetteer,** pages 536–537, lists locations, accompanied by brief descriptions, latitude and longitude, and where to find that location in this book. Flanders is a region in Europe. It is at 51° North, and 3° East, and is shown on a map on page 330.

MAP SKILLS

1. **REVIEW** You want to find the location of the Great Rift Valley. In which part of the Time/Space Databank would you look?

2. **THINK ABOUT IT** What is the relationship between a savanna, a sahel, and a desert?

Where would you look in the Time/Space Databank to find the answer?

3. **TRY IT** Choose any two terms from the Glossary of Geographic Terms. Find examples of these features in the Atlas.

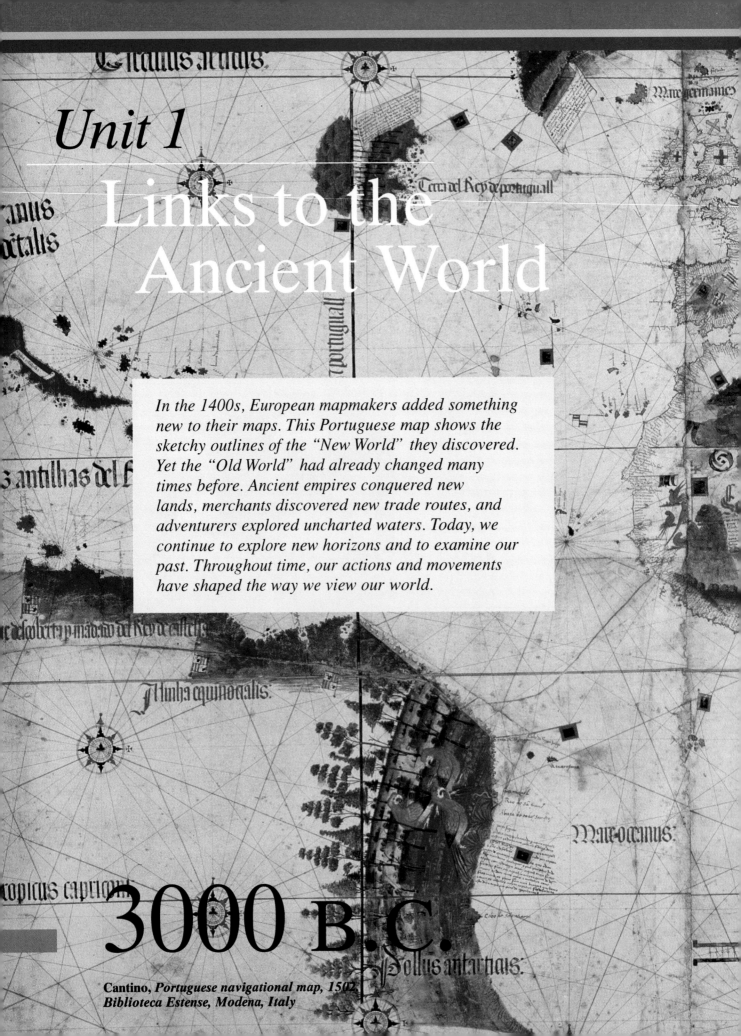

Unit 1

Links to the Ancient World

In the 1400s, European mapmakers added something new to their maps. This Portuguese map shows the sketchy outlines of the "New World" they discovered. Yet the "Old World" had already changed many times before. Ancient empires conquered new lands, merchants discovered new trade routes, and adventurers explored uncharted waters. Today, we continue to explore new horizons and to examine our past. Throughout time, our actions and movements have shaped the way we view our world.

3000 B.C.

Cantino, *Portuguese navigational map, 1502*
Biblioteca Estense, Modena, Italy

Today

Chapter 1

A Changing World View

Roman traders who journeyed to the Far East 2,000 years ago measured distance not in miles but in how far they traveled by camel in an hour. As they approached their destination, they neared the edge of their known world. How the world has changed since then! Today, we travel far into space. We also look back, learning about our past. Our world view expands as we explore distant horizons and the evidence of past worlds.

c. 1000 B.C. We travel back in time by examining the objects ancient people left behind. The writing in this bronze dish tells of a border dispute settled by two rival groups in China.

3000	2000	1000

c. 500 B.C. North African people settle in present-day Nigeria and begin making iron tools.

3000 B.C.

During the 1400s, explorers and traders set sail from Lisbon, Portugal, for the far reaches of the world they knew—Europe, Africa, and Asia. This illustration of Lisbon, drawn about 1590, helps us see what life in the past was like.

c. 1450 Antoine de La Salle includes the discoveries of the Portuguese explorers in his map of the world. Even so, it is far from accurate. Today, radar allows travelers to plot courses across seas, over continents, and into space.

B.C.	A.D.		1000		Today

c. 100 B.C. Merchants use camels to transport goods in the arid regions of Asia and the Middle East.

Today

L E S S O N   1

Connections in the Roman Empire

THINKING FOCUS

How were travel and communication in the Roman Empire different from today?

Key Terms

- electronic communication
- satellite

➤ *What do you know about any of the places on these brochures? How do you know about them?*

aris, Alexandria, Athens. Would you like to visit these cities? What about Sydney, Nairobi, or Moscow? Which of these names is most familiar to you?

You have probably heard of some, if not all, of these places. Even Sydney, Australia, across the vast Pacific Ocean, is now part of the world view of most Americans.

If you had lived in Rome in A.D. 150, your world view would have been quite different. Paris

(then called "Lutetia"), in Gaul; Alexandria, in Africa; and Athens, in Greece, were all part of the Roman Empire. As a merchant or soldier, you might have traveled to these cities.

Sydney? Nairobi? Moscow? These cities did not exist in A.D. 150. More important, the Romans were unaware of cultures in Australia, the Americas, central Africa, and northern Asia. Their limited world view made the world smaller than the one we know today.

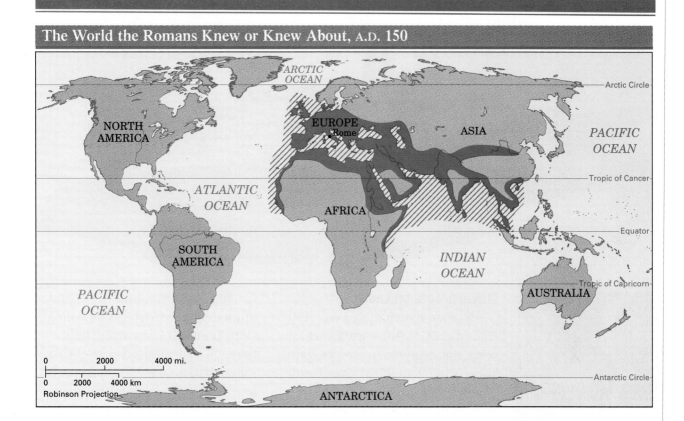

NORTH
AMERICA

ARCTIC
OCEAN

EUROPE
Rome

ASIA

PACIFIC
OCEAN

Arctic Circle

ATLANTIC
OCEAN

AFRICA

Tropic of Cancer

SOUTH
AMERICA

Equator

PACIFIC
OCEAN

INDIAN
OCEAN

Tropic of Capricorn

AUSTRALIA

0   2000   4000 mi.

0   2000   4000 km
Robinson Projection

ANTARCTICA

Antarctic Circle

Travel Then and Now

The Romans of A.D. 150 knew of only a small part of the earth's surface, as you can see on the map above. Yet distances within their known world—for example, from Rome to Lutetia—seemed greater to them than they seem to us. That is because the ways we look at and experience the world have changed greatly since Roman times.

If you had to walk three miles uphill to school, would it seem near or far to you? How about if you took an express train and arrived in two minutes? The longer we must travel to get someplace, the farther away it seems to be.

Travel Within the Empire

In A.D. 150, most people in the Roman Empire knew very little about the world away from home. In fact, peasants and members of the lower classes rarely traveled beyond their village.

Those people who did travel went on foot, on horseback, or in horse-drawn carts. More than 50,000 miles of paved highways connected all parts of the empire to Rome. But travel was slow. The public wagons averaged only 60 miles a day, a distance we can now travel in one hour by car!

Roman merchants and government officials sailed in ships to imperial provinces in Spain, North Africa, or the Middle East. Speed varied, of course, with the winds. The voyage from Sicily, at the southern tip of Italy, to Alexandria in North Africa took six days with good winds. Today, many diesel-powered transport ships follow that same route in less than one-third the time.

▲ *Compare your known world with the world known to the Romans in A.D. 150 (shown in purple). How are they different?*

How Do We Know?

ECONOMICS *Large numbers of Roman coins found in India show that India and Rome carried on extensive trade. Several Roman coins struck in the late A.D. 100s have been found in a port city in modern Cambodia, and 16 Roman coins have been found in the Chinese city of Shansi.*

▲ *Compare the sizes of a modern ocean liner, the* Queen Elizabeth II, *and a Roman sailing vessel from about* A.D. *100. The modern ship measures 963 feet long and the ancient one 120 feet. Hulls of reinforced steel have replaced wooden ones. And with powerful turbine engines, today's captains need not rely on rowers or the wind.*

■ *Describe the main methods of travel within the Roman Empire in* A.D. *150.*

Travel to Foreign Lands

Roman merchants in A.D. 150 traded gold, textiles, glassware, wine, and papyrus for spices, gems, silk, cotton, and fabric dyes from China, India, and Southeast Asia. Routes to the east, whether by land or sea, were long, difficult, and dangerous.

The overland route from Antioch, on the eastern Mediterranean shore, to Luoyang, capital of China, was over 4,000 miles long. Hardly anyone ever traveled the whole way. Goods changed hands in the great trading cities along the route.

Merchants with goods bound for India shipped their merchandise up the Nile to Coptos, where it was transferred to camel caravans for the trip to the ports of the Red Sea. Other goods were shipped from the Persian Gulf. Traders loaded their cargo onto ships for the two-month voyage to India.

Sea travel was hazardous and often delayed. Captains of sailing ships required favorable winds to reach their desired ports. Also, sailors had no navigational charts or instruments, such as the magnetic compass, to help them find their way. Once at sea, travelers commonly fell victim to, and some even died from, storms, sickness, malnutrition, starvation, and dehydration.

Because of the great distances, discomforts, and dangers involved, very few people ever traveled beyond the boundaries of the empire. Most of those who did sought to trade with or invade foreign lands.

Today, all kinds of people travel all over the world for business and for pleasure. Jet planes, cars, trains, and cruise ships carry travelers in comfort and safety where once only brave soldiers and traders dared to go. ■

Communication Then and Now

Just as travel has become easier and faster, communication has improved. At the time of the Roman Empire, messages could be sent only one way—they were hand carried. Messengers crisscrossed the empire carrying correspondence. Often, people asked travelers to deliver letters to faraway places.

Communication was only as fast as the messenger's transportation. Messengers on foot could cover only about 25 miles a day. The official Roman postal service, which used horses or horse-drawn carriages day and night, covered an average of 100 miles a day. Carried over land and sea, a letter that was sent from a general in Rome could take more than 30 days to reach a legion outpost in Britain.

Today, we can contact people in other parts of the world without anyone having to make a journey.

Electronic communication, which includes such inventions as the fax machine, Internet, radio, television, computers, and the telephone, has revolutionized the way we communicate. Communication **satellites** orbit the earth transmitting telephone and television signals. In less than a second, they can relay signals and messages to almost anywhere on earth. Space probes now explore and send back information about our universe.

Through these many scientific developments, our world view has expanded. At the same time, the earth seems to be much smaller than it seemed to the Romans. Today, our frontiers lie in space rather than beyond a distant ocean or unknown continent. ■

◄ *In A.D. 150, the Appian Way (lower left) led Romans to known destinations. Today, communication satellites have greatly expanded our world view.*

■ *How has communication changed since A.D. 150?*

R E V I E W

1. **FOCUS** How were travel and communication in the Roman Empire different from today?
2. **GEOGRAPHY** How do you think a merchant from Lutetia (Paris) would have reached the North African city of Alexandria in A.D. 150?
3. **CRITICAL THINKING** How is space travel today like taking an ocean voyage in A.D. 150?
4. **CRITICAL THINKING** Why would silk clothing have been a sign of wealth in the Roman Empire?
5. **CRITICAL THINKING** Explain this statement: The world shrank on the day when communication no longer depended on transportation.
6. **ACTIVITY** Imagine that you are standing in a major transportation center 1,500 years in the future. Draw a sketch or write a description of the scene. Be sure to include what the destinations might be. Show or describe new methods of travel that you think might exist.

7

A Changing World View

Using Time Zones

Here's Why

Just as there are standard systems that help people around the world communicate about weights and distances, there is also a world standard system to help establish time differences. A time zone map shows the time differences between locations on earth. Because people and information can quickly travel long distances, knowing how to use a time zone map can be a valuable skill.

Here's How

The diagram on page 9 shows that half of the earth's surface is always receiving light from the sun. As the earth rotates on its axis, the part of its surface that receives that light changes. This change provides us with a way to measure time.

The exact time at any place on earth is measured from noon, when the sun is directly overhead. When it is noon for you, the time east of you is a little later, and the time west is a little earlier.

This small difference in time was not very important when people and information traveled slowly. Today, however, people need to communicate immediately with others in distant places. A system of standard time zones was established in

1884, within 10 years of the invention of the telephone.

The earth was divided into 24 time zones, one for each hour of a day, as shown on the map below. Each zone covers about 15 degrees of longitude, the number of degrees the earth rotates in one hour. In some places zone lines are crooked to account for political borders.

The starting point is an imaginary line called the prime meridian, which goes

through Greenwich, England. The time there is called Greenwich mean time or GMT. The time one time zone east of the GMT is one hour later, and the time one zone west is one hour earlier.

The time that divides days is midnight. When it is noon in Greenwich, it is midnight at the International Date Line, which is halfway around the world at the 180th meridian. When you cross the International Date

World Time Zones, 1995

Chapter 1

NIGHT

DAY

6 P.M.

Sun's Rays

Midnight

North Pole

Noon

Earth's
Rotation

North
America

6 A.M.

Line going west, you add a day. Going east you subtract a day.

Find Anchorage, Alaska, on the map below, east of the International Date Line. Suppose you are leaving Anchorage at 6 P.M. to fly to Washington, D.C., and you want to set your watch to the correct Washington time. You can see from the map that you will enter four time zones on the trip. To find out what time it is in Washington when you are leaving Anchorage, add one hour to the Anchorage time for each time zone you enter. To have the correct Washington time, you should set your watch to 10 P.M.

If you fly west from Washington, D.C., to Denver, Colorado, subtract one hour for each time zone you enter. When it is 8 A.M. in Washington, it is 6 A.M. in Denver.

If you fly south from Washington, to Lima, Peru, you do not need to change your watch. Although in different hemispheres, both are in the same time zone.

Try It

Use the time zone map to see what time it is in Montreal, Canada, when it is 8 P.M. in Los Angeles, California. What time is it then in Rio de Janeiro, Brazil? How much earlier is it in Stockholm, Sweden, than in Perth, Australia?

Apply It

Suppose you have friends in New York and in San Diego and you want to call them both on your birthday. If you call at 6 P.M., what time is it in each city?

| −2 | −1 | −0 | +0 | +1 | +2 | +3 | +4 | +5 | +6 | +7 | +8 | +9 | +10 | +11 |

Hours subtracted from Greenwich Mean Time

Reykjavik

Stockholm · Helsinki +2

Moscow · Gorki +4 · Sverdlovsk +5 · Novosibirsk +7 · Irkutsk +6 · Yakutsk +8 · +9 · +10 · +11

London · Berlin +3 · Tashkent +6

Paris · +1

Madrid · Rome · Athens · Tehran +4:30 · Beijing +8 · Vladivostok · Seoul · Tokyo +9

AZORES

Casablanca · Cairo · Tel Aviv · New Delhi · Shanghai · Hong Kong

Dakar · Khartoum +1 · Karachi · Calcutta +5:30 · Bombay · Bangkok · Manila

Lagos · +2 · Nairobi · Singapore +7:30

Accra

Kinshasa · Jakarta

Johannesburg · Perth +8 · +9:30 · Sydney +10 · Melbourne

Sun Time

Riyadh

Prime · Meridian

A Changing World View

L E S S O N   2

The Expanding Horizon

THINKING
F O C U S

How and why did people travel in the years between A.D. 150 and 1500?

Key Terms

- caravan
- stirrups
- lateen sail
- sternpost rudder
- magnetic compass

Isidore of Charax wrote the passage on the right around 10 B.C. for the Roman emperor Augustus. In this first known travel guide, *Parthian Stations*, Isidore describes the trade route from Antioch, on the eastern shore of the Mediterranean Sea, to the borders of India. He names the supply stations and states the distances between them in schoeni *(SKEE nee)*, or the distance people could travel in one hour by camel. Schoeni could vary in length from two and one-half to three and one-half miles, depending on the difficulty of the landscape.

As you read the passage, notice how Isidore points out physical features, such as temples, canals, and villages, to help the traveler follow the route. On the map below, try to find some of the places he mentions.

Then a royal place, a temple of Artemis, founded by Darius, a small town; close by is the canal of Semiramis, and the Euphrates is dammed with rocks, in order that by being thus checked it may overflow the fields; but also in summer it wrecks the boats; to this place, 7 schoeni. Then Allan, a walled village, 4 schoeni. Then Phaliga, a village on the Euphrates (that means in Greek 'half-way'), 6 schoeni.

Who else might have used this particular route, and how would they have traveled? You will learn that, from A.D. 150 to 1500, improvements in transportation encouraged more people to travel. And as travel increased over time, the horizon of people's known world was extended and their world view expanded.

➤ *Compare this map to the maps on pages 522–524 of the Atlas. What has changed? Can you find any of these towns on the modern maps?*

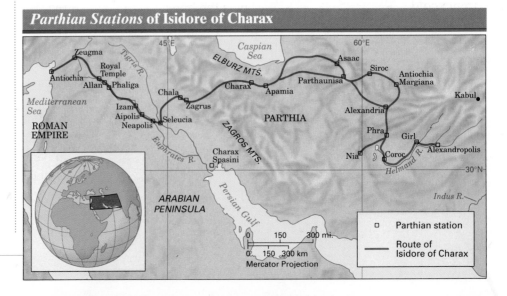

Parthian Stations of Isidore of Charax

Zeugma · Royal Temple · Antiochia · Allan · Phaliga · Chala · Izam · Aipolis · Neapolis · Seleucia · Zagrus · Charax · Apamia · Parthaunisa · Asaac · Siroc · Antiochia Margiana · Kabul · Alexandria · Phra · Girl · Nia · Coroc · Alexandropolis · Charax Spasini

Caspian Sea · ELBURZ MTS. · PARTHIA · ZAGROS MTS. · Tigris R. · Euphrates R. · Helmand R. · Indus R. · Persian Gulf · Mediterranean Sea · ROMAN EMPIRE · ARABIAN PENINSULA

45°E · 60°E · 30°N

☐ Parthian station

— Route of Isidore of Charax

0   150   300 mi.
0 150 300 km
Mercator Projection

10

The Caravan Camel		
Physical Feature	**Advantage**	**Effect**
Hump	stores fat	provides energy for long journeys
Eyelid	protects eye but lets light shine through when closed	able to see during sandstorms
Stomach	in 3 parts, can hold 50 gallons of water	able to make long journeys without water
Legs	strong, can carry up to 1,000 pounds	able to carry freight
Footpads	spread out when camel steps on them	helps with walking in sand

Merchants, Soldiers, Explorers, Pilgrims

Many who used Isidore's guide were merchants. But throughout history, people also have traveled on religious quests, to conquer other lands, and to explore unknown realms. And all travelers depended on the means of traveling available in their time.

Merchants

From about 1100 B.C., merchants trading in arid regions of Asia and the Middle East used camels to transport their goods. The sure-footed animals could carry up to 1,100 pounds and withstand both intense heat and extreme cold.

Traders often used long halters to tie many camels together to form **caravans.** Great caravans of as many as 5,000 camels trudged along various portions of a rugged 4,000-mile route between the Mediterranean Sea and the Chinese capital at Luoyang.

Soldiers

Soldiers and others who also needed swift transportation rode horses. Three inventions improved horseback riding: the stirrup, the bit, and the horseshoe. **Stirrups** are loops that hang down on both sides of a saddle. They hold the rider's feet and make it easier for riders to use their legs to control a horse. By A.D. 400, the Chinese had developed rigid metal stirrups which gave the rider more security in the saddle.

Another invention, the bit, originated in the Middle East, in about 1400 B.C. A bit is a metal piece that fits in the horse's mouth. It is attached to straps, or reins. Pulling on the reins moves the bit and signals the horse to stop or to turn.

The hard, paved roads of the Roman Empire damaged horses' hooves. So to protect their horses, the Romans developed the third invention, horseshoes. At first, Roman soldiers tied an iron plate over each hoof. But by A.D. 100, they nailed on iron shoes.

Though many people traveled on horseback, the most dramatic use of horses was for warfare. For example, the Mongols of central

▲ *For thousands of years, camels have enabled people in dry and desert regions to travel and ship goods over long, difficult terrain. Review the features of the camel that made it suitable for such journeys.*

Across Time & Space

Dates can sometimes reveal the thinking of those who use them. The most common historical dating system in the United States is B.C. and A.D. This system begins the year 1 at the supposed year of Jesus' birth. Thus B.C. means "Before Christ" and A.D. is Latin for "In the year of our Lord." Modern scholars often use C.E. for "Common era" and B.C.E. for "Before the common era."

11

Asia used stirrups to control their horses with their legs so that their hands were free. Experts with bow and arrow, they struck quickly and rode away before their victims could return the attack.

Explorers

Despite fragile ships and the dangers of the open seas, daring explorers set sail to discover what lay beyond the horizon. But, as the Roman Horace wrote in about 65 B.C., "Surely oak and threefold brass surrounded his heart who first trusted a frail vessel to the merciless ocean." Early sailing ships required good weather to reach their destinations. Rigged with rectangular sails, these ships had difficulty sailing against the wind. Also, sailors needed clear skies to see the stars and the shoreline by which they navigated.

Three innovations freed sailors from dependence on the weather: the lateen sail, the sternpost rudder, and the magnetic compass.

Around A.D. 150, a triangular sail known as the **lateen sail** was first used on the Mediterranean Sea. As shown below, the lateen sail enabled ships to sail more easily in any direction, regardless of the direction of the wind.

As early as 200 B.C., the Chinese used the **sternpost rudder** to steer their ships. It was a paddle-like device under the ship that could be moved from side to side. The rudder replaced the steering oar, which was cumbersome and ineffective on large ships. For centuries, sailors were unable to navigate through bad weather. But by the 1100s, the Chinese began to use the **magnetic compass.** A compass needle always points north, so sailors could navigate in any kind of weather.

Such innovations as these revolutionized sea transport.

▼ *Sailing ships travel against the wind by tacking, or often changing directions in a zigzag path. Compare the turning movement of the ship with a lateen sail to that with a rectangular sail. Why was the lateen sail such an important improvement?*

Wind

Wind

Lateen sail

Rectangular sail

Longer voyages became safer and more dependable. Now adventurous sea captains could sail into unknown regions of the seas. More important, they could find their way back.

Pilgrims

As transportation became safer and more reliable, more people began to travel. Pilgrims and adventurers traveled throughout the world and many wrote about their experiences.

From A.D. 629 to 645, Xuanzang *(shoo ahn DZAHNG),* a Chinese pilgrim, journeyed over 5,000 miles from China to India and back to collect Buddhist teachings. He recorded fantastic tales of his adventures. This excerpt describes the Hindu Kush mountains.

Journey of Xuanzang, A.D. 629–645

This mountain pass is very high; the precipices are wild and dangerous; the path is tortuous, and the caverns and hollows wind and intertwine together. At one time the traveler enters a deep valley, at another he mounts a high peak, which in full summer is blocked with frozen ice. By cutting steps up the ice, the traveler passes on, and after three days he comes to the highest point of the pass. There the icy wind, intensely cold, blows with fury; the piled snow fills the valleys. Travelers pushing their way though dare not pause on their route.

Another traveler motivated by religious beliefs was Ibn Battuta, a Muslim. In 1325, Ibn Battuta left his home in Tangier to journey to the Muslim holy city, Mecca, in Arabia. But the sights he saw and the people he met so fascinated him that he devoted the rest of his life to travel.

For 30 years, Ibn Battuta traveled in Arabia, Asia, Africa, and Spain. Like Xuanzang, he recorded many exciting adventures. These accounts shed new light on the world away from home. Describing the Nile River, Ibn Battuta wrote, "This river is most pleasant for navigating, most beautiful in aspect, most productive in fishes, abounding in birds, and its water is most wholesome and pleasant to drink. . . ."

Mapmakers used travelers' information like this to update their own maps of the world. Read A Moment in Time on page 14 to learn more about mapmakers. ■

▲ *Xuanzang's tales of his travels became a popular part of Chinese folklore. What do you think was the most difficult part of his journey? Why?*

◀ *This portrait of Xuanzang, from about A.D. 800, is painted on silk. His backpack is filled with some of the Buddhist writings he brought back to China from India.*

■ *In what ways did travel become easier between A.D. 150 and 1500?*

A Mapmaker

8:47 A.M., August 27, 1500
In the mapmaker's house,
Santoña, Spain

Letter
A letter from Columbus is the source of his information for the southern part of his map.

Globe
It gave the mapmaker a pattern for the northern part of the New World. Now he is adding the southern part to his new map. The map will change the way Europeans view the world.

Dividers
The mapmaker uses this instrument to plot distances on his map. He just read in Columbus's journal that the island of Hispaniola, where Columbus first landed in the New World, is bigger than Spain.

Smudge
Tracing Columbus's map of Hispaniola left a few carbon marks, but the mapmaker will rub them out with bread crumbs.

Rhumb Lines
Carefully drawn from the center circle, they'll be used by pilots to direct a ship's course.

Portrait
The mapmaker used this picture of a saint to connect the Northern and Southern hemispheres. He has no idea how they should be joined, and he hopes people will find his solution clever.

Early Maps

Xuanzang, Ibn Battuta, and other travelers collected a wealth of information. Each new journey provided mapmakers with another small piece of the world. Chinese, Indian, Persian, Arab, African, and Polynesian peoples also used their geographic knowledge to make maps.

The greatest geographer and mapmaker of the Roman Empire was Ptolemy *(TAHL uh mee; 90–168)*. He collected information from travelers to draw a remarkably accurate map of the world the Romans knew or knew about in 150.

In Europe, Ptolemy's work was neglected as the Roman Empire declined. For the next 1,000 years, European maps gave a distorted view of the world. The most common of these are called T-O maps. They show the continents of Europe, Asia, and Africa separated by bodies of water that together formed a "T." An ocean, which is the "O," encircles the three continents.

From the 1200s on, European mapmakers benefited from the study of others. Ptolemy's work, for example, was well known, translated, and thoroughly analyzed in the Muslim world. In the 800s, the astronomer Ahmad al-Faraghani

(ahl fahr uh GAHN ee), working for the ruler of the Muslim Empire, led a team of scientists in measuring a degree of longitude in order to accurately calculate the size of the earth. Technical knowledge also came from the East, and included the astrolabe, compass, and quadrant.

In Spain in the 1100s, Muslim, Jewish, and Christian scholars prepared translations of scientific material on medicine, astronomy, geography, cartography, and mathematics. From there the books were brought to the new universities of Europe. This knowledge helped Europeans explore and map the world beyond their shores. ■

▲ *Many Christian mapmakers put Jerusalem at the center of their maps. Find three or four landmarks that appear on this map and on the map on pages 518 and 519. How do their locations here differ from the map in the Atlas?*

■ *How did travelers and explorers change people's view of the world?*

R E V I E W

1. **FOCUS** How did geographic knowledge increase in the years between A.D. 150 and 1500?
2. **CONNECT** How would the stirrup, the bit, and horseshoes have affected communications by A.D. 500?
3. **GEOGRAPHY** What areas of early maps were most likely to be accurate? Why?
4. **ECONOMICS** Why did traders choose camels instead of horses as pack animals on trade routes through Asia and the Middle East?

5. **CRITICAL THINKING** Explain this statement: Since A.D. 150, the knowledge gathered from many different peoples helped produce changes in travel and communication.
6. **WRITING ACTIVITY** Write a "travel guide" telling someone how to get to a certain place. Use physical features, directions, and estimates of time to describe the route. Do not use mileage, number of blocks, road signs, or other modern conveniences.

L E S S O N   3

Traveling Through the Past

THINKING
FOCUS

How do historians recon-struct the past?

Key Terms

- history
- prehistory
- archaeology
- primary source
- secondary source

➤ *An Aztec artisan crafted this mask by covering the front of a human skull with pieces of turquoise and lignite.*

hen Moctezuma . . . pointed out his great city and all the others standing in the water and on the land around the lake.

That huge . . ., temple stood so high that from [the top] one could see over everything: three causeways leading into Mexico . . . the aqueduct of Chapultepec which supplied the city with the finest water, the wooden bridges built certain distances apart on the three causeways through which the lake water flowed. We beheld on that great lake a multitude of canoes loaded with provisions. We saw how it was impossible to pass from house to house . . . except by drawbridges . . . or in canoes. We saw in those cities . . . oratories all gleaming white and wonderful to behold.

From *Cortés and the Conquest of Mexico by the Spaniards in 1521*

Twenty-seven years after Columbus first landed in the West Indies, a band of Spanish adventurers arrived in Mexico. They had come to find fortunes of gold.

In 1519, the Aztec and their leader, Moctezuma, welcomed Hernando Cortés and 650 explorers to their capital at Tenochtitlán *(tay nawch tee TLAN)*. In the above description of the arrival of the Spanish, Spanish explorer Bernal Díaz gives us a look at the astonishing Aztec city, built over the shallow waters of Lake Texcoco.

Just two years later, Tenochtitlán lay in ruins, its once magnificent buildings burnt to the ground, its causeways and canals filled with rubble. Cortés's army had destroyed the city in his quest to conquer the Aztec.

How do we know about the ruined city, the Aztec, Cortés, and the Spanish conquest? The relic on this page tells us, wordlessly, of the Aztec's skill and artistry. The words of the Spanish explorer Bernal Díaz also speak to us, across almost 500 years, of the glorious city.

Studying the Past

Just as early explorers and mapmakers expanded the world view of their time, historians expand our view of the past. **History** is the record of past human events. To reconstruct history, historians must study nonwritten and written sources. To reconstruct the history of the Aztec, they studied both.

Nonwritten Sources

To study **prehistory,** or history before the development of writing, historians must rely on silent remains, such as fossils, ruins, and artifacts. **Archaeology** is the science of finding and studying these physical remains. Some people wrongly use "prehistoric" to mean "uncivilized," but to archaeologists, "prehistory" is a useful term.

Written Sources

Written sources date back only to about 3200 B.C., when writing was developed in the Middle East.

A wide variety of written materials exists, including scrolls, tablets, inscriptions, calendars, maps, letters, documents, and books.

Primary sources are those written by people who participated in or observed the events they describe. For example, in the last lesson, Ibn Battuta's account of the Nile is a primary source. **Secondary sources** are written after an event, usually with the aid of primary sources. A story that retold Ibn Battuta's experience would be a secondary source.

Historians prefer primary sources, because the people who observed or took part in events usually tell a more accurate story. Historians carefully check the accuracy of every source to make sure they get a true view of the past.

In some cases, careful study of historical evidence leads to changes in our view of the past. For example, a document known as the *Donation of Constantine* gave the Roman Catholic popes power over Italy and western Europe. The document was supposedly written during Constantine's reign (c. A.D. 274–337). In 1440, Italian historian Lorenzo Valla analyzed the text to prove that it was a forgery, written hundreds of years after Constantine's death! ■

▲ *Archaeological teams remove and study tiny pieces of earth bit by bit to reveal clues about the past. The workers below are excavating an ancient tomb in Peru.*

■ *Explain the difference between primary and secondary sources.*

Interpreting the Past

How Do We Know?

HISTORY *In 1978, a Mexico City utility worker struck a stone slab that lay 15 feet below street level. He had discovered the Aztec capital of Tenochtitlán, buried for more than four centuries. Project Great Temple exposed over 5,500 objects created by Aztec laborers and artisans.*

➤ *This page was copied from an Aztec tribute roll, a kind of book with pages made of bark. It shows some of the varied goods that came into Tenochtitlan from the empire: jade beads, birds and feathers, animal skins, and pots of honey.*

Like Lorenzo Valla, a good historian has to be a good detective, evaluating the accuracy and the meaning of all sources. A historian must also be a judge, choosing among conflicting interpretations of the past.

Differing Views of the Past

People's backgrounds clearly affect the way they see an event as well as how they choose to tell the story. For example, in Chapter 16 you will read about the mighty empires of the Aztec and Inca peoples and how they were destroyed by a combination of factors. In the 1500s, the Europeans came with advanced weaponry, horses, and disease. They brought about the downfall of Tenochtitlan *(tehn ouch tiht LAHN)*, the Aztec capital. As you might imagine, Aztec and Spanish primary sources describe these events very differently.

UNDERSTANDING HISTORY

After Cortés's conquest of Tenochtitlán, an Aztec poet lamented the destruction of his city. "The ways are strewn with broken lances," he wrote. "The houses are without roofs." The Aztec poet's name is not known to us, but his words give us a valuable glimpse of Mexican history.

Changing History

History is the study of past events, such as the Spanish conquest of the Aztec. Traditionally, we learn history from the point of view of the winners—in this case, the Spanish. However, hearing an Aztec voice helps us to understand another important part of the story.

The study of history is not just the discovery and listing of facts and events. Historians also attempt to find meaning in those facts and events. But most facts can be interpreted many different ways, so history can never be purely factual. Both the source's and the historian's point of view influence the way history is eventually written.

Future History

Just as history can never be completely objective, a "final" history can never be written. New historians will discover new sources to study and find new questions to ask of the old sources. People will always debate what history means. And as long as people exist, they will be creating history for future historians.

During the 1400s, the Aztecs had seen tremendous advances in the arts, crafts, and learning. Poetry was an Aztec strength. It is not surprising that after the fall of Tenochtitlan, a now-unknown Aztec poet wrote these lines:

> We are crushed to the ground;
> we lie in ruins.
> There is nothing but grief and suffering
> in Mexico and Tlatelolco
> where once we saw beauty and valor.

Compare the Aztec poet's feelings with those of the Spanish soldier and adventurer Bernal Díaz del Castillo. He was with Cortés on his journey and later wrote his memoirs, which also described the fall of Tenochtitlan:

> Some [soldiers] would rob [the Aztecs] of everything they had. We soldiers, on the other hand, who were fighting on the causeways and on land, gained no profit, but plenty of arrows and lance-thrusts and wounds from darts and stones.

Historians must ask when, where, why, and by whom a source was written. The answers to these questions help them evaluate how accurate or biased a source is.

Expanding Views of the Past

History has been called a jigsaw puzzle, with some of the pieces missing. As time passes, new pieces are found. Historians continually revisit the past and reinterpret history in light of new information. In doing so, they change our world view as much as the early geographers who changed the world's map. ■

■ *How do historians evaluate the accuracy of their sources?*

◀ *This Spanish map dates from 1556 and shows Lake Texcoco and the Aztec capital of Tenochtitlan. What reasons do you think the Spanish had for mapping Mexico?*

R E V I E W

1. **FOCUS** How do historians reconstruct the past?
2. **CONNECT** What kinds of primary sources are being created today with the use of electronic communications devices?
3. **HISTORY** Name three sources from which historians have learned about the Aztec civilization.
4. **CRITICAL THINKING** How do you think changing our view of the past affects our world view today?
5. **WRITING ACTIVITY** Choose an event at your school that could have two or more interpretations. Write either an accurate or a biased account of the event. Then exchange papers with a classmate. As a historian, would you use your classmate's account as a reliable primary source? Why or why not? Give examples to support your decision.

A Changing World View

Archaeology: Clues and Connections

*P*ieces of a bowl, broken tools, rusted coins—when archaeologists dig up things like these, they study them eagerly. Everyday items are clues to the lives of the people who used them: What did they eat and drink? How did they travel? Did they play games?

What people throw out tells as much about a society as what people keep. Mountains of garbage give contemporary anthropologists ample material for study.

Get Ready

Gather items for a "trash" bag from your trash at home. Be sure they are "clean" items, because a classmate will study them to find clues about your family. Rinse out any jars, bottles, or cans. Include anything that gives hints about your family's life—pets, number or age of children, hobbies, or work. Cut the labels off magazines and the address portion off letters.

Find Out

Your teacher will hand out one bag of trash to each student. Make a list of the items in the bag you receive. What does each item tell you? Is there any indication of a family pet: An empty dog-food box? A kitty litter bag? What about ages of

◄ Every level of this archaeological site dates from a different time period. Archaeologists dig through the layers, sifting the dirt through a fine screen. In this way they catch even the tiniest clues about the past.

the family members: A baby-food jar? A letter from a Cub Scout leader? Did you find anything that suggests work or a hobby: Computer printouts? Pieces of yarn? *Popular Mechanics* magazine? Does anything reveal the family's size: A giant catsup jar? A jumbo container for laundry detergent?

Move Ahead

Make a chart listing the clues you found. Next to each clue, list what you learned or guessed from it. For example:

Clues	*Facts and Guesses*
cat-food can	pet cat
pieces of yarn	someone knits
baby-food jar	baby in house
sawdust	woodworking

Be sure that every fact or guess is supported by a clue.

Explore Some More

Take a look around the classroom. Suppose it were frozen exactly as it is at this moment. If archaeologists were to dig it up in 1,000 years, what might they conclude? List everything in the room that could be a clue to 20th-century life in your school, in your town, or in the United States.

▲ For what purpose might this Peruvian pottery vessel have been created? Note the stone and shell designs pressed into the clay.

Chapter Review

Reviewing Key Terms

archaeology (p. 17)
caravan (p. 11)
electronic communication (p. 7)
history (p. 17)
lateen sail (p. 14)
magnetic compass (p. 14)

prehistory (p. 17)
primary source (p. 17)
satellite (p. 7)
secondary source (p. 17)
sternpost rudder (p. 14)
stirrups (p. 11)

A. On your own paper, explain why each invention below is important.
1. lateen sail
2. stern-post rudder
3. magnetic compass
4. stirrups
5. satellite
6. electronic communications

B. Answer each question below. Use the key term that is in parentheses in your answer.
1. How did merchants of Asia and the Middle East transport goods overland? (caravan)
2. Why was the invention of writing important to our study of the past? (history)
3. How do historians piece together written evidence of the past? (primary sources)
4. What do "silent remains" contribute to our study of the past? (prehistory)
5. How might we discover and describe a lost city of which there is no written record? (archaeology)
6. Why do we need more than just eyewitness accounts of history? (secondary sources)

Exploring Concepts

A. In this chapter, you read how people in the past expanded their view of the world. Copy and complete the cluster diagram below. Add examples from the chapter of inventions, historical events, and other things that helped expand our world view.

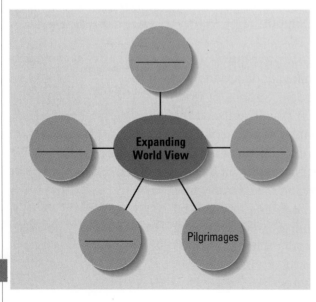

B. Answer each question using information from the chapter.
1. Why did the distance between Rome and Paris, or Lutetia, seem greater in the time of the Roman Empire than it does today?
2. Why was sea travel during the time of the Roman Empire unreliable and dangerous?
3. Compare the speed of communication in the Roman Empire with today.
4. What common role did early soldiers, explorers, merchants, and pilgrims play in expanding the world view of their time?
5. What did travelers such as Ibn Battuta and Xuanzang contribute to mapmaking?
6. How did European geographers benefit from the learning of others?
7. How do historians determine how reliable a primary source is?
8. How do historians affect our world view?
9. Describe how we can "travel" into the past.

Reviewing Skills

1. Use the map at the right to answer the following questions.
   a. When it is 10 A.M. in Seattle, what time is it in Mexico City?
   b. What is the time difference between Detroit and Honolulu?
2. Look at the map on pages 8–9. How many time zones does Africa have? Count from Dakar to Nairobi.
3. Twins are born on a ship. The child who is born first has a birth date one day later than the child who is born last. Where is the ship, and in which direction is it traveling?
4. Suppose you are going to fly from Dallas, Texas, to Paris, France. Your flight is scheduled to arrive in Paris at 7:58 A.M. What could you use to determine the time your watch will show on your arrival in Paris, if you don't reset it during the flight?

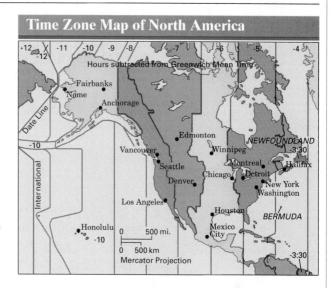

Time Zone Map of North America

Using Critical Thinking

1. A writer has described our world today as a "global village" that has resulted from electronic communications. Based on what you know from the chapter about the limited world view of people of the past and about electronic communications, make an inference about what a global village is. Write a paragraph to explain what led you to this inference.
2. The Romans didn't know that such a place as Australia existed. In fact, they knew nothing of the entire Pacific Ocean. Suppose that somehow a Roman had learned of the existence of the rest of the earth and reported it to the emperor. Imagine the impact such a discovery would have made on Roman society. Now try to imagine what kind of a discovery would have the same impact today. Write a paragraph describing the discovery. Then write another paragraph explaining why you think this discovery would have such an impact.

Preparing for Citizenship

1. COLLECTING INFORMATION The telegraph was one of the first forms of electronic communication. Research the different ways messages were sent before the invention of the telegraph in 1837. Make a notebook that shows as many different methods of communication as you can find. Arrange your notebook from the earliest method to the most recent. Be sure to tell where and when each method was used and how it worked.

2. COLLABORATIVE LEARNING Read about the history of your community or school and discuss it as a class. Locate a primary source that describes an event in your community or school's history. Form committees. Each committee should write its own description of the historical event based on the information in the primary source. As a class, compare the secondary sources written by the committees. Does each secondary source portray the event accurately? In what ways do they differ?

Chapter 2
Empires of the Ancient World

What was happening to the mighty Roman Empire? The Persians challenged its eastern borders. Wave after wave of barbarian tribes swept down from Europe and central Asia. Political quarrels and economic problems forced leaders to split the empire in two. Even so, conditions in the western half of the empire worsened. But the eastern empire—the Byzantine Empire—prospered. Power in the ancient world was shifting to the east.

Barbarian invaders, shown on the bronze clasps above, overran the Western Roman Empire in the 400s. Yet the empire remained strong in eastern areas like Jordan (left).

527–548 Empress Theodora (above), considered the most powerful woman in Byzantine history, rules with her husband Justinian.

	250	B.C.	A.D.		250		500

27 B.C.

C. A.D. 200 Bantu-speaking peoples continue expansion through eastern and southeastern Africa.

300–525 During the Gupta Dynasty, India trades with the Eastern Roman Empire, Persia, and China.

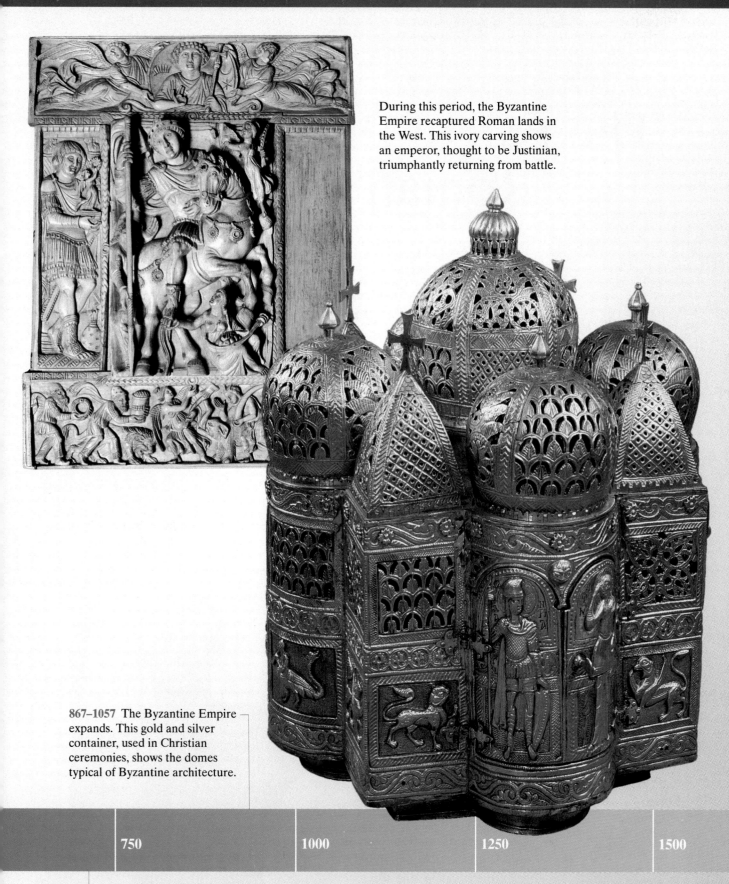

During this period, the Byzantine Empire recaptured Roman lands in the West. This ivory carving shows an emperor, thought to be Justinian, triumphantly returning from battle.

867–1057 The Byzantine Empire expands. This gold and silver container, used in Christian ceremonies, shows the domes typical of Byzantine architecture.

750	1000	1250	1500	

732 Christian forces in France defeat Muslim invaders.

A.D. 1453

250   27   500   476   750   1000   1250   1500

The Fall of the Roman Empire

The world has grown old and lost its former vigor. . . . Winter no longer gives rain enough to swell the seed, nor summer enough to toast the harvest . . . the mountains are gutted and give less marble, the mines are exhausted and give less silver and gold . . . the fields lack farmers, the seas sailors, the encampments soldiers . . . there is no justice in judgments, competence in trades, discipline in daily life.

THINKING FOCUS

What led to the collapse of the Western Roman Empire?

Key Terms

- province
- barbarian

This description, written in about A.D. 250 by one of the Roman Empire's church leaders, foretells the fate of that mighty empire. Within 200 years of the writing of this description, the Roman Empire would suffer great military and economic crises, weaken, and eventually collapse.

The Empire in Prosperity

From 27 B.C. to A.D. 14, Julius Caesar's adopted son Octavian ruled as Rome's first emperor. Octavian was given the name Augustus, which means the revered or exalted one. As emperor, Augustus put an end to the chaos and power struggles that had occurred within the Roman Empire after Julius Caesar's assassination. Caesar and Augustus also expanded the empire by conquering the territory that ran along the Rhine and Danube rivers.

➤ *Roman emperors were often depicted in military dress. The carved figures on the breastplate of Augustus's armor represent a Roman victory over a Persian army.*

Expanding the Empire

Roman conquests of new territory continued under the emperors after Augustus. By A.D. 117, the Roman Empire had reached its greatest size. It extended from Britain in the north to Africa in the south and from Spain in the west to Syria in the east.

The lands and peoples captured by the empire were organized into **provinces,** or territories, of Rome. Rome maintained peace in its provinces by allowing individuals to continue living and working as usual. However, Roman officials did institute Roman laws in these territories. In addition, they appointed governors to rule the provinces and make sure that Roman law was enforced there.

Profiting from the Provinces

Rome benefited from its empire in many ways. Since enemies could reach Rome only by crossing the provinces, these territories pro-

tected Rome by acting as a buffer zone. They also produced food and other goods for the city of Rome. For example, Egypt and North Africa supplied Rome with most of

▲ *As powerful as it was, the Roman Empire did not last. How did its boundaries change as it weakened?*

▲ *Here Egyptian grain is loaded on a barge for shipment to Rome.*

27

Empires of the Ancient World

its wheat. Trade with the provinces brought wealth to Roman citizens. The people in the provinces also paid taxes, which supported the government and the army of about 300,000 men distributed along the empire's frontiers. For a long time, the empire was well fed, strong, and wealthy.

Because Rome was strong, the empire was peaceful and stable, which benefited everyone in it. The government built roads that connected the provinces to Rome. It also funded the construction of aqueducts. Aqueducts were used to pipe drinking water from wells and springs to the people. ■

The Empire in Crisis

The Roman army along the frontiers managed to protect the Romans for many years. But, beginning in A.D. 161, some ene-mies broke across the frontiers to

invade the Roman Empire itself. This became a serious problem for the Romans.

Across Time & Space

The word barbarian *was originally used in the Roman Empire to de-scribe people from out-side the empire who spoke a different lan-guage and had a different culture. Over time, the term* barbarian *has come to mean a person who is uncivilized and warlike.*

▼ *Roman impact on the provinces can be seen in the ruins of a city built by the Romans in Palmyra, Syria.*

Border Problems Increase

Along the empire's central and eastern borders lived tribes of Germanic peoples who were not all content to live peacefully with Rome. The Romans called these peoples **barbarians,** meaning people who speak a different language. Tacitus, a Roman historian from the first century, described the barbarians as having "blue eyes, and reddish hair; great bodies, especially powerful for attack, but not equally patient of hard work."

By the 200s, some of these Germanic peoples had established villages along the Rhine and Danube rivers and were peacefully exchanging goods and ideas with Romans. Some became allies of the Romans. Many barbarian men entered the Roman army and helped to defend the frontiers against invasion by hostile barbarian tribes. In return, they and their families were granted land within the empire and a yearly salary. Some even adopted Latin as their language.

Then, in the late 300s, thousands of barbarians began seeking refuge within the empire to escape the Huns. The Huns, a fierce group of nomadic warriors, were sweeping west from the central plains of Asia, conquering everyone in their path. Roman border patrols were unable to limit the number of barbarians entering the empire during this massive migration. So, many hostile barbarians were actually able to enter the empire's borders and still keep their weapons.

Barbarian invaders reached deep into the empire.

Internal Problems Mount

To complicate the situation further, a struggle for political control was occurring in the empire. From A.D. 193 on, many men tried to claim control of the empire. Many of them were generals who, backed by their armies, took the throne by force. Rivals for the throne began to promise higher salaries to the armies in return for their support, but this strained the empire's treasury.

The combination of barbarian invasions and fighting between Roman armies for control of the empire ruined the countryside. Such unrest made it very difficult for farmers to produce enough food. Food shortages resulted, making available food very costly.

In an attempt to cope with the economic problems of the empire, the government minted more coins. But, because government stores of gold and silver had been reduced, the new coins were filled

▲ *In this early third-century relief, country people wearing typical hooded cloaks bring money to a tax collector who is surrounded by his staff.*

◄ *Ostrogoths wore helmets similar to the one at left in the 500s.*

How Do We Know?

HISTORY *The coin pictured below gives us visual evidence that the barbarians had an impact on the Roman Empire. The coin, from A.D. 8, illustrates Roman Emperor Augustus receiving a child from a barbarian.*

29

■ *Support this statement: The barbarians were both allies and enemies of the Romans.*

with other, less precious metals as well. The new coins weighed the same as the old ones, but they were actually worth less. If merchants had been willing to accept these new coins at their face value, minting such coins might have solved the financial troubles of the empire. But they would not do so. Instead, merchants charged more coins to exact the same value for their goods. ■

The Empire in Transition

When Diocletian became emperor in 284, he made some changes in an attempt to correct the empire's problems. He divided rule over the empire among four men. With two rulers to oversee the east and two to oversee the west, he hoped to make governing the empire an easier task. Each ruler had his own capital and administrative staff. He established four capitals because from Rome alone he could not adequately govern the vast territory belonging to the empire. Diocletian moved his capital from Rome to Nicomedia, a city a few miles south of Byzantium in Asia Minor.

Diocletian hoped that this division of the empire would help prevent civil wars caused by rivals for the throne. He also hoped that it would make the empire easier to manage and defend.

In response to barbarian pressures on the empire, Diocletian increased the size of the Roman army from 300,000 men to 500,000. The increases of both the civil administration and the military meant large increases in government spending. This further emptied the empire's treasury.

The Rise of the East

Diocletian's successor, Constantine, also worked to stabilize the empire. To this end, he decided to establish a stronger eastern capital city. Constantine chose the old Greek trading town of Byzantium as the site for his new capital in 324. Find this city on the map on page 27.

Byzantium possessed great military and economic advantages. With water on three sides and the Balkan mountains on the fourth, enemies would find the city difficult to attack. Its location also made it a perfect stopping place both for merchants traveling overland and for those traveling by sea between Europe and the East Indies.

From 324 to 330, Constantine had Byzantium completely rebuilt

▼ *Look at the map on page 27 to see which tribes took over the Western Roman Empire.*

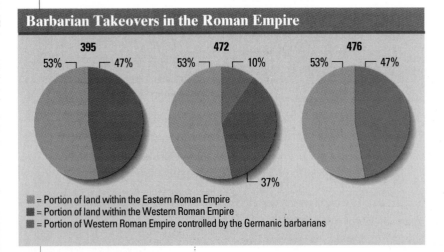

Barbarian Takeovers in the Roman Empire

395	472	476
53% ⌐ ⌐ 47%	53% ⌐ ⌐ 10%	53% ⌐ ⌐ 47%
	⌐ 37%	

■ = Portion of land within the Eastern Roman Empire
■ = Portion of land within the Western Roman Empire
■ = Portion of Western Roman Empire controlled by the Germanic barbarians

to resemble Rome. On May 11, 330, he renamed it "New Rome which is Constantine's City." The people called it Constantine's City. In Greek this is *Konstantinoupolis.* Thus, the city eventually became known as Constantinople.

Constantinople suffered from political quarrels and barbarian invasions, but it was the western half of the empire that suffered most. So, in an attempt to solve these problems, Emperor Theodosius I wrote into his will that upon his death the eastern and western sections of the empire should be declared separate empires. Use the map on page 27 to find the border between the two empires. When Theodosius died in 395, his will officially split the Roman Empire in two. Today, scholars use the term *Roman Empire* for the Western Roman Empire and the term *Byzantine Empire* for the Eastern Roman Empire.

The Fall of the West

The Byzantine Empire prospered for the next 1,000 years. However, the Roman Empire never recovered from its troubles. Spain, Gaul, and North Africa were overrun by barbarian invaders. As shown on the map on page 27, the barbarians set up their own kingdoms. In 410, the city of Rome was raided. By the late 400s, emperors of the Roman Empire were little more than puppets. In 476, a barbarian general overthrew the last of these Roman emperors, bringing the Roman Empire to an end. ■

◄ *The oldest surviving view of Constantinople was created in 1420. How many years earlier had Constantine established the city as Constantinople?*

■ *What did Diocletian do to strengthen the empire?*

R E V I E W

1. **FOCUS** What led to the collapse of the Western Roman Empire?
2. **CONNECT** In what ways might the roads, aqueducts, and buildings that the government funded have improved the living conditions in the provinces?
3. **HISTORY** Why did the government limit the number of barbarians entering the empire at any one time?
4. **ECONOMICS** Why didn't minting more coins solve the empire's economic problems?
5. **CRITICAL THINKING** Why was the Eastern Roman Empire able to survive and prosper while the Western Roman Empire crumbled?
6. **ACTIVITY** Make a list of the problems that led to the collapse of the Roman Empire. Rank the items in your list from most important to least important. Compare your list to those made by other members of your class and defend your ranking.

L E S S O N   2

Acquainted Cultures

It's hard to imagine any benefits arising from war. Yet, all around the Mediterranean, as Romans, Germans, Persians, Arabs, Berbers, and other peoples fought, they also learned from each other. In fact, any encounter between people of different cultures, whether in war or in trade, leads to an exchange of ideas. Thus, the peoples of Rome, Persia, India, and China, being acquainted, or in touch with one another, influenced each other's beliefs, customs, arts, and sciences. Look at the timelines on page 33 to see how these cultures came into contact.

Key Term

• dynasty

▲ *This image of a Sassanid king is made from gold and silver.*

Sassanid Persia

Perhaps no two Mediterranean peoples encountered each other as frequently in battle as did the peoples of the Roman and Persian empires. Two of the major causes of conflict between Rome and Persia were fights about the border between these two empires and disagreement about political control of Armenia. Armenia acted as an important buffer zone between the two powers. It was in the best interest of both Rome and Persia to have some control over the leadership in Armenia. As long as both countries had some control over this leadership, neither one could use Armenia as a base for a full-scale invasion of the other's territory or as a starting point for a surprise attack.

At War

Eventually, Armenia was split between the Romans and the Persians. In the 300s, Armenia was the first country in the world to make Christianity its state religion, and a "golden age" followed. Armenia fell under the rule of the Ottomans, which later proved disastrous. In spite of foreign rule, however, Armenians—who achieved modern-day independence in 1991—have held onto their unique culture and their Armenian Church. There are now some six million Armenians in the world.

From the beginning of the Persian Sassanid **dynasty,** or family rule, in A.D. 224, until its end in 641, the Persians and Romans often fought for control of Armenia. At the same time, the Persians were also busy defending their borders against invasions by barbarians from the plains of Europe and against the Huns from Asia.

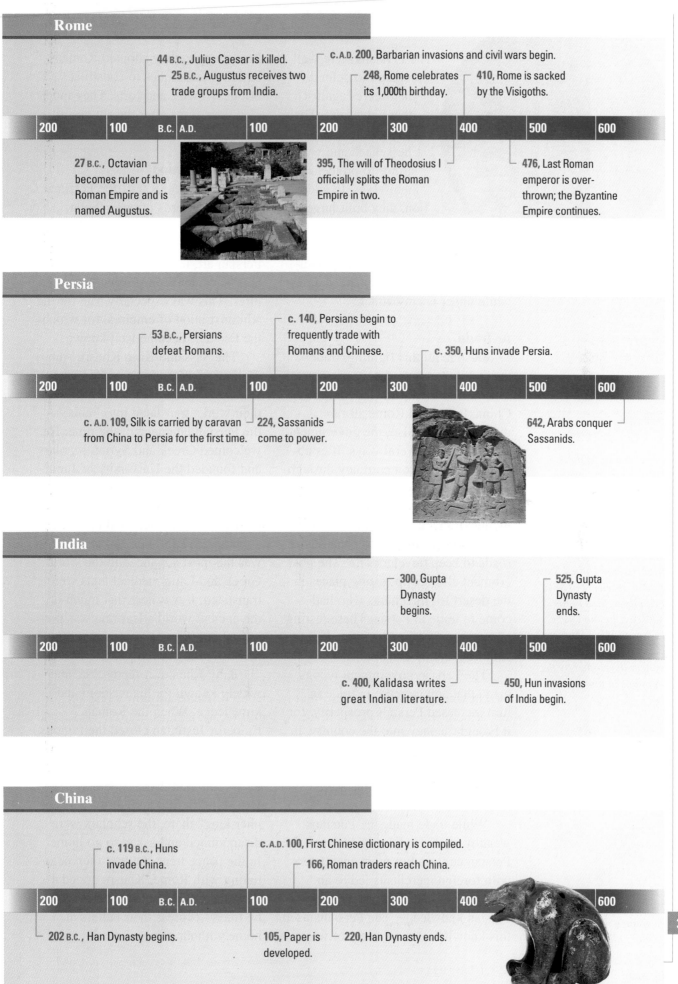

Rome

- **44 B.C.**, Julius Caesar is killed.
- **25 B.C.**, Augustus receives two trade groups from India.
- **C.A.D. 200**, Barbarian invasions and civil wars begin.
- **248**, Rome celebrates its 1,000th birthday.
- **410**, Rome is sacked by the Visigoths.

| 200 | 100 | B.C. | A.D. | 100 | 200 | 300 | 400 | 500 | 600 |

- **27 B.C.**, Octavian becomes ruler of the Roman Empire and is named Augustus.
- **395**, The will of Theodosius I officially splits the Roman Empire in two.
- **476**, Last Roman emperor is overthrown; the Byzantine Empire continues.

Persia

- **53 B.C.**, Persians defeat Romans.
- **c. 140**, Persians begin to frequently trade with Romans and Chinese.
- **c. 350**, Huns invade Persia.

| 200 | 100 | B.C. | A.D. | 100 | 200 | 300 | 400 | 500 | 600 |

- **c. A.D. 109**, Silk is carried by caravan from China to Persia for the first time.
- **224**, Sassanids come to power.
- **642**, Arabs conquer Sassanids.

India

- **300**, Gupta Dynasty begins.
- **525**, Gupta Dynasty ends.

| 200 | 100 | B.C. | A.D. | 100 | 200 | 300 | 400 | 500 | 600 |

- **c. 400**, Kalidasa writes great Indian literature.
- **450**, Hun invasions of India begin.

China

- **c. 119 B.C.**, Huns invade China.
- **c. A.D. 100**, First Chinese dictionary is compiled.
- **166**, Roman traders reach China.

| 200 | 100 | B.C. | A.D. | 100 | 200 | 300 | 400 | 500 | 600 |

- **202 B.C.**, Han Dynasty begins.
- **105**, Paper is developed.
- **220**, Han Dynasty ends.

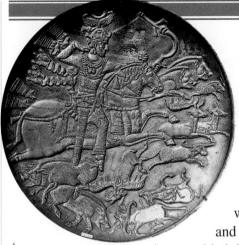

▲ *A Sassanid warrior mounted for battle rides across this silver bowl from c. 364.*

Across Time & Space

"Nothing stops these couriers from covering their allotted stages in the quickest possible time— neither snow, rain, heat, nor darkness." This saying closely resembles the motto of the United States Postal Service, but it was actually written in the 400s B.C. by the Greek historian Herodotus to describe a mail delivery system developed by the Persians in about 500 B.C.

■ *How did Persia become a wealthy trading nation?*

The Persians were well prepared to defend themselves against these attackers. Their soldiers fought on horseback and wore armor to protect themselves. In addition, they built large walls around their towns and fields. These walls enabled them to maintain possession of their food supply and shelter while under enemy attack.

At Trade

Despite all this fighting, trade thrived in Persia for many reasons. The overland trade routes connecting China, India, and Rome all ran through Persia. Also, the government aided trade in several ways. It established one common currency throughout the country so that anywhere in Persia a traveler could use the same money. It maintained the roads and even assigned soldiers to patrol those roads to keep travelers safe. The government also set up resting places in the desert for merchants who had come to trade in Persia. These resting places were equipped with water, supplies, and meeting halls.

The Persian government recognized that any increase in trade in turn increased Persia's prosperity, for it brought money into the country. In addition, the government found a way to make even more money by charging a tax on any goods that were carried in or out of the country.

While trade made the Persians wealthy, it also indirectly enriched the Persian culture. For most encounters with foreign merchants led to an exchange of ideas that increased Persian knowledge. The Persians used this knowledge in a variety of ways.

For example, they adopted Roman building techniques to construct bridges, towns, and forts. They modeled their ships after the single-sail vessels of Greece.

Persian Learning

Since the 500s B.C., the Persians had, in the words of one scholar, "behaved like a great cultural sponge." Over a thousand years of Persian art, learning, and culture nourished new conquerors and cultures. This was especially true for the administration of empires, for which the Persians became well known.

The Sassanid King Khusru Anusharvan *(KOOS roo an a SHAR van)* studied Plato and Aristotle. He had their works translated into Pahlavi, the Persian language of the time. He welcomed Greek and Syrian scholars and founded the University of Jundishapur *(juhn DISH a poor)*. Christians fleeing persecution from other Christians came there and opened up a medical school. For 200 years it was the most advanced in the world. Greek and Latin medical texts were translated. It was here that much of the ancient world's learning was preserved until it was retranslated by the Muslim rulers of the 800s.

King Khusru, it seems, became widely known for his wisdom and knowledge. When the Roman Emperor Justinian closed the famous school of philosophy at Athens and persecuted the non-Christian scholars, Khusru invited them to Persia. Expecting to find a kind of "philosopher-king" there, the scholars were disappointed and asked to go home. In the peace treaty he was then negotiating with Rome, Khusru added a special section so the scholars would be free to express their beliefs at home without persecution. ■

Gupta India

Not long after the founding of the Sassanid dynasty in Persia, a thriving economy and culture began developing in India. The well-run government of the Gupta dynasty existed from A.D. 300 to 467. It maintained the roads to ensure that traders had easy passage to and from India. In addition, the government did not subject its people to heavy taxes, so they had a decent standard of living.

Many of India's merchants also engaged in a prosperous trade with the Eastern Roman Empire, Persia, China, and the countries in Southeast Asia. India sold brassware, ivory, jewels, and even monkeys. The Gupta government profited from this trade by taxing both imports and exports.

The arts and sciences received great attention in this prospering society. Both painting and writing flourished. One of the greatest Indian writers and poets, Kalidasa, describes the results of a battle between the war god Kumara *(koo MAH rah)* and the demon Taraka *(tah RAH kah)* in the following excerpt.

*T*he sun put on a ghastly robe
of great and terrible snakes,
    curling together,
as if to mark his joy
at the death of the enemy
    demon.

Kalidasa, "Kumara's Fight Against the Demon Taraka," c. 400

UNDERSTANDING CIVILIZATION

*T*he civilizations of Rome, Persia, India, and China were all very different. But they shared common traits. According to historians, a civilization is a society that has cities, a written language, specialized jobs, an organized government, technology, and skilled craftspeople.

Not all societies are complex enough to be civilizations. Early hunter-gatherers never settled long enough in one place to build cities or organize a government. They had a distinctive culture, but not a civilization.

Not all societies are civilizations. It depends on how complex they are. Once, Europeans judged that more complex civilizations were more valuable than simpler ones. They used "uncivilized" to mean "inferior." But we know that is not true.

Development

Civilizations first developed as people learned how to increase their food supply. Farming freed people from looking for food. With more spare time, people developed specialized skills. Soon they produced surplus goods as well as surplus food. People traded surpluses for things that they did not have.

People needed places to meet and trade goods, so they built towns and markets. To keep business records, they developed systems of writing and numbers.

Today, trade still plays a major role in the way civilizations grow and change. Through trade, civilizations exchange ideas, inventions, and goods and they learn about each other.

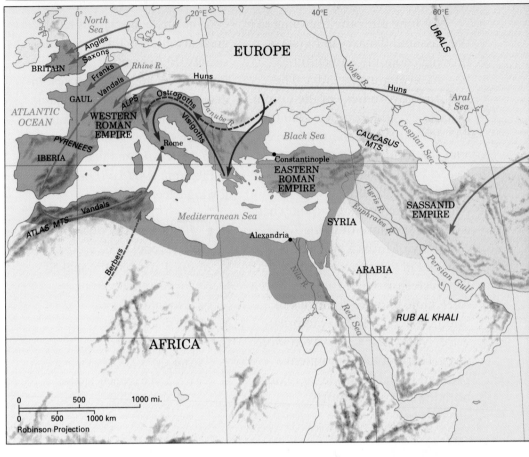

Which invading group attacked both China and the Western Roman Empire?

In the sciences, Indians created a number system, developed the concept of zero, and discovered that the earth rotates on its axis.

However, in 480, Hun invasions began to weaken the prosperous Gupta dynasty. By 525, the Hun invaders had conquered India. They ruled over the people there for the next 200 years. ■

In what ways did India's culture benefit from the prosperity that existed between 300 and 500?

▼ *The Hun invasions of China are documented by these Chinese statues of Huns from the 500s.*

China

To the north of Gupta India lay the vast lands of China. Look at the map on page 37 to find China's boundaries. The Silk Road, a major overland trade route for Chinese silk and other goods, ran through northwest China, Persia, and the Roman Empire. Chinese junks, or ships, also sailed to India to trade their valuable silk and gold for glass and pearls.

The Chinese learned the teachings of Buddhism from Indian traders and missionaries they encountered. Indian ideas also influenced Chinese religious art. Large Chinese statues of Buddha are similar in pose and style to those created by Indian sculptors.

India was not the only area from which China imported goods. From the Middle East, the Chinese imported grapes, beans, and nut trees for their gardens. From Central Asia, they imported horses, which were extremely useful in warfare.

Like India, China was plagued by Hun invaders. In fact, emperors of the Han dynasty, who ruled China from 202 B.C. to A.D. 220, had to fight long and costly wars against the Huns. By 220, the Han dynasty had lost control of China completely. Chinese generals and upper class families, as well as Huns and other invading tribes, then fought each other for control of the country. For the next 360 years, China remained in a state of disunity. ■

■ *What were some of the goods China traded? What are some of the goods they obtained in exchange for these items?*

R E V I E W

1. **FOCUS** In what ways did the peoples of various cultures benefit from their contact with each other?

2. **CONNECT** How might Rome's battles with Persia have contributed to the Western Roman Empire's decline?

3. **CULTURE** In what ways did the peoples of Persia, India, and China influence each other's cultures, and how did they come into contact with one another?

4. **CULTURE** What are some aspects of Chinese culture that were influenced by Gupta Indians?

5. **CRITICAL THINKING** How might the barbarians and Huns have furthered the cultural exchange between Rome, Persia, India, and China?

6. **WRITING ACTIVITY** The cultures of Rome, Persia, India, and China have all influenced the United States. Write about how one of these cultures has influenced our beliefs, customs, arts, or sciences.

37

Empires of the Ancient World

A King's Adviser

Translated and adapted by Hassan Tehranchian

This fable, from Kalilah and Dimnah, originated in India, and from there passed in translation to Arabia and on to Persia. What lesson does the fable teach, and is there any meaning in it for you today?

In Lesson 2 you learned that countries become "acquainted" through trade, war, and cultural exchange. The following fable is an example of that mixing of cultures.

Shanzibah
(SHAN zih bah)
Nanibah (NAN ih bah)

O nce upon a time there was a merchant who owned two bulls, Shanzibah and Nanibah. The merchant and his bulls were on a journey to a faraway land when Shanzibah accidentally fell into a deep hole. After much tugging and pulling, the merchant was finally able to get Shanzibah out and back on his feet. But the poor animal was so injured that he could not travel any farther. So the merchant found a man to take care of Shanzibah until he was better.

The man was supposed to return Shanzibah to the merchant when the bull had recovered. But, after only one day, the untrustworthy man became tired and bored. He left the poor, unhappy animal all alone and returned to the merchant, telling him that Shanzibah had died.

But fortune smiled on Shanzibah and he recovered all by himself, and set out to find food. To his amazement, he came upon a beautiful field that was full of brightly colored flowers and vegetables of all kinds. Shanzibah rested, and ate so well that he soon became healthy again. He felt so lucky and happy that one day, out of pure joy, Shanzibah let out a very loud bellow.

At the same time there was a lion who lived near the field. This lion was the king of many other animals. Although he was strong and brave, he had never seen a bull or heard one bellow before, so when he heard Shanzibah's loud voice he became very frightened. But since the lion did not want the other animals to know that he was afraid, he decided to stay close to home, instead of roaming far and wide all over his kingdom, as he used to.

Kalilah (KAH lih lah)
Dimnah (DIHM nah)

Among the lion's subjects were two clever jackals named Kalilah and Dimnah. One day Dimnah, who was more ambitious and greedy, asked Kalilah, "Why do you think the lion has been staying at home so much lately?"

Puzzled by the question, Kalilah answered, "Why are you so interested in the king? It's really none of our business. We are comfortable and rich under the lion's rule, and besides, we're not friendly enough with the king to give him advice. It would be better to mind your own business and leave the king's alone. . . ."

Dimnah answered cleverly, "Only ambitious and hard-working people reach high positions. If someone works very hard he can raise his position in life. On the other hand, a weak person will cause his own downfall. We should seek higher positions and not be satisfied with what we have now."

"Then," demanded Kalilah, "tell me what you have in mind."

Dimnah explained: "I would like to introduce myself to the lion. He is upset, and I'm sure I can make him happy with my advice. By doing that I will win his confidence."

"But," asked Kalilah, "how do you know that the lion is upset?"

"I know it because I am so intelligent," said Dimnah. "An intelligent man can sense when something is wrong."

"But," answered Kalilah, "how are you going to become an adviser to the lion? You have never served a king before."

Dimnah had a ready answer. "The king's attendants were not given their ranks and positions all at once; they slowly were moved up from lower positions. If I can get close to the lion I will try to understand him and I will be honest and obedient. I will encourage him to act in a way that will help his people. And when I disagree with his plans, I will try, without offending him, to show what will happen if he follows his own plan. I will be so honest and helpful that I will become his most important adviser. When the lion recognizes my knowledge and skill, he will appreciate me much more."

But Kalilah was still uneasy. "If you have really decided to do this," he advised Dimnah, "you must be aware that what you want to do is very dangerous. According to wise men, only foolish men do these three things: become involved in the king's business; taste poison in order to see what it is; and tell secrets to women!"

Dimnah answered, "That is all true. But the one who never takes chances never becomes great. Let me remind you that only a strong and courageous man could do these three things: enter into the king's business; do business by sea; and face one's enemy."

So Dimnah went to court and introduced himself to the lion. The lion asked his attendants if they knew who Dimnah was, and they told him all they knew about Dimnah and his family. The lion remembered Dimnah's father and so was friendly. He asked Dimnah where he lived. Dimnah replied, "I am staying at my lord's court, waiting for a position so that I can prove myself to you. For any servant, no matter how poor he is, can be of some use one day."

The lion was pleased with Dimnah's response and told his

attendants that "a wise man, even if he is of low rank, stands out in a crowd because of his honesty and wisdom."

When he heard this remark, Dimnah became very happy. He realized that he had already impressed the lion, so he dared to suggest, "Let all the subjects present their advice to my lord and show their knowledge openly. If my lord does not know how much knowledge his subjects have, he cannot really benefit from their service. Knowledge is like a seed that is ignored as long as it is hidden beneath the earth. After it grows, people can enjoy taking care of it and gain profit from it. It is important that my lord give his subjects positions based on knowledge and ability, not only on family lineage. He should not prefer careless, unskilled people over learned and wise men. Surrounding himself with friends who have no skills is dangerous. Great things are accomplished by knowledgeable and experienced men; not only by friends or those who stay close to you. Remember, a man who carries a small ruby does not become tired, and the ruby can be very valuable in a time of need. On the other hand, a man who carries a bag of heavy rocks soon becomes tired, and when he is needy his rocks aren't worth anything. And mice, though they live close to people, are hated because they do harm, but a falcon, though it is wild, because of its grace and ability is welcomed by the people, and he even finds himself on the hand of a king."

By the time Dimnah finished talking, the lion had become very fond of him and welcomed his friendship. As time passed, the lion's trust in Dimnah increased.

One day Dimnah asked the lion why he had been staying at home and had given up the joy of hunting. The lion was still trying to hide his fear, but suddenly Shanzibah gave another loud bellow. The noise scared the lion so much his trembling was easy to see. He had no choice but to tell his secret to Dimnah.

"The reason I stay at home is because of this roar. I don't know where it comes from, but an animal with such a loud voice must be very strong and wild, and if he is, then it is not safe for us to live here anymore!"

Dimnah asked if there was anything else besides the roar that frightened the lion, and the lion said, "No."

Then Dimnah said, "It doesn't seem right for my lord not to leave his own land because of a loud roar. Besides, not every powerful voice or large body means something is strong. "What do you mean?" asked the lion. Dimnah explained.

The Fox and The Drum

Once a fox crossing a field saw a drum fall near a tree. The wind caused a branch of the tree to pound on the drum, making a loud noise. The fox, who was impressed by the size of the drum and the loud sound it made, thought it would surely have lots of juicy meat. So the fox tried to tear the drum apart, but he only found a little thin skin. Then the fox told himself, "I should have known that the larger the body and the louder the voice, the less substance it would have."

"I told this story," said Dimnah, "so that my lord would see that he has no reason to be afraid. And, if my lord wishes, I will go to investigate the habits of this wild thing." The lion thought this was a good idea indeed.

When Dimnah came back, the lion rushed to ask him what he had found out. Dimnah reported, "I saw an ordinary bull, without the proud looks that go with great strength."

But this did not comfort the lion. He replied, "What you saw does not prove the bull is weak, either. As you know, a strong wind that can knock down huge trees may not be able to uproot a small bush."

So Dimnah went to Shanzibah and said, "I have been sent by the lion, who has ordered me to take you to him. If you come with me, I will ask him to forgive you for not introducing yourself to him sooner. But if you refuse, I will return at once and report your disobedience."

"Who is this lion?" asked Shanzibah.

"The king of all the wilds," answered Dimnah.

The title "king of all the wilds" terrified Shanzibah. He asked Dimnah whether he would protect him if he went with him. Dimnah promised him he would be safe, so Shanzibah went along.

The lion welcomed Shanzibah warmly. He asked him when and why he had come to the kingdom. Shanzibah told his story to the lion, who liked Shanzibah so much he invited him to stay in the field as his guest. Shanzibah was so thankful he offered his services in return. After testing Shanzibah's knowledge in various ways, the lion decided he could trust him and made him a close friend. Day by day, Shanzibah's rank and position became higher and higher, until he became the lion's most trusted adviser.

Further Reading

The Fables of India. Retold by Joseph Gaer. This book contains beast tales from the *Panchatantra*. It also has tales from two other collections of Indian fables, *Hipotadesa* and *Jatakas*.

Persian Folk and Fairy Tales. Retold by Anne Sinclair Mehdevi. The book includes eleven fables and tales of magic, romance, and adventure.

Tales of India: Magical Adventures of Three Indian Princes. Marie Ponsot, translator. These twelve stories were selected from the *Mabharata*. They tell the story of the epic's hero, Prince Ardjuna, and his brothers.

L E S S O N · 3

The Rise of the Byzantine Empire

THINKING FOCUS

What were some of the accomplishments of the Byzantine Empire?

Key Terms

- mosaic
- commerce

In January 532, Constantinople erupted into riot and flames. As the largest city of the Byzantine Empire, it had 350,000–500,000 people. Taxes were high and city officials took bribes on an everyday basis. There were plans to overthrow Emperor Justinian and Empress Theodora. The Hagia Sophia *(ah YEE uh soh FEE uh)*, the Church of the Holy Wisdom, where the emperors,

supreme heads of the Church, were crowned, had been torched.

Justinian tried but failed to put down what are now called the Nike Riots. As the crowd chose a new emperor, and Justinian was about to flee, Theodora stopped him with the speech below. After hearing it, the Emperor recovered his nerve and gave orders to put down the riots. Within weeks there were over 30,000 dead. The Empire had survived.

> As to the belief that a woman should not be daring among men or assert herself boldly, I consider the present crisis does not allow us to debate that. My opinion is that now is a poor time for flight, even though it bring safety. . . . If now you wish to go, Emperor, nothing prevents you. There is the sea, there are the steps to the boats. But take care that after you are safe, you do not find that you would gladly exchange that safety for death. For my part, I like the old saying that "The Empire is fine burial cloth."
>
> Recorded by Procopius, c. 550

Byzantine History and Culture

Byzantium had been the name of this former Greek colony, founded in 667 B.C. In A.D. 330, the Roman Emperor Constantine built his "new Rome," and named it Constantinople (now called Istanbul). It remained under the control of his heirs until 1453, when the Turks captured it.

While rule in western Europe was decentralized and the population scattered, Constantinople and the great cities of Asia and Africa were thriving.

The borders of the Byzantine Empire changed often over its thousand-year history. The empire fought off Slavs and Bulgars in the west, and Persians in the east. It was held together by Christianity, the state religion, which saw the emperor as God's representative on earth. Slave-holding still existed, but it was forbidden for a Christian to own a Christian slave. Slavery declined in Europe after the fall of the Roman Empire, but slaves continued to be domestic servants. Germanic peoples and Slavs made up the majority of slaves in the Middle East.

In an effort to shore up unity, and for what they thought were the best interests of their faith, the Byzantines forced Christianity on others. Since around 500 B.C., large Jewish communities had existed in Turkey, Mesopotamia, Persia, and Palestine. When the Romans destroyed Judaea in A.D. 70, hundreds of thousands of Jews were shipped off as slaves. Others escaped to set up new lives. By Justinian's time, there were great Jewish centers in what are now Egypt, Spain, France, Germany, Italy, Turkey, and the Balkans.

Justinian's treatment of Jews and other non-Christians (there were then no Muslims) was brutal. Following the anti-Jewish rulings of Church councils beginning in 312, the Byzantines did not allow Jews to build synagogues or join in city life. Justinian forbade Jews to study the works of the rabbis. There were forced conversions and anti-Jewish massacres. Many Jews later moved to more tolerant lands.

Justinian's Contributions

Justinian's passion and effort all went to the church. To glorify the church was to glorify God. To do this, Justinian commissioned religious art and architecture on a grand

scale. He rebuilt Hagia Sophia with columns and walls of polished marble of many colors, and many glittering mosaics. **Mosaics** are colored fragments of glass or quartz embedded in plaster. Read A Closer Look on the next page to see how people restore, or repair, mosaics today. Most awe-inspiring was the Hagia Sophia dome—18 stories high and 108 feet wide. Through its stained-glass windows, light flooded into the church.

In 528, Justinian gave 10 men the task of condensing the 1,600 books of classic Roman law. A year later they came up with a well-organized system of 4,652 laws. The new legal system was called the Justinian Code. It extended the rights of women, children, and slaves, but also called for harsher penalties for crimes. Criminals could have their property taken away, lose an eye or a hand, or even be put to death, depending on their crime. Nevertheless, the laws proved to be very effective at maintaining order.

In fact, Roman law, in the form of the Justinian Code, was so effective that many nations in Europe and Latin America used it as the model for their legal systems.

▲ *Mosaics like these from 547 give us some idea of how the Byzantine emperor Justinian and his empress Theodora actually looked. These mosaics were found in Ravenna, Italy.*

▼ *A gold bracelet from Constantinople.*

43

Conserving Mosaics

Mosaic art once covered floors and walls in the ancient Roman and Byzantine empires. Today conservators in museums work to make sure the mosaics that survive can still be enjoyed.

Solvent—special chemicals sometimes used to dissolve dirt

Animals of the Nile, a mosaic from Pompeii, c. first century B.C.

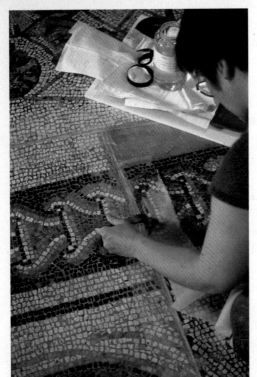

Fine-art jigsaw puzzle is one way to describe a mosaic. Mosaics are made of little bits of colored glass, tile, or stone set into plaster. Over time, the pieces may come loose. To repair mosaics, conservators first cover the pieces with cloth and glue to keep them in place. Then they fix the plaster.

Palette knife—used to work with tiny pieces of mosaic

Spatula—used to separate the mosaic from the wall or floor

Sponge—used to apply water or solvent to the mosaic

Some mosaics get flipped over on their faces so that conservators can clean and repair the backs. After repairs, mosaics can be returned to where they were, or moved to museums for display.

A New Empire

Justinian also considered it his duty to recover Roman lands in the West that had been lost, as he said, "through indolence [laziness]." From 533 to his death in 565, Justinian's armies did regain parts of Spain, all of Italy, and North Africa. But, after his death, some lands were lost again to outsiders. What's more, battling over these lands distracted the Byzantine military and distracted it from another more serious enemy, the Persians. ■

▲ *This is a view of the interior of Hagia Sophia.*

The Persian Threat

Although barbarian tribes ultimately regained some lands in the West, the Persians were a greater threat to the Byzantine Empire. The Persians most closely matched the Byzantines in strength. They were also committed to battling the Byzantines for control of Armenia as well as to regaining control of Turkey, Syria, and Egypt. For 500 years, the Persians and Byzantines fought, but neither ever won an advantage for long.

In the early 600s, the Persians made their move. In a campaign lasting 17 years, they conquered part of Mesopotamia, occupied Asia Minor, and finally took Syria, Jerusalem, and Egypt.

This victory was short-lived. In 627, Byzantine Emperor Heraclius *(hehr uh KLY uhs)* defeated the Persian army. The Persians had to give up all the land they had recently won.

Until 1453, the Byzantine Empire was an important center of **commerce,** or trade, and culture. But constant warfare had weakened both empires. The Persians, in particular, soon had trouble mustering the strength to fight off new invaders. ■

■ *What distinctive elements of Byzantine culture developed under Justinian's rule?*

◄ *This cameo shows a Persian ruler taking a Roman emperor prisoner.*

■ *How did the constant battling between Byzantium and Persia affect the two empires?*

REVIEW

1. **FOCUS** What were some of the accomplishments of the Byzantine Empire?
2. **CONNECT** In what ways was Constantinople like Rome? How was it different?
3. **HISTORY** How has the Justinian Code affected the modern world?
4. **GEOGRAPHY** Why and how did Justinian rebuild Constantinople?
5. **CRITICAL THINKING** Why do you think two countries might battle for centuries over control of a certain territory? What are some of the things people fight about today?
6. **ACTIVITY** Imagine that you have been asked to help revise the laws in your town. In small groups, make a list of laws in existence that you think ought to be changed. Revise each law on your list. Then as a class, vote on the laws to determine which should be added to your legal system.

Chapter Review

Reviewing Key Terms

barbarian (p. 29)   mosaic (p. 43)
commerce (p. 45)   province (p. 27)
dynasty (p. 32)

In each pair of sentences below there are two meanings for one key term. The key term in the first sentence has a different meaning than it does in the second sentence. Explain which sentence describes the key term's meaning as used in this chapter.

1. a. Making laws was the *province* of the Roman emperor.
   b. The captain was assigned to a far-off *province*.
2. a. Caravans kept *commerce* strong.
   b. The Persians and the Indians carried on a vast *commerce* of ideas.
3. a. A family that discovered oil could start a financial *dynasty* in the modern-day Middle East.
   b. Henry Pu-yi was the last ruler of the Manchu *Dynasty*.
4. a. Justinian did not include the *Mosaic* law of the Hebrews in his code.
   b. A popular subject of early *mosaics* was Mary with Jesus.
5. a. The rioters showed they were *barbarians* by burning and looting.
   b. Marcus knew by the strangers' language that they were *barbarians*.

Exploring Concepts

A. Complete the paragraph by writing in each blank an accomplishment of an early civilization. Two have been completed for you.

Historians and other scholars still study the accomplishments of ancient civilizations. Romans are remembered for the _peace they maintained in their provinces_ by allowing people there to live as usual but under Roman law. They are also known for the ___2___ that they built. The Persians are known for the ___3___ they carried on, which enriched their culture. They encouraged trade by establishing a ___4___. Mathematicians today can be grateful to Indians for developing the ___5___. And readers still admire the _poems and folk tales by early Indian writers_. Even today, the Chinese are known in religious art circles for their ___7___, and in commercial circles for their ___8___ trade. The Byzantine Empire influenced modern law with its ___9___ and modern artists with its ___10___.

B. Support each statement with facts and details from the chapter.

1. Rome benefited from having Egypt as a province.
2. Barbarian invasions helped to cause the fall of the Roman Empire.
3. The economies of both India and Persia benefited from safe roads.
4. The Persian navy had the Greeks to thank.
5. Indians made religious and mathematical contributions to other cultures.
6. Law played a key part in the governments of the Roman Empire and the Byzantine Empire.
7. Constantine and Justinian accomplished something similar during their reigns.
8. The Persians were a greater threat to the Byzantine Empire and weakened it more than the barbarians.
9. Julius Caesar's adopted son, Octavian, was a successful ruler when he took over Rome after his father's assassination.

Using Critical Thinking

1. Many ancient cultures have contributed nuggets of wisdom that sound strangely familiar even today. For example, in the first century A.D., a Roman named Pubilius Syrus wrote the following sayings:
   a. The loss that is unknown is no loss at all.
   b. While we stop to think, we often miss our opportunity.
   c. For a good cause, wrongdoing is virtuous.
   d. When fortune is on our side, popular favor bears her company.
   e. It is a consolation to the wretched to have companions in misery.
   f. Practice is the best of all instructors.
   All of these sayings have counterparts in our language today. List the present-day sayings with similar meanings.
2. Perhaps the Romans should have considered the following Chinese proverb from the fifth century B.C. before they expanded their empire: "To go beyond is as wrong as to fall short." Support this statement with an example from your own life or one from current events. Explain your answer.
3. Read a story from or about India from this century. You might choose one by Rudyard Kipling or Rumer Godden, for example. Do you see any similarities between the story and the literature in Lesson 2? What does the story you chose tell you about Indian beliefs, customs, or way of life?
4. Imagine that the towns in your county cannot agree on where the county seat of government should be located. In order to be selected as the "capital" of the county, your town must prove that it has enough important qualities to merit this honor. Write a one-page report boasting about the strengths of your town that will win it the county seat.

Preparing for Citizenship

1. **COLLECTING INFORMATION** The land that was once known as Persia is called Iran today. Look through newspapers and magazines for stories that answer the following questions about the country of Iran: Is the area still a center of trade? Do the people who live there still welcome ideas from other cultures? What is life like in Iran today? Collect everyone's stories and display them on a bulletin board under headings such as "Persia Yesterday, Iran Today," "Trade in Iran Today," or "Iran and Its Neighbors."
2. **ARTS ACTIVITY** Create a three-dimensional mosaic design that is at least six inches wide and eight inches long. You may use colored cellophane, paper, clay, stones, or other materials to develop a mosaic picture. Your creation could show a person from an ancient civilization, a battle, or just an interesting pattern. As you design and create your mosaic, think about the talent, materials, effort, and imagination that ancient people put into their colorful and often large-scale mosaic pieces. Imagine how much time it took to cover an entire wall or floor in a mosaic pattern or picture.
3. **WRITING ACTIVITY** Write a short, humorous dialogue that takes place between a hostile barbarian armed with a knife and a Roman official. The barbarian fears the conquering Huns and wants to take refuge in the empire. The Roman official is not so sure about the idea and insists on filling out certain paperwork before permitting the barbarian to cross the border. Use what you know about immigration and other government procedures today to write the scene.
4. **COLLABORATIVE LEARNING** As a class project, create a multi-cultural display entitled "Cultural Contributions of the Ancient World." Divide into groups of four and have each member choose one of the following ancient civilizations to research: Rome, Greece, India, or China. Write down as many contributions as you can think of for the civilization you have chosen.

Unit 2
The Growth of Islam

Covered in silver and gold, the walls of the house of worship shimmer in the light. The people turn toward the niche in the wall that tells them they are facing Mecca, their holy city. They pray. These Muslims are carrying on a religious tradition that dates to the A.D. 600s. That was when Arabian peoples united behind Muhammad, whom Muslims believe was sent as a prophet with the message of Islam. Within 150 years of his death, Muslims ruled lands from the Atlantic Ocean to central Asia. During the following centuries, Islam continued to spread into Africa, Asia, and Europe.

500

Muslims at prayer, Mashad, Iran. Photograph by Roger Wood

1492

Chapter 3

The Roots of Islam

The Arabian Peninsula is a region of contrasts. By about 1000 B.C., camel caravans crossed the desert, mountains, and grasslands of Southwest Asia carrying trade goods from East to West. Before Roman times, Arab ships had sailed the Red Sea and the Indian Ocean. Arabs of town, oasis, desert, and seaport, all played an important part in the exchange of goods and ideas among Asian, European, and African cultures. The Arabian Peninsula also shared in the religious history of Southwest Asia going back to biblical times. In the 600s, a religious leader named Muhammad brought the message of Islam. United by their belief, the desert Arabs came to rule parts of Asia, Africa, and Europe.

Dried fruits, vital for long desert treks, became important trade goods.

500s Mecca, with its holy sites and its fresh-water well, grows as the most important stop along Arab trade routes. This scenic river valley (above) is near the city of Abha, Saudi Arabia.

500	540	580

c. 550 Japanese rulers allow their subjects to practice the Buddhist faith.

500

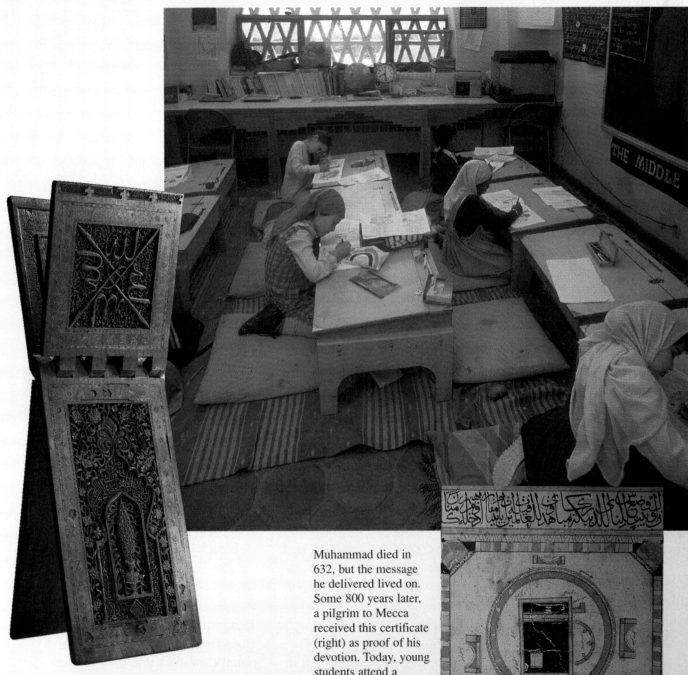

610 Muhammad begins preaching. Muslims believe that he received revelations from God, recorded in the Qur'an. Artists honored the Qur'an by creating this fine wooden stand for it (above).

Muhammad died in 632, but the message he delivered lived on. Some 800 years later, a pilgrim to Mecca received this certificate (right) as proof of his devotion. Today, young students attend a Muslim school in New Mexico (above).

620	660	700

687 In Europe, Pepin II unites the Franks and rules until 714.

661

LESSON 1

Desert Bloom— Caravan Cities

THINKING FOCUS

What different ways of life did people have in the Arabian Peninsula in A.D. 500?

Key Terms

- oasis
- nomad
- tribe
- idol
- pilgrimage

➤ *The ancient caravan routes (above, right) can be seen with a satellite radar photograph, but are invisible to those standing on top of them.*

In 1984, the space shuttle Challenger roared into Earth's orbit. In one of the first uses of "space archaeology," Challenger's radar equipment beamed down microwaves to the southern Arabian Peninsula and digitally recorded any signals that bounced back. Historians were looking for the "lost" city of Ubar. What they saw— invisible to people on the ground— was a thin black line that showed what lay under the surface of the sand. What they found was a line of compacted earth underneath the desert. The compacted earth showed the centuries of beaten-down tracks of trade caravans. The tracks all led to one place.

Historians knew that many ancient peoples burned an incense called frankincense that came from trees in the mountains near the Arabian Sea. Caravans brought the incense through the desert to Ubar, where it was traded and continued its journey to other lands. Could this line in the desert actually be the long-lost Frankincense Road leading to the ancient marketplace of Ubar?

Looking for answers, archaeologists and historians gathered on the site of this ancient village in 1990 and began piecing together clues from the buried fortress and pottery samples that they unearthed. Ubar, once a stop for merchants and travelers, began to reappear slowly from beneath the sand.

Early Arabia

Ubar was only one of the many settlements located in the Arabian Peninsula. Although the Peninsula's Empty Quarter is one of the driest deserts on Earth, the region consists of fertile ranges of mountains and coastal hills that run along the Red and Arabian seas. To the north, the sparse Syrian Desert separates the Peninsula from Palestine and the Mediterranean coast. At its western edges the region borders the Tigris-Euphrates river system. The dry region in the center of the peninsula, however, is dotted with oases. An **oasis** (plural: oases) is a small area in a desert that is watered by springs or wells. Almost all regions except the Empty Quarter receive some rainfall.

At an Oasis

Ubar thrived from around 900 B.C. to A.D. 300. By the 500s, however, the demand for incense had fallen, and Ubar had been destroyed by the collapse of its underground water reservoir. Water determined where people gathered and on what routes they traveled. Journeys were planned from well to well, or oasis to oasis. Towns and cities grew around these sources of water.

Throughout the peninsula's interior, oases attracted families of

▲ *Dates are still raised in groves like this one near the city of Al Ula in Saudi Arabia.*

nomads who were herders. They migrated in regular patterns, following water and grazing land for their camel herds. Their lives revolved around the seasons, as they waited for the rainfall to make the grazing land green. As they traveled, they kept watch for the many wells that had been dug and were maintained to provide water for the people and animals who traveled the land.

Trade Routes, A.D. 570

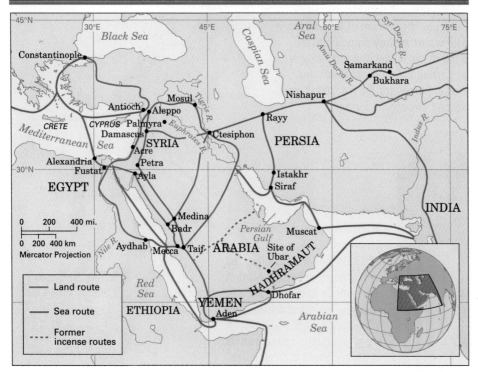

◄ *Arabia was at the center of many early trade routes. Goods from Africa, Asia, and Europe crossed Arabia. If you had been a trader, what routes would you have wanted to travel and why?*

The Roots of Islam

Irrigation Technology

Ever since humans settled down and began raising crops for food, they have been building canals and irrigating fields. The Muslims used science and technology to raise water and move it from one place to another. By organizing resources and spreading knowledge among the many groups that made up Muslim culture, they brought great areas of dry land into agricultural production.

aqueduct

stream

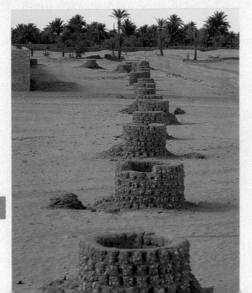

The *noria,* or water wheel, was a Roman invention that spread throughout the Muslim world. Driven by the current of the stream, it was fitted with pots that filled with water as they dipped into the stream. When they reached the top of the wheel, the pots emptied into an aqueduct or channel that carried the water to fields and towns. The windmill first appeared in Persia around A.D. 300. It was later copied in Spain and then spread throughout Europe.

In Algeria, Iran, parts of Oman, Afghanistan, Morocco, and Spain, irrigation was often fed by underground channels that were linked to natural aquifers, where underground water had become trapped. Some of these channels, called *qanats,* stretched more than 40 miles. Shafts spaced along the channel allowed air pressure to keep the water flowing.

At oases, the nomads would often visit towns and villages. Sometimes they came to groves of date trees, or fields of wheat, barley, or other crops. The fields were irrigated from the area's springs or wells. The nomads often brought products such as camel meat and milk to trade. In exchange, villagers supplied the nomads with grain, and city merchants sold manufactured wares, including weapons, carpets, and cloth, as well as goods for trade such as sugar and tea.

Nomadic Life

The nomadic families of Arabia belonged to a group of people who called themselves Arabs after the language they spoke. Some Arabs settled on oases where they lived as farmers. Others lived in villages and were traders or artisans. Farmers and herders supplied these village-dwellers with food and transport animals.

In order to survive in their desert environment, nomads lived in close family groups with grandparents, parents, and children. Families often joined together to form **tribes.** Each tribe was headed by a respected elder called a *shaikh (shayk).* With the help of family leaders, the *shaikh* settled family and tribal disputes.

While the nomads seem to have believed in a Creator, they also believed in lesser gods that they thought influenced their lives. They made **idols** to represent these "sons and daughters of God." They also believed in spirits that could inhabit natural objects and forces.

Among the groups living in Arabia in A.D. 500 were Arabs called *hanif* who believed in one God. Jewish tribes had existed in Arabia for centuries, while Christian tribes had lived in the northern part of the peninsula. Both Jews and Christians earned their livelihoods as farmers, herders, and artisans.

Because water and grazing land were so scarce, feuds broke out occasionally between tribes. Larger tribes sometimes forced payment from smaller tribes to use the oases. For a price, these larger tribes would also protect traders' caravans from danger. ■

■ *Describe the lifestyle of the Arab nomads.*

◀ *Water can be scarce in many regions of Arabia. The* wadis, *or dry riverbeds, will only fill with water after rainfall. However, they can fill so quickly and with so much water, that people have been caught by surprise and drowned.*

Towns and Trade

➤ *The treasury building of Petra, like most of the city, is carved into a mountainside. This treasury is built in the Hellenistic style, a sign of the conquest of Alexander the Great.*

Carrying all kinds of local and exotic goods, merchants crisscrossed Arabia on travel routes stretching between the Mediterranean Sea, the Red Sea, the Arabian Sea, and the Persian Gulf. Some of these merchants chose to stay in the trading centers they passed through, settling and specializing in the trade and transportation of goods. Others became artisans, scholars, and judges. Between A.D. 500 and 600, the Arabian peninsula was inhabited by three types of communities. They were made up of either city-dwellers, people living in agricultural villages, or nomadic tribes. Although each group had a different way of life, they cooperated to make the society run smoothly.

The towns were built along the many trade routes that crossed the Arabian peninsula. Local goods as well as luxuries from Indian Ocean trade routes to the east passed through these villages on their way to Mediterranean lands. As traders crossed the desert, they stopped at the oases for supplies. The Arabs who lived in these oasis villages became leaders among the Arabs throughout the region because of the wealth that such trading brought.

Seaports linked Arabia with Africa and Asia, and travelers and traders came from these continents. Arabs could buy goods and meet people from their own region as well as from distant lands. Various people traveled the desert routes, bringing exotic cloth and fragrant spices from India; ivory, gold, and ebony from Africa; as well as Arabian horses and camels. Many

goods traveled to or from Syrian and other Mediterranean ports as well as across the Red Sea toward Egypt and the port of Alexandria.

Petra

In the northwest corner of the Arabian peninsula are the remains of Petra. A former trading city nestled at the foot of a high cliff, it is now known for its beauty. Attracted by Petra's ample supply of spring water, travelers began stopping at this center as early as 300 B.C. The city took its name from the Greek word for "rock" from which some of its earliest buildings were carved.

In the open-air marketplace, or *suq (SOOK)*, of Petra, wheat, olive oil, wine, hides, slaves, precious stones, and spices were abundantly available. Here, merchants would stock local products and wares, and compete with each other to attract customers to their stalls. ■

■ *Describe the lifestyle of the Arab town-dwellers.*

The Holy City of Mecca

The city of Mecca grew in a well-protected valley at the crossroads of two long-distance trade routes. The routes stretched north and south between Yemen and the Mediterranean, as well as east and west between the Persian Gulf and the Red Sea. Travelers quenched their thirst and watered their animals at Mecca's fresh water well.

A Sacred Meeting Place

Muslims believe that the founding and settling of Mecca is related to the story of Abraham and his son Ishmael. According to Islamic teachings, Abraham and Ishmael built a cube-shaped shrine called the Ka'bah (*KAH buh*) about 4,000 years ago. Islam teaches that Abraham was commanded to build the Ka'bah as a house of worship and a reminder of Abraham's firm belief in one God.

Worshipers honored the Ka'bah and over time placed idols in it for safekeeping. They honored the gods in it by performing religious rituals. Although the Arab tribes still considered themselves to be descendants of Abraham, they introduced the worship of idols to the Ka'bah. By A.D. 500, there were more than 360 different idols in and around it. There were even some Christian pictures placed there. A tradition continued of visiting the Ka'bah and walking around it.

The Quraysh, a local tribe, settled in Mecca sometime before A.D. 500. Their role as keepers of the Ka'bah gave them great prestige and helped them to make treaties with neighboring tribes. This ensured the safe passage of caravans during the months of pilgrimage and travel. A **pilgrimage** is a journey to a sacred site. The treaties prevented fighting and raiding during this time. By A.D. 500, Mecca had become the most successful trade center in Arabia, prospering from the flow of merchants and pilgrims. ■

▲ *The city of Mecca was the location of the Ka'bah, which for centuries has held religious symbols. The city was also a prosperous trade center and an excellent source of fresh water.*

■ *How was Mecca different from other Arab trading cities?*

R E V I E W

1. **FOCUS** What different ways of life did people have in the Arabian Peninsula in A.D. 500?
2. **CONNECT** What contact did the Arabs make with peoples beyond Arabia?
3. **GEOGRAPHY** Why did many families in Arabia keep moving?
4. **BELIEF SYSTEMS** Describe why the Ka'bah was an important site for pilgrims.
5. **CRITICAL THINKING** Do you think religious pilgrimages were necessary for trade to continue? Explain your answer.
6. **ACTIVITY** Use an atlas to describe or show the geography of the countries now within the Arabian Peninsula.

LESSON 2

Muhammad and Islam

Key Terms

- Qur'an
- monotheism
- Islam
- Muslim
- mosque
- Sunna

➤ *Today pilgrims visit the Prophet's Cave on Mount Hira.*

Each year, a Meccan trader named Muhammad would spend a month in quiet thought while inside a desert cave on Mount Hira. In the year A.D. 610, something extraordinary occurred. The first verses of the **Qur'an,** believed by Muslims to be the written record of God's words, were revealed to him at that time.

The story of how Muhammad received these messages was later told by his wife, Aisha *(AY ee shah).* Aisha was the daughter of Abu Bakr, a wealthy trader who was the first person outside Muhammad's family to become a Muslim.

Aisha tells that even before Muhammad's experience in the cave at Hira, he had had "good dreams which came true like bright daylight." Then, in the cave, something more far-reaching happened.

A being he later identified as the angel Gabriel, or Jibril *(juh BREEL)* in Arabic, came to him, telling him to read, or recite. Trembling, Muhammad responded that he didn't know how to read or what to read. "Thereupon [the angel] caught me and pressed me so hard that I could not bear it any more." Three times the angel pressed Muhammad, finally commanding him to

Read! In the name of your
 Lord who created.
Created man from a clot of
 congealed blood.
Read! And your Lord is the Most
 Bountiful.
He who has taught by the pen.
Taught man that which he
 knew not.

Qur'an 96:1–5

The Life of the Prophet

Muhammad was born into the Quraysh tribe around A.D. 570. Orphaned at an early age, he found work in the caravan trade. At 25, he married a wealthy widow in the trading business. This wealth gave him the freedom to visit Mount Hira each year to think.

On one of these visits in 610, Muhammad is believed by his followers to have had a vision of Gabriel. The angel told him to recite in the name of God. Followers of Muhammad believe the angel then told Muhammad the first of many messages from God.

Muhammad's followers believe that in another vision, the angel Gabriel took Muhammad to meet Abraham, Moses, and Jesus in Jerusalem. From Jerusalem, both Muhammad and Gabriel ascended into heaven, where Muhammad spoke to God.

These revelations confirmed both Muhammad's belief in one God, or **monotheism,** and his role as the last messenger in a long line of prophets sent by God. The God he believed in—Allah—is the same God of other monotheistic religions, Judaism and Christianity. *Allah,* the Arabic word for God, is the word used in the Qur'an.

Spreading the Word

Muhammad began to preach, first to members of his family, then to the leaders of his tribe and others. When members of some prominent families accepted Islam, the Meccan leaders became hostile. Failing to convince Muhammad and his followers to give up their beliefs, the Quraysh leaders refused to trade with them, causing the Muslims great suffering. Finally, when Arabs from outside Mecca became attracted to the message during the pilgrimage, the Quraysh leaders plotted to kill Muhammad.

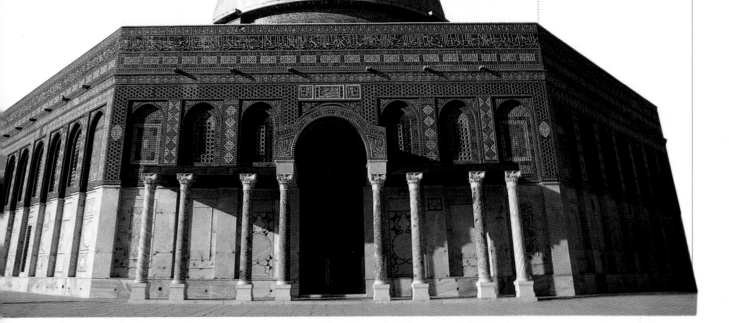

▼ *This monumental building, the Dome of the Rock in Jerusalem, was completed by the Muslims in 691. The rock is believed to be the place from which Muhammad ascended into heaven.*

As you can see from the script on the right, Arabic is written with an alphabet different from English. The passage tells of people who reject the message of Muhammad.

In 622, Muhammad and his followers migrated to Medina, an oasis city about 200 miles north of Mecca. They had been invited and offered safety by the people of the city. This migration to Medina, known as the Hijrah *(HIJ ruh),* marks the beginning of the Islamic lunar calendar. Thus, the year A.D. 622 is also the year 1 A.H. (after Hijrah). Muhammad called the new faith **Islam,** which means "submission" to Allah. Believers in Islam are called **Muslims**—"those who submit to Allah's will."

Returning to Mecca

The Jews and Arabs of Medina welcomed Muhammad and his followers. Their city was on the verge of civil war, and they hoped that Muhammad could unite them. Muhammad hoped that Islam would be accepted by all the people of Medina. Muhammad told the Jews that Islam was not a new religion. The message revealed through him was the same basic message that had been brought by Abraham, Moses, and Jesus, among other prophets. He told them that the true religion is to follow one God and submit to his will. However, some Jewish leaders would not accept Muhammad

as God's latest prophet.

Over the next eight years, support for Islam grew. Resistance to the changes introduced by Muhammad also grew. The enemies of the Muslims, led by the Quraysh, continued to try to eliminate Islam and its followers. The Quraysh, fearing that their power and wealth would be lost, tried to make alliances against the Medinans and their supporters. Eventually, many Arab nomadic tribes and leading Meccans joined the Muslim cause. With their support, Muhammad was able to put together an army of more than 10,000. In 630, this army marched on Mecca and the city surrendered without a battle.

One of the first things Muhammad did was to forgive all those who had opposed Muslims for so long. He also removed the idols from the Ka'bah. Thus the Ka'bah was again dedicated to the one God, as it had been in the time of Abraham. The area around the Ka'bah became the first **mosque,** or Muslim house of worship.

After appointing a Muslim governor, Muhammad returned to Medina. Following the defeat of the Quraysh, many tribes in Arabia decided to join the Muslims. They had waited to see how the contest would turn out. Now they sent delegations to offer allegiance and accept Islam. Muhammad also sent letters to leaders outside Arabia, inviting them to Islam. By the time of Muhammad's death in 632, Islam had encompassed the central and western coastal regions of Arabia. ■

■ *How was the religion of Islam founded, and how did it spread?*

The Teachings of Islam

Muslims believe that the Qur'an is the word of Allah. After Muhammad took over the city of Medina, he began to establish an Islamic community with unique customs.

The Qur'an

Muhammad's revelations occurred from 610 until his death in 632. Although he was not liter- ate himself, Muhammad had his revelations written down by his companions. Many of them memo- rized the whole Qur'an and recited it in his presence. By the time of his death, all the revelations had been compiled into one collection, the Qur'an. In addition, the hadith *(hah DEET),* or words and deeds of Muhammad, were passed down in oral form through several genera- tions, and compiled into authorita- tive collections. Together, the Qur'an and collections of hadith, called the **Sunna,** make up the authentic sources of Islamic beliefs and practices.

▼ *Called to prayer from the minaret (1), Muslims enter the doorway (2), and wash in the ablution fountain (3). They pray under the portico (4), while facing the mihrab prayer niche (5), and listen to an address from the pulpit (6). The mihrab and the pulpit are shown in the photograph at the left.*

The Roots of Islam

For the followers of Islam, the Qur'an completes the earlier revelations of Old Testament prophets and Jesus. The Qu'ran is the final revelation, just as Muhammad is the final prophet.

Islam has close ties to Judaism and Christianity. Many prophets and holy people who are important figures in the Bible are also described in the Qur'an. For example, Abraham is thought to be the father of Jews through his son Isaac. Abraham is also considered to be the father of Arabs through his other son Ishmael.

The Jews' and Christians' holy book, the Bible, is considered by Muslims to be based on God's revelations. But Muslims considered these other religions to be less correct. That is because the Qur'an teaches that the Bible has suffered loss and change with time. Christians and Jews are respected as "people of the book" by Mus-

▼ *All Muslims in good health and with enough money must make a pilgrimage to Mecca once in their lifetime.*

lims, and all their prophets are revered.

The Arabic word Qur'an can be loosely translated as "recitation." In fact, the very first word the angel Gabriel spoke to Muhammad was "Recite." By reciting aloud, many Muslims memorize as much of the Qur'an as they can.

The Sunna

The Sunna were the guiding rules for Islam and were based on the way the prophet Muhammad lived his own life. The most basic of these rules were the Five Pillars of Islam. The principles and commandments behind these five duties came from the Qur'an, but it was in the Sunna that the prophet explained them by his example.

The first of these pillars is the profession of faith. To express their acceptance of Islam, Muslims repeat the phrase, "There is no god but Allah, and Muhammad is his prophet."

The second pillar is prayer. Muslims must pray five times a day. Prayers follow special rituals, including washing before praying, bowing, and then kneeling while praying. Muslims face the Ka'bah in Mecca when praying. Every Friday at noon, Muslims congregate in mosques for prayer and a sermon by the prayer leader.

The third pillar is giving alms, or showing charity to the poor. Muslims must also contribute to public charities, such as the building of mosques and hospitals.

The fourth pillar is the ritual fast during Ramadan, the ninth month of the Muslim year. Ramadan is a holy time, because in this month Muhammad received his first message from Allah. During Ramadan, Muslims must not eat or drink from the break of dawn until the setting of the sun. Muslims hope that their fast, which teaches self-discipline, humility, and sympathy for the hungry, brings them closer to Allah.

The fifth pillar of Islam is Hajj—the pilgrimage to Mecca. All Muslims who can afford it must make the pilgrimage at least once. The pilgrimage involves elaborate rites that take place over many days. Before arriving at Mecca, the pilgrims bathe, cut their hair and nails, and take off jewelry. They then put on a white seamless garment, symbolizing a state of purity. Because Muslims from all over the world make pilgrimage, Hajj is a symbol of Muslim unity and equality. ◼

▲ *Pilgrims circle the Ka'bah in the Great Mosque in Mecca. The heavy black covering that protects the shrine is replaced each year. The cloth covers a single doorway that leads into a room inside the Ka'bah.*

◼ *Why are the Qur'an and Sunna important to Muslims?*

An Islamic Way of Life

The five pillars lay at the foundation of what it is for Muslims to be good human beings in obedience to God's will. But the Qur'an

▲ *This street scene from Essaouira, Morocco, shows a variety of Muslim women's dress. The majority of Muslim women do not cover their faces. Some have abandoned traditional Islamic dress for Western styles. Still others have returned to wearing modern forms of modest dress as an expression of Islamic values.*

■ *How does Islam affect many aspects of daily life for Muslims?*

and the Sunna cover many additional moral standards that a Muslim must live by in his or her everyday life. The Qur'an and the Sunna cover diet, marriage, divorce, business contracts, and even the proper way to clean one's teeth. Muslims are forbidden to eat certain foods such as pork, to drink alcohol, or to gamble. Islam, like most other religions, also prohibits murder and theft.

An Islamic term that is often misunderstood is *jihad (jee HUHD)*. The term means "to struggle," to do one's best to resist temptation and overcome evil. Under certain conditions, the struggle to overcome evil may require action. The Qur'an and Sunna allow self-defense and participation in military conflict, but restrict it to the right to defend against aggression and persecution. *Jihad,* for example, was first carried out against the Meccans who had forbidden Muslims to practice or preach their religion. While Islam forbade forced religious observance in the 600s, most rulers in the world at the time decided what religion their subjects would follow and persecuted those who refused.

In contrast to some other societies of the time, Muslim women were also given clear rights in marriage and the right to an education. They had the right to control the earnings from their work, to make contracts, and to serve as witnesses in court.

Many of these rights have become established law in Muslim countries to the present day. In other places, many of these rights have faded over time and have been replaced by oppressive local traditions. Customs of individual countries, some of them originating before Islam, often have determined women's roles more than Islamic principles.

Islam, like other religions, does influence the everyday lives of believers, from birth to death. Muslim parents chant the profession of faith over each newborn baby. Children use the Qur'an as they learn to read and write.

Many Muslims carry prayer beads that they use during free moments of the day as they think of Allah. Most Islamic prayer beads have 33 beads. Some people use the beads to count off the names of God or to praise God. These customs of both formal and informal worship often develop along regional lines, though in Islam the Qur'an and Sunna help unify practices. When someone is about to die, the Qur'an is recited at the person's bedside. ■

R E V I E W

1. **FOCUS** Find details to support the statement, "Islam, like other religions, is not only a system of beliefs but also a way of life."

2. **CONNECT** In what ways is Islam similar to Judaism and Christianity?

3. **SOCIAL SYSTEMS** How did Islam affect the rights and status of women?

4. **CRITICAL THINKING** Why do you think the Arabs and others in Southwest Asia would have been attracted to Islam? Explain your reason.

5. **ACTIVITY** Interview your classmates or use the encyclopedia to find out what these rituals have in common: Yom Kippur (among Jews), Lent (among Christians), and Ramadan (among Muslims).

Chapter 3

LESSON 3

Early Islam

According to the Qur'an, one day in 632, Muhammad received one of his last messages from Allah: "This day, have I perfected for you your religion and completed my favor to you." Islam teaches that Muhammad was overcome with joy, for he realized that this meant he had accomplished his mission on earth. He had preached and spread Islam throughout the land. Most of Arabia had embraced Islam. He also realized that, with his mission complete, he would soon join Allah in heaven.

Muhammad's success in spreading Islam was due in large part to his strong character. His followers were attracted to his morality, courage, and compassion, perhaps as much as they were attracted to his teaching.

When Muhammad died suddenly in 632 without naming a successor, his followers were stunned. Panic swept the community. Some groups, reasoning that the Muslim community would die without Muhammad, renounced Islam. What would Muslims do without their inspired leader and prophet of Allah? Could someone who was not Allah's prophet guide them?

Abu Bakr *(AH boo BAH kur)*, one of Muhammad's advisers,

offered wise counsel. He stressed the fact that Muslims worshiped Allah, not Muhammad:

> *And Muhammad is no more than a Messenger; all messengers before him have passed away.*
>
> Qur'an, 3:142

Abu Bakr's words restored calm and faith in the hearts of Muslims. The Muslim leaders now had to choose a successor to the prophet Muhammad.

THINKING FOCUS

What challenges did Muslims face after Muhammad's death?

Key Terms

- caliph
- council
- Shiite
- Sunni

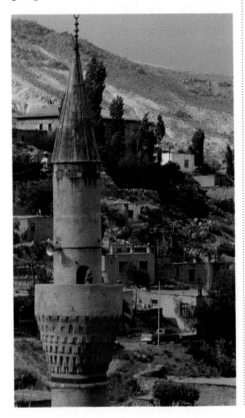

◄ *The teachings of Muhammad lived on after his death. Here a muezzin, or Muslim crier, calls the hour of prayer from the minaret of a mosque in Sille, Turkey.*

65

The Roots of Islam

The First Caliph

➤ *Copies of the Qur'an were often richly decorated. This manuscript page was produced in Egypt during the Mamluk dynasty in the early fourteenth century and is now in the Chester Beatty Library in Dublin.*

■ *How was the problem of Muhammad's successor resolved?*

Soon after Muhammad's death, his most trusted advisers met to choose a **caliph,** an Arabic word meaning "successor." This caliph, Muslims realized, could not give the same kind of spiritual leadership as Muhammad had. The new caliph would not be the prophet of Allah, as Muhammad had been. Rather, he would act as the political and military leader of the Muslims.

Four contenders for the position stood out. Abu Bakr was Muhammad's father-in-law and one of his most respected companions. Two other contenders were Umar and Uthman, Muhammad's long-time friends and advisers. The fourth was Ali, a blood relative. Ali was Muhammad's cousin, his son-in-law, and the father of his grandsons.

An assembly of tribal leaders in Medina chose Abu Bakr as Muhammad's successor. Abu Bakr's first task was to put down revolts by tribes in the area who had renounced Islam after the

death of Muhammad. Thus, he convinced these tribes that the state was still strong. Under Abu Bakr's leadership, the Arabs were united again. The Muslim state began to extend its rule to areas outside Arabia, north into Syria and east into Mesopotamia. ■

The Next Two Caliphs

Abu Bakr, who became caliph at age 59, was caliph for only two years. Before his death in 634, Abu Bakr appointed Umar as his successor. An energetic and spirited leader, Umar encouraged his armies to conquer more lands.

The Muslims were extremely tolerant of those they conquered, as long as they were "people of the book." The Muslims allowed Christians and Jews to keep their churches and synagogues and

promised them security. In fact, some peoples who were persecuted by Persian and Byzantine conquerors, such as the Christians in Egypt and the Jews in Syria, welcomed Muslim rule. They even aided the Muslim takeovers.

Non-Muslims who were not Christians or Jews were also tolerated. Even some other non-Judeo-Christian groups were granted the status of people of the book.

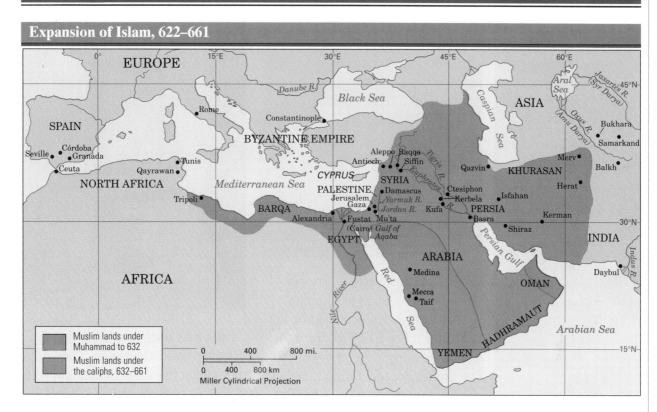

EUROPE

SPAIN

Seville • Córdoba • Granada
• Ceuta

NORTH AFRICA

Rome •

Danube R.

Black Sea

Constantinople •

BYZANTINE EMPIRE

CYPRUS

Mediterranean Sea

Tunis •

Qayrawan •

Tripoli •

BARQA

Alexandria •

Fustat •
(Cairo)

EGYPT

Antioch •

Aleppo • Raqqa
• Siffin

SYRIA
Damascus •
Jerusalem • Yarmuk R.
Gaza • Jordan R.
Mu'ta •
Gulf of
Aqaba

Red

AFRICA

Nile River

Sea

ASIA

Caspian Sea

Aral
Sea

Jaxartes R.
(Syr Darya)

Bukhara •

• Samarkand

Oxus R.
(Amu Darya)

Qazvin •

KHURASAN

Merv •

• Balkh

Ctesiphon •
• Kerbela
Kufa •
Basra •

Tigris R.
Euphrates R.

Isfahan •

PERSIA

Shiraz •

Herat •

Kerman •

30°N

INDIA

Persian Gulf

• Daybul

Indus R.

ARABIA

• Medina

• Mecca
Taif

OMAN

HADHRAMAUT

Arabian Sea

15°N

YEMEN

Muslim lands under
Muhammad to 632

Muslim lands under
the caliphs, 632–661

0   400   800 mi.

0   400   800 km

Miller Cylindrical Projection

In 644, on his deathbed, Umar named a **council,** or an assembly, to choose the next caliph. This council appointed Uthman. He, in turn, continued to conquer other lands and expand the empire. As you can see on the map above, Muslim forces had pushed into North Africa and had completed the conquest of Persia by 661. ∎

▲ *The four caliphs after Muhammad greatly expanded the Muslim Empire. About how many times larger was it in 661 than in 632?*

∎ *Why was the expansion of the Muslim Empire so successful?*

Early Political Division

The state's rapid expansion created challenges for the Muslim government. Culturally different people came under one rule. Communication with remote Medina was hard. The governors relied on local people, often non-Muslims, in the administration. In 656, Uthman was murdered by a number of disgruntled people from the province of Egypt.

This situation threatened the unity of the Muslim state. Ali was the natural choice for leadership, having participated in the election of previous leaders. He had been among Muhammad's most trusted and loyal companions. Muawiya *(mu AH wih ya),* a relative of

Uthman, developed a following in Syria, where he was governor.

Muawiya challenged Ali by demanding that the murderers be punished immediately. He then challenged Ali's right to rule. This forced Ali to oppose him for the sake of unity. Before the two opposing camps came to battle, Ali agreed to negotiate, but talks failed to solve the conflict. Ali ruled for only five years before he was murdered by an angry former supporter. In 661, Muawiya became caliph.

The Shiites

The problem that had caused the civil war remained. Who was Muhammad's rightful successor—

Across Time & Space

The largest Muslim communities today are in South and Southeast Asia, Africa, and the Middle East. In 1995 there were approximately 1.2 billion Muslims in the world. There are about 5 million Muslims in North America.

67

The Roots of Islam

Religious Populations of the World Today

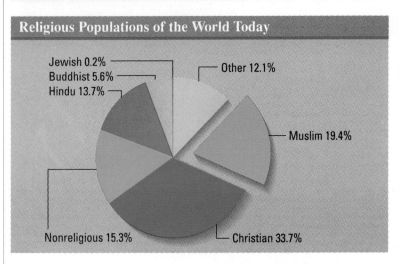

Jewish 0.2%
Buddhist 5.6%
Hindu 13.7%
Other 12.1%
Muslim 19.4%
Nonreligious 15.3%
Christian 33.7%

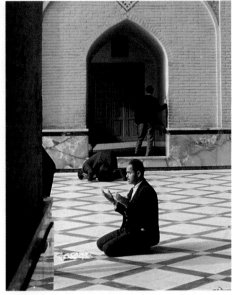

▲ *What percentage of the world religious population is Muslim?*

his descendants, such as Ali, or elected caliphs, such as Uthman?

Ali's followers became known as **Shiites** *(shee EYETZ),* from the Arabic meaning "the party of Ali." The Shiites accepted only members of Muhammad's family as his successors. It was their opinion that Ali should have been chosen over Abu Bakr from the beginning. Later, Shiite scholars denied the legitimacy of the first three caliphs, who had not been blood relatives of the prophet.

The Shiites gave Ali the title of the first Imam, meaning divinely guided successor of Muhammad. This concept of the Imam took on a strong sense of spiritual authority.

The Sunnis

■ *How did the division of Muslims into Sunnis and Shiites come about?*

Those who claim to follow the Sunna, or example of the prophet Muhammad, are known as **Sunni** Muslims. They accept the election of the first four caliphs, called the Rightly-Guided Caliphs. They do not attach the same meaning to the Shiite idea of the Imam. Sunnis emphasize Muhammad's teaching that every individual has a direct relationship with God.

The two groups still exist in the Muslim world today. Sunnis make up more than 80 percent of all Muslims. Iran has the largest number of Shiites. Out of a total population of 60 million, over 90 percent are Shiites.

The differences between Sunnis and Shiites have become public knowledge today, but all Muslims remain united by their common faith in Allah. They also share a reverence for the Qur'an as Allah's word and recognize Muhammad as Allah's prophet. ■

R E V I E W

1. **FOCUS** What challenges did Muslims face after Muhammad's death?
2. **CONNECT** Why were many Muslims fearful after the death of Muhammad?
3. **GEOGRAPHY** How far did the Muslim Empire extend under the four caliphs?
4. **CRITICAL THINKING** Do you think the conflict between

Ali and Muawiya was related to the Muslim state's rapid expansion? Give reasons for your answer.

5. **WRITING ACTIVITY** Assume you are a Muslim soldier on your way to conquer Syria in the year A.D. 635. Write three journal entries that reveal your thoughts about Islam, fighting in battle, or life in the desert.

Chapter 3

Making Parallel Timelines

Here's Why

Most timelines show you dates from a single culture or nation. Some timelines show links between cultural or geographical groups. Parallel timelines show parallels between events and are lined up in parallel.

Some of the events you studied in the Muslim Empire happened at the same time as events in Chapter 2. Parallel timelines help compare different events that happened at the same time.

Here's How

You can make a parallel timeline that helps you see events side by side:

1. Decide what you want to see. You may want to compare the histories of several groups. Or you may have noticed a pattern of events. The timelines below show events in the Muslim Empire and events in other parts of the world.

2. Decide what span of time your timelines will cover. Make sure your timelines are divided into equal and parallel parts. The timelines below cover A.D. 450–700. They are divided into five 50-year segments.

3. Gather dates and information about events for each part of the timeline.

4. Plot the events near the appropriate dates on the timeline. What was going on in the world during the Hijrah?

Try It

Copy the timeline below and plot these events:

- 661, Muslim Empire in North Africa and Persia
- 528, Justinian Code
- 630, Muhammad arrives in Mecca
- 537, New Hagia Sophia in Constantinople

Apply It

Create a parallel timeline. On one part, show events in your own life; on another part, show some significant events that happened in the United States. Find the U.S. dates in a yearbook or an almanac.

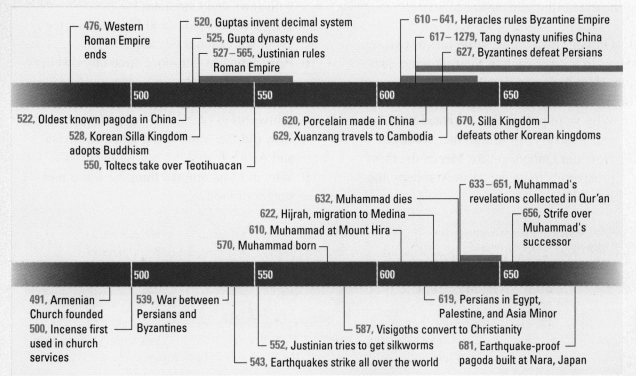

476, Western Roman Empire ends

520, Guptas invent decimal system
525, Gupta dynasty ends
527–565, Justinian rules Roman Empire

610–641, Heracles rules Byzantine Empire
617–1279, Tang dynasty unifies China
627, Byzantines defeat Persians

| 500 | 550 | 600 | 650 |

522, Oldest known pagoda in China
528, Korean Silla Kingdom adopts Buddhism
550, Toltecs take over Teotihuacan

620, Porcelain made in China
629, Xuanzang travels to Cambodia

670, Silla Kingdom defeats other Korean kingdoms

633–651, Muhammad's revelations collected in Qur'an
632, Muhammad dies
656, Strife over Muhammad's successor
622, Hijrah, migration to Medina
610, Muhammad at Mount Hira
570, Muhammad born

| 500 | 550 | 600 | 650 |

491, Armenian Church founded
500, Incense first used in church services
539, War between Persians and Byzantines
619, Persians in Egypt, Palestine, and Asia Minor
587, Visigoths convert to Christianity
552, Justinian tries to get silkworms
543, Earthquakes strike all over the world
681, Earthquake-proof pagoda built at Nara, Japan

The Roots of Islam

Chapter Review

Reviewing Key Terms

caliph (p. 66)
council (p. 67)
idol (p. 55)
Islam (p. 60)
monotheism (p. 59)
mosque (p. 60)
Muslim (p. 60)
nomad (p. 53)

oasis (p. 53)
pilgrimage (p. 57)
Qur'an (p. 58)
Shiite (p. 67)
Sunna (p. 61)
Sunni (p. 68)
tribe (p. 55)

A. The following quotations express the feelings of various people. For each statement, identify the key term most closely associated with it.
1. "With my family always moving to the next pastureland, I look forward to seeing old friends."
2. "I enjoy traveling to religious sites."
3. "They say it's green and fertile enough there to grow crops."
4. "Muhammad taught that the faith was named 'submission to Allah.'"

B. Write one or two sentences telling how each key term below is related to Islam.
1. idol
2. Qur'an
3. monotheism
4. Muslim
5. Sunna
6. mosque
7. council
8. caliph
9. Shiite
10. Sunni
11. tribe

Exploring Concepts

A. Many important events occurred between 500 and 700 in the history of Mecca and Islam. Copy the timeline on your own paper. Then fill in the event that goes with each date.

B. On your own paper, write one or two sentences to answer each of the following questions. Use facts and details from the chapter for your answers.
1. Why were people first attracted to Mecca, and why do they still go there today?
2. How did Quraysh make Mecca the most prosperous trade center in Arabia by the late 500s?
3. What did early nomadic families and townspeople offer each other?
4. What important belief do Muslims share with Jews and Christians?
5. Why did the Sunnis and Shiites disagree about who should be caliph?
6. How did trade introduce Arab city dwellers to other cultures?
7. How did the Quraysh ensure peaceful pilgrimages?
8. How did the Arabs bring Islam to Africa and Asia?
9. Why did Muhammad think he was a messenger of God?

500, Mecca emerges as most important stop along the caravan routes.

622, _____

630, _____

661, _____

500   550   600   650   700

632, _____   633, _____

Reviewing Skills

1. Create a parallel timeline comparing events that took place in the Muslim Empire during the time period from A.D. 630 through 670. You read about the following events in the expansion of the Muslim Empire in Lesson 3:
   - 633, Muslim forces move north into Syria and east into Mesopotamia.
   - 648, Muslim forces push into North Africa.
   - 661, Muslims complete conquest of Persia.

   Find and list dates from Lesson 3 for the following problems of the Muslim government after 630:
   - Muhammad dies suddenly.
   - First caliph Abu Bakr dies.
   - Caliph Umar dies.
   - Caliph Uthman murdered by disgruntled people from Egypt.
   - Ali is murdered, and Muawiya becomes undisputed caliph.

   Plot the dates of all these events from Lesson 3 in the appropriate places on your timeline.

2. When it is 7 A.M. on Tuesday in Teheran, Iran, what time and day is it in New York City? You may need to look at the time-zone map on pages 8 and 9 to find the answer.

3. What would you draw to show the events that took place during several specific times in history?

Using Critical Thinking

1. Think about the geography of Arabia and the people who lived there. Some people were nomadic herders, some were settled farmers, and some were city-living merchants or artisans. Why do you think these three ways of life grew up? How did they work together to create a successful society?

2. Anwar el-Sadat, a Muslim and the late president of Egypt, once said: "There can be hope only for a society that acts as one big family, not as many separate ones." How would the Muslims in A.D. 630 to 660 have responded to this statement?

3. Ali, Muhammad's son-in-law, wrote: "He who has a thousand friends has not a friend to spare; and he who has one enemy will meet him everywhere." How could you apply this to nations today? Give some examples from today's news that support your opinion.

4. Imagine you are a nomad with a family to support living around A.D. 500. You must decide whether to continue wandering or to settle down at an oasis. What is your future plan for you and your family? What are the dangers you face living at that time in history?

Preparing for Citizenship

1. WRITING ACTIVITY You leave your home in Alexandria for the pilgrimage to Mecca. Using the map on page 53 and other atlases, write a letter describing your route, the landscapes and peoples you see as you travel, and any incidents that happen along the way. Describe what you see in Mecca.

2. COLLABORATIVE LEARNING Form small groups of students to build a miniature mosque. You may decide to use cardboard, papier-mâché, or other materials. Have one member do research at the library to find out what the insides of mosques look like. Have another member design a building plan. And have two members collect the building materials. Together, construct the mosque according to your plan.

The Roots of Islam

Chapter 4

The Empire of Islam

To the east in Mesopotamia, the grand city of Baghdad arose. "It will surely be the most flourishing city in the world," boasted the caliph. To the west in Spain, an equally grand city blossomed. "Do not speak to me of the court of Baghdad nor of its magnificence...," wrote a poet, "because there is no place like Cordoba anywhere on this earth." As Muslim influence spread from the Near East to the Atlantic Ocean, these two cities became centers of Muslim trade, art, and learning.

During the 600s, Muslims conquered much of the Middle East. People converted to Islam and built mosques, like this one in Qum, Iran.

c. 650 Muslims conquer Persia and take treasures such as the gold and silver Sassanid dish (above) showing a lion hunt.

| 600 | 800 | 1000 |

768 Germanic leader Charlemagne becomes emperor of the former Western Roman Empire.

635

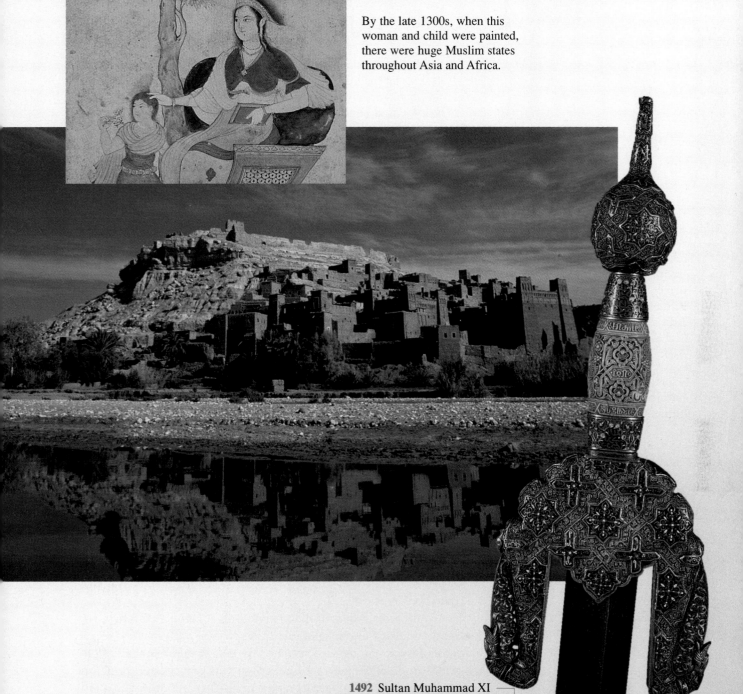

By the late 1300s, when this woman and child were painted, there were huge Muslim states throughout Asia and Africa.

1492 Sultan Muhammad XI surrenders, ending Muslim rule in Spain. His gold ceremonial sword is shown to the right.

1200

1400

1600

c. 1277 Invaders from central Asia conquer China.

1453 The Byzantine Empire falls to the Ottoman Turks.

1492

Medieval Muslim Writings

With the great explosion of learning in Baghdad and Cordoba and the love of Muslims for the beauty of the Arabic language, stories, essays, and poems were a natural way for people to organize what they had learned and to express their feelings. These short pieces on various topics could be used to teach a moral, to send information to friends, to provoke a response from other scholars, or just to express what was in the heart. What values are expressed by these medieval Muslim writings?

The Cadi and the Fly

Al-Jahiz

Al-Jahiz (ahl JAH heeth) was born in the port of Basra about 776, when the city was at its height of cultural and commercial importance. He traced his family roots to East Africa and became a famous figure in Muslim culture. He lived for many years at Baghdad and became a writer, scholar, and adviser at the court of the caliphs. His story titled The Cadi and the Fly *(a cadi is a judge) is a story with a moral, a piece of wise teaching that comes at the end.*

There can never have been a magistrate as sedate, composed, dignified, impassive, self-controlled or precise in his movements as a cadi we had at Basra called 'Abd Allah Ibn Sawwar.

He used to say the morning prayer at home, though he lived quite near the mosque, and then go to his court, where he would wrap his robes around him and sit down without supporting himself on anything as he did so. He sat bolt upright and stock still, neither turning round in his seat, opening his coat, crossing his legs, or leaning on either arm of the chair; he was like a statue.

He would remain thus until the noon prayer compelled him to rise, then sit down again and take up the same posture until the time of the afternoon prayer; having accomplished that, he would remain motionless until sunset, when he would get up, say his prayers, and sometimes (what am I saying? often, rather) return to his seat and deal with a multitude of deeds, contracts, and miscellaneous documents. Then he would say his evening prayer and go home. If the truth be told, he never once got up to go to the lavatory during the whole of his tenure of office: he did not need to, since he never felt like a drink of water or other beverage. Such was his routine all the year round, winter and summer, whether the days were long or short. He never so much as lifted his hand or inclined his head, but limited himself to moving his lips.

One day, when his assessors and the public had taken their place beside him, in front of him and in the gallery, a fly settled on his nose. It lingered there awhile, and then moved to the corner of his eye. He left it

---

In Chapter 3 you learned about the rise and expansion of Islam. These writings are examples of the great cultural flowering that Islam brought to Asia, Africa, and Europe.

cadi (KAH dee), **magistrate** a judge

sedate calm
composed not excitable
impassive showing no emotion

compelled forced

tenure a period of time in a particular position

assessors officials to evaluate property for taxation

alone and endured its biting, just as he had armed himself with patience when it settled on his nose, neither twitching his nostrils, shaking his head, or waving it away with a finger. However, since the fly was becoming really persistent, causing him acute pain and moving towards a spot where it was beyond bearing, he blinked his eyelid. The fly did not go away. This persistence drove him to blink repeatedly, whereupon the fly moved away until the eyelid stopped moving, then returned to the corner of the eye even more fiercely than before and stuck its sting into an already sore spot. The cadi's endurance was weakening and his irritation growing: he blinked harder and more rapidly. The fly went away for a moment, then settled again and became so persistent that our cadi, his patience completely at an end, was reduced to driving it away with his hand: Everyone in court was watching this and pretending not to see it. The fly went away until he dropped his hand, then returned to the charge and compelled him to protect his face with the hem of his sleeve, not once but several times.

The magistrate realized that no detail of this scene was escaping his assessors and the public. When he caught their eye, he exclaimed: "I swear the fly is more persistent than the cockroach and more presumptuous than the crow! God forgive me! How many men are infatuated with their own persons! But God acquaints them with their hidden weakness! Now I know I am but a weakling, seeing that God's most feeble creature has vanquished and confounded me!" Then he recited this verse: "And if the fly should rob them of aught, the gods of the idolaters would be unable to restore it to them. Worshipper and idol are both powerless." [Qur'an, 22:72–73].

endurance the ability to withstand hardship

presumptuous going beyond what is right or proper
infatuated to be so in love as to lose one's reason
aught (AHT) anything

Further Reading

Muhammad: His Life Based on the Earliest Sources. Martin Lings. An engaging narrative of the life of the prophet Muhammad, based on the biography by Ibn Hisham.

Anthology of Islamic Literature: From the Rise of Islam to Modern Times. James Kritzeck. A useful compendium of literature, poetry, tales, historical treatises, and other genres of writing.

The Travels of Ibn Jubayr. R.J.C. Broadhurst. Follow the adventures of a 12th-century Muslim from Spain as he journeys throughout the Mediterranean world on his way to Mecca.

The Disadvantages of Parchment

Al-Jahiz

Al-Jahiz lived at a time when paper had just been brought from China to the Muslim world. Most people still wrote on parchment, animal skins that had been scraped clean and treated for taking ink. In this letter, Al-Jahiz argues to a friend against using it anymore. Paper came to be made at Baghdad by factories along the Tigris River. There, water-powered trip hammers processed the pulp. It was many years before Europe could stop importing paper from the Muslim world and make its own.

What is it to you that all my books are written on China paper or Khurasan paper? Explain why you have pressed on me the advantages of using parchment and urged me to write on hide, when you know very well that parchment is heavy and cumbersome, is useless if it gets damp, and swells in wet weather— so much so that were its sole disadvantage to make its users hate rainy days, and its owners regard a shower as a nightmare, this alone would be reason enough for giving up the stuff. You know very well that on rainy days copyists do not write a single line or cut a single skin.

Parchment has only to get moist, let alone left out in the rain or dipped in water, for it to bulge and stretch; and then it does not return to its original state, but dries noticeably shrunk and badly wrinkled. What is more, it smells worse, is more expensive, and lends itself more readily to fraud: Wasit skins are passed off as Kufa ones, and Basra ones as Wasit ones. You are obliged to leave it to age in order to get rid of the smell and for the hair to fall out; it is fuller of lumps and flaws, more is wasted in scraps and clipping, it turns yellow sooner, and the writing very quickly disappears altogether. If a scholar wished to take with him enough parchment for his journey, a camel-load would not suffice, whereas the equivalent in *qutni* [cotton-fiber paper] could be carried with his provisions.

You said: "You should use parchment because it stands up better to scratching out and correction, and also to repeated borrowing and handling; then unwanted sheets are still worth something, palimpsests can be re-used, and second-hand parchment does the same job as new. Writing-books of *qutni* are of little value on the market, even if they contain the most original texts, the choicest rarities, and the most priceless learning. If you went to sell books of an equivalent number of parchment pages containing nothing but the feeble poetry and the idlest gossip, they would be in much greater demand." And you added: "Hide is entrusted with the accounts of the administrative system, with title-deeds, diplomas, contracts and surveys; sculptors' sketches are made on it, postal pouches are made out of it, and it is used for making bags, lids for jars and stoppers for bottles." You did me a grave disservice when you made me take to using parchment instead of paper, and were the cause of my misfortune when you made me exchange light writing-books for volumes too heavy to hold, that crush people's chests, bow their backs, and make them blind.

cumbersome difficult to handle because of size or weight

suffice to be enough

provisions supplies

palimpsest (puh LIHMP sehst) a manuscript, usually papyrus or parchment, that has been erased and written over many times; often the old writing still shows through

Poems from Muslim Spain

Ibn Sa'id al-Maghribi was born in Granada, Spain, in 1213, but during his life traveled to such places as North Africa, Cairo, Baghdad, and Mecca. He completed a 15-volume anthology of poems that his great-grandfather had begun and which had taken over 100 years to complete. Here are three works by poets from the 11th, 12th, and 13th centuries. The poems give evidence of the water-related technology that eventually spread from Muslim lands to Europe. As you read these poems, ask yourself what water represents in each of them.

Good Deeds At Random

Scatter your good deeds all around, not caring
    whether they fall on those near or far away,
Just as the rain never cares where the clouds pour it out,
    whether on fertile ground or on rocks.

Ibn Siraj, Cordoba
died 1114

The Spinning Water Wheel

How wonderful is the water wheel! It spins around like a celestial
    sphere, yet there are no stars on it.
It was placed over the river by hands that decreed that it refresh others'
    spirits as it, itself, grows tired.
It is like a free man, in chains, or like a prisoner marching freely.
Water rises and falls from the wheel as if it were a cloud that draws
    water from the sea and later pours it out.
The eyes fell in love with it, for it is a boon companion to the garden, a
    cupbearer who doesn't drink.

Ibn al-Abbar, Valencia
died 1260

celestial heavenly, planetary
decreed commanded

boon companion best friend

The Fountain

Oh, the beauty of the fountain, pelting the horizon with
    shooting stars, leaping and jumping around playfully;
Bubbles of water burst out of it, gushing into its basin
    like a frightened snake,
as if it used to move back and forth beneath the earth, but
    when it has the chance, it quickly escaped,
And settled into the basin, happy with its new home, and
    in amazement kept smiling, showing its bubbles.
And the branches hover overhead, about to kiss it as it smiles,
    revealing the whiteness of its teeth.

Ibn al-Ra'i'ah, Seville
flourished in 13th century

hover to float in the air

600   800   1000   1200   1400   1600

635   750

LESSON 1

A Century of Expansion

THINKING FOCUS

How did the Umayyads unite the many lands and peoples of the Muslim Empire?

Key Terms

- empire
- bureaucracy
- emir
- dissent

Muslim soldiers from Arabia attacked Damascus, Syria, in A.D. 635. The Persians and Byzantines had fought back and forth over the territory of Syria for generations. Many inhabitants of Damascus helped the Muslims, expecting their rule to be better than the previous rulers'.

Some soldiers, with their lances, flung small pots of burning oil over the wall, creating smoke and flames that could not be put out. Others loaded catapults with rocks to rain down on the citizens. By nightfall the battle was won. A treaty was drawn up:

> *In the name of Allah, the compassionate, the Merciful. This is what Khalid ibn al-Walid would grant the inhabitants of Damascus if he enters: he promises security for their lives, property, and churches. Their city wall shall not be demolished, nor shall any Muslim be quartered in their houses. We give them the pact of Allah and the protection of His prophet, the Caliph, and the believers. So long as they pay jizya tax, nothing but good shall befall them.*

Expansion Under Umayyad Rule

The Muslim soldiers who fought the Byzantines at Damascus helped to create an **empire,** a number of peoples or provinces ruled by one central authority. After capturing Syria, the victorious Muslim armies went on to conquer Mesopotamia in 637.

By the middle of the 600s, Persia fell to the Muslims. The Muslim Empire then expanded farther to the east by securing the lands that are today known as Turkmenistan, Afghanistan, and Pakistan.

The Umayyads

The Umayyads *(oo MAY yahds)* fought for Islam in these eastern conquests. The Umayyad leader, Muawiya *(mu AH wih ya),* was one of the soldiers who had helped capture Damascus in 635. He had served for 25 years as the Muslim governor of Syria. During that time, Muawiya had built up a devoted army of followers. After the assassination of the fourth caliph, Muawiya had enough support to take control of the empire in 661.

78

Umayyad Changes

Muawiya moved the capital from Muhammad's home, Medina in Arabia, to his own, more central city of Damascus in Syria. From this political and military center, he could control the empire.

Muawiya began the practice of appointing a son as the next caliph. He founded a tradition of continuous rule by one family. The Umayyads ruled for 90 years.

Westward Expansion

The Umayyads were talented military leaders, and during their years in power, 661 to 750, the Muslim Empire expanded. Their armies advanced west into Africa. Soon the Berbers who lived along the northern coast and the Sahara, converted to Islam.

In 711, with the help of the Berbers, the Muslims moved northward across the Strait of Gibraltar (*juh BRAWL tur*).

The Muslims were so determined to conquer the Iberian Peninsula that upon landing at Gibraltar, they burned all of their own boats. Retreat was not possible. Now they could only march forward. The conquest of Spain took seven years or less. The Catholic Visigoths, whose rule was no longer popular with the common people, were not able to raise a large enough army. The persecution of Jews and of Christians who disagreed with the church of the rulers, also helped cause their defeat. In the end, the Muslims drove out the Visigothic leaders. Almost the entire peninsula had become Umayyad territory.

From their bases in Spain, Muslim armies repeatedly crossed the Pyrenees (*PIHR uh neez*) and raided France. In 732, the Muslims confronted Charles Martel and his army of Franks. Martel, whose name means "the Hammer," repeatedly attacked the Muslims.

Martel's troops stopped the Muslims at the Battle of Tours in 732. This battle was one of the most decisive in European history. It determined that Europe would be Christian and not Muslim. Trace the Umayyad conquests and their expansion of the Muslim Empire on the map on page 80. ■

■ *What changes did the Umayyads bring to the Muslim Empire?*

▼ *Buildings in Morocco were often made of dried mud bricks. The same material was used to build walls around Moroccan cities to protect them from enemy attack.*

> Use the map to compare the amount of land under Muslim rule during Muhammad's life and during the time of the first four caliphs with the land ruled during Umayyad times. During which time period did the greatest expansion occur?

Islamic Empire, 661

Conquests, 661–750

0   150   300 mi.

0   150   300 km

Mercator Projection

An Empire of Many Peoples

As the Muslims conquered new lands, the borders of the Muslim Empire expanded far beyond Arabia. Among the peoples conquered by the Arabs were Christians and Jews. The Arabs also conquered people whose religion involved the worship of many different gods.

Treatment of Non-Muslims

Over the centuries that followed, many people in the lands under Muslim rule converted to

Map labels:

45°E   60°E

ASIA

Volga R.   Ural R.

Don R.

CRIMEA   45°N

Black Sea   CAUCASUS MTS.   Caspian Sea   Aral Sea   Jaxartes (Syr Darya) R.   TRANSOXIANA

Tiflis

TAURUS MTS.   Tabriz   Oxus (Amu Darya) R.   Bukhara   Samarkand

CYPRUS   Mosul   KHURASAN   HINDU KUSH

SYRIA   Tigris R.   ZAGROS MTS.   Kabul

Damascus   Euphrates R.   Baghdad   PERSIA   GHAZNA

Jerusalem   30°N

Indus R.

Persian Gulf   INDIA

Medina   Red Sea   ARABIAN PENINSULA

Mecca   Arabian Sea   15°N

Islam. Some rulers forced people to take on Muslim ways. Many Christians and Jews kept their traditional faiths. Spain became known for its mixing of cultural traditions. When non-Arabs began to convert to Islam, they were sometimes not accepted socially by the Arab community. Some Arabs wanted to keep their culture free of outside influ-ences. In time this changed, and a Muslim culture developed that included the customs and traditions of non-Arabs.

The Umayyad Muslims were generally tolerant of people, such as Christians and Jews, who believed in a single God. Muslims consid-ered Jews and Christians to be "people of the book."

Christians and Jews had full religious freedom. They built churches and synagogues, and several were financed by the state. The state did not ask Christians and Jews to perform military service, but it required them to pay a head-tax, called *jizya.* Many Christians, Jews, and other non-Muslims held key positions in government. Everyone paid taxes on the produce from the land and trade. In addition, all Muslims were required to pay *zakat,* the 2.5 percent charity tax.

Many different peoples benefited from Muslim tolerance. Jews lived in Mesopotamia since the 500s B.C. When the Romans destroyed Judaea in A.D. 70, these Jewish communities grew very important. Their academies helped build Judaism as a religion defined by the Torah (the Jewish Bible), the rabbis (teachers), and the synagogue (temple). By 500, scholars had collected a vast amount of learning about the Torah in a work called the Talmud. This text became one of the great cornerstones of Judaism. Sassanid and Christian rulers had persecuted Jews, but Muslim rulers often protected them.

Government

The Umayyad caliph Muawiya patterned his highly organized government on the Byzantine model that he had first seen when he captured Damascus. He even kept some of the Christians in their old government posts. This system of rule and order was a **bureaucracy,** many different departments managed by workers appointed by the caliph or his representatives.

Under Muawiya, the provinces were ruled by **emirs,** or governors, appointed directly by the caliph.

One new emir of Mesopotamia gave his subjects this stern warning:

> I demand obedience from you, and you can demand uprightness from me. . . . Do not be carried away by your hatred and anger against me, it would go ill with you. I see many heads rolling; let each man see that his own head stays upon his shoulders!
>
> Ziyad Ibn Abihi, c. 670
> (zih YAHD IHBN ah BEE hih)

Muawiya encouraged his emirs to rule strictly in order to stamp out **dissent,** or disagreement. Mesopotamia had been a center of resistance to Umayyad rule.

Compare Ibn Abihi's warning with that of the Caliph Omar, who ruled before Muawiya, from 634 to 644. In an open letter to a provincial judge, he wrote,

> Be just between the two opponents in the way you look at them, your fairness and the way you seat them, so that neither the wealthy take advantage because of their class nor the poor lose faith in your justice. . . . Don't hesitate to correct your verdict if you found out that a previous judgment was wrong, because it is never too late to reinstate that which is right, and it is always better than perpetuating [continuing] the wrong. . . . Don't ever be restless or impatient during a dispute. Verily, God multiplies the reward for putting justice where it belongs. And whoever obeys his good intention and disregards the call of his desires, God will take care of his relations with people.
>
> Caliph Omar Ibn al-Khattab
> ruled 634–644

Umayyad Unity

Under the Umayyad dynasty, there was a succession of one caliph after another. There also developed a new Muslim culture for the empire. Abd al Malik *(ahb dul mah LIHK),* caliph from 685 to 705, was influential in shaping this culture.

A Common Language

Abd al Malik declared Arabic to be the official language of the empire. This enabled the Umayyads to bring the diverse cultures of their empire under control. Until Abd al Malik adopted Arabic as the official language, local government workers had been mostly non-Arabic. They had spoken the languages of their local communities. Now all government business and religious affairs were conducted in Arabic. Anyone who wished to participate fully in the culture had to speak Arabic.

A Common Coinage

Not only was the language the same throughout the empire, but the coins the people used were the same too. Muslims borrowed the idea of coinage from the Persians and the Byzantines. The govern-ment began minting coins around 640. Abd al Malik was responsible, around 700, for the first purely Muslim coins. They had no images but were inscribed in Arabic with important quotations from the Qur'an. The coins gave Muslims a symbol of the power of their empire. Having a common coinage also made commerce between parts of the empire easier.

Religious Architecture

One of the first things the Arabs did when they took over a new land was to build a mosque, so they could give thanks to Allah. Muslims throughout the empire could always find a mosque. The mosque would be built from materials that were common to the area.

In 688, during the caliphate of Abd al Malik, North Africa was conquered. In North Africa mosques were made of adobe and wood, because that is what was available for construction. A mosque of this type can be seen on page 116. But the same features that were important to the Islamic religion would be present in every mosque: a minaret, a mihrab, and an ablution fountain. ■

■ *How did Abd al Malik unify the Umayyad Empire?*

◄ *Muslim coins were inscribed with sayings from the Qur'an.*

83

The Empire of Islam

The Umayyad Downfall

The Umayyads conquered many new lands and peoples for Islam. However, by 750, after 90 years of continuous rule, they faced serious economic and political problems.

Many non-Muslim subjects had by this time converted to Islam. After they converted, they paid fewer taxes than they did before they converted. Consequently, as the number of conversions to Islam increased, the amount of tax money available for the empire to spend decreased.

By 732, the Muslim armies were making fewer new conquests. This stopped the flow of captured wealth that had enriched the empire's economy. The decline in tax revenues and the decrease in captured wealth helped contribute to the money shortage the Umayyads experienced. Examine the chart at the left to find how the percentage of the population paying full taxes varied in 727 and 738.

In addition, the Umayyad Empire had gained the reputation of being too much of a worldly kingdom and not interested enough in the religious ideals of the prophet Muhammad. In the last years of the dynasty, the Umayyads' opponents formed secret societies that were devoted to bringing about the downfall of the Umayyads.

One such group, the Abbasids *(AB uh sihdz)*, was named after a family headed by al Abbas. Some historians say that al Abbas was an uncle of Muhammad. The Abbasids started a successful rebellion against the Umayyad rulers from their stronghold northwest of Persia, in a land called Khurasan.

According to some accounts, one of the Abbasid generals, Abdullah *(ahb du LAH)*, invited 80 Umayyad leaders to a banquet. While his Umayyad guests were eating, Abdullah ordered his men to kill them. By 750, the Abbasid family was able to gain control of the Muslim Empire in the East.

Only one of the Umayyads, whose name was Abd al Rahman *(ahbd al rah MAHN)*, escaped from the Abbasids. He leaped out of a window at Abdullah's deadly dinner, swam across the Euphrates River, and fled in disguise. Then he wandered all the way across Arabia and Africa and crossed into Spain. Once in Spain, Abd al Rahman began to unite the warring Muslim groups there and to build a new Umayyad government.

Now the Muslim state was split between two ruling groups, the Umayyads in Europe and the Abbasids in Asia and Africa. Unified rule was over, but Muslim culture continued to grow. ■

Umayyad Tax Revenues, A.D. 727 and 738

▲ *By approximately what percent did the population that paid full taxes decline between the years 727 and 738?*

■ *What political problems led to the downfall of the Umayyad Empire?*

R E V I E W

1. **FOCUS** How did the Umayyads unite the many lands and peoples of the Muslim Empire?

2. **CONNECT** In what ways did the Umayyads carry out the ideals of Muhammad?

3. **ECONOMICS** What economic problems contributed to the collapse of the Umayyads?

4. **CRITICAL THINKING** Since the Muslims did not necessarily encourage people to convert to Islam, why did they bother expanding their empire?

5. **ACTIVITY** Examine some of the coins of your country. What do the images and inscriptions on the coins tell you about your country?

Chapter 4

LESSON 2

The Golden Age

> This island between the Tigris in the east and the Euphrates in the west is a marketplace for the world. All the ships that come up the Tigris will go up and anchor here; wares brought on ships . . . will be . . . unloaded here. It will be the highway for the people. . . .
>
> Praise be to God who preserved it for me and caused all those who came before me to neglect it. . . .
>
> It will surely be the most flourishing city in the world.
>
> Abu Jafar al Mansur, 752

THINKING FOCUS

How did the same wealth that brought the Abbasids power lead to their downfall?

Key Terms

- calligraphy
- faction

▼ *Between which two rivers did Baghdad develop?*

With these words, the second Abbasid caliph described his reasons for building Baghdad as the new capital of the Muslim Empire.

Baghdad, in Mesopotamia, was ideally located to become a world marketplace. It was situated along ancient trade routes serving both the East and the West. Soon Baghdad, somewhat like an island between the Tigris and Euphrates rivers, grew into a huge city that was the center of trade, learning, and government.

River traffic passed up and down the Tigris and Euphrates rivers. On it traveled the produce of the heavily irrigated lands of Mesopotamia. From the plains at the northern ends of the rivers came grain. The old Persian Royal Road still stood, and on it messengers rode from city to city. Camels and carts were loaded at river ports and headed to provincial towns and on to Damascus and Antioch. South of Baghdad, ships sailed to and from China, India, and Africa. Their precious cargoes were traded in Baghdad, throughout the Abbasid Empire, and beyond.

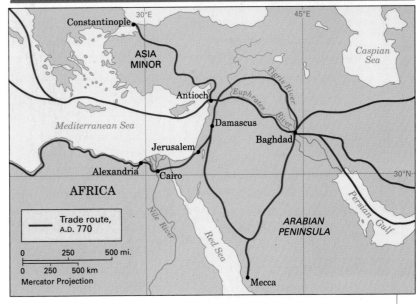

Baghdad: An Ideal Location

Trade route, A.D. 770

0   250   500 mi.

0   250   500 km

Mercator Projection

Constantinople •   ASIA MINOR   Caspian Sea   Antioch   Damascus   Baghdad   Jerusalem   Alexandria • Cairo   AFRICA   ARABIAN PENINSULA   Persian Gulf   Red Sea   Nile River   Mediterranean Sea   Mecca

Under Abbasid Rule

The Abbasids forcibly took over the territories that had been conquered originally during the time of the old Umayyad Empire. This new Abbasid Empire lasted from 750 to 1258.

One of caliph Abu Jafar al Mansur's first actions was to move the capital of the Muslim Empire from Damascus in Syria to Baghdad in Mesopotamia, where the Abbasid family had much support. Mesopotamia was also the richest province in the empire in tax revenues and in agricultural production. It was an ideal location for a capital city.

Once the Abbasids had achieved power, they were able to hold onto it because of their strong standing army. Abu Jafar al Mansur also used the postal communication system that the Umayyads had developed. However, he also used it as a spy network that would relay information about any dissent in the empire back to the caliph's palace.

The Muslim Empire began to absorb the traditions of the many different cultures that were a part of the empire. As the power center of the empire moved farther east, it was no longer possible for

UNDERSTANDING EMPIRE

An empire is a group of peoples or provinces ruled by the strongest one of them. Not all the subjects, or the people, of an empire have the same language, religion, or physical appearance. They do not earn their livings in the same ways, nor might they even live under the same laws. But they do have the same ruler.

The Life of an Empire

Historians have traditionally seen different stages in the life of an empire. An empire usually begins when a number of regions unite under one ruler, either willingly or by force. The beginning period is one of expansion. Soldiers of the empire might conquer other peoples. Appointed governors represent the ruler. The governors often replace the local and provincial administrators and judges.

During the height of an empire, culture and the economy usually flourish. As in many ancient empires, the civilization of the region of the rulers often absorbs some other cultures.

Empires Decline

Political and economic problems often lead to the

weakening and downfall of empires. Regions that have long been part of the empire may rebel against the powers that control them. War may disrupt the empire when region after region breaks free of the control of the nation that once ruled them. While empires can decline, the cultures within them often continue to develop long after the empires have ended.

the Arabs to dominate completely the government, the cultural life, or the economy.

The new culture that developed was Muslim, but it was open to ideas from many different countries and cultures, especially those of Persia. However, the Arabic language continued to be the vehicle of government, education, poetry, and, of course, religion. ■

■ *How did the Abbasids get and keep control of their empire?*

The New Capital of Baghdad

At the heart of this Arab-Persian culture was a city with a strong economy. Baghdad's economy relied on taxes and wealth generated by trade and manufacturing. It was also a city of great science and technology.

The empire was rich in the gold, silver, copper, and iron used in trade. Pearls from the Persian Gulf and precious gems from other Muslim lands were in great demand in the Baghdad market.

The Abbasids preserved and improved the ancient network of wells, underground canals, and water wheels. Food production improved under the Abbasids. Dates, rice, and other grains flourished in the rich soil between the Tigris and the Euphrates. In addition, the Abbasids introduced new breeds of livestock and hastened the spread of cotton.

Traders from Scandinavia to Africa came to Baghdad for the products of its industries as well. Leather goods, textiles, paper, metalwork, and perfumes were produced and sold in the city.

▼ *The Round City was a government complex, with administrative offices and residences for the caliph's relatives. The caliph's palace was topped with a dome, and on top of that was the figure of a mounted horseman, which could be seen from the outskirts of the city. The dome collapsed in a storm in 941, and the entire city was destroyed by the Mongols in 1258.*

Baghdad and the Round City, c. A.D. 820

The Round City (detail)

MARKETS LINING ENTRANCE ARCADES

MOAT

GATES
GUARDS
POLICE
PALACE
MOSQUE

GATES

DEFENSIVE FIELD

MARKETS LINING ENTRANCE ARCADES

Tigris River

Canals flowing from Diyala River

Canals flowing from Euphrates River

The Round City

Palace Gardens

Hospital

Tigris River

0   1 mi.
0   1 km

N
W — E
S

Different markets, according to trades

Urbanized areas

East Baghdad city wall

Residential zone (with traffic)

Government offices, residences of royal children and servants (pedestrian zone)

➤ *This ivory chess piece was presented to Charlemagne, king of the Franks from 768 to 814, by Harun al Rashid, fifth caliph of the Abbasid Empire.*

■ *Why did Baghdad become such an important center of world trade?*

To handle this great volume of business, the Muslims developed something very similar to a banking system throughout their empire. They had no bank buildings yet, but business people invested in long-distance trade, and goods were bought on credit.

Muslim rule unified most of the eastern world. Boundaries were no longer an obstacle. The Muslims introduced a uniform coinage system, which made commerce even easier. Soon brisk international trade brought great wealth to the whole Abbasid Empire and to its rulers.

The caliphs and the upper classes grew rich, and they enjoyed spending their money on lavish homes, fine clothing, and elaborate amusements. Horse racing and polo playing were popular activities. People with leisure time could engage in the sport of falconry—training falcons to hunt other birds which the trainer might eat. Wealthy families invited each other to elegant banquets with entertainment by dancers and poets. Such games as chess and backgammon were played during leisure time. ■

Abbasid Culture

Their great wealth enabled the Abbasids to support the arts and learning. The years from about 800 to around 1000 were a period of high achievement in the areas of art and literature.

➤ *Plaster moldings laced with an intricate leaf design cover the walls and ceilings of this Muslim palace.*

Art and Design

The unique style of Muslim art is unmistakable, because it so often uses Arabic script as its inspiration. Arabic lettering had a special significance for Muslims, because it was used to write down God's words as they had been given to Muhammad. **Calligraphy,** which means beautiful handwriting, flourished under the Abbasids. When used as decoration, the letters were often so fancy that they were almost unreadable. Examples on this and the next page show some of these designs.

Calligraphy and geometric designs, rather than the human form, were common decorations in mosques. The reason Muslims did this was because they were concerned that human images making. These Chinese prisoners won their freedom in exchange for revealing the secrets of papermaking. In time the skill of papermaking spread throughout the Muslim world, making books more available.

The availability of books contributed to the general interest in all types of learning. Caliph al Ma'mun, who ruled from 813 to 833, founded a school in Baghdad called the House of Wisdom (see p. 91). In the school, scholars translated Greek classics in philosophy into Arabic.

These books and thousands of others were brought to Muslim Spain and Sicily from the east. New works were produced in Spain as well. The Abbasid scholars of Baghdad helped preserve Greek classics that might otherwise have been lost or destroyed.

The Abbasids also became famous for their sensitive poetry:

> *You departed
> from my sight
> and entered my thoughts,
> travelled from my eyes
> to my heart.*
>
> Al Abbas Ibn al Ahnaf, c. 800

Many poets and writers from far away flocked to Baghdad, where the caliph welcomed them. ■

◄ In this painting of a coeducational classroom of the time, overseen by a bearded master, some students are reading and writing. The border of the painting is decorated with calligraphy and geometric designs.

Across Time & Space

The craft of papermaking was developed in China around 150 B.C. Paper was made by soaking flattened plant fibers and then allowing them to dry on a screen. The first papermaking factory in the Muslim Empire was built in Baghdad in A.D. 792.

■ *What achievements in culture led to this period being known as the Golden Age?*

would distract worshipers from praying to Allah. Most Muslim scholars agreed that creating images of living things like humans and animals, which have souls, is forbidden. They cautioned against worshiping created images.

Muslim artists often used decorative designs made up of plant patterns. The most common of these floral designs was the arabesque, a winding stem, leaves, and flowers, that formed a spiraling design.

Bookmaking and Literature

In 751, during a raid into central Asia, Abbasids captured some Chinese artisans skilled in paper

Abbasid Achievements in Learning

The interest in reading also extended to learning about science, mathematics, and medicine. The excellent reputation of Muslim scholars spread across the empire into Europe.

The Empire of Islam

Science and Mathematics

Muslim scholars of the Abbasid period were interested in further developing the findings of the ancient Greeks, Africans, and Asians in science, mathematics, and medicine. For example, Muslim astronomers mapped the solar system and believed, long before Columbus's time, that the earth was round.

Modern algebra is based on explorations in mathematics in the early 800s by one of the most famous Abbasid mathematicians, al Khwarizmi *(al KWAH rihz mee)*. Today, we call this type of mathematics *algebra* after the title of one of al Khwarizmi's books, *al jabr*, meaning "the addition of one thing to another."

Medicine

Muslim doctors who lived during the Abbasid reign became skilled at diagnosis and treatment of disease. One doctor, ar-Razi, a Persian-born physician of the 900s, wrote the first accurate description of the diseases that we know today as measles and smallpox. Other doctors performed surgery on patients in clean hospitals that were free to the public. At this time, Muslims were also experimenting with the treatment of disease through herbal medicines. Plants, such as coriander, were used for their medicinal powers. One of the leading Abbasid figures of medicine was Ibn Sina, known in Europe as Avicenna *(av ih SEHN uh)*. In his autobiography Avicenna wrote:

> Medicine is not one of the difficult sciences, and therefore I excelled in it in a very short time, to the point that distinguished physicians began to read medicine with me. I cared for the sick, and there opened up to me indescribable possibilities of therapy which can only be acquired through experience. At the same time, I was also occupied with jurisprudence and would engage in legal disputations, being now sixteen years of age.
>
> Ibn Sina, c. 1000

In addition to law and medicine, Avicenna had a number of other interests—philosophy, mathematics, and astronomy. He also wrote a vast medical encyclopedia called *Canon of Medicine.* It summed up the medical knowledge of the time and accurately described diseases and treatments.

▼ *A window (below) at Princeton University honors Abbasid doctor ar-Razi. Muslims also honored the Greek Aristotle, painted as a Muslim (bottom), for his study of plants, such as coriander, shown at top.*

An Abbasid Scholar

3:20 p.m., February 15, 832
In a study at the Bayt al-Hikmah
Baghdad's new "House of Wisdom"

Bookshelf
Many of the books in the Bayt al-Hikmah have been translated, copied, and bound right here in the building. Calligraphers and artists have beautified these books, too.

Turban
The scholar's turban is wrapped from many yards of fine, cotton muslin. His robe is damask, a specialty of the Damascus weavers.

Stomach
This scholar is hungry. He has been fasting since dawn, because Ramadan is the month for fasting for all Muslims. He is looking forward to sundown, when he will pray and then enjoy dinner.

Ink, Pen and Paper
The scholar writes with a pen that has been cut and trimmed from a reed, ink that has been made from lamp-black and gum arabic, and paper made from cotton fiber in a Baghdad paper factory.

Works
He is taking notes from books on religious and secular subjects, including philosophy, astronomy, mathematics, and medicine. The books are translations from Greek, Hebrew, Syriac, and Persian.

Qur'an
As a sign of respect, the Qur'an has its own stand made of fragrant, carved sandalwood imported from Southeast Asia. The scholar's copy of the Qur'an is illuminated with geometric designs.

91

Interest in treating illness went back to the earliest days of Muslim history. It was the prophet Muhammad himself who stated that Allah had provided a cure for every illness. ■

A Divided Empire

The years 800 to 1000 were a golden cultural period for the Abbasid Empire. The end of this period was also a financially difficult time for the government. Tax money was increasingly important to the caliphs because the Abbasids had lost control of several important trade routes. This hurt Baghdad's economy and led the caliphs to increase taxes to support their costly style of living.

Factions and Revolt

During the same period, several **factions,** or opposing groups, began either to leave the empire for other lands or to take control of distant parts of the empire away from the Abbasids. For example, the Fatimids, who were descendants of the Prophet's daughter Fatima, were unhappy about the costly lifestyle of the Abbasids. The Fatimids felt this lifestyle was corrupt compared to the simple lifestyle of Muhammad.

The Fatimids broke away from the Abbasids by the 900s and then migrated into North Africa. By 969, they had conquered most of North Africa and claimed the city of Cairo as their capital.

Seljuk Turks

Groups continued to break away from the weakened Abbasid Empire and opened it to invasion from outside forces. In 1055, Baghdad was conquered by nomadic Turks from Central Asia, who were descended from a warrior named Seljuk.

These Seljuk Turks captured the weak Abbasid caliph, plundered his palace, and took over the government. The Turks allowed the caliph and those who followed him to remain in Baghdad, but only as religious leaders of Islam. Once in control of the government, the Seljuk Turks took their responsibilities as rulers seriously. They began to govern the empire in the tradition of Islamic law.

The Abbasid-Seljuk Empire continued for 200 years but received its death blow when Baghdad fell to Mongol invaders from central Asia in 1258. Thus ended the Abbasid Empire, which, it is said, began with the violent assassination of nearly 80 Umayyad leaders in 750. Only one Umayyad leader had survived, and that was Prince Abd al Rahman, who had escaped to Spain. ■

This delicate crystal vase, decorated with an arabesque floral design, is from the early Fatimid period in Egypt during the late 900s.

■ *What led to the division of the Abbasid Empire?*

1. **FOCUS** How did the same wealth that brought the Abbasids power lead to their downfall?
2. **CONNECT** In what ways did the Abbasids further develop Muslim culture?
3. **POLITICAL SYSTEMS** How were non-Arabs treated by the Abbasids?
4. **CRITICAL THINKING** How were the Muslim trade routes important in spreading new ideas and knowledge?
5. **ACTIVITY** Write your first name in the center of a sheet of paper. Then work the letters into a design in the way that Muslims make Arabic letters become part of an intricate design.

Origins of Sports and Games

People around the world have always found ways to relax and play. Abbasid rulers enjoyed falconry and backgammon. Find out about these and other games and sports.

Get Ready

Collect a pen, pencil, and notebook. Look for reference books, magazines, or local experts to help you explore the origins of a particular sport or game. You need information about the game's equipment and rules. Also, find out where and how the game originated.

Football is one outgrowth of games that go back centuries. All the related games involved kicking a ball, but the ball's shape and the rules of the game varied.

Find Out

Use your reference materials to find the origins of the game you chose. You may want to show how a game has changed over time. You might want to follow a game to its origins. Some games began as work. The Abbasids, for example, made a sport of hunting with a trained falcon.

Move Ahead

Tape a large sheet of paper to the classroom wall. As you and your classmates share your information, each of you should draw a timeline on this sheet. Each timeline should show the origins of a game and how its rules and equipment changed over time.

Make two lists, one of games that began as recreations, the other of games that grew out of some necessary activity such as work or self-defense.

Explore Some More

Climate, animals, and terrain often affect the development of games. The horse-loving Abbasid rulers enjoyed polo and horse racing. Where did ice hockey develop? Why? Can you think of another sport or game affected by geography?

▼ *Chess has challenged people around the globe for centuries. This Spanish engraving, dating from the late 1500s, shows Arabs playing chess.*

Identifying Main Ideas

Here's Why

When you read, you need to determine what the writer wants you to understand. Identifying the main idea is the key to getting the most from anything you read. For example, if you were asked to tell someone what you read in Lesson 1 about how the Umayyads united the Islamic Empire, you would need to use this skill.

Here's How

The main idea of a paragraph is often stated in a topic sentence. This sentence, which is usually the first or last sentence, tells what the paragraph is about. The other sentences of the paragraph provide facts and details that support the main idea.

In a large section of text, you may find a topic paragraph. Like a topic sentence, a topic paragraph tells you the main idea of the section. The other paragraphs in the section build on and support the topic paragraph.

Look at the summary of Lesson 1 (to the right). In this case, a topic paragraph begins the passage. As you can see from the green highlighting, the passage is about how the Umayyads expanded and unified the Islamic Empire. Supporting details, highlighted in blue, explain how the Umayyads accomplished this.

The main idea of a passage is not always stated in a topic paragraph. For example, if the passage below did not include the first paragraph, you would need to look in the rest of the passage for a common idea or ideas. You would study the supporting details to determine the unstated main idea.

Look back at the passage. The blue highlights the part of each sentence that tells something about how the Umayyads expanded or unified their empire. When you determine what these sentences have in common, you can come up with the main idea of the section.

Try It

Turn to page 83 and reread "A Common Coinage." Write the main idea of that section on your paper. Now list several supporting facts or details that reinforce the main idea.

Apply It

Find a magazine article about a topic that interests you. Identify the topic sentence or topic paragraph of the article. Describe how the other sentences or paragraphs in the article support the main idea.

The Umayyad Empire

In 661, the Umayyads began a 90-year period of rule. During their years in power, from 661 to 750, the Umayyads expanded and unified the Islamic Empire.

Muawiya, the first Umayyad caliph, moved the capital from Medina, in Arabia, to Damascus, in Syria. Muawiya also started the practice of appointing a son as the next caliph. Thus began a tradition of continuous rule by one family.

During their years in power, the Islamic Empire expanded into Africa and present-day Spain and Portugal. In conquered territories, Umayyad Muslims tolerated other religions but gave special privileges to Muslims.

Abd al Malik, caliph from 685 to 705, took other steps to unify the empire. He made Arabic the language of the empire and instituted a common coinage. Mosques built in conquered lands shared a common religious architecture that also provided unity to the empire.

LESSON 3

Islamic Spain

> R *egularly perform thy prayer at the declension [descent] of the sun, at the first darkness of the night, and the prayer of daybreak; for the prayer of daybreak is borne witness unto by the angels.*
>
> Qur'an, 17:80

According to the Qur'an, faithful Muslims are directed to pray at not only these three times of day but also in the afternoon and evening. Mosques were built by the Muslim rulers so that the faithful could answer the Qur'an's call to face Mecca and pray five times every day.

The Great Mosque of Cordoba, Spain, described in A Closer Look on page 97, was begun around 785 by Abd al Rahman. The mosque, completed nearly 200 years later in 976, was a religious, social, and educational center.

THINKING FOCUS

How did Muslim culture influence Spain?

Key Term

- legacy

The Return of the Umayyads

When Abd al Rahman fled to Spain in 750, he discovered that since the time the Arabs and Berbers had invaded Spain from North Africa in 711, rival factions had been competing for control. No group had succeeded for long. Although there were many Muslims in Spain, there was no unified Muslim government.

Uniting Muslim Spain

By 756, the Umayyad forces in Spain, who did not support the new Abbasid caliphate back in Baghdad, accepted Abd al Rahman as their leader. With this Umayyad help, Abd al Rahman was able to establish an independent Muslim kingdom. He made the ancient Roman city of Cordoba his new capital.

◀ *The arches of the Great Mosque of Cordoba are supported by more than 1,000 pillars of marble, jasper, and alabaster.*

95

The Empire of Islam

Abd al Rahman's goals were to unify Spain under a central government, and to protect his realm from Muslim invaders to the south and Christian forces to the north. He succeeded so well that until 1000, there were few invasions.

■ *How did the Umayyads unify and protect Spain?*

Strengthening Cordoba

The high point for Umayyad power in Spain came about 200 years after the first Abd al Rahman, during the 49-year reign of Abd al Rahman III, which was from 912 to 961. He was the first Umayyad ruler of Spain to adopt the title of caliph, rather than simply governor. He patterned his government after the Abbasids' strong, centralized caliphate in the east, in Baghdad.

During his reign, Abd al Rahman III increased the strength of the army. The caliph bought Scandinavian, African, and German slaves to serve in his forces. This vast army protected his kingdom from the same two forces that had threatened the first Abd al Rahman: Christians in the north and Muslim rivals to the south, especially the Fatimids who had started an empire in Africa. ■

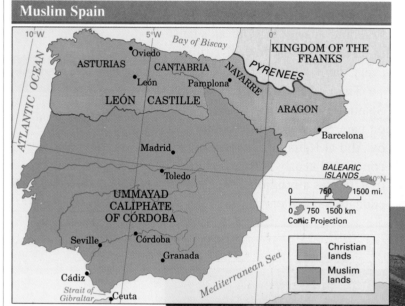

Muslim Spain

Bay of Biscay
ATLANTIC OCEAN
KINGDOM OF THE FRANKS
Oviedo
ASTURIAS
CANTABRIA
PYRENEES
NAVARRE
León
Pamplona
LEÓN   CASTILLE
ARAGON
Madrid
Barcelona
Toledo
BALEARIC ISLANDS
40°N
UMMAYAD CALIPHATE OF CÓRDOBA
0   750   1500 mi.
0   750   1500 km
Conic Projection
Seville
Córdoba
Granada
Cádiz
Mediterranean Sea
Strait of Gibraltar
Ceuta
10°W   5°W   0°

Christian lands
Muslim lands

➤ *Orchards of figs, almonds, and sweet cherries covered the countryside of the Muslim state in Spain. What Spanish cities were part of the Muslim state? What area of Spain was still controlled by the Christians?*

Glory of Cordoba

With his borders well protected, Abd al Rahman III turned his energies toward making Cordoba a thriving cultural center. Prosperous and well run, the city attracted scholars and artists. Many had come from the Abbasid cultural center of Baghdad. The city's most famous attraction was the Great Mosque, the largest of the city's 3,000 mosques. For A Closer Look at the mosque, see page 97.

By 1000, Cordoba was western Europe's largest city with a population of 450,000 people.

The Great Mosque at Cordoba

The great city of Cordoba demanded a great mosque. The building begun by Abd al Rahman I in A.D. 785 eventually became the third largest mosque in the world. Twice the wall facing Mecca was pushed outward. With the third addition, the wall and its jewellike mihrab had almost reached the river, so the fourth extension had to be added onto one side.

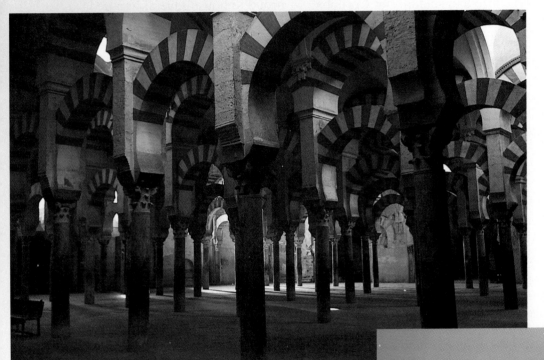

Did you notice that the pillars don't match? The marble and alabaster pillars under the candy-striped arches came from many different Roman buildings. Above this "forest" sparkled a turquoise- and gold-enameled "sky."

Outside, through open arches, rows of fragrant orange trees repeated the rows of pillars inside. The courtyard and mosque, open to each other, allowed Muslims to feel Allah's invisible presence whether they were inside or outside the mosque.

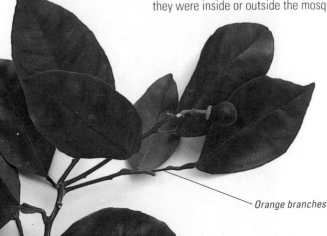

Orange branches

➤ In the 900s, there were two Muslim states, the Umayyads' in the west and the Abbasids' in the east. There were also two Christian empires, those of the Roman Catholic Church in the west and the Eastern Orthodox Church in the east.

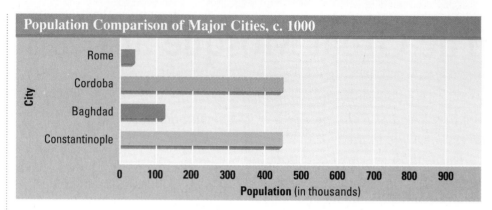

Population Comparison of Major Cities, c. 1000

City | Population (in thousands)
Rome
Cordoba
Baghdad
Constantinople

0 100 200 300 400 500 600 700 800 900

The size and splendor of Cordoba, with its paved and lighted streets and public plumbing in 300 bath-houses, was truly remarkable for a European city of the Middle Ages. Over 100,000 shops and houses filled the city. But it was the 60,000 richly decorated palaces with gardens and fountains, public courtyards, and broad avenues that made Cordoba an urban jewel in Muslim Spain's crown.

A Center of Learning

Poetry and music thrived in Cordoba. Poets and musicians were regarded as important figures in the court of the caliphs, for they produced poems and songs to glorify the empire and its rulers. Cordoba was the cultural and intellectual center of western Islam.

The Muslims brought thousands of books to Spain. New works were written, too. From the 1100s on, Jewish and Christian scholars worked with Muslims to translate these works into Latin. Scholars brought these books back to Christian Europe, where they stimulated the growth of knowledge and learning at the new universities. In the late 900s, the largest of the 70 libraries in Cordoba contained 500,000 volumes. This was at a time when a Christian monastery would have been

proud to house several hundred books. A host of clerks, many of them women, carefully hand-copied 70,000 books a year to satisfy the citizens' literary appetites.

Thousands of men and women attended the university and the law school at Cordoba. Scholars from Baghdad traveled to Spain, bringing knowledge and seeking new ideas. Much of this learning was then shared with western Europe by visiting scholars, merchants, and pilgrims who came to Cordoba. This love of learning was Cordoba's greatest **legacy,** or gift, to cultures and civilizations of the future.

➤ This carved ivory box shows two young men listening to a lute player. The inscription tells us that it was presented in 968 to al-Mughira, a son of Abd al-Rahman III.

The Intellectual Community

Cordoba was a center of learning in which non-Muslims and Muslims from other lands were welcome. One of the first visiting scholars was Abbas Ibn Firnas. He came to teach music but soon began to explore the mechanics of flight. He constructed a pair of wings out of feathers and a wooden frame and made an attempt at flight. Later he went on to build a famous planetarium with revolving planets in Cordoba.

Many non-Muslims played an important part in the intellectual life of Cordoba. For example, Hasdai ben-Shaprut was a Jew who served as court physician, treasurer, and diplomat to Abd al Rahman III.

A Golden Age for Jews

Hasdai ben-Shaprut brought Jewish scholars, philosophers, poets, and scientists to Cordoba and made it the leading center of Jewish culture. Under Romans and Christian Visigoths Jews were persecuted, but under the Muslims in Spain they flourished. Even after civil wars began, the "golden age" of Jewish culture continued for many years. A Jewish-Spanish culture called Sephardic (*suh FAR dihk*) grew up, with the beginnings of its own language, Ladino.

Among the dozens of famous writers and thinkers of Muslim Spain, one stands above all others. Moses Maimonides (*meye MAHN uh deez*) was born in Cordoba in 1135. When an anti Jewish movement took control of the city, he and his family fled to North Africa and to Palestine before settling in Cairo. There he gained a worldwide reputation as a doctor, lecturer, writer, and a scholar-philosopher.

Maimonides was 15 when he wrote his first book. He took large quantities of learning, both sacred and non-religious, and organized them according to logic and reason. His best-known work, *The Guide for the Perplexed,* explained the basic nature and philosophy of Judaism. Other works included material on natural science, medicine, and human psychology.

Muslim Spain fell slowly to rebel factions and advancing Christian armies. When Ferdinand and Isabella reconquered Spain in 1492, they expelled all Jews.

A City of Merchants

Cordoba was also a city of merchants. It supported a great many workshops for leatherwork, prayer carpets, ivory boxes, and other handicrafts. Spanish leather goods and textiles were in great demand throughout Europe. Papermaking, brought from Baghdad, was practiced here also.

Agriculture also flourished. Irrigation enabled farmers to grow new and exotic crops such as figs, almonds, cherries, bananas, and cotton. Over 4,000 thriving markets sold these agricultural and manufactured products. ■

■ *What were the greatest achievements of Cordoba?*

The Loss of Spain

By the 1000s, however, Christian kingdoms to the north were growing in power and began to move southward.

The Reconquest

The late 1000s mark the beginning of a period that Christians call the Reconquest. Knights and

➤ *In 1492, King Ferdinand of Aragon and Queen Isabella of Castile are on their way to the city of Granada to welcome it as part of their united kingdom.*

■ *What were the threats to the Islamic Empire in Spain?*

adventurers from all over Europe journeyed to Spain to fight the Muslims. In 1085, the Spanish Christian ruler Alfonso VI seized the Muslim city of Toledo, whose king was friendly to the Christians. The loss of Toledo marked the point of no return in the battle for Spain.

An Empire Lost

After the attack on Toledo, the rest of Islamic Spain gradually fell to Christian soldiers. The Muslim government dissolved into quarreling factions. Just as the Abbasid Empire had begun to collapse when it could no longer unite its parts, the Umayyad Empire in Spain began to die. The Muslims retreated farther and farther to the south as Christian forces invaded from the north.

Cordoba fell to the Christian forces in 1236, almost 500 years after Abd al Rahman had established it as the capital of his empire. In 1236, the last Islamic kingdom in Spain was that of the Berbers in Granada.

The Catholic kingdoms of Aragon and Castile ruled northern and central Spain. When King Ferdinand of Aragon married Queen Isabella of Castile, their combined kingdoms had enough power to expel the Muslims from Spain entirely. In 1492, the forces of Ferdinand and Isabella of Spain drove out the last Berbers.

Most refugees settled in North Africa, particularly in Morocco where the Berbers had originally come from in 711. Today, 98 percent of the Moroccans are Muslim. The official language is Arabic, but many people speak Spanish. ■

1. **FOCUS** How did Islamic culture influence Spain?
2. **CONNECT** How did the Abbasid Empire influence the start and the development of the Umayyad government in Cordoba?
3. **POLITICAL SYSTEMS** What problems led to the fall of central Islamic governments?
4. **CRITICAL THINKING** How was Cordoba able to become the center of culture for western Europe in the 800s and 900s?
5. **ACTIVITY** Muslims translated many important books of Greek knowledge into Arabic. What English books would you suggest be translated into Arabic? Make a list of books that should be available in Arabic. Tell why each book is significant.

Using the *Readers' Guide*

Here's Why

To find current information about a topic, you need to use reference resources other than encyclopedias, books, or the Internet. Magazines, or periodicals, provide recently written information. Suppose you want to find information about Islam today. How would you find the periodicals you need?

Here's How

The *Readers' Guide to Periodical Literature* is a set of reference books that lists magazine articles by topic. The box below contains two pages from the *Readers' Guide* for the year 1997.

To find an article about Islam, look under the topic **Islam.** There you find a cross reference: *See also* **Muslims.** This reference tells you that more articles about Islam are listed under the heading **Muslims.**

As you can see, there are two other subject headings with *Islam* in the title. These headings also refer you to different subject listings. Where should you look for an article on Islam and Christianity?

If the listings under **Islam** do not have what you want, then look up the heading **Muslims.** There are several subheadings under the subject **Muslims.** One or more articles are listed under each subheading. Each article is a separate entry. An entry includes the name of the article, the magazine that published it, and the date. Then look for that issue of the magazine in the periodicals section of the library.

Try It

Look again at the *Readers' Guide* entries on this page. In what magazines can you find articles about Muslims in Iran? Who wrote each article? What is the title of the most recent article about Muslims in Iran?

Apply It

Think about a special holiday or tradition associated with your ethnic background. Use the *Readers' Guide* to make a list of articles about this topic.

1. Title
2. Joint author
3. Subject heading
4. Author
5. Illustrations, portraits, maps
6. Periodical, volume, page numbers, date

ISAACS, JOHN D.
❶ Spending more, enjoying it less. *The Bulletin of the Atomic Scientists* v53 p19–20 My/Je '97
ISELY, DORIS
❷ (jt auth) See Isely, Bill, and Isely, Doris
ISLAM
  See also
  Muslims
  Pilgrimages to Mecca
ISLAM AND CHRISTIANITY
  See Christianity and other religions
ISLAMIC WOMEN
  See Muslim women
ISLANDS
  See also
  Barrier islands

MUSLIMS ❸
  Indonesia
A multicomplex reality. R.A. Evans and W.R. O'Brien. *The Christian Century* v114 p468–9 My 14 '97
        Iran ❹
Can we coexist with Iran? P. Clawson. il *USA Today (Periodical)* v125 p14–16 Mr '97
A mild renewal of Islamic zeal. C. Roelants. il *World Press Review* v44 p14 My '97 ❺
        Middle East
Elections breed moderation in the Arab world [interview with King Hussein] N. Gardels. *New Perspectives Quarterly* v13 p15–16 Fall '96 ❻

101

Chapter Review

Reviewing Key Terms

bureaucracy (p. 82)   empire (p. 78)
calligraphy (p. 88)   faction (p. 91)
dissent (p. 82)   legacy (p. 98)
emir (p. 82)

On your own paper, write the key term hinted at by each sentence below. Write a different sentence that contains the key term.

1. Opposing groups broke away from the empire and left it weak.
2. Many pieces of Muslim artwork are adorned with beautiful writing.
3. Some emirs did not allow citizens to disagree with them.
4. Scientific discoveries were one of the gifts that the Muslim Empire passed on to other cultures.
5. A ruling governor reported to the caliph.
6. The Muslim Empire government had different divisions that were managed by workers appointed by the caliph.
7. Syria, North Africa, Spain, Persia, and parts of India were among the group of countries ruled by the Muslims.

Exploring Concepts

A. Copy and complete the following outline using information from the chapter.

I. A century of expansion
  A. Expansion under Umayyad rule
  B. _____
  C. Umayyad unity
  D. The Umayyad downfall
    1. _____
    2. _____
II. The golden age
  A. Islam under Abbasid rule
    1. _____
    2. _____
    3. _____
  B. The new capital of Baghdad
    1. _____
    2. _____
  C. Abbasid culture
  D. _____
  E. A divided empire
III. Islamic Spain
  A. The return of the Umayyads
  B. _____
  C. The loss of Spain

B. Decide whether each statement below is true or false. Support your decision in writing, using facts and details from the chapter.

1. The Umayyad rulers made changes that both expanded and unified the Muslim Empire.
2. The rulers of the Umayyad Empire were tolerant and did not discriminate against non-Muslims.
3. A political split helped bring about the downfall of the Umayyads.
4. Under the Abbasids, culture and learning flourished.
5. The way the Abbasids used their great wealth contributed to the downfall of their empire.
6. Because of their different locations, Baghdad and Cordoba had almost nothing in common.
7. The Muslim peoples did not share their culture of knowledge with any other peoples.
8. Both the Abbasid Empire and Islamic Spain declined and were conquered when their rulers could no longer maintain unity among the people.

Reviewing Skills

1. Read the section headed Art and Design on page 88 of Lesson 2. Where in the section does the main idea appear? Write down this main idea. Then list three details or facts that support the main idea.
2. Reread the section headed Strengthening Cordoba on page 96 of Lesson 3. What is the main idea of the section? How can you identify the main idea in this section?
3. Use the *Readers' Guide* excerpt on page 101 to answer the following questions:
   a. In what magazine would you look to find an article describing Muslims in Indonesia? What are the title and the date of publication for the article?
   b. Under what entry would you find information about elections in the Middle East?
4. Use the information in Lesson 2 to make a timeline showing events of the Abbasid Empire. Can you make your timeline into a parallel timeline using events of the Umayyad Empire for the same time period?
5. Taking notes and outlining are two ways of studying. If you were outlining or taking notes on the contents of Chapter 4, what two kinds of information would you be writing down?

Using Critical Thinking

1. An empire is formed when one central authority takes control of several other regions. Being ruled by another country affects the government and way of life of the people. The people also affect the ruling country and the empire. What effects did the Byzantines, Persians, and others have on Muslims and their empire? What positive effects can empires have on progress and on society in general?
2. Baghdad and Cordoba were prosperous, well-run centers of commerce that also became centers of great art and learning. Judging from the example of these two cities, what are two or three comments you can make about places in which art and learning flourish?
3. Arabic was declared the official language of the Muslim Empire. What were the positive effects of this policy? What negative effects can you think of? Keeping both types of effects in mind, do you think English should be declared the official language of this country? Defend your position.

Preparing for Citizenship

1. COLLECTING INFORMATION   Persian and Byzantine coins bore pictures of emperors. Muslim money bore quotations from the Qur'an. Do research to find out what images and words are used on the currency of the United States. Make a scrapbook of the decorations on the money, including drawings and explanations.
2. COLLABORATIVE ACTIVITY   Although mosques do not all look alike, certain features are the same. This is also true for churches and synagogues and other temples. Working in groups of four, prepare an illustrated report on the architecture of these religious buildings. Decide among yourselves who will research each kind of building. One person can find out more about Muslim mosques. Another person can find out about Christian church architecture, the third person should find out about Jewish synagogues, and the other person should find out about Buddhist temples. The group can choose two members to compile the information and write a description of each kind of building. The other two people can illustrate the descriptions. The whole class should decide whether to use the reports in a scrapbook or bulletin board display.

Unit 3

Sub-Saharan Africa

Traders from faraway Europe, Asia, and the Middle East journeyed to the ancient trading empires of Africa seeking gold, ivory, and other exotic goods. They found well-organized states with noble cavalries. The empires fell, but the traditions of the past live on in Africa today. This cavalry brigade, dressed in ceremonial battle gear, parades through Niger just as ancient cavalrymen rode down the trade routes of the early African empires.

500 B.C.

Niger cavalry procession. Agence Hoa-Qui, Paris

A.D. 1700

Chapter 5

West Africa

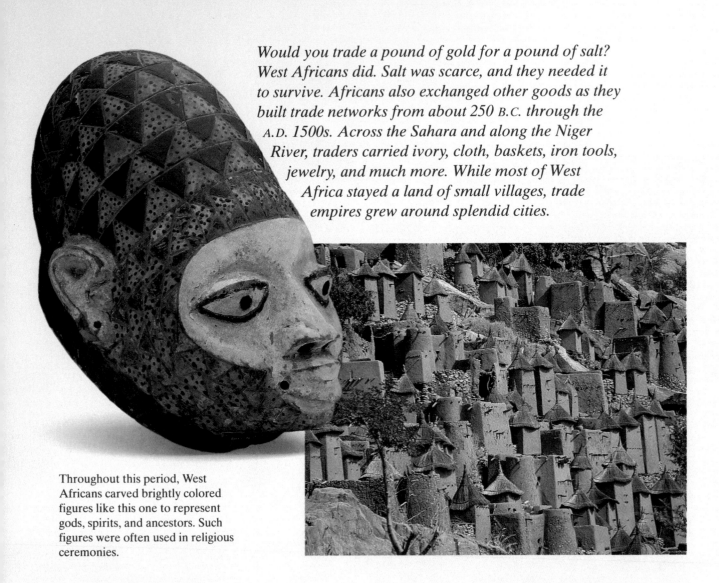

Would you trade a pound of gold for a pound of salt? West Africans did. Salt was scarce, and they needed it to survive. Africans also exchanged other goods as they built trade networks from about 250 B.C. through the A.D. 1500s. Across the Sahara and along the Niger River, traders carried ivory, cloth, baskets, iron tools, jewelry, and much more. While most of West Africa stayed a land of small villages, trade empires grew around splendid cities.

Throughout this period, West Africans carved brightly colored figures like this one to represent gods, spirits, and ancestors. Such figures were often used in religious ceremonies.

A.D. 500–600 The rulers of Ghana store grain in mud huts like these. Built on high, steep land, the huts keep the grain dry and safe from animals.

500

B.C. A.D.

500

500 B.C.

c. 570 Muhammad, founder of the Islamic faith, is born in the Arabian city of Mecca.

Throughout this period, religion, dance, and music played an important part in West African village life. Even today villagers like these Dogon people perform religious dances in traditional clothing.

c. 800–1050 Ghana controls West Africa's rich trade.

c. 1580 The Songhai control West Africa's wealthiest empire, trading for valuable goods like the Ashanti gold badge above.

1000

1500

c. 1500 With 80,000 people, Tenochtitlan is the largest city in the Americas and is more populous than London.

A.D. 1590

LESSON 1

The Roots of Mighty Empires

THINKING FOCUS

What are some of the ways the early West Africans developed prosperous cities in a landscape with such a varying climate?

Key Terms

- savanna
- sahel
- delta

▼ *Although it is as large as the United States, the Sahara has fewer than two million inhabitants.*

I magine being on a trip by van across the Sahara in North Africa. After hours of travel, your guide sets up camp in an oasis. Its palm trees offer a refuge of shade from the sun-baked sand of the desert.

While you're relaxing by a stream, your guide proposes a hike. To those hardy enough for the walk, she promises scenes of lush plant life and full rivers.

You decide to go. The sun-baked sand burns through your sneakers, and rocks cut your hands as you scramble over a hill. Finally your guide leads you into a cave. Here, she says, are the scenes promised.

Paintings cover the cave walls. Images of wide rivers teeming with fish, vast plains of tall grasses, thick forests, and people herding cattle. The guide explains that these scenes were painted thousands of years ago—and that they represent the ancient Sahara. Could that barren desert really have been such a paradise? Were the paintings of real life?

A Land of Many Climates

Dried-up riverbeds as well as cave paintings indicate that in 5000 B.C., the Sahara was indeed a land of flowing rivers, lush green pastures, and forests. However, over time, its climate began to change. By about 4000 B.C., rain fell less often, and average temperatures had risen. As a result, the rivers dried up, and fertile pasture land became bare and bleak. By 2500 B.C., the desert looked much as it does today.

As the desert became drier, many people moved to search for more fertile land. Many Africans journeyed south to West Africa.

Some of those who migrated to West Africa settled on oases located along a strip of grasslands, or **savanna,** on the Sahara's southern border. This region is known as the **sahel** *(suh HAYL)*, or "shore of the desert." Its landscape ranges from desert in the north to scattered vegetation in the south. On the sahel, scant rainfall and occasional oases make some farming possible. There are eight climate zones in Africa. Use the map below to determine the sahel's climate region.

Other Africans went farther south of the sahel to settle in the

▼ *Africa's climate ranges from heavy rainfall in central and parts of southern Africa to scant rainfall in the north.*

Africa: Climate Regions

Climate regions

- Tropical wet (hot and rainy all year)
- Tropical wet and dry (hot, with rainy and dry seasons)
- Desert (dry, either hot or cold)
- Semiarid (short rainy season)
- Mediterranean (hot, dry summer and mild, rainy winter)
- Humid subtropical (hot, rainy summer and mild, rainy winter)
- Marine (cool and wet)
- Highland (climate varies with elevation)

Mercator Projection

109

West Africa

savannas and rain forests of a more fertile area along the Niger River. There they found relief from the barren Sahara. And along the banks of the Niger, they built some of Africa's greatest empires. ■

A New Technology

Although the vast, scorching Sahara made travel difficult, it did not cut West Africa off from traders to the north. Camel caravans regularly traveled across the desert from North Africa to exchange goods and ideas.

From these North African traders, the West Africans learned iron-making technology. Archaeologists have found iron tools near the city of Nok in present-day Nigeria. The artifacts were made by the Nok people, who lived in the area between 500 B.C. and A.D. 200.

The Nok were the first West Africans to make iron. They began working with it as early as 450 B.C. and, in time, had discovered many practical uses for it. For example, by fitting their spears with iron points instead of stone ones, the spears lasted longer. Also, iron tools were better than stone ones for farming. Using iron-making technology, the Nok vastly improved their lives.

To make iron, the Nok placed rocks rich in iron ore in a clay furnace with charcoal. They then heated the mixture to a high enough temperature to liquefy it.

After the wastes were poured off, a chunk of molten iron remained. A Nok iron maker would then shape that soft, red-hot iron into a tool or weapon. This iron-making process is still used today in some parts of West Africa.

In addition to being iron makers, the Nok were also skilled potters. They used clay to build their huts and to make finely detailed sculptures. The clay head shown here illustrates the artistry of the Nok.

Little is known about why the Nok civilization came to an end. The Nok people seem to have begun to move at least by 300 B.C. However, because they shared their knowledge of iron making and pottery with the people they met, we can trace the path they took. ■

An Ancient Trade Center

In 1977, the remains of an ancient city were discovered on the inland delta of the Niger River. A **delta** is a triangular-shaped landform made by mud and silt deposited at a river's mouth. The iron and clay artifacts found among the remains of the city closely resembled the articles made by Nok craftspeople to the east. Thus, archaeologists determined that some Nok people had come to this site. The city, called Jenne-jeno, was inhabited from 250 B.C. to A.D. 1400.

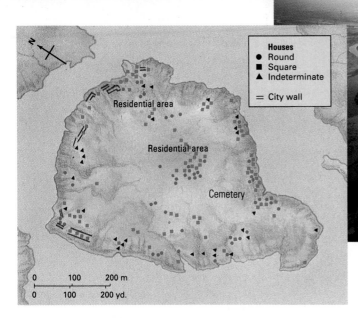

This photograph shows the modern city of Jenne on the left and the ancient city of Jenne-jeno in the upper right-hand box. The illustration on the far left is of ancient Jenne-jeno and is based on the research of archaeologists who uncovered artifacts there.

It lies about two miles from the modern city of Jenne in the Republic of Mali.

As you can see in the photo above, the city was built on a flood plain on the river's inland delta. The Niger flooded this plain yearly, and when the waters fell back, they left behind rich, moist soil ideal for farming rice. Indeed, the first people to settle there were rice farmers, who also raised cattle and fished in the Niger.

In addition, the Niger acted as a natural highway for trade. People carried rice, fish, baskets, and pottery to river cities in the north and brought back salt, copper, and stone. Traders went south on the river to bring back gold.

Traders also traveled over land. In fact, camel caravans eventually linked Jenne-jeno with North Africa. By 800, Jenne-jeno had grown from a small settlement into a bustling trade center of about 10,000 people.

Because the people of Jenne-jeno had such an abundant supply of food and other products, many were free to do other things besides farm. Iron tools, copper and gold jewelry, and clay animals have been unearthed in the city. From these finds, archaeologists have determined that well-trained craftspeople lived there.

Despite its flourishing culture and fine location, by 1400, Jenne-jeno was completely abandoned. Archaeologists do not know why this happened. However, at about this time, the nearby city of Jenne was founded. Perhaps many of the people of Jenne-jeno settled in Jenne, which would make them the ancestors of the people who live there today. ■

■ *How did the people of Jenne-jeno obtain the resources they could not produce?*

R E V I E W

1. **FOCUS** What are some of the ways the early West Africans developed prosperous cities in a landscape with such a varying climate?
2. **CONNECT** What things other than goods were exchanged between North African traders and West African traders?
3. **ECONOMICS** In what ways did the inhabitants of Nok benefit from learning the technique of iron making?
4. **GEOGRAPHY** How did the people of Jenne-jeno adapt to the geography south of the Sahara?
5. **CRITICAL THINKING** What would have been the impact on West Africa if the Sahara's climate had not changed so dramatically?
6. **ACTIVITY** Use the clay head pictured on page 110 to make your own Nok-style sculpture of a human or animal head.

West Africa

L E S S O N   2

The Empire of Ghana

THINKING FOCUS

What effect did trade have on the people of Ghana?

Key Terms

- matrilineal
- patrilineal

Ghana was an ancient agricultural kingdom of the Soninke *(suhn IHN kay)* people with a rich trans-Saharan trade. It began in the southeast corner of what is now Mauritania, along the Senegal River, and later grew along the Niger River. People farmed, built cities, formed social classes, produced art and music, and created trade networks. While agriculture flourished along the rivers, in drier areas people raised livestock. Some moved with the seasons to better grazing land. In the Sahel, on the southern edge of the Sahara, Berber tribes from North Africa raised horses and camels. They led traders and carried goods across the desert by camel to trading towns on the northern edge of the desert. It was a two-month, 1,200-mile trip filled with hardship, yet worth the effort. There was money to be made.

The rulers of Ghana controlled the trade of their kingdom and collected taxes on the salt that came from the north. Large numbers of cavalry and archers made Ghana's army the most powerful in the region. The monarch's power arose from a number of sources: First, he had the loyalty and support of local nobilities. Second, the Soninke religion made him a god to be worshiped. The king's great wealth, however, came from south of the kingdom, from the gold-bearing upper reaches of the Niger and Senegal rivers. This gold (which was in great demand across the Sahara) and its production, trading, and pricing, were all controlled by the king.

➤ *This present-day village in the Sahel is called Chadawanka, in Niger. People still exchange salt for milk or grain at its market.*

A Center of Trade

Ghana was in an ideal position for trade. It lay between the Sahel and Sahara in the north, and the highlands and tropical rain forests in the south. The Senegal and Gambia rivers also helped communication and transport. From the south came kola nuts, palm oil, copper, and gold. From the north, came imported items like ceramics, glass and oil lamps—and, of course, salt.

Under the Soninke kings, Ghana became a wealthy trading empire. The Soninke easily conquered neighboring peoples because their iron weapons were far superior to the stone ones of their opponents. By the late 900s, Ghana controlled more than 100,000 square miles of land and hundreds of thousands of people. Ghana's location—between the northern Saharan salt mines and the gold fields of Wangara to the south—helped it become a major trade center. Traders from both areas had to pass through Ghana to exchange goods. And the empire acquired much wealth from the taxes collected on the goods.

West Africans used salt to preserve and flavor food. They also needed to include a lot of salt in their diet to replace that lost from the body through perspiration.

Salt was scarce in southern Ghana, but gold was not. West African gold became important to Europe, the Middle East, and North Africa, for use as money and in jewelry. Since the supply from the few gold mines in Europe and Asia had been exhausted, gold had to be found elsewhere. The trading

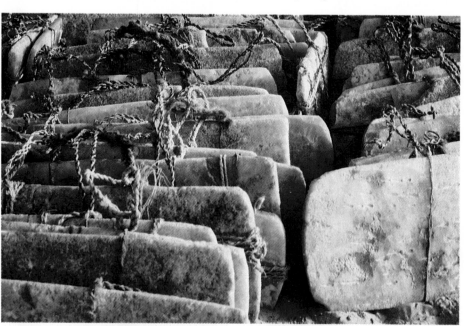

city-states on the northern edge of the Sahara later accumulated so much gold from this trade that they minted gold coins. These coins were used as far away as Egypt and Syria. During the Middle Ages, two-thirds of all the gold circulating in the Mediterranean area had come across the Sahara.

Fortunately, people in Wangara were glad to trade some of their gold for salt from the north. Gold had limited value for them. Tools, for example, could not be made out of the soft metal. But salt was vital to good health. To the people of southern Ghana, salt and gold were of equal value. And so they made the trade in equal amounts—a pound of gold for a pound of salt. You can learn more about the gold and salt trade in A Closer Look on page 114. ■

▼ *In parts of central Africa, salt is still considered to be as valuable as gold.*

Across Time & Space

Salt was also valued in ancient Rome. In A.D. 500, soldiers transported salt on a highway called Via Salaria, or Salt Road. The term salary comes from the Latin salarium, *which means money paid to soldiers to buy salt. Soldiers "worth their salt" were paid a salary.*

■ *What combination of geographic and economic factors made Ghana an ideal trade center?*

113

Trading Gold and Salt

Trading gold and salt was not an easy way to make a living. Merchants risked dying of thirst almost every time they made the 1,200-mile journey across the Sahara. But those who overcame the hardships got rich and brought great wealth to the south Sahara kingdoms.

Gold masks could hide more than faces. Sometimes the gold in molded objects—like masks, jewelry, or coins—was mixed with cheaper metals. To avoid being cheated, merchants liked to trade their salt for pure gold dust.

Gold pendant, Baule tribe, Ivory Coast

The king of Ghana and the small-scale societies of the Berbers kept the Saharan trade routes safe. They considered stealing a serious crime and punished thieves severely. "Neither the man who travels nor he who stays at home has anything to fear from robbers or men of violence" wrote traveler Ibn Battuta.

Pass the salt! For centuries, North Africans have been getting their salt from the Atlantic Ocean, just like the person in this picture. First, they filled shallow pools with salt water. Then they let it evaporate. The piles of moist sea salt dried quickly under the blazing African sun.

Salt

A Diverse Capital

From about 800 to 1050, the gold and salt trade made Koumbi, Ghana's capital, the busiest and wealthiest marketplace in West Africa. Gold and salt were the most sought-after items, but in Koumbi's market people also bought and sold cattle, honey, dates, cloth, ivory, and ebony. In other shops at the market, local farmers sold their produce and craftspeople sold their wares.

Most of the traders in Ghana were Muslims who practiced the religion of Islam. Although Ghana's Soninke kings weren't Muslims, they were tolerant of Islam. Still, they tried to keep Islam separate from the traditional Soninke religion. So they divided many of Ghana's trading towns, including Koumbi, into two sections. One section housed the Muslims, and the other section housed the local people.

A six-mile-long boulevard linked the two sections of Koumbi. The Muslim side had 12 mosques and the homes of Muslim traders. Many of the buildings there were constructed of stone, and some had two stories. This section was also home to the huge Koumbi market.

The Soninke section of the capital looked very different. It was a walled city, and most of its one-story houses were made of wood or clay, with straw roofs. The king lived in this section in a large wood and stone palace.

The king was Ghana's religious and military leader and highest judge. The Ghanaian people came to him to settle their disputes.

> When the king gives [an] audience, . . . he sits in a domed pavilion around which stand 10 horses covered with gold-embroidered cloths. Behind the king stand 10 pages holding shields and swords decorated with gold. . . . At the door of the pavilion are dogs of an excellent breed. . . . Round their necks they wear collars of gold and silver.
>
> al-Bakri, historian, from
> *Book of the Roads and Kingdoms*, 1068

Thus, while administering justice, the king could also demonstrate his great wealth and power. ■

Most modern markets in West Africa are operated entirely by women. The woman in the main picture is selling yams. The baskets below the yam seller were woven by West African women. Why do you suppose they designed them to fit snugly into one another?

■ *How did the two sections of Koumbi differ from each other?*

A New Religion

In the 900s, as trade in West Africa grew more profitable, many Arab merchants came to live in Ghana. With the trading of goods came the trading of ideas. Arab traders brought the first system of

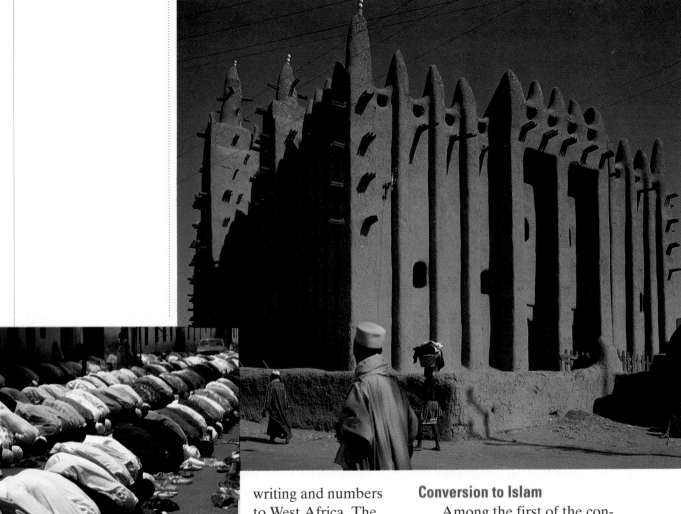

▲ *This mud mosque in Mali is called the Great Mosque. Muslims must pray at a mosque once a week on Fridays. At other times Muslims even pray in the street but always remove their shoes first. Men and women pray separately.*

writing and numbers to West Africa. The Ghanaian kings adopted the Arab writing system and even hired Arabs as government officials to help them take care of trade matters.

By 750, Muslim Arabs had created a huge Islamic Empire in the Middle East. And, as the Arabs gained more influence in West Africa, they taught the people of Ghana about their religion. However, reactions to these teachings were mixed. Although Ghana's Soninke rulers held tightly to their traditional religion, many other government officials and merchants eventually converted to Islam, some spending large sums to build expensive mosques for Muslim worship.

Conversion to Islam

Among the first of the converts to Islam were the Mandinke *(man DIHN kuh)* people from the southern Sahara, who served as middlemen in trade between Arab caravans and Wangara gold miners. The Mandinke formed small trade companies that made contact with many different people. They spread Islamic ideas throughout West Africa.

Many West Africans converted to Islam because it stressed belief in the "brotherhood of all believers." This sense of brotherhood encouraged trust and peaceful trade between people of different nationalities. Muslim traders often extended credit to each other simply because they practiced the same faith.

Traditional Practices

Other Islamic practices were harder for the Ghanaians to accept. Muslims, for example, had their own idea about the succession of kings. In Ghana when a king died, he was not succeeded by his own son but by the son of his sister. This system of tracing succession through the females of the family is known as **matrilineal** succession. Muslims, on the other hand, practiced **patrilineal** succession, in which the throne passes from father to son.

The people of Ghana continued to practice matrilineal succession to determine who inherited family property. This practice was too well established to abandon. Still, many Ghanaians considered themselves Muslims. They were just selective about the ideas they would adopt. ■

■ *In what ways did Ghanaians benefit from their contact with Arab traders?*

A Fallen Empire

Along the northernmost coast of Africa, Berber peoples ruled the region called the Maghreb *(muh GRUHB)*. By the late 1100s they had long been Muslims, and now rival reform movements battled for power. The Almoravids, and later the Almohads, were political and spiritual movements. The wars that followed their rise took large amounts of gold to finance.

Saharan Berbers including the Sanhaja and the Taureg operated the caravans across the desert. By the 900s, the Ghanaians had forced tribute from the Sanhaja's southernmost trading center, Awdaghust *(ah dah GOOST)*. As the Almoravid movement spread, the Sanhaja joined it, and they retook Awdaghust. Then they continued, taking over the lands to the south, conquering Koumbi in 1076.

In 1087, the Soninke regained control from the Almoravids. However, in reestablishing their empire they faced many problems. Some of the states they once ruled had adopted Islam and supported the Almoravids. Others broke away to form separate kingdoms.

King Sumanguru, who wanted to rebuild Ghana's empire, ruled one of these kingdoms. In 1203, he overthrew the Soninke king and took over Koumbi. Meanwhile, a new kingdom to the east called Mali, ruled by the Mandinke, was steadily gaining power. In 1235, the king of Mali defeated Sumanguru and Mali replaced Ghana as the major power in West Africa. ■

■ *How did the brief takeover by the Almoravids lead to Ghana's downfall?*

R E V I E W

1. **FOCUS** What effect did trade have on the people of Ghana?
2. **CONNECT** How did the Nok culture help the Soninke defeat neighboring peoples?
3. **GEOGRAPHY** How did the location of the West African gold and salt mines benefit Ghana?
4. **BELIEF SYSTEMS** What Islamic practice was particularly difficult for the Ghanaians to accept? Why?
5. **CRITICAL THINKING** The Ghanaians who practiced the Soninke religion were tolerant of the Muslims who settled in Ghana. How might Ghana's empire have differed if they had not been tolerant?
6. **WRITING ACTIVITY** Imagine that you are visiting Koumbi in the 1100s. This is your first trip to this part of the world, and you don't speak the language. In your journal, record what you see in each section of the city. What does the marketplace look like? Why do you think the city is divided as it is?

LESSON 3

The Empires of Mali and Songhai

THINKING FOCUS

What events led to the development of the great trade empires of Mali and Songhai?

Key Term

• griot

▼ *Trade still thrives in Mali on the shores of the Niger River.*

In 1235, the Battle of Kirina marked the fall of Ghana and the end of King Sumanguru's reign. But it also meant the rise of the kingdom of Mali and the beginning of King Sundiata's reign. The battle is rich in legends that are retold today.

According to legend, Sumanguru and Sundiata were magicians. Their magic would decide the battle's victor. In the heat of the match, King Sundiata furiously roared at the warriors of King Sumanguru, and they scurried for cover. When Sumanguru bellowed in return, the heads of eight spirits magically appeared above his head.

However, Sundiata's magic was more powerful, and he defeated the spirits. Then Sundiata fixed Sumanguru with his gaze and aimed an arrow at him. The arrow only grazed Sumanguru's shoulder, but it drained him of all his magical powers.

A present-day Mandinke **griot,** or storyteller, finishes the tale:

> The vanquished Sumanguru looked up towards the sun. A great black bird flew over above the fray. . . . "The bird of Kirina," [the king] muttered. Sumanguru let out a great cry and, turning his horse's head, he took to flight.
>
> Recorded by D.T. Niane of Mali, from a griot in Guinea, Africa

To the griot who described this battle, Sundiata was a hero.

Mali Develops a Prosperous Trade

Sundiata became king of the new empire of Mali, which had once been a part of Ghana. And he established its capital at Niani, on the upper Niger.

Sundiata never fought again after Kirina. He relied on his army to extend Mali's boundaries. The king focused on restoring prosperity to his kingdom.

Sundiata first concentrated on improving agriculture. His soldiers cleared land for farming, and they planted rice, yams, onions, beans, grains, and cotton. In a few years, Mali became a productive farming region.

However, as in Ghana, Mali's economy was based on trade. The many years of fighting in Ghana had interrupted trans-Saharan trade—trade that crossed the Sahara. So, once Mali controlled Ghana's gold mines, Sundiata set about restoring the salt and gold exchange with Niani as the kingdom's new trade center.

Sundiata and his successors expanded Mali's trade routes north and east across the Sahara to Cairo, Egypt, and to Tunis in Tunisia. You can locate these cities in the Atlas on the map on page 525. Mali controlled salt mines in the north at Taghaza and copper mines in the east at Takedda.

In addition to the gold mines at Wangara, the people of Mali had discovered a new source of gold at Bure, not far from the new capital on the Niger River. From Bure they easily shipped gold along the Niger to interested traders. The Niger became a busy highway for trading gold and other goods.

Less than 100 years after the victory at Kirina, Mali had become the most powerful kingdom in Africa. By the late 1300s, Mali was three times as large as Ghana had ever been. ■

▲ Onions may have been such an important crop because their strong flavor can be used to season other foods.

■ How did Sundiata and his armies extend Mali's trade empire?

Mansa Musa Enriches the Empire

Mali's greatest ruler, Mansa Musa, succeeded to the throne in 1307. Mansa Musa was a devout Muslim, but he respected all his subjects' beliefs. He allowed those who desired it to worship their traditional gods. However, many of the people who lived in trade centers had been influenced by the Arab traders and had already converted to Islam. Under Musa's rule, conversions greatly increased, mainly due to Mali's expanding trade.

The North African writer, Ibn Battuta, praised the newly converted Muslims for faithfully "observing the hours of prayers, studying the books of law, and memorizing the Qur'an." However, as a traditional Muslim, Ibn Battuta was shocked by some West African customs that survived despite Islamic influence. For example, West African women were quite independent. He also found that people still scarred their faces to show their clan affiliations.

Nevertheless, in accordance with Islamic teachings, some of Mali's rulers made pilgrimages to the holy city of Mecca in the Middle East. Mansa Musa made the 3,500-mile journey in 1324.

According to some accounts, which may have become exaggerated over time, Mansa Musa was accompanied on this journey by as many as 50,000 people—friends, family members, doctors, advisers, and 500 slaves carrying golden staffs. In addition, 80 to 100 camels, each

▲ Mansa Musa in a close-up from the map on the next page.

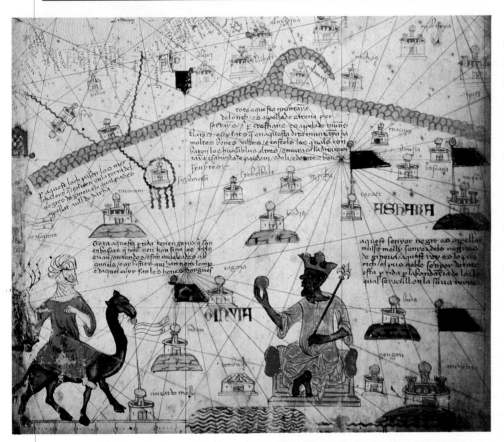

▲ Detail from a map of Mali made in Spain around 1375. Mansa Musa is drawn with scepter and throne, showing he is the equal of European kings.

■ *What effect did West African rulers' conversion to Islam have on the empire?*

Under Mansa Musa, culture and learning flourished in Niani and other trade centers such as Timbuktu. When Musa returned from Mecca, he brought Arab scholars back with him. Mansa Musa invited these scholars to teach in Mali's learning centers. As Muslims, they welcomed the opportunity to instruct their brothers in scholarship and religion.

Likewise, Muslim traders welcomed the opportunity to trade with fellow Muslims in different states. Thus, they helped to increase Mali's trade empire as well as their own profits.

loaded with 100 pounds of gold dust, are said to have traveled with him to Mecca. Hundreds of other camels carried the other supplies.

Mansa Musa's pilgrimage drew the attention of Mediterranean merchants to Mali's economic importance. European mapmakers began to include Mali on maps because of its role in international trade.

Even Mali's borders expanded under Mansa Musa's rule. New land was acquired both peacefully and as the result of war. Most of Mali was divided into states, which were under Musa's control. Some regions were allowed to remain independent as long as their rulers pledged their loyalty and a portion of their wealth to Mali. ■

Power Shifts to Songhai

After Mansa Musa died in 1332, Mali was ruled by a series of kings who were unable to protect its vast territory. Berber nomads attacked caravan routes in the desert and threatened to take Timbuktu. People from the southern rain forests raided Mali's southern border. And in the west, the Songhai on the middle Niger River began to revolt.

The Songhai were a mixture of farmers, traders, fishermen, and warriors who lived along the Niger near the city of Gao. For hundreds of years, the Songhai had fought off Mali's control. Sometimes they succeeded; sometimes they failed.

Under Mansa Musa, Mali ruled Gao and most of the Songhai kingdom for about 50 years. However, when he died, the Songhai stopped

ATLANTIC OCEAN — Mediterranean Sea — 20°E — SAHARA — 20°N
GHANA
Koumbi • — Niger R.
GHANA
Present–day boundary

ATLANTIC OCEAN — Mediterranean Sea — 20°E — SAHARA — 20°N
MALI — MALI
Niger R.
Niani •
Present–day boundary

ATLANTIC OCEAN — Mediterranean Sea — 20°E — SAHARA — 20°N
SONGHAI
• Gao
Niger R.
0 500 1000 mi.
0 500 1000 km
Mercator Projection

paying taxes to Mali. In 1435, a Songhai prince named Sunni Ali declared Gao's independence. Aided by the Songhai warriors, he successfully fought off Mali's attempts to regain the city.

Under attack on all sides after 1400, Mali gradually weakened. Mali's rulers were unable to drive off the invaders. Berbers took over the trade and learning centers of Timbuktu and Walata in the mid-1400s. In 1464, under the guidance of Sunni Ali, the Songhai began conquering their neighbors and expanding their kingdom.

A new Songhai empire thus grew out of a region that had once been part of Mali, just as Mali had grown out of a state in the empire of Ghana. Gao became Songhai's capital and Sunni Ali its king.

Sunni Ali was a Muslim, but he was not a devoted believer. After he died, his son, a non-Muslim, took over the throne. The new ruler was intolerant of Muslims, so many Muslims joined forces to overthrow him. The Muslims wanted a ruler who shared their beliefs. The ruler they supported was Askia Muhammad. In the 1490s, Askia overthrew Ali's son and declared Islam the state religion.

Askia's armies expanded the borders of Songhai and encouraged many non-Muslims to convert. The new king invited Muslim scholars to his empire, and its cities became great centers of culture and learning once again. At the height of its power in the late 1500s, the Songhai empire was larger and wealthier than Mali had ever been. In time, as the number of Muslims and Muslim traders increased, Songhai would become the greatest trade empire of West Africa. ■

▲ *Compare the growth of ancient Ghana, Mali, and Songhai. Note that although a present-day Ghana and Mali exist, there is no longer a Songhai.*

■ *How did Askia Muhammad's strong rule help Songhai become such a great trade empire?*

▼ *Under the leadership of Askia Muhammad, Timbuktu flourished, attracting scholars, traders, and craftspeople from all over the Muslim world.*

Songhai Collapses

Askia's heirs succeeded him to the throne. Over time, however, these rulers created a small but powerful Islamic group at the top of the ruling society. This group distanced itself from people who were not Muslims. As a result, certain states broke away from the empire, resentful of the Muslim kings.

But the major threat to Songhai came from Morocco in North Africa. In 1585, Morocco's ruler

Timbuktu's location at the edge of the Sahara Desert and only eight miles from the Niger River led to the popular saying of the day "Timbuktu, meeting point of the camel and canoe."

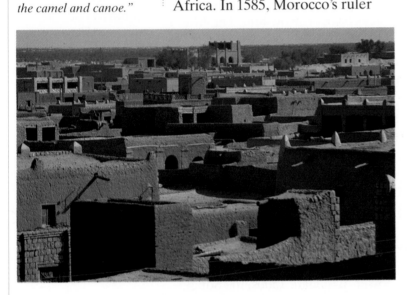

captured Songhai's salt mines in Taghaza. The Moroccan ruler also wanted to control Songhai's source of gold in West Africa. Ownership of both these two important resources would ensure a control of trade. The ruler of Morocco

■ *Why did the ruler of Morocco fight for control of Songhai?*

decided that this was worth fighting for.

In 1590, he sent 4,000 soldiers under Muslim Spaniard Judar Pasha to conquer Songhai. After a five-month-long journey across the Sahara, Pasha arrived in Songhai with only 1,000 men. But his soldiers carried something new to the region, something they had acquired in the Middle East—guns.

Songhai's soldiers outnumbered Pasha's by at least 25,000 men. But swords and arrows were no match for guns. Gao fell, and then Timbuktu, and finally most of Songhai.

Pasha destroyed the gold-producing system. Gradually the North Africans lost interest in making Songhai a colony, although they stayed there another 150 years. What had once been a peaceful, well-organized empire became a series of military camps.

Songhai was the last great trading empire of West Africa. No other West African kingdom ever rivaled its power or strong hold on trade. In the towns and villages, however, people went on paying taxes, providing labor, and showing up for military service. The Songhai monarchs still ruled, but now only in a few of their former lands. ■

R E V I E W

1. **FOCUS** What events led to the development of the great trade empires of Mali and Songhai?
2. **CONNECT** What are some of the things the empires of Ghana, Mali, and Songhai had in common?
3. **ECONOMIC GEOGRAPHY** Why do you suppose all the capitals of the great West African trade empires were located on the Niger River?
4. **CRITICAL THINKING** In what ways were Mansa Musa

and Askia Muhammad alike? In what ways were they different?
5. **CRITICAL THINKING** How might the war with Morocco have destroyed Songhai's gold-producing system?
6. **WRITING ACTIVITY** Sundiata's victory over Sumanguru is the story that *The Lion King* is based upon. Write your own version of this tale. You can set it in any time or place.

Interpreting Proverbs

Here's Why

People sometimes repeat stories or fables in order to teach wisdom or moral lessons. A proverb is similar to the moral of a story; it is a short saying that expresses a well-known truth. Many proverbs can apply to any place in the world and at any time. Others are more specific and reveal something about the particular culture or historical period from which they originated.

If you read a West African proverb, for example, you may learn something about West African culture. You may also learn that West Africans share some values with your own culture.

Here's How

The proverbs in the box below originated among the Ewe tribe of Ghana in West Africa. The proverb about the blacksmith means that when you go to another place, you must learn to behave according to the customs of that place. What clues does the proverb provide about West African

culture? The reference to blacksmiths suggests their importance. Think of a similar saying from your own culture, such as: You can be a big fish in a small pond or a small fish in a big pond.

Now look at the mask on the right, of a European from the west coast of Africa. Think about the second proverb about the hat. One interpretation of this proverb might be that if people want to give you something, you should beware of why they are giving it to you. The proverb gives you a clue that West African culture is a nonwhite culture and that West Africans do not always find white people trustworthy. "Beware of Greeks bearing gifts" is a saying you may know from your own culture that has a similar meaning.

Try It

Examine the last two proverbs. Analyze each of them, asking the same

kinds of questions and using the same kind of thinking applied to the proverbs in Here's How.

Apply It

Your culture has proverbs of its own. Analyze the following proverbs from various cultures, asking questions like those posed in Here's How.

- Haste makes waste.
- A watched pot never boils.
- Anything that can go wrong will go wrong.
- Wisdom is not like money, to be tied up and hidden.

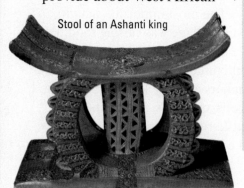

Stool of an Ashanti king

*T*he blacksmith in one village becomes a blacksmith's apprentice in another.

If a whiteman wants to give you a hat, look at the one he is wearing before you accept it.

You do not become a chief simply by sitting on a big stool.

A stump that stays in a river for a hundred years does not become a crocodile.

Ewe Proverbs, Ghana

123

West Africa

L E S S O N   4

Village Society in West Africa

How did the people in the rural villages of West Africa survive in their often unpredictable environment?

Key Terms

• diviner
• ancestor worship
• kinship

➤ *Masked Dogon dancers move to the rhythm of drums.*

The young man waits on a hillside. When the drums begin beating, he and the other Dogon dancers will descend to the village. He will wear the mask of Gomintogo, the antelope.

This is the story the dance will tell: An antelope ate a farmer's seeds. The angry farmer killed the antelope. But then the animal's spirit made the farmer's son very ill. To heal his son, the father made a mask of the antelope. The mask captured the antelope's spirit so that it could no longer harm his son. Soon his son was well again.

Now the young man dances, wearing the wooden mask he has carved himself—an antelope head with jagged horns three feet long. As he dances, he feels the spirits of Gomintogo and his ancestors.

Farming: A Way of Life

Symbols of agriculture often appeared in the religious stories of the early West Africans. Most of these people did not live in the large trading cities of Ghana, Mali, and Songhai. They lived in small villages on riverbanks, on the savanna, or in the rain forests.

The most important activity in every village was raising food. People who fished the Niger River also cultivated gardens. Skilled iron makers and blacksmiths also raised crops, chickens, and goats. Even cattle-raising nomads grew a wheat-like grain called millet.

In the dry regions of the sahel, farmers grew millet and sorghum *(SAWR guhm)*. These grains are well suited to dry climates because during dry periods they remain alive. In the wetter regions south of the sahel, people grew rice, especially in the delta of the Niger.

In the dense West African rain forests, farmers made small clearings and grew edible roots. The people of the rain forests could not raise livestock, however, as the forest was filled with insects that were deadly to herd animals.

West African farmers developed different farming methods to suit the different types of land. The Dogon, for example, who lived on cliffs south of the Niger, found that pools of rainwater formed in crevices among the rocks. Farmers brought fertile soil from the valley below and turned the pools into gardens.

In each area, most farmers grew a small surplus of the crops that flourished in their regions and traded this for the food they could not produce. ■

▲ *Nigerian village women pound palm kernels to extract palm oil, used in making soap.*

■ *How did farming methods differ in different geographic regions?*

Religion, Dance, and Music

*B*ut the year had gone mad. Rain fell as it had never fallen before. For days and nights together it poured down in violent torrents, and washed away the yam heaps. Trees were uprooted and deep gorges appeared everywhere....

That year the harvest was sad, like a funeral, and many farmers wept as they dug up the miserable and rotting yams. One man tied his cloth to a tree branch and hanged himself.

Chinua Achebe, *Things Fall Apart*

Life in the villages of West Africa was often unpredictable. A drought, a flood, or an outbreak of disease could mean disaster. People thought that there were greater powers, or gods, who could protect them from such disaster.

Since earliest times, humans have had religious experiences. These often take vastly different forms. Indigenous religions, or religions that have not been brought by an outside group, flourished in African society. Africans believed that the physical world in which they lived was influenced by a spirit world. Their religion was meant to bring the two together.

Priests and diviners, they believed, helped people interact with the gods. **Diviners** communicated with the spirit world and had healing powers. Diviners also knew how to please the gods through rituals and dancing.

The people of the villages also believed in honoring their relatives through **ancestor worship.** They believed that the spirits of their ancestors lived on after death and could influence the gods in their favor—or punish the living with bad luck, sickness, or even death.

Villagers also tried to contact and please spirits through music and dancing. The Dogon people believed that when a person died,

▲ *Figures such as this one are thought to protect the bones of especially distinguished ancestors.*

125

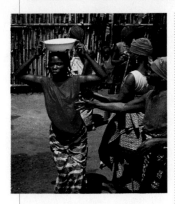

▲ *These women of the Fante tribe from Ghana call spirits with ritual.*

■ *In what ways were the various religions of West Africa similar?*

their spirit needed a place to stay. So they created masks that looked like the person that had died. When a dancer put on the mask, he was able to touch the spirit that lived within it. The masked dancers felt the spirits as they moved to the beat of the drums. ■

Village Life

People who lived in rural villages were members of large related families, or clans. The members of a clan could trace their origins to a common founding ancestor.

Kinship, or family relationship, was the basis of government. The male head of each clan became one of the village chiefs and often one of the religious leaders. Sometimes a council of family elders made up the village government. Within the family, everyone had jobs and responsibilities according to age, skills, gender as well as tradition. Older people were highly respected.

UNDERSTANDING KINSHIP

The settled farming communities of early West Africa were organized around kinship, or blood relationship, and marriage. People were also adopted, and lived among tight-knit, large, multi-generational families, with siblings (brothers and sisters), parents, grandparents, aunts, uncles, and cousins.

A clan was made up of a number of related families. Larger alliances might occur, too, with clans who spoke the same or related languages. Land was owned by the families or clans; it was rare that individuals owned land. The majority of sub-Saharan Africans lived in rural areas, usually in villages of at most a few hundred people. Others, such as the Yoruba people, lived in big cities. But whether in a city or a village, families and clans became one of the most important organizing forces in African society.

Rights and Responsibilities

The village was made up of many clans and families. Clans protected their members and provided for them when they were sick or old. The clans educated members and found work for them. In return for these benefits, members also had responsibilities. For example, if the clan had certain work to be done, or owed a debt to another clan, it was the members' responsibility to pitch in and help. Jobs were handed out according to age and ability. In places out of reach of a state government, clans might ask members to share in defense duties, too.

The Family in Society

In the United States, children are linked to both of their parents' families equally. This is called a bilateral system; in it both sides of a person's family are important.

In other cultures, relatives of one parent may be given more importance. The Ashanti people of modern West Africa are matrilineal. Children inherit property through their mother.

Kinship determines one's position in the family and even in society. This is because the family reflects the customs and traditions of a society.

Slavery

Under extreme hardship, if a clan was in debt or had promised to provide workers, members could be loaned out to fulfill the family's obligations. A clan might temporarily transfer its rights to a member to another clan in return for goods. When the debt was paid, the worker was returned. If the debt was not paid off, however, the status of temporary "slave" became permanent. Even then, individuals were still people, never property. They had only lost their political rights, not their personal rights. Usually the new family would accept them as members. Former slaves' children were not born slaves, nor did one group enslave other groups.

The majority of slaves, however, were captives of war. While today we find slavery unthinkable, historians remind us that for ancient peoples around the world, slavery was an improvement over death after capture. With rising prosperity in the Middle East and Asia after the 700s, slaves came to be in demand. Some African states exported slaves. Between 1200 and 1500, about 2.5 million Africans were taken across the Sahara or the Red Sea bound for slavery. It was not just the labor of the slaves that made them valuable but their skills and talents.

Slaves were used for various jobs. Many military leaders and soldiers were slaves. Some slaves became rich and powerful. Most served as domestic servants or did physical labor, like those who mined copper in Mali. Some slaves became the servants of kings and had power and money but they had no freedom. ■

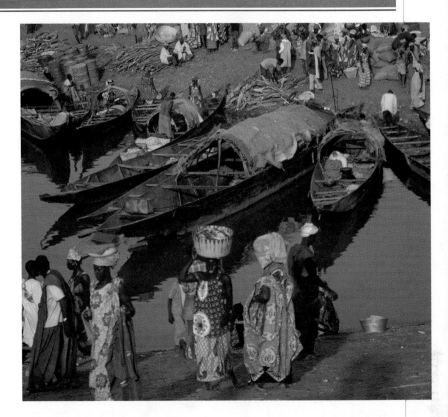

▲ *In current-day Mopti, Mali, goods are traded from boats on the Niger River.*

■ *Why was kinship important in West African village life?*

R E V I E W

1. **FOCUS** How did the people in the rural villages of West Africa survive in their often unpredictable environment?

2. **CONNECT** Many city dwellers in Mali and Songhai converted to the Islamic faith, but most villagers did not. Why do you think the villagers tended to keep to their traditional religion?

3. **BELIEF SYSTEMS** Clans were responsible for their members. What did a clan provide for its members? What were members expected to do in return?

4. **SOCIAL SYSTEMS** What role did the family play in the religious and political life of the village?

5. **CRITICAL THINKING** People in rural West African villages depended on each other for survival. Do you think this is true of people in the United States today?

6. **ACTIVITY** Imagine you are a village leader. One of the village members has damaged another's home. You need to punish the offender and compensate the victim. What exactly do you do to restore harmony?

127

West Africa

The Cow-Tail Switch

Retold by Harold Courlander and George Herzog

West African villagers told stories to teach lessons and for community entertainment. Often, in telling this story about the cow-tail switch, the storyteller would stop before the end. He would then ask the audience to participate by working out the ending. As you read it, think about how you would end this story and what arguments you would make to support your decision.

West African chiefs and other important village leaders often carried symbols of their authority. A decorated cow-tail switch, as in this story, was one of those symbols.

cassava (kuh SAH vuh) an edible root

Ogaloussa (oh gah LOO suh)

manioc cassava

Near the edge of the Liberian rain forest, on a hill overlooking the Cavally River, was the village of Kundi. Its rice and cassava fields spread in all directions. Cattle grazed in the grassland near the river. Smoke from the fires in the round clay houses seeped through the palmleaf roofs, and from a distance these faint columns of smoke seemed to hover over the village. Men and boys fished in the river with nets, and women pounded grain in wooden mortars before the houses.

In this village, with his wife and many children, lived a hunter by the name of Ogaloussa.

One morning Ogaloussa took his weapons down from the wall of his house and went into the forest to hunt. His wife and his children went to tend their fields, and drove their cattle out to graze. The day passed, and they ate their evening meal of manioc and fish. Darkness came, but Ogaloussa didn't return.

Another day went by, and still Ogaloussa didn't come back. They talked about it and wondered what could have detained him. A week passed, then a month. Sometimes Ogaloussa's sons mentioned that he hadn't come home. The family cared for the crops, and the sons hunted for game, but after a while they no longer talked about Ogaloussa's disappearance.

Then, one day, another son was born to Ogaloussa's wife. His name was Puli. Puli grew older. He began to sit up and crawl. The time came when Puli began to talk, and the first thing he said was, "Where is my father?"

The other sons looked across the ricefields.

"Yes," one of them said. "Where is Father?"

"He should have returned long ago," another one said.

"Something must have happened. We ought to look for him," a third son said.

"He went into the forest, but where will we find him?" another one asked.

"I saw him go," one of them said. "He went that way, across the river. Let us follow the trail and search for him."

So the sons took their weapons and started out to look for Ogaloussa. When they were deep among the great trees and vines of the forest they lost the trail. They searched in the forest until one of them found the trail again. They followed it until they lost the way once more, and then another son found the trail. It was dark in the forest, and many times they became lost. Each time another son found the way. At last they came to a clearing among the trees, and there on the ground scattered about lay Ogaloussa's bones and his rusted weapons. They knew then that Ogaloussa had been killed in the hunt.

One of the sons stepped forward and said, "I know how to put a dead person's bones together." He gathered all of Ogaloussa's bones and put them together, each in its right place.

Another son said, "I have knowledge too. I know how to cover the skeleton with sinews and flesh." He went to work, and he covered Ogaloussa's bones with sinews and flesh.

A third son said, "I have the power to put blood into a body." He went forward and put blood into Ogaloussa's veins, and then he stepped aside.

Another of the sons said, "I can put breath into a body." He did his work, and when he was through they saw Ogaloussa's chest rise and fall.

"I can give the power of movement to a body," another of them said. He put the power of movement into his father's body, and Ogaloussa sat up and opened his eyes.

"I can give him the power of speech," another son said. He gave the body the power of speech, and then he stepped back.

Ogaloussa looked around him. He stood up.

"Where are my weapons?" he asked.

They picked up his rusted weapons from the grass where they lay and gave them to him. They then returned the way they had come, through the forest and the ricefields, until they had arrived once more in the village.

Ogaloussa went into his house. His wife prepared a bath for him and he bathed. She prepared food for him and he ate. Four days he remained in the house, and on the fifth day he came out and shaved his head, because this was what people did when they came back from the land of the dead.

Afterwards he killed a cow for a great feast. He took the cow's tail and braided it. He decorated it with beads and cowry shells and bits of shiny metal. It was a beautiful thing. Ogaloussa carried it with him to important affairs. When there was a dance or an important ceremony he always had it with him. The people of the village thought it was the most beautiful cow-tail switch they had ever seen.

Soon there was a celebration in the village because Ogaloussa had returned from the dead. The people dressed in their best clothes, the musicians brought out their instruments, and a big dance began. The drummers beat their drums and the women sang. The people drank much palm wine. Everyone was happy.

Ogaloussa carried his cow-tail switch, and everyone admired it. Some of the men grew bold and came forward to Ogaloussa and asked for the cow-tail switch, but Ogaloussa kept it in his hand. Now and then there was a clamor and much confusion as many people asked for it at once. The women and children begged for it too, but Ogaloussa refused them all.

Finally he stood up to talk. The dancing stopped and people came close to hear what Ogaloussa had to say.

"A long time ago I went into the forest," Ogaloussa said. "While I was hunting I was killed by a leopard. Then my sons came for me. They brought me back from the land of the dead to my village. I will give this cow-tail switch to one of my sons. All of them have done something to bring me back from the dead, but I have only one cow-tail to give. I shall give it to the one who did the most to bring me home."

So an argument started.

"He will give it to me!" one of the sons said. "It was I who did the most, for I found the trail in the forest when it was lost!"

"No, he will give it to me!" another son said. "It was I who put his bones together!"

"It was I who covered his bones with sinews and flesh!" another said. "He will give it to me!"

"It was I who gave him the power of movement!" another son said. "I deserve it most!"

Another son said it was he who should have the switch, because he had put blood in Ogaloussa's veins. Another claimed it because he had put breath in the body. Each of the sons argued his right to possess the wonderful cow-tail switch.

Before long not only the sons but the other people of the village were talking. Some of them argued that the son who had put blood in Ogaloussa's veins should get the switch, others that the one who had given Ogaloussa breath should get it. Some of them believed that all of the sons had done equal things, and that they should share it. They argued back and forth this way until Ogaloussa asked them to be quiet.

"To this son I will give the cow-tail switch, for I owe most to him," Ogaloussa said.

He came forward and bent low and handed it to Puli, the little boy who had been born while Ogaloussa was in the forest.

The people of the village remembered then that the child's first words had been, "Where is my father?" They knew that Ogaloussa was right.

For it was a saying among them that a man is not really dead until he is forgotten.

Further Reading

African Myths and Legends. Kathleen Arnot. These tales are about animals, humans, and superhumans.

Behind the Back of the Mountain. Verna Aardema. These are black folktales from Southern Africa.

The Cow-Tail Switch and other West African Tales. Retold by Harold Courlander and George Herzog. Additional West African tales and legends that have been passed down through oral tradition.

The King's Drum and Other Stories. Harold Courlander. Here are tales from many different peoples of Africa. Each story identifies the tribe it came from.

The Magic Drum: Tales From Central Africa. W.F.P. Burton. The very short stories in this book are similar to fables. They are favorites in the Congo.

Chapter Review

Reviewing Key Terms

ancestor worship (p. 126) matrilineal (p. 117)
delta (p. 110) patrilineal (p. 117)
diviner (p. 126) sahel (p. 109)
griot (p. 118) savanna (p. 109)
kinship (p. 127)

A. Use each word below in a sentence that shows what the word means.

1. griot
2. diviner
3. delta
4. savanna
5. patrilineal
6. kinship
7. sahel
8. matrilineal

B. Write answers to the following questions. You may need to refer to a dictionary.

1. What does the root word *matri-* in *matrilineal* mean? What are some other words that contain *matri-* or a related form?
2. What root word and prefix combine to form the word *ancestor*? What are some other words with the same root? The same prefix?
3. *Sahel* means "shore of the desert." How is this kind of shore similar to that bordering a body of water?
4. What are the different meanings of the adjective *divine* and the verb *to divine*? What root words do they share with *diviner*?

Exploring Concepts

A. Copy the following cluster diagram on your paper. Then fill in the blanks with three important details about each society. Three details are done for you.

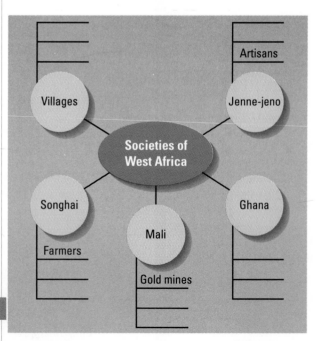

Villages

Songhai

Farmers

Mali

Gold mines

Societies of West Africa

Artisans

Jenne-jeno

Ghana

B. Support each of the following statements with facts and details from the chapter.

1. West Africans created city, regional, and state governments. Some villages fell outside these structures.
2. Despite the hardships of desert travel, West Africa was not cut off from the outside world.
3. The Niger helped Jenne-jeno grow into a bustling trade center.
4. Ghana became a powerful trading empire because of its location and government.
5. Traders brought more than goods to Ghana.
6. The success of Mali's trade empire affected the spread of Islam.
7. Askia Muhammad expanded the Songhai kingdom and advanced the spread of Islam.
8. The nature of West African village life helped shape the people's religious practices.
9. Kinship was the most important element in West African village life.

Reviewing Skills

1. Give one interpretation of the following West African proverb: "When you are carrying beef on your head, you do not use your feet to catch grasshoppers." What does it tell you about West African culture?
2. Give one interpretation of this West African proverb: "You change your steps according to the change in the rhythm of the drum." Can you think of a proverb with a similar meaning? An opposite meaning?
3. Review Understanding Kinship at the bottom of page 126. What is the main idea of this section? What supporting details do you find in the Rights and Responsibilities section? What supporting details do you find in The Family in Society?
4. Suppose you wanted to read an article about the West African trade empires. Where would you look to find the names of magazines that cover that subject?

Using Critical Thinking

1. Ideas are carried along trade routes together with goods and products. Therefore, the direction of trade routes can affect the course of history in very important ways. Suppose trade caravans had been unable, or traders unwilling, to cross the Sahara. How might West African society be different today? What effect might such isolation have had on the spread of religions?
2. Suppose a young person harms another young person. How would the punishment in American society now differ from that in a West African village in the year 1000? Which punishment do you think would be more effective? Why?
3. How did the Nok people make iron, and how did this skill benefit their culture? Do you think the culture you live in would be very different if we did not have metal-working skills? If the world ran out of metal ores completely and our supply of new metal was cut off, how do you think society would be affected? What kinds of adjustments would you have to make in your own life?

Preparing for Citizenship

1. WRITING ACTIVITY In Lesson 3 you read part of the story of the battle between Sumanguru and Sundiata, as told by a modern-day Mandinke griot, or storyteller. The language was colorful and the facts were somewhat exaggerated. Choose a recent event of importance in your life or in the world at large and retell it in the style of a modern-day American storyteller. After you write your story, practice reading it and then telling it aloud.
2. GROUP ACTIVITY Suppose you lived in West Africa in the time of one of the great trade empires, shown on page 121 of this chapter. Would you prefer to live in the exciting capital city of one of the empires, with its great culture, its exchange of people and ideas, and its many goods and services? Or would you prefer life in a small, rural village? Organize a debate on the question and prepare arguments for your side.
3. COLLABORATIVE LEARNING In all the West African cultures this chapter talked about, the importance of cultivating enough food to survive and to trade was stressed. Read through the chapter and list all the foods that were mentioned. Then divide into groups of three or four students. Have each group choose a food (two examples are rice and yams) and find a recipe for it in a cookbook. Then meet with the members of your group to prepare the dish and bring it to school for a potluck lunch.

Chapter 6
Central and Southern Africa

They called themselves Bantu, which means "the people." They spread out from West Africa over 2000 years ago, settling in the grassy savannas and the steamy rain forests of central and southern Africa. Some traveled to the coasts, where they built trading empires. But European traders plundered these empires and took many people away as slaves. Nevertheless, the heritage of "the people" continues. Most central and southern Africans today still think of themselves as Bantu.

During this period, a Bantu group called the Kikuyu became cattle raisers. They used shields like this one to defend their grazing land.

c. A.D. 200 Bantu migrate southward and begin farming and herding. Zulu people living in South Africa today, like this boy, trace their heritage to the early settlers.

500

B.C. A.D.

500

500 B.C.

A.D. 476 A barbarian general overthrows the last emperor of the Western Roman Empire.

Centuries-old traditions continue today. This young Kenyan woman, adorned with gold, bronze, and beads, participates in a ritual celebrating her coming of age.

A.D. 1000–1300 Bantu people called the Shona build the Great Zimbabwe, which means "Houses of Stone" (above). This grand city becomes Zimbabwe's capital and trade center.

1000

1500

Today

A.D. 786 Islamic ruler Abd al Rahman III begins building the Great Mosque in Cordoba, Spain.

A.D. 1300 Mali becomes the largest West African trading empire.

A.D. 1700

L E S S O N   1

The Spread of Bantu

THINKING FOCUS

How did the spread of the Bantu-speaking peoples affect the peoples of east, central and southern Africa?

Key Terms

- ethnolinguistics
- migrate

➤ *Bantu-speaking peoples, such as these Kikuyu women, now live in much of eastern, central, and southern Africa.*

Historians have many ways of studying the past. They can study stories that are passed down orally through the generations, or others that are written down. Music and dance, too, sometimes reflect a culture's history. Finally, artifacts and fossils give us physical proof of past events. In the study of central and southern Africa, however, another tool has proved most useful—language.

Consider the English word "continent." English developed from an old Germanic language, but through learning from the French, English-speaking people adopted the French word "continent" *(kahn tee NAHN).*

French developed from Latin, the language of the Roman Empire.

In Latin, the phrase *"terra continuens" (tayr uh kahn TIHN yoo enz)* means "continuous land." By tracing word histories, we learn how cultures interacted. In east, central, and southern Africa, historians are doing just this with the approximately 800 non-European languages spoken there.

Linguistics is the study of languages, and **ethnolinguistics** is the study of various peoples through their languages. In east, central, and southern Africa, scholars have found four major language families: the Khoisan *(KOY sahn),* Afro-Asiatic, Nilo-Saharan *(NEYE loh suh hayr uhn),* and Congo-Kordofanian *(kohr doh FAN yan).*

Perhaps the best studied languages are from one subgroup of the Congo-Kordofanian language family. These are called Bantu languages. Among different Bantu languages, scholars recognized words and grammatical structures that came from the same source.

Scholars now believe that proto-Bantu, the root language of all the Bantu languages, was the first language spoken by a people who lived in what is now eastern Nigeria or Cameroon between 500 B.C. and A.D. 200. These West Africans are believed to be the ancestors of diverse groups of people in many parts of Africa.

136

Chapter 6

Geography

During this time, most of east, central, and southern Africa was inhabited by various groups of hunting and gathering peoples. Two non-Bantu peoples are the Khoikhoi *(KOY koy)* and the San (Khoisan). Their language has a distinctive "click" sound unlike any other language in the world. For the proto-Bantu speakers, villages eventually became crowded, and some people moved to find additional agricultural lands. They traveled down the Congo River. From the basin of the Congo, they began to branch out. Some **migrated,** or moved to resettle, to the south, some to the east. For the next 2,000 years, descendants of the original proto-Bantu speakers migrated across east, central, and southern Africa where they settled in diverse lands.

Travel Across Africa

The expanse of savanna and dry grasslands that cover much of central and southern Africa provided a travel route, as well as good grazing ranges for domesticated herds. The migrants learned to avoid areas infested with tsetse *(TSET see)* flies that could infect both humans and cattle with a fatal illness.

To the east, the Great Rift Valley extended across the string of Great Lakes and valleys. This fertile valley, some 4,000 miles long and 20–30 miles wide, was formed in prehistoric times by a crack, or rift, in the earth's crust. Stretching north from Mozambique to Jordan in Asia, the valley welcomed migrating groups with its dry grasslands and plentiful water. Because it had few disease-carrying insects, this valley provided an excellent place for cattle to graze and an ideal passageway for travel to the north or south.

Along the equator, in the rain forest area of the Congo Basin, a large variety of animals and people inhabited the dense forest. With the thick undergrowth, travel by foot was difficult. For this reason, people who lived there used the network of rivers for their system of transportation. ■

■ *To which three geographic regions in east, central, and southern Africa did proto-Bantu speakers migrate and why?*

▼ *Compare this map with the one on page 525 of the Atlas. Which present-day countries are now in the regions where Bantu-speaking people migrated?*

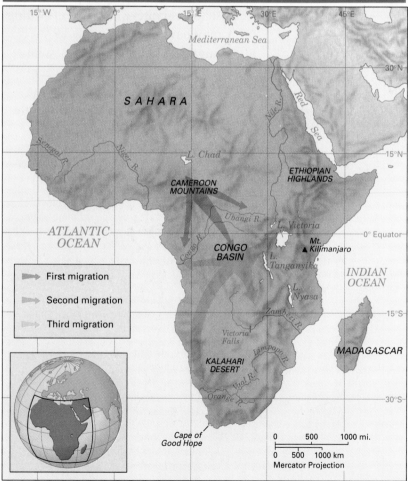

Migration of Proto-Bantu Speakers, 500 B.C.–A.D. 1500

The Spread of Bantu Culture

Across Time & Space

Insects continue to pose a problem in Africa today. The anopheles (uh NAHF uh leez) mosquito, which causes malaria, breeds in areas with standing water. The tsetse fly spreads sleeping sickness, and locusts can destroy a field of crops in minutes.

▼ Use this chart with maps on pages 137 and 525 to trace the order and routes of migrations of the Bantu-speaking peoples.

About 2,000 years ago, proto-Bantu-speaking people lived in what is today the eastern part of Nigeria. They relied primarily on fishing, farming, hunting, and trading. Using iron, they made hoes, spears, axes, and fishhooks that proved to be much stronger and longer-lasting than tools made from stone, wood, or bone. With better tools, they were able to clear more land and grow plentiful crops. They were also able to catch more fish and game than ever before.

As their ability to produce food increased, the proto-Bantu speakers' communities grew. Some scholars believe that overcrowding may have caused people to migrate. Others think that, with their iron weapons and farming tools, the proto-Bantu-speaking people would have met with little resistance from the hunter-gatherers they encountered. Many of the people they met may have adopted the farming methods and language of the Bantu speakers. The Khoikhoi, for example, began to herd cattle. The San, however, were forced out of their normal hunting grounds into the Kalahari desert.

Making New Contacts

As the migrants moved to new areas, they continued to influence the people they met. Some hunter-gatherers may have adopted the migrants' lifestyle when they married into their families. Noting the appearance of similar words in the languages of these groups, scholars believe that the hunters learned not only the language of the farmers but also many customs.

By now, proto-Bantu was giving way to the beginnings of the Bantu languages we know today. We can trace the migrations of these ancient people by observing where Bantu languages are spoken today. They are mostly south of a line drawn from Cameroon on the west coast of Africa to Kenya on the east coast. Today, this language family includes Swahili, Luba, Kongo, Kikuyu, Ruanda, Sotho, Zulu, and Xhosa, and more.

The Bantu-speaking people also adapted to their new environment by taking on the lifestyles of the local people. For example, like the local herders, the Bantu speakers who settled in the Great Rift Valley started to raise cattle. In the Congo Basin rain forest, heavy rains and dense vegetation

Routes of Bantu-speaking Migrants	
Dates	**Migration Routes**
3000–2500 B.C.	along the Sagha River, among others, into the areas around the Congo and Ubangi rivers; some groups move east along the middle of the Congo River into the northeastern parts of the equatorial rain forest
2500–2000 B.C.	some groups move downstream into the areas where the Kwa-Kasai and Congo rivers meet
2000–1000 B.C.	"Savanna Bantu" move east along the southern edge of the rain forest as far as the Western Rift and Great Lakes region (Lakes Victoria, Tanganyika, and Nyasa)
200 B.C.– A.D. 200	from the Western Rift, "Eastern Bantu" move across eastern and southeastern Africa; others spread south into Angola and Zambia or the heart of the Congo Basin

prevented Bantu-speaking farmers from raising crops. So many began fishing instead. They also developed crafts such as weaving, woodcarving, boat-building, and basketry.

From the people they met in east Africa, the Bantu speakers learned how to grow crops that had been brought from Asia, including bananas, new kinds of yams, rice, coconuts, and sugar cane. By A.D. 280, descendants of the Bantu-speaking people were farming near the southeastern coast of Africa, on the fertile slopes of Kilimanjaro and in the highlands around Lake Victoria. By 1400, Bantu-speaking groups populated much of sub-Saharan Africa. ■

Related Bantu Words

| Ethnic Group | Words | |
	person	*people*
Botatwe	muntu	bantu
Swahili	mtu	watu
Tonga	muntu	bantu
Xhosa	umntu	abantu
Zulu	umuntu	abantu

◄ *Ethnolinguists study African history through language. In proto-Bantu, the word for "person" was* mantu *and the word for "people" was* bantu. *Compare the words for "person" and "people" in the present-day languages shown here.*

■ *How did Bantu-speaking groups continue to migrate across Africa?*

Society of the Bantu Speakers

Among Bantu-speaking people, as with all Africans, the family was the basic social and political unit. Families and clans formed villages, and some villages belonged to states and kingdoms. These villages were commonly led by one man or a council of elders. In densely populated areas, some Bantu-speaking people formed empires, such as Zimbabwe.

Some Bantu speakers lived near the edge of the forest, fished, hunted, and cultivated yams, bananas, and grains. Others lived in villages and farmed, traded, made pottery, and kept cattle and goats. The wealth of the villages came from their agriculture. Men, women, and children all worked. Men also herded, hunted, or were artisans, and sometimes performed military duties. Besides their work, women maintained the household and raised the children. ■

■ *Describe the most common political structure among the Bantu-speaking groups.*

R E V I E W

1. **FOCUS** How did the spread of the Bantu-speaking peoples affect the peoples of east, central, and southern Africa?

2. **CONNECT** What did the people of ancient Ghana have that the proto-Bantu-speaking people did not? What effects do you think this had on their descendants?

3. **CULTURE** What changes in lifestyle did the proto-Bantu speakers adopt as they migrated? What changes in lifestyle did the people they meet adopt?

4. **CRITICAL THINKING** In the Indian language Sanskrit, the word for mother is *matar.* In Latin it's *mater,* and in German it's *mutter.* What conclusions might you draw from these similarities?

5. **ACTIVITY** Pick one region of central or southern Africa and collect pictures or draw original ones showing its geography. Then create an illustrated map that shows the geographic conditions the Bantu speakers encountered.

Central and Southern Africa

Making a Vertical Profile

Here's Why

Relief maps use color to show the elevations of landforms. A vertical profile gives a graphic view of the same information. Suppose you wanted to study the early people of Africa. Having a vivid picture of the lands on which these people lived could help you understand them. Could you construct a vertical profile to get this picture?

Here's How

Look at the map on this page. A line has been drawn at 3°S. Use the key to see how the elevation changes along this line. Then look at the vertical profile below the map. It shows the elevations along the 3°S line.

To construct a vertical profile first choose a line along which to draw it— in this case, 3°S. Draw a horizontal line on your paper to represent the profile line. Use the same scale as the map scale. Next look at the map key to see what elevations are represented on the map. Draw a vertical line at one end of your horizontal line. Use the elevation key as the vertical scale along this line. Then use the map to note elevation changes along the profile line. Do this by placing points on the profile to show where and to what degree the elevation changes. Finally, connect the points to complete the profile.

Try It

Construct a vertical profile of the African continent at 15°S. Use graph paper to help you mark elevation segments and place the points of elevation. What is the highest elevation? The lowest?

Apply It

Construct a vertical profile of a location in your state. Use your town as the place to locate your profile line. What is the highest elevation along your line? The lowest?

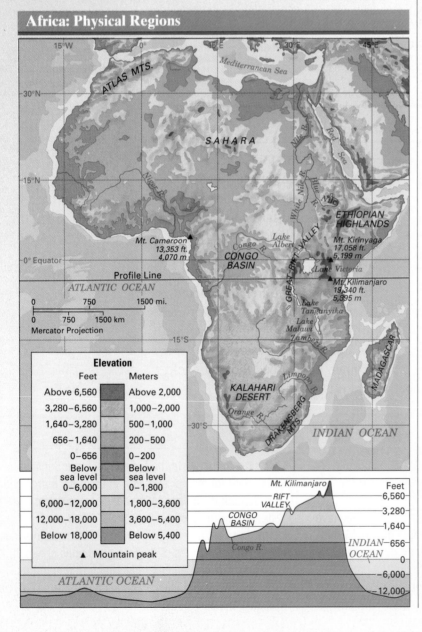

Africa: Physical Regions

Elevation

Feet	Meters
Above 6,560	Above 2,000
3,280–6,560	1,000–2,000
1,640–3,280	500–1,000
656–1,640	200–500
0–656	0–200
Below sea level 0–6,000	Below sea level 0–1,800
6,000–12,000	1,800–3,600
12,000–18,000	3,600–5,400
Below 18,000	Below 5,400

▲ Mountain peak

L E S S O N   2

The Rise of Coastal Trading States

> The last mainland market-town . . . is called Rhapta, a name derived from the small sewn boats. Here there is much ivory and tortoise shell. . . . The people of Mouza . . . send their small ships, mostly with Arab captains and crews who trade and intermarry with the mainlanders of all the places and know their language.
>
> Into these market-towns are imported lances made especially for them at Mouza, hatchets, swords, awls, and many kinds of small glass vessels; and at some places wine and not a little wheat, not for trade but to gain the goodwill of the barbarians. Much ivory is taken away from these places . . . and also rhinoceros horn and tortoise-shell, different from that of India, and a little coconut oil.

This passage, taken from *The Periplus of the Erythraean Sea*, describes trade between the Arab city of Mouza and Rhapta, an East African port. It was written in about A.D. 100 by a Greek merchant. He had been sent by the Romans occupying Egypt to investigate rumors of a booming trade between Indian Ocean ports.

THINKING FOCUS

How did East Africa become part of an international trade network?

Key Terms

- monsoon
- city-state

Sailing with the Winds

This Greek merchant was writing about the Indian Ocean trade network between East Africa, Arabia, India, Ceylon, and the East Indies. Although trading between Arabs and East Africans probably began in about 900 B.C., the Indian Ocean trade network wasn't really established until about 200 B.C. For it wasn't until then that the Arabs learned to use the seasonal winds known as **monsoons** to sail across the Indian Ocean.

Every year without fail the monsoon blows from the northeast between November and March

▼ *Sailors on the Indian Ocean still sail dhows much like those that Arab traders once used.*

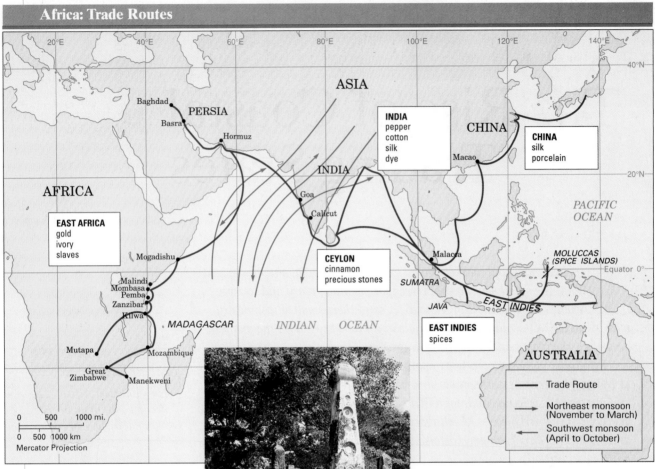

EAST AFRICA
gold
ivory
slaves

INDIA
pepper
cotton
silk
dye

CHINA
silk
porcelain

CEYLON
cinnamon
precious stones

EAST INDIES
spices

0   500   1000 mi.

0   500 1000 km
Mercator Projection

—— Trade Route

→ Northeast monsoon
(November to March)

← Southwest monsoon
(April to October)

➤ *Chinese porcelain plates are embedded in this pillar-tomb from the 1700s, which stands in the ancient trading settlement of Kunduchi in present-day Tanzania. The plates are reminders of the vast trade network that once crisscrossed the Indian Ocean.*

■ *Describe the monsoons and explain why they were so important to the Indian Ocean trade network.*

and from the southwest between April and October. So Arab merchants used these winds to propel their ships, called dhows *(dowz),* from Arabia down the African coast. They could reach Kilwa before the winds died down in March. Then the winds carried them from Kilwa back home again in April. With proper planning, Arabian ships could sail to nearly

any Indian Ocean port, but they had to sail back when the winds changed—or wait a year.

During the short, yearly trading season, the traders would stay with the African merchants. In time they intermarried and settled there. The people on the mainland spoke Bantu languages. After several centuries, their culture merged with the Arabian, Persian, and Indonesian traders', producing the Swahili language and culture. "Swahili" is the Arabic word for "people of the shore." Swahili-speaking people live throughout east and central Africa. ■

The Rise of City-States

Beginning in about A.D. 900, this new immigration of people began to affect the character of the coastal cities. Arab, Persian, and Indian traders came to share in the profits from preparing goods to sell to incoming ships.

In the hundreds of Swahili fishing and farming villages scattered along the coast, people established a complex economic system. Women, children, and a few men worked in the fields, while men and boys fished. Both men and women were traders and artisans.

The Swahili served as the link between foreign traders and inland Africans. One such group of inland Africans was the Shona, who lived in what is now Zimbabwe, between the Zambezi and Limpopo rivers. Find Zimbabwe on the map on page 525. The Shona had found large deposits of gold and other minerals there. By 1100, they were shipping these precious metals from Sofala, a southern port city, to Kilwa and other Swahili ports to be exchanged for foreign goods. Other inland Africans brought ivory, grain, and sometimes slaves to the coastal cities to trade for foreign knives, farming tools, fabrics, and porcelain (*PAWR suh lihn*).

Soon the merchants of one port city were in competition with those of another. There were great riches to be made in import-export trade, and each group of coastal merchants tried to attract a larger share of the business.

At this time, too, many ports became **city-states,** or independent states made up of a city and its surrounding territory. The rulers of the city-states grew rich from trade and from taxes they required merchants to pay on the goods that passed through their port. ■

■ *Describe the importance of city-states in trade between Africa and Asia.*

From Riches to Ruin

The most prosperous city-state was Kilwa, the southernmost port on the Indian Ocean trade route. By 1100, traders in Kilwa controlled the export of gold and ivory from southern kingdoms. The local rulers and merchants became very wealthy from this trade.

The North African traveler Ibn Battuta visited Kilwa in 1331. He described it as "one of the most beautiful and well-constructed towns in the world." He claimed, "The whole of it is elegantly built." In addition to the mosque shown below, Kilwa had a huge

▼ *The Great Mosque at Kilwa was built in the mid-1400s. Although most of it is now in ruins, the domes and cloister recall how glorious the East African city-states once were.*

Central and Southern Africa

palace, vast irrigated gardens, and houses many stories high that were built of stone.

Gedi, a trading town built in the 1300s, also had a mosque, a palace, and large houses built of stone. These houses had bathrooms with drains and overhead basins to flush toilets. In addition, the city was obviously well planned. The streets were not only laid out at right angles, but they had drainage gutters as well.

Then, in 1498, the first Portuguese explorer arrived. His name was Vasco da Gama. The Portuguese government had commissioned da Gama to find a way to sail from Portugal around southern Africa, into the Indian Ocean. They hoped that by developing such a trade route they would seize control of the Far East spice trade. But as Vasco da Gama piloted his ship northward along the East African coast, he realized that controlling East African trade would be quite profitable, too.

In 1505, a well-armed Portuguese fleet attacked Kilwa and then Mombasa. Neither city was able to defend itself against the Portuguese cannon. An observer aboard one of the ships that attacked Mombasa recorded the event. He described how the admiral ordered his men to destroy the city and carry off whatever they wanted. As a result, the observer says, " . . . everyone started to plunder the town and search the houses, forcing doors with axes and bars."

After conquering Kilwa, Mombasa, and other city-states, the Portuguese tried to monopolize trade in East African ports. But they did not have enough ships and men to maintain control over the entire Indian Ocean trade network. And by the late 1500s, Swahili groups had regained control of several ports from the Portuguese.

▲ *The carvings on this doorway from Lamu, near Kilwa, speak of the rich Swahili culture that dominated the coastal city-states of East Africa.*

■ *Who caused the destruction of many East African trading centers, and why?*

*H*e who wants to string pearls
must be an excellent diver;
he who manages to succeed
is a [pearl] diver, a fisherman;
the soul is a vast ocean;
in it there is the treasure-trove
of mother-of-pearl;
he that is afraid of drowning,
[for him] the oyster shells
produce no pearls.

Swahili poem, 1700s

The cities never again saw the prosperity of earlier times. But the unique Swahili culture and language are still a vital part of the African tradition. ■

REVIEW

1. **FOCUS** How did East Africa become part of an international trade network?
2. **CONNECT** How was the growth of trade in East Africa similar to the growth of trade in West Africa?
3. **CULTURE** Who were the Swahili, and how did their culture develop?
4. **CRITICAL THINKING** How might Swahili life in inland villages differ from that in coastal trading towns?
5. **ACTIVITY** Imagine you are a sailor on a merchant ship sailing from India to East African ports in the 1100s. Describe, or map out, the voyage you might make. Include dates, names and descriptions of ports, and cargoes your ship would carry back to India.

144

L E S S O N   3

The Rise of the Zimbabwe State

At its peak around 1400, the stone enclave known as Great Zimbabwe spread over almost 200 acres and held up to 18,000 people. It was the capital city of a major state. Unfortunately only a few records remain of the Shona people who lived in this enclave. There are miles of ruins at Great Zimbabwe, however, that hold much information for archaeologists. In the Shona language, "zimbabwe" means "houses of stone."

There are two large building sites at Great Zimbabwe. One is a hill covered with enormous boulders. Over time, people linked the boulders together with stone walls, making courtyards and narrow passages. The other, is called "the Great Enclosure." Here, a narrow, cone-shaped stone tower rises three stories high. Long corridors gently curve between walls over 15 feet high. Inside the walls are the remains of buildings where the rulers, priests, and artisans of Great Zimbabwe probably lived.

Archaeologists have also found evidence of metal working and trade in copper, iron, and gold. Many gold and copper ornaments were found in the sites—the miner-

THINKING FOCUS

Describe some of the ways the Shona benefited from their decision to settle on the site now known as the Zimbabwe Plateau.

Key Terms

- plateau
- oral tradition
- malaria

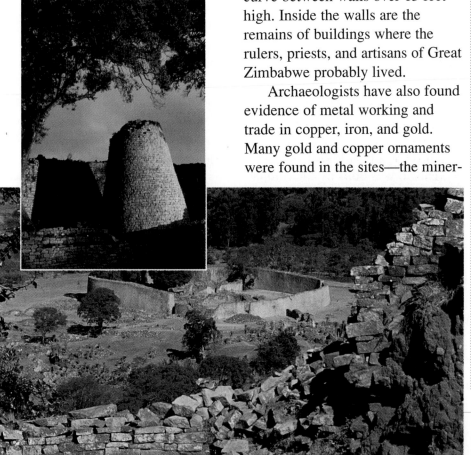

◄ *This view of Great Zimbabwe shows the outside wall that surrounded the king's court and measured more than 820 feet long. The cone-shaped tower rises above the wall.*

al wealth of the lands ruled from Great Zimbabwe. Trading this gold made Kilwa an important Swahili city. Archaeologists also found at Great Zimbabwe items from beyond Africa, including Chinese, Persian, and Syrian artifacts that date back to the 1300s.

▼ *How do the sizes of the empires of Zimbabwe and Monomutapa compare with those of modern African nations?*

The Zimbabwe Kingdom

Extent of Zimbabwe, c. 1400
Extent of Monomutapa, c. 1500

0 250 500 mi.
0 250 500 km
Mercator Projection

The Builders of Great Zimbabwe

ing material and firewood. Also, the plateau was free of deadly tsetse flies. And the earth there was rich in granite, iron, copper, and gold.

People lived at Great Zimbabwe long before the great walls were built. The foundations of the hilltop fortress date back to the A.D. 300s. The population grew, and by the late 1100s the Shona had developed a complex society that included agriculture, cattle herding, mining, metalworking, and trade, as well as political and religious structures.

Some historians suggest that the Shona used diplomacy to rule the small surrounding states. They may have demanded tribute from them in food, gold dust, or ivory. But where did their power come from? The great riches produced by the gold and ivory trade allowed the Shona to maintain their rule and expand their influence. Some historians also believe their power was derived from their priests, who commanded great respect.

The power of Great Zimbabwe was not to last. Historians think that decades of drought or poor crops brought about the state's decline. As people planted fields and grazed cattle year after year, the nutrients in the soil ran out. The people cleared more forests and repeated the process of wearing out the land. People eventually had to move away to better land. ■

How Do We Know?

We know that non-African archaeologists who visited Great Zimbabwe in the 1800s had racist attitudes, because they refused to believe that Africans could have built the impressive site.

■ *Trace the growth and decline of Great Zimbabwe.*

Historians now know that Great Zimbabwe was built by the Shona between A.D. 1000 and 1300. The Shona are Bantu-speaking farmers and cattle raisers who had come to this area in about A.D. 300. They might also have brought mining techniques to the region.

The Shona chose to settle in this area for a number of reasons. The **plateau,** or raised, flat surface of land, had abundant rainfall for crops and plenty of trees for build-

The Gold Mines of Zimbabwe

When the Shona, a Bantu-speaking people, came to the Zimbabwe Plateau, they used gold to make jewelry and other ornaments. But to them, gold was just another metal, like copper or iron. It wasn't as useful as iron, because it was so soft. But coastal traders valued gold highly. The Shona found they could exchange their gold for Chinese silk, Indian glass beads, and fine Persian pottery.

The Search for Gold

The Shona found some of their gold in rivers and streams, but in the 1100s, they began digging to mine gold underground. Archaeologists have found more than 60,000 mine shafts on the Zimbabwe Plateau. They have also discovered that mostly women and children mined these shafts.

The miners built fires next to the large gold-bearing rocks. When the rocks were hot, they threw cold water on them. This caused a sudden temperature change that split the rocks, making it easier for the miners to remove the gold.

The Gold Capital

Through mining and trading gold, Zimbabwe became a wealthy kingdom. By the 1400s, the rulers of Zimbabwe controlled most of the country between the Limpopo River on the south to the Zambezi on the north and from the Indian Ocean west to the Kalahari Desert. Great Zimbabwe was Zimbabwe's capital and trade center.

In the heart of Great Zimbabwe is a large hill where the Shona built a huge granite fortress with 20-foot-thick walls. People lived nearby in clay huts with thatched roofs.

Near the foot of the main hill a thick wall enclosed the king's compound. The significance of the cone-shaped tower is not known to outsiders. At the height of the kingdom in the 1400s, Portuguese historian João de Barros described

◄ *Zimbabwe remains an important producer of gold. Mines such as this one use railroad cars to carry ore from underground.*

147

Central and Southern Africa

the king's complex: "The floors, ceiling, beams and rafters are all either gilt or plated with gold . . ." and there were candlesticks "made of ivory inlaid with gold."

Scholars have learned a great deal about Zimbabwe's past from the ruins and also from the Shona's rich oral tradition. In the **oral tradition,** stories are passed down through time by one generation telling them to the next. An oral tradition preserves the history of a people without written records. ■

The Breakup of Zimbabwe

In about 1450, the chiefs of Zimbabwe's gold-producing provinces declared independence from Great Zimbabwe. One of these groups, a northern group led by King Mwene Mutapa, conquered neighboring kingdoms and formed a new empire called Monomutapa.

But civil wars that began to break out in 1490 weakened Monomutapa. In the early 1500s, the empire split in two. The northern half remained Monomutapa, but a rival dynasty, the Changamire, took over the south.

At the same time, Portuguese traders engaged in friendly trading with Monomutapa. But before long, the Portuguese sought increased wealth and power by taking control of Monomutapa's markets and gold mines. In 1570, they attacked the empire.

However, Portuguese forces had been greatly diminished by **malaria.** Carried by mosquitoes, this disease causes fever and chills, and often death. The Portuguese lost so many soldiers to malaria that their conquest attempt failed.

During the next 100 years, the Portuguese continued to undermine the central government. With civil wars and the disruption of gold production, Monomutapa was seriously weakened. By the late 1600s, southern kingdoms had conquered it. ■

➤ Mwene Mutapa founded and ruled the empire called Monomutapa.

■ Why did the Portuguese undermine Monomutapa?

1. **FOCUS** Describe some of the ways the Shona benefited from their decision to settle on the site now known as the Zimbabwe Plateau.

2. **CONNECT** Describe the trade relationship between the Shona of Zimbabwe and the trading centers on the East African coast.

3. **CULTURE** Why didn't European scholars believe that Africans had built the structures at Great Zimbabwe?

4. **CRITICAL THINKING** Do you think the culture of the United States has an oral tradition? Explain.

5. **ACTIVITY** Imagine archaeologists 1,000 years in the future have discovered the ruins of your school. List three artifacts that the archaeologists might find and explain what the artifacts tell about your culture.

LESSON 4

The Kongo Kingdom

The lone Portuguese ship inched along off the west coast of Africa. It was 1482 and Captain Diego Cão had gone farther south than any other European. But right now his crew needed rest. Cão spotted the mouth of a mighty river and anchored a few miles upstream. Then he and his men stepped ashore.

The Africans there had never seen white men. So, curious, they gathered around the sailors. One rubbed Cão's arm with water, trying to wipe off what he thought was white paint. They offered to take Cão to their king, but he wanted to sail farther south, so he had four servants go for him.

When Cão returned to the river, he found no trace of his servants. Fearing the worst, he captured four local people and sailed for home. But Portugal's King John hoped to impress their king, so he treated the hostages like princes.

About three years later, King John sent Cão and the hostages back to Africa with gifts and letters for their king. Cão's servants were waiting for him with tales of the vast kingdom of the Kongo. Cão returned to Portugal with his servants and a friendly letter to King John from the Kongo king.

Key Terms

- currency
- missionary
- plantation

◄ *This column, left by the Portuguese on the African coast, says the king has "ordered this land to be discovered."*

The Growth of Kongo

Cão was the first European to encounter the Kongo kingdom. Like the Shona people of

Zimbabwe, the people of Kongo descended from Bantu-speaking farmers. Specifically, during the

149

Central and Southern Africa

➤ *Compare this map of the Kongo kingdom with the map on page 525 of the Atlas. What modern nations were once part of the Kongo kingdom?*

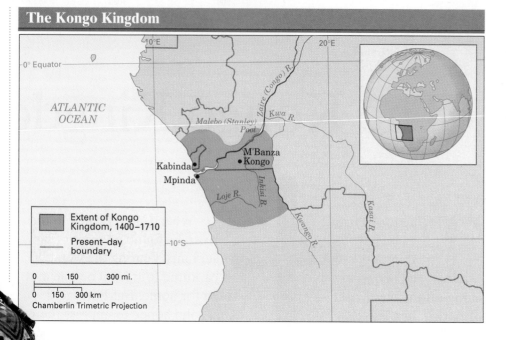

The Kongo Kingdom

ATLANTIC OCEAN

0° Equator

10°E

20°E

Zaire (Congo) R.

Kwa R.

Malebo (Stanley) Pool

M'Banza Kongo

Kabinda

Mpinda

Loje R.

Inkisi R.

Kwango R.

Kasai R.

10°S

Extent of Kongo Kingdom, 1400–1710

Present–day boundary

0   150   300 mi.

0   150   300 km

Chamberlin Trimetric Projection

▲ *This Kongo mask is decorated with cowry shells that were valuable as well as beautiful. Cowry shells were used as money by some African tribes.*

➤ *This carved wooden figure from the Kongo region was used in rituals.*

1300s, two Bantu clans had joined together to form what became the kingdom called Kongo.

By the 1400s, Kongo's king, the Mani-Kongo, ruled six provinces and about two million people. Chiefs appointed by the king controlled each province. Find Kongo lands on the map above.

The People of Kongo

Kongo's royal capital, Mbanza, was built on a fertile plateau surrounded by rain forests, 100 miles east of the coast and 50 miles south of the Congo River. The people of Mbanza lived in straw huts scattered around the walled palace of the king.

Farmers planted millet and sorghum on the land around Mbanza. They gathered bananas, coconuts, dates, and citrus fruits from the surrounding forests, and they made oil, wine, vinegar, and bread from the fruit and sap of palm trees. In addition, the people hunted game for meat.

Trade in Kongo

Mbanza was not only a rich farming area but a prosperous crossroads for trade. The people of Kongo traded with people to the north, east, and west both by land and river. They traded salt from the sea, iron, copper, ivory, and raffia—a fiber made of palm leaves.

As **currency,** or money, the Kongo traders used small seashells, called cowries, from the coast. But when Kongo people began trading with the Portuguese, seashells were the last thing the Portuguese wanted as payment for their goods. They wanted gold. The Kongo region had no gold, so Portugal asked the Mani-Kongo for another form of payment—slaves. To learn more about a Mani-Kongo, see A Moment in Time on page 151. ■

150 ■ *Describe the early development of Kongo.*

A Kongo King

11:47 A.M., May 15, 1544
Mbanza, capital of the Kongo kingdom

Salt
The heavy block, worth its weight in gold, was just presented to him by the governor of one part of the kingdom. The gift proves the governor is still loyal to the king.

Collar
He's wearing his finest African gold for today's tribute ceremony. He wants to show everyone—his subjects and the Portuguese traders— his power and authority. He has to be clever to balance the demands made on him from all sides.

Zebra Skin
The king is pleased that this gift is wrapped in a valuable skin. At the feast after this ceremony, the king will strengthen his ties to the governor by giving him an elegant drinking glass from Venice. The king trades for jewelry with the Portuguese.

Throne
Gleaming with ivory and inlaid gold, his chair is the only seat in the room. The king's men-at-arms stand at attention with their spears. The governors cluster in small groups, waiting for their chance to kneel before the king.

Boots
Of all the European goods the king gets from the Portuguese, these are his favorites. He paid for them with beautiful African cloth he received at last year's tribute ceremony.

151

The Portuguese in Kongo

Portuguese traders developed a prosperous and friendly relationship with the Kongo people. In 1490, the Portuguese king sent teachers and missionaries to educate the Mani-Kongo and members of his court. A **missionary** is someone who goes to a foreign place to teach religion.

Under the missionaries' guidance, the Mani-Kongo converted to Christianity and even sent his son to a missionary school. Later, his son became king and was baptized with the Christian name of Affonso I.

Affonso continued his father's contact with the Portuguese. He adopted many Portuguese customs and encouraged members of his court to attend school. Some even began to wear European clothes and to import European furniture.

However, some people resented the Portuguese influence. They wanted their king to adhere to local traditions.

Nevertheless, the alliance between the Kongo and King John remained strong until the early 1500s. By then Portugal had begun settling the island of São Tomé, 250 miles off the Kongo coast. Most of the settlers were criminals being deported from Portugal. They had little regard for the African people and a great desire to improve their own lives.

When the Portuguese governor of São Tomé discovered that sugar grew well there, he immediately began looking for workers for the large farms, or **plantations.** He knew slave labor would cost the least and thereby leave more money as profit. So the governor turned to nearby Africa to find slaves.

At first, Affonso supplied him with slaves, not realizing that the Portuguese had a different notion of slavery than he did. Enslaving war prisoners was an accepted practice in Africa. But Africans did not mistreat their slaves or separate them from their families, and slaves could eventually earn their freedom. The Portuguese, however, treated slaves like beasts of burden, working them so hard that many died. When this occurred, they simply bought more. ■

> ➤ *An African artisan from the kingdom of Benin, near the mouth of the Niger River, was employed by the Portuguese to carve this salt container from ivory. It represents explorers and their ships. Look at the faces on the carving. How do you think the carver felt about the Portuguese?*

> ■ *What European nation led in the African slave trade?*

Slaves, Guns, and Civil War

The merchants of São Tomé were not satisfied with the limited number of slaves they could obtain from the Kongo. The buying and selling of slaves had become quite a profitable business. And with a new Portuguese colony in South America, called Brazil, the demand for slaves was greater than ever.

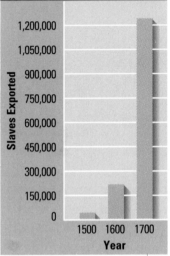

The Portuguese merchants stopped at nothing to get slaves. Since Africans customarily enslaved prisoners they took in war, the merchants tried to get village chiefs to declare war on each other. And since native criminals were punished with slavery, they encouraged crime among the people. The Portuguese also supplied rival villages with guns and even bribed officials to encourage revolts against the Mani-Kongo. They offered European goods and guns to any chief who would supply them with slaves. Some missionaries even became slave traders.

The Kongo rulers were trapped in a tangled web. A chief needed guns for protection from slave raiders. But the only way to get guns was to trade slaves for them.

Desperate to put an end to this problem, Affonso wrote a series of letters to King John. In one, written in 1526, he pleaded:

> Merchants are taking every day our natives, sons of the land and sons of our noblemen. . . . So great is the corruption and licentiousness [immorality] that our country is becoming completely depopulated.

In letter after letter, Affonso asked the Portuguese king to ban slave trade in Kongo. But King John did nothing. And, by 1540, King Affonso had even decided to support the slave trade in order to increase his own wealth and power.

By the 1600s, the Kongo kingdom was breaking apart. The Portuguese pressured Kongo chiefs in the provinces to rebel against the Mani-Kongo. As a result, the chiefs of some provinces declared their independence from the kingdom. Civil wars erupted as villages staged raids against each other to capture slaves and sell them to the Portuguese.

Thus, contact with the Portuguese had a severe and long-lasting effect on the people of Kongo and all of Africa. The Portuguese destroyed Kongo's trade in goods and replaced it with trade in human beings. Kongo lost many strong and able people to slavery. Finally, civil wars sparked by the Portuguese brought an end to the Kongo kingdom. ■

Kongo Slave Trade

Chart: Slaves Exported (y-axis: 0; 150,000; 300,000; 450,000; 600,000; 750,000; 900,000; 1,050,000; 1,200,000) by Year (x-axis: 1500, 1600, 1700)

▲ *Queen Nzinga Mbande (c. 1580–1663), is today a national heroine in Angola. She once worked against the Portuguese. One story says that she called a slave to sit upon when the Portuguese governor refused her a chair.*

■ *Why did civil war erupt in Kongo?*

R E V I E W

1. **FOCUS** How did Kongo change after the arrival of the Portuguese?
2. **CONNECT** Compare the relationship of Portugal and Kongo with that of Portugal and Monomutapa.
3. **HISTORY** Describe the actions of the Portuguese to develop the slave trade.

4. **CRITICAL THINKING** Why do you think King John ignored Affonso's plea for help?
5. **WRITING ACTIVITY** Write a letter from King Affonso of Kongo to King John of Portugal in which King Affonso describes the effects of the slave trade in Kongo and asks King John to put a stop to it.

153

Central and Southern Africa

Trade Between the Kongo and Portugal

> *P*ut all the Guinea countries [African countries along the west coast north of the Kongo kingdom] on one side and only Kongo on the other and you will find that Kongo renders [offers] more than all others put together. . . . No other king in all these parts esteems Portuguese goods so much or treats the Portuguese as well as we do."
>
> Mani-Kongo Affonso I in letter
> to King John III of Portugal, 1540

Background

The kingdom of the Kongo was established in the early 1400s. From its beginning, trade was the key to power in that kingdom. The Kongo kingdom was located at the crossroads of two trade routes. Copper was traded on a north-south trade route; shells and salt were traded on an east-west trade route. The first Mani-Kongo centered his kingdom

➤ *Seated on a throne above his subjects, Affonso, the Mani-Kongo, meets with a representative sent by the king of Portugal.*

154

where these two trade routes intersected. This enabled him to gain control of the distribution of all of these products.

The Mani-Kongo used his control over trade, his army, and his system of administration and justice to hold power over local chiefs. To those who were loyal to him, he gave gifts—trade goods from the far corners of the kingdom. From those who opposed him, he withheld such goods.

Expanding Trade

Soon after the Portuguese arrived in the Kongo in the late 1400s, the Mani-Kongo offered them high-quality copper. In return, he expected that the Portuguese would offer technology, including guns, knives, and cloth. The Portuguese refused to sell the Kongo people goods that would benefit their society. Instead, the Portuguese only traded worthless items such as china, mirrors, and hats. The trade the Portuguese built up with Kongo only benefited the Portuguese.

The decision to trade with the Portuguese had short-term benefits for the Mani-Kongo. In the long run, however, it had serious negative consequences. In the early 1500s, the Portuguese began trading with the Mani-Kongo for slaves. This led to the destruction of the kingdom.

The map of western Africa, created in 1502, reveals how little Portuguese explorers had learned about Africa by this time.

Decision Point

1. For the Mani-Kongo, what were some immediate benefits of trading with the Portuguese? Eventually, what were the negative consequences?

2. Do you think the Mani-Kongo could have foreseen these negative consequences? Why?

3. If the mani-Kongo had refused to trade with the Portuguese, what might have been some of the consequences? Consider both short-term and long-term benefits and drawbacks.

4. Currently the United States trades with many foreign countries, including Japan, China, and South Africa. Look in newspapers and magazines for information about our trade relationships with one of these countries. Discuss some of the short-term and long-term consequences of trading with these nations.

This African mask, made in the Kongo, is covered with cowry shells. These shells were valuable to the Kongo people.

155

Central and Southern Africa

Chapter Review

Reviewing Key Terms

city-state (p. 143)
currency (p. 150)
ethnolinguistics (p. 136)
malaria (p. 148)
migrate (p. 137)

missionary (p. 152)
monsoon (p. 141)
oral tradition (p. 148)
plantation (p. 152)
plateau (p. 146)

A. For each sentence below write whether it is an example of a city-state, an oral tradition, or a currency. Explain your answer.
1. A mother sings songs to her children that she learned as a child.
2. At the restaurant the man pays for his dinner with a gold coin.
3. In addition to a mosque, Kilwa had a huge palace and houses of many stories.

B. Write whether each statement below is true or false. Then rewrite the false statements to make them true.
1. Bantu-speaking people migrated because the climate grew cold.
2. To sail by the monsoons, Arabs left for West Africa between April and October.
3. The Europeans treated African slaves harshly.
4. Christian missionaries taught Africans about Islam.
5. Many of the people in Africa suffered from malaria.
6. No Africans had large cities or well-organized states.
7. Zimbabwe is located on a low plateau.

Exploring Concepts

A. In this chapter, you read about several groups of African people. The chart below compares four of the groups. Copy the chart on your own paper. Then complete the chart using information from the chapter. The first section has been done for you.

Peoples of Central and Southern Africa		
	Occupations	**Additional Information**
Kikuyu	Farming	They lived in villages but not kingdoms.
Swahili		
Shona		
People of Kongo		

B. Answer each question with information from the chapter.
1. What are three kinds of terrain in central and southern Africa?
2. Why do most people of central and southern Africa speak a Bantu language?
3. What products did the city of Rhapta import around A.D. 100? What did Mouza import from Rhapta?
4. How did the Indian Ocean trade between 1100–1500 affect the town of Kilwa?
5. What do we know about the people who lived at Great Zimbabwe?
6. How did the Shona use the gold of Zimbabwe? How did they mine the gold in the 1100s?
7. What products did the people of the Kongo trade with the people around them before the Portuguese arrived?
8. What were the long-term effects of the Portuguese on Monomutapa and Kongo?

156

Reviewing Skills

1. Look at the map on this page. Construct a vertical profile of the land at 20° S. What is the highest elevation shown on your vertical profile? The lowest?
2. Use the following entry from the *Readers' Guide* to answer the questions.
   Monsoons
   Seasonal winds: a blessing or a curse?
   R. A. Borthwick. il maps *Journal of Economic Development* 129:21–7+ Ap '89
   a. What is the title of the article?
   b. Who is the author?
   c. What is the title of the periodical?
   d. On what pages does the article appear?
3. Imagine that African villagers are explaining a truth about life to their children. How might the villagers communicate this truth?

Elevation of Southeast Africa

ZAMBIA
MALAWI
Zambezi River
Mt. Inyangani
8,508 ft.
2,594 m
ZIMBABWE
MOZAMBIQUE
•Bulawayo
BOTSWANA
Limpopo River
INDIAN OCEAN

25°E 30°E 35°E 40°E
15°S
20°S
25°S

Elevation

Feet		Meters
Above 6,560		Above 2,000
3,280–6,560		1,000–2,000
1,640–3,280		500–1,000
656–1,640		200–500
0–656		0–200

0   150   300 mi.
0   150 300 km
Mercator Projection

Using Critical Thinking

1. If you wanted to know whether early African people suffered from sleeping sickness, what information in the chapter might help you to determine this?
2. What were the trading practices of the Arabs of Mouza around A.D. 100? What values of the Arab people do these trading practices reveal? Do you think these values are still important today? Explain your answer.
3. Imagine that you came upon the ruins of Great Zimbabwe. You arrive at a city on a high plateau. You see a tower and a 30-foot wall around the city. Inside the buildings, you eventually discover hidden passages. What would you determine about the Shona's relationships with other groups from these observations?

Preparing for Citizenship

1. COLLECTING INFORMATION   Alex Haley was an African American who traced his family's history back to a village in West Africa. Look in Haley's book, *Roots, the Saga of an American Family,* to find out how he used oral tradition to trace his family's roots.
2. INTERVIEWING Villages of Bantu speakers were commonly ruled by a chief and a council of elders. Interview an official in your city or town. Find out how your town's government is organized. Is there anyone who functions like a chief? Is there any group that acts like a council of elders? If there are, what are their titles and responsibilities?
3. COLLABORATIVE LEARNING Work in committees to research one or two cities in your state or region that were founded as centers of trade. Locate the cities on a map. Find out what products were exported and imported by these cities, and whether this trade is the basis of their economy today. If not, find out how the economy of the city has changed. Each committee should decide what information is important and report it to the class.

Unit 4
Asian Civilizations

Reflect for a moment on this Chinese landscape—the grassy bluffs, the lush trees, the peaceful river, the family quietly taking its leave. For centuries, Asian artists, thinkers, and priests have been fascinated by such moments of calm natural beauty. Yet not all has been peace and beauty in China, Japan, India, and central Asia. Over the past 2,000 years, there have been times of chaos and fighting, and centuries when powerful rulers dominated vast empires.

220

Saying Farewell at Hsün Yang *by Qiu Ying, c. 1495*

1923

Chapter 7

Three Empires

This ceremonial sword belonged to an Ottoman sultan.

The conquerors came from homelands in central Asia. The Mongols swept down and captured lands from China to the Middle East. The Ottoman Turks migrated to Asia Minor and then set their sights on new frontiers. The Mughals trekked over the steep passes of the Himalayas and invaded India. Through strong leadership and tolerance toward the people they conquered, the Mongols, Ottomans, and Mughals built great empires.

1260–1294 Led by Kublai Khan, the Mongol Empire reaches its height. Mongol warriors (left) take control of the Middle East from Egypt.

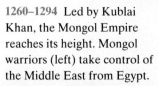

| 950 | 1100 | 1250 | 1400 |

1235 Mali defeats Ghana to become the major power in West Africa.

1096–1291 European Christians fight Arab Muslims for control of Jerusalem and the Holy Land.

997

During the 1400s and 1500s, the Ottomans built a powerful and wealthy empire. Sultan Sulieman wore the jewels at the right on his turban. Sultan Bayezid wore the silk caftan at left as he sat on his throne.

1556–1605 The Mughal Empire prospers under Akbar. In the painting at the right, Akbar directs the building of a fort in his capital.

1550

1700

1850

Today

c. 1600 The Kongo kingdom breaks apart due to civil wars sparked by the Portuguese.

1923

L E S S O N   1

The Mongols

THINKING
F O C U S

How did the Mongols affect Europe and Asia?

Key Terms

- steppe
- clan
- khan

I n the early 1200s, a group of people known as the Mongols began a series of rapid conquests throughout Asia. They would soon control the largest empire in the world. Ibn al Athir wrote about the events of 1220 to 1221, "These Tartars [Mongols] conquered most of the habitable globe and the best, the most flourishing and most populous thereof . . . in about a year."

How were the Mongols able to conquer so much so quickly?

There are several reasons for the Mongol successes. They had outstanding leadership, military skill and, most important, horses. On horseback, the Mongols could advance up to 200 miles a day. Good horsemanship was so important to the Mongols that children, both male and female, learned to ride before they could walk.

► *The Mongols took excellent care of their horses. Here, a Mongol grooms the tail of his horse.*

The Life of Mongol Nomads

The world that horses enabled the Mongols to inhabit was the wide, treeless plains—or **steppes**— of central Asia. To the north lies the Siberian forest and to the south is desert.

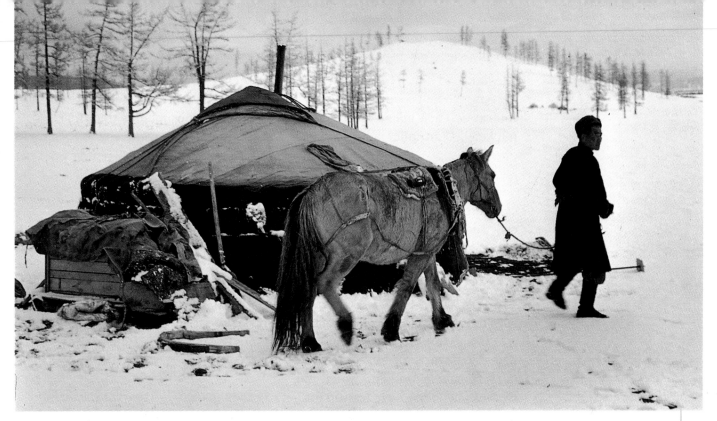

Winter in the steppes is long and bitterly cold, and summer is dry and burning hot. The temperature ranges from –100°F in the winter to 100°F in the summer. The Mongols were nomadic herders who migrated according to the seasons, in search of good grazing land for their flocks of sheep and horses.

Since the Mongols moved so frequently, they didn't have one permanent settlement. Instead, they lived in tents called yurts. Yurts were made of felt, a material made from wool, and so were easily transportable and yet strong enough to offer protection from the extreme weather.

The Mongols traveled in patrilineal family groups called **clans.** Clan members were related by kinship. Clans had a formal leader who was usually the eldest male. They were normally made up of several three- or four-generation family groups. Each clan could trace its descent from an actual or mythical founding ancestor. The tribe united the clans either through kinship or treaty. The Mongol practice of *anda,* or sworn brotherhood, allowed people to swear allegiance to a clan other than the one they were born into. The chart below shows the social organization of the Mongols.

If the reputation of a tribal leader was very impressive, men from other tribes would swear

▲ *Yurts are still used by many nomads on the steppes of central Asia.*

▼ *Mongol social organization was based on family ties, sworn brotherhood, and sworn oaths to leaders. When a man swore allegiance to a new leader, he forswore his blood loyalty to his own clan and to the tribe.*

Social Bonds Among the Mongol

Three Empires

allegiance to him. They would then become the new leader's *nöker,* or followers. Their allegiance to him outweighed any allegiance to clan or tribe.

For all Mongol groups, the need to protect themselves and compete for grazing lands was crucial. To do so, the Mongols developed incredible skill on horseback.

Mongols had such control over their mounts that they could ride long distances using only their feet. Their hands, then, were free to wield weapons in battle. Their exceptional riding skill and their great ability in using weapons while on horseback gave the Mongols a distinct advantage over their less-skilled enemies. ■

Mongol Leadership

Horses also helped the Mongols in another way. Each soldier had at least three or four extra horses carrying food and water. Because he didn't have to stop for fresh food, water, or horses, the Mongol soldier could travel vast distances quickly.

A Mongol soldier carried an array of weapons into battle: two or three bows; three quivers of arrows; and an ax, rope, and sword. His bow was short enough to be used while riding, yet it was strong enough to launch an arrow into a target 350 yards away.

Although clans and tribes often fought with each other, once in a

while a strong leader could unite them all against a common enemy.

The Great Khan

Temujin *(TEHM yoo jihn),* known today as Genghis Khan, was born in 1167. When Temujin was 12 years old, his father, a tribal chief, was murdered by a rival chief. Fearing he would be next, Temujin fled with his mother and brothers. Mothers of princes and rulers played important roles in government. Although it was nearly impossible for very small groups to survive the environment of the steppe, Temujin, with the help of his mother,

■ What effect did the environment of the steppes have on the Mongol people?

Across Time & Space

The present-day country of Mongolia lies between China and Russia. Nearly all the people of Mongolia are descendants of the Mongols, who built an empire in the 1200s.

➤ *The energy of Mongols in battle is shown in this painting from a manuscript page. Notice how the artist has used swirling figures to give a feeling of movement to the scene.*

164

kept the family alive. Thus began his reputation as an intelligent and resourceful leader.

Temujin's reputation continued to grow, and in 1206, an assembly of tribal chiefs elected him the great **khan,** or leader, of the Mongols. They gave Temujin the name Genghis Khan, which means "ruler of all within the seas." He was 39 years old.

Genghis Khan the Warrior

Genghis Khan shaped the powerful Mongol warriors into a tightly structured army. He grouped soldiers into units of 10,000 troops. These units were subdivided into smaller groups of 1,000, 100, and 10. The smaller groups had individual leaders who reported to the group leader above them. This type of military leadership created a clear chain of command within the larger army and helped create order on the battlefield. Genghis further strengthened the Mongol army by incorporating defeated enemy troops who would swear allegiance to the Mongol ruler.

Genghis Khan also devised elaborate signals to be used as communication amid the noise and confusion of battle. Soldiers used drums, horns, shouts, and even bird calls to communicate with each other. Mongol leaders could then direct and organize their troops as situations developed on the battlefield.

Using this highly skilled and structured army, Genghis Khan added vast areas to his empire. The Mongols conquered all the lands between Beijing and the Caspian Sea.

Genghis Khan the Ruler

Although Genghis Khan knew the strength of his warriors, he realized that there were areas where the Mongols were weak. The Mongols lacked a written language. So Genghis used a captured scribe to create a written language for them. He also used the skills of foreign craftspersons and specialists

▲ *The great Mongol ruler Genghis Khan is pictured in this portrait from a Turkish manuscript. Most representations of Mongol rulers come from other cultures.*

Three Empires

■ What qualities did Genghis Khan possess that made him a successful ruler?

to improve his army. From them he learned how to use catapults and gunpowder bombs. These weapons helped the Mongols besiege enemy fortresses.

Genghis respected the knowledge and beliefs of others. During his rule, Genghis Khan opened his empire to foreign travelers.

Missionaries and merchants were allowed to journey through Mongol lands. He also made a series of laws forbidding fighting among tribes. Despite the fact that Genghis Khan introduced several reforms, he is said to have admitted that "man's highest joy is in victory: to conquer one's enemies." ■

The Later Khans

▼ The Mongol Empire grew rapidly and eventually covered much of Asia. Name the four sections that the Mongol Empire was divided into after the death of Genghis Khan.

Genghis Khan died in 1227. In 1229, the empire was divided into four sections, called khanates. His four sons were each assigned a khanate. His third son, Ogodei (*ahg ah DY*), was elected the Great Khan, the overall ruler of the Mongol Empire. One khanate included the eastern part of Europe. Another occupied the middle part of Russia and Central Asia. The third was in Persia, and the khanate

of the Great Khan held China, Mongolia, and eastern Russia.

The growth of the Mongol Empire continued after Genghis's death. China was conquered in 1234. In 1237, Ogodei sent Mongol horsemen to conquer the rest of southern Russia, as well as Poland and Hungary. Upon Ogodei's death in 1241, the Mongol leaders ended their attacks in Hungary and returned to Mongolia to elect

Mongol Empire, c. 1200–1294

Genghis Khan's empire

Expansion under Kublai Khan

Silk Road

0   300   600 mi.

0   300   600 km

Azimuthal Projection

a new Great Khan. This halted the Mongol expansion into Europe.

Kublai Khan

Twenty years later, Genghis Khan's grandson, Kublai Khan, was elected Great Khan. Under Kublai's reign from 1260 to 1294, the Mongol Empire reached its height. The Mongols extended their borders to include eastern Europe, most of the Middle East, China, and the intervening territory. The map on page 166 shows the lands controlled by the Mongol Empire at its height.

Although the Mongol Empire grew, not all Mongol attempts to conquer other lands were successful. Under Kublai Khan, the Mongols tried to invade Japan in 1274 and 1281. Both invasion attempts were stopped by a typhoon, or hurricane, which destroyed most of the Mongol ships.

Like his grandfather Genghis, Kublai developed many programs to help stabilize the empire. Unlike the Chinese, Kublai respected merchants, and under his rule both internal and foreign trade flourished. He also established a postal system with riders covering up to 250 miles a day. Postal stations also served as inns for traveling merchants. Thus, the postal service helped communication and trade.

Breakdown of the Empire

Ultimately, however, the Mongols were better conquerors than rulers. They simply were not able to control the vast area they had won in battle. Communication among the four khanates became increasingly difficult.

UNDERSTANDING CONQUEST

The Romans in the 2nd century. The Mongols in the 12th century. The British in the 19th century. Each group was famous for conquering vast territories and diverse people.

Reasons for Conquest

What motivates one group to conquer another? There are probably as many reasons as there are human needs—security, food, land, wealth, beliefs, and power. The Mongols, for example, originally conquered to gain grazing land. But over time, they conquered to expand their empire's wealth and power base.

The power that accompanies control of territories and people also motivated many Roman conquests. But the desire for security pushed conquest. The Romans fought three wars over Sicily, an island in the Mediterranean Sea. Rome eventually won control of Sicily in 149 B.C.

In the 1700s and 1800s, the British launched a series of conquests to satisfy a need for resources and markets. The British built an empire that ranged around the world to Africa, Asia, North America, and Australia.

Conquest and Empire

Few great empires exist today. The Mongol Empire broke up because of rebellions by conquered peoples and problems in administering such a large area. Throughout history, successful conquests have not guaranteed successful empires.

Three Empires

➤ Timur built Muslim schools and mosques that still stand in the city of Samarkand in present-day Uzbekistan. Note the tigers above the main arch.

▼ This representation of Timur's head was created from his skull by an archaeologist who was also a sculptor.

■ Support the following statement with details: The Mongols were better conquerors than rulers.

Moreover, the Mongols were no longer the fierce warriors who had swept down from the steppes. They began to adopt the social customs, languages, and religions of the people they had conquered. Ghazan Khan, who ruled in Persia, made Islam the state religion and adopted much of the Persian culture. In China, the Mongols accepted Tibetan Buddhism, but they were also influenced by the culture of the Chinese.

By 1300, the unity of the Mongol Empire had disappeared. It was then easy for the conquered peoples of the empire to overthrow their invaders. The Persians drove out the Mongols in 1335, and the Chinese followed suit in 1368.

In 1370, Timur the Lame, or Tamerlane as he is known to Europeans, made a final attempt to build a lasting empire. Timur was a Muslim Turk of Mongol descent. He ruled from Samarkand in what is now Uzbekistan. Timur led successful raids throughout central Asia to Persia and Mesopotamia, Asia Minor, southern Russia, and India.

Timur's empire lasted for 45 years. When he died in 1405, his empire was divided among his sons, as Genghis Khan's had been. His heirs fought among themselves for control, and Timur's fourth son, Shahrukh *(shah ROOK),* won control. After his death in 1447, the empire gradually lost its power. ■

The Impact of the Mongols

Although the Mongols were fearsome warriors who conquered vast territories, that was not their only memorable accomplishment. The Mongols also showed tolerance, or respect, for different religions. They believed that there was truth in each religion. Thus, many

religions existed in their empire, including Buddhism, Christianity, Daoism, Islam, and Judaism.

The Mongols also promoted trade and travel throughout their empire. The Silk Road, which had run from China through central Asia to Mesopotamia and Syria since the time of the Roman Empire, became active again under Mongol protection.

Travelers from both Europe and the Arab world visited the Mongol Empire. The Italian Marco Polo visited the court of Kublai Khan in the late 13th century. He later described his visit, which was the first accurate record of China by a European.

The 14th-century Moroccan writer Ibn Battuta also described the world of the Mongols in a

book about his travels through Africa, Asia, and Europe. The account that Ibn Battuta made of his many experiences throughout Asia is an important historical resource.

In addition to impressing travelers, the Mongol Empire fostered the spread of ideas from Asia to Europe. Military tactics changed, as single knights in heavy armor saw what squadrons of light horsemen could do. Soldiers in formations (provided the supply lines could be kept up) were more powerful than individual knights in battle. ■

▲ *This painting shows travelers on the well-protected Silk Road during the Mongol reign.*

◄ *This statue of a Chinese goddess was made during the Yuan, or Mongol, Dynasty.*

■ *What were the positive effects of Mongol rule?*

R E V I E W

1. **FOCUS** How did the Mongols affect Europe and Asia?
2. **CONNECT** Compare social bonds among the Mongols to social bonds among West African villagers.
3. **CULTURE** What qualities contributed to the Mongols' success as conquerors?
4. **CRITICAL THINKING** Ibn Battuta and Marco Polo traveled freely throughout the Mongol Empire. What does this indicate about Mongol rule?
5. **CRITICAL THINKING** Both Genghis Khan and Kublai Khan made significant contributions to the Mongol Empire. Which of the two was the greatest Mongol leader? Why?
6. **ACTIVITY** Read the poem "Kubla Khan," written in 1798, by the English poet, Samuel Taylor Coleridge. What does the poem tell you about the late 18th-century view of the Mongol Empire?

LESSON 2

The Ottoman Empire

THINKING
FOCUS

How important a factor was leadership in the rise and fall of the Ottoman Empire?

Key Terms

- ghazi
- sultan
- grand vizier
- divan
- janissary
- millet

By the mid-1500s, the heirs of the Roman emperors no longer ran the great city of Constantinople. The Byzantine Empire had fallen. Now the Muslim Empire of the Ottoman Turks controlled the city as part of a larger empire. Muslim culture provided the lifeblood of the city, and the great Hagia Sophia church had become a mosque. But in one sense, nothing had changed: Constantinople was still one of the great trading cities of the world and the center of an empire of many cultures and religions.

In the Great Market of Constantinople, one could find goods from all over the known world. By the mid-1500s, the market covered an enormous area that was enclosed by a high wall with 18 gates. The Great Market had 67 main streets, each named after the guild working there, as well as dozens of side alleys. There were some 3,000–4,000 shops, as well as mosques, warehouses, workrooms, trade schools, and other services. Outside its walls stood a book market, a flea market, and an open food market. At the time, the Great Market of Constantinople had the largest concentration and variety of goods for sale anywhere. The city was located on one of the most important international trades routes in the world. It linked such faraway cities as Antwerp and Zanzibar, Kiev and Samarkand, and even Beijing.

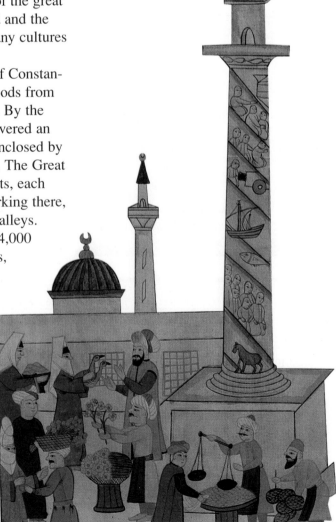

▶ *Flower and spice merchants in the Great Market of Constantinople are shown in this illustration from the 1500s.*

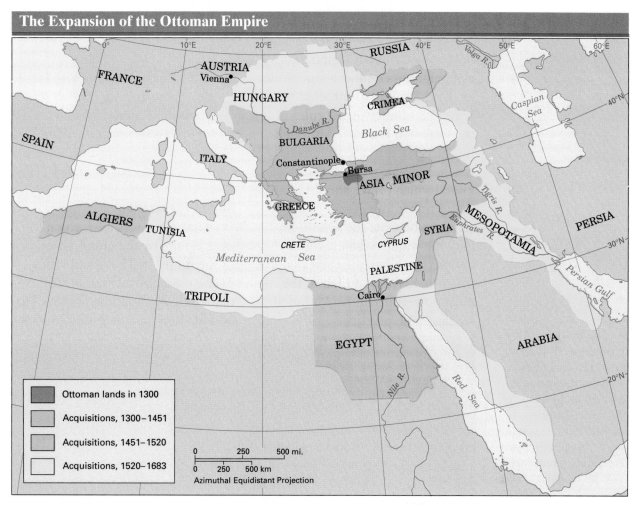

Ottoman lands in 1300	
Acquisitions, 1300–1451	
Acquisitions, 1451–1520	
Acquisitions, 1520–1683	

0   250   500 mi.

0   250   500 km

Azimuthal Equidistant Projection

The Early Ottoman Empire

As a result of the westward movement of the Mongols, many Turkish tribes were driven from their homelands in central Asia. Some of these tribes, who had converted to Islam, settled in Asia Minor and established small states.

Around 1300, one Muslim state was governed by a chief named Osman. Osman and his followers, who became known in the West as Ottomans, were ghazis. **Ghazis** were warriors who fought to expand the frontiers of Islam. As Osman won victories over Christian Byzantine armies, he attracted new followers to his armies.

Osman's armies conquered and united various lands in Asia Minor previously controlled by Byzantium. These conquests formed the core of the Ottoman Empire. Under Osman and his successors, the Ottoman state grew. One of their greatest successes was the capture in 1326 of the Byzantine city of Bursa, which they made the Ottoman capital.

Muslim Ottoman expansion alarmed Christian Europeans, who assembled an army to stop them. But the Ottomans destroyed the European forces in 1389 at Kossovo, in present-day Yugoslavia, and emerged as the most powerful state in the region. In the map above, find this early range of the Ottoman Empire. ■

The Ottoman Empire expanded steadily for four centuries. Use the scale to determine the greatest extent of the empire from east to west.

■ *How did the Ottoman Empire begin and expand?*

171

Three Empires

Rulers and Subjects

In the Ottoman Empire, all campaigns of conquest were either led by the sultan or directed by him. The **sultan** was the ruler of the Ottoman Empire. Although the succession to the sultanship was hereditary, no rules determined which prince should be the heir. Princes fought among themselves to become the sultan. In fact, the winner often killed his brothers to eliminate their possible threat to his power. One of the most powerful sultans, Mehmed, legalized the practice.

> To whichever of my sons the Sultanate may be vouchsafed [granted], it is proper for him to put his brothers to death, to preserve the order of the world.
>
> Ottoman legal code, about 1460

State Organization

The sultan was advised on state affairs by the **grand vizier,** or prime minister. The grand vizier oversaw a political system that extended throughout the empire. He also headed the governing council

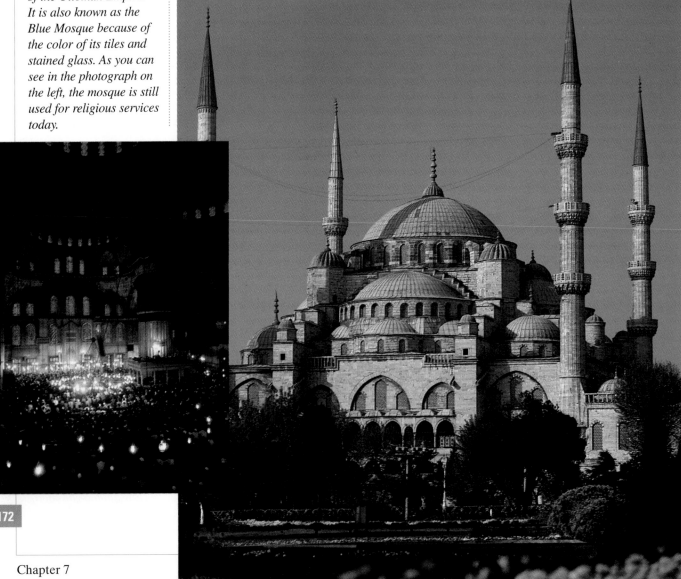

► *The Mosque of Ahmed I symbolized the majesty of the Ottoman Empire. It is also known as the Blue Mosque because of the color of its tiles and stained glass. As you can see in the photograph on the left, the mosque is still used for religious services today.*

called the Imperial Council, or **divan,** which decided legal and personal complaints. As in the Byzantine Empire, the Ottoman Empire based its civil law on religious law.

From the early 1500s and for the following 150 years, high-ranking women held great political power. The Arabic word **harem** means "sanctuary" or "sacred place." To Muslims a harem referred to the women and the private quarters of a family that were their domain. The women of the royal harem controlled political parties, negotiated with foreign powers, and often acted as rulers in place of their sons. They played a very public role, too, as royal patrons to artists and builders. Wealthy women in Ottoman society who were not members of the imperial family could make their own economic and social decisions. They paid for religious buildings, freed their slaves, and did other charitable acts. Some scholars have called this period "the sultanate of women."

The Janissary Corps

Slaves played a unique role in the Ottoman Empire. Many different ethnic groups were slaves—Africans, eastern Europeans, and especially Russians. One kind of slave, however, was highly unusual. Some parents *wanted* their children to become part of the Janissary Corps, for there they might achieve wealth and power. To be a slave of the sultan could be a mark of honor.

The janissaries were recruited from the provinces as boys between the ages of 8 and 15. The Ottomans sent them to Constantinople for education and training. Most janissaries were Christians who were converted to Islam as soon as they arrived in the capital. They were sent either to the army or to the palace school, and many rose to positions of great power. They learned law, languages, mathematics, literature, and religion as well as a trade. They were considered the emperor's personal slaves. They could be trusted to be loyal, with no other claims to allegiance. The grand vizier and many other important officials were janissaries.

Non-Muslims in the Empire

Jews and Christians were tolerated in the Ottoman Empire. They were not forced to convert to Islam, but they did have to pay a special tax.

Non-Muslims were organized into partially self-ruling groups called **millets.** Each group's religious leader was responsible for the actions of his millet. The main millets were Greek Orthodox, Jewish, and Armenian.

Especially for the people of eastern Europe, the Ottoman conquest

◄ *This image shows the Ottoman armies on a campaign. The men in white turbans are members of the elite Janissary Corps.*

▲ *This medal in honor of Doña Gracia Mendes Nasi was made in 1553, the year she settled in Constantinople. She became a heroine to many Jews escaping persecution.*

■ *What highly successful political and educational structures did the Ottoman Empire develop?*

➤ *This map of Istanbul dates from the early 1500s. Hagia Sophia is visible in the upper center of the image.*

brought peace and stability, and Ottoman rule was less oppressive than some of the systems it replaced. Paying the sultan's taxes was preferable to life under the harsh laws of some eastern European lords.

While western European countries were persecuting and expelling their Jews, the Ottomans welcomed them. Some Jews held positions of great power, and by 1553 the Ottoman city of Salonika had some 20,000 Jews. Jews were court physicians, ran printing presses, and carried on international trade. Sultan Bayezid II said, "The Catholic monarch Ferdinand was wrongly considered as wise, since he impoverished Spain by the expulsion of the Jews, and enriched Turkey."

Still, there were many who were persecuted and needed to be saved. One heroine for such a campaign was Doña Gracia Mendes Nasi

(1510–1569), called "La Señora." Doña Gracia's parents had been forced to convert to Christianity in Portugal, where they lived when she was a child. She and her family practiced Judaism in secret. She later married and helped her husband build up an important banking business. Soon widowed and forced out of Portugal by religious persecution, she went to England, then Belgium, Italy, and finally to Constantinople. During her travels, she helped Jews flee from persecution. Doña Gracia patronized scholars and established schools and synagogues in Constantinople, where she could practice her religion openly. In 1556, she tried to organize a boycott of the Italian port of Ancona because they had executed 26 Jews. Today, a synagogue in Istanbul still carries its original nickname, "La Señora." ■

The Empire at Its Height

While the Ottoman Empire absorbed, trained, and employed its newly conquered people, its military conquests continued. The most famous of these conquests was the capture of Constantinople by the Ottoman Sultan Mehmed the Conqueror in 1453.

The New Capital

The Ottoman Turks had tried to take the Byzantine walled city of Constantinople seven times but had failed each time. The city, defended by only 8,000 men, finally fell to Mehmed and his army of 150,000 on May 29.

Sultan Mehmed's victory fulfilled the call from Muhammad some 800 years earlier for the Muslims to conquer Constantinople. The city was called Istanbul by the Muslims and became the new capital of their empire.

The hour was already advanced, the day was declining and near evening, and the sun was at the Ottomans' backs but shining in the faces of their enemies. This was just as the Sultan had wished; accordingly he gave the order first for the trumpets to sound the battle-signal and the other instruments, the pipes and flutes and cymbals too, as loud as they could. All the trumpets of the other divisions, with the other instruments in turn, sounded all together, a great and fearsome sound. Everything shook and quivered at the noise.

Kritovoulos describing the fall of Constantinople, circa 1453

Over the next 100 years, Istanbul became a great international trading city of rare beauty. The Ottomans took care to preserve the existing Byzantine architecture, and they added many new and beautiful buildings. Legend says that Mehmed once caught one of his men trying to remove marble from the floor of a Byzantine church. Mehmed said as he stopped the man, "For you, the treasures and the prisoners are enough. The buildings are mine."

Ottoman expansion continued during the reign of Mehmed's son, Bayezid. The Ottoman navy defeated the strong navy of Venice to extend Ottoman control over the Black Sea area. At the end of Bayezid's reign, he and his successor, Selim, turned their attention to the east. Syria, Palestine, Egypt, and Arabia were added to the empire. With these areas came control of three of the holy places of Islam: Mecca, Medina, and Jerusalem.

Suleiman the Magnificent

The Ottoman Empire reached its height under Selim's son, Suleiman (*SOO lay mahn*), who reigned from 1520 to 1566. His empire stretched from Hungary in the north to Egypt in the south, and from Algeria in the west to Mesopotamia in the east. The capital city of Istanbul, with a population of about 200,000 and growing quickly, was one of the largest cities in Europe at the time. Foreigners called Suleiman The Magnificent because of his power, wealth, and spectacular court life. The Ottoman Empire was one of the richest and most powerful empires in the world. The inscription on the next page was found carved on a fortress in Romania. It dates from 1538. The inscription describes Suleiman's awesome power.

▲ *Beautiful objects were created for Suleiman, including the carved ivory mirror and jeweled water bottle shown above.*

◄ *The official signature of an Ottoman sultan was known as a tugra. Suleiman's tugra, shown at left, was used on official documents during his reign.*

I am caliph in Mecca and Medina. In Baghdad I am the shah, in Byzantine realms the Caesar, and in Egypt the sultan; who sends his fleets to the seas of Europe, North Africa and India. I am the sultan who took the crown and throne of Hungary and granted them to a humble slave.

In addition to being The Magnificent, Suleiman was The Lawgiver to his own subjects. The laws of the empire had been made primarily for a Muslim population. With the rapid growth and conquest of new territories and new peoples, the old legal codes were no longer as useful. Suleiman adjusted the laws to deal with a much larger empire, paying special attention to the fair treatment of non-Muslims. Suleiman's laws remained in use for two centuries.

Suleiman also undertook a massive building program, not only in Istanbul but throughout the empire. Many of these buildings still stand today. They are distinctly Muslim with their domes and minarets. Sinan, Suleiman's architect for 50 years, had been an engineer in the janissaries. As royal architect, Sinan designed over 300 buildings, including mosques, schools, hospitals, and palaces.

In addition, poetry flourished under Suleiman. In fact, next to the Qur'an, poetry was the most important type of literature in the empire. The court poet Baki wrote this poem praising the deceased Suleiman.

➤ *This gold battle standard was carried by Suleiman's armies. Suleiman is shown above in a detail from a 16th-century painting by Nigari. And at the top right, his army reaches the walls of Vienna and then withdraws.*

The infidels of Hungary bowed their heads to the temper of his blade,
The Frank admired the grain of his sword.

He laid his face to the ground, graciously, like a fresh rose petal,
The treasurer of time put him in the coffer, like a jewel.

. . .

This is my prayer: all those who do not weep for you,
Young and old, may their tears be buried in the ground.

May the sun burn and blaze with the fire of your parting;
In grief for you, let him dress in black weeds of cloud.

The world around 1550 seemed to belong to the Ottomans. Until 1683, the Ottoman Empire continued to grow. At its peak, it ran almost three-quarters of the way around the Mediterranean Sea. ■

■ *What were Suleiman's accomplishments?*

Decline of the Ottoman Empire

In the centuries that followed, the Ottoman Empire slowly began to lose both its territories and its military superiority. Although the empire lasted until the 20th century, it never again reached the prominence it had enjoyed under Suleiman.

Several factors contributed to the empire's decline. First, much of the empire's economic strength depended on constant expansion. When the conquests slowed down after 1571, revenues from conquered lands declined. In addition, a new trade route to India (by sailing around Africa) was found. The old trade route through Ottoman territory became less important. Thus, trade revenues declined drastically. The empire underwent considerable financial hardships.

Second, the janissaries began to play a more active and often disruptive role in the government of the empire. Eventually, the sultans lost control over the powerful janissaries. This lack of a strong central leadership had a disastrous effect on the empire. The sultans who followed Suleiman struggled to direct the elaborate political system.

Ottoman rule slowly weakened over the next 350 years. An important defeat happened in 1683. The Ottoman siege of Vienna was turned back with the help of Polish and German troops under Polish King John Sobieski (*sohb YAY skee*).

With the dramatic growth of Europe's commercial, military, and industrial strength, the Ottoman Empire began to disintegrate. Egypt achieved virtual independence in 1805, as did Greece in 1829. France took over Algeria and made it a colony. Russia, with plans to put its navy in the Mediterranean, became an enemy to the Ottomans. From 1853 to 1856, Russia fought the Ottomans for control of the Crimean (*cry MEE uhn*) Peninsula. Russia was defeated when Britain and France, eager to block the Russians, supported the Ottomans. In the 1870s, an uprising against the Ottomans, aided by the Russians, allowed Serbia, Montenegro, and Romania to become independent in 1878. Piece by piece, the Ottoman Empire was crumbling.■

■ *Why did the Ottoman Empire decline?*

R E V I E W

1. **FOCUS** How important a factor was leadership in the rise and fall of the Ottoman Empire?
2. **CONNECT** How did the Mongol Empire and Ottoman Empire compare in their treatment of religious groups?
3. **HISTORY** Why did westerners call Suleiman The Magnificent, while his own people called him The Lawgiver?
4. **CRITICAL THINKING** How did Istanbul represent the best qualities of the empire?
5. **WRITING ACTIVITY** Write a poem or passage praising a former United States leader, as Baki did for Suleiman.

177

LESSON 3

The Mughal Empire

Key Term

• salary

➤ *When invaders such as Mahmud crossed into northern India, they were startled by its lush beauty, as in this countryside near Rawalpinda on the Pakistan-India border.*

The whole country of India is full of gold and jewels, and of the plants which grow there are those fit for making apparel, and aromatic plants and the sugar-cane, and the whole aspect of the country is pleasant and delightful. Now, since the inhabitants are chiefly infidels and idolaters, by the order of God [Allah] and his Prophet it is right for us to conquer them.

These are the reasons that the Turkish Sultan Mahmud of Ghazna gave for his invasions of India. Between 997 and 1030, Mahmud invaded northern India 17 times.

Mahmud had long heard tales about the riches of India from Muslim scholars and merchants who had traveled there. The scholars went to India to study astronomy, medicine, and mathematics. The merchants brought back Indian gold, jewels, and silks. Eventually, soldiers and conquerors traveled to India for less peaceful purposes.

As Muslims spreading the word of Muhammad to unbelievers, the sultan and his followers felt that their invasion of India was both just and holy. A famous Persian epic poet named Firdausi (the pen name of Abul Kasim Mansur)

lived in Ghazna during the time of the Turkish invasions of India. He had a rather different explanation of the sultan's motive, and it wasn't positive:

To plunder their neighbors and gain all themselves Is what men desire, using God as excuse.

On the Eve of the Empire

India's geography—with its forbidding mountain ranges and inviting valleys—both discouraged and attracted invaders. The land falls into three distinct geographic regions. Curving across the far north of India from east to west are the Himalayas, the highest mountains in the world. The Himalayas, 200 miles wide in some places, seem to be perfect natural barriers to foreign invasion. Nevertheless, invaders penetrated the mountains through steep passes, such as the 33-mile-long Khyber Pass, located in the northwest.

South of the Himalayas lie the fertile plains of northern India. Many invaders were attracted to the valleys of the Brahmaputra, Ganges, and Indus rivers, which include some of the richest farmland in the world.

Farther south is the Deccan, or southern plateau. The Deccan forms most of the southern peninsula. It is separated from the north by the Vindhya mountains and a series of other low mountain ranges. This rugged southern region with its mountainous terrain and numerous rivers presented an awesome challenge that few invaders chose to take.

The geographic regions of India helped lead to political divisions, especially between the south and north. Hindu states in the south suffered few foreign invasions. However, in the north, Hindu kingdoms had to compete for power with a succession of invaders. The map below shows the side-by-side existence of regional Muslim and Hindu states by the early 1500s. Muslims, such as

▼ *Look at the physical map of India. Using the elevation legend, describe northern and southern India. Had you been a Muslim invader, where in India would you have settled? Why?*

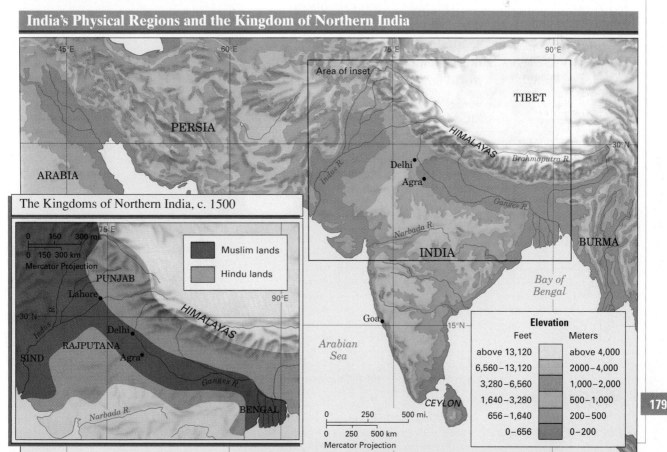

India's Physical Regions and the Kingdom of Northern India

The Kingdoms of Northern India, c. 1500

- Muslim lands
- Hindu lands

0 150 300 mi
0 150 300 km
Mercator Projection

PUNJAB
Lahore
Delhi
RAJPUTANA
SIND
Agra
Narbada R.
BENGAL
HIMALAYAS
Ganges R.
Indus R.

PERSIA
ARABIA
Area of inset
TIBET
HIMALAYAS
Brahmaputra R.
Delhi
Agra
Indus R.
Ganges R.
Narbada R.
INDIA
BURMA
Bay of Bengal
Goa
Arabian Sea
CEYLON

Elevation

Feet	Meters
above 13,120	above 4,000
6,560–13,120	2000–4,000
3,280–6,560	1,000–2,000
1,640–3,280	500–1,000
656–1,640	200–500
0–656	0–200

0 250 500 mi.
0 250 500 km
Mercator Projection

■ *In what ways was northern India a divided country during the 1500s?*

Sultan Mahmud, captured several Indian cities and set up their own governments. In other cities, power remained in the hands of native Hindu princes.

In North India in the early 1500s, many small states competed for more territory. Both Hindu kingdoms and established Muslim states wanted to control the rich agricultural land along the Ganges and Indus rivers. Before the Mughals arrived, an Indo-Muslim political tradition had accepted Muslim overlords in exchange for Hindus' being left alone to rule their own local lands. Hindu society was able to make a place for a Muslim ruling class by adding another caste-like layer at the top of society for them. The Mughals took advantage of these circumstances to build their own empire. ■

Founders of the Empire

The greatest of the Muslim states was the Sultanate of Delhi in north central India. In 1517, a Muslim Turk from central Asia named Babur invaded India. He conquered the Delhi Sultanate in 1526 and went on to found the Mughal Empire.

Babur's Arrival

Related to Timur on his father's side and Genghis Khan on his mother's side, Babur seemed a fitting conqueror and founder of a world empire. Babur had dreamed of reestablishing a great empire in the Mongol tradition. In 1527, he defeated the Rajputs, the strongest Hindu state in India. During Babur's reign, which lasted until his death in 1530, the empire covered most of northern India. His empire was called the Mughal, from the Persian-Indian word for Mongol.

Babur was a wise and kind leader. Like many Mughal emperors who followed him, Babur was

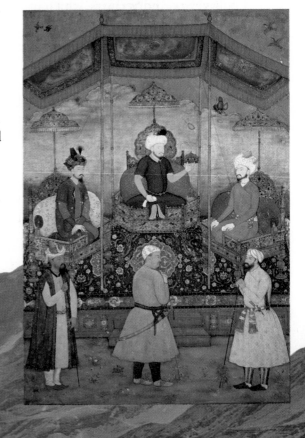

➤ *This painting, on the right, honors the founders of the Mughal dynasty—Timur, Babur, and his son Humayun. Timur wears a turban jewel, like the one above, a symbol of high rank.*

well educated. Throughout his life Babur wrote about the Indian world that he had conquered—its people, animals, landscapes, and customs. But he also seemed genuinely homesick for items from his homeland in central Asia such as good horses, grapes, muskmelons, ice, cold water, good bread and hot baths. Babur wrote in his memoirs, the *Babar-nama*, that "the chief excellency of Hindustan [India] is, that it is a large country, and has abundance of gold and silver."

Akbar the Ruler

Despite his longings for his homeland, Babur remained in India. His grandson, Akbar, who reigned for 49 years (1556–1605) would be remembered as the greatest Mughal emperor.

Akbar's rule began when he was only 13 years old. During his reign the empire expanded to cover most of north and central India and Afghanistan. Look at the map on page 183. Estimate how many miles the empire covered under Akbar.

We know many details about Akbar's life and personality from his biographer, Abul Fazl. For example, we know that "Akbar ate one meal a day—of 40 dishes—and enjoyed ice brought from the mountains." Abul Fazl also tells us that Akbar took great interest in handicrafts. He wrote that Akbar often visited the more than 100 workshops around the palace where crafts and weapons were made.

Perhaps Akbar's greatest political accomplishments were bringing Hindus into the government of the empire and reforming the empire's unfair tax system. Akbar divided the empire into provinces and set up a civil service system to manage its lands. Each job had a salary, or fixed payment, and jobs were given only to qualified men, without regard to their religion. Thus, non-Muslims could enter government service.

Akbar also had the value of land reclassified according to its ability to produce crops. Taxes were lower for those with less productive land. This was fairer than the old system, which made every farmer pay the same rate.

Akbar held a great deal of power, but like other monarchs, he was limited by the power of the nobles, of the cities, and of the army. There were always rebellions or attacks to deal with, and Akbar

▼ *Babur's Mughal army crossed these Himalayas to invade and conquer northern India.*

■ *Evaluate this statement: Religion does not always unify an empire.*

was as skilled a diplomat as he was a military leader.

In Akbar's lands, besides Hindus and Muslims, there were Christians and Jews and many other peoples. Akbar saw that it would not be easy to keep his restless empire together. He abolished the tax on non-Muslims. Whether he truly believed in it, or whether it was only a unifying policy, Akbar developed his own religion for the state. The conflicts between religions prompted him to find a synthesis, or new combination, of all the religions known to him. Born and brought up a Muslim, Akbar turned in 1575 to what he then saw as the essence of all religions. He faced opposition from the Muslim clergy but he proceeded to reduce religious persecution for many of his subjects. Akbar invited scholars of different faiths to his court and sponsored debates on religion.

Akbar the Art Patron

During Akbar's reign, the Mughal court became a center of culture. Akbar invited artists, poets, and musicians to his court and encouraged them to produce works for it.

As trade with the rest of the world continued to grow, there were new influences in art. Some Muslim artists now used naturalism in portraying people and animals, something they had previously kept away from for religious reasons. ■

Inheritors of the Empire

The Mughal Empire continued to grow in size and splendor as Akbar's successors followed his policies. In 1605, Akbar's eldest son Jahangir *(juh hahn GEER)* inherited the throne.

Jahangir continued to expand the empire, and he also sponsored the repair and rebuilding of schools and monasteries. In 1611, Jahangir married a Persian woman named Mehrunissa *(MAIR uh NISS uh)*. She was called "Nur Jahan," or "Light of the World," and she, her father, and her brother dominated Jahangir's court. Nur Jahan's niece, Mumtaz Mahal, married the future emperor. During these years some upper class women studied the arts and sciences. Most women, Hindu and Muslim, generally concentrated on the domestic world, including trades practiced at home such as spinning or weaving. A wide variety of fine Indian textiles became important items of global trade, and their designs were later adapted for factory production.

Jahangir's son, Shah Jahan *(SHAH juh HAHN)*, ruled from 1628 to 1658. Jahan is renowned as the largest Mughal spender and builder. He poured huge amounts of money into construction projects in Delhi, which he made the capital in 1648. The projects included palaces with walls of marble inlaid with precious stones and ceilings of gold and silver.

Shah Jahan also broke with Akbar's religious policies, bringing Mughal laws into closer agreement with some aspects of Muslim law. Shah Jahan also refined Akbar's administrative policies. As the empire grew, productivity rose. The empire's income doubled, and construction projects continued.

Without doubt, Shah Jahan's most famous architectural undertaking was the Taj Mahal. With its inlaid white marble, pointed arches, and domes, the Taj reflects the Mughal style of architecture. To learn more about the splendor of the Taj Mahal, see A Closer Look on page 184.

Only a very wealthy nation could afford such massive building efforts. At one point in the reign of Shah Jahan, "750 pounds of pearls, 275 pounds of emeralds, 5,000 gems from Cathay, corals, topazes, and . . . tubs of uncut diamonds" formed only a part of the Mughal treasury.

But, as time went on, Shah Jahan's spending took its toll on the empire. Shah Jahan added some of the Deccan Hindu states to the Mughal lands. But the cost of military campaigns, combined with huge building projects, seriously drained the treasury. ■

■ *How did the rule of Jahangir and Shah Jahan affect the empire?*

▼ *The Mughal Empire expanded greatly in a relatively short period of time. How much larger was the empire after the death of Akbar?*

The Expansion of the Mughal Empire

Expansion under
- Babur to 1526
- Akbar to 1605
- Aurangzeb to 1707

HINDU KUSH
Indus River
Delhi
Agra
Ganges River
HIMALAYAS
Brahmaputra R.
Narbada R.
Mahandi R.
Godavari R.
Arabian Sea
DECCAN PLATEAU
Goa
Krishna R.
Bay of Bengal
CEYLON
INDIAN OCEAN

0 250 500 mi.
0 250 500 km
Mercator Projection

The Taj Mahal

Mumtaz Mahal was the beloved wife of Shah Jahan. When she died in childbirth in 1631, her heartbroken husband built for her the most glorious tomb in the world—the Taj Mahal.

The rose was her favorite flower. Some say it was a model for the floor plan of the building. Can you see a rose in the design?

From the white marble dome to the precise gardens, every part of the Taj Mahal fits together. Caravans brought rare, colorful jewels from around the world so that the flower designs inside would be the right colors. Craftspeople and architects came from Turkey, Persia, and even Venice, Italy, to work on the tomb.

*Courtesy
Archeological Survey of India
Government of India.*

Mumtaz Mahal

Shah Jahan

Mumtaz Mahal and the Shah were constant companions, even on his military campaigns. He trusted her opinion on everything from art to politics, and showered her with gifts of roses and diamonds. He was so crushed by her death that his beard turned white overnight.

End of the Empire

The empire weakened further under Aurangzeb *(AWR ung zehb),* Shah Jahan's son. Aurangzeb, who ruled from 1658 to 1707, was the last to expand the Mughal Empire. Eventually, shrinking resources, loss of control, and growing disorder reduced its size.

Policy Changes

Although Aurangzeb continued his family's military activities, he made important policy changes.

He reinstated the *jizya,* the tax on non-Muslims. He also prohibited the building of new Hindu temples. Many Hindus rebelled, especially in the Deccan, where a Hindu people called the Marathas vied for power with the Mughals. Aurangzeb spent the last 25 years of his reign fighting rebellion.

Foreign Invaders

Aurangzeb was the last Mughal ruler to reign over a great empire. After his death in 1707, successive rulers continued to lose land to various rebelling factions. Still, the Mughal court at Delhi remained famous for its art and sophistication long after its political power faded.

The final blow to the Mughals would come not from neighboring invaders but from Europeans. They were drawn to India for its pepper and spices and fine cotton textiles. The decline of both Mughal and Hindu states was one factor that allowed Europeans to force their own rules for trade. In the 1700s, a trading company from Great Britain took over the government of an Indian province. Great Britain forced the last Mughal emperor from the throne in 1858. ■

◄ *Aurangzeb, the last great ruler of the Mughal Empire, is shown in this painting from a Mughal miniature album.*

■ *Why did the Mughal Empire decline?*

REVIEW

1. **FOCUS** What factors contributed to the rise and fall of the Mughal Empire?
2. **CONNECT** How were the early invaders of India similar to the early Ottomans?
3. **GEOGRAPHY** How did India's geography affect invasion attempts?
4. **CULTURE** How does the Taj Mahal represent the height of Mughal architecture?
5. **CRITICAL THINKING** Compare and contrast the rule of Akbar to that of other Mughal rulers. Defend the statement that Akbar was the greatest Mughal ruler.
6. **CRITICAL THINKING** Babur, Akbar, Jahangir, Shah Jahan, Aurangzeb—during whose reign would you have liked to live? Why?
7. **WRITING ACTIVITY** You have now read about the rise and fall of three great empires: the Mongol, the Ottoman, and the Mughal. Write an imaginary conversation between the three great emperors: Genghis Khan, Suleiman, and Akbar. Have them discuss what an empire should be like.

Reading Mughal Paintings

Here's Why

By studying art from the past, you can learn about the beliefs, actions, values and customs of people who lived long ago. Art flourished under the patronage of the Mughal emperors. Mughal paintings are rich in information. But first, you must learn how to "read" paintings.

Here's How

Like books, paintings often tell a story. When you study a painting, look for the main idea and identify the major characters. Examine how the painter sets the scene and determine what action is taking place. Then look for cultural details and clues to the emotions of the characters.

Study the painting on the opposite page. This scene by Nar Singh was painted to illustrate Abul Fazl's *Akbarnama,* or history of Akbar.

Akbar's religious and cultural tolerance is the main theme of the painting. The central figure is Akbar, who sits enthroned under a bright red canopy. You may recognize him: on page 182, you saw a painting of his return to Fatehpur Sikri. The key on this page identifies Akbar with the numeral one (1).

The figures who form a circle in front of Akbar are all religious scholars. Find the figures labeled in the key by the numeral two (2). These men are two of the three Jesuit priests whom Akbar had invited to teach about Christianity in 1580. One is Rudolpho Aquaviva, the head of the mission. The other is either the translator Francisco Henriques or the Jesuit priest Antonio Monserrate. The rest of the figures in the circle are thought to be Muslims and Hindus. Outside the courtyard, in the painting's second level, two guards stand watch (3). The bottom level shows horses and passersby (4).

The painting's setting is the Ibadat-Khanah, or House of Worship, located within Akbar's palace at Fatehpur Sikri. Akbar encouraged scholars of diverse faiths to engage in religious discussions at the Ibadat-Khanah. Muslims, Hindus, Christians, Parsees, Zoroastrians, and Jews were all made welcome by Akbar.

This scene shows an evening session at the House of Worship. A heated debate is underway, with participants vigorously discussing the merits and flaws of Christianity and Islam.

In the *Akbar-nama,* Abul Fazl gives a version of what took place that evening. Fazl claims that Father Aquaviva challenged a Muslim

religious scholar to a trial by fire. Fazl says Aquaviva offered to enter a fire holding the Bible if a Muslim scholar would do the same, holding the Koran. Other accounts say that it was actually Akbar or the Muslims who challenged the Jesuits. Although the versions differ, it seems clear that a trial by fire was discussed but rejected.

Now look for important details in the painting. Notice that many of the men hold books, and that books lie scattered on the floor. In this respect, the scene is typical: Akbar enjoyed religious and philosophical debate, and he surrounded himself with learned men.

طراحی لکه کهی ان برزم دران نشان سجایی انست نصاری بنهم وفطرت زولف از دانشوران از اُی بود بادری زولف

The fact that Akbar sits above the others symbolizes the power of the emperor. The architecture, decorations, and beautiful floor coverings show the splendor of the royal court. The absence of women in the painting is significant. Women were excluded from the business of the Mughal court, except as entertainers.

Note how the painter conveys the emotions of the religious scholars and the vigor of the debate. You can see that many of the men are gesturing. This suggests that the scholars were speaking emphatically, and that several conversations were taking place at once.

You have seen how to "read" paintings. Now try to use what you have learned and interpret a painting on your own.

Try It

Look again at the painting of Akbar being welcomed to Fatehpur Sikri, on page 182. What is the painting's main idea, or theme? Who are the major characters? Where does the scene take place, and what is happening in this scene? What cultural information can you gain from examining the painting's details? How does the painter suggest the characters' emotions?

Apply It

Find books that include paintings by American artists of the 1900s, such as Grant Wood, Andrew Wyeth, or John Sloan. Choose a painting that shows an aspect of life in the United States. "Read" the painting, using the approach taught in Here's How.

187

Three Empires

Chapter Review

Reviewing Key Terms

clan (p. 163)
divan (p. 173)
ghazi (p. 171)
grand vizier (p. 172)
janissary (p. 173)

khan (p. 165)
millet (p.174)
salary (p. 181)
steppe (p. 162)
sultan (p. 172)

4. janissary, Ottoman
5. khan, Mongol
6. millet, Ottoman
7. sultan, Ottoman

A. In the following list, each key term is paired with the name of the empire to which it is related. Write a sentence using each of the pairs, showing how they are related. Use the Glossary on pages 543–549 to check your understanding of the meanings.
1. clan, Mongol
2. divan, Ottoman
3. ghazi, Ottoman

B. Write the key term that is described by each sentence below.
1. Both the winter and summer weather of the vast semiarid plain of central Asia was very uncomfortable.
2. The prime minister had other responsibilities in addition to advising the sultan on state affairs.
3. Workers under Akbar were given a fixed payment for their services.

Exploring Concepts

A. The Mongol, Ottoman, and Mughal empires all had strengths that helped them grow and prosper. They also had weaknesses that caused problems or contributed to their declines. Make a chart like the one below. Use all three lessons in the chapter to complete the chart with important strengths and weaknesses of each empire. If a quality was a strength at one time and a weakness at another, write it in both places on the chart.

Empire	Strengths	Weaknesses
Mongol		
Ottoman		
Mughal		

B. Support each statement with facts and details from the chapter.
1. The structure of Genghis Khan's army showed that one of his strengths was his strong ability to organize.
2. Being the son of a sultan of the Ottoman Empire could be dangerous.
3. Janissaries received an excellent education to prepare them for positions in the Ottoman Empire.
4. Mongol and Ottoman rulers usually practiced a kind of religious tolerance in their empires.
5. Suleiman was known both as The Magnificent in other lands and as The Lawgiver to his own people.
6. Modern leaders could learn many lessons about fair and efficient ways to govern their countries from Akbar.
7. Money played an important role in the decline of both the Ottoman and the Mughal empires.

Reviewing Skills

1. This painting shows Akbar crossing the Ganges in 1567 on his prized elephant Uduja. He is pursuing Ali Tuli Khan and Bahadur Khan, two brothers with whom treaties had failed. What does the painting tell about ways of war?

2. What do the painting's details tell about the Ganges? Discuss the river, ways of river travel, the natural setting, and its plants and animals.

3. Akbar agreed with this Sufi proverb: "Religious rituals and prayer are good but the dwelling of the Beloved is not in the mosque, temple, or church; it is in a pure heart." Explain this proverb in your own words.

4. If Mongol rulers had had one modern type of map, they would have known the time in all parts of their empire. What kind of map is that?

Using Critical Thinking

1. Many Mongol, Ottoman, and Mughal leaders encouraged religious freedom. Some did not. How did religious freedom benefit the empires? What happened when it was denied? How is it guaranteed in the United States? How does it benefit us?

2. Shah Jahan had a budget deficit because he spent more than his country produced. Compare his budget problem with that of the U.S. in the 1980s and '90s. Who decided what was spent in the Mughal Empire? Who had responsibility to cut back? Who decides and has responsibility in the U.S.?

3. Reread the description of the Great Market of Constantinople on page 170. What goods do you think one could find there? Where would they have come from? Explain your answers. Do the same for the Mongol and Mughal empires. Which cities might have been their great trading cities?

Preparing for Citizenship

1. **COLLECTING INFORMATION** In small groups, study modern maps of areas once held by Mongols, Ottomans, and Mughals. List the names of the modern countries. Collect news articles about them and discuss together the nature of life in these areas today.

2. **COLLABORATIVE LEARNING** Help your class elect members for a Hall of Fame of Mongol, Ottoman, and Mughal leaders. As a class, make a list of leaders. Working in small groups, choose a candidate for each group to promote. Decide how to present your candidate's qualities. For example, let one member make a poster, one a brochure, one a press release, and so on. Carry out a written and illustrated campaign for a class presentation and election. Post the winning candidates' portraits in a Hall of Fame exhibit.

Chapter 8

China

Throughout this period, scholars wrote using artistic characters. Many characters in Chinese represent whole words. This character, known as yong, means "eternity."

There were troubled times in China after the Han Dynasty fell in A.D. 220. For 360 years, groups battled for power. Still, scholarship survived, and so did beliefs like Daoism and Confucianism. When the Sui Dynasty reunited China in 589, leaders built on such traditions and beliefs to bring the country together. Later dynasties continued to inspire great advances— beautiful works of art, a strong economy, and marvelous new inventions.

617 Taizong (above) continues the Tang Dynasty, a time when art and poetry flower in China. Beautiful ceramic figures like the one at the left are often buried with emperors and nobles.

200   550   900

476 The Western Roman Empire collapses.

1066 Normans from northern France conquer England.

During this period, guard towers along the Great Wall of China (below) and geographical barriers helped keep invaders out of China.

1368 Emperor Taizu founds the Ming Dynasty. This Ming dragon, crafted of gold thread on silk later in this period, was a symbol of imperial power. Many even believed that such dragons protected the emperor.

1250

1600

1950

1450s Johann Gutenberg and other Europeans begin using movable type to print books.

1912

L E S S O N   1

An Emerging Empire

Women gad about in the market place. . . . They go out visiting, to see their relatives, and proceed there by starlight or carrying torches, night after night; they take a large suite with them, setting the street ablaze. . . . maids, messengers, clerks, and footmen. . . . These women also make pleasure trips to Buddhist temples, they go out to watch hunting and fishing, they organize picnics on hills and river banks. They even travel . . . in open carriages with the curtains raised, stopping in every hamlet and town they pass through, drinking toasts, singing, and making music on the way.

Ge Hong, third century

THINKING
F O C U S

What were some of the obstacles to unity in China, and how did Emperor Wen overcome them?

Key Terms

• Confucianism
• Buddhism
• Daoism

➤ *This bronze lamp was found in the tomb of a Han dynasty princess.*

While some women in post Han dynasty China might have been enjoying themselves, the huge majority were doing backbreaking work. They were either working alongside men in the fields, weaving at a loom at home while taking care of children, or even working off the yearly stint of required hard labor for the government. Ge Hong was upset by the city-dwelling, fun-loving ladies, for as the state was falling apart, order and "proper behavior" seemed more and more important.

Lady Ban Zhao *(ban jow)*, the first and greatest of Chinese women scholars, had died in A.D. 116. Ban Zhao was educated in literature, philosophy, business, and politics, and she was given a high position at court. In Han dynasty China, women could still participate in intellectual life. Exceptional women like Ban Zhao could make their mark.

Troubling times followed the overthrow of the last Han emperor, Xian Di *(shehn DEE)*, in A.D. 220. Nomadic horsemen attacked from the north, and landowners refused to pay taxes. Army generals with their troops fought each other for power.

Having survived floods, famine, and plagues, peasants now had no money to buy food or seeds.

Years of Disorder

Emperor Xian Di, the last of the Han emperors, could not solve the many problems of the empire. In A.D. 220, China's first great empire broke apart. China was fragmented into small, competing kingdoms.

Geography Creates Regions

The Han Empire included the area of China shown in orange on the map below. Though the area makes up only one-third of modern China, it was here that most important events in Chinese history took place.

The eastern third of China, the area around the modern cities of Nanjing, Luoyang, and Changsha, has been the center of China's population throughout history. What natural features shown on the map explain why people settled here? The Qin Ling (*chihn lihng*) Mountains divide this fertile area into two regions, northern and southern China.

Before the unification of China under the Han Dynasty in 221 B.C., people living in northern and southern China had almost no contact with each other. Even during the Han Dynasty, only traders, soldiers, or government officials were likely to travel from one region to another.

Barriers Protect the Empire

Geography not only divided China but also protected it from the outside world. In ancient times, the Himalayas to the southwest and the Taklimakan Desert to the west limited Chinese contact with

Across Time & Space

Don't be confused if you see the Chang Jiang written as the Yangzi River on older maps. Chang Jiang is spelled according to the Pinyin system for writing Chinese in our Roman alphabet. In 1958, the Chinese officially adopted Pinyin, replacing older systems.

▼ *The earliest civilizations in China developed along a river, the Huang He. Find the Huang He and the Chang Jiang on the map.*

Division of the Han Empire, A.D. 220–264

80°E · 100°E · 120°E

Huang He

TAKLIMAKAN

WEI

Yellow Sea

Huang He
Luoyang

QIN LING MTS.

Nanjing

Chengdu

30°N

East China Sea

Chang Jiang

Changsha

HIMALAYAS

SHU–HAN

WU

Great Wall

Silk Road

0   200   400 mi.

0   200   400 km
Mercator Projection

100°E · 120°E

➤ *Ban Zhao, charged with teaching manners to the ladies of the emperor's court, writes out some of her rules of conduct. This is an illustration for the scroll* The Admonitions of the Instructress of Court Ladies, *a work from the 200s.*

■ *Find evidence to support this statement: Geographic features made China difficult to unify.*

the civilizations of India, Persia, and other areas. Another natural barrier protected China to the east. What was it? China was vulnerable in the north, however. There, a huge open steppe, or grassy plain, left China open to attack by invaders.

A Period of Unrest

Barbarian invasions and other problems finally brought an end to the Han dynasty. Then tribal invaders, Chinese army generals, and aristocratic families were left to struggle for control of various regions. For about 360 years after the Han Dynasty ended, China was in a state of political disunity.

In the south, large landowners controlled local affairs in most areas. They kept private armies to defend their lands, and they fortified their homes. Many small farmers were forced to give up their land and work the landowners' fields in exchange for food and protection.

Control of the central government changed hands often from 220 to 589. Southern China's economy improved during this time of unrest, however. Good harvests and a growing foreign market for silk

helped the capital city, Nanjing, become a center of commerce. By the 500s, merchants from Southeast Asia, India, and Persia traded in the city.

In the north, various groups of nomads from the steppes invaded China and set up a series of short-lived kingdoms. As these nomadic peoples became accustomed to settled life, they willingly adopted the language, traditions, and government structure of the native Chinese. By 589, descendants of the invaders were fully integrated into northern Chinese culture and society. ■

The Spread of Buddhism

For Chinese in all classes, these were years of uncertainty. During the Han Dynasty, most Chinese had been followers of Confucius.

In **Confucianism,** the roles of men and women were further separated. It focused on having respect for elders, completing duties to the family, and attaining virtue by studying the classics or serving the government.

But after the fall of the empire, people began to turn to **Buddhism,** a system of thought and practice based on the teachings of Siddhartha Gautama, the Buddha or "Enlightened One." It offered the promise of escape from suffering. What do the selections on page 195 from the Buddha's teachings say about how one can escape from suffering?

*L*ike a spider caught in its own web is a person driven by fierce cravings. Break out of the web, and turn away from the world of sensory pleasure and sorrow.

If you want to reach the other shore of existence, give up what is before, behind, and in between. Set your mind free, and go beyond birth and death.

Our life is shaped by our mind; we become what we think. Suffering follows an evil thought as the wheels of a cart follow the oxen that draw it.

Our life is shaped by our mind; we become what we think. Joy follows a pure thought like a shadow that never leaves.

From the *Dhammapada*, translated by Eknath Easwaran

Buddhism originated in India around 530 B.C. Traders and missionaries traveling along the Silk Road introduced the religion to China during the Han Dynasty. However, it attracted few followers then, mostly because it was foreign. Now, in the troubled times at the end of the Han Dynasty, the new religion became attractive.

The Buddha taught that life is a cycle of pleasure and sorrow, of death and rebirth. Suffering, he taught, was a basic part of life. It was caused by paying too much attention to material things in life— to what the Buddha referred to "the world of sensory pleasure."

But a person could escape from suffering, according to the Buddha. Through meditation, he taught, one could achieve enlightenment—a state of complete freedom and peace.

The idea of freedom from the chaos of the earthly world appealed to Chinese people of all classes. It appealed to regional rulers living in constant fear of attack, to landowners worried about crop failure, and to peasants longing for their own plots of land. By the 400s, most regional kings supported Buddhism. Buddhist temples and monasteries thrived throughout China. The Buddhists accumulated much valuable land. They also owned grain mills, and operated hospitals, schools, and inns. ■

▲ *This bronze sculpture of the Buddha was made in the 300s in China. The Buddha sits in a posture of meditation.*

■ *Why did the Chinese find Buddhism more appealing than Confucianism after the fall of the Han Dynasty?*

The Reunification of China

More than 300 years after the Han Dynasty ended, a northern official named Yang Jian reunited the Chinese Empire. He seized power and declared himself emperor of northern China in 581 and then conquered the south by 589. Yang Jian's title was Emperor Wen, and the dynasty he founded is known as the Sui *(sway)* Dynasty.

A National Identity

Emperor Wen's greatest challenge was to reverse the forces that divided China. He used several techniques to do this.

For one thing, he followed ancient Chinese political practices. For example, when his supporters proclaimed him emperor, he accepted the traditional imperial gifts, including red doors for his house and a robe with a red sash—but only after he had refused them three times, as tradition demanded. By following such ancient traditions, the emperor reminded his people of their common history.

Like emperors of the Han dynasty, Emperor Wen organized public works projects. These projects focused people's attention on the common goals of the empire. Using forced labor crews, the emperor built a grand capital city at Changan. Find this city on the map on page 205. He also oversaw the rebuilding of the Great Wall, which had been built around 221 B.C., to protect China from the central Asian nomads who continued to attack the north.

During Emperor Wen's reign, workers began work on the Grand Canal between the Huang He, formerly called the Yellow River, and the Chang Jiang. After the Grand Canal opened in 605, it transported government officials, grain, and silk. Find the Grand Canal on the map on page 205.

Scholarship had been important in earlier Chinese society. Emperor Wen renewed this tradition by founding colleges for the study of the classics. He also set up schools for learning calligraphy, or the writing of Chinese characters, and for accounting and law. Since many ancient manuscripts had been lost after the fall of the Han Dynasty, Emperor Wen collected books from throughout the empire. Scholars organized and classified the texts; then clerks copied them by hand. In this way,

The Great Wall of China extends 1,500 miles from Inner Mongolia to the sea. If a similar wall was built along the border between the United States and Canada, about how far would it extend from the Atlantic to the Pacific Ocean?

Emperor Wen ensured the preservation of the Chinese classics.

The Administrative System

Emperor Wen set up a new system of administration to govern his huge empire efficiently. He created several departments for different government functions. Each department was divided into several smaller offices that performed specific duties. For example, within the Department of State Affairs were six offices. They were responsible for the army, finance, punishments, public works, rites, and civil office.

Officials were classified into nine ranks, or levels. Rank determined salary. Officials of the first rank earned 900 bushels of grain per year, while eighth-ranked officials earned 50.

Emperor Wen ordered local governments to send three worthy men to the capital each year. There they were tested in three areas: general literary ability, mastery of a single classic literary work, and the ability to take action in response to certain situations. Those who performed well on the exams were appointed to one of the lower ranks of government.

To prevent officials from showing favoritism or gaining influence in local affairs, Emperor Wen declared that officials could not serve in their home areas. Traveling inspectors, and often even the emperor himself, visited the provinces to check on local officials.

Three Systems of Thought and Practice

Emperor Wen was a Buddhist. He founded many temples and monasteries, and he encouraged support for them. But he recognized that other Chinese systems of thought and practice could help to strengthen his dynasty.

The emperor knew that Confucianism was an important tradition in Chinese government. So he emphasized the Confucian ideas of good conduct, scholarship, and public service.

Emperor Wen also encouraged **Daoism** *(DOW ihz uhm),* based on the teachings of Laozi, a Chinese philosopher who some say may be legendary. Daoists emphasized living in harmony with nature and being content with life.

By encouraging followers of all three systems, Emperor Wen promoted Chinese unity rather than divisiveness. The unified empire that he created continued under the Tang Dynasty, which followed the Sui Dynasty. ■

▲ *This painting of Emperor Wen is a detail from the scroll* Portraits of the Emperors, *completed during the 600s.*

■ *What steps did Emperor Wen take to reunify China?*

R E V I E W

1. **FOCUS** What were some of the obstacles to unity in China, and how did Emperor Wen overcome them?
2. **CONNECT** How does the fall of the Han Empire compare with the fall of the Roman Empire?
3. **GEOGRAPHY** What were the natural barriers that protected China on the east, west, and southwest?
4. **BELIEF SYSTEMS** Why was Emperor Wen wise to allow the practice of Buddhism, Confucianism, and Daoism in his empire?
5. **CRITICAL THINKING** Why might a country benefit from being strongly unified?
6. **ACTIVITY** You are a public relations expert working for Emperor Wen. You have been asked to promote his campaign to unite north and south China. Design a poster that shows some of the factors that have kept northern and southern China separated. The poster should also explain or illustrate the advantages of unity.

The Great Wall

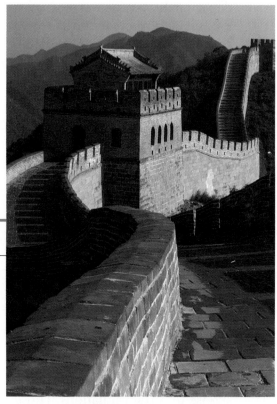

> H*ad the Great Wall not already existed, Yangdi [the second Sui emperor] would certainly have conceived it. As it was, he had to be content with rebuilding it.*
>
> Robert Silverberg,
> 20th-century historian

➤ *The Great Wall still snakes for thousands of miles across modern China. However, the wall that is still standing is not Shihuangdi's wall, but a later version, built during the Ming Dynasty.*

Background

Records show that Yangdi's rebuilding of the Great Wall in 607 required more than a million workers. Over half of them died of overwork or fled the harsh conditions.

The original building of the Great Wall, around 221 B.C., also involved a huge work force. Shihuangdi, the Chinese emperor who conceived of this project, connected shorter walls that had been built along China's northern border centuries before. He also extended the wall for hundreds of miles. The resulting fortified wall was and still is the longest structure on earth.

Before embarking on any massive work, such as the building of the Great Wall of China, a wise decision maker will try to weigh the benefits and the costs of the project. We can look at historical events to try to compare the benefits and the costs of building the Great Wall of China.

Benefits and Costs of the Great Wall

The most obvious benefit of building the Great Wall was protection. The wall helped prevent nomadic horsemen from invading China's farms along the northern border. Also, it kept farmers living along the border from joining the nomads.

Building the Great Wall enabled Shihuangdi to get rid of his

▼ *These coins, which were issued by Shihuangdi, were the standard currency throughout the empire at the time when the Great Wall was being built.*

enemies. He ordered them to work on distant parts of the wall. He also sent soldiers to work on the wall. As a result, the soldiers could not band together and rise up against the emperor.

However, building Shihuangdi's wall is estimated to have required more than 300,000 workers, most of whom were drafted against their will. Thousands of farmers and merchants were required to supply the workers with food, clothing, tools, and shelter. Most of these supplies never made it

to the work sites; bandits roaming the countryside robbed the supply caravans.

The work of constructing the wall was so difficult and living conditions were so harsh that thousands of workers died. Often they were buried in the wall itself. Thus, the Great Wall of China gained the gruesome title of "the world's longest cemetery."

▼ *Sturdy horses, like the one at the left, carried nomads who raided China's northern border. In response, the Great Wall was built, using labor-intensive construction methods as shown. Study the chart for a comparison of the Great Wall's long-range benefits and short-term costs.*

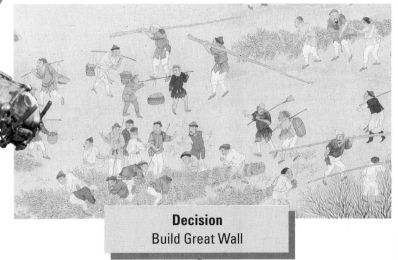

Decision
Build Great Wall

↓

Outcomes

• People are safer	• Many laborers die
• More farmers stay on farms	• People become poorer
• Fewer threats to emperor arise	• Supply caravans often attacked

Decision Point

1. What were the benefits of constructing the Great Wall of China? What were the costs?
2. Do you think these were the only benefits and costs of the Great Wall? Where would you look to find more information about the role of the Great Wall in Chinese history?
3. Based on the information on these pages and any other information you have found,

   do you think the benefits and costs of building the Great Wall balanced out? Explain.
4. Collect information from newspapers and magazines about upcoming plans for large government projects in the United States. Discuss the projected benefits and costs of each project. Decide which projects you would support and which you would oppose.

Heaven My Blanket, Earth My Pillow

Poems by Yang Wan-Li

In the next lesson, you will read about a period of great achievement in Chinese government, trade, science, and art. The poet Yang Wan-Li in many ways symbolized that achievement.

Today our political leaders are usually not poets or artists. In the Song period of Chinese history, which you will study in the next lesson, government officials were also judged on their accomplishments in literature or art. Yang Wan-Li, a respected finance administrator, was also a well-known poet. His poems, like others of the period, express feelings of calm and harmony with nature. As you read, look for examples of these feelings.

Written on a Cold Evening

The poet must work with brush and paper,
but this is not what makes the poem.
A man doesn't go in search of a poem—
the poem comes in search of him.

Evening Lake Scenes

1
The lake seems glued to the sky—
      no banks are visible.
In the middle of the lake, water plants float.
It is evening—geese are forming V's,
      crows are forming flocks;
they land, then fly up again,
      taking a long time to settle for the night.

2
I sit watching the sun set over the lake.
The sun is not swallowed by mountains or clouds:
it descends inch by inch, then disappears completely,
leaving no trace where it sinks into the water.

In the Gorge: We Encounter Wind

Our boat is becalmed in the middle of the river—
the mountains are silent and gloomy at sunset.
Suddenly a clap of thunder sounds in the darkening sky
and the trees along the shore begin to sway.
A powerful wind blows in from the southern sea
and sweeps angrily through the gorge.
The sailors cheer;
    the great drum is beaten.
One man flies to the top of the mainmast.
As a sail unfurls I pull my hands into my sleeves
and watch ripples like goose feathers
    swirl by in the water.

Rain and Cold

I comb my hair and sleep overcomes me:
I dream that all my white hairs are being cut.
I wake up: the wind is leaking through a crack in the window
swinging a spider's web back and forth.

Night Rain at Kuang-k

The river is clear and calm;
    a fast rain falls in the gorge.
At midnight the cold, splashing sound begins,
like thousands of pearls spilling onto a glass plate,
each drop penetrating the bone.

In my dream I scratch my head and get up to listen.
I listen and listen, until the dawn.
All my life I have heard rain,
    and I am an old man;
but now for the first time I understand
    the sound of spring rain
        on the river at night.

Further Reading

Heaven's Reward: Fairy Tales from China. Catherine Edwards Sadler. These stories have been retold for thousands of years in China.

Treasure Mountain: Folktales from Southern China. Catherine Edwards Sadler. These stories tell of greedy officials and noble peasants.

LESSON 2

The Flowering of Chinese Culture

Key Terms

- aristocrat
- meritocracy
- mandate
- currency
- money economy

➤ *Here is a part of the Chinese text of the poem by Li Bo. This landscape, painted in ink on silk, has been attributed to the Tang artist Li Sixun. In an essay on painting, Guo Xi, one of the greatest artists of the Song Dynasty, said that enjoying a landscape painting could be a substitute for wandering through the mountains.*

B eside my bed the bright
  moonbeams bound
Almost as if there were frost on
  the ground.
Raising up, I gaze at the
  moon;
Lying back, I think of my
  old home town.

Li Bo, "Quiet Night Thoughts,"
701–702

If you were to write a poem about a nature scene near your home, how might your poem be like this one? How would it be different? Before you read on, study the painting and reread the poem.

低頭思故鄉
舉頭望明月
疑是地上霜
床前明月光
夜思 李白

The poem was written by Li Bo, the most beloved poet in China's history. He lived during the Tang Dynasty. The dynasty began when Li Yuan, a rebellious lord who had taken power from the Sui emperor, proclaimed himself emperor in 618. The Tang Dynasty was followed by the Song Dynasty, which lasted until 1279. Together, these two dynasties ruled over the most artistically brilliant era in Chinese civilization.

Poetry and painting are two areas in which Tang and Song artists excelled. A favorite theme of both poets and painters was the harmony they saw in the natural world. In the poem you read, Li Bo remembers the place where he grew up. He notes that the moon that he sees in the poem is the same mountain moon that shines on his home town. Nature unites two different times and places in the poem.

Do you think that the painting shown on page 202 expresses the same mood as the poem? The painting shows a mountainous landscape. But notice the person in the foreground. The size of the figure in relation to the landscape seems to suggest that people, or human activities, are not very important when compared with the beauty of the natural world. Nevertheless, the painter chose to place a human figure in the scene. Perhaps the painter is implying that people can live in harmony with nature, provided they recognize their small place in it.

Chinese painters did not simply draw what they saw. They tried to represent the spirit, or essence, of the subject. This feeling of harmony with their subject helped them to create a sense of life in their work. The Chinese landscape painter and poet Wang Wei explained Chinese painting this way:

> Such paintings cannot be achieved by the physical movements of the fingers and the hand, but only by the spirit entering into them. This is the nature of painting.
>
> Wang Wei, from *Introduction to Painting*, 699–759

◄ During the Tang Dynasty, pottery figures such as this fashionable lady were made in molds and painted. A pale, round face was thought to be most beautiful.

▼ Chinese civil service examinations were stamped with seals such as this.

The Civil Service System

Painting and poetry were not the only things the Chinese achieved during the Tang and Song dynasties. They also developed a fair and efficient system of administration.

More Schools for More People

The Sui and early Tang rulers used examinations to find good candidates for public office. But only an **aristocrat,** a member of a wealthy and influential family, could afford to study for the civil service exams. Preparing for the tests took years and meant traveling to special schools in the capital. As a result, aristocrats held most government jobs.

Later Tang and then Song governments recruited civil servants from other classes. It was still difficult for peasants to spend years studying, but during the Song Dynasty nearly half the civil servants came from classes other than the aristocracy.

A System Based on Merit

Officials appointed under earlier dynasties often held their positions for life, even if they were not very good at their jobs. Under the Tang and Song dynasties, civil servants who did their jobs well were promoted. Those who did poorly were demoted or even fired. Such a system, in which people are chosen and promoted on the basis of their performance, or merit, is called a **meritocracy.** The Chinese were the first people to establish a meritocracy. Other countries, such as the United States and France, set up similar administrative systems about a thousand years later.

Power to the Emperor

The Chinese had long believed that each emperor received from heaven a **mandate,** or order to govern. This is why one of the emperor's titles was "Son of Heaven." In theory, the emperor had absolute power. In practice, he had always shared his power with wealthy, landowning families.

Under the meritocracy, aristocrats had less power. They held fewer government positions and risked losing their positions if they did not perform well. Officials who were not from the aristocratic class were grateful for their positions and thus more loyal to the emperor. The emperor trusted them to enforce his laws, even in regions far from the capital. ■

▲ This character used by an emperor of the Song Dynasty means "by order of the emperor." Calligraphy was a subject on the civil service examination.

■ Why did the aristocracy find it more difficult to gain influence under the civil service system?

The Birth of a New Economy

To manage government business efficiently, official inspectors, tax collectors, and messengers needed to travel throughout the empire. To make this possible, the Tang and Song governments built an extensive system of roads and waterways. These, in turn, spurred trade and encouraged the spread of ideas within China.

Better Roads and Waterways

By the late 700s, relay hostels, or inns, with horses and food for traveling bureaucrats were in use along all main roads. Mounted messengers and foot runners carried government mail. One observer of the day wrote, "It took only a few days for all the news from distant places to reach the authorities." The roads also made it possible to move grain, tea, and other goods. Some 9,600 runners regularly supplied fresh seafood to the Tang capital of Changan from coastal cities about 800 miles away.

The government also improved canals and waterways for the growing numbers of sailboats, hand-driven paddle-wheel boats, and rowing ships that used them. The

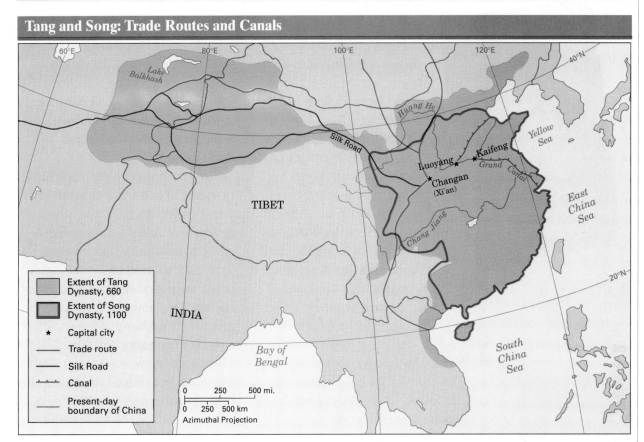

Legend:
- Extent of Tang Dynasty, 660
- Extent of Song Dynasty, 1100
- ★ Capital city
- Trade route
- Silk Road
- ⊢⊢⊢ Canal
- Present-day boundary of China

0   250   500 mi.
0   250 500 km
Azimuthal Projection

government sponsored hostels along the rivers and extended the canal system. By 850, the rivers and canals formed a vast network of about 1,200 miles extending to much of eastern China.

New Crops and Farming Methods

Though built for government use, roads and waterways promoted trade throughout China. At about the same time, Chinese farming became more productive. Around the year 1000, travelers introduced a new, fast-ripening rice from the area that is now Cambodia. Farmers could plant two or sometimes even three crops of this rice each year instead of just one.

Under both the Tang and Song dynasties, the government assigned plots of land to free peasants. Government officials taught farmers to build irrigation ditches and dams with pumps driven by human, water, or wind power. Farmers could then turn dry land into paddies, or wet fields, to grow more rice.

A population shift resulted from this boom in agriculture. Southern China was better suited for growing rice than northern China. As more and more land was turned into rice paddies, more and more people could live on what the land produced. The population of southern China grew steadily. Also, Mongol invasions in the north forced many to flee to the south. Many became tenants on large southern farms. The graph above shows this growth in population.

Farmers soon produced more food than they needed. So they sold the extra food, or surplus, to

Population Change in South China, 500–1500

(Graph: Percent of Total Population vs. Year, 500 to 1500)

▲ *How did the Grand Canal help to unite northern and southern China? What percentage of the total population of China lived in the south around 620? What percentage lived in the south around 1280?*

205

China

This copper plate was used for printing money during the Song Dynasty.

■ *What factors led to a money economy in China?*

people in other regions, using the new roads and waterways to send crops to market. Market towns grew larger in rural areas.

A Thriving Merchant Class

Using this network of waterways, merchants transported products inexpensively in Chinese sailing ships called junks. Junks also carried goods along the coast, as seen from this description of a Song coastal city:

> Merchants from [southern and central provinces] come to this town in seagoing junks to sell such dutiable goods as spices. . . . [Northern] merchants come bringing copper cash, silk thread, silk floss, silk gauze and thin silk, and do an extremely thriving trade with them.
>
> From *The Continuation of the Comprehensive Mirror for Aiding Government,* 1088

Merchants made copper coins with holes in the center

and strung on a string called a *cash.* Usually there were a thousand coins in a cash. In earlier times, bartered goods, such as lengths of silk, had also been used in trading. As trade increased, merchants found it easier to trade in cash.

But cash was heavy. Imagine carrying 50 dollars in coins in your pocket! In 1024, the Song government used an engraved metal plate like the one shown to the left to print the world's first paper **currency.** As cash and paper currency became the most common items exchanged for goods, a **money economy** developed. Money was now the standard by which people judged the value of a bushel of rice or a length of silk.

The business of trade required more shopkeepers, bankers, inspectors, tax collectors, storehouse workers, and others. As a result, the merchant class grew.

Merchants tended to live in cities and towns, where trading activity was greatest. Cities grew in size as rural workers flocked to the cities to fill jobs related to trade. ■

A Continuing Heritage

Although the Chinese prospered through their thriving new trade network, they continued to value their ancient traditions.

The civil service exams, for example, required candidates to study the Confucian classics. The classics became available after the invention of printing in the late 700s,

Inventions in China and Europe

100, Use of writing paper
(*European writing paper–900, from Cairo*)

577, Matches invented
(*European matches–1500s*)

| 100 | 200 | 300 | 400 | 500 | 600 |

200, Fishing reel developed
(*European fishing reel–1650*)

400, Rudder developed
(*European rudder –c.1300*)

about 700 years before the development of printing in Europe.

Historians call this renewed emphasis on Confucian ideas Neo-Confucianism. Writers began to find new meanings in Confucian texts and to relate them to problems of the time.

Respect for the past, however, did not keep the Chinese from moving forward. Between 200 and 1200, new inventions improved life in China. Look at the timeline below. Notice that many Chinese discoveries took centuries to reach the West. Chain drives of the type that were later used in bicycles, for example, were in use in China in 976 in silk-making machinery. When was this invention first used in the West?

Printing

Of all the inventions made during the Tang and Song periods, printing was probably the most significant. By making books, calendars, and government pamphlets available to many more people, printing hastened the spread of knowledge throughout China.

Woodblock printing was the earliest form of printing. The Chinese began to use this method in the late 700s, about 600 years before Europeans learned about it. To make a woodblock print, skilled craftspeople carved raised Chinese characters on a wooden "page." They brushed ink onto this page and laid a piece of paper over it to make a print. The entire process was done by hand.

How long do you think it would take you to carve the words in this sentence onto a block of wood? Chinese scholars spent 21 years carving and printing all 130 volumes of the Confucian classics.

Around 1045, a Chinese commoner named Bi Sheng invented a less time-consuming method of printing using movable type. He cut ideograms, the Chinese characters, out of sticky clay and baked them until they were hard. Then he made each page by placing the necessary characters into an iron frame. This method of printing was very quick and efficient for printing many pages of a work.

By 1100, Chinese scholars used books on law, medicine, mathematics, and science to learn from both the past and the present. New techniques for treating disease or planting crops, for example, spread much more quickly in print than by word of mouth. An observer named Fang Tazong wrote the

▼ *About how long after the Chinese first used matches did Europeans make matches?*

c.8th century, Paper money developed
(*European bank note issued – 1658*)

1041–1048, Movable type developed
(*European movable type – 1450*)

| 700 | 800 | 900 | 1000 | 1100 | 1200 |

976, Bicycle chain drive developed
(*European bicycle chain drive – 1770*)

China

The Chinese first used gunpowder for fireworks during the Tang Dynasty. A Chinese book published in 1044 gives a precise formula for making gunpowder.

➤ *This compass was made by using a magnetic rock called a lodestone. The compass maker cut a thin sheet of metal into the shape of a fish and rubbed it with the lodestone to make it magnetic.*

■ *Find evidence to support this statement: Chinese inventions showed a respect for the past as well as a desire to improve on it.*

following about education in the province of Fujian during Song times:

Every peasant, artisan and merchant teaches his sons how to read books. Even herdsmen, and wives who bring their husbands food at their work in the fields, can recite the poems of the men of ancient times.

Other Inventions

Another important invention was gunpowder, which may have been discovered as early as the 600s. By the 1200s, the Chinese made and used gunpowder in large quantities. A document written in 1221 states: "On the same day were produced 7,000 gunpowder crossbow arrows, 10,000 gunpowder ordinary arrows, 3,000 barbed gunpowder packages and 20,000 ordinary gunpowder packages." In addition, archaeological evidence shows that by 1288 the Chinese had invented guns, which were later copied in Europe.

Another invention made traveling easier. For travel by sea, the Chinese used charts of the stars and a compass they called a "fish."

Chinese astronomers began mapping the stars as early as 300 B.C. Star charts dating from about 940 show many familiar constellations. The "fish" was a piece of metal shaped like a fish that pointed south when floated in water. This description of how sailors used the magnetic fish was written in 1119:

The sailors are sure of their bearings. At night they judge by the stars. In daytime they tell by the sun. When it is cloudy, they rely on the south-pointing needle.

Europeans learned about these inventions during the years that followed the Song Dynasty. These years were a period of Mongol domination in China. ■

R E V I E W

1. **FOCUS** What were the most significant achievements of the Tang and Song dynasties?
2. **CONNECT** How did the civil service system in the later Tang and Song dynasties differ from that of the Sui Dynasty?
3. **CULTURE** What common theme runs through many poems and paintings of the Tang and Song dynasties? How is this theme related to the religious beliefs of the period?
4. **ECONOMICS** How did Chinese agricultural growth

make necessary the development of a money economy?

5. **CRITICAL THINKING** Would you describe your school as a meritocracy? Explain.
6. **ACTIVITY** Assume that you are the inventor of one of the items pictured in the timeline on pages 206 and 207. Describe your invention and explain its purpose to your classmates, who have never heard of such a device. Be sure to point out how your device could improve their lives.

Chapter 8

LESSON 3

China and the Larger World

O n this [New Year's] day all the rulers, and all the provinces and regions and realms where men hold land or lordship under [the Great Khan's] sway, bring him costly gifts of gold and silver and pearls and precious stones and abundance of fine white cloth, so that throughout the year their lord may have no lack of treasure and may live in joy and gladness. . . . I can also assure you for a fact that on this day the Great Khan receives gifts of more than 100,000 white horses, of great beauty and price. And on this day also there is a procession of his elephants, fully 5,000 in number, all draped in fine cloths embroidered with beasts and birds. . . . Let me conclude with one more fact, a very remarkable one well worthy of mention in our book. You must know that a great lion is led into the Great Khan's presence; and as soon as it sees him it flings itself down prostrate before him with every appearance of deep humility and seems to acknowledge him as lord. There it stays without a chain, and is indeed a thing to marvel at.

Marco Polo, from *Travels*

THINKING
FOCUS

What factors caused China to open trade at some times and remain isolated at others?

Key Term

• despot

This detailed account of a day at the Great Khan's court at Beijing was recounted by Marco Polo, a traveler from Venice, Italy. Polo lived in China from 1275 until 1292. The Great Khan in this report was Kublai Khan, a grandson of Genghis Khan.

Although only 17 years old when he arrived in China, Polo served Kublai as an ambassador and in other ways. At the time of his visit, all of China, as well as much of the rest of the world, was under Mongol rule.

◄ *This portrait of Kublai Khan comes from a Chinese manuscript now in Paris.*

209

China

The Mongols in China

While southern China prospered under the Song Dynasty, Genghis Khan made life very difficult for people in northern China. His well-organized and skillful

Mongol horsemen traveled for weeks at a time, making surprise attacks along the Chinese frontier. They learned to use catapults and gunpowder bombs to break through city walls. With few horses and inferior riding skills, Chinese armies were rarely able to defeat the Mongols. In 1234, a few years after Genghis Khan's death, the Mongols completed the conquest of northern China.

A Mongol Dynasty

Kublai Khan was chosen *khan*, or ruler, in 1260. In 1267, Kublai moved his capital from Mongolia to Beijing *(bay JIHNG)* in northern China in order to be closer to his subjects.

Kublai adopted certain Chinese traditions of government to make it easier for him to rule and be accepted by the Chinese. For example, he rebuilt the capital in the traditional Chinese style and declared himself emperor and Son of Heaven. He even founded his own dynasty, called the Yuan *(yu AHN)*, which lasted until 1368.

However, unlike many northern barbarians before them, Kublai Kahn and the Mongols did not try to change Mongol culture so that it became more like Chinese culture. They used some Chinese systems of government, but only to strengthen Mongol rule. The most important government positions were held by Mongols or by other non-Chinese, including Marco Polo. The Chinese themselves were given the least important jobs. Government documents were usually written in Mongolian and then translated into Chinese.

Kublai Khan staged many attacks on the Song Dynasty in southern China. His forces finally overpowered the last group of Song defenders in 1279. Kublai thus became the first ruler to control all of China in over 300 years.

An Interruption in Progress

Although the Mongols maintained the basic Chinese government structure, their occupation of China disrupted economic and social development. It also slowed the remarkable progress of Chinese civilization under the Tang and Song dynasties. Millions of Chinese died during the decades of the Mongol invasions, including about half the population of the North. Some were killed by the Mongol attacks while many more

Mongol warriors, like the one in the upper picture, shot arrows from large bows with force enough to pierce armor. They rode small, sturdy horses like the one shown in the ceramic model above. This ceramic horse was found in a tomb from the Tang Dynasty.

died from outbreaks of disease that often followed the attacks. Once highly populated areas, such as the eastern province of Anhui, were almost empty of people by the time the attacks ended.

Much of the wealth of the Tang and Song dynasties was lost as the Mongols burned cities and used vast areas of fertile farmland as pastures for their horses. They neglected canals and irrigation systems, and fertile fields soon became parched and barren. Many farmers lost their land to the Mongols, and many civil servants lost their jobs.

In the south, the Mongols hoped to win support from the wealthy landowners by letting them keep their lands. However, the Mongols seized land from the peasants, forcing them to seek work as hired hands on large estates. Thus the rich remained rich, while the poor became even poorer.

A Direct Link to the West

The Mongols disrupted Chinese life and culture. However, they strengthened China's links to the rest of the world. Camel caravans traveled throughout the vast Mongol Empire, from Beijing to central Asia to the Black Sea, carrying silks and ceramics for the Western market. The Mongols expanded the Chinese system of postal relays, establishing stations with supplies and horses for travelers who crossed the Asian steppe.

Travelers who crossed the Indian Ocean to China found thriving port cities, such as Guangzhou *(GWAHNG joh)*, sometimes known as Canton, and Fujian *(FOO jihn)*. Merchants, missionaries, and diplomats from the Arab world gathered in southern China's seaports. Through Arab merchants, many goods from the West and from southeastern Asia were traded in Chinese ports.

Increased contacts with the world not only expanded trade in China but also aided the spread of ideas in the West. For example, knowledge of printing and gunpowder probably spread from China to western Asia and then to Europe during the Mongol period. ■

■ *In what ways did the Mongol conquest of China affect the livelihood of most Chinese people?*

The Ming Dynasty

Merchants prospered under Mongol rule. But most Chinese were eager to expel the foreigners who did not appreciate China's traditions. The Chinese rebelled against the Mongol rulers and founded a new dynasty in 1368. The rebel leader and founder of the Ming Dynasty was Emperor Taizu *(ty TSOO)*. The Ming Dynasty continued to rule China until as late as 1644.

Familiar Traditions

Emperor Taizu turned to familiar traditions for help in restoring the empire. He reestablished the civil service examination system and encouraged promising scholars. He undertook public works projects: repairing irrigation systems, building reservoirs, and extensively rebuilding the Great Wall. He helped homeless people by

◄ *Blue and white ceramics such as this Ming vase became the most popular kind of ceramics for trade. Cobalt, used to make the blue color on this vase, was first imported during the Mongol period.*

giving them land in regions left devastated by the Mongols. Unlike earlier emperors, Taizu also seized large estates, abolished slavery, and raised the taxes of the rich. Such measures narrowed the gap between rich and poor.

More Power to the Emperor

Ming rulers made themselves extremely powerful. For example, Emperor Taizu abolished the position of prime minister and controlled all departments of government directly.

While earlier emperors had welcomed open discussion of issues, Ming emperors made decisions in secret councils. Emperor Taizu even created a secret police force to spy on officials. Historians estimate that he accused at least 100,000 people of corruption or treason and then executed them. Such a ruler, who holds absolute power and uses it abusively, is called a **despot.**

The Ming emperors ordered a splendid new capital built on the site of the old Mongol capital of Beijing. During the early 1400s, about one million workers labored to complete the new city. Great walls, 40 feet high, surrounded a central area known as the Imperial City. Here grand halls, courtyards, and gardens provided a costly and lavish setting for the business of government.

A Superior Naval Power

At first, the emperors wanted to show the world the power of the Ming Dynasty. Between 1403 and 1433, court official Zheng He gathered a fleet of ships and made seven voyages to the Middle East and to the east coast of Africa. You can read more about Zheng He in A Closer Look on page 213.

But the Ming emperors soon decided that the rest of the world had little of value to offer China. They forbade further explorations and ended the costly voyages after 1433. They even made it a crime for any Chinese subjects to leave the country by sea.

▼ *The Forbidden City was the innermost square of the Imperial City. It was surrounded by a moat and a high wall. The Forbidden City contained palaces for members of the imperial family, and the Hall of Supreme Harmony, shown below, where the emperor held court. Why do you think that this part of Beijing was called the Forbidden City?*

The Voyages of Zheng He

Fifty years before Europeans began searching for a sea route to the East, Chinese ambassador Zheng He explored the West. His emperor sent Zheng He to collect presents and to display the splendor and power of China. Under these orders, Zheng He sailed to southeastern Asia, India, Arabia, and Africa in the early 1400s.

Zheng He, detail from
a woodcut by Lo Moudeng, 1597

Chinese Pearls

Everywhere he went Zheng He brought pearls and Ming vases to show off China's wealth. Most foreigners had never seen pottery so delicate and beautiful.

Ten times larger than European ships of the period, the junks Zheng He sailed had room for 500 people.

Ming Vase

Zheng He brought back giraffes, zebras, tigers, and ostriches. When they saw the giraffe, people told the emperor Zheng He had brought back a *qilin,* a mythical creature that appeared when the wisest emperor ruled. The emperor is said to have replied, "That is no *qilin,* and I am no wise man."

The Tribute Giraffe with Attendant,
by artist Shen Du, A.D. 1414

213

China

Contact with the World

Until the mid-1400s, Chinese were among the best sailors in the world, visiting Africa and India almost 100 years before the Portuguese rounded the tip of Africa. The emperors, however, stopped financing expeditions and for a time outlawed overseas trade. Invasions from the north demanded their attention and money. Confucian attitudes looked down on merchants, and the bureaucrats resented the growing importance of traders and travelers. Still, goods such as tea and silk were shipped by caravan to central Asia and as far north as Russia, while some ships continued to sail to Southeast Asia and India to trade.

The first European ship to reach China was Portuguese, arriving in 1514. In 1557, the Chinese allowed the Portuguese to set up a trading station on the coast of China at Macao, near Guangzhou. As other Europeans arrived, the Chinese restricted them to certain areas along the coast. Some traders brought Jesuit missionaries with them. The missionaries worked at converting some Chinese to Christianity.

European traders seeking Chinese tea, silk, and porcelain brought with them sweet potatoes and corn from the Americas. They introduced beef and dairy cattle, which the Chinese then raised in the fertile pastures of the south. Increased trade also brought more gold and silver to China.

Throughout the Ming Dynasty, despotic rulers tried to restrict trade. Eventually, the people grew tired of heavy taxation and careless government. In the early 1600s, peasants in the southern regions rebelled against the despots. ■

■ *In what ways did the Ming dynasty affect trade and other contacts with the West?*

▼ *Notice the similarity between the imperial headpiece of this Qing Dynasty empress and that of Kublai Khan on page 209.*

The Qing Dynasty

The Ming ruler sent armies to the south to fight the peasants who were rebelling. A tribal people from the north, known as the Manchus, seized this opportunity to invade northern China. In 1644, they defeated the Ming and began the Qing *(chihng)* Dynasty, which was to last until 1912.

Like the Mongols, the Manchus wanted to keep their tribal traditions. Control of the army was kept in Manchu hands. For governing their subjects, however, the Qing adopted Chinese traditions. The Manchus continued the Ming government structure and civil service system. They even allowed many Ming officials to remain in office. Positions in the local government were filled mostly by Chinese rather than by Manchu officials.

Culture and Population

The Qing rulers also assigned scholars to edit Chinese literary and historical works, including the Confucian classics. The shift from woodblock printing to movable type in the 1500s triggered a boom in publishing and a rising literacy rate. In 1726, they sponsored a famous encyclopedia of 5,020 volumes.

The population of China was about 60 million in 1400. By 1580, it had more than tripled, and it continued to increase rapidly during the Qing Dynasty. By 1850, the population was about 430 million. This population growth was partly due to the nutritious foods introduced during the Ming Dynasty. As population grew, China's territory also increased. During the Qing Dynasty, China doubled in size, expanding north into Manchuria and Mongolia, west into Tibet, and south into what is now Burma and Vietnam. Compare the map on page 533 with the map on pages 522 and 523 of the Atlas to see how China grew.

Cities and Trade

As China's population grew, the cities also expanded. Farmers sold their crops locally to merchants, who transported them to the cities. Peasants found work in small handicraft industries, such as weaving.

The Qing emperors allowed a limited amount of trade between China and other nations through the port at Guangzhou. For the most part, however, the Chinese believed that there was little to be gained by contact with other peoples. They preferred to follow the traditional patterns of Chinese life that had been outlined centuries before by Confucius. ■

What flags can you see over Guangzhou's harbor in this 1847 painting?

What aspects of traditional Chinese government did the Qing retain?

R E V I E W

1. **FOCUS** What factors caused China to open trade at some times and remain isolated at others?
2. **CONNECT** What impact did Mongol rule have on the economic progress of the Tang and Song dynasties?
3. **ECONOMICS** How did the Ming attitude toward foreigners affect trade?
4. **POLITICAL SYSTEMS** Compare and contrast Mongol rule and the Qing Dynasty.

5. **CRITICAL THINKING** Why did invaders from the North not try to replace the Chinese culture with their own culture?
6. **WRITING ACTIVITY** You are a Portuguese trader who has just returned from Macao, China, in 1500, with a shipload of goods. Write a paragraph in which you describe your purchases and explain why you think Europeans will buy them.

Comparing Two Maps of China

Here's Why

No single map can show you everything about a region. Maps have many purposes. Often you learn more by comparing maps than by examining them individually.

For example, you can compare topographic and land-use maps of China. Using the two maps together will help you see how China's physical features affect how people use land in China.

Here's How

Look at the topographic map on this page. It shows physical features such as mountains, deserts, lakes, and rivers. A key explains how colors on the map show elevations.

Study the land-use map of China on the facing page. This map helps you see what types of economic activities are most dominant in different areas of China.

Compare the two maps to see how geographical factors have influenced land use in Beijing. Find Beijing on the topographic map. You can see that a river and a connecting canal link Beijing with both the Yellow Sea and the Grand Canal.

Beijing's elevation is fairly low. Notice that deserts lie to the west and northwest of Beijing and that the land rises to the west and north. Beijing itself lies on the northern edge of the North China Plain. The map shows

that Beijing is approximately 40°N. Its latitude and elevation are much like that of central Illinois.

From the topographic map, you have learned that Beijing has water resources, which could be useful for farming, industry, and trade. Because of its latitude and elevation, you can infer that Beijing is in an area that would be a good place to live, work, and farm.

Now look at the land-use map to see what economic activities are important to Beijing. The map's color coding tells you that Beijing is in an urban and industrial area. Most of the surrounding land is used for farming. Find the city of Tianjin, southeast of

People's Republic of China: Physical Regions

Chapter 8

Beijing. Goods manufactured in Beijing are shipped from port facilities near Tianjin. The photograph to the right helps illustrate the importance of the Grand Canal to these two cities. Beijing's industries clearly benefit from the water transportation routes that link the city to markets in China and abroad.

Try It

Look at the western area of China on the topographic map. Find the Himalayas, the Karakorum Shan (Range), and the Kunlun Shan. These mountains are located in the most rugged area of China.

Now locate China's cities. What areas have few cities?

What geographical features might account for this?

Study the land-use map. What is the main land use in the western half of China? What is the main land use in China's eastern half? What aspects of China's geography explain these differences?

Finally, locate China's urban and industrial areas on the land-use map. What information from the topographic map might help

explain why these urban and industrial areas are located here?

Apply It

Find topographic and land-use maps of your state in an encyclopedia or atlas. Compare the maps. Then write a short report about how information from the topographic map helps explain the locations of cities and land use.

People's Republic of China: Land Use and Resources

217

China

Chapter Review

Reviewing Key Terms

aristocrat (p. 203)
Buddhism (p. 194)
Confucianism (p. 194)
currency (p. 206)
Daoism (p. 197)

despot (p. 212)
mandate (p. 204)
meritocracy (p. 204)
money economy (p. 206)

A. The following quotations describe three systems of thought and practice. Identify the key term by which each of these systems is known.

1. "I am content with my life because I live in harmony with nature."
2. "Through meditation, I can find peace and freedom."
3. "I believe in proper conduct, respect for elders, scholarship, and government service."

B. Identify the term that fits each clue below. Then write a sentence for each term.

1. It means the opposite of "a system in which people trade one kind of goods for other goods."
2. It means the opposite of "a member of a poor family with no influence."
3. It means almost the same as "dictator."
4. It means the opposite of a "system in which people are chosen and promoted without having to do their jobs well."
5. It means the same as "a command from someone who has authority."
6. It means the same as "money."

Exploring Concepts

A. Complete the following outline on your own paper. Fill in all the blank spaces.

Imperial China
  I. An emerging empire
    A. Years of disorder
      1. _____
      2. _____
      3. A period of unrest
    B. _____
    C. The reunification of China
  II. _____
    A. The civil service system
    B. The birth of a new economy
      1. Better roads and waterways
      2. _____
      3. _____
    C. A continuing heritage
  III. China and the larger world
    A. _____
    B. The Ming dynasty
    C. _____

B. Support each of the following statements with facts and details from the chapter.

1. The last Han emperor was faced with serious problems in the year 220.
2. Geography divided China but also protected it from invasion, except in the north.
3. The events following the fall of the Han Dynasty were not all bad.
4. Emperor Wen renewed important traditions and organized projects to focus the people's attention on common goals.
5. Chinese merchants found that paper money was an improvement over the old way of carrying their cash.
6. After 1279, many advances made under the Tang and Song dynasties were undone.
7. For many years, Chinese knowledge, inventions, and art passed to Europeans through Indian Ocean traders, and from overland caravans coming through the Middle East. When the Portuguese found the sea route to the Indian Ocean, this all changed.

Reviewing Skills

1. Look at the map on this page. It shows the location of China's Great Wall and Grand Canal. Parts of the canal were built under different rulers. A connecting canal was built to link Dadu, now Beijing, with the Grand Canal. Look at the topographic map on page 216. Think about China's topography. What geographical facts made it practical for the Chinese to build the canal where they did? What major rivers are linked by the canal?

2. Note the location of the Great Wall on the map on this page. Now find the Great Wall on the topographic map on page 216. The wall was built to prevent invasions. What geographic features shown on the topographic map are also natural barriers? How does the information on this map help explain the location of the Great Wall?

3. Study color coding on the topographic map of China on page 216. Which would show a greater change in elevation, a vertical profile of China at 110° E or a vertical profile of China at 30° N?

4. Beliefs and values of people in ancient China can be understood by studying some of their sayings. What are those sayings called?

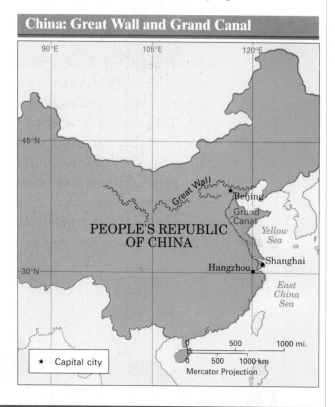

China: Great Wall and Grand Canal

Using Critical Thinking

1. Today, we are affected in important ways by things that were invented in China thousands of years ago. Think of at least three of these inventions you read about in the chapter. Explain how they affect modern people in everyday ways. In your explanation, be sure to mention both positive and negative aspects.

2. The Ming emperor Taizu showed by many of his actions that he was a despot. Citizens of modern nations like ours must constantly be alert to protect themselves from despotic leaders. Recall the despotic actions Taizu took while he was emperor. Then explain how modern citizens can identify leaders who have despotic tendencies.

Preparing for Citizenship

1. **WRITING A REPORT** In the United States, the civil service system is a meritocracy. Most workers in the national government and in many state and city governments belong to this meritocracy. Research the civil service system. Find out how it selects government workers. Then write a report for others who may want to make a career in government.

2. **COLLABORATIVE LEARNING** With your class, plan a large clay or plaster relief map of China. Join in one of these group activities: gather materials; decide which places to show on the map; make the relief map; create labels; prepare a talk to explain the map to visitors. Work out a schedule to show when each task should be finished.

Chapter 9

Japan

A Buddhist monk tends a simple garden of rocks and
sand. A beautiful woman warrior knocks her foe from
his horse. A poet writes three lines about a frog in a
pond. What can these brief moments tell us about Japan
since the 500s? The monk shows religious simplicity.
The woman warrior symbolizes both a love of beauty
and a respect for combat. And the poet reflects a
quiet reverence for nature. Each quality has
played an important role in the unfolding
of Japan's unique history and way of life.

Throughout this period,
Buddhism influenced
life in Japan. The bowl
and whisk are part of
the Zen Buddhist tea
ceremony. With the
whisk, the drinker stirs
and froths the tea.

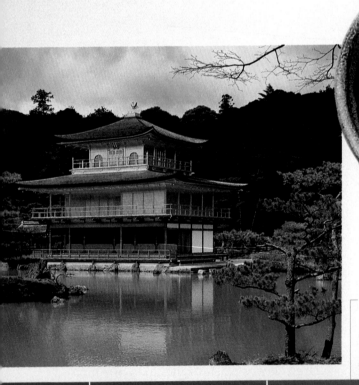

794 Japan's emperor makes Kyoto
the capital. One of the city's loveliest
sights is the Golden Pavilion, built
600 years later as a mountain villa
for Japan's rulers.

| 500 | 700 | 900 | 1100 |

632 Muslim armies begin
building a great empire. By 750,
they control lands from Spain in
the West to India in the East.

Since the 1300s, the Japanese have enjoyed *Noh* drama, featuring a masked dancer on a darkened stage. This wooden *Noh* mask is more than 500 years old.

Toyotomi Hideyoshi, left, becomes Japan's military ruler in 1585. He rises from a peasant background to become a powerful leader.

1800s Ando Hiroshige creates prints like the one above showing a warrior approaching a village in a beautiful setting.

1300	1500	1700	1900

1638–1715 King Louis XIV rules France and drains the treasury with his luxurious lifestyle and many wars.

1854

LESSON 1

Land of the Rising Sun

Key Terms

- isolation
- Shinto

➤ *Izanagi and Izanami
stood together on the
Floating Bridge of
Heaven and held council.
"Is there not a country
beneath?" they asked.
Then they decided to cre-
ate the islands of Japan.*

In the beginning, there was chaos. Then Heaven and Earth began to separate, and gods came to life. In the seventh generation, two gods—Izanagi and Izanami—decided to create a drifting land on the oceans. Izanagi reached down from heaven and thrust a jeweled spear into the ocean. When he withdrew the spear, drops fell from its point, forming the islands of Japan.

This is how the world began, according to Japanese mythology. The myths go on to tell how the next generation of gods struggled for power. The Sun Goddess gave life to everything around her. But her brother, the Storm God, was wild and fierce. He ruined his sister's rice crop and so upset her that she hid in a cave. Without her, heaven and earth went dark.

Other gods brought the Sun Goddess a beautiful bronze mirror and a sparkling jewel to coax her out of the cave. When she came out and told of the Storm God's mischief, the other gods banished him to the earth. His descendants lived on the Japanese islands.

After many years, the Sun Goddess sent her grandson, Ninigi *(nee NEE gee)* to take control of the island of Honshu. As symbols of his divine power, she sent with him her bronze mirror, her jewel, and a

great iron sword. Two generations later, according to legend, Ninigi's grandson Jimmu conquered the Storm God's descendants and in

660 B.C. became the first emperor of Japan. Today, the divine objects described in the legend—the mirror, the jewel, and the sword—are the symbols of the emperor's heaven-sent power.

The Islands of Japan

Millions of years ago, volcanic mountains pushed up out of the Pacific Ocean. The tops of these mountains are the islands of Japan. As you can see from the map on page 224, Japan consists mainly of four large islands—Hokkaido (hah KYD oh), Honshu, Shikoku, and Kyushu (kee OO shoo). Japan also includes many smaller islands.

Together, the major Japanese islands total about 146,000 square miles, about the size of Montana. However, the four main islands are so spread out that their north-south curve covers about 1,200 miles. If the main islands were placed next to the eastern coast of the United States, they would reach from Maine to Georgia.

The Japanese islands lie on a very unstable part of the earth's surface. Each year Japan has more than 1,500 earthquakes, though most are mild. And 60 of its 150 major volcanoes are still active. Typhoons are also frequent in Japan. The heavy winds and rains batter its coasts, flood its valleys, and uproot its trees.

Mountains and hills cover most of Japan, leaving less than 20 percent of it for farming. Japan has few natural resources such as coal, iron, or other minerals. The sea has always been Japan's greatest resource. It provides food for the Japanese as well as transportation routes. Japan's seas have also acted as a natural barrier, keeping Japan in **isolation,** or setting it apart, from much of the world. The seas often shielded Japan from invasion by northern Asian tribes.

Because they live on islands, the Japanese were able to control the flow of people and ideas into their country. As a result, Japanese culture developed with few influences from other countries, except China. ■

Although Japan has few natural resources, its economy today is the second largest in the world. To keep its factories humming, Japan must import 99.7 percent of its oil, 96.3 percent of its natural gas, and 94.7 percent of its coal. It is no longer an isolated nation.

■ *Why is the sea Japan's greatest natural resource?*

◄ *Mount Fuji is the tallest of Japan's volcanoes. Each year, thousands climb to the Shinto shrine on its peak.*

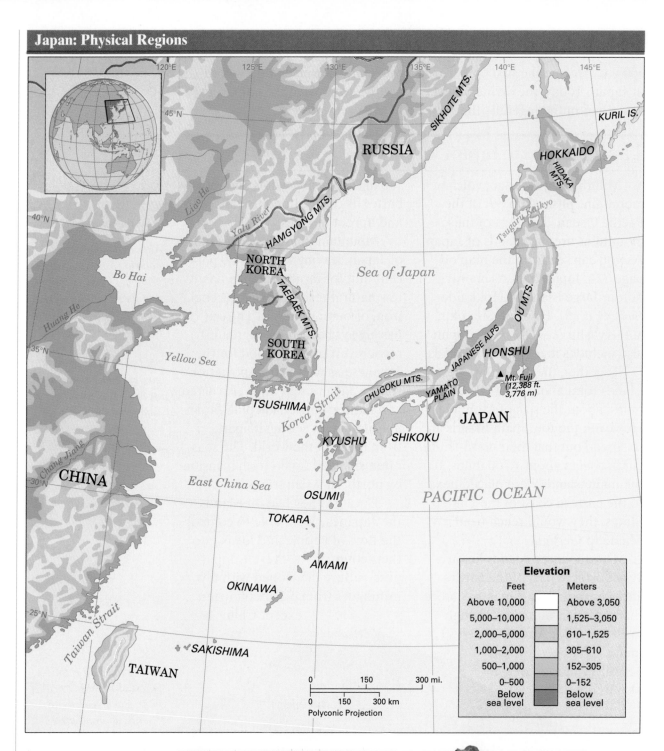

Japan: Physical Regions

RUSSIA

SIKHOTE MTS.

KURIL IS.

HOKKAIDO

HIDAKA MTS.

Liao He

Yalu River

HAMGYONG MTS.

NORTH KOREA

Bo Hai

Huang He

TAEBAEK MTS.

SOUTH KOREA

Yellow Sea

Sea of Japan

Tsugaru Kaikyo

OU MTS.

JAPANESE ALPS

HONSHU

Mt. Fuji
(12,388 ft.
3,776 m)

CHUGOKU MTS.

YAMATO PLAIN

TSUSHIMA

Korea Strait

KYUSHU

SHIKOKU

JAPAN

Chang Jiang

CHINA

East China Sea

OSUMI

PACIFIC OCEAN

TOKARA

AMAMI

OKINAWA

Taiwan Strait

SAKISHIMA

TAIWAN

0   150   300 mi.
0   150   300 km
Polyconic Projection

Elevation

Feet		Meters
Above 10,000		Above 3,050
5,000–10,000		1,525–3,050
2,000–5,000		610–1,525
1,000–2,000		305–610
500–1,000		152–305
0–500		0–152
Below sea level		Below sea level

▲ *On which island is Mount Fuji?*

➤ *Stone spearheads such as this show how people of the Jomon culture lived.*

The Early People of Japan

Despite its isolation, many peoples migrated to Japan. Stone tools and weapons found in Japan show that it has been inhabited for thousands of years.

Among the first people were hunter-gatherers who lived over 10,000 years ago. Other immigrants pushed them north about

200 to 100 B.C.
The Ainu *(EYE noo),* who live on Hokkaido, may be descendants of these hunter-gatherers.

Early Cultures

In about 8000 B.C., people of the Jomon *(JOH mahn)* culture, who probably came from Korea and northern Asia, first appeared in Japan. Ancient accumulations of shells, fishhooks, and harpoon points show that the Jomon were fishers and hunter-gatherers.

About 200 B.C., the Jomon culture was gradually replaced by a new, settled society known as Yayoi *(yah YOY)*. The Yayoi settled in the fertile Yamato plain on the largest island, Honshu.

The Yayoi introduced the cultivation of rice in water, after which rice became Japan's most important crop. The islands' summer rains made the climate ideal.

The Yayoi used metal tools to irrigate and level the land. This development changed the Japanese from hunter-gatherers to farmers.

Between A.D. 200 and 300, an even more complex culture began to replace the Yayoi. Archaeologists call this the "tomb culture." The people of this culture left huge graves filled with such things as bronze mirrors, crowns, and clay figurines of armor-clad warriors and horses. These objects suggest that rulers of this culture were from a respected warrior class.

Early Religion

The religion of early Japan, **Shinto**, revolved around nature.

Shinto teaches that the natural world is filled with divine spirits, or *kami*. The highest-ranking *kami*, the Sun Goddess, came to be identified with Japan's emperor.

Sometime after 400, one ruling warrior clan from the plains of southeastern Honshu became more powerful than other ruling clans. From this family came Japan's first emperor. He was the first of a line of emperors from one family that continues even today. You have read how this family was said to be descended from the Sun Goddess. The idea of the emperor being divine may have been influenced by ideas from China. ■

▲ *These "wedded rocks" are linked by a straw rope. In the Shinto religion, they are associated with the gods who created the islands of Japan.*

■ *How did the lifestyles of the peoples of the Jomon, Yayoi, and "tomb" cultures compare and contrast? How do we know?*

Korea and the Spread of Chinese Influence

By the 800s B.C., native peoples had established small tribal states in Korea, on the Asian mainland across from the Japanese islands. Rice growing had come to southern Korea from China some 2,000 years before. In 108 B.C., northwestern Korea was colonized by Han dynasty China, which set up military posts there. The trade that

followed began a concentrated cultural and commercial exchange between the two areas. In the rest of Korea, three conflicting kingdoms arose, Koryo in the northeast, Paekche *(behk CHAY)* in the southeast, and Silla in the southwest.

Beginning in Koryo in the 400s, Buddhism spread south from China into Korea. The courts took

▲ *The Jomon culture takes its name from its pottery, created by pressing cords into the wet clay.*

■ Why did Chinese cul-
ture spread throughout
Japan?

▼ At Kyongbok Palace in
Seoul, South Korea, the
Hyangwon Pavilion shows
the influence of Chinese
architecture. The Chinese
influence can also be seen
in the Great Buddha Hall
(at bottom), *one of the
largest buildings at Nara,
Japan, built in 745.*

on the new religion at first, then
the nobles, then the common
people. By the 660s, Silla had
unified the country and was sending Buddhist scholars and priests
to Japan.

The powerful Japanese Soga
clan thought Buddhism would
strengthen the government, as it
had in China. They fought to have
it accepted in Japan. In 593, Prince
Shotoku, one of their relatives,
came to rule as regent. He encouraged Buddhism and the spread of
Chinese culture.

Shinto linked the Japanese
to their homeland and their past.
But Buddhism was accepted along
with Shinto because it met spiritual
needs not met by Shinto. Buddhism promised rewards to the
faithful and the good.

After Prince Shotoku's death,
members of the government imposed a series of Chinese-style
changes called the Taika Reforms.
Under this plan, the government

declared that all farmland in the
provinces—areas outside the capital—was the property of the emperor. The land was divided into
small plots, and clan leaders were
assigned to oversee the land in
their territories. In this way the
central government gained more
control over the clans as well as
wealth from taxes on the land.

In 710, the government established a new capital called Nara in
the Yamato plain. Religion and art
flourished in Nara.

Although the Taika Reforms
reduced the power of the clans,
they had little effect on the lives of
the peasants, or poor farm workers. In a collection of Japanese
poems made about 700 and called
the *Man'yoshu*, an anonymous
poet described the hardships he
faced in the countryside:

*H*ere I lie on straw
Spread on bare earth,
With my parents at my pillow,
My wife and children at my
        feet,
All huddled in grief and tears.
Must it be so hopeless—
The way of this world?

As before, small farmers still gave
up part of their harvest. The difference was that after the reforms,
they gave it to government officials
instead of to clan leaders. ■

R E V I E W

1. **FOCUS** How did the geography of Japan influence its
   development?
2. **CONNECT** How is the history of Japan's first emperors
   different from that of China's early emperors?
3. **BELIEF SYSTEMS** Describe the Shinto religion. How is
   it related to the Japanese emperor?
4. **CULTURE** By what means did Prince Shotoku help

spread Chinese culture in Japan?
5. **CRITICAL THINKING** Contrast the effect of the Taika
   Reforms on the landowners and on the peasants.
6. **ACTIVITY** Find Japan on the maps on pages 530 and
   531 of the Atlas. How much of Japan is used for
   crops? What else do the maps tell you? Organize this
   information on the chalkboard.

LESSON 2

A Developing National Culture

L *ady Dainagon is very small and refined, white, beautiful, and round, though in [behavior] very lofty. Her hair is three inches longer than her height. She uses exquisitely carved hairpins. Her face is lovely, her manners delicate and charming.*

Lady Murasaki, *The Diary of Murasaki Shikibu*, c. 980–1015

This portrait tells us a lot about the qualities that were admired at the Japanese court around the year 1000. One important physical characteristic was a woman's hair. People thought the longer her hair, the lovelier the woman.

Because lightness of skin was admired, both women and men covered their faces with white powder. Women even blackened their teeth to heighten the effect. They also shaved their eyebrows and painted false ones high on their foreheads.

Members of the court wore clothing embroidered with gold, silver, and multicolored thread. A woman might wear 12 or more silk robes at one time, all tied with a single sash. The sleeve of each robe would be a different length so that the woman's arm was a rainbow of colors.

THINKING FOCUS

How did moving the capital to Kyoto affect the development of Japanese culture?

Key Terms

- regent
- courtier

◄ *Lady Dainagon might have used hairpins such as these.*

A Court of Refinement

The finely dressed women and men of the court lived in the new capital of Kyoto, then known as Heian. Here they developed a culture of refinement and luxury. The capital that had been established at Nara in 710 was abandoned because the power of the government was overwhelmed by that of the Buddhist clergy. Buddhist temples and monasteries were a center for cultural activity. However, the clergy tried to interfere in politics. After the move to Kyoto in 794, the emperor strictly limited the number of Buddhist temples and monasteries that could be built. In this way he limited Buddhist influences on his government. Moving the capital also had the effect of isolating Kyoto from events in the provinces.

Even before the court moved to Kyoto, nobles of the Fujiwara

▲ *This fragment of a scroll shows a court lady named Kodai no Kimi in her many layers of robes. Their costumes were so heavy that many women found it difficult to move.*

During this relatively peaceful period, Japanese culture flourished. Of the 100,000 people in Kyoto, only about 5 percent were **courtiers,** people who took part in the highly refined social life of the court. Nonetheless, it was these courtiers who created the culture of the period. Japanese literature and customs developed, using language and traditions that the courtiers had adopted from China.

The Kyoto court became one of highly refined manners and tastes, a place where delicacy was valued above all. Every action was thought to carry meaning and every event had great potential. Stories from the literature of the age tell of men falling in love with women after just a glimpse of hair from behind a screen.

The Shingon *(SHIHN gahn)* form of Buddhism was popular among courtiers. Shingon Buddhism involved elaborate ceremonies and rituals and stressed the importance of art and learning. Art, especially poetry and literature, became very important at the court of Kyoto. ■

clan had come to be the most powerful of the emperor's advisers. The Fujiwara were related to the emperor by marriage. To make sure that their power would grow, members of the clan continued to marry into the imperial family. In fact, it became the custom for imperial princes to marry Fujiwara women. Members of the Fujiwara clan served as **regents** for the emperor, exercising power in the emperor's name for most of the time between 858 and 1185. As the Fujiwara clan's power over the imperial family increased, high government offices became increasingly closed to other families. Also, the emperor became much more a religious symbol than a government leader.

■ *What were some of the activities of the courtiers at Kyoto?*

The Literature of the Court

Poetry was the favorite form of writing among Japanese courtiers. They composed short poems for every occasion, and poetry contests were very popular.

The courtiers greatly admired beauty, especially in nature. Their writing expresses a sentimental sadness at the fragile beauty of natural things. This feeling of sadness at the death of beauty is expressed by the Japanese word *aware (ah wah reh)*. What does this poem describe that might arouse feelings of *aware*?

*T*his perfectly still
Spring day bathed in
the soft light
From the spread-out sky,
Why do the cherry blossoms
So restlessly scatter down?

Ki no Tomonori, *Kokinshu*, c. 905

New Writing Systems

One thing Japan borrowed from China was its writing system. Formal writing was in Chinese, and so was early poetry. But because they wanted to express feelings in their own language, the Japanese developed a set of characters called *hiragana* to represent Japanese. *Hiragana* symbols represent syllables rather than words. Compare Chinese symbols and *hiragana* in the chart on this page. Why do you suppose that writing in *hiragana* allowed the Japanese to be more expressive than writing in Chinese? Women, who were not expected to learn Chinese, used *hiragana* to write some of the greatest literature of the age.

Diaries and Tales

After poetry, diaries were the favorite form of writing. These personal accounts help us understand the values of the times. For example, the diary of Murasaki Shikibu, a lady of the Fujiwaras, tells a great deal about the roles of women. Because she was a girl, she was not taught to read or write Chinese. She tells how she found a way to learn:

Writing Styles of Japan

Style	Words (shinto)	(haiku)	Description	Origin
Kanji	神道	俳句	Pictograms of concepts	Writing system adopted from Chinese characters
Hiragana	しんとう	はいく	Phonetic symbols of one syllable each	Writing system originated and simplified in Japan

> When my elder brother Shikubu no Jo was a boy, he was taught to read the Chinese classics. I listened, sitting beside him, and learned wonderfully fast, though he was sometimes slow and forgot. Father, who was devoted to study, regretted that I had not been a son.
>
> Lady Murasaki, *The Diary of Murasaki Shikibu*, c. 980–1015

▲ Hiragana *was developed during the 800s. Another style of Japanese writing,* katakana, *was developed later to spell words from foreign languages.*

The crowning literary achievement of this time was Murasaki's *Tale of Genji*, a long account of the life and loves of a fictional prince. Genji has the virtues valued by the Kyoto court: he is handsome and romantic. But the mood of the tale is often one of sadness. ■

■ *What kinds of literature developed at the court of Kyoto?*

▼ *Two ladies of the court watch as Prince Genji walks in the garden by moonlight.*

Life in the Provinces

Warrior Clans of Japan, 940–1150

Warrior Clans of Japan, 940–1150

Legend:
- Taira provinces
- Taira clan
- Minamoto clan
- Fujiwara clan
- Other clans
- ★ Provincial capital

▲ *What families were in power in the provinces?*

■ *How did life in the Japanese provinces differ from life at the Kyoto court?*

there was in the hands of provincial nobles.

Japan had a long tradition of private ownership of land. In the 600s, clans in the provinces had been unhappy with the Taika Reforms, which had broken up their lands and reduced their power. Taking advantage of the imperial government's involvement with court life, provincial nobles took over more and more land. By 1100, some provincial nobles had acquired large estates that were free of government control.

In order to avoid paying taxes and serving as soldiers in the imperial army, many small landowners gave over their land to the nobles. They ended up as tenant farmers, paying rent in crops for the privilege of farming land owned by the nobles. Others became carpenters or menial laborers on the huge private estates. Most peasants remained as poor and as miserable as ever, spending their days at back-breaking work and their nights in crowded huts.

The Kyoto courtiers were out of touch with all of this. They were isolated in a world of luxury and fine culture at Kyoto. The "dwellers among the clouds," as they were called, probably looked upon lowly workers as barely human. ■

The courtiers were able to live as they did because they were supported by what was produced in the provinces. Farmers paid part of what they grew to imperial tax collectors. Courtiers also collected part of what was produced on their private estates. But caught up in the life of the court, courtiers preferred to ignore the provinces. The responsibility for what went on

---

R E V I E W

1. **FOCUS** How did moving the capital to Kyoto affect the development of Japanese culture?

2. **CONNECT** Why was Buddhism able to coexist with Shinto in Japan?

3. **HISTORY** How did the central government's involvement with court life affect conditions for Japanese farmers?

4. **CRITICAL THINKING** What do you think might have been the eventual result of the isolation of the ruling class at Kyoto?

5. **WRITING ACTIVITY** Imagine that you are a member of the emperor's court at Kyoto. Write a diary entry that describes either clothing worn by courtiers or your daily life at court.

LESSON 3

The Power of the Shoguns

*J*omyo Meishu of Tsutsui . . . was attired in a dark blue hitatare, a suit of black-laced armor, and a five-plate helmet. At his waist, he wore a sword with a black lacquered hilt and scabbard. . . . He let fly a fast and furious barrage from his twenty-four arrow quiver, . . . He abandoned the weapon and fought with his sword.

Anonymous, from
The Tale of the Heike, 1100s

The passage you just read is from a collection of Japanese tales of war. It tells of a warrior monk. Warrior monks, and many more warriors who were not monks, were common in Japan during the 1100s. It was a time when many swords slashed and many arrows struck their marks.

Life for these warriors was clearly quite different from that of the Kyoto courtiers described in *The Tale of Genji*. How had they come to exist in Japan?

THINKING
FOCUS

What impact did samurai values have on Japanese culture and religion?

Key Terms

- shogun
- daimyo
- samurai
- denomination

◄ *This print of two warriors fighting with swords is from a famous series titled* One Hundred and Eight Popular Heroes *from* Shuihu zhuan.

231

Japan

A Warrior Government

As the Kyoto court maintained its isolation, lawlessness spread in the provinces. Rebellions of nobles and even of Buddhist monks were put down by the government.

The central government had long been dominated by the Fujiwara family. But as its income from taxes and its power over provincial nobles decreased, the government came to depend on warlike provincial nobles for help in putting down rebellions. Also, less powerful nobles came to depend on the most powerful clans for protection. It was a dangerous age, one in which men—and even a few women, as this description shows—won fame as warriors:

> *T*omoe was especially beautiful, with white skin, long hair, and charming features. She was also a remarkably strong archer. . . . Tomoe galloped into their midst, rode up alongside Moroshige, seized him in a powerful grip, pulled him down against the pommel of her saddle. . . . She discarded armor and helmet and fled toward the eastern provinces.
>
> Anonymous, from
> *The Tale of the Heike,* 1100s

In the 1100s, nobles of the Taira and Minamoto warrior clans battled for control. By 1185, the Minamoto were victorious. Led by Yoritomo, they set up a warrior government. In 1192, Yoritomo was given the title **shogun,** meaning "great general," by the emperor.

Because Yoritomo didn't want his warriors to be distracted by court life in Kyoto, he made his headquarters at Kamakura, near present-day Tokyo. The emperor continued to live at Kyoto. But the real power resided in the shogun's headquarters at Kamakura.

The Rise of the Samurai

The shogun was supported by the nobles who owned large estates in the provinces. These nobles became known as **daimyo** (DY mee oh). Each daimyo relied on warriors to protect his estate. As reward for their service, the warriors themselves won small pieces of land.

The warriors were called **samurai** (SAM uh ry), which means "those who serve." The samurai became a new class in society— mounted, armored warriors who often held positions as officials in the provinces. You can read more about a samurai warrior in A Moment in Time on page 233.

The Impact of Foreign Invasion

Under the Kamakura shoguns, Japan enjoyed stable rule and trade with China flourished. In the late 1200s, however, Japan was threatened by the Mongols under Kublai Khan. In 1274, when Mongol forces launched an attack from Korea across the Sea of Japan, they had to turn back because of a storm. But in 1281, Mongol forces numbering as many as 150,000 landed on Kyushu.

Cherry blossoms were sometimes used as a symbol for samurai in the literature and art of Japan. A samurai knew that his time on earth was likely to be as brief as the flowering of a cherry tree.

232

A Samurai

10:06 P.M., November 18, 1274
In a manor house on the Japanese
island of Kyushu

Note
He has tucked away the small piece of paper the messenger rushed to him. Our samurai's lord writes that the fierce Mongols will land at Hakata Bay tomorrow morning!

Armor
Made of small, strong iron plates, the suit still lets him swing his sword. Putting it on takes hours, but our samurai expected this battle. He assembled the armor days ago and left it waiting on a stand.

Long Sword
Fired red-hot, folded, and hammered sharp a hundred times, the long blade is called the soul of a samurai. He never goes anywhere without it.

Helmet
The lacquered metal smells of incense, which the samurai burns inside the helmet. He does this so that if an enemy cuts off his head, it will smell sweet.

Mask
It was designed to terrify his enemies and it will. The polished iron face is strong enough to stop a spear.

233

▲ *This beautifully decorated saddle belonged to a shogun of the 1500s. It symbolizes two arts of samurai tradition—the arts of war and peace.*

■ *How were the warrior governments organized?*

The Mongols used crossbows that shot farther than Japanese arrows, and catapults that hurled flaming bombs. But the samurai, relying on their swords, fought fiercely. After 50 days of battle, a great typhoon helped the Japanese achieve victory. The winds and rains rolled over Kyushu, destroying the Mongol fleet. The Japanese called the typhoon the *kamikaze,* or "divine wind," believing that their gods had aided them.

After the Mongols had been repelled a second time, the Kamakura shogunate was plagued by economic troubles caused by the war. The government was unable to reward the samurai for their military services. Angry and resentful, a huge army of samurai marched into Kamakura and burned it to the ground. After a series of battles, a new shogunate founded by the Ashikaga family took over Japan. In 1392, it moved the shogun's headquarters back to Kyoto. There the warriors married into noble families and adopted the ways of the Kyoto courtiers, receiving instruction in etiquette, literature, and music.

The Ashikaga shogunate lasted until the late 1500s through times of peace as well as war. Together, the Kamakura and Ashikaga shogunates make up the period of history, from 1185 to about 1600, known as medieval Japan. ■

Development of Religious Denominations

During medieval times, Buddhism changed to reflect the needs of the Japanese people. Different religious groups, or **denominations,** of Buddhism developed.

Pure Land Buddhism, for example, stressed chanting the name of Amida Buddha. Amida is considered to be a spiritual Buddha who lived many eons ago. Amida was supposed to have established a paradise in the west, beyond the setting sun. His believers would chant his name while watching the sun set. This denomination dif-

➤ *This painting on silk represents the Amida Buddha.*

fered from earlier types of Buddhism in stressing happiness in afterlife rather than finding peace, or enlightenment, in life on earth. It taught that believers would be reborn in a blissful, pure land, or paradise. Amida Buddhism became more popular in Japan as disorder increased in the countryside. It was popular among peasants as well as the upper classes.

One of the most controversial denominations in Japan was founded by the monk Nichiren in the 1200s. Nichiren taught that the only truth was to be found in the Lotus

Sutra, believed to be the Buddha's last teaching. All other denominations were false, he taught, and unless Japan turned from these false religions, it would perish.

Disciples of Zen Buddhism were concerned with individual enlightenment more than national well-being. Zen taught that physical and mental exercise would produce a sudden recognition of the nature of existence.

As the samurai class became important, Zen became more popular. Zen appealed to many samurai, partly because it stressed exacting spiritual and physical discipline as the path to enlightenment. The samurai themselves had been through harsh physical training, and approved the discipline required of Zen converts.

Also, some Zen masters scoffed at book learning and at logic and other mental skills. They taught that enlightenment would come only by breaking away from logic. Zen students were required to sit still while they meditated for hours on seemingly absurd puzzles such as "What is the sound of one hand clapping?" This form of meditation pleased some early samurai warriors who could not read. ■

■ *How was Japanese society affected by Zen Buddhism?*

A Unified Culture

Buddhism greatly influenced the arts of medieval Japan. Zen, for example, stressed the importance of the moment. It taught that a person who is in a hurry to complete something fails to experience the natural world fully. Zen art stressed the process, the way that activities were performed.

This emphasis on process can be seen in arts and ceremonies that developed in medieval Japan and are still practiced today. For example, the tea ceremony was first developed by Zen priests and then adopted by members of the court. As you can see in the pictures below, the tea ceremony has continued into modern times.

Process, in the form of gestures and dance steps, is emphasized as well in Japanese Noh drama, which

▼ *After many years, every movement in a tea ceremony became formalized and took on special meaning.*

A Japanese Tea Ceremony

After rinsing their hands and mouths with water from a wooden dipper, guests crawl through a small passageway to enter the tea room.

The scroll one sees on entering the alcove is a single line of calligraphy, often drawn by a Zen priest. Guests spend some time examining the scroll, clearing the mind in preparation for the ceremony.

The host enters and serves a light meal, which is followed by tea.

Tea bowls are made by hand. Their shape varies according to the time of the year. The "winter" bowl shown here is deeper than a "summer" bowl would be.

In this garden established at a Zen temple about 1450, each detail provides a subject for meditation.

place for meditation. Zen emphasizes severity and restraint, as well as appreciation for simple and natural forms. The rock gardens consist only of rocks and of sand raked in patterns. The rocks are placed so as to suggest natural things, such as a mountain canyon, a beach, or a seascape. Gardeners sometimes search for years for just the right rock to place in a garden.

Flower arranging, incense blending, and painting are other medieval art forms influenced by Buddhism. Most of these art forms are still popular in Japan today. ■

developed from both Shinto and Buddhist forms of worship. A masked dancer, supported by minor players and a chorus, presents a slow dance-drama. The actors wear lavish costumes of gold brocade and vivid colors, but the stage is bare. The script is very poetic, and the plot is simple.

Another form of art that shows Buddhist influence is the Japanese garden. Buddhism teaches that people are a part of nature, and Buddhist gardeners thus find their art in nature. Rock gardens are often found at Zen temples. The gardens are meant to provide a calm, quiet

➤ *Most Noh plays concern an encounter between a troubled spirit and a priest or bystander. People dance the action of the plays and chant to the music of a flute and drum. The demon mask was used in Noh dramas of the 1200s.*

■ *What new art forms developed in medieval Japan?*

REVIEW

1. **FOCUS** What impact did samurai values have on Japanese culture and religion?
2. **CONNECT** Compare and contrast the values and achievements of the Japanese courtiers with those of the samurai.
3. **CITIZENSHIP** Ceremony is important in all cultures. What are some occasions in the United States

where ceremony is important? What formal gestures are used in these ceremonies?
4. **CRITICAL THINKING** Why might Zen Buddhism have appealed to many samurai?
5. **ACTIVITY** Based on what you have learned about the tea ceremony, develop a ceremony or ritual for serving a beverage or food in your classroom.

LESSON 4

Japan: Unified Yet Isolated

General Oda Nobunaga had, by 1591, begun to unify his war-ravaged country. One of his major battles was against a Buddhist monastery whose monks had dared to help an enemy army. He ordered his warriors to destroy all 3,000 buildings of the monastery and kill all 20,000 within. His officers pleaded with him not to do this, but he remained firm.

Nobunaga's forces encircled the monastery. With ferocious cries, they stormed the center, burning the buildings and destroying all within—priceless books and art, monks, soldiers, even children. Nobunaga explained his orders this way:

I have devoted myself to the hardships of warrior life in order that I might restrain the turbulence within the land. [But these monks] are themselves traitors to the country. If . . . they are not destroyed now, they will again become a peril to the nation.

Oda Nobunaga, from
Hoan Nobunaga-ki, c. 1570

This and similar acts of such great violence were not unusual in Japan during the late medieval period. By the late 1400s, both the shogun and the emperor had become dependent on whatever daimyo happened to control the capital.

THINKING FOCUS

Why did the Tokugawa shoguns want to keep Japan isolated?

Key Terms

- succession
- haiku

◄ *Independent warrior clans throughout Japan made constant raids on enemy camps, as seen in this detail from a scroll.*

237

Japan

1185, The Minamoto clan crushes the Taira family and rules from Kamakura.

1274, Mongols make their first attempt to invade Japan.

| 1200 | 1300 | 1400 | 1500 |

➤ *A samurai warrior would have been proud to own this steel sword, which was made in the 1100s. When did Japan take the final step to isolate itself from the West?*

➤ *This statue of Toku-gawa Ieyasu marks his tomb. Ieyasu was from a peasant family, but established a line of rulers.*

▼ *White Heron castle near Kyoto was begun in 1581 by Hideyoshi and completed in 1609 by a member of the Tokugawa clan. To reach it, an enemy would have had to pass through 11 barricades. However, the castle was never attacked.*

An All-Powerful Shogunate

Weakened by court life in Kyoto, the Ashikaga shogunate had been unable to keep control. Warring nobles had nearly destroyed the capital in a struggle for power. In the provinces, various daimyo fought for control.

Wars of Unification

From the midst of this chaos emerged Oda Nobunaga—a powerful leader, fierce and stubborn. Recognizing the limitations of swords and arrows, he armed his troops with muskets, which had been introduced to Japan by Portuguese traders. With his more modern army, Nobunaga soon controlled more than a third of the country.

After Nobunaga's death, one of his generals, Toyotomi Hideyoshi, took control and within five years

conquered all the remaining provinces. When Hideyoshi died in 1598, another power struggle followed. In 1600, Tokugawa Ieyasu *(ih yeh YAH soo)* was victorious. He became shogun in 1603.

The Tokugawa Shogunate

Tokugawa Ieyasu established his shogunate in Edo, now called Tokyo. There he built a nearly indestructible fortress. In 1605, he turned over the shogunate to his son. Ieyasu thus established a line of **succession,** or inheritance, of the shogunate, much like that of a kingship. The Tokugawa shogunate was to last for more than 250 years.

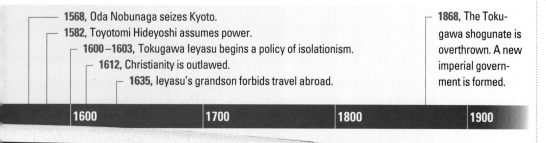

1568, Oda Nobunaga seizes Kyoto.
1582, Toyotomi Hideyoshi assumes power.
1600–1603, Tokugawa Ieyasu begins a policy of isolationism.
1612, Christianity is outlawed.
1635, Ieyasu's grandson forbids travel abroad.

1868, The Tokugawa shogunate is overthrown. A new imperial government is formed.

1600 1700 1800 1900

Under the Tokugawa each daimyo was required to swear an oath of loyalty to the shogun and to give military aid when called upon. In addition, each daimyo had to spend part of every other year in Edo, serving the shogun. The daimyo were forced to leave their wives and eldest sons in Edo when they returned to the provinces.

Foreigners in Japan

When Portuguese traders reached Japan in 1542, they also brought Catholic missionaries.

By the early 1600s, the shogunate saw these foreigners as a threat. The Tokugawa knew of Europe's religious and political wars. They feared the turmoil might spread to Japan. Also, they feared that if the daimyo became rich from foreign trade, they might rebel.

Between 1612 and 1635, therefore, the shogunate issued decrees that outlawed Christianity, restricted travel, and banned virtually all European trade. In effect, Japan was set on a policy of strict isolation from western influences. ■

■ *What steps did the Tokugawa shoguns take to unify Japan?*

UNDERSTANDING ISOLATION

The islands of Japan were cut off, or isolated, from other countries. Even so, in the 1630s, Japan's government felt the need to adopt a policy of political and economic isolation. How were these kinds of isolation different?

Kinds of Isolation

Mountains, jungles, or seas can isolate a culture. This is geographic isolation. For example, the Hawaiian islands were unknown to the rest of the world until Captain James Cook landed there in 1778.

Japan's isolation in the 1630s was deliberate. In America today, the Amish deliberately isolate themselves from the culture that surrounds them. Living in farming communities in Pennsylvania and the Midwest, they practice simplicity as a religiously dictated way of life and do not use modern inventions such as electricity or telephones.

Results of Isolation

Geographic, or deliberate, isolation limits the influences of other cultures and often strengthens the unique qualities of a culture.

Also, isolation limits technological and commercial growth. An isolated culture cannot borrow or adapt the ideas of other cultures. For Japan of the 1800s, the lure of increased trade and new knowledge was to make isolation less attractive than it had been.

239

Japan

Control of the Classes

The shogunate enforced a strict social system designed to preserve a traditional Japan. There were four official classes below the shogun and daimyo. From highest to lowest they were samurai warriors, artisans, peasants, and merchants.

Restrictions on Each Class

To keep the daimyo in line, the shogun made them swear an oath of allegiance. The shogun took away the warriors' lands and instead paid them salaries for their services. The once-illiterate samurai learned to read and write and became educated administrators.

Since artisans didn't threaten the shogun's control, few restrictions were placed on them. They thrived in towns, selling their wares to samurai and merchants.

Peasants made up the bulk of the population. Because they were so numerous, the government placed many restrictions on them. Peasants were forbidden to travel beyond the land on which they worked. Also, tax collectors took about half of their crops, leaving them with just enough to survive.

At the bottom of the social scale were the merchants. Merchants had to live within towns and were excluded from political affairs. Finally, merchants were not allowed to dress lavishly or to live in luxury.

The Rise of the Merchant Class

Despite government regulations, the merchant class prospered. More and more merchants were needed to bring food, cloth, and other goods to Edo. They also traded in other cities where the daimyo and their followers might stop to rest.

Before the Tokugawa era, money was not much used in Japan. But merchants found money much less bulky to carry than the bushels of rice traditionally used for trade. By 1600, gold and silver coins were in use, and by 1700, Japan's economy was based largely on money. Merchants controlled the flow of money by setting prices and charging interest on loans. They grew rich from their trade and their power grew with their wealth. ■

Across Time & Space

In 1996 the tiny, mineral-poor islands of Japan accounted for 17.4 percent of the world's gross domestic product (GDP). GDP is the total value of all the goods and services produced in a country during a single year.

■ *How did Japan's economy change during the Tokugawa era?*

➤ *A daimyo and his samurai warriors make their way to Edo. Daimyo were required to spend part of each year at the shogun's court.*

A New and Different Culture

The merchants had leisure time and money. They spent it on new forms of entertainment that became available in cities. In the late 1600s, areas of cities were set aside as pleasure quarters. There city dwellers could find theaters, teahouses, gambling houses, wrestling, and public baths.

The upper classes officially scorned these amusements as lower-class entertainment. They clung to the traditional arts such as Noh theater and the tea ceremony. Still, they allowed the pleasure centers to prosper and gradually were attracted there themselves.

Some of the new cultural forms, such as Kabuki theater, were long lasting. Kabuki theater had its origins in performances of wandering ballad singers and dancers, who acted out stories by dancing and gesturing. Kabuki, which is still popular today, was a rich blend of music, dance, and mime, and involved spectacular staging and costumes. The plays' subjects ranged from adventures of brave samurai to tales of romance and broken hearts.

Besides plays for the Kabuki theater, new forms of literature also included epic novels about samurai exploits and short poems called **haiku.** A haiku is a poem of three lines that is intended to create a mood or bring about a sudden insight into human existence. A haiku has 17 syllables. The first line has five syllables, the second seven, and the third five. Matsuo Basho, one of Japan's greatest poets, wrote hundreds of haiku, including the following:

 Old pond:
Frog jump-in
Water-sound.

Matsuo Basho, Untitled, 1686

During the 1500s and 1600s, education spread to all classes, to varying degrees, and the economy boomed. When Japan emerged from its self-imposed isolation and reopened its doors in 1854, the West saw a unique and successful civilization. ■

▲ *Small bunraku puppets were often used in plays performed in the cities. Entertainment and everyday scenes were common subjects of prints such as the one below.*

Southeast Asia

In the first thousand years A.D., Southeast Asia was greatly influenced by China and India. Goods and ideas were exchanged in what are now Burma, Thailand, Laos, Cambodia, Vietnam, Malaysia, Singapore, Indonesia, Brunei, and the Philippines. The earliest towns in the region seem to have been started in Vietnam, as shown by the great stone fortifications at Co Lao *(koh LWAH)*. In addition, there were many trade and religious centers around which farmers or fishers lived.

From early times, Hindu ideas and styles spread into the area, affecting Southeast Asian ideas about monarchy, law, religion, art,

■ *What role did the new merchant class play in the development of a new popular culture?*

architecture, and language. The states that grew there were often Hindu or Buddhist or both. Chinese influences were more political and military. The mighty rulers of China forced these states to pay tribute or be taken over.

Outside Influences

China ruled Vietnam as a province from about 100 B.C. to A.D. 900. In addition to using Vietnamese trade networks, China was eager to use the expert sailing skills of the local people to export its silk and spices. The Vietnamese would sail to the islands of Indonesia. Ships from Indonesia carried goods to Malaya. From there, Indian ships would take the goods west. Indian traders often settled in the Southeast Asian ports. At the trading city of Oc Eo (ahk YOH) in Cambodia, archaeologists found ancient Roman coins and Indian jewelry.

Islam first came to Southeast Asia at Perlak, on the northern coast of Sumatra, in the 1290s. It spread gradually through the islands and into the mainland. Many of the port cities and coastal states welcomed Islam not only as a religion, but also as a way of cementing ties with the Muslim traders who came from Arabia and

■ *How did outside influences from China, India, and the rest of the world affect Southeast Asian civilizations?*

Persia. With the profits of trading, some powerful leaders challenged and overthrew the older inland states, whose wealth was based on agriculture. The richest and strongest of the new Muslim states was Malacca, on the west coast of Malaya.

Trade and Resources

Malacca became the center of trade for Southeast Asia in the 1500s. It lay at the junction of the Indian, China, and Java seas. Here traders from as far away as Europe came for cottons and silks, pepper and cloves, perfumes and dyes. When European powers found a direct sea route to Southeast Asia, they began a period of colonization for many Southeast Asian states.

Besides international trade, there was much trade between regions, the coastal areas, the inland regions, and the islands. Southeast Asia is rich in resources. The people's system of agriculture raised enough rice to feed a large population. They domesticated many plants and exported many, including yams. Some plants were used for dyes, others for medicines, and others to eat. Some regions exported timber, oils, resins (a tree product used for inks and varnishes), or minerals. ■

R E V I E W

1. **FOCUS** Why did the Tokugawa shoguns want to keep Japan isolated?
2. **CONNECT** How did the Tokugawa shogunate go about creating stability that had been lacking in medieval Japan?
3. **ECONOMICS** What was the role of the merchants within Japan's early economy?
4. **GEOGRAPHY** How did the geography of Southeast Asia

contribute to its religious diversity?
5. **CRITICAL THINKING** How does the phrase "it takes money to make money" apply to the merchant class under the Tokugawa shogunate?
6. **WRITING ACTIVITY** Write a haiku of your own, following the form explained on page 241. Use a single image from nature as the subject of your haiku.

242

Recognizing Assumptions

Here's Why

Suppose you are planning a party. You choose pizza for food because you assume that most people like to eat pizza. An assumption is an idea that is accepted as fact without proof or demonstration. Often the assumption is so deeply rooted in a culture or in an individual's beliefs that it is not even stated.

For example, look at the picture of court women from *The Tale of Genji*. You might assume that women played a subordinate role in Japan in the 900s. However, you learned in Lesson 2 that Lady Murasaki contributed greatly to Japanese culture, writing perhaps the world's first novel.

Most assumptions can be proven to be either true or false, depending on the actual facts. In either case, you need to be aware of your unstated assumptions in order to correctly evaluate your conclusions.

Here's How

Assumptions that are correct can help you make sound decisions quickly even when you don't have all the facts. Incorrect assumptions, on the other hand, can cause you to make poor and even harmful decisions. Use the following steps to help you identify and evaluate your assumptions.

First, put your assumptions into words. Try to express in words exactly what ideas you accept as facts that influenced your decision or your feelings.

Second, identify the basis of your assumptions. Think about why you hold certain assumptions. Many useful assumptions are based on experience. Others are an unquestioned part of a culture or of certain religious beliefs. Remember that people in different cultures have different values. Be careful not to apply your assumptions to cultures where they are not appropriate.

Third, check your assumptions for accuracy. Be sure you have enough accurate information to test your assumptions. When you test your assumptions against more accurate or more complete information, you may find that they are incorrect.

Try It

Reread The Impact of Foreign Invasion on pages 232 and 233 in Lesson 3. Think about what assumptions you might make about the intensity and outcome of the battle. Then follow the three steps listed in Here's How. How well did the facts bear out your assumptions? On what factors were your assumptions based? What factors did your assumptions leave out?

Apply It

Write a sentence or two identifying the assumptions that might have led to each of these actions. Explain on what the assumptions might have been based.

1. You expect a homework assignment. However, you make plans to go to a volleyball game.
2. You go with friends to a local park and they suggest swimming in a lake you've never been in before. You dive into the water.

243

Chapter Review

Reviewing Key Terms

courtier (p. 228) samurai (p. 232)
daimyo (p. 232) denomination (p. 234)
haiku (p. 241) Shinto (p. 225)
isolation (p. 223) shogun (p. 232)
regent (p. 228) succession (p. 238)

A. Be sure you understand the meanings of the key terms. Then answer each question by writing one or more sentences.

1. How did courtiers influence the culture of Japan between 858 and 1185?
2. What title means "great general"?
3. Which Japanese religion had many denominations?
4. How was a line of succession to the title "shogun" established?

B. Write whether each statement below is *true* or *false.* Then rewrite the false statements to make them true.

1. Japan's seas have kept Japan in isolation from much of the world.
2. The religion of early Japan, Shinto, revolved around ancient feudal rites.
3. The nobles who owned large estates became known as daimyo.
4. In the 1600s, poets in Japan often wrote haiku, poems with exactly 17 lines.
5. Japanese warriors were called samurai, which means "those who rule."
6. From 858–1185, members of the Fujiwara clan were often regents for the emperor.

Exploring Concepts

A. Copy the timeline below on your own paper. After each date, write the importance of the date in the history of Japan. The first entry is done for you.

B. Answer each question with information from the chapter.

1. How did Shinto lead to a political tradition for the emperors of Japan?
2. What role did Korea play in the spread of Chinese culture in Japan in the late 500s?
3. What changes were made by the Taika Reforms? What were the results?

4. What values characterized the court at Kyoto?
5. What task were the clan leaders given under the Taika Reforms? Instead of performing this task, what did they do while the courtiers were preoccupied?
6. How were the Mongols defeated in 1281? What effect did the Mongol invasion have on the Japanese government?
7. What decrees did the Tokugawa shogunate issue between 1612 and 1635? What was the effect of these decrees?
8. When Japan reopened its doors to foreigners in 1854, how had it changed?

593, Prince Shotoku rules and encourages Buddhism.

750   1000   1250   1500   1750

1281, _____

1603, _____

794, _____

1635, _____   1854, _____

Reviewing Skills

1. Turn to page 225 and read the paragraphs in the first column that describe the Yayoi culture. The last sentence of this section is, "These objects suggest that rulers of this culture were from a respected warrior class." What assumption does the author make in this sentence?
2. Read the first paragraph on page 239. The Tokugawa shoguns forced the daimyo to leave their wives and eldest sons at the shogun's court in Edo when the daimyo returned to the provinces they governed. What assumptions did the shogun make about the daimyo?
3. Use an atlas to find out which areas of Japan have few cities. Then look at the topographical map of Japan on page 224. What geographical features might account for the lack of cities in certain areas?
4. You want to summarize the history of Japan on a poster that shows the most important historic events. What graphic device would you use to give visual impact to written facts and dates?

Using Critical Thinking

1. The men and women of the Kyoto court lived very different lives from the rest of the Japanese people. What were the positive effects of their lifestyles at court? What were the negative effects?
2. During the late 1500s, General Oda Nobunaga began to unify Japan. He destroyed a Buddhist monastery and its 20,000 residents because the monks inside had dared to help an enemy army. Do you think his actions were justified? Why or why not?
3. Why did Yoritomo want his warriors to live in Kamakura instead of Kyoto? What do you think he feared might happen if they went to Kyoto?
4. In the early 1600s, the shogunate issued decrees that set Japan on a policy of isolation. When Japan emerged from its isolation in 1854, the West saw a unique and successful civilization. What do you think would happen if the United States began a policy of isolation, including an end to foreign trade, today?

Preparing for Citizenship

1. COLLECTING INFORMATION Japan experiences more than 1,500 earthquakes a year, though most are mild. Find out what causes earthquakes and where the world's major earthquakes occur. To what extent can they be predicted? How do people try to control earthquake damage, especially in cities?
2. WRITING ACTIVITY Japan, an isolated nation, developed a unique and successful civilization. Locate other island nations on a globe. Choose one to study. Find out for how long, and to what extent, this nation was isolated. How much, in spite of isolation, was it influenced by other nations? Write a brief report describing the nation you chose.
3. GROUP ACTIVITY Today most Japanese people live in urban areas. Find out which of the cities mentioned in this chapter are major cities of Japan today. What are Japanese cities like? How are they similar to cities in Western countries? How are they different?
4. COLLABORATIVE LEARNING Work in committees to study different kinds of Japanese arts, such as haiku poetry, the tea ceremony, and Kabuki theater. Using information you find, create a sample of the art form you study. One committee might recite a poem and another perform a skit for the class. As a class, discuss how the art forms of a country help its people take pride in their nation.

Unit 5

Medieval Societies

Today is tournament day, and the squires display the helmets of their knights for all to see. The nobles of the castle gather with the peasants of the countryside to watch the bold warriors. Soon the knights will mount their horses, grab their lances, and demonstrate their battle skills. These are the men who defend the European castles and set out on holy crusades for the glory of their kings and their God.

330

The Showing of the Helms Before the Tournament, from Livre des Tournois du Roi Rene. Bibliotheque Nationale, Paris

1450

Chapter 10
Feudal Europe and Japan

A castle rises high on a rocky mount, defended by massive stone walls. Such fortresses protected people in both Europe and Japan from invaders about 1,000 years ago. The sturdy stone walls, three feet thick, shielded peasants from attack. The peasants paid for their safety by serving the lord of the castle or giving him land. This arrangement, called the feudal system, ruled life in Europe and Japan for centuries.

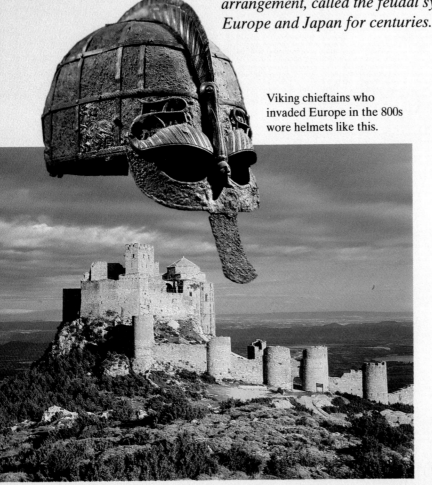

Viking chieftains who invaded Europe in the 800s wore helmets like this.

c. 900–1100 To protect their castles, European landowners build walls with rounded turrets that are difficult to attack. This castle was built along the border of present-day France and Spain.

| 400 | 700 | 1000 |

c. 700 Ghana becomes the first large West African trading empire.

476

Japanese artisans created beautiful war implements for samurai. These sword guards, made in the 1700s, separated the sword handle from the blade.

c. 1100–1854 Like European knights, samurai defend Japanese estates. This samurai armor, made of steel, silk, and bronze, dates to between 1338 and 1573.

1300

1600

1900

c. 1530 The Inca conquer much of South America.

1854

The Story of Roland

Katharine Pyle

Writers of all times revisit historical stories. The work this story is based upon was written in the 1100s. We know that warriors in the time of Charlemagne, the 800s, were not easy to organize and command. By the 1100s, however, loyalty, obedience, and respect for authority were admired traits. Which attitudes are illustrated in this story of Charlemagne?

In this chapter you will read about an age of kings, lords, and knights. "The Story of Roland" is one of the most famous tales from that age.

Charlemagne
(SHAHR luh mayn)

King Charlemagne had a sister Bertha whom he loved above all others of his sisters. Gentle she was, and beautiful, and kind, and Charlemagne thought to marry her to some great noble of his land, or to some foreign Prince or King, for she was worthy of the greatest.

But Bertha loved the young Count Milan. He was of noble birth but poor, and Charlemagne, in his pride, forbade the match.

But Bertha and the Count loved each other so dearly that even their awe of Charlemagne could not keep the two apart, and one night they were married secretly by a wandering priest.

When Charlemagne learned of this, as he needs must, his anger was so great he had the young pair driven from the court. He would not speak of them or hear their names. All were forbidden to give them aid or comfort, and they were even excommunicated by the Pope, at Charlemagne's desire.

And now the young couple were in wretched case. They had no home, and none dared shelter them, or even give them food, lest they bring down the wrath of Charlemagne upon their heads. The two wandered away from court, forlorn and desperate, not knowing what to do, or where to turn, until at last they disguised themselves as beggars, and so begged their way through France and into Italy. There they took shelter in a cave near to the town of Sutri, and in that cave their child was born; a son, whom they named Roland.

The people of the town were kind, and brought them food, and clothing for the babe; but Milan said, "I can no longer bear with pity and with alms. I will go forth to some far country, and will there take service under some foreign King who has no fear of Charlemagne. So I will win a home for thee, and for our babe."

Then Bertha wept bitterly, but would not say him nay, for as long as they stayed in any land where Charlemagne had power they always must keep in hiding, lest he find them out, and wreak his wrath on them.

So Milan bade his wife farewell and journeyed forth. But he did not journey far, for he was drowned in crossing a river there in Italy.

This news was brought to Bertha, and such was her grief that for a time it seemed that she must die with sorrowing. But time went on, and she had still her son, and all her love was turned to him, so that her grief was eased.

And Roland grew to be a lad of noble bearing, strong and tall, and having eyes strangely like Charlemagne's, they were so brightly blue, and clear, and keen as any hawk's.

Now, as it chanced, the Governor of Sutri had married another sister of King Charlemagne, and had a son Oliver of the same age as Roland. Also the two were much of the same height and strength and noble bearing, and he had the same blue eyes, and ruddy coloring, so that those who saw the two boys together wondered much that they should be so like; for no one guessed that they were cousins. Even Roland had not been told of that, nor told that he was a nephew of the mighty Charlemagne of whom he heard so many wondrous tales. His mother feared that if he learned this some harm might come of it.

And Roland's clothes were scarcely more than rags, but the boys of the town had grown to love him, and two who were the sons of merchants begged for him some cloth, and brought it to the cave. The cloth one brought was red, the other brought him white, and out of these Bertha fashioned a tunic for her son.

Full early he became a leader 'mongst the boys, but Oliver would be a leader too. So he challenged Roland to a wrestling match, that they might prove which was the better, and the fittest for the leadership. The place chosen for the contest was a field outside the town, and many came to watch, but Roland told Bertha naught of what was planned.

The two lads, having reached the place, stripped off their outer clothing and stood forth facing each other eye to eye, and foot to foot. Then suddenly, as with one thought they sprang together and seized each other and they wrestled up and down, each striving to throw the other, but neither could succeed. So for a long time they struggled up and down and back and forth. They put forth all their strength and every trick they knew, but neither could best the other. They strove until the sun, that had been high, sank toward the west, and till their breath came whistling from their throats, and till their hearts seemed like to burst.

Then those who were watching cried, "It is enough. Give over! or ye will kill yourselves. 'Tis plain that neither can best the other." But even as they spoke, Roland gave a sudden twist, and shifted his hold, and he caught Oliver by the waist, and threw him down, and held him with his head and back pressed to the earth till Oliver cried, "Enough! I yield me!"

Then Roland drew away and rose, and Oliver too; Oliver said, "Thou art the better one; the fittest for the leadership."

But Roland answered, "Nay, it was by chance I threw thee; thou and I will lead together."

Those who heard shouted with joy of this; and the two lads put on their clothing, and embraced and went away together. And from that very time a friendship sprang up between them, and a love greater almost than that of brothers. It was a love that lasted all their lives, and never changed nor faltered even till that day when both died on the same field of battle.

Now Roland at this time was ten years old, and Charlemagne, his uncle, had become so great and famous that he was to come to Rome and there be crowned as Emperor by the Pope.

The way to Rome led through the town of Sutri, and the King had planned to spend the night there with the Governor.

Roland had gone forth with the other lads to see the Emperor come riding in with all his retinue. The Governor came forth to meet him, and it was a splendid sight.

Roland was standing somewhat apart from all the other boys, and as the King passed it seemed to him that Charlemagne looked at him, kindly, and with more than a passing glance.

And Roland hastened home, and said to his mother, "I have seen King Charlemagne and, mother, he seemed to look at me almost as though he knew me. He is the kingliest man, methinks, of any in the world. I would I were a knight to ride beside him, or a Paladin. How I would love and serve him."

And Bertha said, in a low voice, "He is indeed a man to love and serve, yet he can be cruel, too, unjust and stern."

But Roland heeded not; he said, "My mother, thou hast told me that my father was a knight and of a noble lineage. Why should I not go to Charlemagne and tell him who I am and how I long to serve him? Then, perchance, he would send me as a page to some great house, and I might afterward become a knight, and fight with him in wars."

But Bertha said, "Listen to me, my son. Thou art well grown and wise beyond thy years. Now I will tell thee something thou hast never known. But promise first that thou wilt never tell this thing that I reveal to thee, but keep it secret."

Then Roland promised eagerly, for he was curious to know the secret.

Then Bertha told him that this King he longed to serve was her own brother; told him of how she and her dear husband had been driven from the court, and of his father's death. Last of all she said, "Thou seest now why thou mayst

Paladin high-ranking knight of Charlemagne's court

never go to the King, nor seek his favor, nor in any way reveal thyself to him."

And Roland's face had grown as red as fire, and his eyes blazed with anger, and his hands were clenched until the knuckles whitened. And Bertha, ending her story, wept, not for herself, but for her husband, who was dead and for their son, who must endure this poverty. But Roland said, between his teeth, "The King is feasting even now off yonder with the Governor, while thou, his sister, scarcely hast a crust. But trust me, thou shalt share this feast, my mother"; and he made as if to leave the cave. But Bertha caught him by the sleeve and cried, "What wouldst thou do, my son?"

Roland made answer, "Naught that I should not do," and freed himself, but gently, and went forth, and made his way to the Governor's castle. There he entered in, and came on to the hall where Charlemagne feasted. And many a noble knight was there, and ladies, richly dressed.

But Roland took no heed of them. He came on through the hall and to the King, and said to him, "My mother is hungry, and it is not meet that she should fast while ye have plenty here, and still to spare." And he took up the dish of food that had been set before the King, also his goblet filled with wine, and turned to leave the hall.

meet proper

But those about cried out and rose and would have caught hold of Roland; but Charlemagne hindered them. "Let the boy go," he said, for suddenly he remembered a dream that he had had not long before.

In his dream he had heard his sister Bertha calling him, and she was in deep distress. Then in his dream the love he once had felt for her returned, and he sought everywhere to find her, but he found her not. Then a lad like to the one who had but now gone from the hall, came to him and took him by the hand and said, "Come now with me, and I will take thee to thy sister Bertha, for she is my mother."

Charlemagne went with him in his dream, and so came to a cave and found his sister there, and she was weeping. Then it seemed to him his heart would break with pity for her grief, and he had cried, "Bertha!" and with that cry had wakened, and it was all a dream.

But it was because of that he had let the lad go free, and now he bade the attendants follow him secretly and see which way he went. If it was to his mother, and the food and wine were indeed for her, then they were to bring both son and mother back with them, not with roughness but as though they honored them.

As they were bidden so the attendants did. They followed Roland but so stealthily that he did not know of it, and so came to a cave, and saw him enter there, and afterward they heard him speak and someone answer him. Then they, too, made their way into the cave and saw the Lady Bertha there (but guessed not who she was) and Roland had set the food before her and was urging her to eat; but she would not, and only wept.

When Roland saw the men he thought they had come there for harm, and ran and fetched a staff and made ready to defend his mother. Then the attendants told him that they meant no ill; they had but come to bring him and his mother to the King and that the King intended only good toward them.

Then Roland's heart was lightened, but his mother feared. She feared what Charlemagne might do to them when he discovered she was Bertha. But she rose, and prepared herself as best she could to come before him.

So the attendants brought them back to Charlemagne; and when the King saw that it was indeed his sister Bertha they had brought, he cried aloud, and went and took her in his arms, and there were tears upon his cheeks. And Bertha wept again, but now with joy, and all was forgiven between them.

After that she and Roland were arrayed in garments fitted to their rank, and went with Charlemagne to Rome, and saw him crowned as Emperor. Oliver went with them, riding at Roland's side, and joying in his good fortune.

When Charlemagne returned to France again he brought Bertha and Roland with him, and Roland was trained in all things fitting one of high degree, and he was dear to Charlemagne; so dear, indeed, that none was dearer, not even Charlot the Emperor's own son and heir to France. And Bertha dwelt in the palace, and in time was married to Count Ganelon, the Emperor's counselor and friend.

As for her son, as years went on he came to be the most famous Paladin in all of France, and was beloved alike by high and low; but this was not until years afterward, when Roland had learned the duties of a page, a squire, and then a bachelor, and last of all a knight. And through all this his cousin Oliver was ever his dearest friend, so that a saying rose, "As dear to each other as are Roland and Oliver."

Further Reading

Adam of the Road. Elizabeth Gray Vining. Searching for his minstrel father and his dog, Adam wanders 13th-century England. He meets jugglers, minstrels, pilgrims, and nobles in a journey that shows you the life and customs of the time.

Charlemagne and His Knights. Katharine Pyle. Additional stories about the adventures of Roland and other knights.

Knights in Armor. Shirley Glubok. This art book is based on the collection of armor in New York's Metropolitan Museum of Art. Here you can see exactly what the knights wore.

The Master Puppeteer. Katharine Patterson. A 13-year-old boy in feudal Japan tells his story of everyday existence and life in the theater. The ancient art of Japanese puppetry provides the backdrop for this adventure story.

The Merry Adventures of Robin Hood. Howard Pyle. The book retells the legend of a man who robs from the rich king and gives to the poor peasants.

LESSON 1

Europe After the Roman Empire

THINKING FOCUS

What conditions after the fall of Rome led to the rise of feudalism?

Key Terms

- monastery
- feudalism
- hierarchy
- fief
- vassal
- oath of fealty
- knight

➤ *This Anglo-Saxon box lid from the 700s was carved from whalebone. It shows warriors attacking a fortress. What kinds of weapons can you see in the carving?*

When the barbarian Odoacer took command of Rome in A.D. 476, he removed the powerless emperor Romulus Augustulus. The Western Roman Empire lay like a skeleton fallen in its own useless armor.

To Romans, it must have seemed the end of the world. All along the 10,000-mile border of the empire, there was war. Orientus, a Roman poet in the 400s, wrote:

*S*ee how swiftly death comes upon the world, and how many people the violence of war has stricken. Some lay as food for dogs; others were killed by the flames that licked their homes. In the villages and country houses, in the fields and in the countryside, on every road—death, sorrow, slaughter, fires, and lamentation.

Rise of the Germanic Kingdoms

The fall of Rome marked both the end of the ancient world and the beginning of a new era. Historians call this period, which lasted until about 1450, the Middle Ages, or the Medieval Period. Some have called the early part of this period the "Dark Ages" because little that was written at that time has come down to us. Historians do know, however, that important changes took place in Europe.

New kingdoms were set up in the lands the Germanic invaders had conquered. The map below shows the barbarians' division of rule in Europe. One Germanic group called themselves the Franks, or "the bold." Find the part of Europe where the Franks settled.

A Conquering People

In 481, the 15-year-old warrior Clovis became king of the Franks. He led them for 30 years in wars that widened the boundaries of the Frankish kingdom. Eventually, it included most of what are now France and Germany. Clovis also led the Franks into Christianity. After the collapse of the Western Roman Empire, one of the only ties with the stability of earlier times was provided by the church of Rome. It continued such traditions of the empire as using Latin and making its center in Rome. It supported many of the Roman traditions that Europeans once knew. Laws set up under Christian rulers included many elements of the Roman systems of property ownership and taxation. In addition, a few of the old Roman trade routes still operated.

Elsewhere in Europe, monks formed religious communities known as **monasteries.** There they devoted themselves to preserving the ideas of ancient Rome and Greece as well as church writings.

The church supported Clovis because it wanted to continue to serve Christians in the area ruled by the Franks. In order to do that, the church had to cooperate with

Find present-day France and England on the map of Europe on page 524 of the Atlas. Which Germanic tribes settled in the areas that became France and England?

Barbarian Kingdoms

257

the king. Once Clovis had been baptized and had accepted the support of the church, the leaders of the church encouraged him to spread Christianity. "Every battle you fight is a victory for us," a bishop wrote to Clovis.

A New Royal Family

The sons and grandsons of Clovis were more interested in squabbling among themselves than in ruling the kingdom. A new family rose to power from within the king's household. The Mayors of the Palace, officials of the king, were the kingdom's real rulers.

■ *What important changes took place in Europe after the fall of Rome?*

It was a Mayor of the Palace, Charles Martel, or Charles the Hammer, who defeated Muslim invaders from Spain at Tours, France. Martel's victory against the Muslim armies in 732 meant that northern Europe remained firmly Christian.

In 751, Martel's son, Pepin, asked the head of the church, Pope Zacharias, to recognize him as king. Pepin was the first king to rule with the blessings of the church. King Pepin's son Charles, who was called Charlemagne, would also rule with the church's support. ■

Charlemagne's Empire

Charlemagne was to become more than the king of the Franks. He would become emperor, the ruler of the former Western Roman Empire.

Charlemagne's 48 years of rule, which began in 768, were dominated by war. He fought the Lombards in Italy, the Saxons to the north, the Avars and Slavs to the east, and others, 60 campaigns in all. Charlemagne made his defeated opponents accept the Roman church and swear loyalty to him as their new ruler.

An Emperor Crowned

In 800, Charlemagne marched into Italy to help Pope Leo III put down a rebellion there. Leo knew that he would need Charlemagne's protection and support. On Christmas day, he crowned Charlemagne emperor.

Charlemagne and the pope both knew that only the head of the Eastern Roman Empire at Constantinople could legally claim the title of emperor. But the title fitted Charlemagne well. As emperor, he dedicated himself to strengthening the church and bringing learning to his empire.

An Age of Learning

Although he learned to read and write, Charlemagne still needed men of letters around him. His greatest scholar was a monk from England named Alcuin.

By Charlemagne's time, most of Europe's libraries had been destroyed during periods of war. Very few people knew how to read the few books that were left. Led by Alcuin, Charlemagne's scholars copied by hand these manuscripts to keep them for future ages.

Charlemagne also made sure that religious services were performed the same way throughout Europe. He forced illiterate clergy to become educated, and tried to rid the church of corruption. As Charlemagne grew old, his empire began to unravel. Enemies were

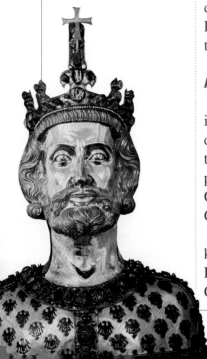

▼ *This gold likeness of Charlemagne at the cathedral of Aachen was made to hold his bones.*

hammering away at its borders. From the east came a people called the Magyars. From North Africa and Spain, Muslims attacked. And from Scandinavia came a group of fearless warriors known as Vikings. The map on page 260 shows these invasions.

But all of this was to be someone else's problem. In 814, at the age of 72, Charlemagne died.

Jews in Medieval Europe

Jews had lived in Europe since Roman times. They lost many rights, however, when the Empire fell and the Christian church began to rule. Charlemagne granted Jews the right to own land in Gaul (France). Jews also had their own courts and freedom of trade and religion.

Many rulers granted Jews rights in exchange for extra taxes. Jewish culture and economy thrived, and many Jews specialized in handicrafts, finance, and navigation. Thus, some Jews created long-distance trade networks organized around Jewish families and relatives in far-away places. Jewish trade networks also grew because Jews were free to move around Muslim lands, while Christians were not. Christian rulers sometimes relied on these Jewish merchants as advisers on international politics and trade.

Jewish culture blossomed in the centers around the Mediterranean and along the Rhone and Rhine rivers. Great Jewish communities in the Byzantine Empire and Rome continued to develop. New Jewish centers arose in Spires, Worms, Troyes, Paris, and Narbonne, in what is now France and Germany. The Jews there created a culture which they called "Ashkenazic" *(ahsh kuh NUHZ ik).* This included customs of religious and daily life as well as the beginnings of a new language— a mixture of Hebrew and Old German called Yiddish. Jewish communities were never very secure, however. Rulers often demanded heavy tributes in money or forced them to leave.

From about 900 to 1100, religious writings, law anthologies, histories, and poetry poured out of Jewish academies of higher learning. One important Jewish scholar was **R**abbi **Sh**lomo (Solomon) ben **I**saac, known as Rashi. He could not attend religious discussions because he had to support his family, so he wrote out his commentaries about the Torah and Talmud. They remain of great importance to Judaism today. Christian scholars, too, still use his work.

Europe After Charlemagne

Charlemagne's son, Louis the Pious, lacked his father's shrewdness and strength. Long before he died in 840, his sons, Lothair, Charles, and Louis, were fighting for control of the empire. For a while, the empire was divided among them, as you can see on the map on page 260. Their kingdoms came apart as landowners became more independent.

As Europe broke up into smaller kingdoms, people looked to local lords to defend them. With the Magyars, Muslims, and Vikings at their borders, the people needed protection.

After Charlemagne's death, the Vikings found Europe falling apart, and ready for the taking. The

▲ *King Solomon reads the Torah, from a late 12th-century Hebrew Bible and prayer book made in France.*

How Do We Know?

HISTORY *Historians know quite a bit about what Alcuin did and thought while he worked at Charlemagne's court. Many of Alcuin's letters to other churchmen can still be read today.*

259

Viking raids

Muslim raids

Extent of Charlemagne's Empire, 814

Where in Europe did Vikings attack?

■ *How did Charlemagne improve learning and the quality of the church in medieval Europe?*

Vikings sailed out of Scandinavia into coastal villages throughout Europe, plundering, killing, burning, and taking prisoners. By the time a local army arrived, the Vikings were gone. In time, they grew bolder, establishing camps from which they raided the countryside. ■

Medieval England

During the 800s, England suffered most at the hands of the Vikings, who launched attacks along the coast. England was saved only by the tough resistance of the Anglo-Saxon king, Alfred the Great. From his base in Wessex, Alfred fought the Vikings for three decades until his death in 899.

A New Ruler

When King Edward, a descendent of Alfred, died childless, the right to the English throne came

260

into question. An English assembly chose Edward's brother-in-law Harold as king. But Edward's cousin William, Duke of Normandy in France, felt his right to the throne was stronger. He said that Edward had promised him the kingdom. He also argued that Harold had sworn to support his claim.

William and his Norman army invaded England. On October 14, 1066, at the Battle of Hastings, William's Norman forces defeated Harold's Saxon infantry.

King William the Conqueror, as he came to be called, was a descendant of Vikings who had settled in France. He had ruled his territories in France with a firm hand and also took firm control of England. He took the land from Harold's followers and, using an arrangement called feudalism, divided it among his own followers.

A New Order

Feudalism was a social and political arrangement that developed in Europe after the fall of the Roman Empire and lasted until about 1200. It was rooted in the people's need for protection against invaders and in landowners' needs for defense. Without Roman administrators or soldiers, small farmers turned to powerful landowners for protection. People received protection in return for service as soldiers or for turning over title and ownership of their land to the larger landowners. With feudalism came new relationships among people. **Hierarchies** developed; they were orders of rank and authority within different classes of people or organizations.

Under the feudal system he established in England, King William ruled all of England. He gave large estates, called **fiefs,** to the warriors who had served him. The new landowners became his subjects, or **vassals.** In exchange for the land awarded to him, each vassal swore an **oath of fealty** to the king. That is, the vassal promised to remain loyal to his lord. He also promised to provide his lord with armed, mounted soldiers, or **knights,** for military duty.

William's vassals, in turn, granted parts of their fiefs to other people. The king's vassals became lords with vassals of their own. These vassals became lords to individual knights. Each vassal swore an oath of fealty to his lord. All levels of society were bound, by loyalty and by need, to their king. ■

▲ *A flag with this design was carried by William the Conqueror's troops at the Battle of Hastings.*

■ *Describe the condition of Europe after Charlemagne's death.*

R E V I E W

1. **FOCUS** What conditions after the fall of Rome led to the rise of feudalism?
2. **CONNECT** Compare and contrast the rule of Charlemagne in western Europe with that of Akbar in India.
3. **CITIZENSHIP** What similarities and differences do you see between the feudal style of governing and our government today?
4. **CRITICAL THINKING** Do you think a law of succession would have prevented the Battle of Hastings? Why?
5. **WRITING ACTIVITY** In the early days of the Middle Ages, Romans and Germanic people lived side by side and influenced each other. In the United States, also, different ethnic groups live side by side. Choose one ethnic group. Describe some of the ways that group has influenced American culture.

LESSON 2

Daily Life in Feudal Europe

Key Terms

- homage
- manor
- serf
- guild

➤ *This cutaway view shows the home of a medieval family and their animals. What would you find most uncomfortable about living in this home?*

*H*is hood full of holes with the hair sticking through,
His clumsy knobbed shoes cobbled over so thickly,
Though his toes started out as he trod on the ground . . .
Two miserable mittens made out of old rags, . . .
He wading in mud almost up to his ankles,
And before him four oxen, so weary and feeble
One could reckon their ribs, so rueful were they.

This description of a medieval peasant is from the poem *Piers the Plowman*, which was written in the late 1300s in England by William Langland. The harsh conditions endured by peasants like the one Langland described in his poem had not improved at all for hundreds of years.

In 1066, the rulers of England changed, but the lives of English peasants remained the same. In the hierarchy of William the Conqueror's feudalism, peasants were at the bottom.

The Feudal System

After the victory at the blood-soaked field of Hastings went to William the Conqueror, life in England changed for many. William planned to rule in peace, using the system of feudalism that was already in place in France.

If you think of feudal society as a house with many rooms, then loyalty was the set of beams that held it up. Vassals paid **homage,** or showed honor, to their lords. The word homage comes from the French word for "man." The vassal was to be the lord's man in body, mind, and spirit.

When an oath of fealty was sworn between a king and a lord or between a lord and a knight, the bond of loyalty was formalized in a ceremony. The vassal knelt before his lord. Placing his hands between the lord's hands, he swore to serve his lord in loyalty and love. Then the vassal and his lord kissed, and the lord gave his vassal a clod of earth symbolizing the fief that the vassal would use. When a vassal died, a lord went through the ceremony with the vassal's oldest son.

In 1066, feudalism was not fully developed in England. William and his Norman lords set about to change all that. William ordered a survey to be taken of the ownership of every bit of land in England. The results of the survey were written in *The Great Domesday Book,* which became a valuable source of information for the king's tax agents. Then William distributed the land as fiefs to his Norman followers. ◼

◼ *Why was loyalty important in the feudal system?*

▼ *These ivory chess pieces from the 1100s show three different classes of medieval society: a knight, a queen, and a member of the clergy—a bishop.*

Life in the Country

William and his Norman lords built fortified castles on their fiefs all over the island kingdom of England. By 1100, several hundred castles had been built throughout the countryside. These Norman fortresses helped to shape the lives of the kings, lords, and knights who made up English nobility.

Nobles

For the lord of a fief, a castle might be home. For others who lived on his land, it was both a

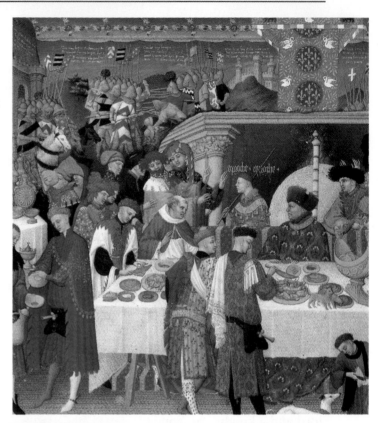

➤ *This painting from* Les Tres Riches Heures du Duc du Berry *shows a rich feast held inside a castle. A lord and his guests, who are other nobles and clergy, are in the foreground. What can you see in the far background?*

center for feudal life and a place of safety during battle. Castle walls were three feet thick. They were built to withstand blows from battering rams and flaming missiles launched from enemy catapults. Windows were mere slits through which the archers could shoot their arrows. A Norman castle was usually a tower built at the top of a hill and surrounded by a deep trench, or moat.

The Norman castle was built for

UNDERSTANDING HIERARCHY

The knight made an oath of fealty to the lord of the manor. The lord swore to be faithful to the more important lord who had granted him his fief. The hierarchy of the feudal society extended from the humblest peasant all the way up to the king.

Hierarchy as Ranking

A hierarchy is a system by which persons or things are ranked one above another. A group of equals, such as the members of a sports team, cannot be considered a hierarchy.

The meritocracy that

Emperor Wen developed in China was a hierarchy with the emperor at the top. Beneath him stood courtiers, administrators, and clerks. Each group, from the administrators up through the emperor, had greater powers than the group below it.

Other Hierarchies

Hierarchies define where people stand in relationship to each other and define their rights and responsibilities. Most workplaces such as offices and factories are hierarchies, with a boss or president

over several rankings of supervisors and workers. Medieval city dwellers and guild members had their own hierarchies.

Slaves were at the bottom of medieval society. They were usually captives of war or kidnap victims. Slavery continued throughout Europe in spite of the teachings of the Church. Gradually, over the centuries most slaves became **serfs.** While slaves could be sold or given away, serfs were required to stay on and work on a piece of land for anyone who owned the land.

Becoming a Medieval Knight

Page	Squire	Knight
• Serving in household • Learning swordplay • Playing chess and other strategy games • Hunting with hawks and falcons • Learning code of courtesy expected of knight	• Acting as personal servant to knight • Learning jousting • Assisting knight in battle • Taking charge of prisoners captured in battle	• Serving lords as warriors • Overseeing land as vassals • Taking part in tournaments
Age 7	**Age 13–14**	**Age 18–22**

security, not for comfort. The lord and lady of the castle usually slept behind a curtain in the main dining hall. Also sleeping in the hall might be a small mob of knights, guests, servants, and dogs. The floor was covered with herbs to keep down the smell of bones and other refuse. On a winter morning, inhabitants would wash by plunging their arms through ice-crusted water in a bucket.

Life in a castle was far from glamorous, and few who lived there were the courteous knights and ladies of legend. A knight was often the landless younger son of a lord's vassal. The lord provided the knight with food, lodging, armor, and a horse in exchange for his services. But between wars the castle's knights fought among themselves or bullied the servants unless the lord of the castle kept an eye on them.

The lady of the castle usually had very little power, except over female servants. Medieval women were supposed to be subject to their husbands and fathers, just as vassals were subject to their lords. However, most of the daily life of the castle was within women's domain. Besides cooking and cleaning, women also managed the making of clothing and medical

▲ *The chart shows the stages that a young man went through before he became a knight. Why do you think it was such a long and rigorous process?*

◄ *This woman of the 1300s wears clothing such as that worn by ladies of English or French castles.*

265

Feudal Europe and Japan

Peasants

The lord's castle might be a cold, drafty fortress. But as you can see in the picture on page 262, even a well-off medieval family lived with its animals.

In the early Middle Ages, farming methods improved in Northern Europe and England. See A Closer Look on page 267 for additional information on advances in medieval farming. But farming was still hard, and both men and women were bound to the plots of land that they tilled for their lords. Some were so poor that they would not even have owned the scrawny oxen described by William Langland. Instead they would borrow oxen from their lord or a neighbor.

The peasant woman produced food and clothing for her own household. William Langland wrote of peasant women's work in *Piers the Plowman:*

In this miniature painting, peasants are shearing sheep and harvesting grain in fields surrounding a castle. Does this picture of peasant life differ from the images conveyed in Piers the Plowman *on this page and on page 262?*

care for everyone in the castle. When their husbands were at war, women took over the **manor,** the castle and entire estate.

Some noblewomen controlled fiefs or became abbesses, who ruled over convents and convent lands. Hildegard of Bingen (1098–1179), a Christian woman raised in a convent, had religious visions. She wrote books, founded convents, and preached throughout Germany. She wrote religious music and poetry. She was also a physician and pharmacologist.

*W*hat they save from
    their spinning they
  spend on house rent,
on milk and oatmeal to make
  porridge
to fill their children when they
  cry for food.
They themselves suffer the
  sting of hunger
and of winter misery, rising at
  night
to rock the cradle in its
  cramped corner,
to card and comb wool, to
  mend and wash,
to scrub and wind yarn, to
  weave rushlights.
It's painful to read or to write
  verses
on the hard lives of women
  who live in hovels. . . .

Medieval Farming

The cycle of changing seasons brought an endless round of work to peasant families. But improvements like the wheelbarrow, horseshoes, and new crops slowly began to soften their harsh lives.

Protecting horses' feet from wear and injury, better horseshoes allowed these strong animals to pull metal-tipped plows. Plowing deeper meant farmers could get at the richest soil, grow more crops, and store food for lean times.

Month by month, this page from a 15th-century French "book of hours" shows the activities of the farm year. Read it left to right and top to bottom. In the January snow, peasants cut the winter wheat they had sowed in September. October found the peasant crushing grapes for wine by foot.

Not the same old bean and pea soup!
New plants like cabbage, parsley and leeks added flavor and nutrition to the boring peasant diet.

Leeks

Parsley

Cabbage

Peas

267

Here Pope Urban II blesses a church at Cluny in the 1000s. The monastery at Cluny in France was established in 910, and was a leader of the reform movement within the church. By the late 1000s, there were about 200 monasteries administered by the center at Cluny.

How did each class help to keep a feudal manor running?

A monk in his study is shown here on an ivory book cover from the Middle Ages.

Clergy

Society in the Middle Ages was described by Alfred the Great as consisting of "men of prayer, men of war, and men of work." Perhaps the men and women "of prayer" had the most comfortable lives of any in the Middle Ages.

The influence of the clergy—from pope, archbishops, and bishops to priests, monks, and nuns—extended to every part of medieval life. Most medieval manors included a small church. From baptism to marriage to burial, the ceremonies of the church guided the lives of medieval men and women.

Also, people at this time saw life on earth as a brief preparation for the eternal life to come. They believed only a few would spend eternity in heaven. Many sinners, people believed, would spend eternity in the flames of hell.

The power to condemn or to forgive sinners made the church a considerable force in medieval society. Many people entered the clergy because of their deeply held beliefs. Others, however, joined the church to acquire status and influence.

Thousands of monks, nuns, and servants also lived and worked in large stone structures. A monastery was a complex community with many different buildings—granaries, breweries, bakeries with huge ovens, wineries, and the abbey church and library.

Inside the library, monks hunched over tall desks and copied manuscripts in beautiful handwriting, or drew illustrations. With the same devotion and care, monks and nuns of the Middle Ages also taught children, fed the poor, cared for the sick, and provided shelter to travelers. Most of the clergy worked long hours and reaped few earthly rewards. Their devotion to the church mirrored a vassal's dedication to his lord. ■

Life in the Town

Not all people lived in feudal manors or monasteries. Peasants seeking freedom, younger sons of nobles seeking a fortune, scholars seeking new ideas, and freed serfs left the country manor for towns.

The Growth of Towns

The walls that rose around a medieval town enclosed a jumble. Narrow, crowded streets turned in on each other. Rough wooden houses shoved up against each other, hardly leaving enough space for light to filter through.

After the Western Roman Empire fell, towns had almost disappeared from Europe. The population of Rome, which remained the largest city in Europe, fell from about one million to only a few thousand.

But in the 1000s, trade and town life began to revive. Linen from Italy, woven wool from Flanders, leather from Spain, and other products were traded in towns in Europe and in countries beyond Europe. And the craftspeople who made these products found ways to control their own trades.

Guilds

Shoemakers, blacksmiths, tailors, weavers, and bakers banded together with others of their trade to form guilds. A **guild** was a union of people who practiced a trade. Guilds for each trade limited the number of people they accepted.

A boy who wanted to work at a trade began as an apprentice. He served a guild member for several years until he mastered basic skills. Then he became a journeyman, or skilled worker. A journeyman received pay for his work. Eventually, if he became skilled enough, he would produce a masterpiece and present it for admission into the guild. Only an expert at his trade was allowed to join a guild.

Christian law, unlike Roman law, put women under the control of their fathers and husbands. Women were responsible for the home, children, and most of the trade goods they produced there, such as textiles or foods. Some, however, were merchants or shopkeepers. A craftswoman might be admitted to a guild if her husband was a member. In Paris and Cologne, embroiderers formed all-female guilds.

Many European Jews also lived in towns because they were not allowed to own land. However, they were not allowed to join guilds, either. Many Jews were therefore merchants. Some were moneylenders, the only trade forbidden to Christians.

The town was where feudalism began to die. Powered by trade, the new commercial way of life that developed in the towns looked beyond the simpler and closed world of manor and village. ■

▲ *The carpenter in this French painting from the late Middle Ages probably belonged to a carpenter's guild.*

■ *Describe the new social order that evolved in medieval towns.*

▼ *This banner was proudly displayed by the boot and shoemaker's guild of a town in Belgium.*

The Forces of Change

Eventually, the feudal monarchy that was established in England by William the Conqueror would also change. After William's death in 1087, the followers he had rewarded with feudal fiefs grew more and more powerful. Their wealth was increased by payments they demanded from towns that grew up on land within their control. Over several generations, the feudal lords' power and wealth grew substantially.

When King John took the throne in 1199, the most powerful landowners had become increasingly outspoken. Then John led England into losing wars and ever-higher levels of taxation. In 1204, John lost all of his lands in the north of France, thus angering those of his vassals who held fiefs in that region.

Also, because of a disagreement between John and the pope, the churches shut their doors to the people of England. Many lords renounced allegiance to John, and a small band of them cornered him in a meadow outside London. In June of 1215, after days of argument, they forced him to affix the royal seal to an amazing medieval document—the *Magna Carta*, or great charter. You can read excerpts from the *Magna Carta* on page 504.

The *Magna Carta* focused on the rights of nobles. It acknowledged the rights of the lords and prevented a king from taking those rights away. It also contained the following condition:

> No free man shall be taken or imprisoned or dispossessed, or outlawed, or banished, or in any way destroyed, nor will we go upon him, nor send upon him, except by the legal judgment of his peers or by the law of the land.

By subjecting the king to the rule of law, the *Magna Carta* became the basis for future reforms. Our own Bill of Rights and the concept of "due process of law" grew out of the *Magna Carta*.

The signing of the *Magna Carta* signaled the beginning of feudalism's decline. The ideas of personal freedom and liberty were now firmly planted. ∎

▲ *This copy of the* Magna Carta *is one of four in England. No one is sure which is the original.*

■ *How did the* Magna Carta *pave the way for a new social system in England?*

R E V I E W

1. **FOCUS** How did the feudal system affect the everyday lives of people in Europe?

2. **CONNECT** How did the Battle of Hastings contribute to the rise of feudalism in England?

3. **BELIEF SYSTEMS** In what ways did the relationship between the clergy and the church resemble the relationship between vassals and their lords?

4. **SOCIAL SYSTEMS** Compare and contrast the life of an apprentice with the life of a serf on a manor.

5. **CRITICAL THINKING** In your opinion, which was the most important class or group of people in feudal times? Why?

6. **WRITING ACTIVITY** The *Magna Carta* guaranteed lords certain rights under laws that even a king had to obey. Think about the elements of respect and consideration that go into running a contented household. Then draw up a household *Magna Carta* to share with the class.

LESSON 3

Two Feudal Societies

The Japanese samurai warrior and the Italian knight on this page face one another across 6,000 miles. Even so, the men are strikingly similar. Like the Italian knight, the samurai rides a horse and wears armor. The samurai's armor consists of lacquered steel plates sewn together with leather strips and fastened across his chest. Although earlier knights had worn heavy chain mail shirts of up to a hundred thousand wire links, this knight is encased in plates of steel.

Both men spent their lives preparing to wage battle for their lords. When the samurai was a boy, he practiced with a long wooden sword and studied martial arts. At 15, he exchanged the wooden sword for a long metal one. The knight, too, began his training young, learning to fight as a page and as a squire.

The samurai practiced Buddhism and Shintoism. The knight prayed to Jesus Christ. But both men followed codes of behavior that stressed loyalty to their lords and serving as examples of virtue to people of lower classes. Despite the miles and years that separate them, the warriors are alike in many ways. Each was a member of a specially trained warrior class that provided protection to people in feudal societies.

THINKING FOCUS

In what ways were feudal Japan and feudal Europe alike and different?

Key Terms

- chivalry
- bushido

▲ *This Italian knight from the 1300s carries a shield with the symbol of Naples, Italy.*

◄ *In this Japanese painting from about 1600, a samurai cleans his sword. Notice that both the knight and the samurai use stirrups. How would stirrups help them in battle?*

271

Similar Societies

Across Time & Space

During the periods of feudalism, massive castles sprang up all over Europe and Japan. In Europe, castles had rounded walls so that ladders would not balance against them and invaders could not get inside. In Japan, the stone walls were curved so they would stay upright through an earthquake. But Japanese castles were palaces—built for beauty as well as protection.

▼ *The Bayeux Tapestry, which was made in the late 1000s by Norman Duchess Matilda and her ladies, is only 20 inches wide but 230 feet long. It tells the story of the Norman Conquest. This section shows William with his Norman lords, some members of the clergy, entertainers, and servants at a banquet.*

In Europe, feudalism developed after the fall of the Roman Empire and especially after Charlemagne's empire collapsed in 814. Lacking a strong central government, landowners came to depend on warrior knights for protection against invaders. These knights became a new class in society.

In Japan of the 1100s, landowners in the provinces depended on samurai warriors to protect their estates and to wage battles against rival clans. In the 1100s, the samurai became an important new class in Japanese society.

Styles of Battle

Frankish warriors of the 700s did not ride horses. The Muslim invaders who threatened France in 732 did ride horses. Therefore, the Franks had great difficulty defeating the Muslims. Later, the Frankish leader Charles Martel granted land to his most trusted warriors and asked them to use income from the land to equip themselves with horses and armor.

When Frankish foot soldiers changed to fighting on horseback, they lengthened the spears they had been accustomed to using into lances. By bracing himself in his stirrups and charging his enemy at a gallop, a warrior could strike a tremendous blow with his lance.

Of course, the armies who fought with Charles Martel and with his grandson Charlemagne continued to be made up mostly of warriors on foot, with only a few mounted knights. But when Vikings and other invaders threatened France, landowners outfitted more and more of their warriors with horses and armor. As a reward for his service as a warrior, a knight was often awarded a fief of land for his own use, thus becoming a vassal to the lord he served.

Japanese samurai did not learn new methods of fighting at the beginning of their feudal period. Japanese armies had included mounted warriors when the ruling clans invaded Japan around A.D 200. But many warriors of the

1100s fought on foot. Samurai also used bows and arrows.

Codes of Honor

Tales of Middle Ages praised knights such as King Arthur's Sir Lancelot:

> You were the [most courteous] knight that ever bore shield! And thou were the truest friend . . . that bestrode horse. And thou were the kindest man that ever struck with sword. And thou were the goodliest person that ever came among [a crowd] of knights, and thou [were] the meekest man and the gentlest who ever ate in hall among ladies.
>
> Thomas Malory, *Le Morte d'Arthur*, 1485

Knights aspired to a code of conduct called **chivalry.** The values of that code were the qualities praised in Sir Lancelot: courtesy, honor, defending the weak, and loyalty to one's lord. Of course, most knights did not live up to these ideals.

The samurai code is today called **bushido** or "the way of the warrior." It required a samurai to give up his life if necessary to protect his lord. If he failed or was captured, a samurai sometimes felt so humiliated by his loss of honor that he would kill himself. Like the code of chivalry, the ideals of bushido included a code of gentlemanly conduct for samurai. Confucian ideas of duty were important in Japan during feudal times. Samurai believed they had a duty to serve as examples of virtue for the lower classes. ■

In this detail from the Handscroll of the Heiji War, painted in the 1200s, warriors defend the gate of a palace.

■ *How did the system of feudalism meet the needs of both medieval Europe and Japan?*

273

Different Societies

■ *Why did feudalism last so much longer in Japan than it did in Europe?*

In Japan, the way of the warrior remained a powerful force in society until 1854. In Europe, feudalism ended 400 years earlier.

Why did feudalism die in Europe? For one thing, growing towns offered alternatives to people who did not want to function within the feudal system. Also, military technology changed in the 1300s. Large armies with new weapons—the longbow in the 1300s and guns in the 1400s—made mounted knights less effective in battle.

Knights were often more interested in overseeing their land than in serving as warriors. Sometimes they refused to fight when asked to perform military service. When feudalism was strong, this would have resulted in a ceremony of public disgrace. Then, a knight who broke his vows was stripped of his armor, piece by piece. His shield was crushed, his spurs cut off, and his sword broken in half. But after about 1400, kings began to rely on paid armies rather than asking knights to honor their feudal obligations.

In Japan, the ruling shoguns eventually forced samurai to become literate and to learn administrative skills. In Europe, however, most knights did not learn these skills. Administrators in European kingdoms were often members of the clergy.

Feudalism in Japan lasted longer than feudalism in Europe partly because samurai who were not warriors became government administrators. Also, Japan sealed itself off from the West between 1635 and 1854, thus preserving its feudal society. But Japanese shoguns adopted Western military technology after 1854.

Just as in Europe, feudalism arose in Japan to fill a need for government and protection. And just as in Europe, Japanese feudalism declined quickly when things began to change. ■

▼ *Part of the wall surrounding this town was originally a castle (top left), built in the 1100s. Compare it with the Japanese castle on page 238.*

R E V I E W

1. **FOCUS** In what ways were feudal Japan and feudal Europe alike and different?
2. **CONNECT** What role did religion play in the belief system of the knight? Of the samurai warrior?
3. **HISTORY** Why did feudalism decline in Europe? In Japan?
4. **CRITICAL THINKING** In the Middle Ages in Europe, a person born into the peasant class had little opportunity to advance upwards. What are some of the ways people today can improve their status?
5. **WRITING ACTIVITY** Write a story about a meeting between a knight and a samurai warrior.

How a Guild Works

Here's Why

Group decisions are effective only when they are accepted and supported by group members. Members of a group need to know how to consider both their short-term and their long-term interests when evaluating group decisions.

You would have needed the skill of evaluating group decisions if you had belonged to a guild in feudal Europe. You need it to be an effective member of a modern group, too, such as a sports team or a scout troop. Do you know how to evaluate and support group decisions?

Here's How

A trade guild benefits its members by making decisions that are good for the group as a whole on a long-term basis. Members of a trade guild are largely dependent upon the guild for their livelihood.

Similarly, the guild depends on the support of its members. The goals of the group may sometimes conflict with the short-term interests of some individual members. When this happens, the individual can either accept the group decision or work to get the decision changed. To disobey the group would probably result in negative consequences over the long term.

Suppose you are a member of a feudal trade guild. Your guild wants you to raise prices on the goods you sell, but you think this will result in a loss of sales for you. What should you do?

You must weigh the negative effects of the price increase on you against the positive effects such a change might have for the entire group. Your reaction to such a decision depends on how the positive and negative effects balance each other. One way to weigh the effects of a decision is to create a chart like the one the students have made in the photograph below.

Try It

Consider the following decisions made by your guild. Make a chart for each decision and then consider what your reaction in each case would be.

1. The guild decides to increase membership dues to support the family of a member who is unable to work.
2. The guild decides to restrict new memberships at a time when it seems there is plenty of business for all.

Apply It

Suppose your study group has decided to meet on the weekend to prepare for a test next week. Make a chart of the advantages and disadvantages of this decision.

Decision:	Should the guild raise prices?	
	Individual	Group
Advantages:	1 More income from sales	More income from members
Disadvantages	1 Loss of ... to hi...	...

Japanese and American Schools

*Y*ou can learn a great deal about another country by finding out about its schools. Education is one way in which a society passes its values and its knowledge to the next generation. What is school like in Japan?

Find Out

Look for answers to each of your questions. If an answer gives you an idea for another question, add it to your list.

Divide your information into two groups: ways in which American and Japanese schools are alike and ways in which they are different. Did you find more similarities or more differences?

▲ *Who cleans your school? In Japan, the students themselves sweep the floors of their classrooms daily.*

➤ *This is the cover of a seventh-grade geography textbook popular in Japan. Japanese seventh graders spend more time on social studies than any other subject except Japanese.*

Get Ready

You'll need a notebook, a pen, and some books or magazines with information about schools in Japan.

Make a list of questions you want to answer: What time does school begin and end for Japanese students your age? Do they have dress codes? What about after-school sports? Do students move from class to class? Does one teacher handle all subjects? What subjects do Japanese schools teach? How much homework do they give?

新編 新しい社会(地理)

276

Move Ahead

Tape a large sheet of paper to the wall of your classroom. Each student should mention a question that he or she asked. Use the questions to create categories on the chart. For instance, some people may have asked about school hours. If so, a student might write on the chart: "Hours in School per Day (or Week)."

Do everyone's answers agree? If not, find out where the information came from. Is one magazine or book more recent than another? Is one author more knowledgeable and respected than another?

When your chart is complete, discuss the information. What Japanese ideas would you like American schools to adopt? Why?

Explore Some More

Choose another area of American life, one you're very familiar with. It might be sports, games, crafts, music, art, or some current concern—animal welfare, the environment, or political campaigns, for instance.

Find out whether the Japanese share this interest of yours. If so, do they pursue it in the same way? If not, can you find out why not?

▲ *May 5, Boys' Day, is a school holiday in Japan. On this day most families fly carp flags outside their homes. The symbol of the carp—a fish that swims against river currents—inspires boys to face life's difficulties with courage.*

◄ *Like Boys' Day, Girls' Day is also a school holiday in Japan. Celebrated on March 3, Girls' Day centers around dolls. Girls display their dolls and hold tea parties where they serve little cakes iced with cherry-blossom frosting.*

Feudal Europe and Japan

Chapter Review

Reviewing Key Terms

bushido (p. 273)
chivalry (p. 273)
feudalism (p. 261)
fief (p. 261)
guild (p. 269)
hierarchy (p. 261)
homage (p. 263)

knight (p. 261)
manor (p. 266)
monastery (p. 257)
oath of fealty (p. 261)
serf (p. 264)
vassal (p. 261)

A. Write whether each of the following statements is true or false. Then rewrite the false statements to make them true.

1. Monasteries were simple town churches in the Middle Ages.
2. Knights were monks and nuns on horseback.
3. Most castles had a hierarchy, or tower.
4. Bushido was the samurai code of loyalty and conduct.
5. A fief was a kind of musical instrument.
6. Feudalism was a religious and economic system of rule in medieval Europe.
7. Knights and their lords sailed to battles on warships called vassals.
8. Serfs were the peasants who lived on a lord's estate.
9. A medieval woman had to take an oath of fealty to her husband at her marriage.
10. A guild was a union of tradespeople.

B. Use each word below in a sentence that shows what the word means.
1. guild
2. manor
3. homage
4. chivalry
5. hierarchy

Exploring Concepts

A. Create an illustrated "people summary" of the chapter by drawing pictures of one person from each lesson as listed below. Write a sentence describing each person you draw.

Lesson 1:
barbarian
Charles Martel
Charlemagne
Pope Leo III
Alcuin
Viking
Alfred the Great
William the Conqueror

Lesson 2:
peasant
monk
Hildegard of Bingen
King John

Lesson 3:
samurai
shogun

B. Support each of the following statements with facts and details from the chapter.
1. After the fall of Rome, Europe became a place of warfare.
2. Viking conquests in Europe were made easier by the weakness of Charlemagne's heirs.
3. Under William the Conqueror there developed a highly organized system for ruling England.
4. Loyalty held English feudal society together.
5. Castles in 12th-century England were built for safety but were not very comfortable for those living within.
6. Peasants led difficult lives.
7. The church played a very important role in the lives of most of the people in Europe during the Middle Ages.
8. In spite of their limited legal state, many European women held great responsibilities in the Middle Ages.
9. Japanese feudalism and European feudalism were different but similar.
10. There were several reasons why feudalism endured 400 years longer in Japan than in Europe.

Reviewing Skills

1. Read the group decision below. Then make a chart that gives both the individual and group advantages and disadvantages of the decision.

   Instead of collecting money to donate to a charity, your class decides to spend several Saturdays helping senior citizens in the neighborhood maintain their houses by raking leaves, painting fences, and hauling away rubbish.

2. Review the section called An Age of Learning in Lesson 1 on pages 258–259. What unstated assumption did Charlemagne make about knowledge and learning?

3. Suppose you are outlining a chapter that compares and contrasts the nature of feudalism in Europe with that of feudalism in Japan. What two kinds of information would you need to find and list in your outline?

Using Critical Thinking

1. In this chapter, you learned how the advent of fighting from horseback and using armor changed the nature of warfare. You also learned about the changes in military technology that permitted armies to defeat mounted knights. What were those new inventions of the 1300s and 1400s? Do you think the country with the most sophisticated weapons always wins a war? Explain your answer.

2. "They worked hard, and they were poor. They had almost nothing to their names, and the little they had was not much use in this world." This bleak description, along with the quotes in the chapter from *Piers the Plowman,* might easily describe the peasants of Europe in the Middle Ages. Do the quotations also describe the plight of some people today? If so, who? Where? How are their conditions similar?

3. Craftspeople in medieval Europe began their apprenticeships when they were very young and worked long hours for no pay while they learned the skills they would need for their life's work. Imagine that you are transported back in time to the Middle Ages. What trade would you be interested in learning to master? Which do you think is more important, the kind of vocational training young people received in the Middle Ages or the general education you're getting now? Explain your answer.

Preparing for Citizenship

1. **COLLECTING INFORMATION** Research what happened on that day in June of 1215 when the powerful landowners made King John of England agree to the Magna Carta. Imagine that you are King John and tell the class about your experience in a way colorful enough to make them feel they are witnessing history.

2. **GROUP ACTIVITY** In two groups, draw hierarchies of your school system and of your town government or a local business. Draw organization charts that show who reports to whom. Your finished products will probably resemble pyramids, with many people at the bottom and fewer on each level as you move toward the top.

3. **COLLABORATIVE LEARNING** In groups of five, plan a five-minute TV documentary on one of these topics: Charlemagne's kingdom, William's conquest and rule of England, life on a medieval manor, or feudalism in Japan. Assign one person to research the subject, one to write the script, one to make simple costumes and scenery, one to prepare the ads, and one to direct the documentary. Each student in the group should also play one of the characters. If possible, videotape the documentary.

Chapter 11

Europe: Rule, Religion, and Conflict

It was the Age of Faith, as the Catholic church dominated much of Europe from 1000 to 1300. As early as the 800s, the church won power from Europe's kings. Then in 1096, the world truly saw the church's might. That year the pope gathered some 45,000 knights, archers, and swordsmen in Constantinople. This massive army hoped to drive the Muslims out of the holy city of Jerusalem. Yet battles over the Holy City would go on for almost 200 years.

Throughout this period, Christians looked toward Jerusalem as their holy city. This map from late in the period depicts the city at the center of the world.

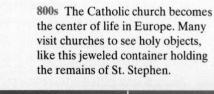

800s The Catholic church becomes the center of life in Europe. Many visit churches to see holy objects, like this jeweled container holding the remains of St. Stephen.

| 650 | 750 | 850 | 950 |

900 Cordoba, the largest city in Western Europe, is the center of western Islam.

726

Crusaders in need of money sacked
and looted Constantinople in 1204.
These bronze horses were among
the valuable objects they took.

1240s Parisians build Sainte
Chapelle in their city. Such
magnificent chapels with costly
stained-glass windows show
the wealth and power of the
French monarchy.

1050

1150

1250

1350

1185 The Minamoto family
unites Japan under its
shogunate rule.

1204

LESSON 1

The Power of the Church

THINKING FOCUS

What aspects of European society did the church dominate from 1100 to 1300?

Key Terms

- clergy
- excommunication
- salvation
- tithe
- university

➤ *This painting shows the building of Chartres Cathedral. The cathedral was so important to the people that even noblemen and their ladies helped haul stones.*

Many townspeople stood on the church steps awaiting the decision about the new cathedral. This decision would affect their town's future. At last the smiling bishop appeared at the doorway to announce the long awaited answer. Yes, a cathedral would be built in their town to the glory of God!

An architect was selected to design the cathedral and supervise the beginning of its construction. The expense would be great since many workers would be needed: stonecutters, woodworkers, carpenters, masons, blacksmiths, roofers, glassmakers, sculptors, and more. For hundreds of men in the town this would become their life's work. For a few it would even mean their death, since there was the possibility of falling from the scaffolding on which the workers stood as they built the walls ever higher.

The townspeople knew it could take as many as 100 years to complete the building of the cathedral. However, it was difficult for them to imagine that their great-great-grandchildren would be as old as they were now when the building was finished.

Why would these people, who lived in western Europe in A.D. 1200, spend so much money, time, and labor to begin building something that they would not even live to see completed? Because the cathedral allowed them to celebrate, in stone and glass, the power of the church and of God in their lives.

A Powerful Church in Europe

Between 800 and 1300 almost all the people of Europe were Christians. Only one branch of the faith existed in Europe, and it was headed by the pope in Rome. The Christian religion was organized in such a way that it was the center of spiritual life and an important political force.

The Church Hierarchy

The church was organized in a hierarchy so that each member of the **clergy,** or ordained members of the church, had a specific rank. The priest of the local church, or parish, had a certain group of duties. These included leading religious services, visiting the sick, and conducting ceremonies such as baptisms and weddings. Many parishes together formed one diocese *(DY uh sihs)*. Heading each diocese was a bishop, who, in turn, had a different group of responsibilities.

The dioceses were united into provinces, or archdioceses, under the authority of archbishops. Cardinals were second in power to the pope. The cardinals also acted as counselors to the pope and eventually were responsible for electing new popes. Leading the entire church was the pope. *Pope* comes from the Latin word for "father."

Monks lived in monasteries headed by abbots and had lives of thought, prayer, and charitable work. The word monk comes from the Greek word *monos* meaning "alone." Although abbots usually answered to bishops, the abbots ran these religious communities and were responsible for their spiritual life. The monks did physical labor to support their communities. Some monks occasionally preached.

Women were not allowed to be priests, bishops, archbishops, or popes. Still, many women were led by their strong belief to participate in other aspects of the church. Many became nuns, who were "Brides of Christ." They swore never to marry and to devote themselves to lives of poverty and charitable work. Abbesses ran their communities, called convents, which sometimes owned the land around them. Thus many abbesses became skilled managers and farmers, as well as spiritual leaders to the nuns. Most abbesses reported to local bishops.

The Church's Influence

The church brought Christianity to many Europeans. It taught that they could help save their souls

▲ *Popes wear miters with peaks in front and back.*

▼ *Chartres Cathedral, built on a hill 50 miles southwest of Paris, is visible for miles around. The tower on the left was not finished for hundreds of years.*

▼ *Hildegard of Bingen wrote music and poetry, tended the sick, preached and ran convents.*

■ *Describe the hierarchy of the church.*

▼ *The jewel-encrusted gold cross reveals the wealth possessed by the church.*

by giving donations to it. In addition, popes, cardinals, and bishops were often nobles with land of their own who left this land to the church when they died. By 1050, the church was the largest landholder in western Europe.

The clergy were often the only members of society who could read and write. Even most kings were illiterate, so they needed bishops, abbots, and clerks to write documents and keep records. Thus the clergy also had the opportunity to advise kings on all sorts of matters.

The career of Abbot Suger *(SOO zhair)* is an example of how religion and politics were often intermingled during this time. Suger was born in 1081 into a peasant family living near Paris. As a boy he showed high intelligence and was selected by his village priest to be educated in a monastery, where his closest friend happened to be the son of the king

of France. In 1108, that friend was crowned King Louis VI of France.

Suger became a monk and, in 1122, an abbot, or leader of his monastery. As Louis's friend and adviser, he worked to increase cooperation between Louis and his nobles by stressing the fact that they shared a common faith. When King Henry of Germany invaded King Louis's lands in 1124, Abbot Suger loaned the king the sacred banner from the monastery to carry into battle. The banner rallied so many French nobles to the king that Henry retreated before the battle began.

From 1147 to 1149, the new king, the son of Louis VI, left his crown with Abbot Suger and appointed him regent to rule his lands while he, the king, was away at war. During these years, Suger developed fairer methods of taxation and prevented a rebellion from taking away Louis's rule. ■

A Power Struggle Between Kings and Popes

Kings and nobles had gained the power to appoint bishops and other officials of the church during the 800s. They sometimes even sold these positions to the highest bidder. In particular, kings rewarded their allies by appointing them to be bishops of the church. The fact that the kings possessed such great power over the church strengthened their authority. Yet, because these church officials appointed by the kings often behaved immorally and quite selfishly, many people lost respect for the church.

Pope Gregory VII

One monk, named Hildebrand, was part of a movement to free the church from the control of kings and nobles. He wanted the church to be free of this control so that the clergy might concentrate on performing its mission of saving Christians. Hildebrand became pope in 1073 and took the name Gregory VII. In 1075, Gregory issued a document stating that the pope was above kings and only the pope could appoint cardinals and bishops. The document warned that government officials who did not obey the pope could be removed from office.

King Henry IV

Henry IV, king of Germany and Italy, considered Gregory's document an attack on his power as king. So, while continuing to appoint bishops in his kingdom, Henry fired back a letter to the pope. In it the king demanded that the pope step down from his office.

But Gregory would do no such thing. Instead, in 1076, he announced the **excommunication** of Henry, thus expelling Henry from the church. Henry was condemned to live as an outcast from the church-oriented society of the 1000s. The excommunication also meant that Henry's subjects were no longer obliged to obey him as their king.

Henry looked for support from his nobles and bishops but found little, because Gregory had also threatened them with excommunication if they supported the king. To save his throne, Henry realized he had to give in to the pope. He then traveled to Italy barefoot during the winter to present himself to the pope as a humble beggar. Gregory kept Henry waiting for three days in the snow outside his castle before finally canceling the excommunication.

Henry IV wears a crown and holds the scepter and the orb and cross, symbols of monarchy. The orb and cross theme is repeated on the top of the crown.

The Treaty

Pope Gregory had won this battle, but the struggle between the kings of Germany and the popes continued until 1122. In that year, church leaders, nobles, and representatives of the king and the pope met in Worms, Germany, where they agreed to a treaty called the Concordat (*kuhn KAWR dat*) of Worms. The king agreed to having the pope select church leaders. ■

■ *Why is the conflict between Henry IV and Pope Gregory significant?*

The Age of Faith

While popes and kings fought for power, the common people of western Europe tried to live their lives according to the principles of the church. The mission of the church was to save the soul of all members so that they would go to heaven after they died rather than hell. This **salvation,** or saving, came through accepting the beliefs of the church, living a moral life, and performing good works.

People also paid one-tenth of the produce from their lands to the church each year. This **tithe** (*tyth*) could be paid in money, produce, or labor. People also had to pay rent to the lord on whose land they farmed.

Daily Life

The church was the center of daily life in every village and town. Church bells announced the time

▲ *People are admitted into the church through baptism.*

➤ *During daily mass, the Last Supper of Jesus and his disciples is remembered.*

▲ *The Catholic church teaches that marriage is the formal union of man and woman as husband and wife in the sight of God. In the 1000s, people married as early as the age of 13.*

➤ *At burial ceremonies a priest offered a blessing for the dead and welcomed the soul into heaven.*

for work, meals, rest, and for mass, the worship service. Churches were also centers of community activity. Often large and sturdily constructed, they served as gathering places for town meetings and as places of refuge during wars or heavy storms. The doorsteps or courtyard of a church might even be where the local farmers' market took place.

Church holidays provided the peasants with relief from their sunup-to-sundown farm labors. On these special days, Christians celebrated events in the life of Jesus and remembered famous saints of the church. After attending mass, the people spent the remainder of the holiday visiting, feasting, and dancing in the church courtyard.

A shared faith gave the church members a sense of community, but it also kept those with different beliefs outside this community. For example, Christians did not accept Jews socially and often even persecuted them. Jews were also generally not allowed to participate in trade. Furthermore, Jews were often required to pay a tax whenever the king demanded.

Religious Orders

Many people in the church wanted a religious life that was less secluded than that of monks living in a monastery. As a result, during the 1200s, several new orders, or religious communities, were formed. These new orders did not shut themselves off from the world as other monks and nuns did. Instead, they lived in the towns and worked to bring Christianity directly to the people.

One new order was founded in 1209 by Francis of Assisi. Francis was born in Italy in 1182, the son of a wealthy merchant. After a carefree youth, he spent a year battling a serious illness. During that time, he had a vision of Jesus that changed him forever.

Francis disowned his father and rejected a large inheritance, making a vow instead to live his life in poverty as Jesus had done. Francis rebuilt churches and served the poor. Many people followed him. He created a new religious order, now called the Franciscans.

Francis was also a talented poet and musician. This is part of one of his poems.

> *B*e praised, my Lord, for all
>   your creatures.
> In the first place for the blessed
> Brother Sun, who gives us the
>   day and enlightens us
>   through you.
> He is beautiful and radiant
>   with his great splendor.
>
> St. Francis of Assisi, from "The
> Canticle of Brother Sun," 1224

The peaceful landscape and gentle animals are symbols of Francis of Assisi's love for nature and all living things. The halo around Francis's head identifies him as a saint. Francis was declared a saint in 1228, two years after his death.

Universities

Until the 1100s, education had taken place within monasteries and bishops' cathedrals. There young men planning to enter the clergy were educated. As European towns grew during the 1100s, people began wanting to get better educated—often still at bishops' cathedrals. This enthusiasm for learning was partly sparked by the flow of knowledge from the Muslim world. The Muslims had important schools in cities such as Cordoba and Baghdad. Muslims and Jews had studied and translated books by Greek, African, and Asian writers, such as the works of Aristotle, which had been lost to Europe after the fall of Rome. European eyes were opened to vast knowledge through Muslim writings and translations.

In Europe, groups of students gathered in towns to study philosophy, theology, medicine, and law under famous teachers. They began to form **universities,** or guilds of students and teachers. Women were not allowed to teach or study at the universities. By the 1200s, universities had replaced monasteries and cathedrals as the popular centers of learning.

287

➤ *The floor plan of a Gothic cathedral is laid out in the shape of a cross. At the front of the cathedral is a crucifix. A crucifix is a cross with the figure of Jesus on it. This one is made of bronze.*

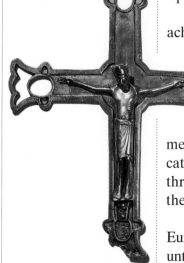

Religious Art

In the painting and sculpture of this time, artists often vividly portrayed events in the life of Jesus, such as the crucifixion. The artists also generally painted Jesus in a highly stylized, as opposed to realistic, manner. Artists stylized their paintings to express their own spiritual beliefs.

However, the greatest artistic achievement of the age was the designing and building of Gothic cathedrals. The word *cathedral* comes from the Greek word meaning "chair." It was in the cathedral that the bishop had his throne, which was the symbol of the power of his office.

Gothic architecture dominated Europe for the 400 years from 1140 until the 1500s. One of the innovations introduced by architects of these cathedrals was ribbed arches, which emphasized the shape of the pointed ceilings. Another was flying buttresses, which were used outside the cathedral to support the heavy structure. Cathedrals were so large and required so much labor to build, that they often took a hundred years or more to finish completely.

Gothic cathedrals were enormous buildings, generally the largest buildings in any community. Their vast interiors were designed to fill onlookers with awe at the power of God. In these masterpieces of design and construction, a variety of artistic elements were combined. Among these were elements such as sculptures of Jesus and the saints; paintings that showed scenes from the life of Jesus; and stained-glass windows, which looked like walls of colored light and usually illustrated stories from the Bible.

For believers, the cathedral, which had an interior or immense open spaces, religious images, and colored light, was the closest thing to experiencing heaven on earth. As Abbot Suger, a pioneer in the design of Gothic cathedrals, wrote of the cathedral of St. Denis, "The entire cathedral is pervaded [filled] by a wonderful and continuous light." ■

■ *How did the church influence European culture between the 1100s and 1300s?*

R E V I E W

1. **FOCUS** What aspects of European society did the church dominate from 1100 to 1300?
2. **CONNECT** How does the hierarchy of the Catholic church compare to the hierarchy of feudal society in western Europe?
3. **BELIEF SYSTEMS** What is excommunication? What role did it play in the struggle between popes and kings?
4. **CRITICAL THINKING** Was Pope Gregory justified in excommunicating Henry? Explain.
5. **WRITING ACTIVITY** Prepare a news story describing the building of a new Gothic cathedral in the late 1100s. Be sure to include quotations from at least three people who would be involved in building or using the church.

L E S S O N   2

The Byzantine Empire

You are a young merchant in the year 1000 seeking your fortune in Constantinople *(kahn stan tuh NOH puhl)*, the capital of the Byzantine Empire. You have endured a 1,500-mile sea voyage from your home in Venice, Italy, to reach this city so rich in works of art and architecture and so busy with commerce. Now, at last, you get your first glimpse of it.

Sailing into port, you see on your left the walls that help protect the city from invaders. Ahead is the Sacred Palace, home of the emperor. Behind it is the towering dome of the great Hagia Sophia *(ah YEE uh soh FEE uh),* a glorious Christian church.

Upon docking, you immediately head up Middle Street, the main street of the capital, which leads right to the palace. This street is crowded with peddlers' canopied stalls. You search the stalls, hurrying past fruit, vegetables, and fish.

Then, quite suddenly, you see what you came for—long rolls of Chinese silk cloth, embroidered in rich threads of gold. You will exchange your gold coins for the cloth. You will then take the cloth back to Venice, where you can sell it for a handsome profit.

THINKING FOCUS

Compare the Eastern Orthodox Church and the Church of Rome.

Key Terms

- literacy
- classic
- patriarch
- icon
- schism

◄ *Constantinople, now called Istanbul, still remains a busy port of trade. The craftsmanship that went into making this silver communion cup was typical of the kind of care artisans took in crafting the goods they sold in Constantinople.*

289

The Roman Empire in the East

Anyone from the West would have experienced wonder upon arriving at Constantinople. Since Constantine had had Constantinople built to be the eastern capital of the Roman Empire, he also had it modeled after Rome. And, like Rome, it became a magnificent center of the Christian faith.

Two Centers of Christianity

Since the time of Jesus' disciple Peter in A.D. 64, the city of Rome had been the center of the Christian faith. According to Christian tradition, Peter was the first bishop of Rome. Christians regarded the pope as the successor to Peter. The pope was the leader of the Christian faith as well as being the bishop of Rome.

In the late 300s, Emperor Theodosius I went one step further. He made Christianity the official religion of the Roman Empire. In addition, when Theodosius I died in 395, his will formally split the empire, leaving half to each son.

Over the next one hundred years, tribes of barbarian invaders captured most of the lands that were controlled by the Western Roman Empire. In 476, one of these tribes, the Goths, overthrew the last emperor of the Western Empire, bringing it to an end. However, the pope and the Roman church still existed in the West. Furthermore, the Eastern Roman Empire, or Byzantine Empire, continued to thrive.

The Byzantine emperor became the head of both the government and the Christian religion in the East. The people of the Byzantine Empire believed the emperor's authority came from God and extended to all matters of church and state. Constantinople became a second center of Christianity.

A Center of Trade

The emperor of the Byzantine Empire ruled with the help of a complex system of advisers and officials. Specialized departments handled different tasks, such as collecting taxes.

Constantinople became a center of world trade. From the lands around the Black Sea came furs and hides, grain, and wine. From Arabia came spices, gems, and silk. And from Africa came ivory and slaves. On the map at left, locate the trade routes used by merchants from these countries.

The empire generated vast amounts of money from trade. The government taxed everything that came through the city.

The Byzantines—those who lived in the Byzantine Empire—sold many of their own products, too. In the rural areas of the empire, farmers produced grapes,

▼ *Why was Constantinople such an ideal port for trade?*

Trade Routes to Constantinople

olives, and wheat for export. In the capital, manufacturers produced glassware, enamel, ivory, and silk.

Attracted by the wealth to be made in trade and industry, people from all over the world came to live in Constantinople. By the year 1000, one million people lived in this thriving city.

Life in the Empire

What was daily life like for the Byzantines? Many of them worked as farmers in rural areas. Craftspersons and traders, who were heavily taxed by the government, lived in the cities. Except for government officials and wealthy merchants, most Byzantines were poor.

Byzantine women had little freedom. They were kept at home, and seldom received any formal education. However, a few women of the wealthy upper classes were educated at home.

The government set up its own schools and libraries, in addition to those run by the church. As a result, there was a higher rate of **literacy**—knowing how to read and write—than in western Europe. At school, the sons of prosperous Byzantine merchants studied the works of famous Greek and Roman writers such as Homer, Virgil, Plato, and Aristotle. These ancient writings were called the **classics.** Even the name of the magnificent church built in 537 during the reign of Emperor Justinian symbolized Byzantine respect for learning. The church was called the Hagia Sophia, which is Greek for "holy wisdom." ■

In this mosaic in the church of Hagia Sophia, Mary and Jesus are receiving a model of the church from Emperor Justinian on the left, and a model of the city from Emperor Constantine.

■ *Why was the Byzantine Empire so powerful?*

291

Europe: Rule, Religion, and Conflict

This Byzantine church in present-day Bulgaria shows the continued use of the rounded arch in Eastern Orthodox architecture. The interior is rich in icons.

The Eastern Church

As the official state religion, Christianity powerfully influenced the lives of the Byzantines. The bishop of Constantinople—called the **patriarch**—dominated the Byzantine church. However, the emperor, the head of both church and state, held more power and authority than the patriarch.

Contrasts with the West

Although the eastern and western churches were both Christian, they differed in many ways. One of these differences was that the Byzantines tolerated much more discussion and debate about religious matters. In the Byzantine church, services were conducted in Greek, the language of the people. The use of their native language allowed the worshipers to become more involved in the service. In the western church, services were conducted in Latin, a language known only to the priests and the well educated.

The architecture of Byzantine churches was also different from that of western churches. Byzantine churches were plainer on the outside, usually featuring a rounded dome, as you can see in the photograph. Their interiors, however, were richly decorated with carvings, painted tiles, and murals. There were **icons** of Jesus and the saints that were nonrealistic, flat images meant to put the viewer in a spiritual frame of mind. Church leaders hoped the faithful would use the icons to worship or honor those religious figures they represented.

Clashes over Authority

Between the years 700 and 1050, the pope still claimed to have authority over the entire Christian church—not just the Church of Rome. However, serious differences of opinion existed between the members of the eastern and western churches. The controversy over icons is one case in point.

Byzantines used icons in many ways. They prayed or lit candles before them or carried them in religious processions. However, some Byzantines thought this devotion to the icons went too far. They feared that people worshiped the icons themselves as gods. Others disagreed, saying that the icons only helped them to worship God better.

In 726, Byzantine Emperor Leo III, fearing that the icons were being worshiped as gods, ordered them destroyed. Many Byzantines refused to comply with the order. From Rome, Pope Gregory III, who was in favor of icons, condemned the emperor's actions. Gregory thought that icons were important for honoring holy people of the past and providing a way for those who could not read to learn about their faith.

As the argument between Emperor Leo III and Pope Gregory III intensified, Gregory made allies of the Franks. Gregory needed the friendship of these Germanic tribes so that they would support and protect him in any war with the Byzantine Empire. In 800, to solidify this alliance, the pope crowned the leader of the Franks, Charlemagne, the only true and holy Roman emperor. Thus, Charlemagne became the first Holy Roman Emperor. However, this action outraged the Byzantines, because they believed that the Byzantine emperor was the only true and rightful Roman emperor.

A Schism in the Church

In 1054, the basic question of who was supreme, the western pope or the eastern patriarch, was still a big issue. The matter finally reached a climax over the question of who was responsible for the churches of southern Italy. When the eastern patriarch, Patriarch Cerularius (*seer u LAIR ih uhs*), lost that argument, he retaliated by closing any churches in Constantinople that celebrated the mass in the western style. At this point, Pope Leo IX of the West excommunicated Patriarch Cerularius of the East, who in turn excommunicated the pope. This led to a split, or **schism,** into two separate churches, the Roman Catholic church in the West and the Eastern Orthodox church in the East. ■

Across Time & Space

The mutual excommunication of the leaders of the Eastern and Roman churches lasted until our century. In 1964, the then-current pope and the patriarch met in Jerusalem. The next year, the two leaders made a formal statement that undid the excommunications.

■ *What factors led to the schism between the churches in the East and West?*

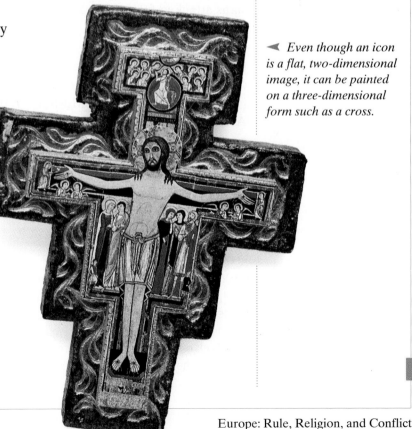

◄ *Even though an icon is a flat, two-dimensional image, it can be painted on a three-dimensional form such as a cross.*

293

The Empire Under Attack

Throughout its long history, the Byzantine Empire endured frequent attacks on its borders. Invaders sought to acquire the empire's great wealth, as well as to acquire the territory itself, because it was so well located for conducting trade with many countries. As a result, emperors had to maintain a powerful military. They also had to build defensive walls around the city of Constantinople.

The Decline of the Empire

The walls protected the city of Constantinople, but they did not protect the empire. After Emperor Justinian extended the empire to its greatest size in the 500s, a period of decline began. In the early 600s, Persians attacked from the east and the south. They took Egypt and marched north, but were unsuccessful in taking Constantinople. Furthermore, in the 630s, Muslim Arabs attacked from the south, capturing the empire's lands in Palestine and Syria.

During the 800s and 900s, the empire again prospered. Trade increased and many of the lost territories were regained by the Byzantines.

An Invasion of Turks

But then in 1071, the invasion of a powerful army of Seljuk Turks threw the Byzantine Empire into decline again. The Seljuk Turks came from Turkestan in central Asia. They were named in honor of Seljuk, their first leader. The Seljuks defeated the Byzantines in 1071 at the battle at Manzikert in present-day Turkey.

The Seljuks continued to capture Byzantine lands, and by 1081 established a new capital in Nicaea *(ny SEE uh)*, only 200 miles southeast of Constantinople. In 1095, the Byzantine emperor sent a desperate message to Pope Urban II. Just 40 years before, the patriarch of the East had excommunicated the pope of the West. Now the Byzantine emperor had no choice but to risk humiliation and plead with the pope for military assistance from the West in order to defend Constantinople against the Turkish invaders. ■

▶ Seljuk Turks ride camelback on the bottom of this colorful ceramic bowl from Persia.

■ *Why did the Byzantine Empire decline in power between the early 600s and late 700s?*

R E V I E W

1. **FOCUS** Compare the Eastern Orthodox Church and the Church of Rome.
2. **CONNECT** Explain why the Eastern Orthodox Church became a separate church from the Church of Rome.
3. **HISTORY** Explain why it was difficult but necessary for the Byzantine emperor to ask for the pope's help in 1095.
4. **CRITICAL THINKING** Do you think Pope Gregory III was justified in condemning Emperor Leo III for his decision to have all icons destroyed? Why?
5. **WRITING ACTIVITY** Use a dictionary to discover the meaning of the word *iconoclast*. Put yourself in the role of Pope Gregory III and write a letter to Emperor Leo III in which you use the word *iconoclast*.

LESSON 3

The Crusades

J erusalem is now held captive by the enemies of Christ and is sub-
jected, by those who do not know God, to the worship of the heathen
[unconverted]. She seeks . . . to be liberated, and [implores] you to
come to her aid.

    On whom, therefore, rests the labor of avenging these wrongs and of
recovering this territory, if not upon you?

THINKING FOCUS

*What were the crusades,
and why were they
important?*

Key Terms

- crusade
- infidel

    Jerusalem is a holy city for
Jews, Christians, and Muslims.
Conflict has sometimes erupted
over possession of Jerusalem and
the right to visit its holy sites. The
crusades were such a period.

    From the 900s, many European
Christians made the pilgrimage to
Jerusalem. The region was stable so
the journey was relatively safe.
After 1070 the region became unstable, and some leaders in Europe
saw a chance to win the Holy Land.
In 1095, Pope Urban II spoke to an
audience and inflamed his listeners
with the words above. Many replied, "God wills it! God wills it!"
They began preparing for holy war.

◄ *While leading a
religious council in
Clermont, France,
Pope Urban II called
on his fellow Christians
to free the Holy Land
from the Turks.*

295

Europe: Rule, Religion, and Conflict

Christian lands, 1080
Muslim lands, 1080
→ First Crusade, 1096–1099
→ Second Crusade, 1147–1149
→ Third Crusade, 1189–1192
→ Fourth Crusade, 1202–1204

0   150   300 mi.
0   150   300 km
Azimuthal Equidistant Projection

▲ *Look at the map to determine which of the crusades used a water route.*

The Crusades Begin

This campaign was actually the first of eight wars Europeans fought to win the Holy Land from the Muslims. These wars, called the **crusades,** occurred between 1096 and 1270. Four of the eight crusades involved Europeans in major warfare. Those who fought were called crusaders, because they vowed to "take up the cross."

The Christians' Motives

Winning the Holy Land from the **infidels** *(IHN fih duhlz),* or non-Christians, was Pope Urban's most obvious motive for war. He

also wanted to reunite the Western and Eastern Christians under his rule. Becoming allies to the Byzantines might aid this cause. At home, Urban also wished to turn the European knights away from infighting and to put their energy into Christian service. For their sacrifices, the knights would be granted the land they conquered. This appealed to the younger sons of many nobles because only the first-born son could inherit a father's feudal lands.

Historians estimate that some 45,000 crusaders left western

Europe to fight in the First Crusade. About 4,000 of those were knights, who were happy to at last be able to employ their fighting skills. The rest of the crusaders were foot soldiers, archers, and cooks. Women and priests also traveled with the men of the army.

Peasants had any of several good reasons for going on the crusade. One reason was that the church promised immediate salvation in heaven to anyone killed while helping to recover the Holy Land for Christians.

A second reason was that a peasant could be free of the bonds to his feudal lord while on a crusade. In other words, if a peasant left on a crusade, the lord of the manor would accept that as a reasonable excuse for the peasant not to pay his rent. The crusades also offered peasants an adventure.

The March to Jerusalem

The crusaders first made their way by foot and on horseback to the important city of Constantinople. The Byzantine emperor's daughter wrote about this as follows:

> F ull of enthusiasm and ardor they thronged every highway . . . Like tributaries joining a river from all directions they streamed towards us in full force.
>
> Anna Comnena, c. 1097

From Constantinople the crusaders marched to Nicaea, the Seljuk capital, conquering it in June 1097. Then they swept eastward across Turkey. There, in 1098, they established the first of their crusader states.

The Crusader States

Crusader states were small outposts that were run like feudal kingdoms in Europe. The crusaders chose kings of these states, though these kings had no more power than a feudal lord.

The crusade now swept southward towards the Holy Land. In July 1099, the crusaders reached Jerusalem. The crusaders slaughtered its Muslim and Jewish inhabitants and made the city the capital of another crusader state.

Now the crusaders controlled a narrow strip of land about 500 miles long but only about 50 miles wide. This left them vulnerable along the outer strip to continued threats from Muslim forces. They built huge castles on the eastern border to better cope with these threats. Knights lived in these castles. To learn more about these knights of the crusades, look at A Moment in Time on page 298.

For now, the Christians had regained the Holy Land. Pilgrims could come to Jerusalem. Fulcher of Chartres wrote, "Now we who were westerners have become easterners. He who was Italian or French has in this land become a Galilean or Palestinian." ■

▼ *This cross belonged to a crusader from the first crusade. Roundels, or curved panels, with Arabic inscriptions from the Koran were hung in Hagia Sophia after the Turks turned it into a mosque.*

■ *Why did the Christians want to recapture Jerusalem?*

A Crusader

3:32 P.M., October 20, 1192
In a field outside Temitz, Austria

Sword
This weapon is useful for fighting on foot. On his return trip, he has been attacked by German townspeople who think he might rob or kill them, as some knights have.

Chain Mail
The knight's head-to-toe suit of interlocked metal rings is heavy, hot, noisy, and hard to keep clean.

Pebble
He picked this stone off the floor of the Church of the Holy Sepulchre in Jerusalem. Filled with good luck, it's very precious to our knight.

Shield
Designed as a personal sign, his shield identifies him to friend and foe on the battlefield.

Letter
A commander near Jerusalem wrote this letter to a king in northern Germany. Our knight cannot read the letter, which complains of a water shortage.

Spices
These gifts will amaze his friends in England. Black pepper is unknown in his district; sugar is a once-in-a-lifetime treat.

Quilted Body Suit
Protecting him against the chain mail, this suit hasn't been washed or removed in eight and a half months.

Bandage
The knight's arrow wound is dressed with a sophisticated, soothing ointment, applied by an Islamic doctor.

Muslims Regain the Holy Land

During the 1140s, about 40 years after the First Crusade, the Muslims began to overpower the crusader states. The Church urged the people to renew the battle.

The Second Crusade, which lasted from 1147 to 1149, proved unsuccessful. Instead of fighting against the Muslims, armies led by King Louis VII of France and King Conrad III of Germany fought among themselves. Then Muslims almost wiped out the crusader army in Turkey. The small number of men who did make it to the Holy Land could not manage to live peacefully with the local Christian lords, who feared that the newcomers would attempt to set up a new government. While the crusaders argued among themselves, the Muslims continued to recapture lands.

Saladin's Rise to Power

In the late 1100s, Saladin was the leader of the Muslim forces. Saladin had been just a young Muslim schoolboy in Damascus when Christian knights laid siege to his city during the Second Crusade. But Saladin, whose name means "honoring the faith," would become a towering figure in the Muslim world, the greatest leader against the Christian crusaders.

As a young man Saladin served in the army of Syria, a country to the east of the crusader states. When the Syrian army took control of Egypt, south of the Holy Land, the caliph gave Saladin the job of running the government.

Because he was a strong leader, Saladin was able to unite the many small Muslim groups surrounding

the crusader states. He became the supreme leader of both Egypt and Syria in 1171.

The Horns of Hattin

Saladin led the Muslims in a siege of Tiberias, the capital city of one of the crusader states near the Sea of Galilee. Knights of the Kingdom of Jerusalem, the southernmost crusader state, headed north to free Tiberias from Saladin. Christians and Muslims met in a decisive battle in July 1187.

The crusader army of about 20,000, including 1,200 knights in full armor and chain mail, was exhausted from marching all day in the desert. So six miles from Tiberias the crusaders camped in a small valley between the Horns of Hattin, twin mountain peaks. During the night the Muslim cavalry, outnumbering the Christian crusaders by several thousand, surrounded the crusaders.

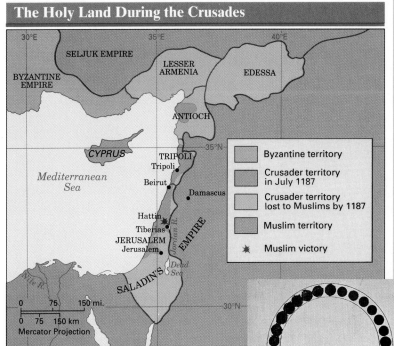

The Holy Land During the Crusades

Byzantine territory

Crusader territory in July 1187

Crusader territory lost to Muslims by 1187

Muslim territory

★ Muslim victory

▲ *The portrait of Saladin painted in 1180 is thought to be the only image of him that still exists. Find the lands on the map controlled by Saladin and his forces.*

299

Jerusalem was taken by the Christians in 1099. The Muslims recaptured the city in 1187. This French illustration from the 1300s depicts a battle for control of Jerusalem.

Just before dawn, the Muslims set fire to the dry grass that surrounded the valley, and the wind blew the flames up to where the crusaders were encamped. The Muslims charged behind the flames, boxing in the crusaders.

After the fire died down, few crusaders escaped death or captivity. Most of the crusader foot soldiers were sold into slavery. But Saladin also had a tremendous sense of honor. He guaranteed the safety of fleeing pilgrims, released husbands from captivity, and gave gifts to widows and orphans.

Saladin had decisively defeated the crusaders. With no opposition left, Saladin retook Jerusalem, and within three months, he had retaken almost all of Palestine. Use the map on page 299 to identify lands held by Muslims.

The Crusade of Kings

When news of the loss of Jerusalem reached western Europe, the pope is said to have died of grief. His successor, Pope Gregory VIII, called for a Third Crusade, which came to be called the Crusade of Kings. Three kings responded to the call: Emperor Frederick I of Germany, King Richard of England, and King Philip II of France. In 1189, these kings and their armies began preparations to regain Jerusalem from Saladin and the Muslims.

From the beginning, this crusade went badly. The 70-year-old Frederick drowned in 1190 while swimming across a river in Turkey. Most of Frederick's army was so discouraged that they returned to Europe.

Richard, who would later be nicknamed "the lion heart," was a military genius famous for his great courage in battle. But he had an unstable character—generous one moment and violent the next. Philip, a skilled politician, was no warrior but was an expert in planning sieges.

In April 1191, Philip began a siege of Acre, a key city on the coast. Richard joined Philip for the siege in June. The following month, the Muslims surrendered and Philip headed back for France. After occupying Acre for a few weeks, Richard became impatient when peace negotiations with Saladin were going slowly. Richard ordered the execution of all 2,700 Muslims within the city's walls.

Richard and Saladin

During the next year, Richard and Saladin fought many battles. Richard regained some territories but failed to regain Jerusalem. Each leader made various peace proposals, and in September 1192, the two leaders signed a five-year treaty. Under this treaty, the crusaders could keep their cities along the coast from Jaffa north, and pilgrims could once again freely visit the holy places.

The Fourth Crusade

In 1198, Pope Innocent III called a crusade that proved to be disastrous to the Byzantine Empire. In this Fourth Crusade, the crusaders decided to head east by the Mediterranean Sea rather than by land. The merchants of Venice saw this as an opportunity to strengthen their trade routes. They convinced the crusade leaders to use force if necessary to install the Venetians' choice for the next Byzantine Emperor.

When the crusaders reached Constantinople, where the emperor lived, they kept their promise, but the people rebelled against this imposed ruler. The crusaders then seized Constantinople and pillaged it. Later historians have referred to this incident as "the Sack of Constantinople."

For three terrible days, the crusaders burned libraries; desecrated churches; and stole many valuable works of art, jewels, and gold. They then shipped their bounty back to Venice. In the selection below, you can read a Greek historian's eyewitness record of the pillaging.

> How shall I begin to tell of the deeds done by these wicked men? They trampled the images underfoot instead of adoring them. They threw the relics of the martyrs into filth. . . , They broke into bits the sacred altar of Santa Sophia, and distributed it among the soldiers. When the sacred vessels and the silver and gold ornaments were to be carried off, they brought up mules and saddle horses inside the church itself.
>
> Nicetas Choniates, 1204

The spirit of the crusades had been lost. The "enthusiasm and ardor" that Anna Comnena had seen in the first crusaders had been replaced by a hunger for wealth. ∎

▲ *This Egyptian leather shadow puppet showing archers in a river boat celebrates a victory over the crusaders.*

■ *Were the crusades successful? Explain.*

The Crusades Affect the West

Since these wars did not achieve their stated purpose, Christians might say they ended in failure. Jerusalem, the "center of the earth," remained in the Muslims' control. Constantinople, the jewel of the Byzantine Empire, was ravaged. People lost respect for the crusaders because of the abuses inflicted upon innocent people.

In Europe, the crusades proved to be a particular disaster for one group—the Jews. Crusaders considered both Jews and Muslims to be infidels. So at the same time that the crusaders set out to fight Muslims in the East, they slaughtered both the eastern and western Jewish population. The crusaders destroyed a number of Jewish towns along the Rhine River.

In some ways, though, western Europe did benefit from the crusades. First, trade, which was

Across Time & Space

Over the centuries, many Arabic words have come into common use in English. Arabic terms for products or ideas that have become part of the English language include tariff, sugar, rice, lemon, pistachio, and cotton. With the crusades, most Europeans got their first taste of sugar, citrus fruits, and many spices.

301

▲ *Christians brought this reliquary, or container for relics, from Turkey to Italy in the late 1000s. They believed it held part of the finger of St. Nicholas, which would have made it a holy vessel. The crusaders carried many relics back to western Europe when they returned from the crusades.*

■ *How did the crusades benefit western Europe?*

already growing, expanded as a result of the crusades. As the crusaders passed through Europe, they brought with them a need for goods and services. Business in European towns boomed. In the lands of the Muslim Empire, there was a much higher standard of living. Some crusaders were determined for Europe to have the paved and well-lit streets and other civic improvements of those lands.

Crusaders also brought back many of the luxury goods available in the East—silk, spices, and pearls—and European demand for these fineries grew. The Italian cities of Venice, Pisa, and Genoa negotiated special trade treaties with Muslim rulers. In some cases, they were the sole suppliers of certain goods. In 1277, by special treaty with Muslim Sicily, the Venetians learned glass making.

A second effect of the crusades was a great transfer of military technology. Battles with the more advanced Muslims taught the Europeans about new and better weapons and tactics. It is possible that this is how gunpowder came to Europe.

Third, some scholars say that European poetry and music grew after the crusaders heard Arabic love poetry and music. In literature,

chivalry developed a concept called "courtly love." Women received the benefit of this literary style, in which they were seen as holy, pure, and good. This contrasted with the general view of women as weak and inferior.

A fourth effect of the crusades was on the church itself. These wars strengthened the church's desire to spread Christianity and to eventually overwhelm the Muslim Empire. The church also came to see exploration as one of the most useful ways to spread Christianity around the world.

A fifth effect of the crusades was to strengthen Europe's national governments. Thousands of feudal lords were killed, and many landowning families went bankrupt paying for their knights' voyages. Thus their lands returned to the monarchs, whose power grew.

Finally, and perhaps most important, many Europeans now had their eyes opened wide to the world. Before the crusades, most had seen little beyond the next village. Now they knew about life in the Holy Land, other parts of Europe, and the Mediterranean. They now knew there were other ways of doing things—sometimes better ways. And, in some cases, they were willing to try them. ■

R E V I E W

1. **FOCUS** What were the crusades, and why were they important?
2. **CONNECT** Why did the crusades prove disastrous for the Byzantine Empire?
3. **BELIEF SYSTEMS** Why have so many wars been fought over the region called "the Holy Land?"
4. **CRITICAL THINKING** How did the motives of the first crusaders differ from those of the last crusaders?

5. **CRITICAL THINKING** How does using the label "infidel" to describe members of other faiths affect the way people behave toward one another?
6. **ACTIVITY** Prepare a chart of the four major crusades. For each crusade, give the dates when it occurred, the major participants, and the major events that occurred during the crusade.

Drawing Conclusions

Here's Why

Historical maps provide information about the past. Some of this information may be straightforward, such as boundaries or routes. Sometimes, however, you need to use the facts to answer more complicated questions. When you use pieces of information to figure out another idea, you are drawing a conclusion.

Here's How

Look at the map of trade routes in A.D. 1200. It shows products traded and trade routes. You can use one piece of information, products traded, to draw a conclusion about Chinese economy and society.

The products traded from eastern China were perfume, silk, and porcelain. You know that these are products that people need to manufacture, and they are not raw materials, such as iron ore or sheep. Because they are manufactured goods, some complicated technology was probably needed to make them. You can conclude that Chinese society around 1200 had some complex technology.

Try It

Now look at the goods traded from Europe. Based on that information, what conclusions can you draw about European society around 1200? What kinds of goods were they and what was required to produce them? Draw a conclusion about the kinds of technology that might have been available in Europe.

Apply It

Do some research to find out more about making silk and wool. See how the two processes compare, and what kinds of technology were needed. Then look at the conclusion that you drew about European society. How can you find out whether it was correct?

Trade Routes, c. A.D. 1200

Legend

- The Silk Road
- Other land routes
- Sea routes
- Direction goods were traded
- Mongol Empire
- Holy Roman Empire
- Silk
- Spices
- Perfumes
- Glassware
- Precious stones
- Cotton
- Wool
- Elephants
- Ivory
- Porcelain
- Metalware
- Horses

Chapter Review

Reviewing Key Terms

classic (p. 291)
clergy (p. 283)
crusade (p. 296)
excommunication (p. 285)
icon (p. 292)
infidel (p. 296)

literacy (p. 291)
patriarch (p. 292)
salvation (p. 285)
schism (p. 293)
tithe (p. 285)
university (p. 287)

A. The key terms in each group are related in some way. Write a sentence or two showing how the words in each pair or group are related to each other.
1. clergy, salvation
2. excommunication, patriarch, schism
3. crusade, infidel
4. classics, crusade, university
5. icon, schism

B. Each phrase below is related to a key term as it is used in the chapter. Write a sentence that includes each phrase and the key term to which it relates. The first one has been done for you.
1. money, produce, or labor: A tithe, or one-tenth of a person's income, could be paid in money, produce, or labor.
2. paintings and figures
3. Aristotle, Plato, Homer, and Virgil
4. Byzantine schools and churches
5. theology, philosophy, law, and medicine
6. "full of enthusiasm and ardor"
7. worship services, weddings, baptisms
8. belief, moral life, good works

Exploring Concepts

A. On your own paper, copy and complete the timeline using information from the chapter. Then write a summary of the chapter based on the dates and events in this timeline.

B. Write a sentence to answer each question using information from the chapter.
1. How did the crusades help bring about the end of the Byzantine Empire?
2. How did the crusades reflect the power of the church in Europe?
3. What positive effects did the crusades have on trade, warfare, and outlook in western Europe?
4. In what way did Christians look upon the crusades as a failure?
5. How did the establishment of religious orders and universities help expand the church and the community?
6. Describe three ways in which the church was the center of community life in Europe around 1000.
7. Why did King Louis the VI appoint Abbot Suger as regent in 1147?
8. How were Byzantine churches different from western European churches?
9. Summarize the dispute over icons between Leo III and Gregory III.

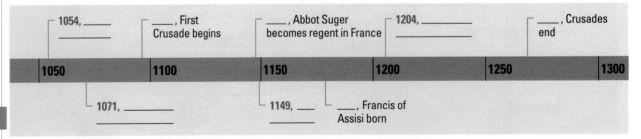

1054, _____ _____ | _____, First Crusade begins | _____, Abbot Suger becomes regent in France | 1204, _____ _____ | _____, Crusades end

1050 | 1100 | 1150 | 1200 | 1250 | 1300

1071, _____ _____ | 1149, _____ _____ | _____, Francis of Assisi born

Reviewing Skills

1. Look at the map on page 142. Your business, located in Alexandria, is planning to send a ship from the Red Sea to Southeast Asia, stopping along the way in India. The voyage one-way to Asia will take four months. The wool you are shipping has arrived late, so your ship won't reach the Indian Ocean until December. Use the map and a calendar to estimate when the ship will arrive in Southeast Asia. Form a conclusion about when the ship will return.

2. The map on page 290 shows trade routes in the eastern Mediterranean during the Byzantine Empire. Venice-to-Trebizond is the longest route under Byzantine control. Now look at the map on page 205. The Silk Road was the longest trade route in the Tang lands. How long is each? Draw a conclusion about trade, government, or transportation technology as you compare Byzantine and Tang trade routes.

3. Look at the map of Baghdad on page 87. What conclusions can you make about Baghdad's dependence on water.

Using Critical Thinking

1. "Many feudal Europeans, most of whom had never traveled beyond the next village, now had their eyes opened to the wide world." Write one or more paragraphs to answer the following questions about the above quotation. Is it a statement of fact, opinion, or reasoned judgment? Why? Given the information in the chapter, what might the statement mean? Is it supported by information in the chapter? How?

2. The beginning of Lesson 2 talks about some of the trade that existed between western Europe and the East before the crusades began. The Seljuks invaded the Byzantine Empire in 1071. That same year, they seized Jerusalem and prevented Christians from entering the city. What effect did the actions of the Seljuk Muslims have on the beginning of the crusades? How did they influence trade between East and West? Write a paragraph or two describing the Seljuk influence and the effect of the crusades themselves on international commerce.

Preparing for Citizenship

1. WRITING ACTIVITY Imagine that you work for King Henry IV as a clerk. As such, you are a member of a very special group of people: you are one of the few individuals in western Europe at this time who can read and write. The king has asked you to record the story of his excommunication by Pope Gregory. Write two or three paragraphs describing this event.

2. ARTS ACTIVITY In the library, find books on European, Byzantine, or Muslim arts and crafts from the period between 1000 and 1300. Choose one style and find a picture that represents that style. For example, it could be a picture of enameled jewelry or embroidered cloth, a carving, a mural, a painting, or a sculpture. Draw a picture of your own that is similar in style to the picture you are looking at.

3. COLLABORATIVE LEARNING Divide into groups of three to four people each. As a group, gather and present visually as much information as you can about the people of Europe and the lands around the Mediterranean from 1000 to 1200. Your presentation should consist of a variety of visuals, such as maps, timelines, charts, or graphs, or any combination of those formats. It also can include written notes, but it should not simply be a report. One person from each group should explain the group's project to the class.

Europe: 1300-1600

A traveler passing through the city gates of Florence one day in the 1400s remarked that this was a city "in which much money was to be made and many were making it." But something new was happening here as well. Florence, Italy, was a center for a revolution in arts and ideas that swept through Europe. Europeans began to think more about life on earth than about life after death. They found new ways to paint, to look at life, and to worship. Explorers even pushed out the horizons of the known world.

1300

Map of Florence by Vincenzo Catena, c. 1480.
Museo di Firenze, Florence.

RVCANO

S.FRANCESCO

SMINI
ATO

BELLO
SGUA
RDO

S.FELICE

PORTA
S.PIER
GATT
OLINI

1600

Chapter 12

The Renaissance

From the 1300s to the mid-1600s, Europe went through a renaissance, or "rebirth." People broke from bonds of the church and feudal structures. Scholars and artists studied the ideas of classical Greece and Rome. Writers told stories of everyday people. Paintings burst with life. To many Europeans, this was the beginning of the modern world.

1434 Cosimo de Medici (above left) begins his rule of Florence, Italy. The wealthy Medicis support architects who design the city's impressive buildings (above).

| 1300 | 1350 | 1400 | 1450 |

1370 Mongol leader Timur begins a series of raids through central Asia.

1420 The Chinese build the Great Temple of the Dragon in Beijing.

1300

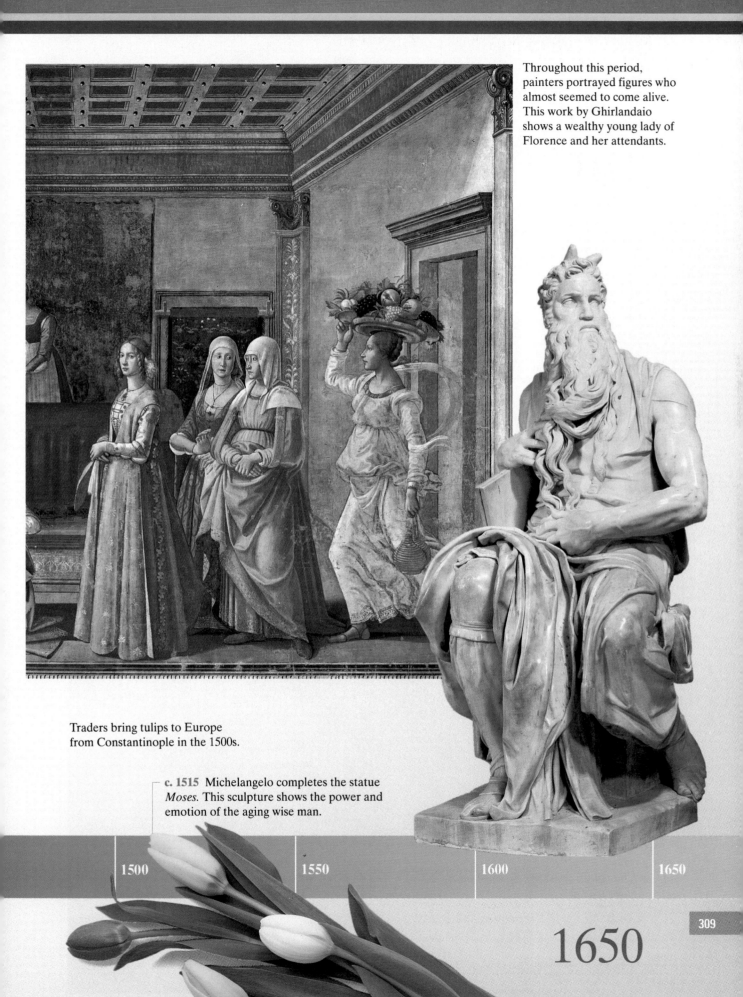

Throughout this period, painters portrayed figures who almost seemed to come alive. This work by Ghirlandaio shows a wealthy young lady of Florence and her attendants.

Traders bring tulips to Europe from Constantinople in the 1500s.

c. 1515 Michelangelo completes the statue *Moses.* This sculpture shows the power and emotion of the aging wise man.

1500　　1550　　1600　　1650

1650

L E S S O N   1

Europe at the End of the Middle Ages

THINKING

F O C U S

How did the problems of the 14th century bring about changes in European society?

Key Terms

- plague
- monarchy
- heretic
- individualism

R ing-a-ring o' roses,
A pocket full of posies,
A-tishoo! A-tishoo!
We all fall down."
The words may be a little different, but you probably still recognize this children's rhyme: "Ring-Around-the-Rosie."

As common as this verse is, few people know that it describes one of the most destructive events of the Middle Ages—the Great Plague. The **plague** was a disease that swept like wildfire through Europe beginning in 1347. It was first seen in China in 1331 and in 15 years had spread across Asia to the Black Sea. People later called it the Black Death, because black spots formed under the skin from internal bleeding.

A rosy rash and sneezing were also symptoms of the disease. People carried bunches of herbs called "posies" in their pockets to try to ward off the illness. Millions of people "fell down" and died as wave after wave of the Black Death struck.

The plague spread quickly, infecting rich and poor alike. On the next page is an Italian man's description of the helplessness he felt as the disease spread.

► *The plague overwhelmed Europe during the 1300s. In this painting, The Triumph of Death, by Francesco Traini, a hunting party comes across the coffins of three plague victims. The monk at the far left reminds the hunters of how fleeting life is.*

The Great Plague, 1346–1353

Advance of the Plague

- By December 1346
- By December 1347
- By June 1348
- By December 1348
- By June 1349
- By June 1350
- By December 1350
- By December 1351
- By December 1353
- Areas of minor plague infection

North Sea
Baltic Sea
50°N
Dublin · Lancaster · Durham
Leicester · York
Bristol · London
Hamburg
Calais · Cologne
Liège
Würzburg
Nuremberg
Vienna
Paris
Angers
Strasbourg
ATLANTIC OCEAN
40°N
Zurich
Bordeaux · Milan · Venice
Avignon · Genoa
Marseille · Pisa · Florence
Siena · Dubrovnik
Barcelona · CORSICA · Rome
Valencia · SARDINIA · Naples
Seville
Mediterranean Sea
Messina
SICILY
Athens
Black Sea
Constantinople
ASIA MINOR

0   250   500 mi.
0   250   500 km
Azimuthal Equidistant Projection
0°   10°E   20°E   30°E

I do not know where to begin describing its relentless cruelty; almost everyone who witnessed it seemed stupefied [stunned] by grief. . . . I, Agnolo di Tura, known as the Fat, buried five of my children with my own hands. . . . Nobody wept for the dead, since each was awaiting death; and so many died that everyone thought that the end of the world had come.

▲ *The Great Plague began in Asia and was carried to Europe by the fleas on black rats. These rats lived on trade ships that traveled between Asia and Europe. In Europe the plague moved from south to north, along trade routes.*

Europe in Crisis

During the 350 years before the plague, the population of Europe had more than doubled in size. Because the agricultural techniques of the Middle Ages were fairly crude, farmers had trouble growing enough food for the large population. Then disaster struck. Unusually heavy rains fell during the years from 1315 to 1319, causing the farmers' grain to rot in the fields. Thousands of people starved to death.

When the plague struck in 1347, it devastated many areas already weakened by the famine. Look at the map above, and follow the progress of the plague as it swept across the continent. The

▼ *Many Europeans used "remedies" for the plague. Two popular remedies were pomanders, which were oranges stuck with cloves, and peeled onions. Neither worked, however.*

population recovered in most areas from the 1347 outbreak. New outbreaks of the plague hit Europe in 1360 and 1374. By the late 1300s, one-fourth to one-third of the population of Europe had died. In some towns, over 50 percent of the people died.

After the plague, there were too few people. There were not enough people to harvest the crops or produce all the necessary goods.

Because there were fewer people to do work, peasants demanded better wages and lower rents. Landlords resisted peasant demands. Like others before them, many peasants moved to towns or villages. There they hoped to find a better life, free from the control of the landlords.

Some landlords passed laws to force peasants to work for their traditional wages. Throughout Europe, bitter resentment brewed as landlords tried to enforce those laws. Many peasants joined forces to storm and burn manor houses. As peasants broke their ties with landlords, the feudal system began to falter.

These economic and social crises chipped away at the foundations of medieval society in the 1300s and 1400s. Conditions were ripe for great social change. ■

▲ Neither rich nor poor was spared from the plague. These woodcuts from The Dance of Death *by Hans Holbein show death visiting a poor farmer and a scholar.*

■ *How did the plague affect the society and economy of western Europe?*

W Joan of Arc is still celebrated as a heroine who helped save France from the English, as shown in this French statue.

Rise of Central Governments

During the Middle Ages, power rested in the hands of nobles who owned feudal estates. But from the 1100s to the 1300s, the power in Western Europe had begun to shift from the nobles to kings. These kings were attempting to form **monarchies,** or strong central governments ruled by a king or queen. Monarchies in countries like England and France began to gain power and authority. Kings and queens collected taxes, raised armies, and ruled their subjects through central governments.

However, the increasing power of some kings was not well received by everyone. Revolts by many nobles against kings and contests between kings for territory produced war. These wars raged almost constantly in the 1300s and 1400s. The longest war of the later Middle Ages was the Hundred Years' War. This war began in 1337, when the king of England claimed to be the rightful king of France. The French king resisted, and war lasted on and off for another 116 years. Finally in 1453, the French troops defeated the English.

Joan of Arc

At the point during the war when French fortunes had sunk to their lowest, a young woman helped bring about a remarkable reversal. Joan of Arc grew up in the small French village of

Donremy. Like most peasants, she never learned to read or write.

Joan left home in 1429 at the age of 17. She insisted that she had received messages from God telling her to help drive the English out of France. Joan asked one of the French nobles to let her speak to Charles, heir to the throne.

Charles decided to test Joan. He had one of his nobles sit on the throne while he stood with the rest of the court. When Joan entered, she went to Charles, although she had never seen him before. This helped convince Charles that Joan spoke the truth.

Charles gave Joan soldiers and supplies and sent her off to Orleans. At this town in northern France, the English and French had been engaged in a fierce battle for several months. Before she left, Joan dictated a message for the English leaders. She hoped to persuade them to leave France without further bloodshed:

> Surrender to the Maid [Joan] sent hither by God the King of Heaven, the keys of all the good towns you have taken and laid waste in France.

The letter did not convince the English to surrender. Instead, the 17-year-old Joan rode off to Orleans to fight bravely alongside her soldiers. Joan defeated the English at Orleans and went on to win four other battles against them.

Joan was captured in May 1430. The English army and the Church tried her as a witch and a **heretic,** or one who speaks beliefs different from the accepted church opinion. Her sentence: to be burned at the stake. Joan was only 19 years old when she died.

New Ways of Fighting

The Hundred Years' War was a turning point in medieval war technology. Horse-mounted knights in heavy armor could not survive the armor-piercing arrows shot from the newly developed longbows.

With the crusades and revived trade routes, Europeans learned about Greek, Roman, Indian, Chinese, and Muslim war technology. During the crusades, the Muslim armies had used hand grenades and flame throwers filled with naphtha, a naturally occuring petroleum byproduct. The Chinese had long used gunpowder for fireworks and signals.

The introduction of guns and gunpowder to Europe in the 1320s made the biggest impact on how wars were fought there. By the 1320s, cannons were being made for besieging and bombarding forts and castles. Smaller cannons led to hand-held cannons, and beginning in the 1400s, soldiers carried long handguns known as harquebuses (*HAHR kuh buhs uhs*) into battle.

During the 1300s, rulers also began to raise large armies by hiring professional soldiers. ■

◄ *Warfare changed greatly during the Hundred Years' War. New weapons, such as the longbow and the cannon, made both the knight and the castle obsolete.*

Across Time & Space

Twenty-five years after Joan of Arc was executed, the Catholic Church decided that Joan had not been a witch. Five centuries later, on May 16, 1920, Joan of Arc was declared a saint by the Roman Catholic Church.

■ *Why did the feudal system begin to crumble?*

Trade and Commerce

In spite of the famine, plague, and wars of late medieval society, manufacturing and trade flourished. Goods and services were more in demand than ever.

In Europe, large-scale manufacturing and commercial activity was centered in the towns rather than in the countryside. Towns, especially those on the rapidly developing intercontinental trade routes, were prosperous, bustling with people buying and selling food and goods.

Town society was made up of merchants, shopkeepers, and artisans who were socially above the laboring class and below the nobility. This commercial class tended not to rely heavily on the church for guidance. Instead, they focused on achieving earthly success and wealth. While women were kept out of government and some guilds, their work as merchants, shopkeepers, and artisans was crucial to both family and town economy.

Some of the most prosperous and powerful towns in Europe were Florence and Milan, in Italy. The country's location made trade easier with Asia, Africa, and the rest of Europe.

Italian traders bought and sold fine woolens, colored cottons, and silk woven with gold and silver threads. They also traded wines, furs and leather, jewels, ivory, and metals. They traded spices, too—salt from the coast of France, and cinnamon and peppercorns from the islands of Southeast Asia.

Some of the wealthiest Italian merchants were bankers and moneychangers. Over 500 different currencies were in use in Europe at the time. For a fee, moneychangers would exchange Portuguese coins for French, or Italian coins for English.

▼ *The commercial class became increasingly powerful during the 1300s and 1400s. Members of this class tended to be concerned with making money. They made their money by trading such goods as silk, linen, saffron, and salt.*

Bankers could afford to lend some of their own money. Some banking families were so rich that they even lent money to kings and popes.

International trade brought many upper-class and commercial class Europeans into contact with new ideas and exotic goods from faraway places. Many worked for themselves and earned money to support their families. This freedom to work for one's self, along with the lure of money and success, changed the values of medieval society. **Individualism,** the idea that each person should be free to develop and pursue his or her own goals, became an important value for many of the people of the time. ■

■ *How did medieval values change as trade and commerce grew?*

UNDERSTANDING RELIGIOUS PERSECUTION

Religious persecution is practiced when people of one faith deny those of another the right to their own beliefs. Sometimes, persecution takes the form of denying other people their right to justice, property, or life.

As Christianity in Europe grew stronger, it taught that members of other religions were to be converted, by force if necessary. In the Crusades, many Jewish communities in Europe were slaughtered by Crusaders. Some Crusaders claimed they were trying to strengthen Christianity, but many simply looted and killed in a superstitious frenzy. When Black Death broke out, many Christians blamed Jews for it, leading to more deadly attacks on Jewish communities. Rulers often expelled the Jews from their countries, as did the English in 1290, the French in 1306, 1322, and 1394, and the Spanish in 1492.

Causes of Persecution

Throughout the ages, and especially in Europe in the Middle Ages, people believed in superstitions. These are beliefs or practices that come from ignorance, fear of the unknown, or trust in magic or chance. Many people in troubled times look for scapegoats, too. Scapegoats are people or things that are falsely blamed. Some medieval women who did not fit traditional roles were accused of being witches and burned.

Effects

Christians drove out Jews and other non-Christians from medieval European society. They forbade them to own land, to practice a trade or a profession, or to bear arms. Jewish long-distance trade networks were broken. In 1215, a Church council forced Jews to wear special badges to set them apart from Christians. Can you think of any examples of religious persecution today?

REVIEW

1. FOCUS How did the problems of the 14th century bring about changes in European society?

2. CONNECT How did the Black Death help weaken feudal arrangements?

3. HISTORY How did changes in warfare in the 1300s help to change European society?

4. CRITICAL THINKING How did trade help to change the attitudes some Europeans had of the world?

5. WRITING ACTIVITY Pretend that you are living in Europe during the 1350s. Write two or three entries in your diary describing the events taking place in your area.

The Renaissance

LESSON 2

The Italian Renaissance

Key Terms

- Renaissance
- republic
- mercenary
- humanism
- realism

*I*t is wrong to rinse your mouth and spit out wine in public . . . to carry your toothpick either in your mouth, like a bird making its nest, or behind your ear.

Refrain as far as possible from making noises which grate upon the ear, such as grinding or sucking your teeth.

It is bad manners to clean your teeth with your napkin, and still worse to do it with your finger.

A man . . . will take care not to get his fingers so greasy as to dirty his napkin with them, because the sight of it would be unsavory to others.

Anyone whose legs are too thin, or exceptionally fat, or perhaps crooked, should not wear vivid or parti-colored [multi-colored] hose, in order not to attract attention to his defects.

It is not polite to scratch yourself when you are seated at table. You should also take care, as far as you can, not to spit at mealtimes, but if you must spit, then do so in a decent manner.

Your conduct should not be governed by your own fancy, but in consideration of the feelings of those whose company you keep.

A man must . . . not be content to do things well, but must also aim to do them gracefully.

Giovanni della Casa, from
The Book of Manners, 1558

➤ *During the Renaissance, wealthy people began to eat from plates and to use knives and forks. During the Middle Ages, people did not use utensils, and ate from a common plate.*

These are some of the social do's and don'ts of a new age as listed in an Italian manners book. A new way of living and thinking was taking hold in Europe as the Middle Ages died out. During this new age, called the Renaissance *(rehn ih SAHNS)*, people began to focus on refinement, personal achievement, and learning.

The Birthplace of the Renaissance

The word **Renaissance** comes from a Latin word that means re-birth or revival. The term is used to describe a renewed attention to ideas from classical Greek and Roman culture. This renewal occurred first in northern Italy and then spread through Europe between the 1300s and mid-1600s.

Italian City-States

During the late Middle Ages, the government of Italy was different from those of other countries in Europe. In France and England, for example, strong central governments were forming. However, at the beginning of the Italian Renaissance, Italy was made up of about 250 small states. Most of these states were ruled by cities and were called city-states. Some of the cities were small, but others, like Venice and Milan, had as many as 100,000 people. Look at the map on this page to see how Italy was divided at this time.

Each Italian city-state was independent. All had formed when townspeople began to free themselves from the control of feudal landlords in the 1100s. Some Italian city-states had a republican form of government. A **republic** is a government whose head of state is not a monarch. These cities were not republics like the U.S., as only a few people got to vote, and the cities were mostly run by a few rich families. Other city-states were ruled by a tyrant, or absolute ruler. These tyrants often passed on their jobs to their children, just like kings. Some even ruled so-called "republics," but controlled the elections.

Italian City-States, 1454

SAVOY
MONTFERRAT
ASTI
SALUZZO
GENOA
Verona
Milan
MANTUA
MILAN
MODENA
FERRARA
Bologna
SAN MARINO
LUCCA
Pisa
Florence
FLORENCE
Siena
Urbino
SIENA
Assisi
CORSICA (Genoa)
PIOMBINO
Rome
PAPAL STATES
Naples
SARDINIA (Aragon)
Adriatic Sea
Tyrrhenian Sea
Mediterranean Sea
KINGDOM OF THE TWO SICILIES (Aragon)
VENETIAN REPUBLIC
Venice
Po R.
Adige R.
Arno R.
Tiber R.
Garigliano R.

0   100   200 mi.
0   100   200 km
Mercator Projection

10°E   15°E   45°N   40°N

The Ruling Class

Florence's ruling class was made up of about 800 of the city's wealthiest families. They were aristocrats or merchants and bankers who often led the major guilds. To maintain their control, members of the ruling families often excluded others from government and guilds.

These families lived in luxurious palaces that often took up an entire city block. They used their wealth to beautify their cities by hiring architects to design and build palaces. Inside these palaces, each family usually had an elaborate court of attendants. The court included family members and political advisers, as well as leading artists and scholars.

▲ *The Italian city-states were often ruled by powerful families. This was especially true of Florence. This guild shield illustrates the trade that made Florence wealthy: wool.*

▲ *This French engraving shows Niccolò Machiavelli as a young man.*

■ *Why did the Renaissance begin in northern Italy?*

➤ *The figure in this painting is probably Cardinal Bessarion, who was seen by people of the Renaissance as a model humanist. The cardinal was honored for being devoted to both scholarship and public service.*

The ruling families often struggled among themselves for control of their city. In the 1430s, the Medici family dominated the ruling class of Florence. The Medicis were a talented and ambitious family who controlled an international network of banks in Europe.

City-states also competed with each other for land and power. Frequently they fought to control international trade markets. To defend the city-states, the rulers gathered large troops of **mercenaries,** or paid soldiers. The thirst for power and wealth led to many murders, riots, feuds, and battles within and among city-states.

One of the great political thinkers of the Renaissance was Niccolò Machiavelli (*MAK ee uh VEHL ee;* 1469–1527), who lived in and worked for Florence. His book, The Prince, is a discussion of how a leader should govern his people. In medieval times, the job of government was to administer justice. Machiavelli—having studied ancient Rome—thought the job of government should be the state's growth and expansion. Machiavelli advised his prince to ignore whether actions were good or evil, and to judge them on their benefit to the state. A ruler might be cruel or merciful, generous or deceitful, all to better the state. What do you think of his ideas? ■

The Renaissance and Life

Life in the Italian city-states changed the way some residents viewed the world. Though very religious, these residents concentrated more on this life than on heaven or hell. In doing so, they hoped to understand people and their world better.

In particular, these Italian scholars turned to the works of the ancient Greeks and Romans as their guides. Many of these classics had been reintroduced into Western Europe by Europeans who came into contact with Byzantine and Arab scholars. European scholars of the Middle Ages had studied some of the classics to deepen their religious faith. Renaissance scholars added to this and now studied to expand their knowledge. Scholars spent many hours learning Greek and Latin in order to read the Greek and Roman sources. They wanted to recreate the spirit of classical arts, literature, and philosophy. Because they studied the classics, or the humanities, they were called humanists. Their concern with the classics was called **humanism.**

During the Middle Ages, many Christians saw themselves as sinful creatures struggling to get into heaven. But humanists did not see people as sinful. They thought people had dignity, worth, and the ability to achieve almost anything. Religion was important to humanists, but they stressed that life on earth was also meaningful.

Renaissance humanists focused on three ideas of the Greeks and Romans. The first was individual worth. The humanists were impressed by the ideas of Romans such as Virgil, and Greeks such as Socrates. These men felt that humans could improve themselves through study and reflection.

The second idea that impressed the humanists was a strong commitment to public service. They read how the Greek aristocrat Pericles had revitalized Athens with public buildings like the Acropolis. They learned how Cicero, a member of a wealthy Roman family, had fought bravely for the Republic of Rome. In a similar spirit, wealthy Italian families spent much of their money constructing public buildings like the Ospedale degli Innocenti, an orphanage in Florence. They also adopted the idea of public service to encourage the arts. As an example, these wealthy families helped to support artists and writers so that all the citizens of the community could enjoy artistic and literary works.

The third idea the humanists encouraged was the development of a variety of skills and talents. They thought people should be well-rounded in their knowledge. They admired individuals like Archimedes *(ahr kuh MEE deez)*, who had been a scientist, a mathematician, and an inventor. Humanists saw no limits to what people could achieve. ■

▼ *Renaissance humanists studied the works of ancient Greek philosophers such as Plato, whose bust is shown here.*

■ *What were the basic beliefs held by Renaissance humanists?*

The Flowering of Arts and Learning

The new excitement about human potential spilled over into many areas of Renaissance life. It helped to stimulate great artistic and intellectual achievements across the European continent.

The Italian Leonardo da Vinci *(duh VEEN chih)* was one of the greatest figures of the Renaissance. As an artist, he is known

for the *Mona Lisa* and many other paintings. He was also one of the greatest scientific thinkers of his day. As you can see in A Closer Look at Leonardo's Notebook on pages 320 and 321, Leonardo was curious about how things worked. With his strong desire to learn and his many talents, Leonardo was the ideal Renaissance man.

Da Vinci's Notebooks

Leonardo da Vinci had done everything. At least that's what the people of his time thought. Everybody knew of his successes in painting, medicine, military engineering, and even costume design. What they didn't know was that all his life Leonardo had been writing and drawing even more astonishing ideas in his private notebooks. Looking through these notes, we can see his exciting imagination at work.

Using a quick hand, Leonardo sketched birds in flight. Look at how the top sketches show artistic illustrations of birds soaring in the sky. Then see how he has made the lower drawings more technical. Leonardo seems interested in how wings move up and down. What is he working toward?

Humans had wanted to fly for thousands of years. Leonardo came amazingly close to making that possible. The sketches above and to the left show that he had figured out how wings work and had designed a flying machine. The only problem is that humans don't have strong enough arms to power his invention.

320

Leonardo drew his design for a parachute around 1485. But the first air-to-ground jump wasn't made until 1797—more than 300 years later!

It looks like a car, but Leonardo actually designed this "horse-less carriage" for use in combat. He was trying to solve the problem of horses getting scared and panicking in the noise of battle.

Leonardo's backward signature and his self-portrait at age 60—the only picture of him in existence

He always planned to write a book. Some historians think that's why Leonardo wrote more than 4,200 pages of notes backward—to prevent people from stealing his ideas. But he had so many ideas to write about that he never had time to organize them for publication.

The Renaissance

Renaissance Literature

Italian writers Francesco Petrarch *(PEH trahrk)* and Giovanni Boccaccio *(boh KAH chee oh)* were two of the first Renaissance humanists. Examining ancient Greek and Roman manuscripts during the 1300s, they discovered letters written by Roman politicians and books written by Greek philosophers. They adapted the clear and graceful style of these Roman and Greek writers.

Literature was one area where Renaissance thinkers excelled. New ideas, new technology for making books, and a growing readership inspired new writers. Some of our greatest works of literature are from the Renaissance.

One literary genius was

▼ *Many Florentines thought this building would collapse. Because Brunelleschi studied Roman architecture and used his knowledge of mathematics to design a dome similar to those built by the Romans, the building has stood for over 500 years. Note how the style of this church differs from that of the Gothic cathedrals of the Middle Ages, shown on page 283.*

Miguel de Cervantes *(suhr VAHN tehz*; 1547–1616), a Spanish poet, playwright, and novelist. He was also a diplomat, a soldier, and for five years, a captive of pirates. His greatest work is the story of Don Quixote *(kee HOH tay)*, a slightly befuddled old gentleman who thinks he is a medieval knight, and who sets out to rid the world of evildoers. Cervantes' work is both funny and thoughtful, and has been a favorite of readers since it was written.

Renaissance Architecture

Classical styles also influenced Renaissance architects. Florence architect Filippo Brunelleschi *(broo nuh LEHS kee)* built a Roman-style dome on top of the Florence Cathedral, shown at left. Brunelleschi had a good grasp of mathematics and was the first artist known to use linear perspective. Linear perspective is a system that gives a flat surface the feeling of space and depth. Examine the medieval and the Renaissance paintings on the next page, and compare the use of perspective.

Renaissance Art

Greek and Roman styles also influenced many Renaissance artists. Like the ancient artists, Renaissance painters and sculptors wanted to show people and nature as they really were. Such **realism** is evident in sculptures such as the *Moses* by Michelangelo on page 309. Like many artists of the Renaissance, Michelangelo studied anatomy so that he could sculpt and draw the human figure realistically.

Renaissance artists depicted subjects other than religious ones. They created realistic portraits, battle scenes, and country and street scenes using a new technique of mixing paints with oil. Oil paints could be blended easily because they dried slowly. These paints allowed artists to add more subtle colors to their paintings. ■

▲ Perspective gives a painting a sense of depth. Notice how the people in the painting from the Middle Ages, shown on the left, all appear to be in one place. In the Renaissance painting, shown on the right, some people appear close while others appear far away.

Wealth and the Renaissance

Why did the Renaissance begin amongst the wealthy? Upper-class Italians had enough money to allow them to enjoy their leisure time. This leisure provided them with time to study the ideas of the ancient Greeks and Romans. These upper-class Italians were also highly literate and thus could easily learn about Renaissance ideas.

In addition, increased trade had brought wealthy Italians into contact with other peoples and ideas. Trade had also provided them with money to spend on art.

Not everyone in the city-states felt the influence of the Renaissance. Scholars, painters, and art supporters realized that they were participating in something new and exciting. But life for the average worker remained much the same. Because they could neither read nor afford art, workers were more concerned with making a living than with learning about Renaissance ideas. ■

■ How did Renaissance humanism lead to achievements in the arts and sciences?

■ How important was wealth in fostering the Renaissance?

Reading a da Vinci Sketch

Here's Why

A technical drawing shows how an object works or how it can be built. Knowing how to read a technical drawing will help you to understand how objects are designed and produced.

The roasting spit below (left) was drawn by Leonardo da Vinci some 500 years ago. You read this drawing just as you would a modern technical drawing.

Here's How

The model in the photograph below (right) is based on the drawing. The chimney has been left uncompleted so you can see some interior parts. Technical drawings will not always be accompanied by models. This time, however, the model will help you to understand the drawing.

Look at the drawing, especially at the gears and the fanlike part in the chimney. Notice that the focus of the drawing is to show how all the elements work together to turn the spit.

Now concentrate on how the drawing describes the working of the spit. Use the labels on the photograph to help you.

Find the part that is labeled "Airscrew." The airscrew operates from the draft caused by the fire. As the airscrew moves, it turns the lantern gear. The lantern gear turns the crown gear, which in turn moves the pulley. The pulley, connected to the spit, then turns the spit.

The turning motion of the airscrew is rotational, or around and around. The gears change the motion to a direction that can turn the spit. Otherwise, the design would not be functional.

Da Vinci introduced many practical features into this design. First this design saves the time of turning the spit by hand. Also, since the spit turns slow or fast depending on the size of the fire, the design provides a way to control the evenness of the cooking.

Try It

Turn to A Closer Look on pages 320 and 321. Study the drawings and model of the automotive wagon. Explain how the drawings provide information about the design.

Apply It

Use your school or community library to find a technical drawing related to a career or hobby. Describe the focus of the drawing and the information the drawing provides about the design.

Airscrew

Lantern gear

Pulley

Crown gear

Spit

LESSON 3

Renaissance Life

Early in the morning of July 2, 1442, the people of Florence have turned out to salute their city and its patron saint, John. Shops are closed, but peddlers line streets selling fat cherries, golden peaches, and lion-shaped sweets.

As you pop a cherry into your mouth, your eyes move toward the crowd gathering around the jugglers and acrobats on the corner. How gaily everyone is dressed! The ladies' pale silks shimmer. The gentlemen's long cloaks of red, black, or peacock-blue velvet glow in the bright sunlight.

The parade is a wonderful sight. Bishops in long, flowing robes lead the street procession. Trumpeters and drummers in formation play rousing tunes while flagbearers march in step.

The most exciting part of the festivities is the *palio,* a horse race held in Florence's largest square. The crowd gathers to cheer for their favorite riders as they gallop bareback over the rough stone streets. The street curves dangerously close to buildings and spectators. Riders risk their lives to make the hairpin turns that lead to the finish line and glory. The winner of the race basks in the applause of the crowd. The losers limp home with broken spirits and sometimes broken bones.

THINKING FOCUS

How did each of the social classes contribute to the Renaissance in Italy?

Key Terms

- patrician
- patron
- dowry

The Renaissance City

The cities of Renaissance Italy were colorful, lively places. Florence was a typical Renaissance city. The twisting streets were crammed with tall, narrow buildings with shops on the street and living quarters above. The entire city seemed to tumble over itself.

▲ *In* The Race of the Palio in the Streets of Florence, *Di Francesco showed the excitement of Florence's race.*

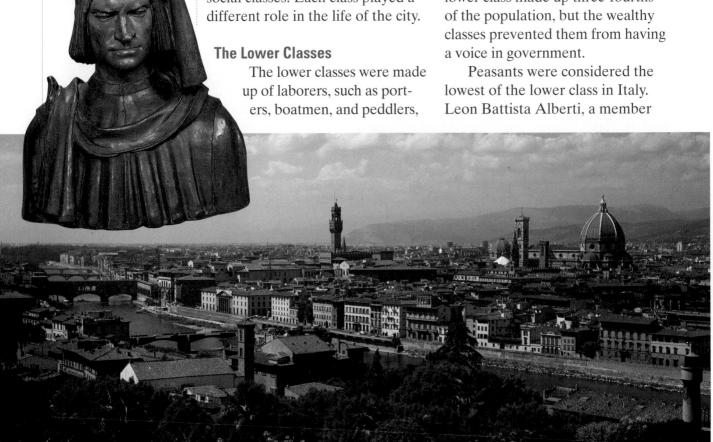

The streets of a Renaissance city were often very muddy. To prevent their skirt hems from dragging in mud, women wore platform shoes.

What were some of the advantages and disadvantages of living in a Renaissance city?

Renaissance Florence was a bustling, prosperous city. Lorenzo di Medici was an important person in the city.

The palaces of wealthy citizens stood next to the run-down houses of the lower class. Large, open plazas, or squares, stood in the shadows of giant cathedrals and public buildings.

In the 1400s, Florence was one of the largest cities in Europe, with over 38,000 people. Another 200,000 people lived in the countryside around Florence.

Cities were the showcases of Italian city-states, and residents worked hard to make their cities beautiful. New streets were paved and straight and were built much wider than the old alleyways of the Middle Ages. The city government strictly limited the height of new houses so that light and air could reach street level.

The city of Florence was quite prosperous. One 15th-century traveler, when entering one of the 11 gates of Florence, remarked that it was a city "in which much money was to be made and many were making it."

But Florence was also very crowded. Overcrowding often led to friction between city dwellers. Violent feuds between families were common. Assassinations, ambushes, and bloody riots disturbed the peace of the streets and the business of the marketplace.

At night, the gates of the walled city were closed, and a curfew was enforced. Only the police, government officials, and those with special passes were allowed to be out on the streets of Florence after dark. ■

From Peasant to Patrician

The residents of Italy's thriving cities belonged to many different social classes. Each class played a different role in the life of the city.

The Lower Classes

The lower classes were made up of laborers, such as porters, boatmen, and peddlers, who had no association with the powerful guilds. In Florence the lower class made up three-fourths of the population, but the wealthy classes prevented them from having a voice in government.

Peasants were considered the lowest of the lower class in Italy. Leon Battista Alberti, a member of one of Florence's oldest families of merchant bankers, referred to farmers as "ploughboys who had grown up among the clods." In spite of prosperity in the cities, Italian peasants remained poor.

Commercial and Upper Classes

The commercial class of the cities consisted of shopkeepers and artisans. Many of them worked for the minor guilds, which included blacksmiths, leather tanners, carpenters, and butchers.

A person could move up in society, especially from the middle to the upper class, but it was not easy. Many members of the commercial class worked long and hard to gain wealth and success but never changed classes.

The **patricians** were at the top of the social ladder. Some were the descendants of medieval noble families. Most were merchants and business people who ran the highly prosperous major guilds. These guilds included cloth manufacturers, bankers, doctors, and lawyers.

Patricians and their families controlled the wealth and government of Italian cities. Some patricians also felt it was their duty to give financial support to local scholars and artists. As **patrons,** they gave money to creative individuals. The artists, in turn, often paid tribute to their patrons in their art.

The First Ghettos

In Renaissance times, Christians still barred Jews from most occupations and from owning land. Many Jews turned to finance, as it was one of the few pursuits open to them. Some Jews were touched by the new learning and formed small groups of poets and philosophers. In Venice, however, in 1517, the city ordered all Jews to live in a particular neighborhood, where they could be gated in behind walls and controlled. Approved by the Church in 1555, this system of forced segregation spread throughout Europe. Inside the ghettos, as they were known, Jews still managed to carry on their own community life, with markets, hospitals, and courts, and their remarkable, high level of education for all. ■

▲ *Isabella d'Este was a member of a family that ruled Mantua, an Italian city-state. She was a patron to some of the finest artists and writers of the Renaissance.*

■ *Describe the people who made up the lower, middle, and upper classes in Renaissance Italy.*

The Importance of Family

Patricians also felt a strong obligation to their families. The family was the center of patrician life, and family members had strong loyalties to each other.

The family was so important in Renaissance Italy that Leon Batista Alberti wrote a *Book of the Family* in 1432–1434. In his book he offered rules for family members to live by. Alberti advised families to own houses rather than to rent them. All branches of the family should live together and take their meals together. He also advised keeping the family business within the family.

True to Alberti's advice, the wealthy families lived in large, high-walled palaces, some of which covered a whole city block. Grandparents, aunts, uncles, and cousins shared a central courtyard, a chapel, and a dining hall.

How Do We Know?

HISTORY *Some women were able to move ahead in Renaissance society. Artemisia Gentileschi (GEN tuh LESS kee) was a talented artist. She wrote in a letter to Galileo, "I have seen myself honored by all the kings and rulers of Europe."*

The Role of Men

Boys of patrician families began learning about the family business at an early age. After completing school, they were sent to other countries to learn about international business. After years of training, they would return to the family business.

Men also married with the good of their businesses or families in mind. Often, marriage joined the social and political fortunes of two families. Parents chose suitable mates for their children and arranged the terms of the marriage.

The Role of Women

Members of the bride's family had to provide a **dowry** when she married. The dowry could be money, land, servants, or any other valuable property. Girls whose families could not afford dowries often remained unmarried and were sent by their families to convents.

Following the Roman model, upper-class Renaissance men expected women to confine their activities to the care of the house and the children. Middle- and lower-class women continued to work in trades and prospered with the rise of the economy.

For all women who could read—and many now learned how—the world of books opened up their minds to new ways of thinking, including thinking about their own situation. Cassandra Fedele *(fuh DEL ay)* was famous as a public speaker in Venice and a lecturer at the University of Padua. The French poet Louise Labé *(lah BAY)* requested in her 1555 book that women make their mark by writing:

> If any woman becomes so proficient as to be able to write down her thoughts, let her do so and not despise the honor but rather flaunt it instead of fine clothes, necklaces, and rings. For these may be considered ours only by use, whereas the honor of being educated is ours entirely.

■ *Why was the family so important in Renaissance life?*

REVIEW

1. **FOCUS** How did each of the social classes contribute to the Renaissance in Italy?
2. **CONNECT** How were Italian Renaissance cities different from medieval towns?
3. **HISTORY** Why did peasants and women benefit so little from the Renaissance?
4. **CRITICAL THINKING** What were some advantages and disadvantages of being a tradeswoman?
5. **WRITING ACTIVITY** Write two descriptions of life in an Italian Renaissance city. In the first, imagine that you are a wealthy trader. In the second, imagine that you are a poor dockworker. How do your descriptions differ?

LESSON 4

Renaissance in Northern Europe

Pieter Brueghel the Elder *(BROO guhl)* was a successful artist born in Flanders about 1530. Flanders is now part of the countries of France and Belgium.

Brueghel is best known for his paintings of peasants. His painting *The Peasant Dance,* shown below, is a fine example of the Renaissance art of northern Europe.

The subject of the painting is a village celebration. Brueghel portrays peasants as real people. Some are fat, some have missing teeth, and some have big noses. Like many painters of the Renaissance, Brueghel relied on colorful, vivid detail and realism.

Brueghel's peasants are dancing, drinking, kissing, and talking. Look at the strain on the face of the bagpipe player and the expression in the eyes of his friend, who is trying so hard to get his attention.

Like Italian Renaissance artists, Brueghel painted people as they really were. He showed their flaws as well as their strengths. Such honesty makes his paintings sparkle with life and emotion.

THINKING FOCUS

How was the northern European Renaissance different from the Italian Renaissance?

Key Term

- secular

◄ The Peasant Dance *by Pieter Brueghel illustrates the style of northern European painting.*

329

The Renaissance

The Spread of Ideas

The Renaissance ideas that inspired Brueghel began to spread to northern Europe in the late 1400s. How did these ideas move from Italy to countries such as France, Germany, England, and Spain?

Trade and Travelers

One way was through travel. Italian businessmen had offices in cities throughout Europe. Whether in Geneva or London, they lived in Italian Renaissance style. They carried this style as they moved through Europe while trading. Other Europeans began to appreciate the Italians' emphasis on wealth, beauty, and personal achievement. The map below shows the major trade routes of Europe. Which of the cities do you think felt the greatest impact of the Italian Renaissance?

While Italians were traveling through Europe, other Europeans made journeys to Italy. Artists such as Brueghel came to Italy to study art. Scholars came to the great library at the Vatican in Rome. And many foreign visitors came to see Rome's ancient ruins.

Words and Books

Renaissance ideas also spread by way of the printed word. Many people had experimented with ways to print type. Then, between 1438 and 1454, Johannes Gutenberg (GOOT en burg), a German, invented and perfected a movable type printing press. Because books could now be printed quickly with

▼ *How did the European trade routes affect the spread of Renaissance ideas?*

Trade Routes

Hand-drawn type   Block type   Movable type

machines, they were cheaper to buy. Books became available to thousands of people. The presses printed everything from the Bible to Greek and Roman classics. By 1500, between 9 and 12 million books had been produced by about 1,000 printers in Europe. The literacy rate began to rise steadily as interest in learning grew.

The book trade then became a major part of trade fairs. Churches, universities, and also individuals bought books printed in many languages. Works by classical and humanist writers were translated and circulated all over the European continent.

Monarchs, Scholars, and Artists

As humanism spread, royal courts of the north, such as those of France and England, began to develop an interest in learning

and the arts. Kings and queens eagerly supported the humanist scholars and artists. For example, King Francis I of France brought Leonardo da Vinci and many other Italian artists and scholars to his court. French writer and physician François Rabelais *(rah BLEH)* summarized the outlook of the new age:

> *Light and dignity have been restored to the art of letters. Now all branches of science, so long extinct, have been reestablished. . . . The world now is full of scholarly men, learned teachers and ample libraries.*
>
> Francois Rabelais,
> *Gargantua*, 1535

Renaissance values and ideas had become firmly rooted in northern Europe by the mid-1500s. ■

During the Middle Ages, books were hand printed. At first, Europeans printed books by using block printing. In this technique, letters are carved on a block of wood, the block is inked, and the ink is transferred onto paper. For the later movable-type press, a printer joins individual letters together in a case and then inks them. Cases of movable type were easy to put together. Letters could also be reused.

■ *How did the ideas of the Italian Renaissance spread to northern Europe?*

Ideas and Ideals

The Renaissance humanism of northern Europe was not simply Italian humanism transplanted. Northern humanism had a character of its own. During the Middle

Ages, feudalism had been stronger in northern Europe than it had been in Italy. As a result, the northern Europeans with the most money and power were nobles and

➤ *Royal courts, rather than the homes of the wealthy, were the center of Renaissance learning in northern Europe. Here, Francis I of France listens to a lecture in his court.*

■ *Did northern humanism stress the spiritual or the secular? Explain.*

▼ *In this detail from the Ghent altarpiece, Jan van Eyck painted Jesus in a realistic, lifelike way.*

royalty, not members of the patrician families. Thus, nobles and royalty became patrons of the arts as were the patrician families in Italy. Renaissance learning in northern Europe centered on the royal courts rather than in the homes of great families.

Northern humanism also differed from Italian humanism in the role of the church. Because northern Europe had fewer large towns to act as cultural centers, the church played a larger, more active role in northern culture. Northern Europeans, like the Italians, valued **secular,** or nonreligious ideas, such as individual achievement and progress. But northern Europeans also emphasized the importance of spiritual life.

Thus, northern humanists studied more than the philosophy and literature of ancient Greece and Rome. Students also learned Greek and Hebrew so they could read ancient Bibles and understand how early Christians practiced their religion.

As northern Europeans began to absorb the ideas of humanism, some began to question the way that church leaders interpreted the Bible. Specifically, humanists

thought church leaders put too much emphasis on ceremony and ritual.

One of these scholars, Desiderius Erasmus *(ih RAZ muhs),* a Dutch priest and 16th century humanist, wanted to reform the church. He believed that church teachings should be easy for everyone to understand, and that everyone should be able to read the Bible, not just the clergy. Erasmus traveled across Europe and wrote dozens of books, mostly on religion. His works were widely published and read, thanks to the new technology of printing. ■

Achievements

More than just the quest for knowledge and learning spread from Italy. The changing style of the arts and sciences also found its way to northern Europe.

Arts and Literature

Many northern artists expressed religious themes in their work, but they began to represent both people and nature more

realistically. Look at the painting at left by the Dutch artist Jan van Eyck. Note how realistic the figure in the painting looks.

Realism was also important to the humanist writers of northern Europe. They wrote about religion, politics, and the behavior of their fellow human beings.

Sir Thomas More was an English statesman, scholar, author,

and a friend of Erasmus who lived from 1478 to 1535. Based on the Renaissance concept of the individual worth, More proposed that all men should be treated equally.

In his most famous book, *Utopia*, More described the rules of a society in which all men are equal and everyone works together to achieve happiness:

> *T*he second rule of nature is to lead a life as free of anxiety and as full of joy as possible, and to help all one's fellow men toward that end.
>
> Sir Thomas More,
> *Utopia*, 1516

This theme of tolerance was continued by Michel de Montaigne *(mawn TAYN)*, a French writer who felt that no man should be put to death for his beliefs.

Some Renaissance writers tried to entertain as well as educate their audiences. William Shakespeare, born in England in 1564, was a poet, an actor, and a master playwright. Shakespeare's characters are full of life, wit, and passion. They reveal the strengths and weaknesses of people from all walks of life. Many plays are built around historic figures, such as Julius Caesar and the kings of England.

The following passage reflects Shakespeare's attitude toward life and art:

> *A*ll the world's a stage,
> And all the men and
>   women merely players.
> They have their exits and their
>   entrances,
> And one man in his time
>   plays many parts . . .
>
> William Shakespeare,
> *As You Like It*, 1599

Medicine

The achievements of the northern Renaissance were not limited to the arts. Medicine also made advances. In Switzerland, Paracelsus, a physician and chemist, discovered a new way to treat illness. He treated his patients with tiny doses of poisons to destroy diseased tissue.

The surgeons of the 1500s often had to treat injuries caused by firearms and cannons. Ambroise Paré, a French surgeon, developed bandages to replace the common practice of the time of cauterizing, or burning, the edges of a wound. He also was the first to use thread to close a wound. Paré's attitude toward his medical skills might be described as evidence that he was a humanist in the northern tradition: "I treated him, God cured him." ■

▲ *Marguerite of Navarre (1492–1549), a French queen, was a patron of learning and literature.*

▲ *William Shakespeare, shown above, wrote many of the most famous works of the Renaissance.*

■ *Describe some of the achievements of the northern Renaissance.*

R E V I E W

1. **FOCUS** How was the northern European Renaissance different from the Italian Renaissance?

2. **CONNECT** How did feudalism in northern Europe make the character of the Renaissance different in the north than in Italy?

3. **CULTURE** How did the scholar Erasmus represent northern humanism?

4. **CRITICAL THINKING** Why was the printing press an important part of the Renaissance?

5. **WRITING ACTIVITY** Imagine that you live in Paris in the early 1500s. You have a sister or brother who lives in Florence whom you write to regularly. Write a letter to her or him discussing the changes that the Renaissance has brought to life in your city.

333

Chapter Review

Reviewing Key Terms

dowry (p. 328)
heretic (p. 313)
humanism (p. 319)
individualism (p. 315)
mercenary (p. 318)
monarchy (p. 312)
patrician (p. 327)

patron (p. 327)
plague (p. 310)
realism (p. 322)
Renaissance (p. 317)
republic (p. 317)
secular (p. 332)

A. Write a sentence or two using each pair of words. The sentences should show how the words are related.

1. mercenary, republic
2. patrician, patron
3. Renaissance, realism

B. Each key term can be used to describe a fact about the time in history covered in the chapter. Use each key term in a sentence that gives a fact about this time.

1. plague
2. monarchy
3. individualism
4. Renaissance
5. secular
6. humanism
7. realism
8. dowry
9. heretic

Exploring Concepts

A. During the Renaissance, many individuals developed their skills and talents. Copy the chart on your own paper. Note the information given. Using information from the chapter, add one contribution for each person.

	Name	Contribution
Leaders	Joan of Arc	
Writers	Petrarch and Boccaccio	
	Erasmus	
	Sir Thomas More	
	Shakespeare	
	Louise Labé	
Artists	Michelangelo	
	Brunelleschi	
	da Vinci	
	Brueghel	
Inventors and Scientists	Gutenberg	
	Paré	
	da Vinci	

B. Support each statement with facts and details from the chapter.

1. One of the major changes brought about by the Renaissance was the development of a new sense of individualism.
2. The plague ravaged Europe and directly affected the state of feudal society.
3. Greek and Roman art, literature, and philosophy played important roles in the development of Renaissance ideas and ideals.
4. Ruling families were a very important feature of the Italian city-states.
5. During the time of the Renaissance, there were great artistic and intellectual achievements across the European continent.
6. The population of Italian Renaissance cities included three social classes.
7. Life in an Italian Renaissance city had many advantages and disadvantages for all classes of the population.
8. Renaissance ideals did not apply to all people.
9. The ideas of the Renaissance were spread in a variety of ways.

334

Reviewing Skills

1. Study the da Vinci drawing of a printing press at the right. The type bed is at the top of the incline. When the press is moved down by turning the operating lever, the type bed is pulled up the incline by a rope tied to the geared axle on the left. Releasing the lever lets the type bed roll down the incline so new type can be put in. Is the press up or down here? What advantages does a wheeled type bed have?

2. Reread Religious Persecution on page 315. How does superstition play a part in religious persecution?

3. If you wanted to find a recent magazine article about Joan of Arc, Leonardo da Vinci, or the city of Florence, where would you look?

Lever

Press

Type bed

Incline

Using Critical Thinking

1. The invention of a printing press with movable type was a great advancement. What might your classes in school be like if a printing press with movable type had not been invented?

2. Ideas of the Renaissance were spread through travelers on business and by way of the printed word. Review highlights in the history of communication by looking up "Communication" in an encyclopedia. Compare and contrast the ways that ideas were communicated in the Renaissance period with the ways that new ideas are communicated today.

Preparing for Citizenship

1. **WRITING ACTIVITY** Reread the description of Brueghel's painting *The Peasant Dance* on page 329. Pretend that you are a young peasant living in the 1500s. Write a brief essay about Brueghel's painting expressing your feelings about the way the artist has portrayed the characters.

2. **GROUP ACTIVITY** With three classmates, plan a panel discussion on the topic "Should Artists Be Supported by Patrons?" Two classmates take the position that patrons have always been needed for art to flourish. The other two argue that no other profession is given financial support, so why should artists be supported?

3. **COLLABORATIVE LEARNING** Review the information about the Renaissance cities and the different social classes in Lesson 3. Divide into groups of four to eight students each. Each group will be responsible for dramatizing a scene from everyday life at that time. Assign the following tasks to members of the group:
   (1) write the scene,
   (2) get costumes and act out the scene,
   (3) design and create the scenery,
   (4) gather props and prepare advertisements of the production.
   When all preparations have been completed, present the minidrama.

Chapter 13

Reformation and the Scientific Revolution

Handwritten papers nailed to a church door . . . a telescope aimed at the stars . . . an apple falling from a tree: each played a part in a great era of change that swept across Europe. Christian leaders such as Martin Luther and John Calvin tried to reform the Catholic church. Scientists such as Nicolaus Copernicus and Galileo helped launch a scientific revolution.

1319 *The Madonna and Child with Saints* by the Italian artist Simone Martini shows a scene approved by Catholic leaders. Reformers questioned the power of the Catholic church.

1300   1400   1500

1492 Christian forces drive out the Moors, the last Islamic kingdom in Spain.

1302

The Italian astronomer Galileo (1564–1642) used the telescopes above to study the stars and planets. Catholic leaders persecuted Galileo for supporting the idea that the earth travels around the sun.

SCUOLA DI SUSTERMANS
RITRATTO DI GALILEO
106

1619 The German astronomer Johannes Kepler publishes a book explaining how the planets orbit the sun. This pen-and-ink drawing from the book tells how to predict the position of the planets.

1600 1700 1800

1556–1605 In India, Mughal emperor Akbar practices religious tolerance, integrating Hindus into his empire.

1687

The Decline of Church Authority

THINKING FOCUS

What challenges did the Catholic church face between 1300 and 1500? Why?

Key Terms

- council
- indulgence

> *We are obliged by the faith to believe and hold . . . that there is one Holy Catholic and Apostolic church, and that outside this church there is neither salvation nor [pardon] of sins. . . . Of this one and only church there is one body and one head—not two heads, like a monster. . . . Furthermore we declare, state, define and pronounce that it is altogether necessary to salvation for every human creature to be subject to the Roman [pope].*
>
> Pope Boniface VIII,
> *Unam Sanctam,* 1302

King Philip IV of France knew that this latest decree from the pope was a response to the king's most recent challenge to the Catholic church. He had ordered the clergy to pay taxes. Pope Boniface VIII replied by issuing a strong statement of his authority—the *Unam Sanctam.*

Furious, King Philip ordered his men to arrest Boniface at his family home in Anagni, Italy, and bring him back to France for trial. Though the aged pope died before he reached France, the king had succeeded in humiliating him. He had also damaged the authority of the once powerful church.

The church drew its authority from people's faith. Millions of Europeans were now Christian, and the great majority of them followed the leadership of the pope.

➤ *Ornate, gold-encrusted crosses such as this one created in the 1300s reveal how wealthy the church had become.*

Conflicts over Power

Between 1100 and 1300, the office of the pope was extremely powerful. Indeed, during this time, the Catholic church had become increasingly involved in political matters, helping to hold Europe together. By the end of the 1300s, however, monarchs who resented the pope's interference had risen to power. King Philip IV was one of many who refused to bow to the pope's authority.

Challenges from Monarchs

The cardinals, the highest ranking clergy under the pope, were responsible for electing a new pope when the old one died. In 1305, the cardinals attempted to restore harmony between the French monarchy and the church by electing a Frenchman as the new pope. This did improve the relationship between the French monarchy and the office of the pope. But then the new pope, Clement V, did something that angered the monarchs of other European countries. He moved the pope's residence to Avignon *(ah vee NYAWN)*, France, to keep it safe from fighting going on in Italy.

The pope's residence remained in Avignon for 70 years, during which time seven popes were elected. The rulers of such countries as England, Germany, and the Italian city-states thought that these popes were dominated by France. Although this was not entirely true, the monarchs nevertheless resented what they saw as France's overwhelming influence over the church. As a result, the church was less respected and lost some of its power to influence rulers.

In 1376, Pope Gregory XI moved the pope's residence back to Rome. When he died in 1378, Urban VI, an Italian extremely unpopular with the French, was elected pope. In protest the French cardinals elected a Frenchman, Clement VII, who returned the pope's residence to Avignon. Pope Urban VI, however, refused to step down from office. Now the church had two popes!

This split, known as the Great Schism, weakened the church's authority. Many people, not knowing which pope to follow, lost faith in the church's ability to provide spiritual leadership.

Corruption Within the Church

Bishops and other top-ranking clergymen decided it was up to them to restore unity and dignity

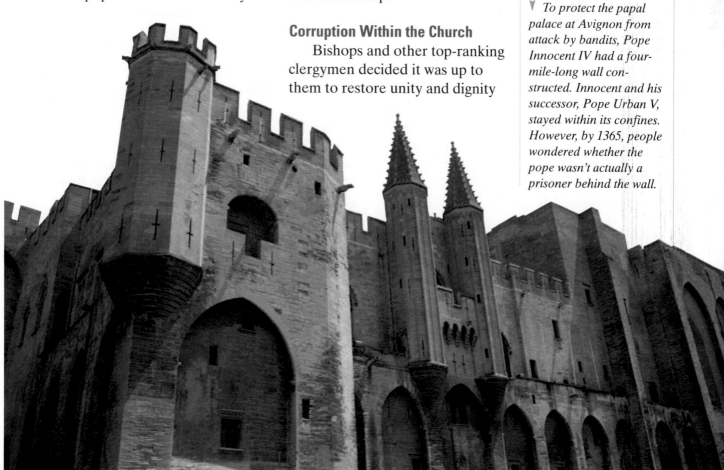

▼ *To protect the papal palace at Avignon from attack by bandits, Pope Innocent IV had a four-mile-long wall constructed. Innocent and his successor, Pope Urban V, stayed within its confines. However, by 1365, people wondered whether the pope wasn't actually a prisoner behind the wall.*

to the church. During the 1400s, they created a series of **councils,** or groups of church leaders, which met to rule on matters of church law and faith. These councils became much more powerful than the pope. One council, the Council of Constance, finally reunited the church under one pope in Rome in 1417. Thus ended the Great Schism.

Although the councils reunified the church, they did not help it regain its former power. In time, the councils came to be controlled by the European monarchs.

The church collected taxes, property, and court fines to support itself. Some ambitious people were attracted to its wealth and used its money and power to further their own ends. Some clergy also sold **indulgences** to believers who felt they had sinned. These certificates, issued by the pope, were said to reduce or cancel punishment for a person's sins. With the wealth they obtained, some popes and higher clergy lived like princes.

Furthermore, clerical positions were often sold to the highest bidder, regardless of a person's background. This practice resulted in some clergy who were immoral, uneducated, or even illiterate. As such practices continued, corruption increased in the priesthood. Many people questioned the spiritual leadership of the clergy. ■

■ *How did the conflict between kings and popes lead to the Great Schism?*

The Call for Church Reform

The church had a long tradition of reform. Reformers called for changes among the clergy, including a return to the spiritual ideals set forth in the Bible. By the 1300s, however, many of the clergy had become corrupt. Many people were outraged by the behavior of the church. Others believed the church expressed the true meaning of the Bible. Those who spoke out against church practices were sometimes branded as heretics. The church punished heretics with excommunication or execution.

Challengers of the Church

John Wycliffe, a scholar at Oxford University in England, was one such challenger of the church. In his writings in the late 1300s, he declared that monarchs should rule over the church in their own kingdoms. He also translated the Bible from Latin into English, which threatened the clergy's power. Since the clergy was among the small percentage of the population able to read Latin, people depended on it to interpret the Latin Bible. If the Bible could be taught and read in English, people could interpret its meaning themselves.

Wycliffe was not the only reformer who defied the church. His ideas also influenced John Hus,

▼ *Nicholas Ridley and Hugh Latimer were two Protestant martyrs burned at the stake for heresy in 1555.*

an eastern European priest. In fiery sermons, Hus spoke out against the practice of selling indulgences and called for reform. He went to the Council of Constance for a debate, but was instead burned at the stake as a heretic. This example kept many people from voicing their disagreements with the church.

Spiritual Movements

Spiritual movements also formed in response to the problems of the church. These groups wanted to express religious feelings in their own way. Mystics believed that people could experience God directly in their hearts. They also believed that both men and women could experience God. Margery Kempe and Catherine of Siena were two well-known mystics.

From Philip IV of France to John Wycliffe of London to the mystics of the 1300s and 1400s, people questioned the church's authority. They paved the way for Martin Luther, whose ideas would change the church forever. ■

▲ *Catherine of Siena claimed that she "was chosen and sent on to this earth in order to right a great scandal." That scandal was the Great Schism.*

*T*hen the Archbishop said to [Margery Kempe]: "I have received bad reports about you. They tell me you are a very wicked woman." And she replied: "Sir, they tell me that you are a wicked man. . . ."

Then an important cleric in a furred hood said: "Hold your tongue: talk about yourself, and leave him alone. . . ."

Then the Archbishop said to her: "You will swear that you will neither teach the people in my diocese, nor argue with them."

"No sir, I will not swear that," she said, "because I shall talk about God . . ."

Straight away an important cleric produced a book, and quoted St. Paul against her, saying that no woman ought to preach.

She in reply said: "I am not preaching, sir, I do not get up in a pulpit. I only use conversation and holy talk and I intend to do that as long as I live."

From *The Book of Margery Kempe*, c. 1432

■ *What church doctrine did the early reformers oppose?*

R E V I E W

1. **FOCUS** What challenges did the Catholic church face between 1300 and 1500? Why?
2. **CONNECT** Why might it be said that the church reformers of the 1300s and 1400s were carrying out the spirit of the Renaissance?
3. **HISTORY** How did corruption within the church contribute to its loss of authority among the people?
4. **BELIEF SYSTEMS** What basic principle did early religious reformers emphasize?
5. **CRITICAL THINKING** Find evidence from the lesson to support this statement: Power corrupts. Do you think this generalization always holds true? Explain.
6. **ACTIVITY** Enact a scene where a monarch and a pope discuss which is more important, the church or the state. Each side should come with its own advisers, split equally between supporters and critics.

L E S S O N   2

Martin Luther and the Reformation

Key Terms

- Protestant
- Reformation
- pamphlet

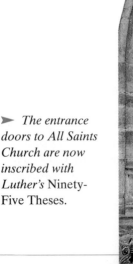

➤ *The entrance doors to All Saints Church are now inscribed with Luther's* Ninety-Five Theses.

Martin Luther, a priest and professor at the University of Wittenberg, approached All Saints Church in Wittenberg on October 31, 1517. Quickly he nailed some papers, handwritten in Latin, to the church door.

No crowd gathered to see what Luther was doing. However, on the outskirts of Wittenberg, people were gathering around Johann Tetzel, a Dominican monk. Tetzel had been authorized to preach indulgences, for which people donated money.

It was against such practices that Luther was protesting in the papers he nailed to the church door. In these papers, his *Ninety-Five Theses,* Luther explained his objections. He saw the practices as proof of how corrupt the Catholic church had become. Luther challenged the church to defend itself. He read over one thesis:

Why does not the Pope, whose riches are at this day more ample than those of the wealthiest of the wealthy, build the one Basilica of St. Peter's with his own money, rather than with that of poor believers?

Luther's *Ninety-Five Theses* were really an invitation to scholars to debate certain church issues. He had no idea that his challenge to the church would capture a growing movement of protest and change that would sweep Europe.

Luther Questions the Church

Martin Luther was born on November 10, 1483, in Eisleben, Germany. Luther's father, a hard-working miner, wanted his son to be a lawyer. So in 1501, Luther began studying law at the University of Erfurt.

A Man of Faith

One day in 1505, Luther was caught in a thunderstorm and thrown to the ground when a bolt of lightning struck nearby. Like most men and women of his time, Luther believed that God could come to the aid of humans. In the storm he cried out, "Help, St. Anne, and I'll become a monk." True to his word, that same year Luther ceased studying law and joined the monastery in Erfurt.

Luther was a model monk, and in 1507, he was ordained a priest. A year later, Luther was selected from among his peers to teach at the University of Wittenberg.

A New Religion

As a monk Luther had struggled to understand the true nature of godliness. The church taught that the performance of religious ritual and good deeds was necessary to ensure the soul's salvation. Luther worked hard to satisfy the church and save his soul. But he worried that his actions might not satisfy God.

◄ At the University of Erfurt, Luther became known for his long and serious talks. His friends nicknamed him "the philosopher." This engraving depicts Luther as he looked at this time.

Across Time & Space

Reform is not restricted to either the Middle Ages or the church. In the 1950s and 1960s, Martin Luther King, Jr., led a social reform movement in the United States seeking racial equality. Under the leadership of this Baptist minister named for Martin Luther, the movement for civil rights gained wide support from blacks and whites. His policy of nonviolent protest helped curb racial injustice in the South.

◄ *Johann Tetzel sold so many indulgences that some people made fun of him in a popular rhyme: "As soon as money in the box rings, The soul from Hell's fire springs."*

Luther's fears vanished, however, when he read St. Paul's letter to the Romans: "He who through faith is righteous shall live" (Romans 1:17). To Luther, Paul's message seemed clear: the path to God is through faith alone. Forgiveness was not something the church could grant, nor was it something individuals could achieve on their own. Instead, it was given by God to each person who accepted Him. This theory became known as justification by faith, meaning that a person could be made just, or good, by his or her faith in God.

Luther's belief in justification by faith led him to question the Catholic church's practice of selling indulgences. He objected not only to the church's greed but to the very idea of indulgences. He did not believe the Catholic church had the power to pardon people's sins. Rather, Luther taught that

salvation could be achieved only through God's mercy. No one needed to seek or buy salvation through the church.

By nailing his theses to the church door, Luther was not acting as a heretic. He was simply inviting other scholars to respond to his ideas in a debate, an ordinary method of learning at universities of his day.

At first, no one accepted Luther's invitation. Over the next few years, however, his *Ninety-Five Theses* sparked a religious movement to reform the Catholic church. Because the reformers were protesting against what they felt to be the abuses of the Catholic church, they came to be known as **Protestants.** And because they wanted to reform the Catholic church, that is, improve it by making changes, their movement is known as the **Reformation.** ■

■ *How did Martin Luther's beliefs conflict with church doctrine and practices?*

▼ *Luther claimed that his burning the bull was purely symbolic; in reality he thought it was the pope himself who should have been burned.*

The Reformation Begins

Luther's *Ninety-Five Theses* were soon translated from Latin into German. Within a year, his

ideas were known throughout Europe. As one historian put it, they spread "as if angels from heaven themselves had been their messengers." Encouraged by this success, Luther wrote hundreds of essays between 1517 and 1546, in which he stressed justification by faith and criticized church abuses.

Finally, in 1520, Pope Leo X issued a bull—a statement of the pope's authority—condemning Luther and banning his works. Defying the pope, Luther publicly burned the bull. The break with the church was then complete. In January 1521, Pope Leo X excommunicated Luther.

However, Charles V, the Holy Roman Emperor, decided to give

344

Chapter 13

Luther one final chance. In 1521, at a meeting in Worms, Germany, the emperor demanded that Luther recant, or take back, his teachings. Facing church officials and an excited assembly of people, Luther refused. He said in part:

> I do not accept the authority of popes and councils. . . . My conscience is captive to the word of God. I cannot and I will not recant anything. . . . Here I stand, I cannot do otherwise. God help me. Amen.

A near riot broke loose. Luther strode out, his hands raised high in triumph. Yet the emperor later declared him an outlaw whom anyone could kill without punishment.

Fortunately for Luther he had a powerful friend in Frederick the Wise, Prince of Saxony. The prince arranged a pretend kidnapping of Luther and hid him away for about a year in the castle at Wartburg. Here, Luther translated the Bible from Greek into German. His translation allowed the German people to read the Christian Bible without having to rely on the interpretation by the priests.

Luther continued to write works in which he attacked the church or discussed books of the Bible. His teachings eventually led to a separate "Lutheran" church. This and other Protestant churches would continue to oppose the Catholic church. ∎

◄ *Turn this woodcut portrait of Luther upside down to see what his opponents thought of him.*

∎ *How effective were the church's responses to Luther's teachings?*

▼ *Many people feared that the art of printing, new to Europeans, came from the devil. But by 1500, there were more than 1,000 print shops in Europe.*

Protestantism Spreads

Why did Luther's ideas, which challenged the centuries-old Catholic church, succeed? First, many people longed for a simpler, more direct relationship with God. Second, the times were changing. Trade was increasing, and many people felt a new individualism and nationalism. The new ideas around showed that change was possible.

The printing press, developed in Europe about 1450, also contributed to Luther's success. Printed **pamphlets** containing unbound essays could spread new ideas quickly to many people. By 1523, about a million copies of Luther's pamphlets were in circulation. The printer in A Moment in Time on page 346 is typical of the craftsmen who ran the early presses.

As the Reformation spread, it gained the support of European peasants. In 1524 and 1525, arguing that everyone was equal under God, a group of poor German peasants took up arms against their wealthy landowners. Known as the Peasants' War, this revolt was badly organized and lacked strong leadership. Government armies quickly crushed the uprising.

The peasants were surprised and disappointed to discover that Martin Luther did not support them in the Peasants' War.

A Printer

4:29 P.M., August 24, 1620
Great Hall, Northumberland House, London

Eyes
He can read both English and Latin backward and forward. When he started working for the king's printer at age 14, it was hard for him to read the backwards-facing metal type.

Arms
The printer's arms ache from lifting the heavy iron plate of the press hundreds of times since 7:00 this morning.

Beard
He keeps his London-style beard neatly trimmed. After a country childhood, he enjoys city entertainments like seeing plays by Shakespeare.

Woodcut
Pages with pictures, like the one he just took off the press, are still carved in one piece. Most pages are made with movable type that will be taken apart as soon as all the books are printed.

Title Page
The book's title, *Novum Organum,* and its author's name, Francis Bacon, are surrounded by fancy pictures.

Paper
This sheet was thrown away because a young apprentice mixed up a *p* and a *q*. On this page Bacon says printing, gunpowder, and the magnet have changed the world.

Apron
He tries to keep his clothes free of ink, but our printer is called the "dirty-hands" apprentice. His friend, the "clean-hands" apprentice, gets to handle the paper.

In the pamphlet *Against the Robbing and Murdering Hordes of Peasants,* Luther criticized the rebels for seeking economic gain in the name of God. As a result, Luther lost the support of many social reformers.

However, Luther's ideas became popular with the German princes. Luther did not believe that the church should own property. He also thought that rulers should appoint clergy members. Thus, Luther favored a more powerful role for rulers and a weaker church authority.

Many German princes who wanted freedom from the pope's authority favored Protestantism. Others remained Catholic because they depended on the support of the pope. Eventually, the differences between these German princes erupted in war. From 1546 to 1555, war raged between the Catholic and Protestant princes.

Finally, in 1555, a compromise, called the Peace of Augsburg, was reached. This compromise permitted each German prince to decide which religion would be allowed in his state. Most rulers of northern Germany chose Protestantism, and most in southern Germany remained Catholic. Many people had to move to states that allowed them to practice their own religion.

Lutheranism in Central Europe

Roman Catholic

Lutheran

By 1560, the Reformation was established in Germany and, as you can see on the map above, in much of the rest of Europe. Compare this map with that on page 529 of the Atlas showing the distribution of religions in the world today. What other countries can trace their religious roots to the ideas of the Reformation? ■

▲ *In what countries did Lutheranism become established by 1555?*

■ *Why did Protestantism spread throughout Germany between 1517 and 1560?*

REVIEW

1. **FOCUS** What was Luther's role in the Reformation?
2. **CONNECT** What similar task did John Wycliffe and Martin Luther undertake? What was the purpose of their work?
3. **HISTORY** How did Gutenberg's invention help spread Protestantism?
4. **POLITICAL SYSTEMS** How did Luther's reforms affect political events in Germany?

5. **CRITICAL THINKING** How do you think Martin Luther would have advised the European peasants to handle their problems with their landowners?
6. **ACTIVITY** Think of a topic you would like to debate. Then write out your position on the topic and post it on your class bulletin board. As in Martin Luther's time, invite other students to debate your viewpoint and exchange ideas.

Reformation and the Scientific Revolution

Identifying Patterns

Here's Why

Writers use different patterns to organize what they write. The chart on this page identifies four text patterns and gives clues for each. You will find examples of all four patterns in this chapter. Recognizing the patterns while reading helps improve your understanding.

Here's How

The section Challenges from Monarchs on page 339 is an example of a chronological or time-related pattern. This pattern describes events in the order in which they happened. Notice that several dates are used: "in 1305," "in 1376," and "in 1378." Dates and phrases that describe time periods, such as "for 70 years," are clues that the pattern is chronological. Words that describe time relationships—before, after, during—are clues too.

A cause-and-effect pattern shows what events made other events happen. Sometimes this pattern begins with the effect and then explains its causes. The section Corruption Within the Church on page 339 is an example of a cause-and-effect pattern. The first sentence alludes to the schism in the church. The rest of the paragraph describes actions taken by the bishops to restore the unity of the church.

Look for the cause-and-effect pattern in the paragraph that focuses on how corrupt practices severely weakened the church (page 340). The cause is the sale of indulgences to raise money. The effect is that some officials kept the money for themselves.

Spatial patterns describe people, places, things, and events. Such a pattern shows the relationship of the characteristics being described. The description of Luther and Tetzel on page 342 is an example of spatial organization.

Compare-and-contrast patterns show similarities and differences between two subjects. On pages 346–347 is a description of two groups' reactions to Luther's ideas. It contrasts the reactions of some social reformers with that of the German princes.

Writers use all of these patterns to organize their work. Often, especially in long passages, you will find a combination of several of these patterns.

Try It

Turn to A New Religion in Lesson 2. Tell what organizational pattern is used in this section. Explain how you identified the pattern.

Apply It

Find an article in a magazine or newspaper that uses one of the organizational patterns explained on this page. Name the pattern and explain how you identified it.

Pattern	Definition	Clue Words
Chronological	Tells the order in which events happened	as soon as, at last, first, second, third, next, then, before, after, finally, while, by 1565, until 7 P.M.
Spatial	Describes people, places, things, or events	above, across, beside, behind, below, beyond, east, farther, in front of, inside, lower, near, next to, north, outside, south, under, within, west; names of places
Cause-and-effect	Tells what events caused others	as a result, because, consequently, if, nevertheless, since, so, therefore, then
Compare-contrast	Compares or contrasts events, ideas, people, and so on	although, by contrast, by comparison, compared to, relatively, similarly, unlike

Chapter 13

LESSON 3

Era of Reformation

H ere's an imaginary scene that might have occurred in 1560. A young Frenchman arrives in Geneva, Switzerland, and enters a Calvinist church—a plain wooden structure one story high. Inside, the people sing a hymn in French.

Looking around, the young man compares this church with the Catholic church he attended as a boy. Absent are brightly colored stained-glass windows, candles, ornate statues, paintings on the walls. The young man sees just one cross, a plain wooden one that hangs above the small altar table.

When the singing stops, the minister delivers a sermon on the importance of living a virtuous life.

The entire service is simple but serious, and the young man feels comfortable in this church.

THINKING FOCUS

What effect did the Reformation have on religion in Europe?

Key Terms

- predestination
- Counter Reformation
- inquisition

◄ *Like Luther, Calvin was a persuasive writer and speaker who united many religious reformers.*

Calvin and the Reformation

In the early 1500s, reform spread throughout Europe. Three of Martin Luther's ideas became the center of debate. One idea was justification by faith. The second was the idea that the Bible was the only authority for Christians, rather than the laws of the Catholic church or papal bulls. The third was a belief in a priesthood of all Christians, denying the special powers that priests had in the Catholic church.

Around 1517, when Luther posted his *Ninety-Five Theses,* Ulrich Zwingli, a Swiss priest working in Zurich, brought the Reformation to that city. He urged Christians to study the Bible on their own and deepen their faith.

After Zwingli's death, John Calvin, a Frenchman educated in law, continued to teach the ideas of the Reformation. Forced to flee France in 1534, where the Catholic church had been harrassing

349

Calvinist churches did not allow ornamentation to distract worshipers. This Dutch Calvinist church was built in the early 1600s.

■ *What religious ideas and practices were important to Calvinists?*

▼ *Can you list some of the beliefs or practices central to each of these church traditions?*

Protestants, Calvin moved to Switzerland. The city of Geneva soon became the center for a movement called Calvinism.

Calvinism differed from other movements of the Reformation in one important way. Calvin taught that God had already chosen, or predestined, a special group of believers for salvation. This theory is known as **predestination.** Luther also accepted predestination but thought that people could never know whom God had chosen.

Calvinism emphasized being devoted to God and leading a disciplined life. According to Calvinists, a person who could maintain such conduct was probably a member of God's chosen group.

Calvinist church services were plain. No images of saints hung on the walls; no organ accompanied the singing. Nothing appealing to the senses interfered with what the worshiper experienced as his or her spiritual link to God.

Calvinists also followed a strict code of moral behavior. Fortune-telling, gambling, and even dancing at social gatherings were all pro-

hibited. Councils elected by church members enforced this code of behavior, as well as other laws of the Calvinist church. By the time Calvin died in 1564, Calvinism had taken root in many places including Scotland, France, and Bohemia.

While Protestant reformers did not aim to change women's roles in society, their actions had that effect. The reformers did not think that women were equal to men, but the Reformation and other social changes did introduce new ideas about family life that gave women a more important role. With changing ideas about marriage and women's roles, the family became a more loving, spiritual relationship.

When convents were closed, many women lost the safety of all-female communities. Since the Protestant clergy could now marry, however, the wife of a minister became an important person. Protestants also favored public education, with both boys and girls learning reading, arithmetic, writing, and religion. ■

Other Protestant Movements

One Protestant group, called the Anabaptists, lived by an even stricter moral code than that of the

Calvinists. The Anabaptist movement began in Zurich around 1525 among a group of dissatisfied followers of Zwingli. They believed that the state was made up of sinners. Therefore, true Christians should withdraw from the state and form a separate community.

Both Catholics and Protestants openly opposed the Anabaptists. They resented the Anabaptists' claim that members of all other religious groups were sinners. Anabaptists were widely harassed,

Major Churches During the Reformation

Religion	Time Founded	Founders	Administrators
Roman Catholic	500s	Popes	Pope, Councils, Bishops
Lutheran	1529	Martin Luther	Congregation, Local Rulers
Church of England	1534	Henry VIII	King of England
Calvinist	1546	John Calvin	Presbytery (Council of Elders)

and many were executed. Survivors fled to Poland and Holland.

Not all religious reform movements had religious causes. In 1533, Henry VIII of England argued with the pope that he should be allowed to have a divorce, even though it was against church rules. To get his way, Henry persuaded the English parliament to declare England independent of all foreign authorities, including the pope. The following year, parliament's "Act of Supremacy" recognized the Church of England as a separate body with the monarch of England as its head on earth. Religious practices changed slowly, however. Not until Henry's son, Edward VI, became king in 1547 did Protestant practices gain a strong following in England.

Although these reform movements had different beliefs, they shared the same basic motivation: the desire to bring about changes in the church. And because those changes were not coming from within the church, the reformers created their own churches. ■

■ *Find evidence to support this statement: Some Protestant groups wanted to make political as well as religious reforms.*

The Catholic Church's Response

During the 1400s, many priests recognized that reforms needed to be made. They realized that selling indulgences was corrupt, and they protested against such abuses.

Reforms came slowly. However, as more and more people left the Catholic church to join the Protestant movement, Catholic leaders urged Pope Paul III to assemble a general council to discuss church reform. The Council of Trent, held from 1545 to 1563, set two main goals: to rid the church of abuses and uphold traditional Catholic beliefs. This movement

UNDERSTANDING REFORM

The leaders of the Reformation first tried to change the Catholic church from within. Reform means to change an existing institution.

Participants in a revolution, on the other hand, seek to destroy or replace an existing institution. Therefore, the actions of the colonists in America against the English in 1776 were a revolution, not a reform movement.

Issues and Leaders

Reform movements start because people want to improve some aspect of society. In the mid-1800s, many people wanted to reform the United States voting system to allow women to vote. Leaders of this reform movement, such as Susan B. Anthony, campaigned for women's rights for more than 70 years. In 1920, the Nineteenth Amendment to the U.S. Constitution guaranteed women's right to vote.

The Results of Reform

Sometimes the changes brought about by reform movements go beyond what the reformers had in mind. For example, Luther's religious reformation helped to further the existing climate of questioning that led to many social, political, and scientific changes during the following 300 years.

Christian Churches in Europe, 1600

▲ *Most Anglicans lived in England in 1600. Anglicans are members of the Church of England.*

■ *In what ways did the Catholic church try to reform from within?*

ihts), as the members of the society were called, took vows of poverty and of obedience to the pope. The Jesuits were noted for their educational and missionary works.

In addition to encouraging the spread of Catholicism, church officials tried to halt the spread of Protestantism. Officials in Rome revived the **Inquisition**—a church court to judge, convict, and punish heretics. Both Catholics and Protestants used death and torture in their battle for supremacy.

In Spain, Ferdinand and Isabella used the Inquisition to consolidate their new Spanish state, which had been slowly conquered from the Muslims. In 1492, after using torture, burning, and forced conversions, Ferdinand expelled all Jews from Spain. It had been a center of Jewish and Muslim culture for over 700 years (see pages 95–100). Portugal's Inquisition followed this example four years later.

The church officials also established the *Index of Prohibited Books.* Prohibited books included works by Calvin and Luther.

The Counter Reformation helped to correct many church abuses. However, it could not stop the spread of Protestantism. Never again would a single church dominate all of Europe. ■

within the church became known as the **Counter Reformation.**

Reacting to Protestants

To help purify itself, the church also encouraged the founding of new orders, or special religious groups. One new order was the Society of Jesus, founded by a Spanish priest named Ignatius Loyola in 1540. Jesuits *(JEHZ oo*

R E V I E W

1. **FOCUS** What effect did the Reformation have on religion in Europe?
2. **CONNECT** In what ways were the religious beliefs of Zwingli and Calvin similar to Martin Luther's beliefs?
3. **GEOGRAPHY** Suppose you were a follower of Martin Luther living in Spain in 1600. Use the map on this page to determine where you could go to live among people who shared your beliefs.

4. **CRITICAL THINKING** Why do you think the Anabaptists were persecuted by other Protestant groups?
5. **CRITICAL THINKING** In your opinion, was the Counter Reformation successful? Explain your answer.
6. **WRITING ACTIVITY** Write a brief essay defending the Catholic Church against the changes of the Reformation.

LESSON 4

Scientific Revolution

C learly, by 1543, Nicolaus Copernicus, the Polish physician and astronomer, did not have much longer to live. For years, Georg Joachim, his young assistant, had begged Copernicus to publish his revolutionary theories on planetary motion. Copernicus theorized that the sun, not the earth, was the center of the universe. Copernicus claimed he needed more time to provide mathematical and factual support for these theories. But, on his deathbed, he agreed to publish.

Copernicus died later that year. But on the day he died, Joachim brought him the first copy of his work, *On the Revolution of the Celestial Spheres*.

The publication of Copernicus's theory began a movement that would change people's view of the world. Theories that had been accepted for hundreds of years would be challenged by scientific experiment and observation.

THINKING FOCUS

What was the Scientific Revolution?

Key Terms

- Scientific Revolution
- scientific method
- hypothesis

◄ *In Ptolemy's system, the earth is circled by water, air, fire, and seven planets—including the moon and sun. The plan shown here illustrates Copernicus's sun-centered theory.*

353

New Visions of the Natural World

The new Protestants encouraged Bible reading. They taught reading to many people, and thus spread learning and ideas through books. By promoting literacy skills and questioning authority, the forces of the Reformation directly affected the Scientific Revolution.

Copernicus was one of the first European scientists to question theories about the universe. For instance, educated Europeans accepted the theory of Egyptian astronomer Ptolemy that stated that the earth was at the center of the universe.

The Universe

After years of observation and mathematical research, Copernicus concluded that the universe was sun-centered. Drawings demonstrating Copernicus's theory appear on the preceding page and on page 516 of the Minipedia. According to this theory, the planets, including earth, revolve around the sun in circular orbits. The German astronomer Johannes Kepler later proved that the planets' orbits were oval.

Protestant and Catholic leaders alike opposed Copernicus's theory.

The Protestants claimed that the Bible said the earth stood still. The Catholics claimed that the earth and its human beings—not the sun—held the central place in the universe. In 1610, the Catholic church declared that all followers of Copernicus were heretics.

The Human Body

While Copernicus and Kepler explored the universe, Flemish physician Andreas Vesalius explored the human body. His observations challenged the works of Galen, a second-century physician whose theories were widely accepted. Vesalius's thorough dissection of the human body enabled him to describe human anatomy much more accurately. Vesalius's book stimulated new research in the field of anatomy. Some results stemming from continued research are discussed in Making Decisions on pages 358 and 359.

Vesalius and Copernicus questioned and reevaluated accepted theories. Their emphasis on careful observation of the natural world marked a new era in scientific thinking, a period that became known as the **Scientific Revolution.** ■

▲ *In order to carry out his experiments and make drawings such as this, Vesalius sometimes stole the bodies of people who had been hanged.*

■ *How did the scientific discoveries of Copernicus offer a new view on the world?*

Galileo and the Church

The Italian astronomer and physicist Galileo continued the work of Copernicus. He greatly admired the Polish astronomer's genius. Like Copernicus and Vesalius, Galileo recognized the importance of relying on observation rather than blindly trusting classical authorities.

Through observation and experimentation, Galileo tested the theory of falling bodies. This theory, which held that heavy objects fall faster than lighter objects, had been accepted since about 300 B.C. Galileo made his own observations by dropping objects of various weights and shapes from different heights. He then developed a mathematical formula showing that all bodies—no matter what their shape or weight—would fall at the same speed.

Galileo also applied his method of observation to astronomy. In 1609, he developed a telescope that was larger and more powerful than any made before. Galileo was the first person to observe sunspots, Jupiter's moons, and Saturn's rings. He also provided new information about the rough, crater-marked surface of our moon, which had previously been considered smooth.

Galileo's observations of one planet, Venus, provided strong support for Copernicus's theory. But when Galileo argued the point in his *Dialogue Concerning the Two Chief World Systems,* the Catholic church reacted. Because the idea of a sun-centered universe went against Catholic beliefs, the publication was placed on the *Index of Prohibited Books.* The inquisition in Rome condemned Galileo in 1616. Threatened with torture, Galileo, now an old man, denied his belief in Copernicus's ideas.

But his spirit was not broken. Upon leaving his trial, he is believed to have said of the earth, "but still it moves." Galileo spent the remaining eight years of his life under house arrest on his estate near Florence, where he continued his scientific activities.

The church's victory was short-lived. By the late 1630s, the theory of the sun-centered universe was well established, and the age of science was under way. ■

How Do We Know?

HISTORY *Church officials banned books whose ideas threatened the church's power and authority. By reading the books listed in the* Index of Prohibited Books, *modern scholars have determined which ideas the church considered to be most dangerous.*

■ *Why was the Catholic church threatened by Galileo's ideas?*

▼ *Using this compound microscope, Robert Hooke examined cork, snowflakes, and tiny organisms, such as the tick. His drawings were published in the book* Micrographia *in 1645.*

The Scientific Method

The Scientific Revolution was pioneered by Copernicus, Vesalius, and Galileo. Many other thinkers and writers also contributed to its success.

Francis Bacon

One such thinker was Francis Bacon, an English philosopher. In his book *Novum Organum,* published in 1620, Bacon stressed the importance of observation and experimentation leading to the statement of general principles about the natural world. This way of doing scientific research is now known as the **scientific method.**

A key part of this process, according to Bacon, was forming a hypothesis. A **hypothesis** is an assumption that can be tested by investigation. For example, Robert Hooke, an Englishman who developed the compound microscope in 1665, hypothesized that a microscope with two lenses could produce a clearer image of a magnified object.

This hypothesis was then tested by an experiment, and the results were recorded. Hooke experimented by adjusting and readjusting the placement of the lenses. Then he made accurate drawings based on his observation of the

▲ *Isaac Newton was praised by the English poet Alexander Pope in the following rhyme: "Nature, and nature's laws lay hid in night/ God said, 'Let Newton be!' and all was light."*

➤ *Newton's studies of how light passes through a prism helped explain how rainbows are formed.*

■ *What was revolutionary about the scientific method?*

magnified objects. Finally, the collected data were analyzed and a conclusion was drawn. Hooke's data indeed revealed that objects could be more closely observed using a microscope with two lenses.

Bacon's method helped others in the Scientific Revolution organize and formulate their research. The scientific method is still at the core of scientific research.

Isaac Newton

Sir Isaac Newton, English scientist, astronomer, and mathematician, also used the scientific method. Many scientists before Newton made observations and recorded data. However, Newton's biggest contribution was in providing an explanation for the universe that was very large in scope. His great ability lay in interpreting data and drawing accurate conclusions about the nature of the universe.

Born in 1642, the year Galileo died, Newton expanded and perfected many of Galileo's theories. Like Galileo, Newton was fascinated by falling objects. According to the story, while in the country one day, Newton saw an apple fall from a

tree branch. He hypothesized that there must be some force pulling the apple to the ground. He further hypothesized that the same force that pulls an object to earth keeps the moon and planets in orbit around the sun. After much observation and many experiments, Newton announced that a force called gravity holds the universe together. He described this theory and many others in the *Mathematical Principles of Natural Philosophy* published in 1687.

During the Reformation and the Scientific Revolution, people began to reexamine their spiritual and physical worlds. Freed from having to rely on accepted theories and beliefs, they sought new answers to old questions. This searching set the stage for further reformation in the 18th and 19th centuries. ■

REVIEW

1. **FOCUS** What was the Scientific Revolution?
2. **CONNECT** What did the new scientific thinkers and the leaders of the Reformation have in common?
3. **BELIEF SYSTEMS** Why was the publication of Vesalius's findings considered revolutionary?
4. **SCIENCE** How did Newton use the scientific method?
5. **CRITICAL THINKING** Which scientific achievements do you think were more important, those of Copernicus or those of Galileo? Explain.
6. **ACTIVITY** Use Bacon's scientific method to answer the following question: Which weighs more, a pound of apples or a pound of lettuce?

Making Hypotheses

Here's Why

You know that a hypothesis is an explanation, based on known facts, that can be tested as more facts become available. To develop a hypothesis, you gather all the information you can about a question or a problem. The hypothesis then becomes the basis of any further testing. You can test a scientific hypothesis through observation or experimentation, as discussed in Lesson 4.

Other subjects, such as history, also invite hypotheses. Some hypotheses about history can never be proved or disproved because of lack of evidence. However, you can continue to test a hypothesis when you find new information.

Suppose you want to explain why the church lost so much of the power it once had. You have read many facts about this in the chapter. You could use these facts to form a hypothesis.

Here's How

Look at the diagram below. It shows the steps involved in making a hypothesis.

The arrows indicate that each step leads to the next. To formulate a hypothesis of your own, follow these steps in order:

1. **Define the question.** You could ask, for example: What was the primary cause of the decline in church authority between 1300 and 1500?
2. **Gather evidence.** Read through the chapter and list events that caused the church's authority to decline. Your list may look something like this:
   - Secular rulers gained power.
   - The Great Schism caused confusion.
   - Corruption existed within the church.
   - Many groups were asking for reform in the church.
3. **Examine the clues.** Analyze the list. Can the clues be placed under a particular heading? How might the ideas be summarized?
4. **Make a hypothesis.** One example of a hypothesis that shows the primary cause of the decline in church authority be

tween 1300 and 1500 is this: The church did not use its power wisely.
5. **Test the hypothesis.** You can test your hypothesis by reading more about the topic, either in your textbook or in outside sources.

Try It

Now form a hypothesis of your own that answers this question: Why did the Calvinists have such a strict code of behavior? Use what you have learned about the Calvinists in Lesson 3 to complete steps 2–4.

Apply It

Formulate a hypothesis which answers this question: Why do some seventh grade students. make excuses about late homework assignments? Use the five-step process to work out your hypothesis. Write down the facts you used to develop your hypothesis. When you learn new facts about the question, examine them and be prepared to alter your hypothesis to account for the new information.

Making a Hypothesis

I. Define the question. → 2. Gather evidence. → 3. Examine the clues. → 4. Make a hypothesis. → 5. Test the hypothesis.

Scientific Discoveries

> I n all corners of the world, I sought for the true and experienced arts of medicine. Not alone with doctors; but with barbers, surgeons, learned physicians, women, magicians, alchemists . . . , with the wise and the simple, I [gathered information] for a foundation of medicine which should be unspotted by fables or babble.
>
> Paracelsus, a Swiss physician, 1493–1541

Background

In 1543, Flemish scientist Andreas Vesalius did a shocking thing. He published a book about human anatomy, showing detailed pictures of the bones, muscles, and organ systems. In doing so, he admitted that he had performed dissections. In those days, dissecting the human body was forbidden by the major religions—Judaism, Christianity, and Islam.

The Scientific Revolution, fueled by the courage of Galileo, Vesalius, and others, created an intellectual climate in which people began to question even the oldest and most accepted ideas. Doctors and scientists rejected what they could not prove to be true and formulated new theories based on their observations of the world.

For example, in 1796, English physician Edward Jenner made an observation about smallpox, a disease that terrorized Europe.

Milkmaids— young girls who milked cows—rarely contracted the disease. Jenner found that these girls had previously suffered from cowpox, a disease similar to smallpox, but much milder. Victims of both diseases developed infected sores on their skin.

Jenner did an experiment to find out if injecting a person with fluid from a cowpox sore prevented the person from contracting smallpox. A young boy volunteered to be the guinea pig. Several weeks after injecting the boy with fluid from a cowpox sore, Jenner injected the boy with material from smallpox sores. Jenner, the boy, and the boy's mother waited anxiously to see if the boy would come down with smallpox, but the boy remained healthy. By recognizing that cowpox and smallpox were related and conducting a daring experiment, Jenner had found a way to protect people from smallpox.

➤ *Vesalius made drawings such as this one to show the parts of the body.*

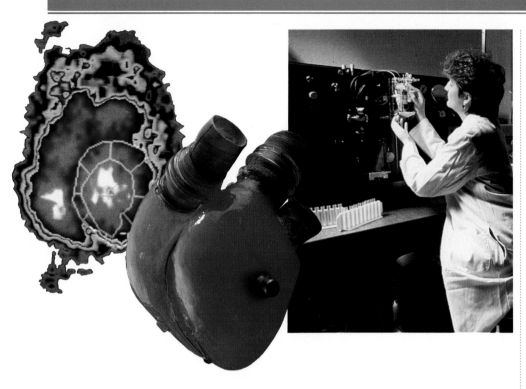

Magnetic resonance imaging produces pictures of the human body that enable doctors to pinpoint problems before surgery. Today, doctors are also able to use artificial hearts and cell-separation techniques to save lives.

Knowledge and Responsibility

Jenner's discovery was not easy for people to accept at first. Even physicians found it unsettling to think of injecting people with material from infected sores. Was Jenner taking too many risks? Was he sure that injections could do no harm? Should people wait for more proof before submitting themselves to Jenner's procedure?

Decision Point

1. What were the risks and benefits of Jenner's treatment for smallpox? Do you think Jenner was right to test his procedure the way he did? Why?

2. If you had been alive in Jenner's day, would you have wanted to undergo Jenner's treatment? What would you want to ask him before you agreed to the procedure? List the questions you would ask before making this decision.

3. Suppose a researcher discovers a drug that helps cure heart disease. Its side effects are not yet fully known or understood. What information could help you decide whether this new drug should be given to patients? How could you find this information?

What should a doctor do with a new medicine that could save people's lives?

Withhold it for further tests	Make it available to a select group	Make it available to anyone
• Advantages • Disadvantages	• Advantages • Disadvantages	• Advantages • Disadvantages

Reformation and the Scientific Revolution

Chapter Review

Reviewing Key Terms

council (p. 340)
Counter Reformation (p. 352)
hypothesis (p. 355)
indulgence (p. 340)
inquisition (p. 352)
pamphlet (p. 345)
predestination (p. 350)
Protestant (p. 344)
Reformation (p. 344)
scientific method (p. 355)
Scientific Revolution
 (p. 354)

A. Write whether each of the following statements is true or false. Then rewrite the false statements to make them true.
1. Martin Luther was a leader in the Counter Reformation.
2. The Reformation was the Catholic movement to improve the Protestant church.
3. The scientific method involves a series of logical steps used in scientific research.
4. Councils of church leaders were created to meet and rule on matters of church law and faith and to restore unity and dignity to the Catholic church.
5. During the Scientific Revolution, accepted theories about the nature of the universe were challenged.

B. Write a sentence or two using the three terms in each group. The sentences should show how the terms are related.
1. indulgences, Protestant, predestination
2. Protestant, Reformation, inquisition
3. scientific method, hypothesis, Scientific Revolution

Exploring Concepts

A. In every age there are individuals who have a strong effect on historical events. Copy the chart below. Then fill in the boxes with the names of individuals who were important participants in this historical period. Add more boxes if necessary. Then choose two names from each category and summarize the contributions of each.

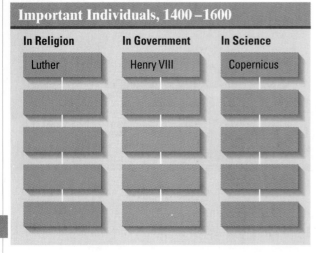

Important Individuals, 1400–1600

In Religion	In Government	In Science
Luther	Henry VIII	Copernicus

B. Support each statement with facts and details from the chapter.
1. The *Unam Sanctam* eventually led to a lessening of the authority of the Catholic church.
2. Many Catholics were confused by the French cardinals' election of Clement VII to the office of pope.
3. Some clergy engaged in corrupt practices, which further weakened the authority of the church.
4. Copernicus and Newton reached conclusions that changed previous ideas of how the universe worked.
5. The Council of Trent was an important part of the Catholic church's attempt to reform itself.
6. Scientists of the 1500s and 1600s and religious reformers questioned accepted theories and beliefs.
7. In addition to Martin Luther, there were other individuals and groups who broke away from the Catholic church.

Reviewing Skills

1. What system is used to organize the text sections The Reformation Begins and Protestantism Spreads on pages 344–347? Explain what clues you had.
2. Copernicus believed that the sun was the center of the universe and the earth only one of the planets that revolved around the sun. However, he refused to publish the mathematical work and records of observation that supported his hypothesis until he knew that he was near death. Use the five-step process to formulate a hypothesis that explains why Copernicus did not publish his findings earlier. Read Lesson 4 to review the facts. Explain how your hypothesis accounts for all the facts you list.
3. Reread the quotation from Pope Boniface's *Unam Sanctam* on page 338. What was Pope Boniface's bias?
4. You are reading Protestant and Catholic primary sources on the Reformation. What factors can you think of that might affect factual reporting from both Protestant and Catholic sources?

Using Critical Thinking

1. The events of history are like a chain of causes and effects. What action of King Philip IV caused Pope Boniface VIII to issue the *Unam Sanctam?* What action did Philip take as a result of the pope's decree? What effect did Philip's action have on the Catholic church? If Philip IV hadn't responded to the *Unam Sanctam* as he did, what role might the church play in our lives and government today? Why?
2. "The pen is mightier than the sword" is an old saying. What does it mean? How would you apply the saying to the actions of Martin Luther?
3. Copernicus's theory on planetary motion was strongly opposed by certain leaders of his day. Suppose that a theory that is in direct opposition to a widely accepted scientific theory was proposed today. Do you think it would meet with the same kind of opposition? Why?
4. Modern Americans enjoy many important rights, including the freedom of religion and the freedom of speech. If the people you learned about in this chapter had these two rights, do you think the events in the chapter would have been any different? Explain what you mean.

Preparing for Citizenship

1. GROUP ACTIVITY Look at the map of world religions on page 529 of the Atlas. Choose one of the religions shown. Research its development and prepare a timeline showing dates of important events in its history. Display the timelines in the classroom. Also look for and display newspaper and magazine articles about that religion.
2. INTERVIEWING Interview a minister, a priest, a rabbi, or someone else in a religious role. Ask questions such as these: Why did you choose this profession? What type of schooling is required? What do you especially like about your work? What are some disadvantages? Present your information in brief talks called "Meet ____."
3. COLLABORATIVE LEARNING Meet with your class to plan a Living History in which important people introduced in this chapter discuss their contributions and achievements. Which people made the most important contributions? Use the chart you completed in Exploring Concepts as a guide. Select students for the following tasks: role-play the historical figures; write their scripts; make costumes and props; design and construct scenery; and make posters advertising the presentation. Then present the Living History.

Chapter 14

The Age of Exploration

Gold, silver, and silks glimmered in the North African sun. The fragrance of spices filled the air. The year was 1415. Portugal's Prince Henry, then a crusader, marveled at the riches in the city of Ceuta. These sights gave Henry a dream—to control the rich trade with Africa and Asia. The same dream sparked many adventurers of the 1400s and 1500s. Time after time, they risked voyages on uncharted waters to reach the valuable goods of Africa and Asia.

Throughout this period, explorers brave high waves, storms, rocky shallows, and their crews' fears that sea monsters lurk in the ocean.

1292 After 17 years in China, traveler Marco Polo returns to Venice and tells Europeans of China's wonders. A later geographer uses Polo's accounts to draw this map.

| 1250 | 1300 | 1350 | 1400 |

c. 1400 Chinese trading ships sail to the Middle East and eastern Africa.

1250

During this time, scholars and sailors worked to improve the tools of navigation. Their work paved the way for many advances, like this sextant of the 1700s.

1400s and 1500s Monarchs like England's Queen Elizabeth (above) finance exploration in hope of gaining great riches.

| 1450 | 1500 | 1550 | 1600 |

1526 Babur founds the Mughal Empire in India.

1600

LESSON 1

Travel, Trade, and Exploration

THINKING FOCUS

Why did explorers in the 1400s risk their lives to explore parts of the world that were unknown to them?

Key Terms

- monopoly
- balance of trade
- bullion

➤ *This print of Vasco da Gama is based on an unknown artist's painting.*

*T*he seas rose towards the sky and fell back in heavy showers which flooded the ships. The storm raging thus violently, the danger was doubled, for suddenly the wind died out, so that the ships lay dead between the waves, lurching so heavily that they took in water on both sides; and the men made themselves fast not to fall from one side to the other; and everything in the ships was breaking up, so that all cried to God for mercy.

Gaspar Correa,
from *Lendas da India*, 1561

That is how the Portuguese chronicler Gaspar Correa recorded the dramatic events of Vasco da Gama's voyage. The Portuguese explorer sailed around the Cape of Good Hope at the southern tip of Africa to India in the late 1490s.

The voyage took tremendous courage. At one point, da Gama's four ships lost sight of land for 96 days. The sailors thought they were lost. The crew was panic-stricken with fear, and murmurings of mutiny worried the captain.

But da Gama did not turn back, despite storms, sickness, and food shortages. He reached India in May 1498, after 14 months at sea. In 1499, when he finally returned to Portugal, only 44 of the original 170 sailors still survived.

Finding the Way

Great advances in mapmaking helped explorers like Vasco da Gama. Between the late 1200s and 1500, geographers began to produce a more accurate picture of the world. They also developed new theories about its shape and size. And new information gathered by earlier world travelers and traders about the riches of far-away places kindled the desire for travel and exploration.

Early Exploration

Many people knew more about the world than the Europeans did. These included groups from China, India, Southeast Asia, Africa, and the Middle East. The Europeans' interest in exploration now grew. The crusades had shown many people the wider world. Towns were growing, as was trade. Also, the new universities brought advanced learning from Asia and Africa to the attention of Europeans. Marco Polo's written account of his travels was a popular book.

Firsthand observations, like those you have read about from Marco Polo and Ibn Battuta, also provided some mapmakers with valuable information. By the 1300s, pilots were using coastal charts, or portolans, that had been prepared according to information supplied by trading ship captains. These charts showed the sailing courses, ports, and anchorages that were mainly used by traders in the Mediterranean Sea. Portolan charts eventually surpassed earlier maps in accuracy and reliability.

Although the quality of Portolan charts was improving all the time,

travelers needed still better maps. The slow development of understanding of ancient and medieval learning was starting to make a difference in travel to western Europeans.

This map from 1493 locates sailing routes and anchorages along the West African coast as well as cities and kings in West Africa.

New Old Learning

The ancient observatory at Alexandria, the imperial geographers of Abbasid Baghdad, even the Byzantine sea traders gathered knowledge of geography, cartography, astronomy, and navigation. From the 1100s on, some translations of their work began filtering through to western Europe. Eventually it spread through the growing university towns of Paris, Padua, Oxford, and others. The T-O maps of medieval European cartographers showed the three known continents separated by T-shaped bodies of water and encircled by an O-shaped ocean. T-O maps were small and did not accurately represent locations. For an example of a

Across Time & Space

Mapmaking has come a long way since the rediscovery of Ptolemy's Geography. *Airplanes make it possible to photograph large areas from the air and then map them. Artificial satellites can send pictures of still larger areas, even the whole earth.*

The Cape of Good Hope can still be difficult to sail around today.

T-O map, see page 15 in Chapter 1.

In 1400, a patron brought to Florence the ancient text *Geography,* by the geographer Ptolemy *(TAHL uh mee).* It was then translated and circulated. Written 1,250 years earlier, in A.D. 150, it contained a remarkably accurate map of the world known to the Romans at that time.

Most people still believed in Ptolemy's idea of how the heavens operated, too. The earth, which was round, was at the center of the universe. The planets revolved around it. Arab, Persian, and other Muslim mathematicians created advanced calculations in order to be able to predict the locations of the planets. These calculations were necessary if one had to plot a course at sea without landmarks. Surprisingly, Ptolemy's system worked well for a thousand years. Our current understanding of how the planets revolve is now some 400 years old, and there are new discoveries all the time. ■

■ *What developments between the late 1200s and 1500 spurred European interest in exploring the world?*

Meeting the Demand for Goods

In the 1300s and 1400s, many traders were willing to risk their lives for the wealth they would receive by satisfying the demand in Europe for luxury goods. Items such as eastern silks, cotton, dyes, and gems could be sold at high prices. The demand for spices was especially strong. Find out more about the spice trade in A Closer Look on page 367.

Goods from the East were brought by camel caravan or ship.

▼ *Which Italian ports were located at the western end of the east-west trade routes?*

Eurasian Trade Routes Before Europe's Age of Exploration

0 500 1000 mi.
0 500 1000 km
Lambert Azimuthal Equal-Area Projection

—— Trade route

The Spice Trade

Europeans wanted more spice in their lives. Tired of bland food, nobles used spices to lend their dishes an exotic flavor. Spices were expensive because they were rare and passed through many hands on their way to market. The demand for tasty products pushed out the boundaries of the known world, as explorers rushed to find new routes to the spice lands.

Pepper plant, pepper berries, and dried peppercorns— native to India

One of the earliest known spices, pepper became popular because its fiery bite overpowered the taste of spoiled food.

Marco Polo in Pepperland shows the explorer helping to harvest the precious berries. Marco Polo tasted pepper for the first time in the East and brought some back to Europe in the 13th century. At one time in England, peppercorns were so valuable they were counted out one by one, and used as money.

Cinnamon—native to the island of Sri Lanka

Cloves —dried flowerbuds of a tree from Southeast Asia

Merchants, sailing ships like this one, traded Arabian frankincense for Indian pepper.

Peppercorns in meat

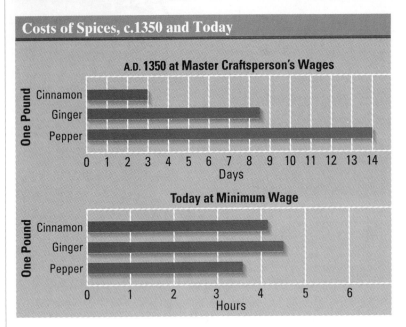

Costs of Spices, c.1350 and Today

A.D. 1350 at Master Craftsperson's Wages

One Pound

Cinnamon	
Ginger	
Pepper	

0 1 2 3 4 5 6 7 8 9 10 11 12 13 14
Days

Today at Minimum Wage

One Pound

Cinnamon	
Ginger	
Pepper	

0   1   2   3   4   5   6
Hours

▲ *This chart compares the amount of time it would have taken to earn enough money to buy these luxury items in 1350 with the amount to time it takes today. Which item is now the most expensive?*

■ *How did Europeans obtain goods from the East?*

Along the way to ports such as Antioch and Alexandria the goods changed hands many times. Each trader covered only a portion of the route and then sold his cargo to the next trader.

Each trader in the long relay through Eurasia raised the price in order to make a profit. Thus, by the time a piece of silk reached the Mediterranean, it might cost more than 100 times its original price.

In the bustling Mediterranean ports, cargoes from the East were loaded onto Italian merchant ships for the passage to Europe. Italian port cities such as Venice and Genoa played a key role in east-west trade.

Because their location was central to Mediterranean markets, the Italian city-states had long been home to the best seafarers, navigators, and shipbuilders in the West. Moreover, Italian merchants had long been involved in overseas trade with commercial centers in Muslim countries. As a result, Italian cities had flourished since the 1100s.

Venice was all-powerful in the eastern Mediterranean, while Genoa dominated western Mediterranean trade in the early 1300s. However, in the late 1300s, the two cities waged war to determine which of them would command trade on the Black Sea and the Aegean Sea. Despite some crushing defeats in battle, Venice maintained a **monopoly,** or complete control, over trade with the East. ■

Carrying Christianity Across the Sea

Europeans sought goods and profit, but they also wanted to spread Christianity among non-believers in other parts of the world. Some Christian explorers also hoped to find a mythical king named Prester John, who was rumored to rule a Christian kingdom in Africa or Asia. According to legend, Prester John had successfully defended his kingdom from Muslim attack. From the 1100s on, the Portuguese spent great amounts of time, energy, and resources looking for this potential ally in the fight against the Muslims.

The Spanish and Portuguese had long been waging religious warfare against Islam. Since the early 700s, Muslims had invaded and occupied much of Spain and what would later become Portugal. Many battles were fought against the Muslims, but they were not finally driven out of southern Spain until 1492.

These religious wars influenced Spanish and Portuguese exploration. If people in newly discovered regions converted to Christianity, Spain and Portugal would have new allies in the fight against Islam. This was one reason missionaries usually accompanied the expeditions that explored or settled new regions.

Missionaries used education to convert the nonbelievers to Christianity. In the 1600s, Jesuit missionaries in China studied Chinese language and culture to better understand the people they wanted to convert. They also helped teach the Chinese and Europeans about each other's civilizations.

However, other missionaries were not so gentle. Some used torture to subdue nonbelievers in foreign lands. For instance, 16th-century missionaries in Central and South America forced native inhabitants to work on church-owned farms. This outraged many Christians. Bartolomé de Las Casas, a defender of the rights of the natives, wrote a book on acceptable methods of conversion. An excerpt from his work follows.

*H*earers, especially pagans, should understand that the preachers of the faith have no intention of acquiring power over them through their preaching. . . . [They] should understand that no desire for riches moves [preachers] to preach. . . . In speaking and conversing with their hearers, especially pagans, the preachers should show themselves so mild and humble, courteous and . . . good-willed that the hearers eagerly wish to listen and hold their teaching in greater reverence.

Las Casas, *The "Only Method" of Converting the Indians*, 1530s

While missionaries on exploratory expeditions sought to make new converts, many of the explorers leading these expeditions were searching for new gold markets. If Spanish and Portuguese explorers could find new sources of gold, their governments might be able to break up the Venetian monopoly on trade. ■

◄ *This 1422 painting is of a Jesuit missionary-astronomer who predicted an eclipse of the sun in China. The Chinese ruler ordered the missionary to teach his people Western science.*

■ *What role did religion play during the new era of European exploration?*

Searching for New Markets

The Venetians delivered their cargoes of spices and other eastern goods by land or by sea to cities throughout Europe. In exchange for the eastern imports, Europeans exported wool, linen, timber, tin,

The Age of Exploration

copper, lead, and guns. Above all, some European countries needed gold to buy imported goods.

Portugal and Spain were active participants in east-west trade. However, the total cost of the goods Portugal imported was often higher than the total value of the goods it exported. Thus, the Portuguese government frequently owed a trade debt to other governments. Portugal had to pay these governments to maintain the **balance of trade,** or the difference between the total value of exports and the total value of imports. European trading countries demanded payment of debts in gold, which often took the form of **bullion.** Bullion was gold that had been melted and then molded into ingots, or bars, of specific weights.

As eastern imports increased, the Portuguese government needed more gold to pay for the goods. Portugal and Spain obtained most of their gold from North African traders at high prices. These traders had bought the gold from central and southern African gold producers and then carried it by caravan across the Sahara. Portugal wanted to bypass the North African traders and deal directly with the source, the gold producers. By trading directly, they could obtain gold more cheaply. So, in 1419, Portuguese explorers began sailing south along the west coast of Africa in search of gold markets.

Portugal needed gold, but it also needed good farmland and workers to cultivate the land. Nobles wanted to claim farmland in overseas regions to increase their wealth. And traders were eager to find new supplies of agricultural produce to sell in Portugal.

Eventually, some Portuguese began to hope for an even greater reward than gold and land: a sea route to the East. If they sailed directly to India and China, Portuguese traders could buy goods at their source and sell them in Europe at huge profits. Portugal could then break the Italian monopoly on east-west trade. Finding a sea route to the East and establishing a direct trading connection became the goal of many European explorers. ■

▲ *Gold bullion is still used by countries today to pay debts and to settle accounts.*

■ *Why did Portugal want to find new markets?*

R E V I E W

1. **FOCUS** Why did explorers risk their lives to explore parts of the world that were unknown to them?
2. **CONNECT** Travelers in the age of exploration began to view the world in new ways. How was their view of the world similar to that of thinkers during the Reformation and the Scientific Revolution?
3. **ECONOMICS** Why did the Portuguese want to find new sources of gold?
4. **BELIEF SYSTEMS** What did European Christians hope to achieve by exploring unknown lands?
5. **CRITICAL THINKING** Many "explorers" "discovered" places that were already thoroughly known to the people who lived there. What are the real meanings of the words "explore" and "discover"?
6. **ACTIVITY** Hide a book or other object. Then draw a map that could be used to direct someone to the object's discovery. Be sure to indicate the proper positions and directions of things and places indicated on your map. Finally, see if a friend can use the map to find the object.

L E S S O N 2

Adventure and Profit

Prince Henry of Portugal, or "Henry the Navigator" as he was known, was a leader in the early years of European exploration. In 1453, a historian described him as a curious and adventurous man.

The noble spirit of this Prince was ever urging him both to begin and to carry out very great deeds. . ... He had also a wish to know the land that lay beyond the isles of Canary and that Cape called Bojador [BAHJ uh dawr], for that up to his time, neither by writings, nor by the memory of man, was known with any certainty the nature of the land beyond that Cape. . . . It seemed to him that if he or some other lord did not endeavor to gain that knowledge, no mariners or merchants would ever dare to attempt it, for it is clear that none of them ever trouble themselves to sail to a place where there is not a sure and certain hope of profit.

Gomes Eannes de Azurara, from *Discovery and Conquest of Guinea*, 1453

Prince Henry was determined to overcome the fear surrounding Cape Bojador. And the unknown beyond the Cape fascinated him.

THINKING
FOCUS

How did Prince Henry's center for navigation help establish Portugal's trading empire in the 1500s?

Key Terms

- caravel
- capital
- colony

◄ *Prince Henry leads troops against the Muslim city of Ceuta in this painting from the 1400s. While in Ceuta, Henry became intrigued by descriptions of Africa's wealth.*

Prince Henry, Navigator

Henry could not guarantee that Portugal would profit from his exploration along the west coast of Africa. But he could vouch that gold and other luxury goods could be found in Africa. In 1415, he had been a crusader in the Muslim port city Ceuta *(SAY oo tah)* in North Africa. He had seen vast quantities of gold, silver, and grain, magnificent silks and tapestries, and fragrant spices. Camel caravans from sub-Saharan Africa brought these sumptuous goods to Ceuta.

The Age of Exploration

This astrolabe dates to 1532. G. Hartmann, the name of the maker, is inscribed on it.

This woodcut of a mapmaker in his study shows the tools he used. The lodestone shown on the small, round table had magnetic properties and so served as a compass.

■ *Why was Prince Henry of Portugal nicknamed "the Navigator"?*

Henry hoped to find the source of African gold by sailing south along the coast. He hoped to find new markets and new goods for Portugal as well. Perhaps he would even find the legendary Prester John or new believers for the Christian faith.

Henry was an unusual man—intensely religious and fascinated by the mystery beyond known boundaries. When he left Ceuta, he did not return to Lisbon and the luxurious life of a prince. Rather, Henry sailed to the small town of Sagres *(SAH greesh)*

on Cape St. Vincent, the southernmost point of Portugal. There, on the rocky, windswept peninsula, Henry established a center for navigation and exploration. He summoned shipbuilders, mapmakers, sea captains, and instrument makers from all over Europe to live and study in Sagres.

Henry also invited sailors, travelers, and scholars from Europe, Africa, and the Middle East to share their geographical knowledge. He financed expeditions to West Africa. Bit by bit, Henry's scholars added information to the maps developed at Sagres. ■

Preparations for Sailing

Explorers needed more than improved maps to find their way to unknown destinations in Africa and beyond. Out on the open sea, they had only the sun, moon, and stars to guide them. Ocean-going seafarers also had to deal with unpredictable winds and unseen

currents that could send them far off course. They didn't know what hardships lay ahead of them or how long it might take to get to their destination.

Prince Henry's experts improved and adapted for navigation such instruments as the compass

The smooth hull enabled the caravel to travel fast and withstand rough seas. Its shallow depth allowed in-shore exploration.

Triangular lateen sails, copied from the Arab dhows, allowed the caravel to sail into the wind on a zigzag course. Some caravels used lateen sails in combination with square sails.

The rudder in the center of the stern enabled the caravel to make sharp turns and steer more easily than a ship with a rudder on one side.

and the astrolabe, which is used to determine latitude. They also devised methods that would help guide a ship when it sailed out of sight of land. For example, they designed mathematical tables that could be used to determine latitude from the angle of the North Star or the sun's elevation. A cross-staff measured this angle. A sailor held the long shaft of the cross-staff to his eye and pointed the instrument heavenward. He then moved the crosspiece until the horizon was at one end and the star was at the other. The sailor measured the angle that the cross-piece formed and used the mathematical table to determine his location's latitude.

Henry also required his sailors to keep accurate accounts of all the things they saw while sailing along a coastline. This information was added to information brought by travelers and scholars invited to Sagres to make maps more accurate.

In addition, Henry's ship designers built a new kind of ship better suited to voyages on the open sea. The ships used for coastal trade had square sails and steering oars. These ships were hard to maneuver on the open sea and had difficulty tacking, or changing course, with the wind.

Prince Henry's ship designers borrowed the best features from other sailing vessels to create the swift and maneuverable **caravel,** which is pictured above. This vessel was large enough to hold the supplies for a crew of about 20. One Venetian seaman called it "the best ship that sailed the seas." The caravel became the standard ship of explorers of the 1400s and 1500s.

▲ *The caravel's ability to sail into the wind meant the vessel also had the ability to return its passengers home. Explorers going out in a caravel were more willing to risk longer voyages.*

▼ *Prince Henry could not improve the food his explorers ate on their voyages. Foods like the cheese, salt pork, and oats shown here often spoiled as a result of the ship's dampness.*

On the open ocean, strong winds and currents made ships travel much faster than they did in the calmer areas along the shore. Speedier passage meant ships could travel farther on fewer supplies. ■

The Portuguese Explorations

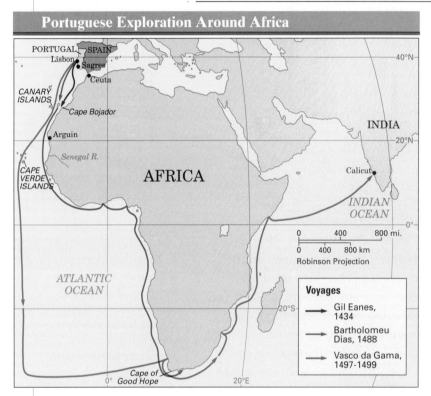

Portuguese Exploration Around Africa

Voyages
→ Gil Eanes, 1434
→ Bartholomeu Dias, 1488
→ Vasco da Gama, 1497–1499

▲ *Find Cape Bojador on the map. Do you think it was primarily a physical or mental barrier to the Portuguese explorers? Why was rounding the cape so important?*

Even with these technological advances, it took many years and many voyages before the seafarers of Portugal became experts on the open sea. The first expeditions down the African coast, organized and financed by Prince Henry, probably began around 1419. The goal of these voyages was to round the dreaded point of land called Cape Bojador, just south of the Canary Islands.

Arab geographers called the waters there the "Green Sea of Darkness" because of violent waves and currents, frequent fogs, strong winds, and dangerous shallows. Beyond Bojador was the unknown, feared by even the most daring and skillful seafarers. In 1453, the chronicler Azurara explained why no ship had ventured beyond Cape Bojador.

> T he mariners said] that beyond this Cape there is no race of men nor place of inhabitants . . . and the sea [is] so shallow that a whole league from land it is only a fathom [six feet] deep, while the currents are so terrible that no ship having once passed the Cape, will ever be able to return. . . .
>
> Gomes Eannes de Azurara, from *Discovery and Conquest of Guinea*, 1453

By 1433, Henry had sent 15 expeditions to pass the cape, but each one returned to Sagres without success. Finally, in 1434, a Portuguese captain named Gil Eanes *(zhil YA nihsh)*, rounded Bojador and landed on the African coast south of the cape. The barrier of fear had been broken.

Year by year, Henry sent ships farther down the African coast. In 1448, the explorers established the first Portuguese trading post at Arguin. Merchants there exchanged wheat, cloth, and glass beads for African gold, slaves, pepper, and ivory. By the time Prince Henry died in 1460, 25 caravels a year carried goods between Portugal and West Africa.

Later Portuguese rulers continued to support exploration of the West African coast. As the expeditions pushed down the coast, some rulers began to think it might be possible to sail all the way around

Africa to the East. In 1485, the king of Portugal, Dom João *(zhwown)* II, announced that his ships would soon open up the sea route to India.

The king's hunch proved correct. In 1488, Bartholomeu Dias rounded the Cape of Good Hope at the southern tip of Africa. In 1498, Vasco da Gama became the first European to sail around Africa and reach the city of Calicut in India, proving the existence of a sea route to the East. ■

◄ *With this bronze figure, a West African artist "recorded" Portuguese exploration of his land. How do you think it reflects the West Africans' impression of the Portuguese explorers of the 1500s?*

■ *Why did the Portuguese want to explore the west coast of Africa?*

Commerce and Colonies

Long-distance voyages like those of da Gama and Dias were expensive and risky. Explorers needed huge sums of money to build ships and equip their expeditions, which often lasted several years. Thus, the first problem most explorers faced was finding someone to finance their voyages.

Investing in Overseas Trade

Prince Henry, a wealthy member of the royal family, paid for his early projects with his own money. However, eventually it became clear that trade with Africa could be highly profitable. Then Portuguese kings and wealthy merchants were willing to contribute **capital,** or money and materials, to finance later voyages. But the large fleets that sailed to the East after da Gama's first voyage in 1498 required more money than the Portuguese could supply.

To finance these longer voyages, Portuguese investors turned to foreign bankers in southern Germany and the Italian city-states of Genoa and Florence. In exchange for their investment, the

bankers became part owners of the valuable cargoes. When their agents sold the goods in Europe, the bankers often received more than twice as much money as they had invested.

Establishing Colonies

The Portuguese lost a large percentage of their profits to foreign investors. But Portugal profited from exploration by establishing **colonies,** or settlements of their own citizens, in the lands they explored.

Prince Henry's voyagers had discovered several uninhabited islands off the coast of West Africa between 1419 and 1470. Among these were Madeira, the Cape Verde Islands, and São Tomé *(sown tuh MAY).* The Portuguese sent settlers to these islands to grow sugar and wheat for export back to Portugal.

Crusaders had created a demand for sugar in Europe after tasting it in the Middle East during the 1000s. As a result, Italian merchants established huge farms, called plantations, on several

The Age of Exploration

Mediterranean islands and grew sugar. These merchants brought slaves from Russia and Africa to the islands to cultivate and harvest the sugar.

During the 1400s, Portuguese explorers bought, traded, and

The sugar obtained from sugar cane stalks such as these remained a luxury throughout the 1700s. Sugar was often listed with diamonds among the gifts given to European monarchs.

■ How did Portugal profit from the colonies it established off the coast of West Africa?

captured African slaves. Many of these slaves were shipped to Europe. Many others were sent to Portuguese colonies to work on the sugar plantations. Frequently, colonists enslaved the islands' native inhabitants and forced them to work on the plantations.

The European demand for sugar, however, soon exceeded the supply the plantations could produce. Sugar could, therefore, be sold in Europe at a very high price. Since the price paid for the sugar far surpassed the cost of growing it, plantation owners made great profits. They used these profits to buy more slaves and expand their sugar plantations. As a result, by 1550, the

island of São Tomé was producing 30 times as much sugar as it had produced in 1530.

Trading in the East

The early Portuguese traders were also active in the East. In the early 1500s, they established naval bases and trading stations at strategic locations along the eastern spice routes. They hoped to ruin the Venetian spice trade by preventing Arab and Indian merchants from carrying spices overland to Egyptian and Syrian ports.

Meanwhile, Portuguese fleets brought gold and Indian cotton to trade in busy spice ports such as Malacca, on the south coast of Malaysia. These important trade ports are shown on the map of trade routes on page 366.

Although Portuguese explorers conquered important port cities such as Malacca, Goa in India, and Hormuz in the Middle East, they never completely cut off the Venetian spice trade. Many Arab and Indian merchants continued to use traditional routes to trade with Venetian merchants in the Mediterranean. However, Portugal's conquests in the East and in the Atlantic enabled it to control a large part of eastern trade for nearly 100 years. ■

R E V I E W

1. **FOCUS** How did Prince Henry's center for navigation help establish Portugal's trading empire in the 1500s?
2. **CONNECT** Why did Prince Henry want to find a new source of African gold for Portugal?
3. **HISTORY** Why weren't technological advances enough to launch the new era of European exploration?
4. **ECONOMICS** Why was the tiny island of São Tomé important to the Portuguese?
5. **CRITICAL THINKING** If you were a Portuguese ruler in the 1400s, would you support exploration? Why or why not?
6. **ACTIVITY** Make a timeline of the explorers of the great age of European discovery. Add other explorers by looking at "Exploration" on page 514 in the Minipedia.

376

LESSON 3

Exploring the Americas

Columbus's plan was so exciting, and hiring on as a ship's boy seemed like such a good idea at the time. You were ready for an adventure. But how could you have known that it would be like this?

You work hard, the days are monotonous, and you're not sure if you will ever see home again. It's been 52 days since you left Spain, but there's no land in sight. . . .

The last grains of sand slip through the sandglass. Another half hour gone. You turn the glass. Ring the bell. Make your mark. One more mark to go, then your four-hour watch is over.

Waves rock the ship. Sleep is impossible now. Whoever sees land first will receive 10,000 maravedis.

Enough to change your life, at least for a little while.

A dark twig bobs in the foamy water. A small flock of birds passes overhead, moving southwest. The captain must be right. Land must be near. The sun on the water hurts your eyes as you strain to make out a tree, a hill, a sandy beach. Nothing. Just green sea.

The glass is empty. You turn the glass. Ring the bell. Make your mark. Rodrigo takes over the glass. The new watch charts the speed of the bobbing twig in the green sea.

There's space on deck in the shade of the mast. A short nap might stop the burning in your eyes. Maybe later you'll lower a line and catch a fish for dinner. You close your eyes and dream of home.

THINKING FOCUS

What role did Christopher Columbus's voyages play in the colonization of North America?

Key Term

- circumnavigation

◀ *When the sand measuring the last half-hour of a seaman's watch ran out of the glass, he'd call the next men on duty: "On deck, on deck, gentlemen mariners of the starboard watch . . . shake a leg!"*

Christopher Columbus

Like the boy described above, but about 30 years earlier, Christopher Columbus probably began his seafaring career as a ship's boy.

Although very little is known about his early life, most scholars think that Columbus was born in Genoa, Italy, in 1451.

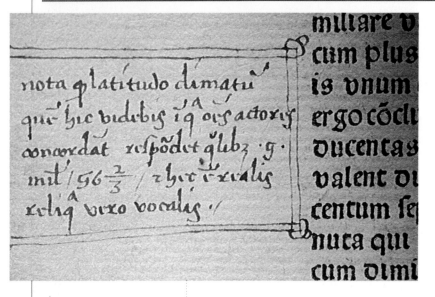

▲ *Columbus's notes in a geography book (now in a Seville library) show that he forgot that his and al-Faraghani's "miles" were different lengths.*

▼ *Both Columbus and Magellan sailed west. Which one found a westward route to India?*

While still a young man, Columbus became a seaman on Genoese merchant vessels. When he was 25 years old, Columbus was shipwrecked off the coast of Portugal. By good fortune, he landed close to Sagres and Prince Henry's center for navigators. Columbus decided to stay. For eight years Columbus read books about geography, history, and travel. He studied the charts of Portuguese pilots who had sailed to

Africa's west coast. He calculated that the distance from Spain to Asia would be no more than 4000 miles. It is, in fact, about 15,000 miles, with the Americas in between. Columbus misunderstood the unit of measure used in 861 by the Muslim astronomer al-Faraghani, when he calculated the earth's circumference (and fell short by less than one mile!).

In 1484, Columbus asked the Portuguese rulers to finance his voyage. When they refused, Columbus turned to King Ferdinand and Queen Isabella of Spain. They rejected his idea at first, but finally, in 1492, agreed to pay for the expedition.

On August 3, 1492, Columbus set sail from Palos, Spain, with three ships and 88 men. After eight weeks at sea, the crew feared that they would never see land again. They were afraid that the strong east winds would prevent them from sailing back home. On September 24, Columbus made the following entry in his journal.

European Exploration

> *I am having trouble with the crew, . . . complaining that they will never be able to return home. They have said that it is insanity and suicidal on their part to risk their lives following the madness of a foreigner. . . . I am told by a few trusted men (and these are few in number!) that if I persist in going onward, the best course of action will be to throw me into the sea some night.*
>
> Christopher Columbus,
> from his journal, 1492

Despite this threat of mutiny, Columbus stayed on course. Two hours after midnight on October 12—two very long months after they'd set sail—land was sighted. At dawn, the sailors went ashore. They named the new land San Salvador and claimed it for Spain.

San Salvador is a small island in the Bahamas, located about 50 miles off the east coast of Florida. Columbus thought he had landed on an island off the coast of Japan or China. Columbus also visited two other islands: Cuba, which he believed to be part of China, and Hispaniola. People knew within 30 years of his expedition that Columbus had not discovered a westward route to India. But people continued to call the native inhabitants of America "Indians" and the islands he reached the "West Indies."

The name "America" was chosen by Alsatian geographer Martin Waldseemüller *(VAHLT say myoo lur)*, when he laid out a new map of the world in 1507. Amerigo Vespucci *(vehs POO chee)* made voyages after Columbus, and while Columbus died forgotten, Vespucci wrote a best-selling book about "the New World." ■

How Do We Know?

HISTORY *On his maps in the early 1500s, Waldseemüller named America after Amerigo Vespucci. The mapmaker thought that Vespucci had discovered the North American mainland in 1497. When he found out that Columbus had arrived first, "America" had already been printed in thousands of books.*

■ *Why did Columbus continue to explore the islands in the Caribbean and the coasts of South and Central America?*

▼ *Exports of gold and silver from the New World were very important to Spain. By law, one-fifth of the silver and gold mined in the regions claimed by Columbus belonged to the king of Spain.*

The Spanish in the Americas

Columbus made four voyages in all, to the Caribbean and the coasts of South and Central America. After his first, the Spanish rulers acted quickly to prevent their chief rivals, the Portuguese, from profiting from his discovery. The Spanish asked Pope Alexander VI to grant them control of navigation and settlement in the regions Columbus had visited.

The pope had drawn an imaginary line from north to south in the Atlantic. All land and sea west of the line would belong to Spain, and all land east of the line would belong to Portugal. In 1494, the rulers of the two countries signed the treaty of Tordesillas *(tawrd uh SEE yuhs)* to establish this boundary.

Rumors that the lands were rich with gold and silver attracted many Spanish adventurers to the Americas. Wherever they found riches, Spanish conquerors killed

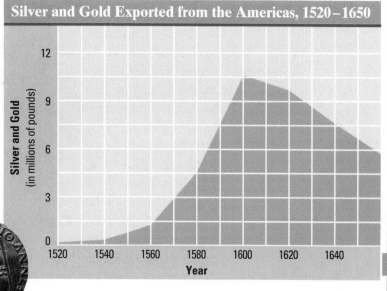

Silver and Gold Exported from the Americas, 1520–1650

Y-axis: Silver and Gold (in millions of pounds) — 0, 3, 6, 9, 12

X-axis: Year — 1520, 1540, 1560, 1580, 1600, 1620, 1640

The Age of Exploration

the local people and stole their treasures. In the 1540s, the Spanish discovered silver deposits in Peru, on the Pacific coast of South America. They opened mines and forced the Indians to work in them.

Spain also sent explorers and colonizers to the new territories. Eager for profit, the colonists set up plantations to grow sugar cane, tobacco, and other crops for export to Europe. These plantations required great numbers of laborers to plant, harvest, and pack the crops. The Spanish colonists forced the Indians to do the work. These workers were poorly fed, overworked, and beaten by the Spanish. Many died from this abuse.

Even more death, however, was brought to many Native Americans through the introduction of European diseases. Europeans, Africans, and Asians had endured centuries of plagues, and those who had survived developed immunities. Their bodies were able to fight off these diseases. Native peoples, however, had no such immunities, and the diseases spread like wildfire. There were nearly 80 million native people in North and South American when Columbus arrived. Probably more than 75 percent had died by 1600.

Some Spanish priests, who attempted to convert the native peoples to Christianity by gentle means, tried to enforce laws designed to protect the Indians. However, these priests were few in number, and rarely succeeded. ■

■ *Why was it necessary to create laws designed to protect the Indians from the Spanish colonists?*

Europeans in North America

Spain was only one of many European countries that explored the Americas. Around the year 1000, almost 500 years before Columbus's voyage, Vikings led by Leif Ericson landed in Newfoundland and explored part of the coast of North America. In the 1480s, Basque and other European fishermen fished and whaled near the coast of Canada.

The English were the first to send an organized expedition in Columbus's wake. In 1497, the Italian John Cabot, sailing for England, reached Newfoundland, which he thought was part of Asia. On a second voyage, he explored the coast of North America. When the English began to establish colonies in North America in the 1600s, they claimed possession of the areas Cabot had visited.

In 1513, Vasco Núñez de Balboa, sailing for Spain, crossed the Isthmus of Panama and saw the Pacific Ocean. From 1519 to 1521, a Spanish fleet under the command of Ferdinand Magellan made the first **circumnavigation,** or voyage around the earth. You can trace that voyage on the map on page 378.

By 1521, Balboa and Magellan had proved that a huge, newly discovered continent blocked the westward route to Asia. Explorers who followed were determined to find a way around or through that continent.

➤ *In this engraving, Magellan holds the world and uses a navigator's instrument to plot a course.*

The hope of finding such a route, called the Northwest Passage, drew Europeans across the Atlantic. In 1524, King Francis I of France sent an expedition to America. The Italian commander of the voyage, Giovanni da Verrazano, sailed from the coast of present-day North Carolina north to Newfoundland. Another expedition was led by the French explorer Jacques Cartier. In 1535, he sailed up the Saint Lawrence River to the future site of Montreal, Canada. Verrazano and Cartier's voyages gave the French a claim to part of North America.

In the late 1500s, the Europeans realized that the vast continent offered a wealth of resources: land, timber, minerals, fur, and much more. Colonists from England, France, and Holland began to arrive in North America to farm, search for gold, trap animals for fur, or seek religious freedom. The native population in North America was not taken advantage of as rapidly as in the Spanish colonies. Northern colonists had no need for cheap labor. But as more settlers claimed American Indian land, the Indians were pushed westward.

As colonies and trading empires were established in North America, the importance of Mediterranean trade with the Far East declined. Sugar raised on Caribbean island plantations became the main export of the North American colonies. Because of the rising demand for sugar, the focus of trade in Europe shifted from the Mediterranean nations to nations along the North Atlantic that had colonized the New World. Thus, in the 1600s and 1700s, Holland, France, and England became the major powers in European commerce. ■

◄ *John White, the English governor of an American colony, painted watercolors depicting American Indian life. This man is wearing ceremonial body paint.*

■ *What was the result of France's search for the Northwest Passage?*

R E V I E W

1. **FOCUS** What role did Christopher Columbus's voyages play in the colonization of North America?

2. **CONNECT** How were the goals of Prince Henry and Columbus similar? How were their goals different?

3. **CRITICAL THINKING** Review the maps on pages 374 and 378. Which of the five explorers, in your opinion, was most important? Why?

4. **ECONOMICS** How did Europe's exploration and colonization of North America affect Mediterranean trade?

5. **CRITICAL THINKING** Do you think the harsh treatment of native peoples was a necessary result of European exploration? Explain why or why not.

6. **ACTIVITY** Trace the map of North America in the Atlas on page 526. With different-colored markers, trace the routes European explorers followed between 1497 and 1550 in their search for the Northwest Passage. Then try to "discover" the actual Passage, which was not conquered until 1906.

The Age of Exploration

Reading a Wind and Current Map

Here's Why

Wind and ocean currents affect many things from the weather and climate to ocean transportation. Maps like the one shown here describe the flow of these currents around the world. Of course, Vasco da Gama did not have such a map when he sailed to India in 1498. Knowing how to read this map, however, can help you understand some of the conditions da Gama faced on his voyage.

Here's How

The map on this page shows the major ocean currents of the world and the prevailing winds around the world in July. Locate Portugal on the map. Then follow the line that shows da Gama's route to India.

Now look at the arrows on the map that show wind currents. These arrows represent prevailing winds, or winds that usually blow from the same direction. Wind currents in the Northern Hemisphere tend to move in a clockwise direction. In the Southern Hemisphere, winds tend to move counterclockwise.

Focus your attention on the Atlantic Ocean. You will see that winds moving clockwise in the Northern Atlantic would have helped move da Gama's ships south to a point about midway down the

coast of Africa. Here, the wind moves in a counterclockwise direction. These winds would have slowed the progress of the ships.

To see how the winds affected the rest of the voyage, look at the arrows showing wind direction in the Indian Ocean. The winds blow from Africa's west coast toward the east. This means that the wind was blowing with the ships as they crossed the Indian Ocean.

Besides the wind, da Gama depended on ocean currents to move his ships along. Like the wind, water tends to circulate clockwise in the Northern Hemisphere and counterclockwise in the Southern Hemisphere.

Look back to the Atlantic Ocean near Portugal. As you can see, da Gama's ships would have started off their voyage by being carried down the coast of Africa, first by the Canary Current

Prevailing Winds and Ocean Currents

and then by the Guinea Current.

About halfway down the coast of Africa, however, da Gama would have encountered the Benguela Current. This current runs in the opposite direction of the route of da Gama's ships. What current affected the ships after they went around the tip of Africa?

For the final leg of the voyage, da Gama's ships crossed the northern Indian Ocean. The currents in this portion of the Indian Ocean change direction in response to strong seasonal winds called monsoons. From April to October, monsoons blow from the southwest, creating a current that flows in a clockwise direction. From November to March, monsoons create a current that runs in a counterclockwise direction. Since da Gama completed this last leg of the voyage in May, we can

assume that he was helped by both the wind and ocean currents in the northern Indian Ocean.

Try It
Look back at the map on page 378 that shows the routes taken by Christopher Columbus from Portugal to the Americas. Use that map with the one below to describe how wind and ocean currents affected one of the voyages.

Apply It
Suppose you wanted to sail from a port about halfway down the western coast of North America to the Philippines, and then back. Assume that you are making the voyage during the summer. What route would you take in order to use wind and ocean currents to speed your voyage? Suppose you wanted to sail from the tip of Florida to the coast of West Africa and back. What route would you take?

The Age of Exploration

The Audience

C. Walter Hodges

As you have learned in this chapter, the dream of wealth and the lure of riches drove Columbus and other explorers like him. They undertook journeys of unknown dangers and uncertain outcomes to pursue that dream. But they needed financial support. As you read this story, play the role of the audience— the King or Queen. Would you support Columbus? Why or why not?

In Lesson 3 you learned about Columbus's appeal to Ferdinand and Isabella. Here is an imaginative recreation of his second appearance before that King and Queen.

The town was taken, the Moors were driven out, the wars were at an end. Now, now at last there must be time to hear Columbus. Now at last the victorious Sovereigns would give him ships to sail in quest of his new horizon.

He went to his friend Alonzo de Quintanilla and implored him to obtain audience for him soon. The Accountant-General promised to do so, and on the following day Columbus was summoned into the presence of Their Majesties.

Father Juan Perez, Luiz de Santangel and I went with him to the audience. The antechamber was full of people, little groups talking in low voices, Court officials, men and women with petitions to present. Presently an usher called the name of Columbus, and he went in.

Ferdinand and Isabella were seated on a low dais, surrounded by the councillors and members of the Royal Household. Prominent among them was Fernando de Talavera, recently made Archbishop of Granada, the King's most trusted adviser. Near the dais, a little to one side, was a table at which were seated the Court notaries. There was a subdued light in the room, a feeling of many people gathered in a warm silence. Their dresses seemed to melt into the rich colors of the surrounding tapestries. A blade of sunlight dazzled upon the helmet of a soldier, and its reflection nodded in an opposite corner of the room.

From the table a little man rose halfway to his feet and read from a paper:

"Señor Christopher Columbus of Genoa, making application to Your Majesties for ships to seek out certain lands which he claims to stand yet undiscovered beyond the seas."

Having gabbled his formality he sat down again. The Queen smiled gently at Columbus and inclined her head towards him.

Then the King spoke:

"Señor Columbus is well known to us, I think; but if I remember rightly his proposals were examined by a Special Commission some years ago. Was it not so?"

"At Salamanca, sire."

"And the Commissioners rejected them," continued the King, "on the grounds that you could not bring forward sufficient evidence in support of your theory. Again, was it not so? And was not the Archbishop of Granada here in charge of that Commission?"

Columbus looked across at Talavera, and said nothing. The King continued:

"But since you bring your case again before us, señor, we must presume that you have fresh evidence in support of it. Or that you have fault to find with the method by which it was previously examined."

"Sire, it is not with the method but with the verdict that I have fault to find," said Columbus. "I believe that the members of the commission were all men of great renown for learning and scientific knowledge. But the greater their learning the greater was their error. They were wrong in their conclusions, and I dispute their verdict."

"And what says the Archbishop to that?" asked the King. Talavera shrugged.

"What can I say, sire, more than Señor Columbus has said? The men whom I assembled numbered among them some of our greatest scholars. Upon my word the hearing was fair and unprejudiced. Señor Columbus has his project much at heart, and it is natural that he should disagree with our findings upon it. Indeed I am sorry. But if he can bring forth further evidence . . ." He was silent. The King looked questioningly at Columbus. "Can you do that, señor?"

Columbus seemed for a second to be tongue-tied. Then he said, rather slowly:

"I can bring forward a few more traveler's tales, more strange reports; what else had I to do in all these years but to seek and collect them wherever they were to be found? I have no more real proofs than you have heard already. Nor will any man have, until he goes to find them where they exist beyond the horizons of the Ocean itself. Only give me my ships sire, and I will bring you proof enough."

There was whispering among the company, and someone laughed softly. But the King was obviously impatient. Drumming with his fingers on the arm of his chair, he said:

"We do not doubt your personal sincerity, señor. But you have heard the Archbishop. Without fresh evidence we cannot think it would be justifiable to re-open the inquiry."

Suddenly the Queen spoke.

"My Lord," she said, "perhaps Señor Columbus has not been quite fair to himself. He says he has no further proofs to bring. But since his proposals were first rejected by us he has faced much adversity without foregoing his convictions. Also he has made many friends who believe in him, men whose opinions should carry some weight. If constancy of itself is proof of nothing, at least it has the merit to be heard, even a second time."

The King looked at her and smiled slightly.

"I stand rebuked, madam," he said. "Certainly, if Señor Columbus wishes to speak, he shall be heard."

Again Columbus bowed; and he began to speak, at first slowly, then with increasing force.

"It is true what I have said. The evidence you have previously examined is still the only evidence I have to offer. But, sire, upon that very evidence I am willing to venture my life. I have shown you maps, drawn up not only by me, but by some of the greatest authorities ever known to have studied the mysteries of the Western Ocean; and I have offered to follow those maps till I have found a way for you across that ocean to the very shores of the Indies. I repeat, to do so is to venture my life; and not only my life, but the reputation I have spent so much of it to build. I can offer no other guarantee. But if Your Majesties will give me three ships, and accept the hazard, then it must be, if God so wills it, that according to all the known laws of science we shall find those shores that I have promised you, and Spain will become as wealthy as she is now victorious."

The King interrupted: "Spain is victorious, but she is also poor. The wars against the Infidel have drained the treasury dry. You say you demand three ships only. But what you really ask is for ships, men, provisions, cannon, ammunition, a thousand things, for a voyage lasting perhaps a year, perhaps even longer. It may be, as you yourself suggest, that I shall never see those ships again. Where is the money to come from?"

"From the Indies, sire!" cried Columbus, "where there is wealth enough in one province to beggar the combined treasuries of all Europe! This is testified by Marco Polo and Sir John Mandeville, and many other travellers from the East. They have seen kingdoms where swineherds fasten their rags with belts of gold and where the little street boys play in the mud with pearls. They have seen with their own eyes the princes of India riding in procession upon elephants whose thick hides are inset with jewels patterned like a carpet, whose tusks are carved to the fineness of lace, and whose ears are hung with bells of silver and gold which chime with every step in confused and wonderful harmonies! They say these beasts would seem like gods of splendor were it not for the splendor of the kings who ride them, under the tinkling and perfumed canopies that shade them from the sun. Is there another nation in Europe that would not gamble three ships for all that treasure? I tell you, for the people who first discover the Western way to the Indies, a thousand ships will not suffice to carry home the riches they will find, not even though their holds are crammed so full they spill upon the decks! All this I offer to Spain. But there is little time for Spain to choose. My plan is no secret. It is talked of everywhere, and is plainly written down for anyone to study. Am I the only man to consider the undertaking? Perhaps even now in Portugal, or France, or England, they are preparing ships for just such a voyage as mine. Perhaps in a few years the Atlantic will be an open road. Perhaps some other man, not I, will sail the ship that opens it. If this should happen it will be God's punishment for my pride, for I have lived all these years dreaming of the pride I should have when I, the first, shall strike the Spanish flag into the soil of the Indies.

"I have only one thing to add. Upon the floor here between us is a carpet. It is an Indian carpet such as has great value for us in Europe. The merchants who trade in such things grow richer every year. And from whom are they obtained? Not from the Indians. They are bought from the Muslims of Aleppo and

Alexandria, who alone control the channels of trade with the Far East. Thus, though you have driven the Infidel out of Spain, you must still buy in his bazaars and pay the price he asks. And as your ships return home from the Muslims of Aleppo they may be plundered and sunk by the Muslim pirates of Barbary, and their crews sold into slavery. Will you pay that price, and still not grant three ships for a venture such as mine?"

It was plain, long before he finished speaking, that Columbus held the imagination of the Court. Even those who could not believe him to be more than a half-crazy fanatic were moved by the forcefulness of his address. After his concluding words the assembly became aware of its own hesitancy, kept awkwardly silent and waited for the King to establish them again in their former opinions. But the King himself was hesitant. He cleared his throat and looked round at the Archbishop of Granada, and somehow it began to be clear, even from this, that Columbus had made his mark. In a moment the silence was relieved by the mutterings of conversation, and when at last the King spoke it was to make certain the good opinion in which the petitioner now found himself. The King inquired if Columbus had with him the papers and other material relating to the expedition, particularly of the estimated cost. Columbus produced two closely written scrolls, saying that the greater bulk of the material was at his lodging.

"Then señor," said the King, "if you will deliver it this evening to my secretary, I will see that the Council meets to discuss the matter within the next day or two, and I promise that it shall have every consideration."

More than this Columbus could not have desired. His joy was evident to everyone, and we, his friends, standing in the doorway of the room felt that at last his success was assured.

Our hopes were high. But in a few minutes they were to be brought down even lower than before! Where success had seemed certain, failure became inevitable out of the mouth, as it were, of Columbus himself. For, as we were about to leave the audience, the Archbishop spoke suddenly:

"Señor Columbus has stated his requirements for the expedition," he said, "but nothing for himself. Before the matter goes to Council we should know what reward he proposes to ask for his services. Supposing," he added, "that they are fruitful."

To this the King immediately assented, and the Court again waited for Columbus to speak. After a moment's hesitation he made the following demands:

"Firstly, my lords, I request that I receive a knighthood and the title of First Admiral. Secondly, if the expedition is successful, that I should be accorded the hereditary vice-regency of all the lands I may discover. And thirdly, that I receive a tenth part of all the revenues obtained from them."

The entire audience was aghast. No one had expected such extravagant demands. When he finished speaking Columbus found himself the center of a silence so deep that it seemed as though a blanket of deafness had enclosed the room. Not even the voice of anger could find itself. At last the King spoke, quietly, his words magnified by the hush.

"Can you not moderate those terms, señor?"

Columbus spread his hands. "They are reasonable, my lord," he said.

"Reasonable indeed!" a thick red-faced man spluttered out suddenly, unable to hold his wrath. "They are outrageous, monstrous, an insult! Has not this crazy adventurer the wits enough to know his place before the nobility of Spain? What is he but a weaver's son from the gutters of Genoa, and he demands to be made an Admiral and a knight! A peddler of inaccurate maps! He, an Admiral! And since when did tradesmen receive knighthoods? He should be whipped for his impertinence!"

"Sire," cried Columbus, addressing the King. "From whom should Spain most proudly accept her Empire: from the hands of a tradesman, or from her own Admiral, duly appointed by the State?"

The King shrugged his shoulders and said:

"Very well, señor. The Council shall consider the matter."

The audience was at an end. Columbus bowed and walked quickly from the room. We, his friends, went with him into the bright evening street through the crowd of idle soldiers at the gate. Here we parted company, no one saying a word.

Further Reading

Argosies of Empire. Ralph Bailey. Here are stories of sailors who explored the world's sea routes before Columbus.

Columbus Sails. C. Walter Hodges. The rest of Columbus's story by the writer of "The Audience." A sailor and a monk describe his story.

He Went with Vasco da Gama. Louise Andrews Kent. This is a story of how da Gama sailed around the Cape of Good Hope to reach the Indies. It also tells the story of Portuguese history.

I Challenge the Dark Sea. Olive W. Burt. Based on the life of Henry the Navigator, this story describes how Henry's support of science above superstition paved the way for many of the discoveries of his time.

Son of Columbus. Hans Baumann. Columbus's youngest son sails with his father and tells the story of his fourth and final voyage to the New World.

Chapter Review

Reviewing Key Terms

balance of trade (p. 370)
bullion (p. 370)
capital (p. 375)
caravel (p. 373)
circumnavigation (p. 380)
colony (p. 375)
monopoly (p. 368)

A. Each of the sentences below has words in italics that describe a key term. Read each sentence, and replace the words in italics with the correct key term from the list above.

1. Spain, Portugal, England, and France founded *settlements of their own citizens in foreign lands they explored.*
2. Portugal paid its foreign debts in *bars or blocks of gold.*
3. Spanish explorers in South America searched for gold so that Venice's *complete control of business activity* might be destroyed.
4. Ferdinand Magellan of Spain made the first *voyage around the earth.*
5. Prince Henry's ship designers created a *swift and easily maneuverable ship that could sail on the open sea.*
6. Portugal had to pay other countries to maintain the *difference between the total value of exports and the total value of imports.*
7. The rulers of Spain contributed the *money and material* to finance Columbus's voyage.

B. Write a sentence or two using each pair of words below. The sentences should show how the words are related.

1. bullion, monopoly
2. caravel, circumnavigation
3. capital, colony

Exploring Concepts

A. Copy the following chart on the age of exploration on your paper. List one or more reasons for each historical fact.

Historical Fact	Reason
1. Knowledge about the world grew (1200–1500).	Maps, travelers' tales
2. Portuguese exploration became easier.	
3. Spanish mistreated natives of Central and South America.	
4. Christianity spread.	
5. Portuguese sugar plantations were profitable.	

B. Tell why each statement below is false using facts and details from the chapter.

1. From 1200 to 1500, geographers had no idea of the size and shape of the world.
2. Vasco da Gama reached Mexico in May 1498.
3. Ptolemy's map was of little use to European mapmakers.
4. Few Europeans wanted to buy goods from the East during the 1200s and 1300s.
5. Venice and Genoa were isolated from profitable trade with the Middle East.
6. Jesuit missionaries in the 1600s were not interested in understanding the Chinese people whom they wanted to convert.
7. Prince Henry of Portugal had little interest in exploring other lands.
8. Spain had no colonies in the Americas.
9. Only Spain explored North and South America.

Reviewing Skills

1. Look at the wind and ocean current map on pages 382 and 383. In what direction do the prevailing winds blow in the Pacific Ocean off the eastern coast of South America? Would you expect this for wind currents in this area of the world? Why?
2. Look again at the map. Would it be difficult to sail from Australia to the southern tip of South America? Describe the winds and currents and their directions on such a voyage.
3. Suppose you are a partner in an English trading company in the early 1500s. Your company has just voted to finance an expedition to find the Northwest Passage. What are the advantages and disadvantages of such a decision? How did you vote?
4. If you wanted to find out how terrain helped people decide how to use land, what two types of maps would you compare?

Using Critical Thinking

1. As in Columbus's time, some people today argue that the exploration of the solar system and the universe is a waste of time and money. If you agree with these people, explain your reasons. If you do not agree, write down some arguments that could be used to convince them that they are mistaken about space exploration.
2. An old saying states that the people of one generation build on the accomplishments of the generations who lived before them. Explain how this saying was true of the European explorers between 1200 and 1500. Then discuss how the saying applies to the generations living today.
3. Prince Henry and Christopher Columbus both reached important goals in their lives. Examine and compare the lives of Prince Henry and Christopher Columbus. Think of what character trait or traits may have helped them succeed. Now think about goals you want to reach sometime in your future. How could you use one of the traits that helped them succeed to achieve your goal? Explain your answer.
4. Suppose you could travel back in time and live in Europe during the age of exploration described in this chapter. Would you like to live during that era? If so, what things would you like to do? If not, why not?

Preparing for Citizenship

1. **ARTS ACTIVITY** Choose an event from each lesson of this chapter that interests you. Draw or paint a picture to illustrate each event. You may want to select one of these: Vasco da Gama's voyage to India; Bartolomé de Las Casas defending the rights of native people to the King of Spain; Prince Henry's shipbuilders inspecting their first caravel; sailors on a ship in the "Green Sea of Darkness" near Cape Bojador; enslaved Africans working on a sugar plantation on Madeira; Cabot, Verrazano, or Cartier searching for the Northwest Passage.
2. **COLLABORATIVE ACTIVITY** Meet with your class to plan a book of mini-biographies of people you learned about in this chapter. Have each biography explain how the person was involved with European exploration. First, decide on a title for the book. Then, choose groups to do the following jobs: research and write an introduction and the biographies; illustrate the biographies and design a cover; photocopy the biographies and bind them together in a book; distribute copies of the finished book to other classes in your school. Have all the groups work together to produce your book.

Unit 7

Civilizations of the Americas

Richly colored, this South American weaving is made of tropical bird feathers. What was it for? Archaeologists think it is an Inca cape of the A.D. 1400s, perhaps worn by priests. Such objects, left by small groups or great civilizations, tell of life in the Americas before 1500.

1800 B.C.

Detail of a feathered poncho with cotton base, Inca culture, north or central coast of South America, 15th century. The Textile Museum, Washington, D.C., 91.7.

A.D. 1572

Chapter 15

Early American Civilizations

A prehistoric bone, a spear, a carved jade figure—all are clues in an age-old mystery: What were the earliest Americans like, those who settled North and South America between about 40,000 B.C. and A.D. 1300? Ancient tools and bones found by archaeologists help trace the paths of these first settlers. Carvings and sculptures, ornaments and massive temples show how later groups farmed, hunted, fought, and worshiped. All of these objects help unravel the mysteries of prehistoric America.

During this period, hunters migrated as far as southernmost South America. In Texas's Bonfire Cave archaeologists have found weapons and bones from about 13,000 to 10,000 B.C.

1200–400 B.C. The Olmec people build a great civilization in Mexico. Religion is important to the Olmec, who carve jade religious figures like the one shown here.

| 2000 | 1500 | 1000 | 500 |

1800 B.C.

563 B.C. Religious leader Siddhartha Gautama, later called the Buddha, is born in India.

During this period, the Maya built great pyramid-temples, like this one at Chichen Itza in Mexico.

Tiwanakans abandon their great city between A.D. 1100 and 1300. They leave behind traces, such as gold ornaments of condors and other religious figures.

A.D. 250–900 Mayan culture reaches its height in Mexico and Central America. Brilliant Mayan wool and cotton are treasured trade goods. The sculpture (above) shows a Mayan noblewoman weaving.

| B.C. | A.D. | | 500 | | 1000 | | 1500 |

A.D. 312 Roman Emperor Constantine becomes a Christian. Before the century ends, Christianity is the empire's official religion.

A.D. 1300

L E S S O N   1

Origins

THINKING
F O C U S

Describe the development of early communities in the Americas.

Key Terms

- hunter-gatherer
- extinct
- sedentary

➤ *Many mammoths stood as tall as 14 feet at the shoulder. Their tusks grew to more than 13 feet in length.*

His heart was beating fast. Was it excitement or fear? Today, as a young man, he would finally join the hunt.

The men had sighted a herd of mammoths. Now they would try to drive the mammoths toward a steep ravine. Armed with flint-tipped wooden spears, they hoped to force some of the huge beasts off the cliff.

The boy gasped when he saw the mammoths. They were at least three times his height. Giant, curved tusks jutted from their jaws.

He tightened his grip on his spear. With a signal from his father, he rushed with the others toward the animals, startling them into a full run.

The mammoths pounded toward the cliff, but most of them veered to avoid the edge. One turned too late. When the hunters found their reward at the bottom of the cliff, the boy's eyes gleamed with pride. He had left the camp a boy; he would return a hunter.

Migrants from Asia

Archaeologists believe the first people to come to the Americas were hunters such as those described above. These hunters traveled across the Bering land bridge, which connected Siberia and Alaska during several Ice Ages. Native American creation tales teach that humans were created in North America.

Today, the Bering land bridge is under water. But this was not the case between about 33,000 and 10,000 B.C. During those years, glaciers one to two miles thick covered much of the northern hemisphere. So much water froze into ice that the ocean level dropped, exposing the 50 miles of land between Asia and North America.

Animals wandered across the land bridge to graze on the plants growing on each continent. From time to time, hunters from east Asia followed the animals across to North America. Over thousands of years, hunters and animals traveled south to the warmer forests and grasslands of North and Central America. Follow their migration routes on the map on page 398. By 10,500 B.C., people were living at Monte Verde in South America.

Archaeologists traced the path these early migrants took by studying ancient bones and artifacts, such as tools, pottery, and ornaments. They have discovered tools dating from 32,000 to 17,000 B.C. that are very similar to ancient stone tools found in Asia. In 1998, archaeologists found evidence that humans may have also migrated to the Americas by boat. ■

▲ *Islands between Siberia and Alaska are the parts of the Bering land bridge that are still above water.*

■ *Describe a migration of Asians to the Americas.*

Early Hunter-Gatherers

The hunters who migrated to North America made their own weapons and tools. They pounded pieces of stone into sharp points and attached them to long wooden spears or bones. As the hunters learned more about working with stone, they developed improved tools, like those shown below. Some of these tools have sharp edges, which means other stones were used as chisels to chip off one or both edges of the stone. Sharp points such as these were an improvement over the points used earlier in Asia. These improved points have been found at hunting sites, along with the bones of hundreds of animals apparently killed in one hunt.

These people moved from place to place following big-game animals. They hunted huge tusked mammoths like the one shown on page 396, mastodons, ground sloths as big as modern-day elephants, sabre-tooth cats, and bison. Usually they hunted these animals in groups of 20 to 50 people, since it took several spear points to kill a big-game animal.

The hunters also stalked smaller animals, such as bears, deer, foxes, and turkeys. And they gathered nuts, wild berries, and other foods from plants. Because these people obtained their food by hunting wild animals and gathering fruits of wild plants, scholars call them **hunter-gatherers.**

▼ *Early hunter-gatherers used points like these as tools and weapons. Each one could fit easily in your hand.*

Early American Civilizations

By dating bones of big-game animals, archaeologists have established that the big game had died out by 8000 B.C. No one is certain why they disappeared, or became **extinct.** Some experts think that as the last Ice Age ended at about 8000 B.C., the climate grew warmer and drier. The grass fields where animals grazed turned brown and dried into dusty deserts. The lakes where hunter-gatherers fished, shrank or dried up. And as food and water supplies dwindled, so did the great herds. Others think the hunters killed off too many of the big animals when they developed better hunting methods. ■

■ *What did early hunter-gatherers eat, and how did they get their food?*

▼ *While the first Americans were migrating into South America, sheets of ice covered most of what is now Canada. How did this affect the migration routes of these people?*

Early Farmers

As the big game died out in the Americas, the hunter-gatherers adapted to their changing environment. They hunted smaller animals and gathered food within a smaller area than they had before. As they began to spend time in one place, they adopted a more **sedentary,** or settled, lifestyle.

To support this new lifestyle, the hunter-gatherers developed new tools. Those who lived near water wove nets and fashioned harpoons to catch fish. To store the food they gathered, they wove baskets from plant fibers. Using rocks, the hunter-gatherers crushed nuts and seeds into coarse meal to make flat cakes something like tortillas (*tawr TEE yuhs*).

As people searched for food closer to where they lived, they noticed that many of their food plants grew in the same places year after year. They probably saw plants sprout from discarded seeds. Eventually, they found they could grow their own plants using seeds from wild plants.

They probably also noticed that their plants grew best in open, sunny areas, so they began to create clearings with their stone axes. To plant their seeds, these first farmers used long, sturdy digging sticks. They harvested plants by hand. Gradually, as would happen all over the world, the hunter-gatherers became food producers. In the chart on page 399, you can see how their lives changed as

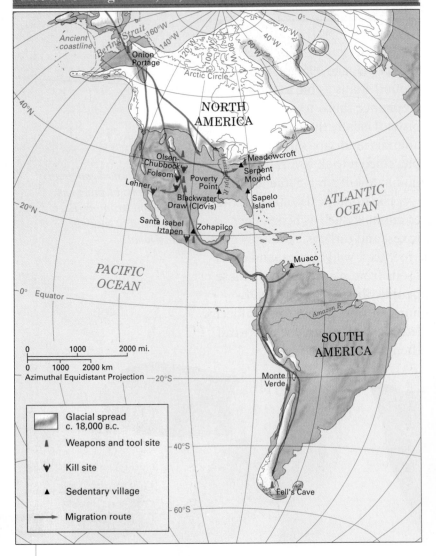

Routes of Migration, 18,000–500 B.C.

Ancient coastline
Bering Strait
Onion Portage
Arctic Circle
NORTH AMERICA
Olsen-Chubbock
Folsom
Lehner
Poverty Point
Blackwater Draw (Clovis)
Meadowcroft
Serpent Mound
Sapelo Island
ATLANTIC OCEAN
Santa Isabel Iztapan
Zohapilco
Muaco
PACIFIC OCEAN
Equator
Amazon R.
SOUTH AMERICA
Monte Verde
Fell's Cave

0   1000   2000 mi.
0   1000   2000 km
Azimuthal Equidistant Projection

Glacial spread c. 18,000 B.C.
▲ Weapons and tool site
▼ Kill site
▲ Sedentary village
→ Migration route

Life in the Americas

	Hunter-Gatherers, c. 12,000–8500 B.C.	Sedentary Villagers, c. 8500–500 B.C.
Food	Some large game, but primarily smaller animals, such as moose and bear; fish; wild plants; and limited cultivated plants	Cultivated crops, including maize (corn), beans, squash, and chili peppers; domesticated animals, such as sheep, goats, and llamas; and some small wild game
Homes	Portable and easy to assemble (probably made of animal hides and wood)	Sturdy, built to endure over time (hardwood frames and foundations)
Tools	Projectile points, axes, scrapers (made of stone), wooden mortars, grinding stones, and small implements (made of shell and bone)	Cultivating tools, such as digging sticks and simple hoes; cooking pottery; weaving looms; and polished stone tools

◄ *What clues can you find on this chart to indicate that the people in the Americas lived a more settled life after about 8500 B.C.?*

Pinto beans

Acorn squash

Kidney beans

Raspberries

Walnuts

Pecans

Chili peppers

Sunflower seeds

Banana squash

they began to rely more heavily on farming.

Farmers in regions now known as Mexico, Peru, and Bolivia began growing maize (corn), beans, and squash around 8500 B.C. These new foods were especially important because people could eat them fresh, or they could dry them and store them for later use.

People also domesticated wild animals that roamed near their settlements. In early Bolivia and Peru, for instance, people raised llamas and alpacas for food and wool. They also used such animals to transport heavy loads.

Freed from the demands of constant hunting, people had time for other activities. They used their free time to build durable dwellings and to perfect their crafts and toolmaking. They also built special structures for religious ceremonies. Religion became a community-wide activity, and religious events became social events as well.

As the settlers worked in their fields, good farmland became important, and people created permanent homes in fertile areas where they settled. Neighboring farmers began sharing duties and dividing up tasks. Some settlers developed specialties and traded tasks or goods with their neighbors. Thus, their simple settlements grew into established villages. As the villages prospered, their populations increased. These early communities became the basis for the first civilizations in the Americas. ■

■ *How did hunter-gatherers become food producers?*

R E V I E W

1. **FOCUS** Describe the development of early communities in the Americas.
2. **CONNECT** In what ways did the arrival of the early migrants in America differ from the arrival of the European explorers?
3. **GEOGRAPHY** What do you think caused big-game animals and hunters to migrate as far as South America?
4. **ECONOMICS** What did having a surplus of food enable

the early hunter-gatherers to do?
5. **CRITICAL THINKING** How did the lifestyle of hunter-gatherers differ from that of early farmers?
6. **ACTIVITY** Look at the chart, Life in the Americas, on this page. On a separate sheet of paper, create a third column with a heading that describes your lifestyle, for example, Urban Dweller, and the year. Then list your food, home, and tools under this new heading.

399

Early American Civilizations

L E S S O N   2

The Olmec

THINKING
F O C U S

What evidence suggests that the Olmec civilization was complex?

Key Terms

- elite
- hieroglyph

▼ *Huge stone heads such as this were first unearthed in 1862. They weigh 18 to 24 tons and stand 6 to 10 feet tall.*

"*A*bout a league and a half's distance [four and a half miles] from a sugarcane hacienda (hah see EHN duh), on the western slopes of the Sierra de San Martin, a worker on this hacienda who was clearing jungle noticed on the surface of the ground what he took to be the bottom of a huge pot lying upside down. He told the owner of the hacienda of this discovery, and the latter ordered this object to be unearthed. . . . As a work of art, it is, without exaggeration, a magnificent sculpture. . . ."

This notice appeared in 1869 in a bulletin of the Mexican Geographical Society. The news it told introduced the modern world to a mysterious ancient world, one of the first American civilizations, the Olmec of Mexico.

The object was a colossal head, carved from stone. It was taller than a person and weighed several tons. Archaeologists wondered about the person with the helmet and stern face. Was he a king, a soldier, a priest, or some combination of the three? More mystifying, how had the Olmec obtained the massive stone that was used in the sculpture?

Archaeologists knew there were no large boulders in the area where the Olmec had settled. The closest stones were about 50 miles away in the Tuxtla (*TOOST luh*) Mountains. The Olmec must have brought the stones from the mountains. But how had they managed to move these huge stones?

After studying the geography of the area, archaeologists found an answer to their question. The Olmec probably rolled the huge slabs of rock on logs or dragged them 25 miles on wooden sleds down the mountainsides to a tributary of the Coatzacoalcos (*koh aht suh koh AHL kuhs*) River. Then they must have floated their cargo on rafts to the Gulf of Mexico and along the coast to the Tonala River. There they battled their way upriver 12 miles to their site at La Venta.

A Fertile Environment

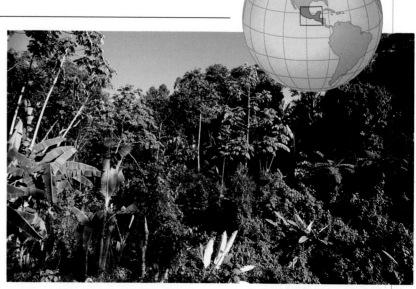

Archaeologists now think that the Olmec civilization developed around 1200 B.C. It occupied the region from the Gulf of Mexico on the north to the Tuxtla Mountains in the south. The two major centers of the Olmec, La Venta and San Lorenzo, were built on rivers. La Venta, in fact, was located on an island in the Tonala River.

The Olmec home was a challenging land of rivers and jungle. Heavy rains caused the rivers to flood each year. And because of the tropical climate, much of the land was swampy and covered with dense jungle. Whenever farmers cleared the land, the jungle sprang back almost overnight.

But the Olmec adapted to the land. The floods deposited fertile soil ideal for raising their squash, gourds, beans, avocados, peppers, and maize. And the rivers provided game such as crocodiles, fish, shellfish, and aquatic birds.

The Olmec also learned to farm the jungle. They cut down and burned one section of thick

jungle vegetation and planted there for several years. Then they moved on and cleared the next section of jungle for farming.

The Olmec even developed a calendar of their growing seasons. They used the calendar to track the passing of the seasons, so they knew when to sow and harvest each crop. In addition to the food they raised or caught in the rivers, the Olmec ate deer, wild pigs, pheasants, and wild monkeys from the jungle.

Thus, the Olmec became efficient producers of their own food. Soon they even had surpluses, or extra supplies, of food. In turn, their population grew rapidly. And as their population increased, the Olmec developed the class system, rituals, and networks of trade that are features of a complex society. ■

▲ *The region the Olmec occupied is shown on the locator map above. The lush jungle vegetation seems to swallow up everything. In fact, the tangled vines that grew over Olmec ruins hid them for centuries.*

◄ *This aerial view of southeastern Mexico shows the jungle rainforest that lies in the lowlands near the Gulf of Mexico.*

■ *What environmental factors helped the Olmec develop a complex society?*

Elite and Commoners

Archaeologists believe that at its height, the Olmec population numbered tens of thousands of people and covered from 6,000 to 7,000 square miles. That is slightly less than the area of New Jersey. These people were probably divided into at least two classes of society—the upper, or **elite,** class and a lower class, the commoners.

Early American Civilizations

The colossal heads were monuments to honor the Olmec rulers. The great stone faces of Mount Rushmore in South Dakota are 10 times larger than the Olmec heads. They pay tribute to four U.S. presidents.

■ *What do the artifacts found at Olmec burial sites reveal about Olmec society?*

■ *What role did priest-kings play in Olmec society?*

▼ *These jade figurines were found buried in this arrangement in 1955 at La Venta.*

This idea is based on inferences about the carving and moving of the giant Olmec heads.

In general, when archaeologists find evidence such as the giant Olmec heads, they conclude that hundreds of workers must have labored to carve and move these monuments. These laborers were probably directed by a smaller group of supervisors. They, in turn, followed the dictates of a single ruler or group of rulers. Such a division of labor suggests that the Olmec divided their society into distinct classes of people.

Archaeologists believe that many of the massive heads found at sites in La Venta are probably heroic portraits of Olmec leaders. Each helmet is marked with unique symbols that probably represent the different ruling families.

Olmec burial sites provide further clues about the different Olmec classes. Some burial sites consist of simple, crudely prepared graves that contain few or no ornaments. These are most likely the graves of commoners. At other sites, elaborate stone tombs contain intricately carved figures and finely crafted ornaments made from jade, amethyst, and other semiprecious stones. Some even contain mirrors that were made from iron ore. These tombs probably belonged to members of the elite class. ■

Power and Religion

Olmec rulers were priest-kings who came from the ranks of the elite. They were not only brave warriors and civil leaders, they were also religious leaders. The Olmec believed that the priest-kings were direct descendants of their gods. They also believed the priest-kings had the power to ensure that the gods would protect them from their enemies. And they looked to the priest-kings to influence the gods to send good weather for their crops.

The Olmec had as many as 15 gods, but the jaguar-man was probably the most important god. It represented the mystery of life and death. The Olmec made small jade sculptures of jaguars and other images of gods to use in their religious rituals.

They performed these rituals in an attempt to please their gods. Many ceremonies took place at stone altars, which were adorned with intricate carvings. The priest-kings sacrificed animals, and even human beings, as offerings to their gods. They often sacrificed soldiers captured in battle to demonstrate their own power as warriors. Archaeologists have discovered knives, axes, and other sharp tools that may have been used in these sacrifices. ■

Trade and Competition

For the Olmec, jade was extremely valuable. They obtained jade and other raw materials for their crafts by trading with people in nearby regions. Olmec-style pottery, statues, and cave paintings have been found in Mexico, Guatemala, and El Salvador. This suggests that the Olmec traveled to these places to find and trade for resources. Archaeologists have found both Olmec artifacts and **hieroglyphs,** written signs that represent concepts and objects, as far as 500 miles from the Olmec area.

Archaeologists have also found scenes of war carved on stone monuments. This suggests that the Olmec sometimes fought neighboring tribes—and each other—for materials and control of trade routes.

This competition for resources may have caused the destruction of Olmec civilization. In fact, evidence of vandalism has led archaeologists to conclude that the Olmec center of San Lorenzo was purposely destroyed around 900 B.C.

After San Lorenzo, La Venta seems to have become the center of Olmec art and religion. But mutilated and buried stone heads found at La Venta suggest that it, too, was destroyed by enemies around 400 B.C. After eight centuries of growth, the Olmec civilization, the first civilization of the Americas, was in decline.

Regional Powers

As traders and keepers of religious centers, the Olmecs transferred many elements of their culture to the growing civilizations around them.

Beginning around 200 B.C., a strong empire and a great city grew in the Valley of Mexico called Teotihuacan *(tay oh tee wah KAHN)*. Lasting until around A.D. 650, Teotihuacan attracted people from the countryside to city life, with broad streets, markets, plazas, temples, palaces, and apartments. The city also had waterways, reservoirs, sewers, and slums. Irrigated fields surrounded the city, but in its center stood two gigantic, pyramid-shaped temples, now called the Temples of the Sun and Moon.

After Teotihuacan's fall, people from northern colonies moved back into the central region, bringing with them a group called the Toltec. The Toltec later came to rule lands north and west of the Valley of Mexico. They passed on legend and lore to the Aztec. ■

▲ *Jade figures like this axehead were more valuable than gold to the Olmec. Jade figures have been found as far as 500 miles from the Olmec's territory. The jade had been used in trade.*

■ *How did Olmec competition for goods and trade routes affect their civilization?*

| R E V I E W |

1. **FOCUS** What evidence suggests that the Olmec civilization was complex?
2. **CONNECT** In what ways were Olmec farming techniques better than those of the early farmers?
3. **SOCIAL SYSTEMS** How did archaeologists determine that the Olmec probably had at least two social classes?
4. **SOCIAL SYSTEMS** In what ways were the priest-kings important to Olmec society?

5. **CRITICAL THINKING** How might the course of Olmec civilization have differed if it had never developed a trade network?
6. **WRITING ACTIVITY** Imagine that you and your family are in the Americas in 1200 B.C. searching for a new place to settle. Write a paragraph describing the type of area that you are looking for, including the sources of food and the climate. Also describe what your lifestyle would be like there.

The Maya

THINKING

In what ways were the Maya an advanced civilization?

Key Terms

- stele
- codex

➤ *The seven-inch-tall ceramic ballplayer at top right is part of the religious art of the Maya. Real players on the losing side sometimes became sacrifices to the gods. The large Mayan temple, on the right, was built between A.D. 600 and 800. Artist Frederick Catherwood, who accompanied explorer Stephens, painted this view of the Mayan temple.*

*I*t is impossible to describe the interest with which I explored these ruins. The ground was entirely new. . . . We could not see ten yards before us, and never knew what we should stumble upon next. The beauty of the sculpture, the solemn stillness of the woods, disturbed only by the scrambling of monkeys and the chattering of parrots, the desolation of the city, and the mystery that hung over it, all created an interest higher, if possible, than I had ever felt among the ruins of the Old World.

With these words, John Lloyd Stephens described his discovery in 1839 of a ruined city in the jungles of Central America. Among the ruins and tangled vines, he found a temple with a broad stairway that was inscribed with thousands of strange symbols. He also found a ball court watched over by six enormous stone parrots. And he found heavy stone columns carved with images of jaguars, birds, serpents, and men in fabulous feathered headdresses. Stephens had no idea who the builders of this city were, but he was sure he had found evidence of a magnificent civilization.

A Growing Civilization

Stephens had discovered the ruins of Copan, an ancient Mayan city. Like the Olmec, the Maya settled in a fertile region. Notice on the map on page 405 that this region stretched south along an extended finger of land that is surrounded by water.

The 125,000 square miles that the Maya occupied contained both highlands and lowlands. The highlands in the south ran along a mountain range that included active volcanoes. A long rainy season and deep, fertile soil made this area good for farming.

The lowlands were located in the central and northern part of the region. Some lowlands were covered with dense tropical forests with fertile soil. Others had only rough, dry grass or cactus and were not good for farming. But they were rich in the limestone the Maya needed for building and in the flint they used in stonework.

Archaeologists think the Maya may have begun farming the fertile areas of the lowlands as early as 1800 B.C. Between 1800 and 500 B.C., the Maya established small farming villages. They gathered food from the forests and also raised crops. Between 100 B.C. and A.D. 200, some of the villages grew into cities with impressive palaces and pyramids. Mayan artisans carved huge stone figures and pillars to adorn their cities.

During the height of Mayan civilization, between A.D. 250 and 900, about three million people lived in Mayan cities scattered through the region. Look at the map at the above right to find the major cities.

Mayan cities were built around religious centers. At the heart of

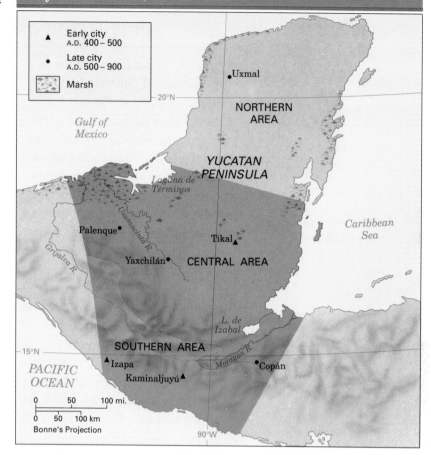

Mayan Civilization, A.D. 300–900

▲ Early city
A.D. 400 – 500

● Late city
A.D. 500 – 900

Marsh

Gulf of Mexico

•Uxmal

20°N

NORTHERN AREA

YUCATAN PENINSULA

Laguna de Términos

Palenque•

Usumacinta R.

Tikal▲

Grijalva R.

Yaxchilán•

CENTRAL AREA

Caribbean Sea

L. de Izabal

15°N

SOUTHERN AREA

▲Izapa

Motagua R.

•Copán

PACIFIC OCEAN

Kaminaljuyú▲

0   50   100 mi.

0   50   100 km

Bonne's Projection

90°W

the city, the Maya usually built tall limestone pyramids that were surrounded by large, open plazas. At the top of the pyramids they built temples. The Mayan priest-kings climbed the steps of the pyramids to perform religious ceremonies at these temples. ■

▲ *Find Copan on the map. Look at the Copan ball court below. Guess the size of the buildings by comparing them with the car in the background.*

■ *What were Mayan cities like?*

An Economy Based on Agriculture

■ *What techniques enabled highland and lowland farmers to become more efficient?*

▼ *Mayan farmers built flat terraces on the slopes of the highlands to stop topsoil from being washed downhill. They built canals that descended the hills. The canals were an efficient way to provide water for irrigating the crops in the terraces.*

As the population of Mayan cities increased, farmers had to produce more food. To meet this demand, they devised ways to farm hillsides and other land that they had not been able to farm before. You can see in the diagram below that the Maya built flat terraces into the slopes of the highlands. In the wet lowlands, they built raised fields to improve drainage and, thus, water fields without flooding them. In densely forested areas, they burned off vegetation to clear land.

In the hot, dry region of the lowlands, where the soil was thin, the Maya used yet another technique. They scooped rich soil from the banks and the bottom of rivers and spread this over the rocky plains to create farmland. They also dug canals and moats to bring water to dry areas. Using these techniques, the Maya grew their crops of maize, beans, avocados, melons, and squash.

As the Maya became more efficient farmers, they developed a surplus of food. They traded their excess food and other products with other peoples living in Central America and Mexico. Mayan traders carried their goods on foot or in dugout canoes to places as far away as present-day Mexico City. In this way, they obtained things they could not produce themselves. For instance, they traded salt, honey, finely decorated cotton, and jaguar pelts with people in regions we know today as Guatemala and Honduras. In return, they received jade, brightly colored bird feathers, and cacao beans. From jade they carved jewelry and statues. They used the cacao beans to make chocolate and also as a form of money in trade. ■

High ground

Irrigation channel

Topsoil
Small, smooth gravel
Large, coarse gravel
Clay
Cobblestone base

Limestone mountainside

Drainage channel

Field of level soil

Embankment

Priests as Kings

The Maya worshiped many gods and believed their gods controlled the sun, rain, and other elements of nature. They sought to please the gods, hoping in return they would be blessed with good weather and bountiful harvests. They also worshiped their rulers, because they believed their rulers could influence the gods.

The Maya told about their rulers in hieroglyphs painted on tomb walls and carved into stone **steles,** or columns. One such ruler, named Pacal, began ruling the city-state Palenque at the age of six, with help from his mother. In A.D. 65, when he turned 12, he became king in his own right. During his 68-year reign, the city of Palenque flourished.

From pictures carved on the walls of Pacal's tomb, scholars have concluded that Pacal, like other Mayan rulers, was a priest as well as a warrior and ruler. As priests, Mayan kings sacrificed food, animals, and even human beings to please the gods. Sometimes the priest-kings pierced their own skin and shed their own sacred blood in the belief that this would keep their society healthy and productive. ■

◄ This Mayan death mask from about A.D. 700 was fashioned out of pieces of jade cemented together. The eyes are made of seashells. The Maya covered their king's face when he went to live with the gods.

■ *What do we know about Mayan rulers?*

Mayan Achievements

The Mayan civilization developed many cultural achievements, such as a number system and a writing system of hieroglyphs like those on the stele at the right. The priest-kings also created two calendars to record and plan their years. To learn more about the Mayan calendars, read A Closer Look on page 408.

The number system enabled the priest-kings

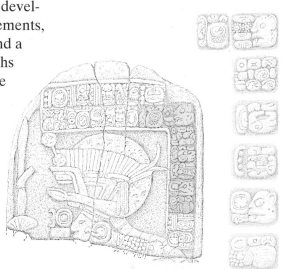

◄ Mayan hieroglyphs are read from left to right, top to bottom. Scholars think this stele describes a person named Jaguar Claw, who is about to be sacrificed. The person shown here is probably the ruler of the Mayan city of Dos Pilas.

407

The Mayan Calendar

Why do people have good days and bad days? Why do crops grow well one year and poorly the next? The Maya believed it was because different gods ruled each day. By consulting their two calendars and using the right mathematics, Mayan priests knew which gods ruled which days. Then the priests had to figure out what influence the gods would have.

On the 260-day religious calendar, each day was given a name and a number. The name *Imix* meant "water lily," and represented the ocean. *Ik* was named for the wind, and *Akbal* was named for the darkness of night.

Historians use the diagram above to explain the 260-day religious calendar. Each name and each number was a divine being—two gods for every day. When you turn the wheels, you discover that the same name and the same number only fall together once every 260 days. Then the cycle starts all over again.

1 Imix—the New Year's day of the Mayan 260-day year

Dates were skillfully carved in Mayan hieroglyphs like these

Mayan priests interpreted the mood of the gods. If the gods on a particular day were grouchy—look out!

The other Mayan calendar was based on the earth's orbit around the sun and had 365 days like ours. Each of these days had a god, too. This calendar had 18 months of 20 days each, plus 5 extra days. It was considered bad luck to do anything on those 5 days, so people did very little. They didn't even eat!

to record information about astronomical events. The detailed astronomical charts and tables that they made using this system are quite accurate. Their system was based on the number 20 instead of 10, which is the basis for our decimal system. As you can see at the top of this page, they used dots and dashes to represent numbers and even had a symbol for zero.

To record important dates and events in the lives of their rulers, the Maya developed hieroglyphs. Each hieroglyph represents a sound. When the pictures are put together, they can make up part of a word or a whole word. Some hieroglyphs represent ideas, such as "life" or "happiness." Others represent objects like "corn" or "water."

The Mayan priest-kings used hieroglyphs to write record books, each of which was known as a **codex.** Archaeologists have studied the three existing codices and deciphered part of them to learn about religious ceremonies, astronomy, and Mayan calendars.

The codices reveal that the Maya had two calendars. They used them to determine the best time to plant crops, hunt, and perform religious ceremonies. The Mayan priest-kings developed the

calendars from their close observations of the movements of the sun, moon, and stars.

Mayan cultural achievements also included the magnificent architecture of their cities and beautiful works of decorative art. For example, Mayan artisans made jewelry out of jade, gold, and shells. King Pacal, in his tomb at Palenque, was found wearing a life-size mosaic mask made from jade. He also wore jewelry of jade and mother-of-pearl. The Maya were also accomplished weavers, and they communicated nonverbally through their weaving designs. (See Exploring Nonverbal Communication on pages 410–411.)

These are only some of the achievements of the ancient Mayan civilization. The Mayan culture has survived, however, unlike many other early American cultures. Today, Mayan people live in Guatemala, Belize, and parts of Mexico. ■

The Mayan Number System

									Positional Values
								••	x 400
						•	▬	••••	x 20
◈	•	••••	▬	▬•	▬•••	◈	▬•	▬•	x 1
0	1	4	5	11	19	20	126	1092	

▲ *In the Mayan number system, symbols represented basic numerical values. Find the bar above that equals 5. Vertical positions also indicated that the basic value was multiplied by a certain number (1, 20, 400, and so on). Thus, the representation above for 1,092 translates into this equation: 12 + (14 x 20) + (2 x 400) = 1,092. Translate the representation for 126 into a numerical equation.*

■ *Describe the Mayan writing and number systems.*

R E V I E W

1. FOCUS In what ways were the Maya an advanced civilization?

2. CONNECT What agricultural techniques made Mayan farming more efficient than Olmec farming?

3. BELIEF SYSTEMS What did the Maya worship? What important role did the priest-kings play in the Mayan religion?

4. CULTURE How have archaeologists learned so much about King Pacal?

5. CRITICAL THINKING Why was the invention of a number system important in Mayan society?

6. WRITING ACTIVITY Write a message for a classmate using your own hieroglyphs. First, write out the message you want to send. Then create simple pictures for each sound, word, or idea you want to get across. Remember, when someone looks at your picture, they will need to be able to guess the sound, word, or idea it represents. Trade messages, and decipher them.

Nonverbal Communication

Mayan weaving contains messages, but only people who can recognize and understand its colorful symbols can read them. For centuries people have used various kinds of nonverbal communication to convey their thoughts to others.

Get Ready

Get a notebook, a sketch pad, and a pencil. List several forms of nonverbal communication: facial expressions, gestures, and codes using symbols or sounds. Include some visual arts, such as Mayan weaving or another art form that communicates through colors and symbols. Choose one form.

Sign language Charades

➤ *Using a traditional back-strap loom, this Mayan woman weaves patterns used in her village for generations. For the Mayan weaver, snakes symbolize the earth, toads symbolize saints, and eagles symbolize life and death.*

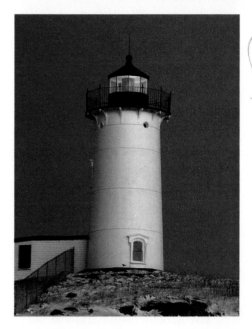

Or do people need special knowledge in order to understand them, as they would for the signals of the basketball referee?

Move Ahead

Display your sketches of nonverbal messages on the bulletin board. Try to "read" the messages your classmates drew. Can they "read" yours?

Did you find any nonverbal signs that had more than one meaning? For instance, waving is a way of saying "Good-bye." But waving very forcefully or with a downward movement of the hand can mean "Go away!"

Explore Some More

Be alert to all forms of nonverbal communication in your everyday life. Notice a traffic officer stopping traffic or signaling it to move on. Sometimes families have special signals too. For example, some parents ring a bell or flash a porch light to call children home.

You are going to explain and illustrate an example of nonverbal communication. You may need reference books to help you with this exploration. Sports and art magazines can also be good sources of ideas.

Find Out

Make a list of messages that can be delivered using the form of nonverbal communication that you chose. For instance, you might list the various messages that a basketball referee can deliver through gestures: personal foul, traveling, or time out. Draw simple sketches to show how some of these messages would be expressed.

What are the limits of the form of nonverbal communication you chose? What kinds of messages could not be communicated using this form?

Are your examples of nonverbal communication easy to understand, like a smile or a shrug?

◄ Its beacon flashing in the night, this lighthouse transmits information to incoming sailors about conditions close to shore.

◄ Wandering in a foreign city, how can you find the local train station or a place to exchange money? These signs, which use international symbols, will help guide you.

▼ Many deaf people use American Sign Language to communicate. Combining hand signs, body movements, and facial expressions, this language is as expressive and complex as spoken English. Below is the sign for the letter "h".

LESSON 4

The Tiwanakans and the Moche

THINKING FOCUS

In what ways did the Tiwanakans and Moche adapt to the land?

Key Terms

- altiplano
- adobe

You've worked your way to the top of a magnificent peak high in the Andes. The air is thin but clear at 12,000 feet. A large condor circles the high, flat, and barren plateau called the **altiplano.** Its wings catch the dry wind blowing across the sun-baked rock. As you scan the vast stone wilderness, you glimpse a huge lake surrounded by snow-covered mountains.

This is the land of the ancient Tiwanakans *(tih WAHN ah kahns),* a civilization that prospered from 300 B.C. to A.D. 1200. At its height, the Tiwanakan culture occupied 1,500 square miles from the plateaus of Peru and Bolivia down the southern coast of Peru and into northern Chile.

About 400 years after the Tiwanakan culture began, another culture, called the Moche *(MOH chay),* developed along the northern coast of Peru.

The Moche homeland was very different from the altiplano. North along the Pacific coast of Peru is a thin strip of desert where rain almost never falls. The land is stark, with barren foothills that rise into the Andes. Small rivers flowing down the Andes to the ocean irrigate the sparse vegetation. These river valleys were home to the Moche from about A.D. 100 to 700, when Moche culture flourished.

As the Tiwanakans adapted to the cold, high plateaus, the Moche adapted to the dry desert coast. To survive, both had to develop efficient farming techniques.

Adapting to the Land

The Tiwanakans and Moche developed different ways to grow their crops that were well suited to their different environments. Look at the cross-sectional map below to get a sense of the terrain and elevation in the Tiwanakan and Moche regions.

Tiwanakan Adaptations

On the high plateau where the Tiwanakans lived, the nights are cold and the daylight sun is scorching. Water is scarce, except near the lakes. The Tiwanakans channeled water to their fields from nearby Lake Titicaca and from other lakes. They dug broad irrigation canals to enable water to flow around large raised beds of soil.

To make the soil beds, the Tiwanakans built a cobblestone base and covered it with a thick layer of clay. They poured on top of this three layers of gravel, each finer than the next. Finally, they covered the entire mound with a rich layer of soil. These raised beds provided a quality of both irrigation and drainage that today's technology cannot surpass.

The canals around the beds not only provided water for the plants but also protected them from the killing nightly frosts. Water and algae in the canals absorbed the sun's heat during the day and then radiated that warmth throughout the chilly nights.

The Tiwanakans could not grow maize, beans, squash, and other warm-climate crops. Instead, they grew hardy crops such as potatoes and grain suited to the cool climate.

Moche Adaptations

Because the land was too dry for farming, the Moche had to invent ways to get water to their crops. Using mud as their building material, the Moche constructed miles of aqueducts to carry river water to their fields. At least one of these channels was 70 miles long. Many are still in use today.

The Moche also found a way to grow crops on the steep slopes of the Andes foothills. They terraced the slopes into flat beds like steps of a giant staircase. In these fields the Moche grew corn, beans, peanuts, hot peppers, and squash. They also gathered shellfish from the sea and rivers and ate llama and guinea pig. ■

■ *Describe the methods the Tiwanakans and Moche used to bring water to their farmlands.*

▼ *Melting snow from the Andes forms a river that created the Moche Valley (previous page, left) leading into the Pacific coast. The Moche lived alongside the river. The environment below is called an "altiplano," or high plain. It is a windswept plain with a lake. Compare the elevation of the Moche and the Tiwanakans.*

Lake Titicaca

Tiwanaku
(12,645 ft./ 7,857m)

ALTIPLANO

▲ *This four-cornered, brightly dyed Tiwanakan hat is made of llama wool. Hats like these were used by all for extra warmth at high elevations.*

➤ *Viracocha was the Tiwanakans' god of the sky and creation, and was often shown as the condor god with snake hair, as in this sandstone image.*

Living and Working

As the Tiwanakans improved their farming methods, their harvests grew in size. Their population also increased, and soon social classes began to form. Moche civilization also shows evidence of social classes.

Tiwanakan Lifestyle

Among the Tiwanakans, as in other early civilizations, the common people performed the hard labor. They also paid two types of taxes to support the government. They gave part of the food they harvested to the state and spent time each year working for the state. The women usually worked as weavers, and the men helped to build and maintain the raised fields and roads.

The Tiwanakan rulers ordered many miles of roads to be built to connect the villages and to make trading easier. To further promote trade, the government supplied llamas as pack animals in trade caravans and patrolled the roads to protect caravans from attack.

The llama caravans brought tropical fruits, wood, monkeys, and colorful bird feathers from the jungles of Bolivia. From Chile and Peru, they carried seafood, corn, hot peppers, copper, and gold dust. Outbound caravans hauled potatoes, grains, locally crafted textiles, pottery, and jewelry.

The holy city of Tiwanaku was the center of both trade and religion. Pilgrims came to worship at the Gateway of the Sun in this holy city. Archaeologists who have studied this carved gateway and other Tiwanakan carvings have deduced that the Tiwanakans honored the condor. This is not surprising, since great numbers of stately condors must have soared over Tiwanaku, seeming to watch over its land and subjects.

The condor is also associated with the ruling elite. Perhaps like the Maya, the Tiwanakans thought their rulers could influence the gods and, out of respect, treated them much like gods. Artisans crafted fine jewelry, crowns, pottery, and vivid textiles to honor them. What happened to these strong, creative people? How did their civilization come to an end?

Between 1100 and 1300, the city of Tiwanaku was abandoned.

Those who lived in and around Tiwanaku resettled in small groups on the mountainsides.

Archaeologists disagree about why people deserted the city. Some think a drought destroyed the city's fragile agricultural system. Others speculate that Lake Titicaca may have flooded and made the nearby fields unusable. Still others believe that outsiders invaded the city. Whatever the reason, by 1400, all that was left of Tiwanakan culture were ruins high in the Andes.

Moche Lifestyle

The ancient city of Moche was the civic and religious hub of the Moche civilization. It was located on Peru's Pacific coast in the midst of irrigated farmlands.

Much like the Tiwanakans, the Moche probably used great numbers of laborers from the lower class to do their work. These workers dug and maintained aqueducts and built great pyramids and temples. To build temples, the Moche mixed river mud and straw to form bricks called **adobe** (uh DOH bee).

Most commoners farmed or fished and hunted for food. Priests, artisans, warriors, and engineers were members of the elite. The 1987 discovery of the tombs of the "Lords of Sipan," the richest tomb found in the Americas, has added to our knowledge of Moche crafts.

◀ The figure at left is a Tiwanakan condor god made of a beaten sheet of gold. The one-foot tall Moche pot below is decorated with the ruler's head at the top of the vessel. Examine each artifact carefully. What does each imply about that civilization, its people and their beliefs?

The Moche did not have a system of writing, but Moche pottery recovered from tombs reveals much about their culture. Clay figures and painted pottery jars show people farming, cooking, weaving, and giving birth. These ceramics tell of war and sacrifice, of glorious rulers and many gods.

Some experts think that the Moche culture was absorbed by other Andean cultures. Others believe the Moche were conquered by outsiders. But the truth remains unknown. In about 600, the Moche abandoned their city and moved to nearby areas. Six hundred years later, the Tiwanakans would do the same. ■

■ *Compare and contrast Tiwanakan and Moche lifestyles.*

R E V I E W

1. **FOCUS** In what ways did the Tiwanakans and the Moche adapt to the land?
2. **CONNECT** What did the Tiwanakan lifestyle have in common with other early civilizations in the Americas?
3. **CULTURE** What does Moche pottery tell us about Moche culture?

4. **CRITICAL THINKING** In what ways were the Moche and the Tiwanakans similar?
5. **ACTIVITY** The condor was an emblem of a Tiwanakan god. What symbols do we use in our society to represent important things? Make a list of modern symbols such as the American eagle and the American flag. Tell what each symbol represents.

415

Early American Civilizations

Recording Information

Here's Why

You may have made use of reference books, magazines, newspapers, or computer databases in the library or on the Internet. To make the most effective use of such sources, you need to develop the skill of taking and organizing notes. Taking good notes will help organize your information and make the task of writing a report easier. It will improve the quality of your reports.

Suppose you had to prepare a report about how the ancient Maya lived. Would you know how to take notes and organize them for your report?

Here's How

As you begin to gather information for your report, skim several general sources. This will give you an idea of some of the key topics and subtopics. You might begin by reading about the Maya on pages 404 through 409 of this book. Another general source would be an encyclopedia. From these general ideas, develop several questions you want your report to answer. For example, you might decide to answer these questions: What did Mayan houses look like? What were they made of? How were they made? Revise and add to these questions as you do further reading for your report.

Once you have several questions to answer, begin the note-taking process. Writing your notes on 4" x 6" cards will make it easy for you to keep track of your information and organize it.

The text shown on the computer screen in the illustration is an example of a source you might use for notes. It tells about the homes of the Maya. This will be a subtopic in your report. Write the name of the subtopic on the first line, as shown on the sample note card at the top of the next page.

On the note card under the subtopic name, list important details from the text. If you are listing many details about a subtopic, use a separate card for each category. Look again at the sample note cards. Notice that one card has information about how the Mayan huts were divided for use. What category of details does the other card contain?

As you make notes, be sure that you paraphrase what you have read. This means you must write the

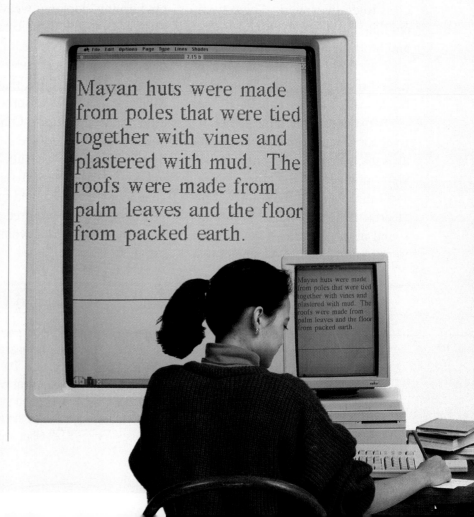

5. Mayan Huts
Single room
Partition divides sleeping area from living area

5. Mayan Huts
Walls of poles covered with mud
Palm leaf roofs
Packed earth floors
The Mayans, p. 15

notes in your own words. Reread the information about Mayan huts shown on the computer screen below. Notice how this information has been condensed to three short phrases on the note card. The card simply notes the main ideas from the sentences.

Paraphrasing will help you to take notes more quickly and efficiently. It will also help to ensure that the report you turn in is your own work. You should copy directly from a source only if you want to use an exact quotation.

If you plan to include a quotation in your report, be sure you have copied the spelling, punctuation, and grammar from your source precisely. On your note card, be sure to put quotation marks at the beginning and the end of the quotation, so that you will be able to tell it from your paraphrased notes.

On each note card, include information about just one subtopic. If the source you are using includes information on more than one subtopic, put the information on separate cards. Keeping the information on different subtopics separate will make sorting your note cards much easier.

After you have written all of the details about one subtopic from a single source, write the source information on the card. Source information includes the source title and the page number on which you found the information. By recording this information, you make it easy to refer to the source again.

When you finish writing note cards, you might want to use a number-coding system to help organize your cards. Assign each subtopic a number, and write that number on any cards with notes about that subtopic. For example, the number 5 on the note cards above indicates that both cards contain information about the subtopic "Mayan huts."

You could also code your note cards with color. Use a magic marker of a different color to highlight each subtopic, or use note cards of different colors for each subtopic.

Try It

Turn to Lesson 3, page 406. Find the paragraph that begins with the sentence "As the Maya became more efficient farmers, they developed a surplus of food." Write a note card summarizing the information in the paragraph. Be sure to include a subtopic, notes that are paraphrased, and source information.

Apply It

Suppose you were writing a report about one of the groups you have read about in this chapter. Prepare five or six note cards on the material you find for your report. Remember to include the source of your information on each card. Organize your note cards using one of the methods mentioned in Try It.

Early American Civilizations

Chapter Review

Reviewing Key Terms

adobe (p. 415)   hieroglyph (p. 403)
altiplano (p. 412)   hunter-gatherer (p. 397)
codex (p. 409)   sedentary (p. 398)
elite (p. 401)   stele (p. 407)
extinct (p. 398)

A. Use a dictionary to find the origins of the following words. On your own paper, write one or two sentences explaining how each word got its meaning.

1. hieroglyph
2. altiplano
3. adobe
4. codex
5. stele
6. extinct

B. Each sentence below includes one or two key terms. Rewrite each sentence. Do not use any of the key terms in your new sentence.

1. Hunter-gatherers followed mammoths and other animals that have long been extinct.
2. The development of farming enabled people to adopt a sedentary way of life.
3. Fancy, complicated tombs found at Olmec burial sites probably belonged to members of the elite class.
4. The people who live on the altiplano today live a sedentary way of life, farming and keeping small herds.
5. Translating a Mayan codex requires tremendous dedication.

Exploring Concepts

A. The diagram below should show ways that each of the two groups, hunter-gatherers and sedentary villagers, adapt to their environment. Copy the diagram on your paper, and fill in four behaviors and characteristics of both hunter-gatherers and sedentary villagers. Use information from the chapter to complete the diagram.

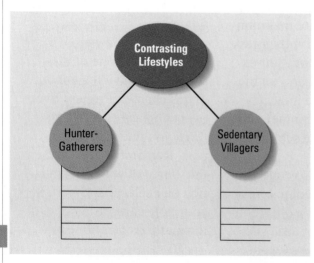

B. Write a sentence giving a piece of archaeological evidence that supports each statement below. The first one has been done for you.

1. People first came to the Americas from Asia. Answer: Tools found in South America are very similar to stone tools from the same time period found in Asia.
2. Olmec society was divided into classes.
3. In their rituals, Olmecs sacrificed people and animals.
4. Many ancient American cultures worshiped animals.
5. The Olmec traded with people as far away as 500 miles.
6. Mayan priest-kings developed two calendars, an understanding of astronomy, and a number system.
7. Food surpluses led to increasingly complex societies and cultures.
8. The Tiwanakans built raised beds of soil for farming that provided an exceptional quality of irrigation and drainage.

Reviewing Skills

1. Find the heading Moche Adaptations on page 413. Read the first two paragraphs that appear under the heading. Write a separate note card explaining each paragraph. Be sure to write your notes in your own words.
2. Read the paragraphs that appear under the heading Moche Lifestyle on page 415. Write a note card for each paragraph explaining the information, again in your own words. What subtopics will you need? How many note cards will you need to use to explain the information?
3. Suppose you wanted to find out if any recent articles have been written about the Mayan civilization of Central America. What subject headings might you look under in the *Readers' Guide to Periodical Literature* to find information about the Maya? What subject headings might you look under to find information about the areas of Peru, Bolivia, and Chile once inhabited by the Tiwanakan and the Moche?
4. Suppose you were reading a difficult primary source account of an exploration of a Mayan ruin in the jungles of Central America. What would help you better understand a passage from this account?

Using Critical Thinking

1. In what ways were the Olmec, the Mayan, the Tiwanakan, and the Moche civilizations similar? If you can identify major differences between the civilizations, do so. If not, explain why. Were there no major differences, or do you not have enough facts to make a comparison?
2. Some of the civilizations described in the chapter had class systems. For each society, list evidence of a class system. Then explain whether you think a class system is the only explanation for this evidence and why. If you think the evidence might point to some different kind of system, describe it.
3. When the Olmec civilization vanished, there were few clues as to why. State one hypothesis given in the chapter to explain the Olmec's disappearance. Describe evidence that supports that hypothesis. How would you further test that hypothesis?

Preparing for Citizenship

1. **ARTS ACTIVITY** Research the Olmec or Mayan civilization's artifacts, art, and hieroglyphs in the library. Then use a variety of symbols like these to create a poster. Show things you like and are interested in, something interesting you have done or that you hope to do. Or you might show some skill or ability you have.
2. **COLLABORATIVE LEARNING** Form a group of three or four people. In your group, choose one of the artistic or engineering feats that was accomplished by one of the civilizations from the chapter. Then figure out a plan for accomplishing this feat. The task to be performed can be the creation of an artistic work such as one of the huge stone heads the Olmec created, a land engineering project such as raised beds or terraces, or a water transportation project involving the creation of aqueducts or irrigation canals. As a group, make a list of questions you will need answered in order to plan the project. Then have each group member research the answers to assigned questions and present those answers to the group. This will require estimation and hypothesis-making. Have the group figure out a way to present the plan to the whole class as clearly and in as much detail as possible. Then have each group member complete the presentation of his or her information and conclusions according to the group's plan.

Two American Empires

Floating gardens of sunlit yellows, reds, and greens—in the 1300s and 1400s, the Aztec created such gardens on the swampy land outside their capital in Mexico. By the 1100s, the Inca were engineering terraced fields in the high, cold mountains of South America. Until the 1500s, these two powerful empires ruled vast lands in the Americas. It seemed as though they would rule forever, but then strange invaders appeared from the East.

During this time the Inca rule a vast empire and craft striking works of art, like this gold and turquoise knife handle.

c. 1300 The Aztec settle on an island in Lake Texcoco, Mexico. Their empire grows rich and powerful, and artisans craft works like this two-headed turquoise serpent.

1200	1300	1400

1230

c. 1330s Bubonic plague, or Black Death, hits Asia and then Europe.

Throughout this period, the Inca wove colorful works of art. Many had everyday uses, such as this combination child's doll and good-luck charm.

The Inca ruled an empire of about 13 million people during the 1500s. Their ruins stand today. The "baths of the Inca" above were used by Inca priests for religious ceremonies.

1521 Spanish conquerors, led by Hernando Cortés (right), defeat and plunder the mighty Aztec Empire.

1500

1600

1700

1518 Traders begin sending shiploads of African slaves to the West Indies.

1572

L E S S O N   1

The Aztec

Key Terms

- chinampa
- alliance
- calpulli
- tribute

➤ *The eagle on a prickly pear cactus is an important symbol in Mexican history. The eagle shown here was used on a plan of Tenochtitlan from the 1500s. Today, the eagle symbol forms the center of the Mexican flag.*

According to legend, the Aztec received this command from the god Huitzilopochtli *(wee tsee loh POHCH tlee)*. "Go where the cactus grows, on which the eagle sits happily . . . there we shall wait, there we shall meet a number of tribes and with our arrow or with our shield we shall conquer them."

The Aztec were a band of hunter-gatherers living on a small island in northwestern Mexico, when their god summoned them to leave their homeland. Guided by Huitzilopochtli, they journeyed through deserts and over steep mountains. They fought hunger and thirst, hoping at every turn to see the promised sign, an eagle perched on a prickly pear cactus, eating a snake. There was no time to grow food, so they ate fly eggs and snakes to survive. There was no time to weave cloth, so they wore animal skins for clothing.

They journeyed through the fertile lands of tribes that were larger and stronger. These tribes looked down on the Aztec, calling them Dog People because of their barbarian ways. They did not allow the Aztec to settle. Besides, the Aztec still had not seen the sign.

After 200 years of wandering, the Aztec came upon the promised sign. They found the eagle on a small, swampy island in Lake Texcoco in the Valley of Mexico. They named their new home Tenochtitlan *(tay nawch tee TLAHN)*, "Place of the Prickly Pear Cactus." There they started to build a powerful empire.

Building an Empire

No one knows exactly why the Aztec came to the Valley of Mexico. Perhaps they were attracted to the valley's climate and fertile soil. Its high altitude gives the valley a mild climate. By the time the Aztec arrived in the Valley of Mexico in the early 1300s, powerful tribes had already claimed the most fertile lands in the area. So they settled on a soggy, uninhabited island in Lake Texcoco. The island was about 12 miles square in size.

Expansion of the Aztec Empire

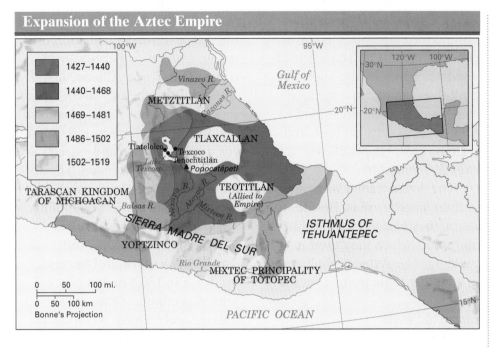

Legend:
- 1427–1440
- 1440–1468
- 1469–1481
- 1486–1502
- 1502–1519

METZTITLÁN
TLAXCALLAN
Tlatelolco
Texcoco
Tenochtitlán
Popocatépetl
Lake Texcoco
TARASCAN KINGDOM OF MICHOACAN
Balsas R.
Nexapa R.
Atoyac R.
Mixteco R.
SIERRA MADRE DEL SUR
YOPTZINCO
Rio Grande
MIXTEC PRINCIPALITY OF TOTOPEC
TEOTITLÁN (Allied to Empire)
ISTHMUS OF TEHUANTEPEC
Gulf of Mexico
Vinazco R.
Cazones R.
PACIFIC OCEAN
0   50   100 mi.
0   50   100 km
Bonne's Projection

◄ The Aztec Empire expanded greatly over a 92-year period. During what periods did it expand the most?

Adapting to the Land

The future looked grim for the Aztec. Because the land on their island was mostly swamp, they couldn't grow crops such as corn for food or cotton for clothing. Also, the timber and stone they needed to build huts was scarce on the small island.

The Aztec, however, learned to use what was around them to their advantage. They used reeds and mud from the swamp to make huts. They caught and ate birds and fish that lived on the island or in the water around it. From the tribes around them, the Aztec learned a method of farming that was especially suited to the swampy areas in which they lived.

This way of farming made use of **chinampas,** or "floating gardens." Chinampas are narrow strips of land about 300 feet long and 15 to 30 feet wide, almost completely surrounded by canals. The Aztec built these floating gardens around their central city. They used the rows of canals to tend the chinampas by boat. Look at the pictures of the floating gardens below. On these floating gardens, Aztec farmers were able to produce such vegetables as corn, squash, chili peppers, beans, and tomatoes.

▼ The Aztec were able to turn swampy ground into usable farmland with chinampas. Notice the types of soil that were piled in layers. Which layer do you think would have been most fertile? In the photograph at left, modern farmers are tending chinampas in south central Mexico.

Wooden stake
Fresh mud
Dirt and vegetation
Canal
Lake bed

The Aztec used the canals around the chinampas to travel by canoe to the city of Tenochtitlan and to nearby islands. They also built three great causeways, or raised roads, to the mainland so they could also travel back and forth on foot. One causeway was over five miles long.

The Aztec traded with peoples in these nearby areas. Besides food items, they also obtained timber and stone, which they used in building. The Aztec had succeeded in adapting to their environment.

Rising to Power

The Aztec not only adapted to the land, they also found ways to get along with their neighbors. According to Aztec legend, more powerful and more civilized tribes forced the Aztec to serve as soldiers in their armies. From these more powerful tribes, the Aztec learned to be skilled warriors.

As the number of Aztec warriors increased, so did the Aztec reputation for military skill. In 1428, the Aztec formed an **alliance,** or union, with two other powerful tribes. This Triple Alliance increased Aztec military strength, and they began to build a huge empire that would one day cover the southern third of Mexico and extend into what is today Guatemala. The Aztec empire covered an area about 375 miles wide and 315 miles long.

One of the greatest rulers of the empire was Ahuitzotl *(ah WEE soh tl)*. From 1486 until his death in 1502, he led Aztec armies in conquest throughout Mexico and Central America. He launched lightning-quick attacks that took his enemies by surprise. Ahuitzotl also oversaw the completion of the pyramid of the Great Temple, which he dedicated to the god Huitzilopochtli.

When Ahuitzotl died in 1502, his nephew, Moctezuma, became the new ruler. Like Ahuitzotl, he led his warriors into battles of conquest. Under his rule, which lasted until 1520, the empire reached its greatest size, with a population of about 25 million people. ■

■ *How did the Aztec adapt to their swampy environment?*

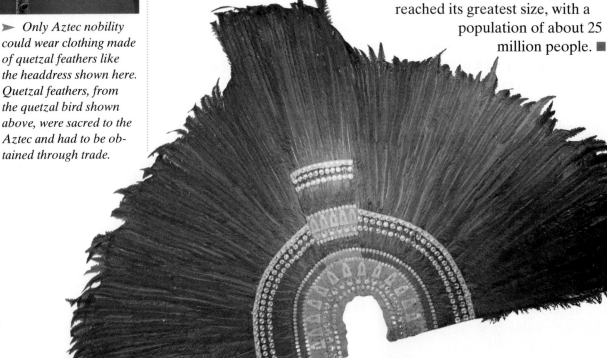

➤ *Only Aztec nobility could wear clothing made of quetzal feathers like the headdress shown here. Quetzal feathers, from the quetzal bird shown above, were sacred to the Aztec and had to be obtained through trade.*

Living in the Empire

As the empire expanded, Aztec society became more complex. An intricate class structure had developed over a period of more than 200 years.

Social Classes

The Aztec lived in large settlements called **calpullis.** Families of different social ranks—nobles, commoners, serfs, and slaves—lived in each calpulli. They all shared the land of the calpulli.

Commoners made up the majority of the Aztec population. They farmed their calpulli land but were also required to farm the nobles' land. While the men of the calpulli worked in the fields, the women cooked and wove cloth and cared for the younger children. At about age 10, commoner boys were sent to a school run by the calpulli, where they learned, among other things, Aztec religion and history.

Aztec commoners had to pay tribute to the government. **Tribute** was a kind of tax paid in goods or services. Tribute could be paid in crops, in handmade items such as jewelry or clothing, and by work on state projects, such as temples, canals, and dams.

Like commoners, serfs had to work the land, but they could not own it. Serfs made up about one-third of the Aztec population.

Slaves occupied the lowest rung of the Aztec social ladder. Many slaves were captives of war. Others were Aztec who had committed crimes or who had not repaid debts.

The nobles were the smallest class, but they controlled the other classes. Nobility was hereditary, and members of the noble class served as government officials, priests, and warriors. Nobles lived off tribute paid by commoners and conquered peoples.

The Mexican painter Diego Rivera painted Great Tenochtitlan *from 1929 to 1945. It shows his imaginative view of the color, excitement, and people in an Aztec market. The statue below helps us know what Aztec commoners actually looked like.*

Conquered peoples made up the majority of those living in the Aztec Empire. The Aztec allowed each conquered tribe to keep its own religion, language, social structure, and customs.

But not all aspects of Aztec rule were so positive. Most of the wealth of the empire was made up of tribute paid by subject, or conquered, tribes. Many tribes were forced to give up so much of their food as tribute that they lived on the brink of starvation. The endless demand for tribute made subject tribes resent Aztec rulers.

Trade and Markets

Aztec merchants lived in separate calpullis. They traveled throughout the empire and beyond to bring back exotic goods such as colored feathers, jade, and cocoa for the nobles. The merchants employed many carriers, usually slaves, who walked in long caravans carrying heavy loads for trips of 250 miles or more.

Merchants sold many of their goods in city markets throughout the empire. The marketplace was an important center in Aztec cities. The Spanish explorer Hernando Cortés later reported that more than 60,000 people visited the city market daily in Tlatelolco *(tlah tehl OHL koh)*.

The Aztec Universe

The Aztec believed that the world was alive with spirits. Every aspect of nature had been created by the self-sacrifice of the spirits of wind and rain, or rocks and corn, and more. These spirits still lived in nature. The Aztec believed that humans must live by the rules of

the spirits, or the universe would be destroyed.

The Aztec gods represented these spirits who controlled the world. They were more like African gods than Greek or Roman gods. The Aztec gods did not share human characteristics, did not marry or have children, and did not have emotions. The gods required prayer, thanksgiving, rituals, and sacrifices to keep the world from destruction.

The Aztec dealt with the gods in their everyday lives, in the fields and on the lakes. They respected nature. An early Spanish missionary named Bernard de Sahagun *(sah hah GOON)* recorded that when Aztec women cooked corn, "first of all they breathed upon [the corn]. . . . In this way it would not take fright; thus it would not fear the heat."

Cultural Achievements

From archaeologists' findings, we know the Aztec built elaborate palaces, temples, and government storehouses out of stone and brick. We have also recovered many everyday objects, including jewelry, pottery, carvings, and even the remains of sacrifices. We also know Aztec craftworkers produced beautiful feather headdresses, stone sculptures, and jewelry set with precious stones.

Perhaps the most important Aztec artifacts that archaeologists have discovered are the Aztec codices, or codes. Each codex is a kind of book, with pages made from bark. The pages open and close like folding screens and include brightly colored hieroglyphs.

At one time there were hundreds of these books. Unfortunately, Spanish missionaries and settlers in the Aztec region burned many of the codices. Other books rotted in the humid climate. From the few that remain, historians have learned about aspects of Aztec life. What kind of scene is on the codex page shown below? ■

■ *Describe the different classes in Aztec society and the effect that tribute had on each of them.*

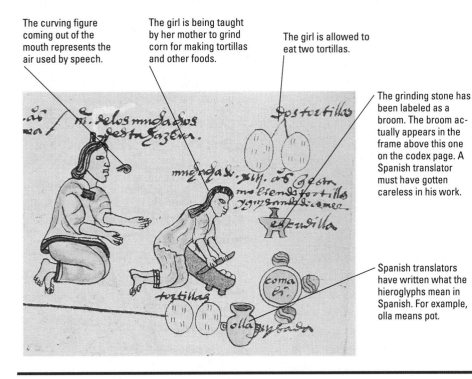

The curving figure coming out of the mouth represents the air used by speech.

The girl is being taught by her mother to grind corn for making tortillas and other foods.

The girl is allowed to eat two tortillas.

The grinding stone has been labeled as a broom. The broom actually appears in the frame above this one on the codex page. A Spanish translator must have gotten careless in his work.

Spanish translators have written what the hieroglyphs mean in Spanish. For example, olla means pot.

◄ *This codex page shows some of the tasks that Aztec girls learned to perform.*

Fighting for the Gods

The everyday lives of all classes of Aztec society revolved around religion. Many Aztec gods are depicted in the codices.

The two most important gods in the Aztec world were Huitzilopochtli, the god of the sun and of war, and Tláloc *(tlah LOHK),* the god of rain. The Aztec especially feared the god Huitzilopochtli, because he could destroy the world whenever he wanted.

Human Sacrifices

The Aztec held many religious ceremonies throughout the year. At these occasions, Aztec priests offered sacrifices to the gods to help ensure good harvests. Human sacrifice was common. When the Temple of the Sun in Tenochtitlan was dedicated to the sun and rain gods, the Aztec sacrificed as many as 10,000 people.

The reasons for the human sacrifices are still not clear. Many historians believe that the Aztec used these human sacrifices to frighten their enemies. Most of the people sacrificed by the Aztec were captives of war. The Aztec believed that whatever one's station in life, if he were sacrificed he would become a divine being. Many victims went willingly. A sacrificed warrior would live happily forever, they said, like a hummingbird. Some scholars think that the Aztec arranged wars to capture sacrifices for the gods.

▼ *The rain god Tláloc was one of the major Aztec gods. This is only one of many different Aztec representations of the god.*

427

▲ This Aztec codex page shows different types of Aztec warriors. Notice how the warriors carry shields. Warriors' shields were made from quetzal feathers and would have resembled the feather shield shown above.

■ *How were war and religion linked in Aztec culture?*

War and Religion

The Aztec's reasons for war, however, were not strictly religious. They wanted to control the Valley of Mexico, so they waged war on any tribes who resisted their rule. As the number of people in the empire grew, the Aztec required more land to grow crops and more tribute to support the expanding government. To meet this demand for resources, they conquered more and more tribes.

The Aztec needed a well-trained army to keep expanding. At the calpulli schools, the boys learned ruthless fighting methods and became strong warriors. When the Aztec attacked a city, they killed warriors and townspeople alike. They plundered homes and captured victims for sacrifice.

Aztec warriors fought without fear of death. They believed their deaths would help keep the world going.

*I n the midst of the plain
my heart craves death
by the obsidian edge.
Only this my heart craves:
death in war.*

From an Aztec codex

Warriors also fought hard because the more captives they took, the higher their social rank would be. The ruthless tactics of the Aztec helped them build an empire. But like their ever-increasing demand for tribute, their cruelty led to deep resentment among subject tribes. Later, Spanish adventurers would use this resentment to their advantage. ■

R E V I E W

1. **FOCUS** What methods did the Aztec use to build their large empire?
2. **CONNECT** What did the Moche, the Tiwanakan, and the Aztec all have to overcome in order to farm?
3. **HISTORY** Why was the Triple Alliance important?
4. **CULTURE** What do the Aztec codices tell us about Aztec life?
5. **CRITICAL THINKING** Did the Aztec use the tribute system wisely? What changes would have improved the system?
6. **ACTIVITY** Study the codex pages shown on page 427 and on this page. Choose an aspect of everyday life in the United States and then draw your own codex page to describe it.

LESSON 2

The Inca

The young Inca and his fellow workers walked up to the next boulder to be moved. It was as tall as three men. Working side by side, the men wrapped a thick rope around the massive rock. At the leader's signal, they gripped the rope and began to pull. The young man grunted. His muscles strained and the palms of his hands burned. Sweat poured down his face. Slowly the boulder inched closer to the fortress. Finally, the leader signaled them to stop.

The man sat down to rest. He watched as other workers pounded and sculpted the boulder with big stone hammers. Then, with a mixture of sand and water, they all rubbed the rock until it was very smooth on four sides. When joined, the squared boulder would fit tightly with the others.

The Inca built the massive stone fortress of Sacsahuaman *(sak sa wah MAN)* during the 1400s. It was built just north of their capital city Cuzco in western South America. The fortress not only protected the Inca from their enemies but survived several powerful earthquakes. This is a remarkable fact, since the Inca used no mortar to join the boulders together. The fortress was one of the many technological achievements of the Inca, who conquered and ruled one of the largest empires in the Americas.

THINKING FOCUS

In what ways were the Inca a technologically advanced civilization?

Key Terms

- vertical economy
- terrace farming

▼ *Inca stonework was so finely made that a piece of paper cannot fit between two stones.*

Rising to Power

■ *What was the extent of the Inca Empire?*

▼ *The Inca Empire grew over about a 200-year period. Between what two geographic features did the empire develop?*

The Inca competed with other tribes for control of the fertile Cuzco Valley. By 1230, they controlled the area shown in red-violet on the map below.

The Cuzco Valley lies in the Central Andes, a land of very diverse terrain. Mountains surrounding the valley reach heights of more than 22,000 feet above sea level. Rivers cut deeply into these mountains as they plunge north toward the Amazon River. Bare, windblown plateaus lie above the tree line of the fertile valley.

Very little is known about the early history of the Inca. Unlike the Olmec and the Maya, the Inca had no writing system. Their history was passed down orally from one generation to the next by "official rememberers" called quipu camayocs. Because of this oral tradition, legend, myth, and fact overlapped in Inca history.

We do know that it was not until 1438 that the Inca began to gain dominance over the Cuzco Valley. The seventh ruler of the Incas, Pachacuti *(PAH chah koo tee),* whose name means "he who transforms," launched a sweeping campaign of conquest. First, the Inca armies took over the smaller states in and around the Cuzco Valley. Next, they marched into the Andes highlands and conquered other tribes there.

By 1525, the Inca Empire covered most of what is now Ecuador, large areas of modern-day Peru and Bolivia, and parts of modern-day Argentina and Chile. The map shows the greatest extent of the Inca Empire. How many miles did it extend from north to south?

The Inca called their powerful empire Tihuantinsuyu *(tee wahn teen SOO yoh),* or the "Land of the Four Quarters," because they believed they had conquered the entire world. At its height, the population of the Inca Empire reached about 13 million. ■

Expansion of the Inca Empire

Inca territory acquired by
- c. 1230
- c. 1400
- 1438–1463
- 1463–1471
- 1471–1493
- 1493–1525
- Inca road

0   200   400 mi.
0   200   400 km
Mercator Projection

Conquering and Controlling

How were the Inca able to conquer and control so many different peoples so far away from their capital? Superior organizational and administrative skills are a large part of the answer.

Conquering a Region

The Inca ruler first sent scouts to the region he wanted to take over. The scout judged the fertility of the region's land and the strength of its armies and defenses, and memorized its geography. Then the ruler and his military advisors devised a plan of attack based on the scout's report. Before attacking, though, the Inca ruler sent ambassadors to the enemy tribe to try to persuade them to join the empire peacefully. Usually, the tribes refused, and then the massive Inca armies attacked.

Once they conquered a region, the Inca made certain that it stayed under their control. They held both local religious idols and local princes hostage in Cuzco to discourage rebellion. The Inca also forced members of conquered tribes to join their army. The Inca offered rewards to new soldiers who proved successful in battle to ensure their loyalty. These rewards were taken from newly conquered areas.

The Inca stationed troops throughout their empire. If an uprising occurred far away from Cuzco, the Inca ruler could easily send a messenger to his army in that region to put it down. The rebellious people were then relocated closer to Cuzco or to another area where Inca rulers could keep a close eye on them. When tribes were peaceful, the Inca allowed the local rulers to stay in power. They also held feasts and festivals for loyal subject tribes.

The Inca also used other methods to maintain control of subject peoples. They made the Inca religion the official religion of the empire and they required all of their subjects to learn Quechua *(KEHCH wuh)*, their native language. This helped promote unity in the empire.

Organizing the People

Inca rulers totally controlled the lives of their peoples. The Inca believed that their ruler was lord of all things—the land, the animals, the water, and the people. Everything belonged to him. A rigid social structure helped the emperor exercise this control.

The Inca had two classes—the nobility and the commoners. Most of the people in the empire were commoners. They lived in cramped adobe huts and worked the land from sunrise to sunset. This work was their tribute to the government. The nobles lived off the tribute but also served as governors of Inca subject tribes, political advisers, and public administrators. Government administrators organized huge public projects. Those commoners not needed for farming had to pay tribute by helping with these projects.

One such project was a highway system that spanned the

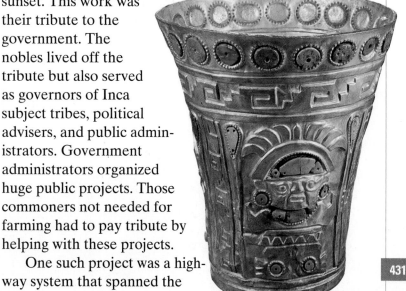

▲ *One of the first steps in organizing an area is to find out what exists there. The Inca used counting devices called quipus to keep track of everything from soldiers to food.*

▼ *Tribes conquered by the Inca generally had well-developed cultures of their own. This ceremonial cup was created by the Chimu people of northwest Peru.*

431

Across Time & Space

The Inca built many rope bridges that spanned steep-cliffed canyons and crossed over fast-flowing rivers. Today, many Inca descendants still rely on rope bridges. They often spin as much as 20,000 to 30,000 feet of rope from grass to build or repair their bridges.

■ *What methods did the Inca use to control their empire?*

▼ *The llama was very important to the Inca. Its wool, shown here, was spun into thread, which was used to make beautiful fabrics like the weaving below. These fabrics were used by all levels of society.*

length of the empire. Roads were built in the highlands and along the coast. When necessary, the roads included tunnels, causeways, and stone or even rope bridges. Built to quickly move the Inca army, the highways also helped transport crops and other goods throughout the empire. Scholars estimate that the Inca built nearly 10,000 miles of roads.

Under Inca rule, the commoners had few individual freedoms. They weren't allowed to travel without government approval. The government also decided when and whom they married. Marriage was encouraged, because only married couples were assigned plots of land

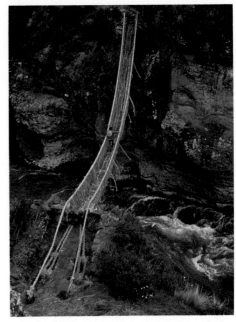

from which goods for tribute could be raised. ■

Working the Land

Though they enjoyed little freedom, Inca subjects rarely went hungry. The Inca's clever farming techniques allowed them to make full use of their varied lands. In addition, their strong organizational skills made them efficient producers and distributors of food.

Once the Inca conquered a region, they took total control of the land. They sent administrators, who were members of the nobility, to evaluate the geographic resources of the region. Then they divided the region's farmland into three parts. The commoners harvested one part of the farmland for government workers, one part to support Inca religious leaders, and one part for themselves.

The farmland varied greatly from region to region because the Inca Empire lay in and around the Andes. Some valleys lie as high as 8,000 feet above sea level. Others are only a few hundred feet above sea level.

Because soil, temperature, and other conditions change as altitude increases, only certain crops could be grown in

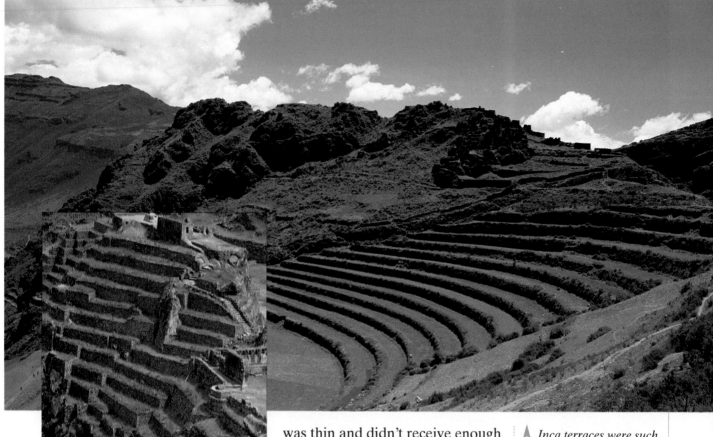

Inca terraces were such an effective farming technique that they are still used in modern-day Peru.

certain areas. In the low valleys, farmers grew maize (corn), beans, and squash. In the mountains, they raised llamas and alpacas for wool and meat. This growing of crops according to the height of the land is called a **vertical economy.**

The Inca were able to grow surplus amounts of food by using very productive farming techniques. One of these techniques was **terrace farming.** The soil on the mountain slopes in the highlands was thin and didn't receive enough rainfall. The Inca carried topsoil and gravel from the more fertile lowlands to the hillsides. There, they packed it into narrow farming terraces like the ones pictured above. To protect against drought, the Inca constructed elaborate canal systems for irrigation.

The government built huge warehouses to store surplus food in case of emergencies such as crop failure or war. The quipu recorded how much food was stored and where it was stored. Because the government distributed food and goods to the people, free trade and huge markets like those the Aztec enjoyed did not exist in the Inca Empire. ■

■ *Why was Inca agriculture so productive?*

Praying to the Ancestors

Not all of the commoners worked to produce food for the empire. Some commoners helped to build massive cities. To learn more about an Inca city, see A Closer Look on page 434.

Other commoners paid their tribute by making pieces of art and

Two American Empires

Machu Picchu

Almost touching the clouds, the Inca city of Machu Picchu sits one and a half miles high on a mountaintop in Peru. Forgotten for hundreds of years, Machu Picchu was rediscovered in 1911 by explorer Hiram Bingham, who wrote: "It fairly took my breath away."

Clearing away the vines covering the city, Bingham searched for clues to its inhabitants. He made drawings of objects he found, like this knife with its little man pulling a fish on a rope.

Bingham thought that Machu Picchu must have been a special religious city because of the fine stonework. Archaeologists now think it may have been a kind of vacation resort for Inca nobles.

Climbing stairs was a way of life for the people who lived here. Over 3,000 steps connect the levels of the city and the farming terraces. Machu Picchu could only be reached by a log bridge on a sheer cliff. If enemies threatened, citizens could simply draw back the bridge.

Many mysteries about Machu Picchu remain. When, exactly, did people live here? Why were more women buried here than men? Historians still study Bingham's discoveries, like this jar which may have held a corn drink, to try to find answers.

jewelry from precious metals. Many of these precious works of art were placed in the palaces of dead rulers as well as the temples of the gods. In order to assure that their crops would grow, the Inca prayed to both gods and ancestors. They believed that there was life after death, and that dead rulers and nobility played a role in deciding the fate of the empire.

When an Inca ruler died, the Inca mummified, or preserved, his body. His relatives looked after his palace and estate. They believed the mummy's spirit would harm them if they didn't. The Inca believed mummies spoke to the living and to each other through priests. Mummies were brought out of their palaces for important ceremonies held during the harvest and planting seasons. A Spanish chronicler in the 1500s witnessed one of these ceremonies.

*T*hey sat them [the royal mummies] all down in a row, in order of seniority, and the servants who looked after them ate and drank there. . . . In the fire they burned the food they had set before the mummies to eat; it was the same meal that [the family] themselves ate.

Inti, the god of the Sun, was the most important god of the Inca state. In all major cities of the empire, the Inca built temples for Inti, whom they portrayed as a golden disk with a human face. The Inca made animal or special food sacrifices to their gods. Only in times of crisis, such as flood or famine, did the Inca sacrifice humans.

Priests performed these sacrifices. In fact, priests played a large role in Inca everyday life. In Cuzco, the priests began each day with prayers, offerings to the gods, and predictions of the future. They predicted the future by "reading" the remains of animal sacrifices or flames in a fire. No matter how small the issue, Inca rulers often based their decisions on predictions of the priests.

The Inca were optimistic about the world and their place in it. They believed that, under the rule of their divine king, their empire would continue into eternity. The arrival of the Spanish, however, would prove them wrong. ■

▲ *Fine gold jewelry, like this necklace, was placed in the palaces of dead rulers. Inca children were often buried with dolls like the one below.*

■ *Why were mummies important to the Inca?*

R E V I E W

1. **FOCUS** In what ways were the Inca a technologically advanced civilization?
2. **CONNECT** How did the Inca method of conquering other tribes differ from the Aztec method?
3. **GEOGRAPHY** How did altitude and terrain affect Inca agriculture?
4. **SOCIAL SYSTEMS** What was everyday life like for the common people who lived in the Inca Empire?
5. **CRITICAL THINKING** Why do you think the Inca worshiped their ancestors?
6. **ACTIVITY** Choose a city that you feel best illustrates life in the United States. Make A Closer Look for the city you chose using photographs from magazines.

Analyzing Elevation

Here's Why

You already know about topography, the natural surface features of the land. If you plan a bicycle route to avoid hills or to go around a lake, you are considering topography.

Studying topography doesn't only provide information about possible routes. Topography can also help you explore cultures and history. For example, you can learn about the Inca culture by analyzing the elevation of the Inca Road.

Here's How

Suppose you want to go from Lima to Jauja on the Inca Road. The map below uses color to show different ranges in elevation, or height above sea level.

Elevation is part of the topography of a region. The key beside the map shows the elevations represented by each color.

From Lima, you travel south for about 35 miles. The elevation during this portion of your trip is low and unchanging.

Now you turn to the east, toward Huarochiri. In the 45 miles to Huarochiri, you climb first to an elevation of over 5,000 feet and then to over 10,000 feet. This is higher than Mount St. Helens in Washington.

In Huarochiri, you continue east and soon reach an elevation of over 15,000 feet. This is higher than Mount Whitney in California.

As you leave Huarochiri, the elevation drops to the 10,000-foot range. In the 50 miles between Huarochiri and Jauja, you are never below 10,000 feet and are often as high as 15,000 feet.

Try It

Suppose you wanted to travel from Nazca to Cuzco, going through Andahuaylas, on the Inca Road. Use the map to trace your route. Use the vertical profile to describe the topography that you would encounter.

Apply It

Locate a topographic map of your state in an atlas. Use the map to describe a bicycle or hiking route between two areas that show either a very great or very small change in elevation over 50 miles.

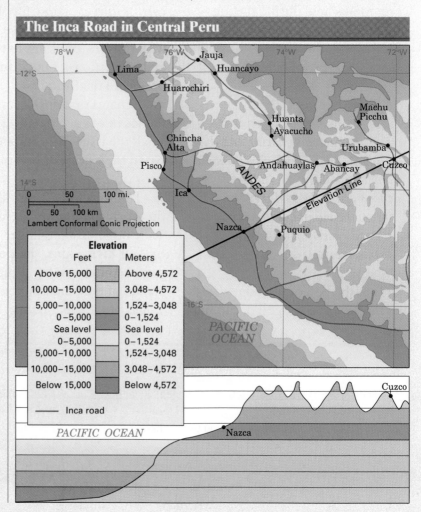

The Inca Road in Central Peru

Elevation		
Feet		Meters
Above 15,000		Above 4,572
10,000–15,000		3,048–4,572
5,000–10,000		1,524–3,048
0–5,000		0–1,524
Sea level		Sea level
0–5,000		0–1,524
5,000–10,000		1,524–3,048
10,000–15,000		3,048–4,572
Below 15,000		Below 4,572
——— Inca road		

LESSON 3

The Arrival of the Spanish

THINKING FOCUS

Why were the Spanish able to take over the Aztec and Inca empires so quickly?

Key Terms

- conquistador
- civil war

▲ *This drawing from a codex shows the Aztec view of the arrival of the Spanish.*

A thing like a ball of stone flies out of their bellies and flashes sparks and rains fire. . . . If the ball hits a tree, it blows away in splinters, as though a magician had blown it away from inside. Their battle dress and their arms are all made of iron. . . . They are carried on the backs of stags wherever they like to go. Their skin is white, as though made of chalk. . . . Their dogs are great monsters with flat ears and long tongues which hang out."

An eyewitness account of
the Spanish arrival, as told to
Bernardo de Sahagun, 1528

Hernando Cortés, the Spanish **conquistador,** or conqueror, landed on the shores of central Mexico in April 1519, seeking adventure and wealth. With him were over 550 men, 16 horses, 14 cannons, and a few dogs. He was greeted by messengers of the Aztec ruler Moctezuma. Wanting to show the Aztec his power, Cortés had the ships' cannons fired. The Aztec were stunned. They rushed back and reported to Moctezuma.

This was the first time the Aztec had seen cannons or horses or men with white skin. According to Sahagun's account, which was based on reports by Aztec who had been with Moctezuma: "When Moctezuma heard this report, he was seized with fright. His heart grew weak to the point of faintness. . . . And despair overcame him."

437

The Empires Weaken

The Spanish appeared on American shores in the early 1500s. At that time, **civil war,** or fighting between parts of the empire, plagued both the Aztec and the Inca.

In the Aztec Empire, a number of subject tribes began to rebel against their harsh Aztec rulers. Led by the Tlaxcalans, these rebel tribes put up a bitter struggle. Infuriated, Moctezuma launched huge attacks against them.

Rebellion was so widespread that the Aztec were forced to fight in many areas at once. Because their armies were spread so thinly, they won few battles. Also, waging so many battles caused war costs to soar. There were few resources left for making new conquests.

Increasing war costs, decreasing tribute from new conquests, and a famine in 1505 prompted Moctezuma to demand more tribute from his subject states. This demand led to even more resentment and rebellion among subject tribes.

The Inca were also facing internal unrest when Spanish adventurers, led by Francisco Pizarro, arrived in 1532. When the Inca ruler died in 1525, his two sons, Huascar *(WAHS kahr)* and Atahualpa *(ah tah WAHL pah),* fought each other for the throne. The northern half of the empire supported Atahualpa, and the southern half supported Huascar. After three years of bloodshed, Atahualpa emerged as the ruler of a greatly weakened empire. ■

■ *How were the internal problems of the Aztec and Inca empires similar, and how did they contribute to their downfall?*

Old and New Worlds Clash

Because of internal division, the Aztec and Inca could not keep out the Spanish invaders. When the Spanish saw the wealth of the two American empires, they set out to conquer them.

Cortés Conquers the Aztec

When Moctezuma first learned of the Spanish arrival, he believed that Cortés might be Quetzalcoatl *(keht sahl koh AHTL),* an ancient god come to reclaim his earthly kingdom. He welcomed the strangers into Tenochtitlan, saying, "It appears that our Lord has returned to his country. Go hence and receive him worthily."

But he soon learned he had made a grave mistake. Within days, Cortés took Moctezuma hostage. Moctezuma ordered vast

How Do We Know?

HISTORY *Much of what historians know about the Aztec comes from Spanish translations of Aztec codices. The Spanish often added descriptive captions to explain what the hieroglyphs meant.*

➤ *This painting, called* Cortés Enters Mexico by the Street of San Antonio Abad, *was painted in 1698 by the Spanish artist Miguel Gonzalez. It is one in a series of five panels painted to record the Spanish conquest of Mexico.*

amounts of gold and silver brought to the palace. But the foreigners stayed. Moctezuma remained a prisoner. Many people blamed him for the Spanish takeover.

Some people blamed an Aztec slave girl named Doña Marina by the Spanish and called "La Malinche" *(lah mah LEEN chay)* by the Aztec. She translated the Aztec language, Nahuatl *(naw WAT uhl),* to Mayan. A shipwrecked Spaniard named Aguilar *(ah GWEE lar),* whom Cortés rescued, then translated from Mayan to Spanish. With La Malinche and Aguilar at his side, Cortés was able to negotiate with the Aztec. In modern Mexican vocabulary, a *malinchista (mah leen CHEES tah)* is someone who betrays one's country or friends.

Six months later, one of Cortés' deputies massacred thousands of Aztec people, triggering a rebellion. Moctezuma died in the rebellion, but sources disagree as to who killed him—the Spanish, or his own people. After the rebellion the Aztec drove the Spanish out.

The remaining Spanish escaped to a Tlaxcalan camp. The Tlaxcalans hated the Aztec, so Cortés persuaded them to help him. Other tribes eagerly joined the army.

In May 1521, with a huge army behind them, the Spanish laid siege to the Aztec capital. They blocked boat traffic and stranded the city without supplies. Then an epidemic broke out among the Aztec.

Finally, on August 13, 1521, with most of their warriors dead from disease, starvation, or war wounds, the Aztec gave up. Thousands of them were enslaved, but most fled to the countryside.

Pizarro Conquers the Inca

The Inca Empire ended similarly 11 years later when the Spanish conquistador Francisco Pizarro arrived. Leading about 150 men, Pizarro landed in Tumbes on the northern coast of the Inca Empire in early 1532. The Spanish assured Inca messengers that they wished only to admire the empire. The Inca ruler Atahualpa then allowed the Spanish to advance as far as his military stronghold in Cajamarca.

Pizarro decided on a quick, brutal attack. He called for a meeting with Atahualpa, but waited safely behind and sent a Spanish monk in his place. The monk offered Atahualpa a Bible and told the chief to give up his beliefs. Outraged, Atahualpa threw the Bible to the ground, saying, "I will be no man's tributary. . . . As for my faith, I will not change it."

When the monk reported that the Inca chief could not be converted, Pizarro and his troops attacked, killing more than 5,000 Inca. Atahualpa was taken prisoner. The Inca gave Pizarro 24 tons of gold and silver as a ransom for Atahualpa, but he was not released. The Spanish later strangled him.

▲ *This image shows the Aztec view of the war against the Spanish invaders. Notice the difference in weapons and armor used by the Aztec and the Spanish.*

▼ *This standard was carried by Hernando Cortés on all his campaigns in the New World. Notice that the Madonna is the central image.*

Two American Empires

In February 1536, Manco Inca, the last heir to Huascar's throne, led an army estimated at 200,000 Inca to Cuzco. But the Inca siege soon failed because most supplies had been used up in the civil war. Manco Inca retreated with his army into the Andes. There they held out until 1572, when the Spanish finally defeated them. ■

Two Empires Destroyed

Scholars give many reasons for the rapid Spanish conquest of the Aztec and Inca empires. First and foremost, disease brought by the Europeans had a disastrous effect on the Aztec and Inca. Smallpox and measles, which the Aztec and Inca had never been exposed to, spread rapidly through their empires. Not only did disease drastically reduce their armies, it killed off many leaders, leaving the Aztec and Inca even more vulnerable.

Second, the Spanish took advantage of the weakened and rebellious state of the American empires. They used resentful subject tribes to guide them through unfamiliar territory and to help them win their battles. The Spanish turned on the subject tribes once their goals were achieved.

Third, the Spanish weapons were technologically superior. They fought with cannon and crossbow, as well as spears and swords made of iron. The Aztec, with bronze and copper shields, stone knives, and woven-cloth armor, were no match for them.

Finally, the Spanish and the Aztec came from drastically different cultures. They had different ways of living and believing. Moctezuma believed that Cortés might have been a god and allowed him to walk freely into the capital city. Cortés, on the other hand, saw the Aztec culture as something pagan to be destroyed and replaced by the Christian faith.

The two groups even fought by different rules. The Aztec usually

➤ *These portraits at right and above show the Spanish conquistador Francisco Pizarro, who conquered the Inca empire, and the last Inca ruler, Atahualpa. The Inca used rope slings, similar to those above, as weapons against the Spanish invaders.*

fought only to take captives for sacrifice. The Spanish, however, fought to kill.

The Spanish conquest devastated the Aztec and Inca populations. Spanish nobles took over the land and forced the Aztec and Inca into slavery. As slaves, they labored on farms and in silver mines. In some areas more than 90 percent of the population died as the result of the Spanish takeover. The chart on this page shows the population decline among the Aztec and the Inca after the arrival of the Spanish.

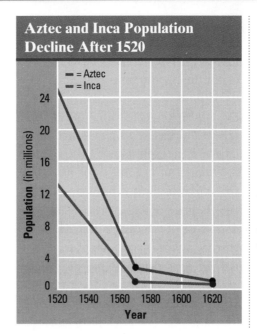

Aztec and Inca Population Decline After 1520

◄ *Note the dramatic drop in both the Aztec and Inca populations after the Spanish arrived.*

UNDERSTANDING EPIDEMICS

It attacked people, beat them down all over the city and killed enormous numbers. Those afflicted lay about helpless, like corpses on their beds. . . . If they tried to move they cried out in pain." A Spanish chronicler describes the effects of a smallpox epidemic that killed millions of Aztec and Inca in the 1500s. An epidemic is a highly contagious disease that infects many people at the same time. Because of the numbers they affect, epidemics disrupt societies and help shape history.

The Spanish had built up immunity, or resistance, to diseases like the measles and smallpox. Native Americans had no immunity to the diseases, which devastated their peoples.

Epidemics in History

Major epidemics have had significant impact on other civilizations. An outbreak of the bubonic plague, or Black Death, swept through Europe in the 1300s. Nearly half the population of Europe died. Due to the plague, life in both cities and the countryside was hard hit. Trade and production slowed, and governments found it difficult to raise money.

Epidemics Now

Epidemics still occur today. In late 1997, over 1.6 million people in the world were living with Acquired Immune Deficiency Syndrome, or AIDS. Researchers are looking for a cure, but experts predict that by the end of the year 2000, over 60 million adults will have been infected with HIV (the virus that causes AIDS). No one knows what the full impact of the epidemic will be in this country, but in some parts of Africa, entire villages have been wiped out.

In general, epidemics are much rarer today. Medicines now exist that prevent the diseases that devastated the Aztec and the Inca. But the discovery of such drugs came too late to prevent epidemics from playing a role in the conquest of the New World.

441

The Aztec and Inca, however, responded differently to the invaders. The capture of Tenochtitlan meant the end of Aztec civilization, because the city had been the center of Aztec life. When it fell, they ceased all resistance and allowed the Spanish to take over their land and people.

An anonymous poet described the feelings of the Aztec just after the Spanish conquest in 1521:

> There is nothing but grief and suffering
> in Mexico and Tlatelolco,
> where once we saw beauty and valour.
> Have you grown weary of your servants?
> Are you angry with your servants, O Giver of Life?

The Inca, on the other hand, did not give up after their capital city was conquered. Resistance to Spanish rule continued for 40 years. Some scholars believe this is because the Inca rulers took much better care of their subject tribes. They provided their subjects with both food and land. By spreading their culture, religion, and language throughout their empire, the Inca bonded their subjects together.

The Spanish destroyed temples, artwork, and anything else that represented Inca culture. But Inca traditions survived. Today, some 20 million Inca descendants still speak Quechua, celebrate ancient religious ceremonies, and farm in small villages. The Inca people below live much as their ancestors did. ■

■ *Which of the following contributed most significantly to the defeat of the Aztec and Inca empires: disease, civil war, cultural differences, or Spanish military strength? Defend your answer.*

➤ *Both the Aztec and the Inca continued to exist after the Spanish conquest. The people in the near photo are descendants of the Aztec. Those to the far right are descendents of the Inca.*

R E V I E W

1. **FOCUS** Why were the Spanish able to take over the Aztec and Inca empires so quickly?
2. **CONNECT** Why did civil wars occur in the Aztec and Inca empires?
3. **HISTORY** Spaniards wrote most accounts of the conquest. Why do you think it would be hard for historians to reconstruct the truth about what happened?
4. **CRITICAL THINKING** Do you think the defeat of the Aztec and Inca by the Spanish could have been prevented? Explain.
5. **WRITING ACTIVITY** Write a news broadcast describing either the arrival of Cortés in the Aztec Empire or the arrival of Pizarro in the Inca Empire.

Chapter 16

Identifying Values

Here's Why

Do you sometimes wonder why people act as they do? If you can identify the values that underlie their actions, you may better understand those actions.

When the Aztec and the Spanish conquistadors first faced each other in 1519, they knew nothing about each other's values. As the painting below shows, the Aztec welcomed Cortés with gifts, as they would a returning hero or a god. Compare the weapons carried by the Aztec and by the Spanish soldiers. What does this suggest to you?

The reasons why the Spanish were able to conquer the Aztec within two years are complex: technical advantages of cannons and muskets over stone knives, political instability of the Aztec Empire, and a disastrous outbreak of smallpox among the Aztec.

If the Aztec and the Spaniards had known more about each other's values, that might not have been enough to change the outcome of the battles. However, from your viewpoint, looking back into the past, you can see how their values influenced their actions.

Here's How

Turn to page 440 and read the section Two Empires Destroyed. Identify statements that refer to values of the Spanish and the Aztec. Explain the differences in values and how these might have affected their actions. For example, look now at the statement,

"The two groups even fought by different rules." The Aztec valued the taking of captives in battle; the Spanish did not. Therefore, the Spaniards who were captured frequently escaped and could fight again. Because of the differences in values, the Aztec were more likely to die on the battlefield.

Try It

Use the text on pages 431, 432, and 442 to identify values of the Inca. List those you think affected the Inca's responses to the Spaniards.

Apply It

Write down the values you and your classmates hold in common on these topics: air pollution, environmental waste, diet, clothes, exercise. Compare your list with others'.

The Legend of the Lake

Retold by Douglas Gifford

Although the Conquistadors destroyed much of the Aztec and Inca civilizations, the people live on. Sometimes that living is more in memory than in reality, as in this Inca legend.

Lake Titicaca, the largest freshwater lake in South America, lies nearly 4,000 meters up on the Altiplano. There it straddles the border between Bolivia and Peru. To the Inca, the lake was a holy place. According to legend, it was there that the children of the Sun first descended to earth. This story, set in a region where earthquakes are still a common occurrence, tells how the lake first came into being.

Long ago in the high plains lay a vast, rich city built by a proud and arrogant people. They were so pleased with their city and so satisfied with their progress that they would never admit that any improvement was possible. "We are the lords of all creation," they said loftily, "and all people must obey us. There is no city like ours in all the world."

One day a group of ragged Indians arrived in the city. Although they looked poor, they soon began to attract attention to themselves by prophesying that the city would be destroyed. "Prepare," they told the people, "for ruin will come by earthquake and flood and fire. The smell of death is on this city!"

"What nonsense," scoffed the city people. "Why don't you go away? We are the greatest of all people. Look at our buildings. There are none like them in the world. Look at our water system and irrigation. Where will you find any to equal them? We are a modern, progressive race: we know how to deal with floods and earthquakes. Go away with your old wives' tales."

The ragged band of Indians persisted in their warnings and eventually, tired of their nagging, depressing voices, the city people had them flogged and thrown out of the city. Only the priests were anxious.

"These were holy men," they said, "and who knows, they may be right. Perhaps they can see further than we can."

Some of the priests took the Indians' words so seriously that they, too, left the city and retired to their temple on the hill. There they lived as hermits, cutting themselves off from the city people completely.

"Look at them," mocked the city people. "What good do they think they are doing up there? All they can do is preach; they've never done an honest day's work in their lives. If anyone is doomed it is they. That hill is the very place for lightning to strike. How we'll laugh when that happens."

Then, one peaceful afternoon, one of the city people saw a small red cloud on the horizon. At first he could not tell whether it was a real cloud or just a puff of smoke from a burning house but it grew larger and larger. Soon it was obvious that it was a real cloud and that there were others massing together with it, red clouds and dark clouds the color of lead. When night came there was no darkness, for the sky and the earth below were lit up by a glaring red light from the clouds. An eerie silence hung over the whole land.

Suddenly, there was a flash and a rumble, then an ear-splitting crash as the earth jolted violently. Many of the buildings stood firm, for they had been well constructed of stone but almost immediately a red rain started to pour from the clouds and the earth shook again, more violently even than before. Building after building crashed to the ground and the red rain grew to a continual cloudburst. The carefully constructed water and irrigation systems were completely destroyed; mountain rivers were jolted from their courses and a great flood rose over the buildings of the city.

Today the great Lake of Titicaca covers the proud city. Not one of its mocking inhabitants survived and it is said that some died with their unbelieving smiles still on their faces. Only the priests in their humble straw huts were saved. Their temple on the hill stood firm against the earthquake and the hill itself rose above the flood waters. Today it is the Island of the Sun.

The ragged prophets, too, survived for they watched sadly from a high place as the waters rose and the city was destroyed. Some of their descendants became the Callawayas, the wise men of the valleys by the Altiplano, travelling doctors and healers famous for their skills.

Further Reading

The Captive. Scott O'Dell. A young seminary student joins a Spanish expedition to the New World. He joins the Maya and assumes the identity of a Mayan god.

The Feathered Serpent. Scott O'Dell. This book continues the chronicle begun in *The Captive*.

Temple of the Sun. Evelyn Lampman. This is a story of how the Aztec Indians tried to resist being conquered by Cortés.

Warriors, Gods and Spirits from Central and South American Mythology. Retold by Douglas Gifford. A collection of stories about Central and South American peoples.

Chapter Review

Reviewing Key Terms

alliance (p. 424) conquistador (p. 437)
calpulli (p. 425) terrace farming (p. 433)
chinampa (p. 423) tribute (p. 425)
civil war (p. 438) vertical economy (p. 433)

The following sentences contain clues to the key terms. On your own paper, write the key term each sentence suggests. Then use the key term in a different sentence.

1. Fighting between different parts of the empire was a problem for both the Aztec and the Inca empires.
2. Inca living at different altitudes grew products and raised livestock suited to different altitudes and conditions.
3. In the Aztec Empire, nobles lived off a kind of tax that could be paid to them in goods and services.
4. The Aztec converted swampy land to floating gardens.
5. Aztec families of different social ranks lived in each settlement.
6. Cortés and Pizarro were Spanish conquerors who conquered the Aztec and Inca.
7. To enlarge their empire, the Aztec formed a union with other tribes.
8. In order to grow crops at high altitudes, the Inca carried rich topsoil from low areas and packed it into flat-topped mounds of earth in the higher areas.

Exploring Concepts

A. Copy and complete the following outline using information from the chapter.

I. The Aztec
   A. Building an empire
   B. _____
   C. Fighting for the gods
II. The Inca
   A. Rising to power
      1. _____
      2. _____
   B. _____
   C. Working the land
   D. _____
III. The arrival of the Spanish
   A. _____
   B. Old and new worlds clash
   C. Two empires destroyed
      1. _____
      2. _____
      3. _____

B. Support each of the following statements with facts and details from the chapter.

1. Both the Aztec and the Inca used imaginative farming methods to grow crops.
2. Historians have a different way of learning about early Aztec history than they do about early Inca history.
3. The Inca Empire was larger than the Aztec Empire.
4. The Inca and Aztec behaved differently when they conquered other tribes.
5. The Inca used various methods for maintaining control over conquered tribes.
6. Everyday life differed for Inca nobility and commoners.
7. The Aztec and the Inca had different reasons for human sacrifice.
8. More social classes existed in the Aztec Empire than in the Inca Empire.
9. The Inca engaged in ancestor worship.
10. Conquistadors conquered the Aztec and the Inca for many of the same reasons.

Reviewing Skills

1. Refer to the map of the Inca Road on page 436. Use this map to trace a route from Chincha Alta to Andahuaylas. Then describe what this route is like as if you were telling a group of travelers what they can expect.
2. Study the overall network of roads shown on the map of the Inca Road. In general, do you think it is easier to travel east-west or north-south on the Inca Road? Explain your answer.
3. Find the heading Rising to Power on page 424. Reread this part of the chapter and explain what values the Aztec seem to have learned from neighboring tribes.
4. Tell how each of these sections of Lesson 1 helps to identify the moral values of the Aztec people:
   Social Classes—pages 425 and 426
   Human Sacrifices—pages 427 and 428
   War and Religion—page 428
5. How were different attitudes toward conquered peoples in the Aztec and Inca empires shown?
6. Before the arrival of the Spanish in the Inca Empire in 1532, the Inca were confident that their empire would continue on into eternity. Form a hypothesis to explain this belief. Be sure to give evidence from the chapter to support your hypothesis.
7. If you were planning a trip from one side of the Andes to the other and you wanted to see where mountain peaks and valleys were located, what kind of map would you use?

Using Critical Thinking

1. Both the Aztec and Inca solved the major problem of feeding their people in spite of poor farming conditions. Modern farmers have also had to solve problems to grow crops. For example, the dry climate in the American Southwest presented problems, so farmers developed ways to irrigate crops. How does this solution compare to that of the Aztec and Inca?
2. The Aztec government allowed only certain goods to be sold in each market. There might have been one market for feathers and jewels and another market for slaves. Evaluate how this system might affect store owners and shoppers today in your community if all the shoe stores were in one area, sporting goods stores in another area, bookstores in still another, and so on.

Preparing for Citizenship

1. **WRITING ACTIVITY** Write a report in which you compare the way the Inca emperors ruled with the way our leaders govern today. For example, how would each type of leader accomplish large building projects such as the construction of roads, sewage treatment plants, or large public monuments?
2. **COLLABORATIVE LEARNING** The Aztec created beautiful hieroglyphic books called codices that told about various aspects of Aztec life. Create a codex to tell about life in your school. As a class, decide which aspects to include, such as school sports, the art department, the choir or chorus, the band or orchestra, the school newspaper, and various clubs such as language clubs. Then break into small groups to cover each aspect. Each group should decide what each member will contribute. One might research the various school departments for ideas about what to draw; another might draw the hieroglyphs; another might write translations of the hieroglyphs. All the codices can then be bound into a book for the whole class to use.

447

Unit 8
Europe: 1600-1789

The 1600s and 1700s were the Age of Monarchs, when powerful kings ruled Europe. Witness the splendor of Louis XIV's magnificent palace at Versailles, France, shown on these pages. But power and splendor would bring their own destruction. How long would subjects pay the high taxes needed to support a lavish royal court? New ideas began to spread. A government that does not serve its people must be overthrown, one writer insisted. In the late 1700s, such ideas began coming to life.

1600

Versailles, by Pierre Patel, 1668

1789

Chapter 17

European Rule and Expansion

"*I have loved war too much,*" *confessed King Louis XIV of France. The period after the Reformation was a stormy time in Europe. Catholics and Protestants fought for their beliefs. Kings plotted against their enemies. Nations battled for land. Meanwhile, European explorers tested uncharted waters and claimed new lands. In time, the Europeans carried their disputes across the ocean to the New World.*

During the 1500s, Spanish officials in the Americas forced Indians to work on farms and in mines. This emerald-studded cross was made of gold mined in the Americas.

1498 Portuguese explorers make Goa, a port in India, a center for trade and Catholic missionaries. This painting shows St. Francis Xavier sailing into Goa in 1542.

1400	1475	1550

1505 Portuguese ships attack key African ports and try to control East African trade.

1400

King Charles I of England, shown with Queen Henrietta, lost a power struggle with Parliament. He was beheaded for treason in 1649.

In the 1700s, the kings of France held grand parties at the palace in Versailles. Women dressed in the latest fashions, such as this silk and lace gown from about 1770.

1661–1715 King Louis XIV outlaws the Protestant faith and wages war against England and Spain. This portrait of the king was painted on the lid of a snuffbox.

1625

1700

1775

1635 The Japanese shogunate bans European trade.

1763

L E S S O N   1

The French Monarchy

Key Terms

- prime minister
- absolute monarch
- divine right

➤ *All three of Catherine's sons became kings of France. Catherine was the mother and unofficial adviser of Francis II, Charles IX, and Henry III.*

Within weeks after the wedding, it became known as the "scarlet nuptials," because of the amount of blood that had been spilled. But at first it had seemed like a chance to unite French Catholics and Protestants.

In 1572, Henry, King of Navarre, arrived in Paris to marry Marguerite, the sister of the Catholic king of France, Charles IX. Henry was a leader of the French Huguenots *(HYOO guh nahts),* or French Protestants, a small but fast-growing group that some Catholics feared would eventually control the government.

One person who had much to lose if the Huguenots gained power in France was Catherine de Medici, the mother of the bride. But Catherine was also the niece of the Pope, the widow of the French king, Henry II, and the mother and adviser of King Charles IX. She pressured her son to have one of the Huguenot leaders killed so that the others would flee Paris.

King Charles submitted to the pressure and ordered a few of his nobles to commit murder. When the plot failed, Charles's nobles spread rumors that Huguenots were seeking revenge against all Catholics.

The following morning, St. Bartholomew's Day, Catholics who

were convinced the Huguenots were about to kill them murdered hundreds of Huguenots in their beds. The Huguenots fought back, but in one month's time 20,000 Huguenots died. Henry, the new husband of the king's sister, was spared on the condition that he renounce his Protestant faith and become a Catholic.

Religious Wars Divide France

Since the Reformation began in 1517, Christians had a choice of being Protestant or Catholic. Making the choice often involved serious consequences, even death.

After convincing his French in-laws that his conversion to Catholicism was sincere, Henry returned to Navarre in 1576. There he resumed his leadership of the Huguenots and his membership in the Protestant church.

In 1589, Charles IX's brother, King Henry III of France, was dying without a direct descendant. The dying king named his sister's husband as his successor. Henry of Navarre became King Henry IV of France.

Henry's Second Conversion

But Catholics refused to allow a Protestant to rule France. So Henry took religious instruction, converted to Catholicism, and was crowned at Chartres Cathedral.

Both Catholics and Huguenots claimed Henry had given up his faith for political gain. But Henry replied, "I wish to give peace to my subjects, and rest to my soul."

The Edict of Nantes

In 1598, Henry met with Protestant leaders in Nantes (*nants*), France. Together they created a document known as an edict, or order, that gave Protestants the same civil rights as Catholics:

> *A nd we permit those of the so-called Reformed religion to live and dwell in all the towns and districts of this our kingdom and the countries under our rule, without being annoyed, disturbed, molested.*
>
> Edict of Nantes, 1598

In 1610, a religious fanatic who did not agree with the edict assassinated Henry IV. ■

▲ *The Edict of Nantes allowed Protestants such as the Huguenots of Lyon to build a church and worship openly.*

■ *Why did Henry IV issue the Edict of Nantes?*

Cardinal Richelieu Builds the Monarchy

At the time of Henry IV's death, his son, Louis XIII, was only nine years old. Louis XIII depended upon a council of advisers. By 1624, the king's chief adviser, or **prime minister,** was a cardinal named Richelieu *(RISH uh loo).*

From 1624 to 1642 he ruled France for Louis XIII.

Gaining Power for the King

Richelieu was both a cardinal of the Catholic church and a brilliant politician. His goals were to

European Rule and Expansion

▲ *These three views of Richelieu were painted as a study in preparation for a sculpture of him.*

■ *Why did Richelieu want to limit the nobles' power?*

make the king the undisputed ruler of France and to increase the power of France in Europe.

Richelieu did not want the nobility to share the king's power. In 1626, he ordered the army to destroy the nobles' castles, except those border and coastal castles needed for defense against invasion. He felt that their castles gave the nobility too strong a power base.

Richelieu thought that the Huguenots also threatened the king's power. He personally led the French troops in taking the Huguenots' weapons. But he allowed the Huguenots to keep their freedom of worship.

Waging War on Spain

In the 1630s, Richelieu turned his attention to the Thirty Years War, involving France in this conflict. This war had started in 1618 as a religious dispute between the Catholic and Protestant nations of Europe. By the 1630s, it had become a political battle to obtain land.

Richelieu commanded the French Catholic forces to fight the Spanish Catholic forces. Since Spain and its territories in the Netherlands nearly surrounded France, Richelieu was worried about the possibility of Spain invading France. He was also anxious to increase French landholdings. Although France acquired more land through these battles, Richelieu had to triple taxes between 1635 and 1638 to finance the war. ■

Louis XIV Reigns Supreme

▲ *A Huguenot cartoon shows King Louis XIV, the "Sun King," as the "Sun Avenger" out to bring death to all Protestants.*

When Louis XIII died at age 42 in 1643, his son, Louis XIV, was only 4 years old. For 18 years, he was advised by Cardinal Mazarin, who had succeeded Richelieu as prime minister. When Cardinal Mazarin died in 1661, Louis—then 22 years old—announced that he would rule without a prime minister, although he would have advisers.

Louis was an **absolute monarch,** an all-powerful king. For the next 54 years, he devoted himself to his task eight hours a day (and often longer), controlling everything from court etiquette to troop movements. He described the position of monarch in a letter to his son:

I n a well-run state, all eyes are fixed upon the monarch alone. . . . Nothing is undertaken, nothing is expected, nothing is done except through him alone.

Louis XIV stated the theory that he ruled by **divine right,** that his power came from God and he was responsible only to God. Louis XIV's great power earned him the title "the Sun King."

Nobles and Huguenots

The nobility of France could have challenged Louis's power. But in 1661, Louis began to build a new palace near Paris. Find out about Louis's life at Versailles (*vuhr SY*) by studying A Closer Look on the next page.

Morning at Versailles

All France revolved around the palace at Versailles, and life at Versailles revolved around King Louis XIV. Every morning a crowd of nobles gathered anxiously outside the king's bedroom. Inside, the ceremonial "Rising of the King" was beginning.

If the king woke up in a bad mood, the news spread throughout the palace in minutes.

The best time to ask the king a favor was early in the morning.

At about 7:45, royal fire starters and the royal watch winder entered the bedroom. They were followed by the royal wig maker, who brought the king's early-morning wig from the royal wig room.

At 8:00, when the clock rang, the valet approached the king, who pretended to still be asleep and officially woke him. Then the two top doctors entered with Louis's childhood nursemaid, who gave him a kiss.

At 8:15, the most privileged nobles and priests entered to watch Louis get dressed. To be in this group was the highest honor at Versailles. Whoever was the king's favorite noble at the time got to hand the king his shirt.

This chest held the king's clothes for the day

Dette Nationale

Le temps present veut que chacun supporte le Grand Fardeau &c.

➤ *This print, made in 1789, the year of the French Revolution, calls for everyone (from left to right), the peasants, the clergy, and the nobility, to share in the great burden of taxes.*

Louis invited many nobles to come live with him in his palace at Versailles. There he could keep the nobles under watch while entertaining them with frequent banquets and festivals.

The other challenge to Louis's power might have come from the Huguenots. For in 1685, he abolished the Edict of Nantes. Since Louis was convinced he ruled by God's authority, he believed that his first duty as ruler was to uphold the Catholic faith. Therefore, he made it illegal to be Protestant in France. Nearly 200,000 Huguenots moved to other countries.

Peasants

Louis wanted to make France the greatest military power in Europe. Thus, he increased taxes to finance wars against England and Spain.

Peasant farmers had the most difficulty paying taxes, since they also paid rents to their landlords for use of the land they farmed. The peasants lived in fear of bad harvests that would limit their produce and leave little money for taxes. Many of the peasants' noble landlords lived at Versailles with the king and were out of touch with the peasants.

By 1715, at the end of Louis XIV's 72-year reign, wars had killed many Frenchmen and the government was bankrupt. On his deathbed, Louis XIV confessed, "I have loved war too much." ■

■ *In what ways did Louis XIV govern as an absolute monarch?*

R E V I E W

1. **FOCUS** What part did religion play in French history?
2. **CONNECT** In what ways were Louis XIV's idea of divine right and the beliefs of the Incas about their ruler alike?
3. **POLITICAL SYSTEMS** How did Cardinal Richelieu increase the power of the monarch?
4. **HISTORY** Compare the ways in which Louis XIII and Louis XIV ruled France.
5. **CRITICAL THINKING** Was building the palace at Versailles an appropriate use for the tax money that Louis XIV collected from the people? Why?
6. **WRITING ACTIVITY** Look at the political cartoon on this page. Write a paragraph describing your impressions of the situation in France in 1789.

Predicting Consequences

Here's Why

When you read a mystery novel, you constantly think about what will happen next. The same thing can happen when you read history. When you read about Henry of Navarre as you did in Lesson 1, you wonder what will happen next. The French Catholics resist Henry, and you wonder who will win.

Knowing the result of one struggle can help you predict what might happen in a similar struggle later. Could you have predicted what Henry would do to become king of France?

Here's How

To predict consequences accurately, follow these steps:

1. **Review the facts stated.** In Lesson 1, you read that Henry of Navarre first converted to Catholicism to save his life after the St. Bartholomew's Day Massacre. Then he became a Huguenot again. You also learned that only a Catholic could rule France and that Henry was next in line to become king.

2. **Add other knowledge and experience.** This information may come from your own experience or from something you have read. As you know, Catholics and Protestants behaved violently toward each other at this time. The engraving below of Henry's assassination several years later helps illustrate the depth of religious feeling. Notice the assassin climbing up on the wheel to attack Henry.

3. **Make a prediction.** Use what you know and your additional knowledge to decide what you think will happen. Henry had previously converted to Catholicism for political reasons, so you can predict that Henry might do the same thing again.

4. **Check for accuracy.** You can check your prediction by further reading.

Predicting Consequences

1. Review the facts stated.
2. Add other knowledge and experience.
3. Make a prediction.
4. Check for accuracy.

Try It

Read the first sentence in the Huguenots and Nobles section of Lesson 1. Follow the first three steps in Here's How to predict a possible consequence after Louis XIV revoked the Edict of Nantes. After you finish reading the section, write a statement analyzing the accuracy of your prediction.

Apply It

Write a sentence predicting how your classmates might respond to each of these situations. Use the four steps to make each prediction.

1. You and a friend enter the same essay contest and you win first place.
2. The administration decides to cancel the end-of-the-year school party because too many students have not turned in their missing assignments.

LESSON 2

The English Monarchy

THINKING FOCUS

What events led to Parliament's becoming a major power in the English government?

Key Terms

- Parliament
- commonwealth
- constitutional monarchy

"At last he laid down his head, stretched out his hands as the sign, and the executioner let drop the hatchet." This event in 1649, described in a book of memoirs by Sir Philip Warwick, had until then been thought impossible. The king of England, Charles I, had been tried and executed for betraying his own country.

The members of **Parliament,** an elected group of representatives, did not have any constitutional authority to sentence the king to death. However, backed by the soldiers nicknamed "Roundheads," they did have the military power to do so. The story of how the English Parliament became so powerful begins at least 100 years before the execution of the king.

▲ *By signing this blank piece of paper, Charles's son gave Parliament the freedom to set its own terms for sparing the king's life. But they beheaded the king instead.*

The Reign of Elizabeth I

The 45-year reign of Elizabeth, which began in 1558 when she was 25, is known as the Elizabethan Age. One of the subjects in Queen Elizabeth's kingdom was William Shakespeare. He wrote poetry and plays in an atmosphere that was open to literary creativity.

Elizabeth, the lords and ladies of her court, and the common people of London all responded enthusiastically to the very lively though sometimes violent works of Shakespeare. But he was only one of many who produced and dedicated works of literature to the queen.

The Church of England

When Elizabeth I became queen of England in 1558, she took over a kingdom divided by religion. Her half-sister Mary, an older daughter of Henry VIII, had ruled England before her. Mary, who was a Roman Catholic, opposed the way her father had broken away from the pope's Catholic church and started a separate English church. Mary tried to reimpose Catholicism on England. She put non-Catholics on trial for heresy and had some of them executed. Other Protestants fled, nicknaming the queen "Bloody Mary."

Elizabeth was the daughter of Henry VIII's second wife and had been raised a Protestant. When Elizabeth became queen, she made the Church of England the official state religion. It followed a middle ground between Catholicism and Calvinism. However, Elizabeth persecuted Catholics and tortured and executed a number of Catholic priests.

The Spanish Armada

In the 1580s Elizabeth decided to support the Dutch Protestants in their war against Spain. To put a stop to that, the Catholic ruler of Spain, Phillip II, decided to invade England with an armada, or armed fleet, of 130 warships.

The big Spanish ships, however, were slow. The English ships were faster and easier to maneuver. Also, English guns shot more rapidly.

The armada entered the English Channel between England and France on July 30, 1588. In the first few days, the English captured and destroyed only a few Spanish ships. Then on August 8, before dawn, the English set eight of their own unmanned ships on fire. A favorable wind carried the fire ships toward the Spanish fleet. Astonished, the Spanish cut anchor and sailed out to sea.

As the Spanish fled, the English pursued them and badly damaged the Spanish fleet. A violent storm finished off the armada.

▲ *Elizabeth I is painted in her coronation robe with crown, orb, and scepter. The orb is a globe of gold topped by a cross, signifying the rule of Jesus over the world.*

Even before the Magna Carta was accepted in 1215, monarchs summoned nobles to advise them in making laws. By the 1500s, this group, Parliament, had become a part of the English government.

Parliament was made up of two houses. Members of the House of Lords were titled members of the nobility who by birthright received an invitation to attend Parliament. The House of Commons was made up of landowners, merchants, and lawyers elected to serve in Parliament whenever the king called it into session. Parliament could disapprove taxes or laws that the monarch wanted. In addition, Parliament could suggest new laws. ■

▲ The Spanish used a crescent formation to fight the English at sea. But the English were victorious and made medals like this to remember their victory.

■ *What were some of Elizabeth's accomplishments as the queen of England?*

Only half of the original 130 ships made it home. Spain, which had been a sea power since the voyages of Columbus in the 1490s, ruled the seas no longer.

The Power of Parliament

Before Elizabeth could use any funds from the English treasury to fight the Spanish Armada, she needed approval from Parliament.

The English Civil War

Elizabeth I died in 1603 without an heir. The crown passed to her Protestant cousin James, who had ruled Scotland since 1583 as an absolute monarch. James wrote, "The state of monarchy is the supremest thing on earth."

Monarchs Oppose Parliament

James and Parliament quarreled when he wanted to raise taxes. They again argued when he wanted to arrange a marriage between his son, Charles, and a Catholic princess of France.

After Charles became king of England in 1625, he simply dismissed Parliament whenever it opposed him. He also persecuted the Puritans, who were another Protestant religious group that wanted simpler forms of worship than the Church of England had.

In 1628, Charles wanted to increase taxes for a war with Scotland to force them to belong to the Church of England. Before the Parliament would grant its consent to another tax increase, its members insisted that Charles approve the Petition of Right. This petition made it illegal for the king to imprison citizens, such as the Puritans, without cause. Desperate for money, Charles agreed to the Petition of Right. But the following year, he dismissed Parliament again when it refused to approve more war funds. For the next 11 years, Charles ruled alone and did not call Parliament.

In 1640, Charles needed money to fight the Scots, who were invading England. He was forced to accept Parliament's demands to get the money. By now, Puritan candidates had gained power in Parliament. They introduced laws to make the king call Parliament into session every three years.

In 1642, Charles made a final effort to assert his power. He ordered the arrest of five powerful members of the House of Commons. To defend itself, Parliament took control of the army. Charles fled north with his own army, and Parliament took over the central government. The clergy and most of the nobles, who benefited from Charles's religious policies and taxes, supported the king. Puritans and many merchants supported Parliament. Thus began the English Civil War.

Cromwell Leads Parliament

The war lasted seven years until Oliver Cromwell, a devout Puritan and a brilliant military leader, led Parliament's forces to victory. At the end of the war in 1649, Parliament put Charles on trial. They accused him of treason, charging "that by a tyrannical power he had endeavoured to overthrow the rights and liberties of this people." Charles claimed that, because he was king, no court had authority over him. Nevertheless, Parliament found him guilty and ordered him beheaded.

For the next four years, Cromwell and a Parliament dominated by Puritans ran the government. The leaders called the nation a **commonwealth,** because the government was a group working for the common good of all people.

However, in 1653, Cromwell was angered by the failure of Parliament to adopt proposed reforms. He responded by dismissing Parliament and abolishing the commonwealth. He then formed a new government, called the Protectorate, gave himself the title Lord Protector, and continued to rule England.

Cromwell ruled much like a military dictator. He imposed his Puritan values on England, limiting freedom of the press and enforcing strict moral standards. He

A memorial locket picturing Charles I contains a piece of linen stained with his blood.

prohibited gambling, horse racing, dancing on the village greens, fancy dress, and going to the theater. Because of such harsh policies, the public hated him as much as they ever hated Charles. However, Cromwell still controlled the military.

This is a portrait of Charles I in three poses. Studies of this type were usually done in preparation for a sculpture of the model.

461

1624–1649 Charles I

1649–1658 Oliver Cromwell

1658–1660 Richard Cromwell

1660–1685 Charles II

1625

1650

■ *Why did Charles I and Parliament quarrel?*

When Cromwell died in 1658, his son, Richard, attempted to run the country. But Richard did not have the leadership ability to manage the new government, and in 1659, Parliament took sole control of the government. By that time, the English were weary of political and religious conflict but were still in need of a leader. So in 1660, Parliament invited Charles, the son of the executed king, to return from exile in France to become King Charles II. ■

The Glorious Revolution

Historians call this return to monarchy the Restoration. It was not an absolute monarchy, however. When Charles II became king, the authority to govern was divided more equally between the monarch and Parliament.

A Period of Uncertainty

After what happened to his father, Charles II knew better than to try to force Parliament to do as he willed. He ruled England peaceably for 25 years. During his reign, many people rejected the Puritan ways that had dominated the country under Cromwell's rule. Parliament restored the Church of England as the state church and passed laws restricting the religious practices of Puritans, preventing them from assembling in groups of five or more persons.

After Charles II died in 1685, he was succeeded by his brother,

King James II. However, at the age of 25, James had converted to Catholicism. Many in England feared that he would try to make England Catholic again. He did appoint Catholics to public office, against Parliament's wishes. He also stationed soldiers near London to scare Parliament.

To many, it looked as if James was preparing to rule as an absolute monarch. However, the people were willing to put up with James, because they expected that eventually he would be succeeded by his Protestant daughter, Mary. Mary had been raised a Protestant by James's first wife. Then, in June 1688, James's second wife, a Catholic, had a son. Because males succeeded to the throne before females, the new heir to the throne would be Catholic.

Parliament was unwilling to govern in partnership with another

Across Time & Space

Today, about 75 percent of the French people are members of the Roman Catholic Church, and just 2 percent are Protestant. In England at present, 85 percent of the people are Protestant, and only 13 percent are Catholic.

1685–1688
James II

1702–1714 Anne

1700

1689–1702 William; 1689–1694 Mary

1714–1727 George I

1725

Catholic king.

A group of lords invited Mary, daughter of James II, whom they had originally hoped would become their monarch, to become the new queen. They also asked Mary's husband, the Protestant William of Orange, to be their king. William was the ruler of the Netherlands.

William arrived on English shores with an army of 14,000 soldiers and was welcomed by the English people. King James II, powerless, fled to France without putting up a fight. This became known as the Glorious Revolution because power changed hands without blood being shed.

A Constitutional Monarchy

Although William and Mary became joint rulers of England in 1689, they did so only after agreeing to accept Parliament's Bill of Rights. This document limited the power of the English monarch in a number of ways.

First, the monarch could appoint to public office only persons who were acceptable to a majority of Parliament. Second, the monarch could not keep an army in peacetime, nor could he suspend any laws without the consent of Parliament. Third, Parliament was required to hold regular meetings so that the king could never govern without Parliament. Finally, a Catholic could no longer become king of England.

With the passage of this Bill of Rights, Parliament finally had direct political power over the government of England, making England a **constitutional monarchy.** A constitutional monarchy is one in which the monarch's power is limited by law. ■

▲ King Louis XIV ruled France for 72 years. During that time England had nine leaders.

■ What was the Glorious Revolution, and why was it so named?

R E V I E W

1. **FOCUS** What events led to Parliament's becoming a major power in English government?

2. **CONNECT** How did the power of the English monarchs in the 1600s and early 1700s compare with the power of the French monarchs during the same period?

3. **HISTORY** Why did Parliament want William of Orange, rather than James II, to be king?

4. **CRITICAL THINKING** In what ways is a constitutional monarchy different from an absolute monarchy?

5. **WRITING ACTIVITY** Study the portrait of the young Queen Elizabeth I on page 459. Imagine you have just written a book of poems dedicated to the queen. Write a flattering description of the queen that could serve as an introduction to the book.

European Rule and Expansion

L E S S O N   3

European Expansion

Key Terms

- encomienda system
- mercantilism
- charter

➤ *This illustration shows how slave revolts were handled on board ship and suggests the extreme violence associated with slave trade.*

Shielding their eyes from the blazing African sun, the men from the Portuguese ship approached the chief of the tribe. After an exchange of greetings and some gifts, the ship's captain got down to business: Did the chief have any slaves to sell? Yes, there were slaves.

With a signal from the chief, guards brought the slaves forward, chained to each other at the wrists. The captain inspected them carefully to find the healthy ones, for only healthy ones would survive the trip back to Lisbon. Then he pointed to the ones he wanted, and the barter began. When the dealing was finished, weapons and trinkets were exchanged for human beings, and families were separated forever.

On board ship, the slaves had to lie on planks that were stacked between the decks. Each was in a space only two feet by five feet. They were allowed to walk around the deck once each day for exercise. They ate twice a day if there was enough food. Those who rebelled on the way were killed by being tossed overboard. One out of six died anyway from disease, spoiled food, or starvation.

Slave trade was only one part of a trading empire that linked the small country of Portugal to colonies in Africa, South America, India, and China. In the 1400s, Portugal's Prince Henry, known as the Navigator because of his interest in sea exploration, led all other European monarchs in setting up an overseas empire.

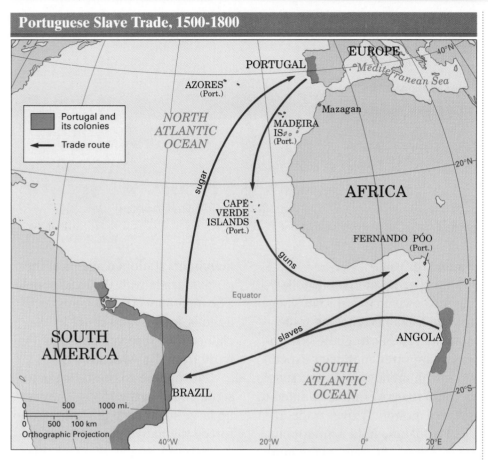

Portuguese Slave Trade, 1500-1800

Legend:
- Portugal and its colonies
- → Trade route

(Map labels) EUROPE, PORTUGAL, AZORES (Port.), Mazagan, MADEIRA IS. (Port.), NORTH ATLANTIC OCEAN, CAPE VERDE ISLANDS (Port.), AFRICA, FERNANDO PÓO (Port.), Equator, SOUTH AMERICA, slaves, ANGOLA, SOUTH ATLANTIC OCEAN, BRAZIL, sugar, guns, Mediterranean Sea

Scale: 0 500 1000 mi. / 0 500 100 km / Orthographic Projection

◄ *The exchange of goods and slaves among Africa, South America, and Europe formed a triangle of trade.*

▼ *The Portuguese brought back cinnamon, peppercorn, and cloves from the Indies.*

Growth of the Portuguese Empire

The Portuguese wanted to establish a sea route to the Indies. Most Europeans at that time used the term *East Indies* to refer to India and the islands southeast of it. The Portuguese were tired of relying on Italian merchants who, since the Crusades, had dominated trade in spices and other products from the East Indies.

The Portuguese also wanted to spread Christianity. By the mid-1200s, Muslims had been expelled from Portugal. The Christian government was eager to spread the Catholic faith to new lands.

Exploring the Seas

On their early voyages in the mid-1400s, Portuguese explorers cautiously hugged the west coast of Africa as a way of directing their course. By 1488, explorers had rounded the southern cape, or tip, of Africa and headed up the east coast. The Portuguese exploration voyages reached India in 1498.

In 1500, a Portuguese ship captain supposedly drifted off course and landed on the east coast of South America in an area known today as Brazil. However, he may have been secretly exploring lands south of where the Spanish had been. The Portuguese laid claim to a large area of South America for their king. On the map above, estimate how close Africa and South America are to each other.

3,250

465

European Rule and Expansion

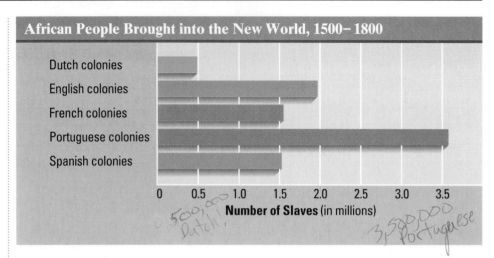

African People Brought into the New World, 1500–1800

Colony	Number of Slaves (in millions)
Dutch colonies	
English colonies	
French colonies	
Portuguese colonies	
Spanish colonies	

Number of Slaves (in millions)

0,500,000 Dutch,   *3,500,000 Portuguese*

➤ *All countries having colonies in the New World imported slaves to the Americas. The largest percentage of the slaves were brought to Brazil by the Portuguese. Which country was second in bringing slaves to the New World?*

■ *Why did the Portuguese seek new trade routes to the Indies?*

Setting Up Trade

Portuguese merchants following the newly mapped routes began to establish a far-reaching trade network. The Portuguese government supported merchant expeditions with money, ships, and sailors, because the government wanted to set up a monopoly over trade. If the Portuguese held a monopoly, the government could make more money. The government got a share of the profits made by merchants, so when merchants made more money, the government also made more money.

The Portuguese set up their first trading posts along the west coast of Africa. Portuguese merchants stationed agents at the posts to trade with the local people. The merchants traded items such as guns, knives, and cloth. In exchange they received gold and ivory from the Africans.

Portuguese colonists began to settle Brazil in the 1530s. They set up large sugar cane plantations and forced the native people to work on them. Many native people died from diseases brought by the Europeans, such as smallpox and measles. As the native population dwindled, Portuguese traders brought slaves from Africa to Brazil. These slaves were then forced to work on the plantations in place of the natives. ■

Expansion of the Spanish Empire

From 1492 to 1504, Columbus made four voyages to and from the Americas. During each voyage, he explored and claimed islands, including those now known as the Bahamas, Cuba, and Haiti. He called these islands the West Indies and the inhabitants Indians.

The Encomienda System

News of Columbus's discoveries attracted many Spanish explorers to these new lands. By 1550, Spain controlled Mexico, Central America, part of South America, most islands in the Caribbean, and part of what is now the southwestern United States.

The Spanish government ruled with the **encomienda** *(ehn koh mee EHN dah)* **system,** named after a Spanish word meaning "to entrust." Under this system, a Spanish colonist received from his government the grant of a group of Indians who had to work for him. In exchange, he was entrusted to house and feed the Indians and instruct them in the Catholic faith. For their part, the Indians were expected to mine and farm the land and to pay tribute.

However, many Indians died from the hard labor, as well as from the diseases carried by the Spaniards. In fact, so many Indians died that the Spaniards, like the Portuguese, eventually imported slaves from Africa to replace Indian laborers.

Mercantilism

The Spanish and Portuguese governments both followed an economic policy called **mercantilism** *(MUR kuhn tee lihz uhm)*. According to this policy, a country set up colonies for the purpose of obtaining raw materials and developing new markets that would trade only with the ruling country. The colonies provided the ruling country with the raw materials they produced. Likewise, the colonies bought manufactured goods from the country that ruled them.

By 1600, vast amounts of silver had been shipped back to Spain. When the supply of precious metals declined, the Spaniards concentrated on agriculture as a source of income.

Slavery and Race

Spanish slave traders bought sugar, tobacco, and cotton and shipped them to Spain. There they traded these agricultural products for manufactured goods, such as cloth and guns. Then the traders took these goods to Africa and exchanged them for slaves to bring to the Americas. This "Triangle Trade" lasted from 1520 to 1800. European traders shipped as many

as 12 million slaves from Africa to the mines and plantations of the New World.

As you have already read, many different forms of slavery have existed throughout the world in many different cultures. The Triangle Trade grew from a desire for cheap labor in the Americas. More and more enslaved Africans were brought to the Americas, and slavery itself again changed.

As Europeans colonized and traded in slaves, they came to divide the peoples of the world into those who were "white" and those who were "colored." Soon they came to think that dark skin color meant "inferior." In time, racism, the dividing of people according to skin color, came to dominate many parts of the Americas. Great Britain led the campaign to abolish slavery in the early 1800s. The U.S. abolished slavery in 1865. Brazil was the last country in the Americas to abolish slavery, in 1888. ■

▲ *The Spanish used slaves to mine gold during the 1500s in South America. Slave laborers on plantations produced cash crops such as sugar, tobacco, and cotton (below).*

■ *Describe the encomienda system and the policy of mercantilism.*

European Rule and Expansion

▶ *A painted cotton wall hanging from India, done in the 1600s, shows the Portuguese in India. The Portuguese can be identified by their European dress.*

▲ *This coat of arms of the East India Company includes the Latin motto "God shows the way."*

Dutch, English, and French Competition

Because they were busy with civil and national wars, the Dutch, English, and French lagged behind Portugal and Spain in developing overseas trade and establishing colonies. However, beginning in about 1600, the Dutch began taking control of Portuguese colonies along the African coast, in the East Indies, and in China. They also began setting up new colonies in North America.

Trade in the East

Not only did the Dutch take over many of Portugal's colonies, they also took over Portugal's trade routes. The Dutch, English, and French founded large trading companies. Private investors joined together to finance these companies, such as the East India Company. They could invest more money than the government or an individual alone could afford.

Furthermore, the government granted **charters,** official documents that gave companies the right to do things that normally only a government would do. They could maintain an army and navy, declare war, and govern new territories. The Portuguese, more limited in power, were no match for these well-equipped rivals.

In 1662, the English won trading rights to Bombay, an important colony on the west coast of India. In 1690, they founded another major colony, Calcutta, on the east coast of India. Meanwhile, in 1674, the French set up a post near Madras on the Indian south coast. England and France then battled each other throughout the next century for control of trade in

India. In 1763, British troops decisively defeated the French forces.

Colonies in the West

Spain's hold over its colonies in the Americas proved strong. Therefore, the other European powers began to establish colonies away from the Spanish on the Atlantic coast of North America.

England was the first to establish a North American colony. In 1607, the English made a permanent settlement at Jamestown. The London Company, granted a charter by King James I, provided the money for the ship and crew. Some people came to seek wealth, while others, such as the Puritans, came to escape religious persecution. By 1763, the British colonies had nearly two million inhabitants. Under mercantilism, people in the colonies exchanged raw materials, such as tobacco and furs, for manufactured goods from Britain, such as cooking utensils, tools, and cloth. Colonists were not allowed to manufacture any product that Britain could sell to them.

The Dutch also settled in North America. In 1624, they founded New Netherland, which covered parts of today's states of New York, New Jersey, Connecticut, and Delaware.

Many colonists in New Netherland made a living by trapping animals and selling the pelts to merchants. The furs were shipped to the Netherlands to be made into hats and coats for the Dutch. However, the Netherlands and England competed for the fur trade. In 1664, the Dutch lost New Netherland to England,

▼ *The English boasted the sun never set on their Union Jack flag. A jack is a small flag flown at the front of a ship on a jack, or a staff.*

UNDERSTANDING COLONIALISM

Colonialism did not begin with the Portuguese in Africa in the 1400s. The Greeks established colonies along the coast of Italy in 750 B.C.

Why Colonies Existed

Colonialism is a policy in which one country forcibly takes control of the people and land of another country, known as its colony. The ruling country often uses the colony as a source of wealth.

A colony is a separate country; however, a colony is not a separate nation, because it does not govern itself.

During the 1800s, Europeans explored and claimed land in Africa's interior. Parts of Africa were ruled by Italy, Belgium, France, Britain, Germany, Spain, and Portugal. By 1914, the only independent countries left in Africa were Liberia and Ethiopia.

Colonialism Runs Its Course

In the early 1900s, many African colonies began to demand self-government. In 1975, Portugal, the last European country with holdings in Africa, gave up its colonies. The last British colony, Hong Kong, returned to Chinese control in 1997.

In the Western Hemisphere, most colonies won their independence in the 1700s and early 1800s. In many cases the struggle for independent status involved a colony in a war with the ruling country. Freeing its colony meant a loss of economic benefits to the ruling country.

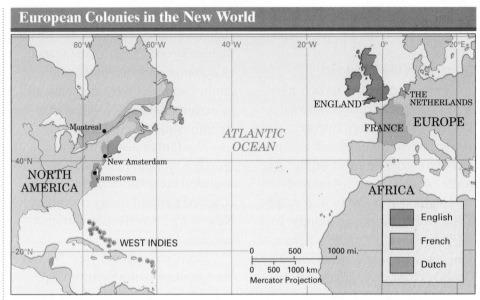

European Colonies in the New World

The colonies increased the territory of the monarchs and produced new resources for Europe.

when English warships entered the harbor of New Amsterdam and demanded the city's surrender.

In 1608, England's other rival, France, founded its first North American settlement of Quebec in present-day Canada. Later, Louis XIV did not allow Huguenots to settle there, because he wanted colonists to be loyal to the king and to the Catholic faith. Although sparsely populated, French territory included all the land along the Mississippi River Valley down to the Gulf of Mexico.

Conflict in the West

Native Americans still controlled the vast lands of North America. However, conflict

■ *Why did the Dutch, English, and French settle in North America?*

between the English and French spilled into their territory. In 1756 the two world powers fought in the Americas as well as Europe and Asia. The French and Indian Wars, or the Seven Years' War, were fought in what are now New York and Pennsylvania, and the Canadian provinces of Ontario, Québec, New Brunswick, and Nova Scotia.

The English finally defeated the French in 1763. As a result, the American colonies felt less dependent militarily on the English, who had been protecting them from the French and the Indians. Now, the American colonists began to question the rules of mercantilism which limited their rights to trade and manufacture. ■

R E V I E W

1. **FOCUS** Why did European nations establish colonies throughout the world?

2. **CONNECT** Compare the way the French and English monarchs felt about religious minorities in their colonies.

3. **GEOGRAPHY** What valuable resources did the Spanish export from South, Central, and North America?

4. **ECONOMICS** Why did the Dutch, English, and French set up trading companies?

5. **CRITICAL THINKING** Was the encomienda system a good way to manage Spain's colonies in the New World? Why?

6. **WRITING ACTIVITY** Suppose that you have been asked to establish a colony for your country. What type of site would you choose? How would you manage the colony? What would you do if natives already lived on the site? Write a proposal discussing these three issues.

Identifying Stereotypes

Here's Why

A stereotype is an over-simplified idea about a group of people. For example, "Scandinavians are blond" is a stereotype. It is oversimplified. Not all Scandinavians are blond.

Because they are often based on partial truths, stereotypes can be hard to recognize. You may have some oversimplified and only partly true ideas about people from a certain country or of a certain race, religion, age, or sex. Some stereotypes, such as that of blond Scandinavians, may be harmless; others are not. During the 1500s, Europeans made slaves of the peoples of Africa and the Americas. Because these Europeans accepted the stereotype of Africans and Indians as less than human, they did not treat them as fellow humans.

Relating to people as individuals rather than as members of groups will help you to overcome stereotypes. Many of the events described in this chapter would not have been possible if people of the 1500s and 1600s had been able to recognize and overcome the stereotypes they held about people of certain religions or people of certain races.

Here's How

The picture below shows an American family from the 1960s packing its car for a vacation. What does the picture tell you about the stereotypes people had about boys and girls at that time? Notice that the girl holds a doll; the boy, a baseball bat. Like her mother, the girl wears a skirt and dressy shoes. The boy wears clothing more suitable for play. Some stereotypes that this picture suggests are that boys play active games and girls wear pretty dresses and play quietly with dolls.

Try It

What stereotypes about sex roles did people have during other periods in history?

Look through this textbook for pictures of men or women. Think about what the men and the women are doing in the pictures. Notice that many pictures include no women at all.

What stereotypes about sex roles do the pictures represent? Write a paragraph about one or two of the most interesting examples. Compare your observations with those of your classmates.

Apply It

Much of the humor in television situation comedies is based on stereotypes. Make a list of stereotypes that you see in a show you watch. Discuss your list with others in your class.

Chapter Review

Reviewing Key Terms

absolute monarch (p. 454)
charter (p. 468)
commonwealth (p. 461)
constitutional monarchy (p. 463)
divine right (p. 454)

encomienda system (p. 467)
mercantilism (p. 467)
Parliament (p. 458)
prime minister (p. 453)

A. Rewrite the sentences below using key terms in place of the underlined words.

1. A <u>ruler who believes in doing whatever he or she wants</u> has complete freedom of rule and answers to no one.
2. Louis XIV ruled by believing in <u>God-granted power</u>.
3. The <u>members of an elected group of representatives</u> made the laws in England.
4. England was called a <u>government where people governed for their common good</u>.
5. A <u>system that allows foreigners to take over and enslave locals</u> must have been hated by the local people.
6. Under a <u>government where a king or queen rules a country</u>, power is restricted by a constitution and laws.

B. The statements below are false. Rewrite them to make them true.

1. A ruler owes allegiance first to the prime minister who appoints him or her.
2. Colonies receive more benefits than the ruling country under mercantilism.
3. The only reason that governments granted charters to private investors was out of a desire to help businesses grow.

Exploring Concepts

A. Copy and complete the following chart on your own paper.

People	Main Religions	Countries Fought	Lands Colonized
French	Catholic Protestant (Huguenot)	England Spain	N. America India Africa
English			
Spanish			
Portuguese			
Dutch			

B. Answer each question with information from the chapter.

1. Henry IV of France took an important step for religious freedom. What was it?
2. Richelieu wanted to increase the king's power. How did he do this?
3. Louis XIV ruled by divine right, with no prime minister. What was the form of government?
4. Was Elizabeth considered a successful Queen of England? Explain.
5. What did Charles I do when Parliament would not approve his requests for money?
6. What was it called when William arrived to take over England and James II fled? Why?
7. Why did Portugal encourage exploration?
8. Were the Spaniards in the Americas fair or unfair rulers? Explain.
9. Why did the English, French, and Dutch establish colonies away from Spain's in North America?

Reviewing Skills

1. Read the first paragraph in the text section on page 458 of Lesson 2 that begins with The Reign of Elizabeth I. Predict what actions Elizabeth will take to solve the religious problems in England. Explain the stated facts and other knowledge that you used to make your prediction.
2. Under the encomienda system, the Spanish government gave Spanish officials grants of land with power over all the Indians who lived on it. What might you predict could happen when a person has this much power over other people?
3. How did the Spanish government view Indians? How might that have made it easier for the Spanish to adopt a policy of giving away Indians with land grants?
4. When there is a struggle for power in a war or over succession to a throne, people often view those on the other side in a stereotyped way. How might this make it easier for one side to fight the other?
5. Read pages 452 and 453. How did the religious values of the leaders of France affect the citizens of France? How did these values make it hard for the people to understand each other?
6. When reading about the actions of a character in a story, what skill would you use to guess what will happen?

Using Critical Thinking

1. When kings were absolute monarchs they caused much bloodshed and turmoil. Do you think it is possible for an absolute monarch to be a wise, fair, honest king or queen? Would an absolute monarchy work in today's world? Explain your opinion.
2. When a Spanish official received land and the Indians living on that land, he was expected to provide something in return: to care for them and teach them Catholicism. Evaluate the strengths and weaknesses of this system. Do you think people would want to live under this system today?
3. Choosing a religion in the 16th century was a dangerous business. If your choice was not the accepted religion, you might face death. Think about why some people chose to practice unpopular religions they knew might endanger their lives. Were they stereotyped because of their religious choices? Are all people the same who practice a certain religion?

Preparing for Citizenship

1. **WRITING ACTIVITY** Imagine you live in England during the Glorious Revolution. Today you witnessed the arrival of William of Orange accompanied by 14,000 soldiers. A group of lords invited him to rule peacefully with his wife, Mary, the Protestant daughter of James II. Describe the scene and express your thoughts about this revolution.
2. **COLLABORATIVE LEARNING** Your class will stage two debates set in England in 1642. Both debates will present the Puritans and merchants who support Parliament against the nobles and clergy who support King Charles. But the two debates will have different outcomes: the first debate will stage the actual outcome—the English Civil War; and the second debate will stage an imaginary outcome—peace. Divide the class into four sections. The first two sections' debate will lead to the actual outcome. The other two sections will "rewrite" history and show a peaceful outcome. In each section, have some students research the information (or create new ideas for the peaceful outcome), some moderate the debate, and some do the actual debating. You might create simple costumes and a painted mural background for your debates.

473

Chapter 18

The Enlightenment

To enlighten *means "to shine a light on." During the 18th century, the time known as the Enlightenment, great thinkers did just that. They shed new light on old ideas by using their powers of reasoning and helped bring about great change. Scientists made great discoveries. Inventors created marvelous new machines. Revolutionaries even overthrew kings and built new governments with the inspiration of Enlightenment ideas.*

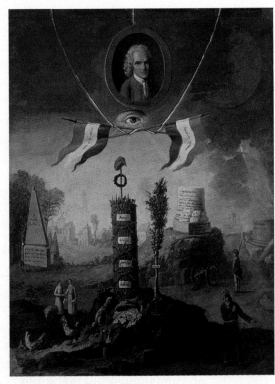

Jean Jacques Rousseau (right) comes to Paris and meets Enlightenment thinkers in the 1740s. Rousseau's ideas help spark the French Revolution.

1717 At the age of 23, the writer Voltaire is jailed for making fun of the French government. Voltaire goes on to become a great Enlightenment thinker.

1700	1720	1740

1733 Georgia becomes Britain's 13th colony along North America's Atlantic coast.

1700

1776 Thomas Jefferson, influenced by Enlightenment ideas, writes America's Declaration of Independence. Also an inventor, he later creates this polygraph, which copies a letter as the original is written.

1789 A revolution begins in France. In 1793, revolutionaries execute King Louis XVI and later his queen, Marie Antoinette (above).

1760

1780

1800

1750s Slaves are Africa's major export, replacing gold.

1784 The British government takes control of India from the British East India Company.

1800

LESSON 1

A New Order of Ideals

How did the Age of Enlightenment reflect a spirit of optimism?

Key Terms

- reason
- Age of Enlightenment
- philosophe
- contract
- natural right

➤ *Enlightenment thinkers were fascinated by the universe. Scientists had shown that the movements of the planets and stars were orderly and predictable. This painting from 1765 by Joseph Wright shows people studying a model of this orderly universe.*

The 1700s must have been an exciting time in which to live. Everywhere in Europe, philosophers and scientists tried to solve old problems with a new approach. These thinkers believed that **reason,** or logical thought, was the key to understanding the world and creating a perfect society. The belief in the power of reason to change the world was first seen in science. During this Age of Reason, one scientific discovery seemed to follow on the heels of another. Whole new fields of science were born. In France, Antoine Lavoisier's *(lah vwah ZYAY)* experiments led to the invention of chemical equations and, eventually, to the study of modern chemistry. Charles Coulomb *(KOO lahm)* invented several instruments for measuring electrical and magnetic forces. Pierre Laplace developed a theory about the origin of the solar system.

Some people found the era threatening, as many long-held beliefs were disproved. But others looked to the future with confidence. They hoped that, just as reason helped people understand the physical world, so it could help them understand their social and political world. Once people understood this human world, they could then improve it. Governments could be changed to better serve the people. Poverty, intolerance, and injustice could be ended. In this new age, anything seemed possible. This spirit of optimism spoke for the century, which was named the **Age of Enlightenment.**

Roots of the Enlightenment

This new way of thinking about the world had its roots in the Renaissance. Beginning in that period, a number of European traditions came under examination. The philosophy of humanism paved the way. Renaissance humanists believed in the dignity and potential of the individual. They argued that people could improve their world by understanding it and changing it.

Many Renaissance thinkers began to reexamine critically a number of long-held beliefs. The growing European exploration and understanding of the world helped call into question the belief that the ancient civilizations had been superior to modern Europe in all ways. Humanists began to realize that they had surpassed the Greeks and Romans in exploration, trade, and science. They began to believe in progress. Perhaps advances in learning and science would improve life. ■

▲ *During the Scientific Revolution, scientists learned a great deal about the physical world. Using a telescope like the one shown, Isaac Newton studied the universe and helped change people's views of the world during the Enlightenment.*

European Philosophers

European thinkers during the 1600s and 1700s hoped that they could use reason to achieve progress in other areas besides science. Made up of members of the aristocracy and middle class, these thinkers called themselves **philosophes** *(fee luh ZAWFS),* from the French word for philosophers.

Both the Catholic and Protestant churches and many monarchies of Europe distrusted the philosophes. In order to solve problems, the philosophes made proposals that challenged traditions and promised to give more power to individuals. Neither the churches nor the monarchies of Europe were willing to give up their power. They censored and even imprisoned the philosophes to discourage these thinkers from trying to spread their new ideas. The most famous philosophe was François Marie Arouet *(a REH),* known by his writing name, Voltaire *(vohl TAIR).*

Voltaire

Although he was born into a middle-class family, Voltaire knew firsthand about the injustices of his day. While in his twenties, he had been arrested and jailed for being the supposed author of verses making fun of the government. In his thirties, he was beaten and

■ *How did the idea of individualism lead to the Enlightenment?*

▼ *Voltaire was one of the most versatile of the Enlightenment figures. Here the artist Hubert has drawn the many faces of Voltaire, from writer and philosopher to spokesman for democracy.*

During the 18th century, philosophes spread their ideas through salons, books, and pamphlets. Salons, such as the one shown above, were held one day a week in the home of a weathy woman. Here philosophes would read their work to the audience.

➤ *Not only did women become important in salons, they also became professional artists.* Lady at Her Dressing Table *is a miniature painting by Rosalba Giovanna Carriéra, who lived from 1675 to 1757.*

■ *What changes did the philosophes want to make in society?*

jailed for remarks made to a French nobleman. These events made a deep impression on Voltaire. He fought all his life for freedom from censorship and for the rights of the individual.

Voltaire worked especially hard against religious intolerance. He saw that intolerance led to violence. He urged people to be tolerant of each other's beliefs:

By what right could a being, created free, force another to think like himself? . . . Tolerance has never brought civil war; intolerance has covered the earth with carnage.

The *Encyclopédie*

Another of the philosophes, Denis Diderot *(DEE dih roh),* spread the ideas of the philosophes

and the new scientific knowledge. He spent more than 20 years writing and editing the *Encyclopédie (ahn sy kluh PAY dih).* Diderot hoped the *Encyclopédie* would help ". . . change the general way of thinking." The first volume, published in 1751, was followed by 21 others, and over 160 authors contributed. No such vast collection of learning had existed before the *Encyclopédie.* By 1789, nearly 16,000 copies had been sold, and people all over Europe and America learned about the ideas of the philosophes.

Both the government and the church recognized that the *Encyclopédie* was a powerful voice for change. The French king banned the *Encyclopédie,* and the pope placed it on the *Index of Prohibited Books.* ■

New Ideas about Government

Among the thinkers whose ideas were included in the volumes of *Encyclopédie* were three philosophes—John Locke of England, Baron de Montesquieu of France, and Jean-Jacques Rousseau of Switzerland. These three men concerned themselves with the question of what the best form of government was.

In *Two Treatises of Government* (1690), Locke wrote that government was a **contract,** or agreement, between the people and their ruler. The people allowed the ruler power as long as he or she governed fairly. Locke believed that if a ruler did not honor this contract, then the people had a right to overthrow the ruler.

Locke was willing to accept a monarch as ruler as long as he or she protected the rights of the people. Locke considered these **natural rights**—the rights every person was entitled to by nature—to be life, liberty, and the protection of property.

Baron de Montesquieu thought that government worked best when the power of the monarch was limited. Montesquieu argued that good government was best divided into three equal branches—legislative, executive, and judicial. If government were not divided, he feared:

> There would be an end of everything, were the same man or the same body . . . to exercise those three powers, that of enacting laws, that of executing the public resolutions, and of trying the causes of individuals.
>
> Montesquieu,
> *The Spirit of the Laws,* 1748

Rousseau criticized the idea of an absolute monarch even more strongly than Montesquieu. Rousseau believed that the people should participate directly in the government they elected:

> The deputies of the people . . . are not and cannot be its representatives. . . . Every law the people have not ratified [approved] in person is null and void—is, in fact, not a law.
>
> *The Social Contract,* 1762

Like Locke, Rousseau believed that government was a contract between the rulers and the people. He argued that the people could cancel the contract if they believed the government was not serving their needs. However, they could not sever the contract for trivial reasons. ■

▼ *Rousseau was an important philosophe during the Enlightenment. This playing card from the 1700s shows Rousseau dressed as a champion of democracy.*

■ *How were Locke, Montesquieu, and Rousseau alike and different in their philosophies of government?*

REVIEW

1. **FOCUS** How did the Age of Enlightenment reflect a spirit of optimism?

2. **CONNECT** Why do you think the philosophes were critical of Louis XIV's absolute monarchy?

3. **HISTORY** What role did the *Encyclopédie* play in spreading the views of the philosophes?

4. **CRITICAL THINKING** How was the focus of the Enlightenment different from the focus of Renaissance humanism?

5. **WRITING ACTIVITY** Imagine that you have just been at one of the famous salons in Paris in the 1700s. Write a brief description of what you heard.

The Enlightenment

LESSON 2

Ideas in Action

Key Term

• enlightened despot

➤ *Voltaire, the figure on the left in the engraving, often provided advice to Frederick the Great, shown at right.*

H e [the king] should often remind himself that he is a man just as the least of his subjects." With these words, Frederick II of Prussia, shown here with Voltaire, defined the new type of leader envisioned by the philosophes. An avid reader of the philosophes, Frederick especially admired Voltaire. Frederick even invited Voltaire to come live at his court. Voltaire must have thought highly of Frederick as well, for he called him the "Philosopher King." Eventually they quarreled, but not before Frederick had adopted many of the ideas of the philosophes. In an essay, he wrote:

I f [a king] is the first judge, the first general, the first financier, the first minister of the nation . . . it is in order to fulfill the duties which these titles impose upon him. He is only the first servant of the state, obliged to act with fairness, wisdom, and unselfishness, as if at every instant he would have to render an account of his administration to his citizens.

Essay on the Forms of Government, 1788

Attempts at Reform

Frederick wanted to use his power and wisdom to improve the lives of his people. Because Frederick supported the ideals of the Enlightenment while remaining an all-powerful ruler, or despot, he is called an **enlightened despot.** But

Frederick was not the only European monarch to adopt Enlightenment ideals. Catherine the Great of Russia and Joseph II of Austria were also enlightened despots of the late 1700s. Locate the areas they ruled on the map on page 481.

Reform in Europe

Frederick made important changes in Prussia during his rule from 1740 to 1786. His interest in recent scientific advancements resulted in the use of new crops, such as potatoes and clover in Prussia. He also encouraged the use of new planting methods and new equipment, such as crop rotation and iron plows.

As an enlightened ruler, Frederick also worked to increase religious tolerance. He welcomed Catholics into Lutheran Prussia and gave them nearly full equality. He even built a large Catholic church in Berlin and once said that he would erect a mosque if Muslims came to Prussia.

Under Frederick's rule, Prussia's legal system was vastly improved. The laws were simplified, and Frederick worked to ensure just sentences by trying to end the bribing of judges.

Elsewhere in Europe other enlightened despots supported reforms. In Russia, Catherine the Great ruled from 1762 to 1796. She tried to modernize Russia by importing architects, musicians, and intellectuals from western Europe. When the French government banned Diderot's *Encyclopédie,* Catherine offered to publish it. Catherine also restricted cruel punishment of serfs and allowed some religious tolerance.

Most progressive of all the enlightened despots was Joseph II of Austria, who ruled from 1780 to 1790. Determined to improve life for his subjects, he abolished serfdom and allowed peasants to own land. He taxed all classes equally and offered complete religious freedom to all faiths.

The Failure of Reform

Although these monarchs tried up to a point to help their people, most of the gains they made were small or short-lived. In Prussia, Frederick was intolerant of Jews. He made Jews pay special taxes, and tried to keep them from holding government offices. In Russia,

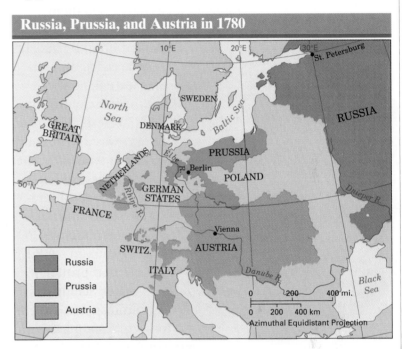

Russia, Prussia, and Austria in 1780

a peasant revolt caused Catherine to strengthen oppression of the serfs. And in Austria, nearly all of Joseph's reforms were reversed after his death at the age of 49. Nobles regained their privileges, and peasants lost their rights.

It was clear that the European nobility, who held the power and the money, were not going to give up their favored position easily. Since a monarch's power depended on the nobility's support, enlightened despots found it difficult to fulfill Enlightenment ideals. Montesquieu described this interdependence between the monarch and the nobles in a brief phrase: "No monarchy, no nobility; no nobility, no monarchy." ■

▲ *The rulers of Russia, Prussia, and Austria all tried to use the ideas of the philosophes when governing their countries. Where were these countries in relation to France?*

■ *Why were the reforms of enlightened despots largely unsuccessful?*

The Enlightenment

Influences in America

Leaders of the British colonies in North America adopted Enlightenment ideas with more success. Two leaders, Thomas Jefferson and Benjamin Franklin, had studied European ideas and traveled in Europe. The philosophes' ideas impressed them.

Like the philosophes, Jefferson and Franklin had a wide range of intellectual, political, and scientific interests. Jefferson was a writer and a student of the classical languages, literature, and architecture. Franklin—a talented printer, writer, scientist, politician, and inventor—corresponded with many of the philosophes.

Since the mid-1760s, Jefferson, Franklin, and other British colonists in North America had been enraged by attempts to raise taxes. Parliament wanted the colonists to pay a share of the expense from fighting the Seven Years' War with France. The colonists disagreed. Since they were British citizens, they reasoned, they should not be taxed unless they were represented in Parliament.

Convinced that their rights were being violated, the colonists made a bold decision. In 1776, they decided to reject British rule. Then Thomas Jefferson headed a committee to draft a Declaration of Independence. On July 4, 1776, the Declaration was formally adopted.

In this document the colonists declared that "governments are instituted among men" to secure "certain inalienable rights, that among these are life, liberty, and the pursuit of happiness." These guaranteed rights follow directly from Locke's belief in natural rights.

The Declaration also stated that "governments [derive] their just powers from the consent of the governed." Therefore, when a government fails to respect the people's rights, "it is the right of the people to alter or to abolish it and to institute new government." This again echoes Locke's belief that the people have a right to overthrow a king who violates the contract between subjects and ruler. The American Revolution would be fought to defend these declarations of Enlightenment thought. ■

▲ *Some Americans, such as Franklin, were influenced by Enlightenment thought. Here Franklin, at right, is shown on a snuff box with Rousseau and Voltaire to illustrate that all three shared many of the same ideals.*

■ *How does the Declaration of Independence reflect the influence of Enlightenment thinkers?*

Antoine Lavoisier, a generous man/ scientist died during this because of his spot in Parliament. He named oxygen and came up w/ the Law of Conservation. Oxygen was to be ~~called~~ "dephlogisticated air."

The French Revolution

In 1787, France's government was deeply in debt from supporting the colonists during the Revolutionary War. Poor harvests in 1788 led to food shortages, rising food prices, unemployment, and starvation. But still the government continued to collect taxes from the poor, while French nobles paid almost no taxes. The anger of the French people grew.

In 1789, King Louis XVI, needing money to pay off his debts, decided to raise taxes. He called a meeting of the Estates General. The Estates General was made up of representatives from three groups of people, or estates. The First Estate was the clergy, the Second Estate was the noblility, and the Third Estate included everyone else. Members of the Third Estate had virtually no power in the government but paid almost all the taxes.

A Struggle for Power

On June 17, 1789, the representatives of the Third Estate broke away from the Estates General and formed a new group called the National Assembly. They swore to meet separately until France became a constitutional monarchy. Some members of the First and Second Estates joined them. In need of a unified group to have new taxes passed, Louis gave in to the Assembly's demands. He then urged the rest of the nobles and clergy to join the Assembly.

In July 1789, Louis gathered troops near Paris. The people of Paris feared that he was going to seize power from the Assembly and go back to his old methods of absolute rule. In retaliation, on July 14, a crowd stormed the Bastille, a fortress-prison that held arms and a few prisoners. They tore down the prison, took the weapons, and liberated its prisoners. This event marked the beginning of the French Revolution. The French woman in A Moment in Time on page 484 is part of a group that is presenting the demands of the people to King Louis XVI.

Waging a Revolution

In August 1789, the Assembly began drafting a new constitution. They adopted the Declaration of the Rights of Man and of the

▲ The poor in France paid almost all the taxes. This French cartoon from the 1700s shows a poor person carrying a noble and a churchman.

▼ Governor De Launay (center) is arrested by the angry crowd during the storming of the Bastille.

Parisian Market Woman

*7:19 P.M., October 5, 1789
In the royal clock room of the
palace at Versailles*

Eyes
She's amazed by the
bright, white room
decorated with real
gold. Never in her life
did she dream that she
would be demanding
the king's help.

Apron
She had no time to change
before she joined the huge
march to see the king. She
sells the fish her husband
catches, and a fishy smell
clings to her clothes.

Stomach
She's hungry, very hungry.
It's not just because she
hasn't eaten since early
morning today. It's been
weeks since she's been
able to put bread on her
family's table.

Hand
Trembling with excitement
and fear, she is holding
her skirt to bow to her
king. She wishes her
hands weren't so chapped
from her hard daily work.

Pamphlet
Tucked under her apron, a
crudely printed page de-
mands, "We want
bread!" In the market
people say that the king's
army is not letting wheat
wagons into Paris.

Skirt
Her hem got caked with
mud on the rainy 12-mile
march from Paris to Ver-
sailles. The angry marchers
waited for hours at the
gates of the palace before
a small group of women
was allowed inside.

Citizen. At the top of their list of natural rights, they placed "liberty, property, security, and resistance to oppression." They wrote that "the source of all sovereignty [power] resides essentially in the nation" rather than the king. Read more from the Declaration on p. 506.

In the next few years, the Assembly began numerous reforms in France. The nobility and clergy now had to pay taxes. In 1791, the Assembly established a constitutional monarchy. In 1792, Louis plotted with the rulers of Austria and Prussia to overthrow the new government. The plot was discovered. In September, the people ended the monarchy, and France became a republic. Louis was guillotined for treason in January 1793.

After Louis' death, disorder and violence swept through France. This Reign of Terror lasted almost a year. Anyone suspected of treason or hostility to the revolution was imprisoned and, sometimes, executed. More than 18,000 men, women, and children were killed.

The revolutionary period ended when General Napoleon Bonaparte seized control of the government in 1799. He defeated the Austrians and convinced the other European powers to make peace. Although the revolution had been bloody, it marked a turning point for France.

The Declaration of the Rights

◄ *The artist Jacques Louis David drew this pencil sketch of Marie Antoinette on the way to the guillotine during the Reign of Terror.*

of Man prompted Olympe de Gouges *(duh GOOJ)* to write a Declaration of the Rights of Woman in 1791. The following year, in Britain, Mary Wollstonecraft echoed her call. In 1791, the French National Assembly gave Jews and Protestants full and equal rights. In Berlin, German Jewish philosopher Moses Mendelssohn sparked a new reform movement within Judaism. He asked Jews to remain Jewish but to share in the culture of the nations they lived in.

Yet for both Christian women and Jews, the French Revolution brought few real changes. To them, the Revolution meant a new way of looking at the world—as future citizens with full rights still to be obtained. ∎

Across Time & Space

The storming of the Bastille is celebrated in France on Bastille Day. Observed on July 14, it is France's most important national holiday. This day of remembering freedom and independence, much like the Fourth of July in the United States, is traditionally celebrated with parades, music, and dancing.

∎ *How are the reforms that took place during the French Revolution representative of Enlightenment ideals?*

R E V I E W

1. FOCUS How did the ideas of the Enlightenment affect governments in Europe and America?

2. CONNECT How did the enlightened despots in Europe differ from the constitutional monarchs in Britain?

3. ECONOMICS What were some of the economic and agricultural crises that helped to bring about the French Revolution?

4. CRITICAL THINKING Montesquieu wrote: "No monarchy, no nobility; no nobility, no monarchy." What do you think he meant by this statement?

5. WRITING ACTIVITY Imagine you have participated in the events in France of July 14, 1789. Write a letter in which you describe your day to a friend.

LITERATURE

To the Assembly for Protection

Elizabeth Powers

Fifteen-year-old Marie Therese Charlotte began writing the story of her life in a journal when she and her family were imprisoned in revolutionary France. The daughter of Louis XVI and Marie Antoinette, Madame Royale, as Marie Therese was known, gives us an eyewitness account of the French Revolution. This story is from The Journal of Madame Royale, *a book based on the real journal kept by Marie Therese. What are Madame Royale's feelings about the French Revolution?*

In Lesson 2 you read about both liberation and terror during the French Revolution. The following story recreates a part of that stormy period.

Roederer (reh DRAIR)
Tuileries
(TWEE luh reez)

Mme Madame

M. Monsieur

At midnight on the ninth of August, Attorney General Roederer and others came to my father and warned him that there would be another march on the Tuileries. He urged my father to take his family to the National Assembly hall that adjoined the Tuileries and had been, in fact, the indoor riding school of the palace. There we would be under the protection of the deputies. My father left the room without answering.

My mother sent a message for Mme de Tourzel to awaken my brother and me and bring us to her. We came, along with kind Mme de Lamballe who had been safely out of the country but who had returned from England to be with my mother in her bad moments.

It was so hot that the leaves had fallen off the trees, and my mother had not been able to sleep.

Now she said, "This is a conflict of forces. We have come to the point where we must know which is going to prevail—the King and the Constitution, or the rebels."

At this point there was shouting and booing in the garden and drummers were beating the call to arms. M. Roederer put his head out of the window. He said, "My God, it is the King they are booing! What the devil is he doing down there? Come quickly, let us go to him!" He and his men ran down the stairs.

My father was brought back, out of breath and red in the face. It seems he had gone down to rally his guards, but when he got there he did not know what to say, so he only made matters worse. Some artillery men had even dared to turn their cannon against their King!

My poor father. I remembered then what I had heard my mother say once to Mme Campan, her first lady of the bedchamber: "The King is not a coward; he possesses an abundance of passive courage, but he is overwhelmed by an awkward shyness, a mistrust of himself, which proceeds from his education as much as from his disposition. He is afraid to command, and above all things, dreads speaking to assembled members. He lived like a child, and was always ill at ease under the eyes of Louis XV until the age of twenty. This constraint confirmed his timidity."

After M. Roederer returned with my father he pleaded, "Sire, your Majesty has not five minutes to lose."

My mother said that we had a strong force in the palace but he answered, "Madame, all Paris is on the march." Then he turned to my father, who was sitting staring at the floor, and asked permission to escort us to the Assembly.

My father raised his head and looked at M. Roederer. Then he turned to my mother and said, "Let us be going." As he rose to his feet, my aunt came from behind his chair and said, "M. Roederer, will you answer for the life of the King?"

He said yes, that he would walk in front, but that there should be no one from the Court, and there should be no other escort than the members of the department who would surround the Royal Family, and the men of the National Guard who would march in line on both flanks as far as the National Assembly.

"Very well," my father said. "Will you give the orders?"

My mother said, "What about Mme de Tourzel, my son's governess? And Madame de Lamballe?"

Yes, he said. They could come, too.

When we reached the bottom of the great staircase my father stopped and said, "What is going to happen to all the people remaining up there?" No one answered.

Mme Campan had remained in my mother's apartments. We learned later that some men with drawn sabres rushed up the stairs, seized her and thrust her to their feet. But some of the Queen's other waiting women threw themselves at the ruffians' feet and held their blades away from her. Just then someone called from the bottom of the staircase, "What are you doing up there? We don't kill women." Her assailant quitted his hold on her and said, "Get up; the nation pardons you."

When we were under the trees we sank up to our knees in the piled up leaves. "What a lot of leaves," my father remarked, "they have begun to fall very early this year."

My brother, holding my mother's hand, was amusing himself by kicking the leaves against the legs of the persons walking in front of him. My aunt was holding tight to my hand and Mme de

Lamballe (lah BAHL)

Tourzel and her daughter were supporting Mme de Lamballe who was trembling so she could hardly walk.

When we reached the hall, my father made an address. He said: "I have come here to prevent a great crime from being committed, and I am convinced that I could not be in a safer place than in your midst, gentlemen."

The president of the Assembly replied that the King could depend on the firmness of the National Assembly, but that they were sworn to defend with their lives the rights of the people and the constitutional authorities. They also said that it was against the rules for them to proceed with their debates with us there.

They then took us to the minute-writer's office. This room was so low the grown-up people could not even stand up straight. It had two or three stools and a bench, and an iron grating separated it from the hall. Not a breath of air could enter, and we were compelled to spend eighteen hours in this steaming cubbyhole.

All at once the boom of the gunnery was heard and men were saying it was coming from the Tuileries. Then someone shouted, "Here come the Swiss Guards!" Soon we heard the rattle of gunfire. There were shouts and cries coming from outside and inside now, saying that the King's Swiss Guards had fired on the people—had lured the citizens and then shot them down. There were curses and shouts demanding the death of the King.

My father sent an order for the Swiss Guards to cease firing, but before morning more than a thousand lives had been lost.

All at once, to our horror, we saw some of the faithful guards and nobles being chased into the Assembly hall by rogues who struck them down without mercy. They brought in my father's own servants who, with the utmost impudence, gave false testimony against him, while others boasted of vile things they had done. These were followed by looters who triumphantly strewed silverware, cashboxes, letters, even our toys, and anything else they could pick up over the desk of the president of the Assembly.

We listened as men mounted the tribune to lie about and denounce my mother and father. They cried, "Death to the Austrian woman!" "Death to the King!" and "Death to the Aristocrats!" We heard my father, the King, deposed and his veto abolished.

At last some one brought us food and water. My mother took a glass of water; my father ate; my brother and I fell asleep. My mother did not break her fast until we were taken to the Convent of the Feuillants, which had been confiscated and where bedrooms were made up for us. Next day we were taken back and heard the King and Queen branded as oppressors of the people. We heard them discuss what should be done with the King and where he should be kept.

Feuillants
(fuh YAHNTS)

For three long days we listened until it was declared that the King was suspended from his functions and a new municipal government, the Commune, was formed.

It was decreed that the Temple was the only place to ensure our safety. We were to be conducted there "with all the respect due to misfortune." The attorney for the new Commune, M. Manuel, was to accompany us. The Temple—so-called because in olden days it had been the fortress of the Knights Templar—was as sinister-looking as the Bastille. It consisted of a small castle with a round tower at each corner, narrow windows, and an inner court which, we would find, the sun hardly ever reached. We were to live in this fortress.

Towards three in the afternoon, Manuel, accompanied by Petion, came to take the Royal Family away. They made us all get in a carriage with eight seats. Then they crowded in with their hats on their heads, shouting "Long Live the Nation!" They had the driver go slowly, as throngs pressed themselves against the carriage, shrieking, spitting, and hurling insults. They had the cruelty, too, to point out to my parents things that would distress them—for instance, the statues of the kings of France thrown down from their pedestals, even that of Henri IV, before which they stopped and compelled us to look.

We learnt that the guillotine, the official instrument to cut off people's heads, had been set up in the Place du Carrousel.

Further Reading

Fear No More. Hester Chapman. This story is about the mysterious life and death of Louis Charles, the son of Louis XVI.

Jacobin's Daughter. Joanne S. Williamson. This story about the French Revolution focuses on its leaders and the conflicts among the political factions of the time.

Marie Antoinette, Daughter of an Empress. This biography focuses on the life of the woman who was queen of France in the 18th century. It also tell the story of her mother, the dominating Maria Theresa, Empress of Austria.

Victory at Valmy. Geoffrey Trease. This is an adventure story that takes place in the early days of the French Revolution.

LESSON 3

Economic Changes

THINKING
FOCUS

How did the agricultural and industrial revolutions change life in Britain during the 1700s?

Key Terms

- agricultural revolution
- crop rotation
- enclosure
- industrial revolution
- capitalist

➤ *Gleaners are seen hard at work in this painting by Jean François Millet. Gleaning was backbreaking labor. But some families could not grow enough on their small plots for their own needs. So they gleaned to survive.*

The British farm women bent over to gather the gleanings, or the grain remaining on the ground after harvest. These women and their families before them had gathered gleanings from these fields, which were owned by an aristocratic family, for hundreds of years. The women's families farmed small plots of land. But they depended on gleanings because their own lands were simply too small to provide their families with enough food.

But these were perhaps the last gleanings that the women would ever collect. Parliament had decreed that large landowners could fence in and redistribute the land. The women and those like them had staged demonstrations, complained, argued and pleaded, but with no result.

Where would they go in the spring? Perhaps their families would go to the city to look for work. Perhaps they could be hired hands for a wealthy neighbor. Neither future appealed to them. They wanted things to stay the same.

The Agricultural Revolution

ce n'est pas un révolution, c'est un transition!!
um, I don't understand, the Ag. ⊙ was Paleolithic/
Neolithic era...

The French Revolution was not the only revolution that occurred during the 1700s. In Britain two different revolutions would change life in Europe forever.

The first major change took place on farms. By the end of the

1700s, British farmers had learned how to increase the amount of food they could grow by using a number of new methods. These new methods were so significant that together they are called the **agricultural revolution.**

C'est très faux!

The agricultural revolution began in Britain in the 1500s. It started slowly and gathered momentum in the 1600s. By 1750, when the population of Britain began to grow rapidly, the changes were well under way. Experimentation resulted in more food to feed a hungry population.

Crop Rotation

In medieval Britain, farmers had used a three-field system when planting their crops. Each year, they would plant one field with wheat or rye and another with barley or oats. They would not plant any crop on the third field, allowing the soil to rest. The next year they would switch which crops were grown in which field. Under this system, called **crop rotation,** the soil in a field rested every third year.

Beginning in the 1500s, British farmers introduced changes in crop rotation. In the 1600s, they began to grow new crops, such as turnips or clover, on the field that had previously been left unplanted. Such crops actually nourished the soil, making it more fertile. Now fields were productive every year instead of lying unused every third year.

Turnips and clover also increased the amount of fodder, or food for animals, that was grown. The new crop rotation allowed farmers to raise more cows, sheep, and horses than before, making meat more plentiful. More animals also meant more manure, an important soil fertilizer. The more fertile soil produced more food.

Farm Tools

Another change in farming during the 1700s was the use of more efficient farming tools. One such tool was the horse-drawn seed drill pictured above. Developed by Jethro Tull in the 1730s, the drill planted evenly spaced seeds at a consistent depth and immediately covered them with soil. Space was left between rows so that the ground could be broken by a horse-drawn hoe. In this way the soil absorbed more air and water, helping plants grow better.

Enclosure

Perhaps the most significant change accompanying the agricultural revolution was **enclosure** of land—breaking up large unfenced common fields into smaller, fenced-in plots. Traditionally, peasants held their land scattered equally in the three fields in their village. Once the grain in one field was harvested, poor farmers could collect gleanings from the lands. Once the gleaning was finished, villagers could pasture their animals on the stubble. They also had

Across Time & Space

Historians are not sure why the population of Britain increased during the 1700s. One reason for the increase was that fewer people were catching the plague and dying.

491

The Enlightenment

common rights to village pastureland and meadowland. Without these sources of food, farmers had trouble providing for their families.

But during the 1600s and 1700s, large landowners began buying up the holdings of small landowners and then fencing in, or enclosing, the land. Once the land was enclosed, the owner could farm it any way he liked. Landowners introduced new agricultural techniques, which boosted the amount of food produced on the same amount of land. But many peasants were left without land of their own. They bitterly resented enclosure but could not stop it. Deprived of land, many headed to cities to find work. ■

■ *What developments changed agriculture in Britain?*

The Industrial Revolution *or transition?*

As the population of Britain grew, the demand for goods, such as clothing, also increased. British manufacturers could not meet this demand using only the traditional method of making cloth by hand. In response, inventors began producing machines that could manufacture goods faster and more cheaply. Some were operated by people who had been driven off the land by the agricultural revolution. These improvements brought about an **industrial revolution,** a change in the way goods were produced and the way people lived.

New Technology

Like other Enlightenment figures, British inventors hoped to apply scientific principles to the problem of producing more goods. Many inventions in the 1700s affected the textile industry. Prior to the 1700s, spinning and weaving had been done with spinning wheels and hand looms. In 1733, John Kay invented a flying shuttle, a mechanical loom that allowed one person to do the work of two.

With the flying shuttle, workers used up thread so quickly that a better machine was needed for spinning. In 1764, James Hargreaves invented the jenny, a device that spun eight spools of thread at once. Between 1750 and 1800, England went from importing 3 million to 50 million pounds of raw cotton per year to make cloth.

▼ *Adam Smith's idea of specialization of labor can be applied to making shoes. By specializing in a particular step, each worker becomes faster at it. Also, dividing the process into simple steps opens the door to mechanization. The cotton gin (right), invented by Eli Whitney in 1793, separated cotton fiber from seed 50 times faster than workers could do it by hand.*

Specialization of Labor

Process of Making a Pair of Shoes

Cutting pieces → Fitting, shaping → Attaching sole, heel → Trimming, finishing

Pairs of Shoes Made in a Six-Hour Period

■ = Setup between steps

Hours: 0, 1, 2, 3, 4, 5, 6

1 pair of shoes per person

8 pairs of shoes or 1.6 pairs per person

Capital and Labor

Capital and labor, or money and workers, were two of the important elements in the industrial revolution. The British government encouraged individuals called **capitalists** to invest their money in new industries. Competition among individual producers led them to produce the best product at the cheapest price. It was important for producers to do this, so that they would have the most customers and make the greatest profit.

A British economist named Adam Smith wrote about some of the changes in the economy. Smith showed how having workers specialize in a task could increase the number of goods they could produce. The chart on page 492 illustrates Smith's argument.

Conditions of Life

Although the new industries provided jobs, they damaged the living and working conditions of many laborers. Workers—even children under 10 years of age—spent 12 or 14 hours, six days a week, performing monotonous tasks. Some children were crippled by unsafe machines.

The increase in the number of people in British cities caused new problems. So many people burned coal for heat that the skies turned black with smoke. Charles Dickens described the intense overcrowding and dirtiness of these cities:

> *I*t was a town of machinery and tall chimneys, out of which interminable [never ending] serpents of smoke trailed themselves for ever and ever. . . . It had a black canal in it, and a river that ran purple with ill-smelling dye, and vast piles of buildings.
>
> Charles Dickens, *Hard Times*

For better or worse, the industrial revolution made Britain the workshop of the world. ■

▲ *The first steam-powered loom was invented by Edmund Cartwright in 1786. Early power looms were most effective for weaving tough cotton fibers.*

■ *What conditions contributed to the growth of industry in the late 1700s?*

R E V I E W

1. **FOCUS** How did the agricultural and industrial revolutions change life in Britain during the 1700s?
2. **CONNECT** How did crop rotation in Britain during the 1700s differ from that used during the Middle Ages?
3. **ECONOMICS** How did an increase in the population during the 1700s help bring about changes in agriculture and industry?
4. **CRITICAL THINKING** If you had been a British peasant in the late 1700s, would you have preferred to remain a farmer or work in a textile factory? Explain.
5. **WRITING ACTIVITY** Referring to the text and a dictionary, write a definition of *capitalist* in your own words, and give an example from the present or the past.

Industrial Growth

> *The city's destiny and expanse finally bred a sense of captivity. . . . Its ugliness finally obscured its grandeur; the wretchedness of most of its inhabitants mocked the luxury of the few. In the workers' quarters it was a sink of vice and disease. . . . It was crowded with rootless, anonymous strangers.*
>
> Richard D. Altick, 20th-century historian

▼ *The textile factory below was one of the first examples of industrial growth in England. Notice the huge machines in this cloth factory. Modern industrial growth often results in other community projects, such as schools, museums, and shopping centers like the one at the right.*

Background

The English agricultural and industrial revolutions led to higher living standards and new expectations and desires. Thousands of people moved from rural areas to cities in search of work and a brighter future. The cities, however, were not ready to accommodate them. London, Birmingham, and other English cities were filled with people desperate for work. As described in the quote at the top of this page, poverty and overcrowding made these industrial cities places that bred despair.

On the other hand, industrialization affected the people in some very positive ways. Because of improvements in agricultural technology, food production increased. The increase in the number of new industries gave people a wider choice of how to make a living.

In cities, people were exposed to music, art, and other forms of culture that were less available in the countryside. Nevertheless, debates raged over whether the advantages of industrialization actually outweighed the disadvantages.

Concerns About Growth

The same debate rages today. When a major industry considers opening a plant or large office in a small or medium-sized community, some people in the community are for such growth; others are against it.

Those who welcome the new facility promote it with a number of arguments. For one thing, new industry creates new jobs. Its owners and the people who move to the town to work at the new facility will pay taxes to the town. These taxes can be used to build new schools, repair streets, and improve city services. The larger population will attract other new businesses: restaurants, hotels, clothing stores, groceries.

Those who do not want the new industry in their community have other arguments. A larger population will require more city services, such as more teachers, wider streets, more sewers, and larger police and fire departments. To get enough money to pay for all this will involve increasing taxes, at least at first. Opponents also argue that heavier traffic may lead to congestion, confusion, and frustration. Life may become more hectic and less enjoyable for the people in the town.

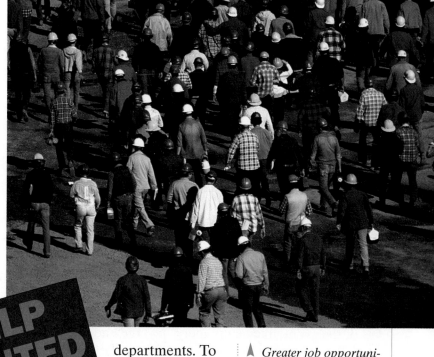

HELP WANTED

▲ *Greater job opportunities result from industrial growth.*

Decision Point

1. What goals and values would cause residents to support the bringing of a new industrial facility to their community? What goals and values would cause these residents to oppose the idea?

2. Suppose a manufacturing company plans to build a new factory in your town or city. What do you think you would want to know about this new facility? Where could you find the information you want?

3. Imagine that a new industry is going to be based in your community. What one problem could this help to solve? (Consider unemployment, young people leaving the community, inadequate support for local businesses.)

4. What is one problem that a new industry in your area might create? Can you think of a way to prevent this problem from arising and still allow the industry to develop in your area?

Presenting Primary Sources

Here's Why

You will probably speak to groups several times while you are in school. If you know how to prepare an interesting oral report, your presentations will be less stressful and more well received.

One way to make oral reports more accurate and interesting is to use primary sources. As you know, primary sources are documents that are produced at the time of the event, like newspaper articles. Many people you have read about in this chapter left written accounts of events that occurred during their lifetimes. Benjamin Franklin, for example, is well known for his fascinating autobiography. John Locke, Jean Jacques Rousseau, Adam Smith, and Voltaire also wrote extensively about events and ideas of their time. Suppose you wanted to make an oral report about one of these people. How would you use primary sources to make your report interesting?

Here's How

You can use primary sources in any of several different ways. You would not use all of these methods in one report, but using any one of them will certainly improve your report.

1. Use a primary source to limit your topic. For example, a specific journal entry could become the basis for an oral report about Benjamin Franklin.
2. Use quotations from a primary source to help bring your report alive. For example, you could frame your report with quotations at the beginning and the end. Or you could use quotations throughout the report to support specific points.
3. Broaden the perspective of your report by using several primary sources. For example, if you were preparing a report about the Constitutional Convention, you might choose quotations from the writings of Thomas Jefferson, Benjamin Franklin, and John Adams.

Review the steps below for preparing and presenting an oral report. Think about how you might use primary sources as you work your way through the steps.

Try It

Use the steps listed below to prepare an oral report about one of the people mentioned in Here's Why. Be sure to use primary source materials that will spark your listeners' interest.

Apply It

Find examples of primary sources used in oral reports on radio or television. Explain how the reports used those primary sources.

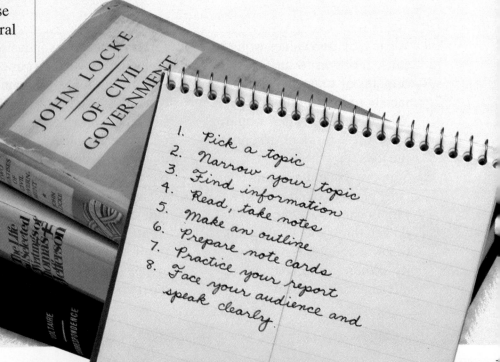

1. Pick a topic
2. Narrow your topic
3. Find information
4. Read, take notes
5. Make an outline
6. Prepare note cards
7. Practice your report
8. Face your audience and speak clearly.

LESSON 4

After the American Revolution

After the North American colonists over-threw Britain's authority, government in the new nation was founded on the Articles of Confederation. Adopted in 1777, the Articles only loosely united the 13 states. Each state was like a separate country, with its own government, army, trade, and currency.

Many leaders, including George Washington, felt that the nation needed a more powerful central government than it had. They hoped that such a government would unite the states. The leaders also believed that the natural rights of the people had to be outlined to protect the freedoms that had so recently been won. In 1787, the leaders of the nation met to provide the nation with a new and responsive government.

What Enlightenment ideals did the founders of the government of the United States share with the philosophes?

Key Terms

- checks and balances

◄ *George Washington was unanimously approved as president of the Constitutional Convention held at Philadelphia in 1787.*

A New Constitution

We the people of the United States, in order to form a more perfect union, establish justice, insure domestic tranquility, provide for the common defense, promote the general welfare, and secure the blessings of liberty to ourselves and our posterity, do ordain and establish this Constitution for the United States of America.

497

▲ *The three branches of the U.S. Government are also separated physically in Washington D.C.—the executive White House (top right), the judicial Supreme Court (top left), and the legislative Capitol (bottom).*

How Do We Know?

HISTORY *In 1792, British author Mary Wollstonecraft extended the theory of natural rights to include women. In her book* A Vindication of the Rights of Women, *she stresses the importance of education in bringing about equality between men and women.*

■ *What ideas in the Constitution are similar to the ideals of the philosophes?*

The quote you just read begins the Constitution. It expresses the purpose of the document. The influence of the Enlightenment can be clearly seen in the first three words, "We the people." Americans had come to believe in Locke and Rousseau's theory that government is basically a "social contract" between the people and their ruler.

The Constitution goes on to identify the branches of government and to define these branches' roles. The three branches were the legislative, executive, and judicial. The framers of the Constitution wanted to keep any one of the branches of government from becoming too powerful. As the French philosophe Montesquieu had written, "It is necessary from the very nature of things that power should be a check to power."

Those writing the Constitution developed a system of **checks and balances** between government power centers. For example, the president can veto, or refuse to pass, bills passed by the Congress. But if Congress passes the bill again by a two-thirds vote, it becomes law.

Similarly, the president can nominate judges to the Supreme Court, but the Senate can refuse to approve the persons chosen by the president. The Supreme Court can also cancel laws that have been passed by Congress if they are judged to be in conflict with the Constitution. ■

We the People

UNDERSTANDING PROGRESS

When Alexander Hamilton, one of the delegates at the Constitutional Convention, tried to convince Americans to ratify the Constitution, he used a typical philosophe argument. The government of the United States would be better than past governments, he argued, because "the science of politics . . . like most other sciences, has received great improvement." Much like other thinkers of the Age of Enlightenment, Hamilton believed in progress. What is progress? And how do we measure progress?

What Is Progress?

Progress implies improvement, or forward movement toward a desirable goal. Although progress involves change, not all change involves progress. When the Roman Empire broke up, most of western Europe became isolated from the learning and culture of the larger world community. The Middle Ages were certainly a time of change but, in many ways, not a time of progress.

How Is Progress Measured?

Progress is not always easy to measure, because in some societies it occurs for some people but not for others. Ancient Greece is often considered a model of political, economic, and social progress. But this progress applied only to free white men, not to women or slaves. The opening up of the American West brought progress to pioneers but certainly not to American Indians.

Is Progress Always Good?

The philosophes of the 18th century looked forward to a perfect world. They did not realize that progress often has a cost. For instance, although the Industrial Revolution provided many people with jobs and goods, it also brought pollution, oppressive working conditions, and overcrowding to the cities. It is important to evaluate progress in terms of its benefits as well as its costs.

The Enlightenment

Around the World in 1790

■ *What was happening in the United States at this time that was so unusual?*

▼ *The Statue of Liberty has been a symbol of liberty, freedom, and democracy for over a hundred years.*

While Americans chose to form their own nation and to govern themselves, we should remember that this was an extremely unusual step for those times. With the adoption of the U.S. Constitution in 1788, Americans chose for themselves a system of government based on Enlightenment ideals and lessons learned from history. In the Constitution as in the French Declaration of the Rights of Man and the Citizen, are ideas from the *Magna Carta*, and the English Bill of Rights.

Yet most people around the world had no idea of these changes. When the power of the Indian Mughal emperors fell in the 1770s, European trading companies established treaties that often led to colonization. As their power grew, the British took over more and more Asian lands. When Britain won the Seven Years' War in 1763, it became the world's largest and most powerful empire.

In China, Emperor Qianlong ruled an empire closed to outside influences and threats. During his reign, China came to be the most populous and largest nation on earth. China also ruled parts of Vietnam and Burma. In Japan, the Tokugawa clan still ruled as shoguns.

Society was also closed to outsiders, except for trade with the Dutch.

Europe's demand for the high-quality silks, cottons, lacquers, porcelains, rugs, and eventually tea that came from Asia, had to be paid for in gold and silver. That came either from Spanish-American mines or Africa's Gold Coast. In Spanish America, many people worked in mines in order to support this trade. Others worked on large cattle-ranching estates, also owned by the Spanish.

For the great majority of people around the world, ideas of full citizenship, equal rights, freedom of speech and belief, and democratic decision making, would have been extremely foreign. It was in British North America and France, however, that large segments of the merchant or middle class, working class, and peasantry began to believe in democratic republicanism.

The American experiment meant democracy on a scale that had never been tried before. The Constitution created by these early Americans gave them and continues to give us today the opportunity to reform and change our government, ensuring that in all ages it is "of the people, by the people, and for the people." ■

R E V I E W

1. **FOCUS** What Enlightenment ideals did the founders of the government of the United States share with the philosophes?

2. **CONNECT** What were the similarities between the Constitution and the Declaration of the Rights of Man and of the Citizen?

3. **HISTORY** How did the United States Constitution reflect a belief in progress?

4. **CRITICAL THINKING** How does the separation of powers into three branches of government, and checks and balances among those branches, help to guarantee freedom?

5. **WRITING ACTIVITY** Imagine that you are an immigrant arriving in the United States in the 1800s. Write a description of why you left your home and what you hope to find when you arrive in the United States.

Chapter Review

Reviewing Key Terms

Age of Enlightenment (p. 477)
agricultural revolution (p. 490)
capitalist (p. 493)
checks and balances (p. 498)
contract (p. 479)
crop rotation (p. 491)

enclosure (p. 491)
enlightened despot (p. 480)
industrial revolution (p. 492)
natural right (p. 479)
philosophe (p. 477)
reason (p. 476)

A. Rewrite each sentence. Use a key term in place of the phrase in italics.

1. Sir Isaac Newton used *logical thought* to discover the laws of motion.
2. Joseph II was an *absolute ruler who supported the ideals of the Enlightenment.*
3. The framers of the Constitution developed *a system of maintaining a balance of power between the three branches of government.*
4. *Breaking up large open, common fields into smaller, fenced-in plots* was an important part of the agricultural revolution.
5. *People willing to invest their money in new industries* were essential to the industrial revolution.

B. Write a sentence or two for each pair of words showing how the words are related.

1. Age of Enlightenment, philosophe
2. contract, natural right
3. agricultural revolution, crop rotation
4. industrial revolution, capitalist

Exploring Concepts

A. Copy the diagram and fill in the names of the people or documents.

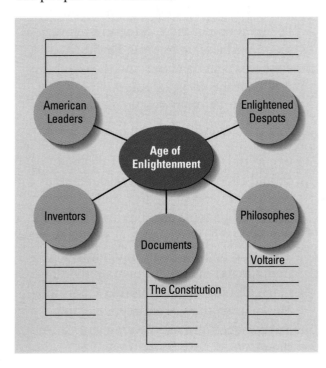

B. Support each statement with facts and details from the chapter.

1. Many of the philosophes hoped to discover a better way to govern.
2. Both Martin Luther and Thomas Jefferson challenged authority in order to make positive changes in their world.
3. Frederick II admired Voltaire and adopted many of his ideas.
4. During the reign of Joseph II, many Austrians were freer than ever before.
5. The Declaration of the Rights of Man and the Citizen included ideas from the writings of John Locke and Jean-Jacques Rousseau.
6. One of the effects of the agricultural revolution was an increased supply of workers for the Industrial Revolution.
7. Ideas expressed by the philosophes can be found in American government.

Reviewing Skills

1. Reread the section in Lesson 3 entitled The Industrial Revolution. Choose one invention that would make a good oral report. What would you want to cover in your report? Make an outline. What primary sources might you use? Indicate in your outline where you would use information from primary sources.

2. Turn to Lesson 3, page 490. Find the section of the lesson with the heading The Agricultural Revolution. Use note cards to take notes summarizing the information found in this section. Remember to include subtopics, the source of information, and your page references.

3. You have to give an oral report on a recent event that occurred in your city, state, or country. What might you use as a source of information for your oral report?

Using Critical Thinking

1. In 1764, Voltaire wrote: "In general, the art of government consists in taking as much money as possible from one class of citizens to give to another." He was referring to the way that the king of France taxed the Third Estate. Does this statement describe government in the United States today? Why?

2. People living during the Age of Enlightenment believed that poverty, intolerance, and injustice could be ended. But we still have those problems today. What can citizens of this century do to help end them?

3. Inventions such as the flying shuttle greatly changed the British textile industry. Goods were produced more cheaply and quickly, but under terrible working conditions. Think of other inventions that have had a profound effect on other industries. Name some positive effects of those inventions. Name some negative effects.

Preparing for Citizenship

1. GROUP ACTIVITY Stage a panel discussion between philosophes and enlightened despots. You may portray Locke, Voltaire, Catherine the Great, or other figures from the chapter. Your purpose should be to include the points that the two groups agreed on, but also show how they differed. You may want to consult other resources such as biographies or the encyclopedia for additional ideas.

2. WRITING ACTIVITY Analyze a part of the Declaration of Independence to find ideas from the philosophes. On the left half of a large poster, write passages from the Declaration. On the right half, write the name of the philosophe on whose ideas the passage is based.

3. COLLABORATIVE LEARNING As a class, choose a recent period from history and put together a three-volume encyclopedia of the thinking from that period similar to Diderot's *Encyclopédie*. Each volume will be about one of these categories: government, business, or science. Decide as a class what the page size and the cover design of the encyclopedie will be. Team up with three other people. Divide the team into two pairs. Each pair is responsible for providing an illustrated article in one of the three categories. Each pair should choose a topic and research it in periodicals, encyclopedias, and other resources. The topic may be related to people, ideas, events, inventions or discoveries. Then one person should summarize the findings and the other illustrate the summary. Get together with other teams who have chosen the same category, bind all the pages into one volume and cover them.

Time/Space Databank

Primary Sources   504
  Excerpts from the *Magna Carta*   504
  Excerpts from the English
    Bill of Rights   505
  Excerpts from the Declaration
    of the Rights of Man
    and the Citizen   506
  Declaration of Independence   509

Minipedia   513
  Heraldry   513
  Exploration   514
  World History Timelines   515

Atlas   518
  World: Political   518
  World: Physical   520
  Eurasia: Political/Physical   522
  Middle East: Political/Physical   524

Africa: Political/Physical   525
North America: Political/Physical   526
South America: Political/Physical   527
Pacific Rim: Political/Physical   528
World: Religions   529
World: Languages   529
World: Vegetation   530
World: Climate   530
World: Population   531
World: Land Use and Resources   531
The World: A.D. 750   532
The World: A.D. 1492   533

Glossary of Geographic   534
  Terms
Gazetteer   536
Biographical Dictionary   539
Glossary   543

★ ★ ★ ★ ★ ★ ★ ★ ★ ★

Excerpts from the

Magna Carta (1215)

The *Magna Carta* brought constitutional monarchy to England by limiting the power of the rulers. Since the time of William the Conqueror, the law of the land held that ordinary people had rights; the *Magna Carta* made that law official. It established that no one is above the law, even the king. This is called the rule of law. The *Magna Carta* also balanced the monarch's power by putting the right to tax people into the hands of the people's representatives. It set the rights of private property so that kings or lords could not simply take away others' property. The *Magna Carta* also set a system of justice that called for proper trials and juries. Here are some excerpts from the *Magna Carta* (1215).

---

freeman someone with the rights and privileges of a citizen
gravity seriousness
saving except for
freehold property held for life
villein a kind of serf
wainage agricultural tools
bailiff officer of the law
chattels personal, movable property

A *freeman* shall not be fined for a small offense, except in proportion to the **gravity** of the offense; and for a great offense he shall be fined in proportion to the magnitude of the offense, **saving** his **freehold;** and a merchant in the same way, saving his merchandise; and the **villein** shall be fined in the same way, saving his **wainage,** if he shall be at our (i.e., the king's) mercy; and none of the above fines shall be imposed except by the oaths of honest men of the neighborhood.

No constable or other **bailiff** of ours [i.e., the king] shall take anyone's grain or other **chattels** without immediately paying for them in money, unless he is able to obtain a postponement at the good will of the seller.

No sheriff or bailiff of ours [i.e., the king] or any one else, shall take horses or wagons of any free man, for carrying purposes, except on the permission of that free man.

The king cannot seize people, put them in jail, or expel them from the kingdom without a fair trial with a jury, according to the law.

No free man shall be taken, or imprisoned, or banished, or in any way injured, nor will we go upon him, nor send upon him, except by the legal judgment of his peers, or by the law of the land.

Neither we nor our bailiffs will take the wood of another man for castles, or for anything else which we are doing, except by the permission of him to who the wood belongs.

To no one will we sell, no one will we deny or delay, right to justice.

Excerpts from the

English Bill of Rights (1689)

Almost 500 years after the *Magna Carta* was signed, the English Bill of Rights extended more individual rights to English citizens. In the Glorious Revolution of 1689, England's new king and queen had to accept the English Bill of Rights before they could take the throne. This law guaranteed basic freedoms, like the freedom from cruel and unusual punishment, the freedom for members of parliament to speak openly, and the freedom of parliament to meet often and without the influence of the crown. The Bill of Rights established the principle that the monarchy was limited by the parliament. Now the ruler was simply another official in the service of the state. Here are some excerpts from the English Bill of Rights (1689), in which the parliament declares.

That the **pretended** power of suspending of laws or the execution of laws by regal authority without consent of parliament is illegal.

That the pretended power of dispensing with laws or the execution of laws by regal authority as it hath been assumed and exercised of late is illegal.

That the **levying** money for or to the use of the crown by **pretence** of **prerogative** without grant of parliament for a longer time or in other manner than the same is or shall be granted is illegal.

That it is the right of the subjects to petition the king and all commitments and prosecutions for such petitioning are illegal.

That the raising or keeping a standing army within the kingdom in time of peace unless it be with consent of parliament is against law.

That the subjects which are Protestants may have arms for their defence suitable to their conditions and as allowed by law.

That election of members of parliament ought to be free.

That the freedom of speech and debates or proceedings in parliament ought not to be **impeached** or questioned in any court or place out of parliament.

That excessive bail ought not to be required nor excessive fines imposed nor cruel and unusual punishments inflicted.

And that for **redress** of all **grievances** and for the amending, strengthening and preserving of the laws parliament ought to be held frequently.

pretended supposed

levying raising *pretence* a right that is claimed without basis in law *prerogative* an exclusive right or privilege

Parliament limits the power of the king to raise or keep an army. Now the monarch needs the parliament's agreement to do this.

impeached challenged

redress setting right; correcting
grievances complaints or protests

505

Excerpts from the

Declaration of the Rights of Man and of the Citizen *(1789)*

The Declaration of the Rights of Man and of the Citizen was strongl[y] influenced by the English Bill of Rights, the writings of Rousseau, and the American Declaration of Independence. The rule of law is supporte[d] in the French Declaration, and France's rulers now lead only by the agreement of the nation. To balance power, the Declaration establishes a national assembly which will also control the country's taxation. Also se[t] down in the Declaration are the right to private property and the right t[o] a fair trial according to the law. For those who believed in the French Revolution, the Declaration of the Rights of Man and the Citizen (1789) was practically a holy document.

---

calamities disasters
solemn serious
inalienable cannot be removed or transferred to others

grievances complaints or protests
incontestable unquestionable
redound contribute
auspices protection

imprescriptible cannot be removed

The representatives of the French people, organized as a National Assembly, believing that the ignorance, neglect, or contempt of th[e] rights of man are the sole causes of public **calamities** and of the corruption of governments, have determined to set forth in a **solemn** dec[-] laration the natural, **inalienable**, and sacred rights of man, in order tha[t] this declaration, being constantly before all members of the social body, shall remind them continually of their rights and duties; in order that th[e] acts of the legislative power, as well as those of the executive power, may be compared at any moment with the objects and purposes of all political institutions and may thus be more respected; and lastly, in order that the **grievances** of the citizens, based hereafter upon simple and **incon-testable** principles, shall tend to the maintenance of the constitution an[d] **redound** to the happiness of all. Therefore the National Assembly recognizes and proclaims, in the presence and under the **auspices** of the Supreme Being, the following rights of man and of the citizen:

1. *Men are born and remain free and equal in rights. Social distinc[-] tions may be founded only upon the general good.*

2. *The aim of all political association is the preservation of the nat-ural and **imprescriptible** rights of man. These rights are liberty property, security, and resistance to oppression.*

3. *The principle of all sovereignty resides essentially in the nation. No body nor individual may exercise any authority which does not proceed directly from the nation.*

4. *Liberty consists in the freedom to do everything which injures no one else; hence the exercise of the natural rights of each man has no limits except those which assure to the other members of the society the enjoyment of the same rights. These limits can only be determined by law.*

5. *Law can only prohibit such actions as are hurtful to society. Nothing may be prevented which is not forbidden by law, and no one may be forced to do anything not provided for by law.*

6. *Law is the expression of the general will. Every citizen has a right to participate personally, or through his representative, in its formation. It must be the same for all, whether it protects or punishes. All citizens, being equal in the eyes of the law, are equally eligible to all dignities and to all public positions and occupations, according to their abilities, and without distinction except that of their virtues and talents.*

7. *No person shall be accused, arrested, or imprisoned, except in the cases and according to the forms prescribed by law. Anyone **soliciting**, transmitting, **executing**, or causing to be executed, any **arbitrary** order, shall be punished. But any citizen summoned or arrested **in virtue of** the law shall submit without delay, as resistance constitutes an offense.*

8. *The law shall provide for such punishments only as are strictly and obviously necessary, and no one shall suffer punishment except it be legally inflicted in virtue of a law passed and **promulgated** before the **commission** of the offense.*

9. *As all persons are held innocent until they shall have been declared guilty, if arrest shall be deemed **indispensable**, all harshness not essential to the securing of the prisoner's persons shall be severely repressed by law.*

10. *No one shall be **disquieted** on account of his opinions, including his religious views, provided their **manifestation** does not disturb the public order established by law.*

Liberty means that people are free to do anything as long as it does not harm others. People have the right to pursue their own goals, as long as they recognize that other people have the same rights, too.

soliciting trying to get
executing carrying out
arbitrary not limited by law
in virtue of according to

promulgated put into effect by formal announcement
commission carrying out

indispensible absolutely necessary

disquieted troubled; made anxious
manifestation presentation

People have the right to speak, write, or publish their thoughts freely. The law may set limits to this freedom of speech, and people must respect the limits of the law.

11. *The free communication of ideas and opinions is one of the most precious of the rights of man. Every citizen may, accordingly, speak, write, and print with freedom, but shall be responsible for such abuses of this freedom as shall be defined by law.*

12. *The security of the rights of man and of the citizen requires public military forces. These forces are, therefore, established for the good of all and not for the personal advantage of those to whom they shall be intrusted.*

13. *A common contribution is essential for the maintenance of the public forces and for the cost of administration. This should be equitably distributed among all the citizens in proportion to their means.*

duration length of time

14. *All the citizens have a right to decide, either personally or by their representatives, as to the necessity of the public contribution: to grant this freely; to know to what uses it is put; and to fix the proportion, the mode of assessment and of collection and the **duration** of the taxes.*

15. *Society has the right to require of every public agent an account of his administration.*

16. *A society in which the observance of the law is not assured, nor the separation of powers defined, has no constitution at all.*

inviolable unable to be broken or changed

indemnified compensated

17. *Since property is an **inviolable** and sacred right, no one shall be deprived thereof except where public necessity, legally determined, shall clearly demand it, and then only on condition that the owner shall have been previously and equitably **indemnified**.*

★ ★ ★ ★ ★ ★ ★ ★ ★ ★

The Declaration of Independence

In Congress, July 4, 1776

The unanimous declaration of the thirteen united States of America

INTRODUCTION*

When, in the course of human events, it becomes necessary for one people to dissolve the political bands which have connected them with another, and to assume, among the powers of the earth, the separate and equal station to which the laws of nature and of nature's God entitle them, a decent respect to the opinions of mankind requires that they should declare the causes which impel them to the separation.

In the Declaration of Independence, the colonists explained why they were breaking away from Great Britain. They believed they had the right to form their own country.

powers of the earth *other nations*
station *place* **impel** *drive*

BASIC RIGHTS

We hold these truths to be self-evident: That all men are created equal, that they are **endowed** by their Creator with certain unalienable rights; that among these are life, liberty, and the pursuit of happiness; that, to secure these rights, governments are instituted among men, **deriving** their just powers from the consent of the governed; that whenever any form of government becomes destructive of these ends, it is the right of the people to alter or to abolish it, and to institute new government, laying its foundation on such principles, and organizing its powers in such form, as to them shall seem most likely to effect their safety and happiness. **Prudence,** indeed, will dictate that governments long established should not be changed for light and **transient** causes; and accordingly all experience hath shown that mankind are more disposed to suffer, while evils are sufferable, than to right themselves by abolishing the forms to which they are accustomed. But when a long train of abuses and **usurpations,** pursuing invariably the same object, evinces a design to reduce them under **absolute despotism**, it is their right, it is their duty, to throw off such government, and to provide new guards for their future security. Such has been the patient sufferance of these colonies; and such is now the necessity which **constrains** them to alter their former systems of government. The history of the present King of Great Britain is a history of repeated injuries and usurpations, all having in direct object the establishment of an absolute tyranny over these states. To prove this, let facts be submitted to a candid world.

The opening part of the Declaration is very famous. It says that all people are equal. Everyone has certain basic rights that are unalienable. That means that these rights are so basic that they cannot be taken away. Governments are formed to protect these basic rights. If a government does not do this, then the people have a right to begin a new one.

endowed *given* **deriving** *receiving*
prudence *wisdom* **transient** *temporary*
usurpations *seizing powers unjustly*
absolute despotism *complete and unjust control* **constrains** *forces*

Forming a new government meant ending the colonial ties to the king. The writers listed the wrongs of King George III to prove the need for their actions.

*Titles have been added to the Declaration to make it easier to read. These titles are not in the original document.

Colonists said the king had not let the colonies make their own laws. He had limited the people's representation in their assemblies.

assent agreement inestimable immeasurable formidable causing fear compliance giving in to a request or a demand

The king had made colonial assemblies meet at unusual times and places. This made going to assembly meetings hard for colonial representatives.

In some cases the king stopped the assembly from meeting at all.

annihilation complete destruction convulsions disturbances endeavored tried

The king stopped people from moving to the colonies and into new western lands. *hither here appropriations grants judiciary powers system of law courts*

The king prevented the colonies from choosing their own judges. Instead, he sent over judges who depended on him for their jobs and salaries.

tenure term multitude large number harass bother, cause trouble

The king kept British soldiers in the colonies, even though the colonists had not asked for them.

render make jurisdiction authority quartering providing housing for mock false imposing forcing depriving taking away

The king and Parliament had taxed the colonists without their consent. This was one of the most important reasons the colonists were angry at Great Britain.

★　★　★　★　★　★　★　★　★

CHARGES AGAINST THE KING

He has refused his assent to laws, the most wholesome and necessary for the public good.

*He has forbidden his governors to pass laws of immediate and pressing importance, unless suspended in their operation till his **assent** should be obtained; and, when so suspended, he has utterly neglected to attend to them.*

*He has refused to pass other laws for the accommodation of large districts of people, unless those people would relinquish the right of representation in the legislature, a right **inestimable** to them, and **formidable** to tyrants only.*

*He has called together legislative bodies at places unusual, uncomfortable, and distant from the depository of their public records, for the sole purpose of fatiguing them into **compliance** with his measures.*

He has dissolved representative houses repeatedly, for opposing, with manly firmness, his invasions on the rights of the people.

*He has refused for a long time, after such dissolutions, to cause others to be elected; whereby the legislative powers, incapable of **annihilation,** have returned to the people at large for their exercise; the state remaining, in the mean time, exposed to all the dangers of invasions from without and **convulsions** within.*

*He has **endeavored** to prevent the population of these states; for that purpose obstructing the laws for the naturalization of foreigners; refusing to pass others to encourage their migration **hither,** and raising the conditions of new **appropriations** of lands.*

*He has obstructed the administration of justice, by refusing his assent to laws for establishing **judiciary powers.***

*He has made judges dependent on his will alone, for the **tenure** of their offices, and the amount of payment of their salaries.*

*He has erected a **multitude** of new offices, and sent hither swarms of officers to **harass** our people and eat out their substance.*

He has kept among us, in times of peace, standing armies, without the consent of our legislatures.

*He has affected to **render** the military independent of, and superior to, the civil power.*

*He has combined with others to subject us to a **jurisdiction** foreign to our constitution and unacknowledged by our laws, giving his assent to their acts of pretended legislation:*

*For **quartering** large bodies of armed troops among us;*

*For protecting them, by a **mock** trial, from punishment for any murders which they should commit on the inhabitants of these states;*

For cutting off our trade with all parts of the world;

*For **imposing** taxes on us without our consent;*

*For **depriving** us, in many cases, of the benefits of trial by jury;*

★ ★ ★ ★ ★ ★ ★ ★ ★

For transporting us beyond seas, to be tried for pretended offenses;

For **abolishing** the free system of English laws in a neighboring province, establishing therein an **arbitrary** government, and enlarging its boundaries, so as to render it at once an example and **fit instrument** for introducing the same absolute rule into these colonies;

For taking away our charters, abolishing our most valuable laws, and altering fundamentally the forms of our governments.

For suspending our own legislatures, and declaring themselves **invested** with power to legislate for us in all cases whatsoever.

He has **abdicated** government here, by declaring us out of his protection and waging war against us.

He has **plundered** our seas, ravaged our coasts, burned our towns, and destroyed the lives of our people.

He is at this time transporting large armies of foreign **mercenaries** to complete the works of death, desolation, and tyranny already begun with circumstances of cruelty and **perfidy** scarcely paralleled in the most **barbarous** ages, and totally unworthy the head of a civilized nation.

He has constrained our fellow-citizens, taken captive on the high seas, to bear arms against their country, to become the executioners of their friends and brethren, or to fall themselves by their hands.

He has excited domestic **insurrection** among us, and has endeavored to bring on the inhabitants of our frontiers, the merciless Indian savages, whose known rule of warfare is an undistinguished destruction of all ages, sexes, and conditions.

RESPONSE TO THE KING

In every stage of these oppressions we have **petitioned** for **redress** in the most humbles terms; our repeated petitions have been answered only by repeated injury. A prince, whose character is thus marked by every act which may define a tyrant, is unfit to be the ruler of a free people.

Nor have we been wanting in our attentions to our British brethren. We have warned them, from time to time, of attempts by their legislature to extend an **unwarrantable** jurisdiction over us. We have reminded them of the circumstances of our emigration and settlement here. We have appealed to their native justice and **magnanimity;** and we have **conjured** them, by the ties of our common kindred, to **disavow** these usurpations, which would inevitably interrupt our connections and correspondence. They, too, have been deaf to the voice of justice and of **consanguinity.** We must, therefore, **acquiesce** in the necessity which **denounces** our separation, and hold them, as we hold the rest of mankind, enemies in war, in peace friends.

---

abolishing getting rid of **arbitrary** tyrannical **fit instrument** suitable tool **invested** having

The colonists felt that the king had waged war on them.

abdicated given up **plundered** robbed

The king had hired German soldiers and sent them to the colonies to keep order.

mercenaries hired soldiers **desolation** misery **perfidy** treachery **barbarous** uncivilized **insurrection** revolt

The colonists said that they had asked the king to change his policies, but he had not listened to them.

petitioned requested **redress** relief **unwarrantable** unfair **magnanimity** generosity **conjured** requested earnestly **disavow** turn away from **consanguinity** kinship **acquiesce** agree **denounces** condemns

The writers declared that the colonies were free and independent states, equal to the world's other states. They had the powers to make war and peace and to trade with other countries.

rectitude moral rightness *absolved* freed *allegiance* loyalty *levy* declare *contract* make *mutually* together

The signers pledged their lives to the support of this Declaration. The Continental Congress ordered the Declaration of Independence to be read in all the states and to the army.

★ ★ ★ ★ ★ ★ ★ ★ ★

INDEPENDENCE

*We, therefore, the representatives of the United States of America, in General Congress assembled, appealing to the Supreme Judge of the world for the **rectitude** of our intentions, do, in the name and by the authority of the good people of these colonies, solemnly publish and declare, that these United Colonies are, and of right ought to be, FREE AND INDEPENDENT STATES; that they are **absolved** from all **allegiance** to the British crown, and that all political connection between them and the state of Great Britain is, and ought to be, totally dissolved; and that, as free and independent states, they have full power to **levy** war, conclude peace, **contract** alliances, establish commerce, and do all other acts and things which independent states may of right do. And for the support of this declaration, with a firm reliance on the protection of Divine Providence, we **mutually** pledge to each other our lives, our fortunes, and our sacred honor.*

John Hancock

NEW HAMPSHIRE
Josiah Bartlett
William Whipple
Matthew Thornton

MASSACHUSETTS
John Adams
Samuel Adams
Robert Treat Paine
Elbridge Gerry

NEW YORK
William Floyd
Philip Livingston
Francis Lewis
Lewis Morris

RHODE ISLAND
Stephen Hopkins
William Ellery

NEW JERSEY
Richard Stockton
John Witherspoon
Francis Hopkinson
John Hart
Abraham Clark

PENNSYLVANIA
Robert Morris
Benjamin Rush
Benjamin Franklin
John Morton
George Clymer
James Smith
George Taylor
James Wilson
George Ross

DELAWARE
Caesar Rodney
George Read
Thomas McKean

MARYLAND
Samuel Chase
William Paca
Thomas Stone
Charles Carroll of Carrollton

NORTH CAROLINA
William Hooper
Joseph Hewes
John Penn

VIRGINIA
George Wythe
Richard Henry Lee
Thomas Jefferson
Benjamin Harrison
Thomas Nelson, Jr.
Francis Lightfoot Lee
Carter Braxton

SOUTH CAROLINA
Edward Rutledge
Thomas Heyward, Jr.
Thomas Lynch, Jr.
Arthur Middleton

CONNECTICUT
Roger Sherman
Samuel Huntington
William Williams
Oliver Wolcott

GEORGIA
Button Gwinnett
Lyman Hall
George Walton

Heraldry

Symbols of heraldry

Parts of a coat of arms

- Crest
- Mantling
- Helmet
- Supporter
- Shield
- Motto

The displaying of arms

Coats of arms were first displayed on the shields of knights. Later, arms appeared on flags, clothes, and other possessions.

Symbols used on a coat of arms

Coats of arms were developed during the 1100's as a way to help a knight's followers recognize him on the battlefield. The colors, designs, lines, and *cadency* (status) symbols shown below became standard and were used in different combinations according to specific rules.

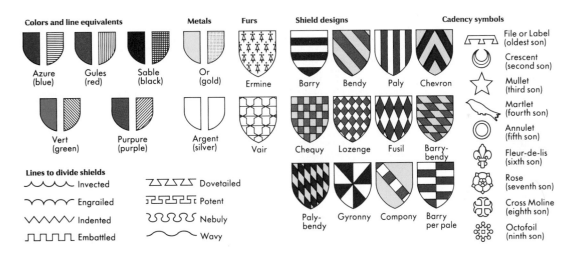

Colors and line equivalents

- Azure (blue)
- Gules (red)
- Sable (black)
- Vert (green)
- Purpure (purple)

Metals

- Or (gold)
- Argent (silver)

Furs

- Ermine
- Vair

Shield designs

- Barry
- Bendy
- Paly
- Chevron
- Chequy
- Lozenge
- Fusil
- Barry-bendy
- Paly-bendy
- Gyronny
- Company
- Barry per pale

Cadency symbols

- File or Label (oldest son)
- Crescent (second son)
- Mullet (third son)
- Martlet (fourth son)
- Annulet (fifth son)
- Fleur-de-lis (sixth son)
- Rose (seventh son)
- Cross Moline (eighth son)
- Octofoil (ninth son)

Lines to divide shields

- Invected
- Engrailed
- Indented
- Embattled
- Dovetailed
- Potent
- Nebuly
- Wavy

Kinds of charges

A charge is a symbol of an object or figure that appears on a shield. Animals are among the most popular charges.

- Swords
- Ship
- Tower
- Unicorn
- Lion
- Dragon
- Arms
- Wolf's head
- Tortoise

Patterns of family relationships

Two or more arms were sometimes combined on one shield in order to show family relationships. The earliest methods of *marshaling,* as this procedure is called, are shown below. The arms of two families are placed side by side or one within the other.

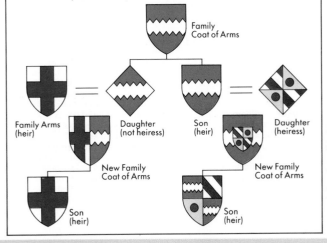

- Family Coat of Arms
- Family Arms (heir)
- Daughter (not heiress)
- Son (heir)
- Daughter (heiress)
- New Family Coat of Arms
- New Family Coat of Arms
- Son (heir)
- Son (heir)

Famous ancient and medieval explorers

Explorer	Nationality	Main achievements	Date
* Alexander the Great	Macedonian	Reached Afghanistan, western India.	c.331 B.C.-326 B.C.
* Eric the Red	Norwegian	Sailed to Greenland from Iceland.	c.982
* Ericson, Leif	Norwegian	Probably the first European to reach mainland North America.	c.1000
* Ibn Batuta	Arabian	Traveled through the Middle East and India; visited China and the East Indies.	1325-1354
Odoric of Pordenone	Italian	Traveled in Turkey, Iran, across central Asia, and in the Indian and South Pacific oceans.	c.1314-c.1330
* Polo, Marco	Italian	Visited Sri Lanka, China, India, Iran, and Sumatra.	1271-1295
* Pytheas	Greek	Sailed from the Mediterranean Sea to the North Atlantic Ocean.	c.300 B.C.
Rubruck, William of	Flemish	Traveled through central Asia to Mongolia.	1253-1255
Zhang Qian	Chinese	Traveled from China to central Asia.	128-126 B.C.

*Has a separate biography in WORLD BOOK.

Explorers of the great age of European discovery

Explorer	Nationality	Main achievements	Date
* Balboa, Vasco Núñez de	Spanish	Led expedition across Isthmus of Panama; sighted Pacific Ocean.	1513
* Cabeza de Vaca, Álvar Núñez	Spanish	Explored Gulf Plains from Texas to Mexico.	1528-1536
* Cabot, John	Italian	Sailed across the North Atlantic to what is now Canada.	1497-1498
* Cabot, Sebastian	Italian	Explored South American coast to the Río de la Plata.	1526-1530
* Cabral, Pedro Álvares	Portuguese	Reached Brazilian coast; sailed around Africa to India.	1500-1501
* Cartier, Jacques	French	Sailed up the St. Lawrence River.	1535
* Columbus, Christopher	Italian	Made four voyages to the West Indies and Caribbean lands.	1492-1504
* Coronado, Francisco de	Spanish	Explored the American Southwest.	1540-1542
* Cortés, Hernando	Spanish	Conquered Mexico.	1519-1521
* Da Gama, Vasco	Portuguese	First European to reach India by sea.	1498
* De Soto, Hernando	Spanish	Explored American Southeast; reached Mississippi River.	1539-1542
* Dias, Bartolomeu	Portuguese	First European to round the Cape of Good Hope.	1487-1488
* Drake, Sir Francis	English	First English explorer to sail around the world.	1577-1580
* Frobisher, Sir Martin	English	Searched North American coast for a Northwest Passage.	1576-1578
* Magellan, Ferdinand	Portuguese	Commanded first globe-circling voyage, completed in 1522 after his death.	1519-1521
* Oñate, Juan de	Spanish	Explored American Southwest.	1598-1605
* Orellana, Francisco de	Spanish	Explored Amazon River.	1541
* Pizarro, Francisco	Spanish	Conquered Peru; founded Lima.	1531-1535
* Ponce de León, Juan	Spanish	Explored Florida.	1513
* Verrazano, Giovanni da	Italian	Searched for a Northwest Passage.	1524
* Vespucci, Amerigo	Italian	Sailed to the West Indies and South America.	1499-1504

*Has a separate biography in WORLD BOOK.

Famous explorers of Africa

Explorer	Nationality	Main achievements	Date
Bruce, James	Scottish	Rediscovered source of the Blue Nile.	1770
* Burton, Sir Richard	English	Explored Arabia and East Africa; reached Lake Tanganyika.	1853-1858
Caillié, René	French	Explored western Africa; crossed the Sahara.	1826-1828
Clapperton, Hugh	Scottish	Explored northern Nigeria and Lake Chad region.	1822-1827
* Emin Pasha	German	Explored east-central Africa.	1878-1892
Laing, Alexander Gordon	Scottish	Explored Niger River Basin; reached Timbuktu.	1822; 1826
* Livingstone, David	Scottish	Traced upper course of the Zambezi River; reached Victoria Falls and Lake Ngami.	1849-1873
* Park, Mungo	Scottish	Explored course of the Niger River.	1795-1797; 1805-1806
Speke, John Hanning	English	Reached Lake Tanganyika and Lake Victoria.	1858
* Stanley, Sir Henry	Welsh	Explored the Congo River.	1874-1889

*Has a separate article in WORLD BOOK.

Explorers of Australia and the Pacific Ocean

Explorer	Nationality	Main achievements	Date
Bougainville, Louis Antoine de	French	Led first French expedition around the world.	1766-1769
Burke, Robert O'Hara	Irish	One of the first explorers to cross Australia from south to north, with William John Wills.	1860-1861
* Cook, James	English	Explored South Pacific.	1768-1779
* Dampier, William	English	Explored coasts of Australia, New Guinea, and New Britain.	1691-1701
Eyre, Edward John	English	Explored southern coast of Australia.	1840-1841
Jansz, Willem	Dutch	First known European to sight and land in Australia.	1606
Stuart, John McDouall	Scottish	Made six trips into the interior of Australia.	1858-1862
Sturt, Charles	English	Explored southeastern Australia; reached Darling River.	1829-1830
* Tasman, Abel Janszoon	Dutch	Sailed to Tasmania and New Zealand.	1642
Warburton, Peter Egerton	English	Crossed Australia from Alice Springs to Roebourne.	1873
Wills, William John	English	One of the first explorers to cross Australia from south to north, with Robert O'Hara Burke.	1860-1861

*Has a separate article in WORLD BOOK.

Extracted from the Exploration article in *World Book.* Copyright © 1998 by World Book, Inc.

Major developments

WORLD BOOK illustrations by Tak Murakami

Muhammad, the founder of Islam, began preaching about 610.

Under Justinian I, Byzantine scholars organized a great code of Roman law during the 500's.

The Chinese invented the magnetic compass about 1100.

Notre Dame Cathedral was completed in Paris in 1250.

The first books printed in Europe with movable type appeared in the mid-1400's.

Yuan Dynasty (1279-1368)

Song Dynasty (960-1279)

Christopher Columbus reached America in 1492.

Toltec and Aztec Empires (900-1521)

Abbasid Caliphate (750-1258)

The Italian poet Dante Alighieri wrote the *Divine Comedy* in the early 1300's.

Tang Dynasty (618-907)

Byzantine Empire (395-1453)

| 500 | 750 | 1000 | 1250 | 1500 |

Between 300 and 1500, new civilizations appeared in Africa and the Americas. In the Middle East, the Muslim Arabs rose to power and conquered a huge empire by the mid-700's. In the 1200's, Mongol warriors swept through Asia, creating one of the largest empires in history.

WORLD BOOK map

Important dates

300's-mid-1000's The Ghana Empire, the first great black empire in western Africa, existed as a trading state.

527-565 The Byzantine Empire reached its greatest extent under Emperor Justinian I.

622 Muhammad, prophet of Islam, fled from Mecca to Medina. His flight, called the Hegira, marks the beginning of the Islamic calendar.

732 Charles Martel and the Franks defeated invading Muslims in fighting in west-central France. The victory prevented the Muslims from overrunning Europe.

750 The Abbasids became the caliphs of the Islamic world.

800 Pope Leo III crowned Charlemagne, ruler of the Franks, emperor of the Romans.

c. 988 Vladimir I (also spelled Volodymyr) established

Christianity among the East Slavs, ancestors of the Belarusian, Russian, and Ukrainian people.

1054 Rivalries between the church in Rome and the church in Constantinople resulted in their separation as the Roman Catholic Church and Eastern Orthodox Churches.

1192 Yoritomo became the first shogun to rule Japan. Shogun rule lasted until 1867.

1215 English barons forced King John to grant a charter of liberties called Magna Carta.

1279 The Mongols gained control of all China.

1300's The Renaissance began in Italy.

1368 The Ming dynasty began its nearly 300-year rule of China.

1453 The Ottoman Turks captured Constantinople (Istanbul) and overthrew the Byzantine Empire.

World, History of the

Major developments

Nicolaus Copernicus proposed in 1543 that the sun is the center of the universe.

Michelangelo completed painting the ceiling of the Sistine Chapel in the Vatican in 1512.

William Shakespeare wrote many of the world's greatest dramas between 1590 and 1616.

Charles Darwin published his theory of evolution in 1859 in *The Origin of Species*.

European Colonial Expansion in Africa and Asia (1870-1914)

Latin-American Wars of Independence (1791-1824)

French Revolution (1789-1799)

Revolutionary War in America (1775-1783)

Industrial Revolution (1700-mid-1800's)

Manchu Rule of China (1644-1912)

Tokugawa Shogunate in Japan (1603-1867)

Mogul Empire (1526-1707)

Ludwig van Beethoven composed many of his greatest symphonies between 1800 and 1815.

Alexander Graham Bell invented the telephone in 1876.

Voyages of Discovery (1400's-1500's)

Ottoman Empire (1326-1922)

Renaissance (1300-1600)

| 1500 | 1600 | 1700 | 1800 | 1900 |

European colonial empires had spread over much of the world by the late 1800's. The largest empires of the period belonged to Great Britain, France, and Germany.

- Belgium
- France
- Germany
- Great Britain
- Italy
- Netherlands
- Portugal
- Spain

Important dates

1500's The Reformation led to the birth of Protestantism.

1519-1521 Ferdinand Magellan commanded the first globe-circling voyage, completed in 1522 after his death.

1521 The Spanish conquistador Hernando Cortés defeated the Aztec Indians of Mexico.

1526 Babar, a Muslim prince, invaded India and founded the Mogul Empire.

1588 The Royal Navy of England defeated the Spanish Armada, establishing England as a great naval power.

1644-1912 The Manchus ruled China as the Qing dynasty.

1776 The 13 American Colonies adopted the Declaration of Independence, establishing the United States of America.

1789 The French Revolution began.

1815 Napoleon Bonaparte was defeated in the Battle of Waterloo, ending his attempt to rule Europe.

1853-1854 Commodore Matthew Perry visited Japan and opened two ports to U.S. trade, ending Japan's isolation.

1858 Great Britain took over the rule of India from the East India Company after the Sepoy Rebellion.

1865 Union forces defeated the Confederates in the American Civil War after four years of fighting.

1869 The Suez Canal opened.

1871 Germany became united under the Prussian king, who ruled the new empire as Kaiser Wilhelm I.

1898 The United States took control of Guam, Puerto Rico, and the Philippines following the Spanish-American War.

Major developments

WORLD BOOK illustrations by Tak Murakami

Sigmund Freud developed psychoanalysis about 1900.

The Wright brothers made the first successful airplane flights in 1903.

Albert Einstein published his special theory of relativity in 1905.

World War I (1914-1918)

Alexander Fleming discovered penicillin in 1928.

The first computers were developed in the 1930's and 1940's.

The British Broadcasting Corporation made the world's first TV broadcasts in 1936.

World War II (1939-1945)

The Soviet Union launched the first artificial satellite in 1957.

Space Age (1957-   )

Vietnam War (1957-1975)

Korean War (1950-1953)

Researchers developed the first successful recombinant DNA procedure in 1974.

1900   1925   1950   1975   2000

The wealth of nations can be compared on the basis of each country's *gross domestic product* (GDP). The GDP is the value of all goods and services produced within a country in a year. The developing countries of Africa and Asia have the lowest GDP per person.

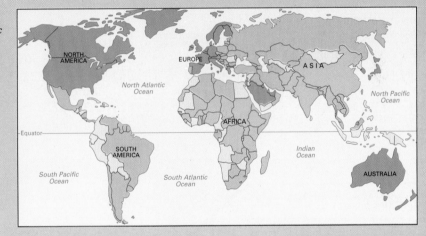

High GDP per person

Medium GDP per person

Low GDP per person

Very low GDP per person

WORLD BOOK map;
1991 GDP estimates.

Important dates

1914 The assassination of Archduke Francis Ferdinand of Austria-Hungary started World War I.

1917 The Bolsheviks (Communists) seized power in Russia.

1933 Adolf Hitler became dictator of Germany.

1939 Germany invaded Poland, starting World War II.

1941 The Japanese attacked Pearl Harbor, and the United States entered World War II.

1945 The United Nations was established.

1945 The first atomic bombs used in warfare were dropped by U.S. planes on Hiroshima and Nagasaki.

1945 World War II ended in Europe on May 7 and in the Pacific on September 2.

1949 The Chinese Communists conquered China.

1950 North Korean Communist troops invaded South Korea, starting the Korean War.

1957 The Vietnam War started when South Vietnamese rebels attacked the U.S.-backed South Vietnamese government.

1969 U.S. astronauts made the first manned moon landing.

1989-1990 Democratic reforms spread across Eastern Europe, and several non-Communist governments replaced Communist dictatorships.

1990 East Germany and West Germany were reunited, ending the division of Germany that had begun soon after the end of World War II.

1991 The Communist Party of the Soviet Union lost control of the Soviet government, and the Soviet Union ceased to exist.

WORLD: *Political*

ABBREVIATIONS

BOS. AND HERZ.
    Bosnia and Herzegovina
CEN. AFR. REP.
    Central African Republic
DEN. Denmark
FR. France
GR. Greece
IT. Italy
N. North, Northern
NETH. Netherlands
N.Z. New Zealand
PORT. Portugal
S. South
SP. Spain
U.A.E. United Arab
    Emirates
U.K. United Kingdom
U.S. United States
W. Western

—— National boundary

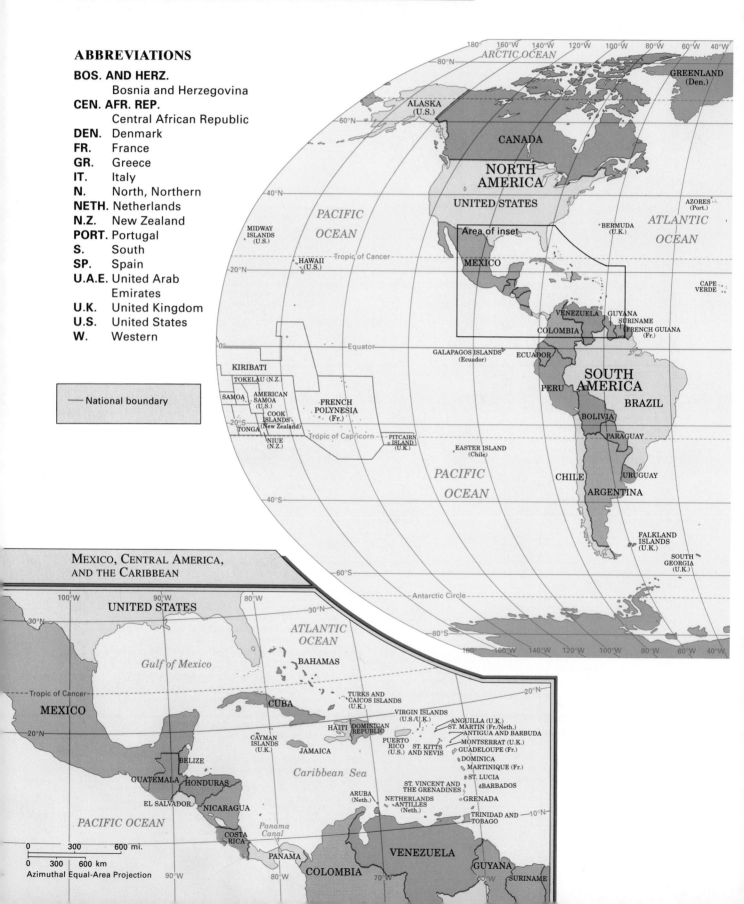

MEXICO, CENTRAL AMERICA, AND THE CARIBBEAN

Azimuthal Equal-Area Projection

Scale at Equator

0   1000   2000 mi.

0   1000   2000 km.
Robinson Projection

EUROPE

0   300   600 mi.

0   300   600 km.
Azimuthal Equal-Area Projection

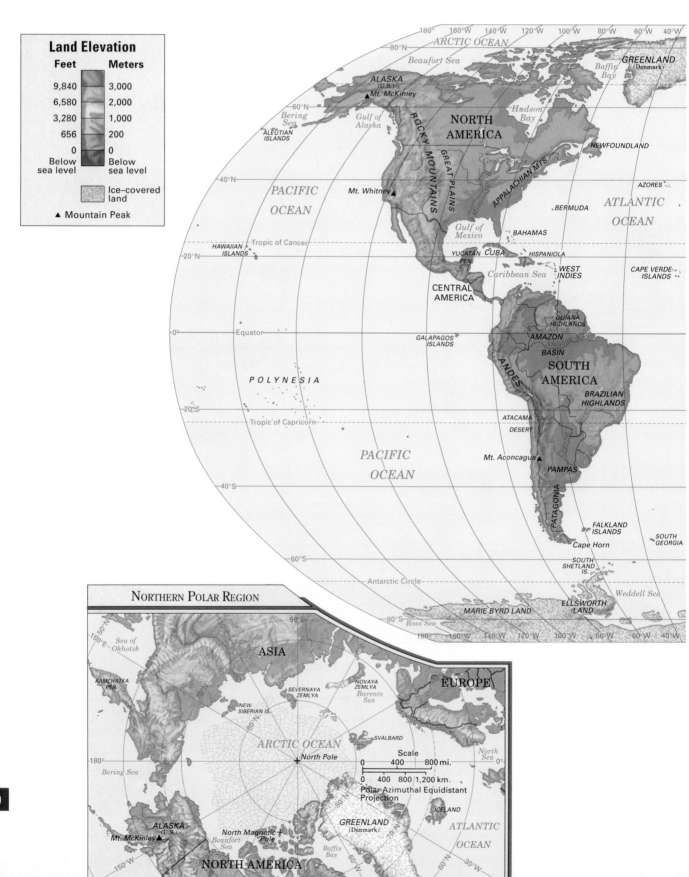

Land Elevation

Feet	Meters
9,840	3,000
6,580	2,000
3,280	1,000
656	200
0	0
Below sea level	Below sea level

Ice-covered land

▲ Mountain Peak

ARCTIC OCEAN
Beaufort Sea
GREENLAND (Denmark)
Baffin Bay
ALASKA (U.S.)
▲ Mt. McKinley
Bering Sea
Gulf of Alaska
ALEUTIAN ISLANDS
Hudson Bay
NORTH AMERICA
ROCKY MOUNTAINS
GREAT PLAINS
APPALACHIAN MTS.
NEWFOUNDLAND
Great Lakes
AZORES
BERMUDA
ATLANTIC OCEAN
PACIFIC OCEAN
Mt. Whitney ▲
Gulf of Mexico
BAHAMAS
Tropic of Cancer
HAWAIIAN ISLANDS
YUCATAN PEN.
CUBA
HISPANIOLA
WEST INDIES
CAPE VERDE ISLANDS
CENTRAL AMERICA
Caribbean Sea
GALAPAGOS ISLANDS
GUIANA HIGHLANDS
AMAZON BASIN
Equator
SOUTH AMERICA
POLYNESIA
ANDES
BRAZILIAN HIGHLANDS
ATACAMA DESERT
Tropic of Capricorn
Mt. Aconcagua ▲
PAMPAS
PACIFIC OCEAN
PATAGONIA
FALKLAND ISLANDS
SOUTH GEORGIA
Cape Horn
SOUTH SHETLAND IS.
Weddell Sea
MARIE BYRD LAND
ELLSWORTH LAND
Ross Sea
Antarctic Circle

NORTHERN POLAR REGION

Sea of Okhotsk
ASIA
KAMCHATKA PEN.
NEW SIBERIAN IS.
SEVERNAYA ZEMLYA
NOVAYA ZEMLYA
Barents Sea
EUROPE
SVALBARD
Bering Sea
ARCTIC OCEAN
North Pole
North Sea
Scale
0   400   800 mi.
0 400 800 1,200 km.
Polar Azimuthal Equidistant Projection
ALASKA (U.S.)
Mt. McKinley ▲
North Magnetic Pole
Beaufort Sea
GREENLAND (Denmark)
ICELAND
ATLANTIC OCEAN
Baffin Bay
NORTH AMERICA

20°W 0° 20°E 40°E 60°E 80°E 100°E 120°E 140°E 160°E 180°

ARCTIC OCEAN

SVALBARD
SEVERNAYA ZEMLYA
NOVAYA ZEMLYA
NEW SIBERIAN IS.

80°N

Barents Sea

Arctic Circle
ICELAND

SIBERIA

60°N

North Sea
BRITISH ISLES

EUROPE

URAL MOUNTAINS

ASIA

Lake Baikal

KAMCHATKA PEN.

Sea of Okhotsk

Mt. Blanc ALPS
PYRENEES
CARPATHIANS
BALKAN PEN.

CAUCASUS MTS.
Black Sea
Caspian Sea

GOBI (DESERT)

40°N

Sea of Japan

HOKKAIDO

HONSHU

Strait of Gibraltar
MADEIRA IS.

Mt. Ararat

Mt. Damavand

KUNLUN SHAN
PLATEAU OF TIBET

Huang He

East China Sea

SHIKOKU
KYUSHU

ATLAS MTS.
CANARY IS.

Mediterranean Sea

HIMALAYAS
Mt. Everest
THAR DESERT

Chang Jiang

TAIWAN

20°N

SAHARA

NUBIAN DESERT

ARABIAN DESERT

Persian Gulf

DECCAN PLATEAU

HAINAN

SAHEL

Red Sea

Arabian Sea

Bay of Bengal

South China Sea

PHILIPPINE ISLANDS

MICRONESIA

PACIFIC OCEAN

0°

SUDAN

AFRICA

GREAT RIFT VALLEY

Niger River

Lake Victoria

Mt. Kirinyaga
Mt. Kilimanjaro

SRI LANKA

MALAY PEN.

SEYCHELLES

INDIAN OCEAN

NEW GUINEA

MELANESIA

CONGO BASIN

ATLANTIC OCEAN

MADAGASCAR

20°S

KALAHARI DESERT

GREAT SANDY DESERT

AUSTRALIA

NULLARBOR PLAIN

Darling R.

NORTH ISLAND

Prime Meridian

Cape of Good Hope

TASMANIA

SOUTH ISLAND

40°S

N
W   E
S

Scale at Equator
0   1000   2000 mi.
0   1000   2000 km.
Robinson Projection

60°S

Cape Adare

QUEEN MAUD LAND
ANTARCTICA

ENDERBY LAND
AMERICAN HIGHLAND

WILKES LAND

Ross Sea

80°S

20°W 0° 20°E 40°E 60°E 80°E 100°E 120°E 140°E 160°E 180°

SOUTHERN POLAR REGION

90°W
SOUTH SHETLAND IS.
SOUTH GEORGIA

PACIFIC OCEAN

60°S
150°W

ANTARCTIC PENINSULA

ELLSWORTH LAND

MARIE BYRD LAND

70°S

Ross Sea

Weddell Sea

ATLANTIC OCEAN

30°W

0°

TRANSANTARCTIC MOUNTAINS

South Pole
POLAR PLATEAU

ANTARCTICA

QUEEN MAUD LAND

Cape Adare

180°

Scale
0   400   800 mi.
0   400   800   1,200 km.
Polar Azimuthal Equidistant Projection

South Magnetic Pole

WILKES LAND

150°E

AMERICAN HIGHLAND

ENDERBY LAND

30°E

521

EURASIA: *Political/Physical*

NORTH AMERICA

Reykjavik ✷ ICELAND
Norwegian Sea
Arctic Circle

ATLANTIC OCEAN

Trondheim
SWEDEN
NORWAY Helsinki ✷ FINLAND
Oslo ✷ Stockholm Tallinn ✷
Gulf of Bothnia ESTONIA

Barents Sea
Murmansk •
White Sea
RUSSIA
Ob River

St. Petersburg • *Lake Ladoga* *Volga River*
Edinburgh *North Sea* Copenhagen Riga ✷ LATVIA
UNITED KINGDOM DENMARK Gdansk LITHUANIA Vilnius ✷
Dublin Amsterdam Berlin Minsk ✷ BELARUS
IRELAND The Hague NETH. GERMANY POLAND Warsaw ✷
London BELG. Bonn Prague CZECH REP. Kiev ✷ UKRAINE
Brussels LUX. SLOVAK REP. *Vistula* MOLDOVA
Paris ✷ *Rhine River* LIECH. Vienna Bratislava HUNG. Chisinav ✷
Bern ✷ SWITZ. AUST. Budapest ✷ ROMANIA
FRANCE *ALPS* Venice CRO Zagreb ✷ Belgrade ✷ Bucharest ✷
MONACO SAN MARINO BOS. YUGO. BULGARIA Sofia ✷
ANDORRA CORSICA (Fr.) *PENNINES* Sarajevo FYR Skopje MACE.
Barcelona SARDINIA (Italy) Rome ✷ ITALY ALB. Tirane ✷ GREECE
PORTUGAL Madrid ✷ SPAIN *Tyrrhenian Sea* Athens ✷
Lisbon ✷ BALEARIC ISLANDS (Sp.) SICILY (Italy) *Ionian Sea* *Aegean Sea*
MALTA

Moscow ✷ Samara •
Don River Kharkhiv •
Volgograd •
Sea of Azov
Black Sea GEORGIA Tbilisi ✷
CAUCASUS MTS.
ARMENIA Yerevan ✷ Baku ✷
Istanbul • AZERBAIJAN
Ankara ✷ KURDISTAN
ASIA MINOR TURKEY *Tigris* *ELBURZ MTS.*
Nicosia ✷ SYRIA *Euphrates R.* Tehran ✷
CYPRUS Beirut ✷ Damascus ✷ Baghdad • *ZAGROS MOUNTAINS* IRAN
LEBANON Jerusalem ✷ Amman ✷ IRAQ PLATEAU OF IRAN
ISRAEL JORDAN
Kuwait ✷
KUWAIT *Persian Gulf*
BAHRAIN QATAR Abu Dhabi ✷
Riyadh ✷ U.A.E. Muscat ✷
SAUDI ARABIA OMAN
Mecca • *RUB AL KHALI (DESERT)*
Red Sea
Sanaa ✷
YEMEN
Aden • SOCOTRA (Yemen)
Gulf of Aden

URAL MOUNTAINS
Novosibirsk •
Irtysh River
Astana ✷
KIRGHIZ STEPPE
KAZAKHSTAN *Lake Balkhash*
Aral Sea *Caspian Sea*
UZBEKISTAN Almaty •
Tashkent ✷ Bishkek ✷
PAMIRS KYRGYZSTAN
TURKMENISTAN Dushanbe ✷ *KUNLUN*
Ashgabat ✷ TAJIKISTAN
HINDU KUSH *HIMALAYAS*
Kabul ✷ Islamabad ✷
AFGHANISTAN *Indus River* New Delhi ✷ NEPAL Kathmandu ✷
PAKISTAN *THAR DESERT* *Ganges R.*
Karachi • **INDIA**
DECCAN PLATEAU
Mumbai (Bombay) •
Arabian Sea *WESTERN GHATS* *EASTERN GHATS*
Channai (Madras) •
LACCADIVE ISLANDS (India) SRI LANKA
Colombo •
Male •
MALDIVES

AFRICA
Mediterranean Sea
Prime Meridian
Tropic of Cancer

Equator

INDIAN OCEAN

N
W ✦ E
S

Legend:
✷ National capital
• Major city
— National boundary

0   400   800 mi.
0   400   800 km.
Robinson Projection

522

90°E 105°E 120°E 135°E 150°E 165°E 180° 165°W 150°W 135°W 120°W

ARCTIC OCEAN

75°N

NORTH
AMERICA

60°N

Yenisey River

SIBERIA

Lena River

STANOVOI RANGE

Amur River

Bering Sea

Sea of
Okhotsk

SAKHALIN

180°

45°N

ALTAI MTS.

Irkutsk

Lake Baikal

DA HINGGAN LING

Ulaanbaatar

MONGOLIA

Harbin

KURIL ISLANDS

Vladivostok

Sapporo

GOBI (DESERT)

SHAN

Beijing

N. KOREA
Pyongyang

Sea of
Japan

Huang He

Seoul
S. KOREA

JAPAN

Tokyo

PLATEAU
OF
TIBET

PEOPLE'S REPUBLIC
OF CHINA

Jiang

Yellow
Sea

Osaka

30°N

Brahmaputra R.

Thimphu
BHUTAN

Chang

Shanghai

East
China
Sea

PACIFIC

BANGLADESH
Dhaka

Xi Jiang

Taipei
TAIWAN

OCEAN

Calcutta

MYANMAR
(BURMA)

LAOS

Guangzhou
MACAO
(Port.)
HONG
KONG

Hanoi
Gulf
of
Tonkin

HAINAN

Philippine

15°N

Bay of
Bengal

Vientiane
Yangon
(Rangoon)

Mekong R.

Da Nang

Sea

THAILAND

VIETNAM

ANDAMAN
ISLANDS
(India)

Bangkok
CAMBODIA

Manila

PHILIPPINES

NICOBAR
ISLANDS
(India)

Phnom
Penh

Ho Chi Minh City
(Saigon)

South China
Sea

Bandar Seri
Begawan
BRUNEI

MALAYSIA
Kuala Lumpur
MALAYSIA

Singapore
SINGAPORE

BORNEO

0°

SUMATRA

INDONESIA

CELEBES

NEW GUINEA

Java Sea

Jakarta

JAVA

Arafura Sea

15°S

Timor
Sea

AUSTRALIA

90°E 105°E 120°E 135°E 150°E 165°E

MIDDLE EAST: *Political/Physical*

EUROPE

ASIA

Black Sea

Bosporus

Caspian Sea

Istanbul

Sea of Marmara

Dardanelles

PONTIC MOUNTAINS

Ankara

ARMENIA

Murat River

Lake Van

Izmir

Tuz Lake

TURKEY

Aegean Sea

TAURUS MTS.

Lake Urmia

KURDISTAN

ELBURZ MTS.

Teheran

DASHT-E-KAVIR (DESERT)

Nicosia North Cyprus

Aleppo

Tigris River

CYPRUS

SYRIA

Euphrates River

PLATEAU OF IRAN

Mediterranean Sea

LEBANON

Beirut

Damascus

Baghdad

DASHT-E-LUT (DESERT)

Jordan River

SYRIAN DESERT

ZAGROS MOUNTAINS

IRAN

ISRAEL

Tel Aviv

Jerusalem

WEST BANK

Amman

IRAQ

Alexandria

Port Said

Dead Sea

Gaza

Suez Canal

NEGEV DESERT

JORDAN

AN NAFUD (DESERT)

KUWAIT

Kuwait

Persian Gulf

QATTARA DEPRESSION

Cairo

Gulf of Suez

SINAI PEN.

ARABIAN DESERT

Gulf of Aqaba

Strait of Hormuz

(Oman)

Gulf of Oman

EGYPT

Nile River

Manama

BAHRAIN

Doha

QATAR

UNITED ARAB EMIRATES

Abu Dhabi

Muscat

S A H A R A

Medina

Riyadh

LIBYAN DESERT

Tropic of Cancer

Lake Nasser

Red Sea

SAUDI ARABIA

OMAN

Jidda Mecca

AFRICA

RUB AL KHALI (DESERT)

N

W   E

S

HADRAMAUT

Arabian Sea

Sana

Bab el Mandeb

Aden

YEMEN

Gulf of Aden

SOCOTRA (Yemen)

INDIAN OCEAN

⊛ National capital

● Major city

— National boundary

0   200   400 mi.

0   200   400 km

Lambert Conformal Conic Projection

524

AFRICA: *Political/Physical*

EUROPE

ASIA

Strait of Gibraltar

Tunis
★ Algiers
Casablanca ● ★ Rabat
Marrakech ● ★ ATLAS MOUNTAINS
MOROCCO

TUNISIA
Tripoli ★

Mediterranean Sea

Suez Canal

Alexandria ●
QATTARA DEPRESSION
★ Cairo

MADEIRA ISLANDS (Port.)

CANARY ISLANDS (Sp.)

WESTERN SAHARA (Morocco)

ALGERIA

LIBYA

EGYPT

S A H A R A

AHAGGAR MOUNTAINS

TIBESTI MOUNTAINS

Tropic of Cancer

MAURITANIA
Nouakchott ★

MALI

NIGER

CHAD

NUBIAN DESERT

NILE BASIN

Cape Verde

Dakar ★ SENEGAL
Banjul ★ GAMBIA
Bissau ● GUINEA-BISSAU
Conakry ★ GUINEA
Freetown ★ SIERRA LEONE
Monrovia ★ LIBERIA

Timbuktu ●
S A H E L

Niamey ★
Bamako ★ BURKINA FASO
Ouagadougou ★

BENIN

● Kano
NIGERIA
★ Abuja

● N'Djamena

SUDAN

SUDAN
Khartoum ★

ERITREA
★ Asmara

Bab el Mandeb

Gulf of Aden

DJIBOUTI ★ Djibouti

AMHARA
★ Addis Ababa

PLATEAU

ETHIOPIA

SOMALIA

Red Sea

White Nile R.
Blue Nile R.

Nile River

CÔTE D'IVOIRE
GHANA
TOGO
L. Volta
Porto-Novo ● ● Lagos
Abidjan ★ Accra ★ Lomé ★

CAMEROON
★ Yaoundé
Malabo ★
EQUATORIAL GUINEA

CENTRAL AFRICAN REPUBLIC
Bangui ★

UGANDA
Lake Albert
Kampala ★

KENYA
★ Nairobi

● Mogadishu

SÃO TOMÉ AND PRINCIPE
★ São Tomé

Libreville ★

ANNOBÓN (Equatorial Guinea)

GABON

REP. CONGO

CONGO BASIN

Zaire River

Kasai R.

Brazzaville ★ ● Kinshasa
CABINDA (Angola)

DEMOCRATIC REPUBLIC OF CONGO

Kigali ★ RWANDA
Bujumbura ★ BURUNDI
Lake Victoria

SERENGETI PLAIN

L. Tanganyika

TANZANIA
● Dar es Salaam

ZANZIBAR

GREAT RIFT VALLEY

MITUMBA MTS.

INDIAN OCEAN

Victoria ★ SEYCHELLES

ATLANTIC OCEAN

Equator

ASCENSION (U.K.)

Luanda ★

Cuanzo R.

KATANGA PLATEAU

● Lubumbashi

ANGOLA

MALAWI
★ Lilongwe
Lake Malawi

MORONI COMOROS
Moroni ●
MAYOTTE (Fr.)

ST. HELENA (U.K.)

ZAMBIA
Lusaka ★
L. Kariba
Harare ★
Zambezi R.
Victoria Falls

ZIMBABWE

MOZAMBIQUE

Mozambique Channel

MADAGASCAR

Antananarivo ●

Port Louis ★ MAURITIUS
RÉUNION (Fr.)

NAMIBIA
NAMIB DESERT
Windhoek ★

OKAVANGO BASIN

BOTSWANA

KALAHARI DESERT
Gaborone ★

Limpopo River

Pretoria ★
Johannesburg ● ★ Maputo
Mbabane ★ SWAZILAND

Maputo

Orange River
Vaal R.

LESOTHO
Maseru ★ ● Durban

SOUTH AFRICA

GREAT KAROO
DRAKENSBERG MTS.

Cape Town ★
Cape of Good Hope   Cape Agulhas

Tropic of Capricorn

N
W   E
S

⊛ National capital
● Major city
— National boundary

0   400   800 mi.
0   400   800 km
Azimuthal Equal-Area Projection

525

NORTH AMERICA: *Political/Physical*

ASIA

ARCTIC OCEAN

EUROPE

Bering Strait

Bering Sea

Beaufort Sea

Arctic Circle

BROOKS RANGE

Yukon River

QUEEN ELIZABETH ISLANDS

ELLESMERE ISLAND

GREENLAND (Denmark)

ALASKA RANGE
Fairbanks

Anchorage

BANKS ISLAND

VICTORIA ISLAND

Baffin Bay

BAFFIN ISLAND

KODIAK ISLAND

Gulf of Alaska

Mackenzie River

Great Bear Lake

Labrador Sea

ALEXANDER ARCHIPELAGO

QUEEN CHARLOTTE ISLANDS

COAST MOUNTAINS

Great Slave Lake

UNGAVA PENINSULA

LAURENTIAN SHIELD

Hudson Bay

LABRADOR

VANCOUVER ISLAND

Vancouver

Puget Sound

Seattle

ROCKY

Edmonton

CANADA

Calgary

NEWFOUNDLAND

PRINCE EDWARD ISLAND

CAPE BRETON ISLAND

Portland

Lake Winnipeg

Winnipeg

MOUNTAINS

St. Lawrence River

Quebec

Montreal

Ottawa

Bay of Fundy

Boston
Cape Cod

San Francisco

COAST RANGES

SIERRA NEVADA

Great Salt Lake

Salt Lake City

Snake R.

BLACK HILLS

Minneapolis

Milwaukee

Lake Superior

Lake Michigan

Lake Huron

Lake Ontario

Lake Erie

New York

ATLANTIC OCEAN

Missouri River

Chicago

Detroit

Cleveland

Toronto

APPALACHIAN MTS.

Philadelphia

Denver

Omaha

Baltimore

Washington

Los Angeles

San Diego

MOJAVE DESERT

Colorado River

Kansas City

Indianapolis

St. Louis

Ohio River

Louisville

Nashville

Charlotte

Cape Hatteras

BERMUDA (U.K.)

GRAND CANYON

Wichita

UNITED STATES

Phoenix

Red River

Fort Worth

Atlanta

Birmingham

PACIFIC OCEAN

Rio Grande

Ciudad Juárez

Chihuahua

Austin

San Antonio

Mississippi River

Houston

New Orleans

Jacksonville

Cape Canaveral

Tropic of Cancer

BAJA CALIFORNIA

Gulf of California

SIERRA MADRE OCCIDENTAL

SIERRA MADRE ORIENTAL

Monterrey

Miami

Nassau

BAHAMAS

Cabo San Lucas

MEXICO

PLATEAU OF MEXICO

Guadalajara

Mexico City

Veracruz

Puebla

YUCATÁN PENINSULA

Havana

CUBA

Santiago de Cuba

CAYMAN ISLANDS (U.K.)

JAMAICA

Kingston

Port-au-Prince

HAITI

DOMINICAN REPUBLIC

Santo Domingo

PUERTO RICO (U.S.)

San Juan

VIRGIN ISLANDS (U.S., U.K.)

ANGUILLA (U.K.)

ST. KITTS AND NEVIS

DOMINICA

ANTIGUA AND BARBUDA

GUADELOUPE (Fr.)

Roseau

MARTINIQUE (Fr.)

Castries ST. LUCIA

ST. VINCENT AND THE GRENADINES

Kingstown

Bridgetown

BARBADOS

Acapulco

ISTHMUS OF TEHUANTEPEC

Belmopan

BELIZE

Caribbean Sea

NETHERLANDS ANTILLES (Neth.)

ARUBA (Neth.)

St. George's

GRENADA

Port-of-Spain

TRINIDAD AND TOBAGO

GUATEMALA

Guatemala City

San Salvador

EL SALVADOR

HONDURAS

Tegucigalpa

NICARAGUA

Managua

MOSQUITO COAST

Lago de Nicaragua

San José

COSTA RICA

ISTHMUS OF PANAMA

Panama City

PANAMA

SOUTH AMERICA

N
W   E
S

⊛ National capital
• Major city
— National boundary

0   400   800 mi.
0   400   800 km
Azimuthal Equal-Area Projection

Gulf of Mexico

Equator

526

SOUTH AMERICA: *Political/Physical*

CENTRAL
AMERICA

Caribbean Sea

*ATLANTIC
OCEAN*

Barranquilla
Cartagena
Maracaibo
Caracas

*Gulf
of
Panama*

LLANOS
VENEZUELA

Orinoco River

Georgetown
Paramaribo

Medellín

Angel Falls

GUYANA

Cayenne

Bogotá

GUIANA HIGHLANDS

SURINAME
FRENCH
GUIANA
(Fr.)

MALPELO
(Colombia)

COLOMBIA

OCCIDENTAL MTS.

Cauca R.

Magdalena River

Rio Negro

AMAZON

River

Amazon

Belém

Equator

Quito
ECUADOR

Guayaquil

*Gulf of
Guayaquil*

Iquitos

Manaus

BASIN

Solimões River

Javari River

Madeira River

Tapajós River

Xingu River

Fortaleza

GALÁPAGOS
ISLANDS
(Ecuador)

Trujillo

PERU

A
N
D
E
S

BRAZIL

São Francisco River

Recife

Lima

Cuzco

PACIFIC
OCEAN

Arequipa

Lake Titicaca
La Paz

BOLIVIA

Sucre

ALTIPLANO

PLATEAU OF
MATO GROSSO

Brasília

BRAZILIAN

HIGHLANDS

Salvador

Paraguay River

Belo Horizonte

Antofagasta

ATACAMA DESERT

GRAN CHACO

PARAGUAY

Tropic of Capricorn

SAN FÉLIX
ISLAND
(Chile)

SAN AMBROSIO
ISLAND
(Chile)

Asunción

São Paulo

Parana River

Rio de Janeiro
Santos

Salado River

Paraná River

Pôrto Alegre

JUAN FERNÁNDEZ
ISLANDS
(Chile)

CHILE

A
N
D
E
S

Córdoba

Rosario

URUGUAY

Valparaíso
Santiago

Buenos Aires

Montevideo

Rio de la Plata

Concepción

ARGENTINA

PAMPAS

Colorado R.

Bahía Blanca

Valdivia

*ATLANTIC
OCEAN*

Gulf of San Matías

N
W   E
S

PATAGONIA

Comodoro Rivadavia
Gulf of San Jorge

⊛ National capital

• Major city

— National boundary

0   400   800 mi.
0   400   800 km
Azimuthal Equal-Area Projection

*Strait of
Magellan*

FALKLAND
ISLANDS
(U.K.)

TIERRA
DEL FUEGO

527

SOUTH GEORGIA
(U.K.)

Cape Horn

Drake Passage

PACIFIC RIM: *Political/Physical*

ARCTIC OCEAN

Arctic Circle

RUSSIA

ALASKA
(U.S.)
• Anchorage

60°N

Bering Sea

60°N

ASIA

KAMCHATKA

CANADA

NORTH
AMERICA

• Vancouver
• Seattle

• Ottawa

MONGOLIA

SAKHALIN

PACIFIC
OCEAN

Beijing ✴
NORTH
KOREA
✴ Pyongyang
Vladivostok
KURIL IS.
(Russia)

UNITED
STATES

San
Francisco

Washington ✴

PEOPLE'S
REPUBLIC
OF CHINA

Hanoi

✴ Seoul
SOUTH
KOREA
✴ Tokyo

JAPAN

• Los Angeles

30°N

Shanghai

East
China
Sea

RYUKYU
IS.(Japan)

MEXICO

30°N

Taipei

VOLCANO IS.
(Japan)

MIDWAY ISLANDS
(U.S.)

Tropic of Cancer

Mexico City •

BAHAMAS

HONG
KONG

TAIWAN

Philippine
Sea

WAKE ISLAND
(U.S.)

• Honolulu

HAWAII
(U.S.)

CUBA
HAITI

LAOS
VIETNAM
THAILAND
CAMBODIA

Manila

NORTHERN
MARIANA
ISLANDS
(U.S.)

MARSHALL
ISLANDS

GUATEMALA
EL SALVADOR

BELIZE
HONDURAS
NICARAGUA

PHILIPPINES

GUAM (U.S.)

MICRONESIA

Kolonia

Majuro

COSTA RICA
PANAMA

Bogotá •

Kuala
Lumpur
MALAYSIA
SINGAPORE
BRUNEI

PALAU

FEDERATED STATES
OF MICRONESIA

Tarawa

Equator

GALAPAGOS IS.
(Ecuador)

COLOMBIA
ECUADOR • Quito
Guayaquil

Yaren

INDONESIA

NEW
GUINEA
PAPUA
NEW GUINEA

NAURU

TUVALU

KIRIBATI

PERU

Jakarta

Arafura
Sea

SOLOMON
ISLANDS

Funafuti

TOKELAU
(N.Z.)

POLYNESIA

Lima ✴

INDIAN
OCEAN

Timor
Sea

Port
Moresby

Honiara

SAMOA

Great
Barrier
Reef

VANUATU

AMERICAN
SAMOA
(U.S.)

WALLIS AND
FUTUNA IS. (Fr.)
Apia
Port-
Vila
Suva
TONGA
NIUE
(N.Z.)
COOK
ISLANDS
(N.Z.)

FRENCH
POLYNESIA
(Fr.)

SOUTH
AMERICA

Gulf of
Carpentaria

Coral Sea

FIJI

Nuku'alofa

GREAT
SANDY
DESERT

NEW CALEDONIA
(Fr.)

Tropic of Capricorn

EASTER I.
(Chile)

CHILE

MACDONNELL
RANGE

PITCAIRN I.
(U.K.)

Valparaíso •
Santiago

30°S

AUSTRALIA

Great
Australian
Bight

• Sydney
Canberra ✴

NORFOLK I.
(Aust.)

KERMADEC
ISLANDS
(N.Z.)

PACIFIC

30°S

TASMANIA

NEW
ZEALAND

Auckland •

✴ Wellington

OCEAN

Tasman
Sea

CHATHAM IS.
(N.Z.)

Scale at Equator

0   1000   2000 mi.

0   1000   2000 km

Miller Cylindrical Projection

60°S

60°S

Antarctic Circle

✴ National capital

• Major city

— National boundary

ANTARCTICA

120°E   150°E   180°   150°W   120°W   90°W

WORLD: *Religions*

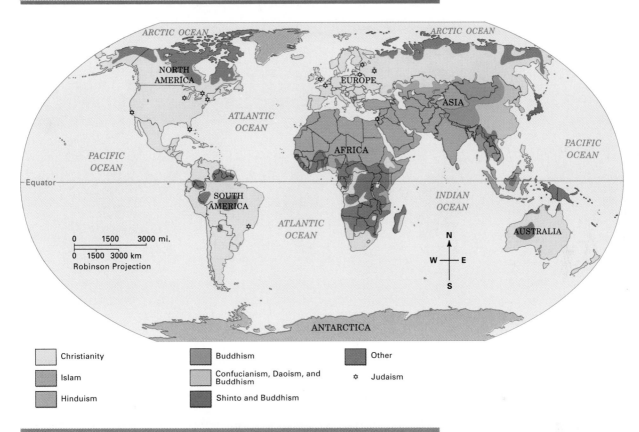

	Christianity		Buddhism		Other
	Islam		Confucianism, Daoism, and Buddhism	✡	Judaism
	Hinduism		Shinto and Buddhism		

WORLD: *Languages*

	Indo-European (includes English, Spanish, Hindi)		Dravidian		Semitic (includes Hebrew, Arabic)
	Sino-Tibetan (includes Chinese, Burmese)		Malayo-Polynesian (includes Hawaiian, Pilipino)		Other
	Ural-Altaic (includes Finnish, Hungarian, Turkish)		Amerindian (includes Inuit, Iroquoian, Quechua)		
	Japanese and Korean		African (includes Yoruba, Swahili)		

WORLD: *Vegetation*

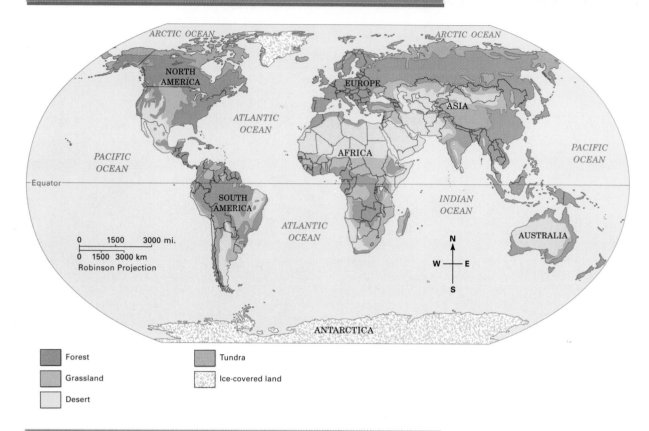

Forest

Grassland

Desert

Tundra

Ice-covered land

WORLD: *Climate*

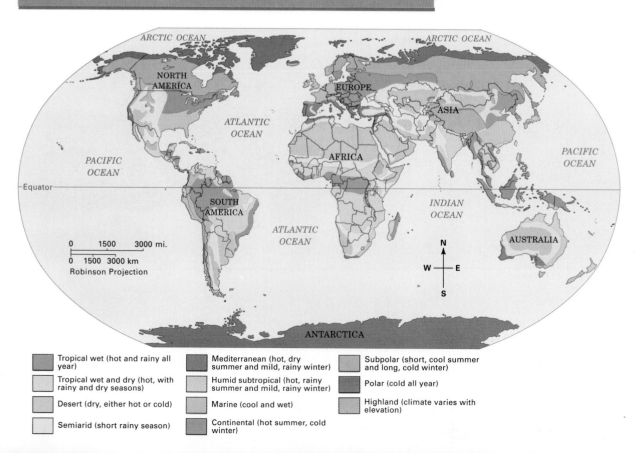

Tropical wet (hot and rainy all year)

Tropical wet and dry (hot, with rainy and dry seasons)

Desert (dry, either hot or cold)

Semiarid (short rainy season)

Mediterranean (hot, dry summer and mild, rainy winter)

Humid subtropical (hot, rainy summer and mild, rainy winter)

Marine (cool and wet)

Continental (hot summer, cold winter)

Subpolar (short, cool summer and long, cold winter)

Polar (cold all year)

Highland (climate varies with elevation)

WORLD: *Population*

UNITED
KINGDOM

EUROPE

FRANCE

GER. POLAND

UKRAINE RUSSIA

ASIA

ITALY

ROM.

S. KOREA

SPAIN

IRAN

CHINA

JAPAN

PAKISTAN

NORTH
AMERICA

UNITED STATES

MEXICO

COLOMBIA

SOUTH
AMERICA

BRAZIL

ARGENTINA

EGYPT

AFRICA

NIGERIA

KENYA

SOUTH AFRICA

INDIA

BANGLADESH

VIETNAM

INDONESIA

AUSTRALIA

NEW
ZEALAND

In millions

Less than 10

10-20

20-100

More than 100

Each country's size in the cartogram represents the size of its population compared
with those of other countries in the world. Based on information in *Statistical
Abstract of the United States 1995*.

WORLD: *Land Use, Land and Ocean Resources*

ARCTIC OCEAN

ARCTIC OCEAN

NORTH
AMERICA

EUROPE

ASIA

ATLANTIC
OCEAN

PACIFIC
OCEAN

AFRICA

PACIFIC
OCEAN

Equator

INDIAN
OCEAN

AUSTRALIA

SOUTH
AMERICA

ATLANTIC
OCEAN

0   1500   3000 mi.

0   1500 3000 km

Robinson Projection

N

W   E

S

ANTARCTICA

◼ Farming	◼ Little land use	⬥ Natural gas	🐟 Fishing
◼ Grazing	🪨 Coal	ⓒ Copper	
◼ Forests	⚒ Iron	◗ Gold	
◼ Urban and industrial	⛏ Oil	▲ Tin	

THE WORLD: *A.D. 750*

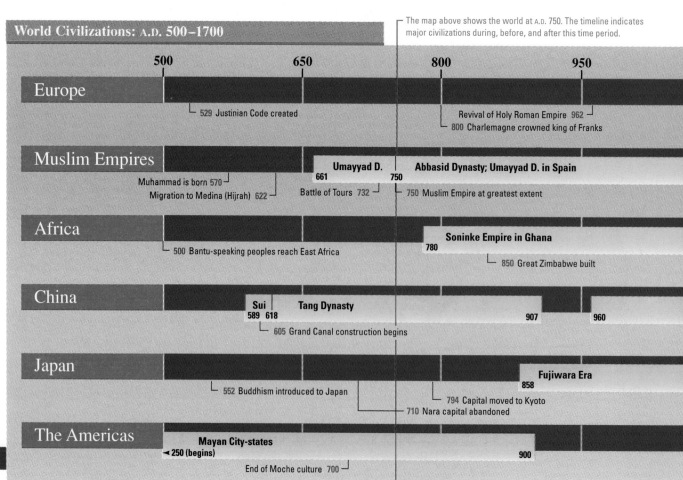

The map above shows the world at A.D. 750. The timeline indicates major civilizations during, before, and after this time period.

World Civilizations: A.D. 500–1700

	500	650	800	950

Europe
- 529 Justinian Code created
- Revival of Holy Roman Empire 962
- 800 Charlemagne crowned king of Franks

Muslim Empires
- Muhammad is born 570
- Migration to Medina (Hijrah) 622
- **Umayyad D.** 661
- Battle of Tours 732
- **Abbasid Dynasty; Umayyad D. in Spain** 750
- 750 Muslim Empire at greatest extent

Africa
- 500 Bantu-speaking peoples reach East Africa
- **Soninke Empire in Ghana** 780
- 850 Great Zimbabwe built

China
- **Sui** 589 618 **Tang Dynasty** 907 960
- 605 Grand Canal construction begins

Japan
- 552 Buddhism introduced to Japan
- **Fujiwara Era** 858
- 794 Capital moved to Kyoto
- 710 Nara capital abandoned

The Americas
- **Mayan City-states** ◄ 250 (begins) 900
- End of Moche culture 700

THE WORLD: *A.D. 1492*

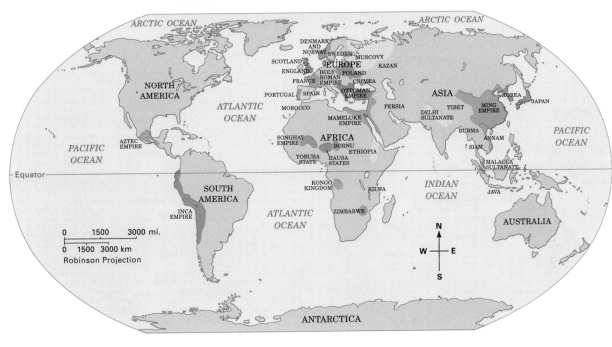

The map above shows the world at A.D. 1492. The timeline indicates major civilizations during, before, and after this time period.

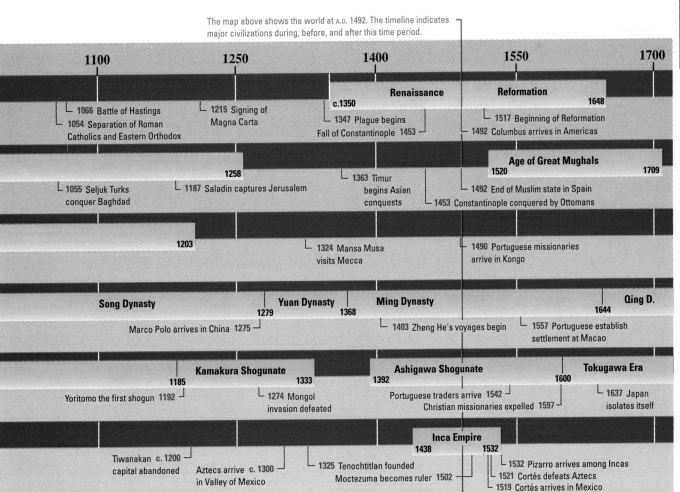

1100	1250	1400	1550	1700

Renaissance c.1350 — **Reformation** 1648

1066 Battle of Hastings
1054 Separation of Roman Catholics and Eastern Orthodox
1215 Signing of Magna Carta
1347 Plague begins
Fall of Constantinople 1453
1517 Beginning of Reformation
1492 Columbus arrives in Americas

Age of Great Mughals 1520 — 1709

1055 Seljuk Turks conquer Baghdad
1258
1187 Saladin captures Jerusalem
1363 Timur begins Asian conquests
1492 End of Muslim state in Spain
1453 Constantinople conquered by Ottomans

1203
1324 Mansa Musa visits Mecca
1490 Portuguese missionaries arrive in Kongo

Song Dynasty — **Yuan Dynasty** 1279 — 1368 **Ming Dynasty** — **Qing D.**
Marco Polo arrives in China 1275
1403 Zheng He's voyages begin
1644
1557 Portuguese establish settlement at Macao

Kamakura Shogunate 1185 — 1333 **Ashigawa Shogunate** 1392 — **Tokugawa Era** 1600
Yoritomo the first shogun 1192
1274 Mongol invasion defeated
Portuguese traders arrive 1542
Christian missionaries expelled 1597
1637 Japan isolates itself

Inca Empire 1438 — 1532
Tiwanakan c. 1200 capital abandoned
Aztecs arrive c. 1300 in Valley of Mexico
1325 Tenochtitlan founded
Moctezuma becomes ruler 1502
1532 Pizarro arrives among Incas
1521 Cortés defeats Aztecs
1519 Cortés arrives in Mexico

GLOSSARY OF GEOGRAPHIC TERMS

cape
a narrow, curved area of land extending into an ocean or lake

(river) mouth
the place where a river flows into a lake or ocean

sea level
the level of the surface of the ocean

volcano
an opening in the earth, usually raised, through which lava and gasses from the earth's interior escape

harbor
a sheltered area of water, a safe docking place for ships

flood plain
flat land near the edges of rivers formed by mud and silt deposited by floods

strait
a narrow strip of water connecting two large bodies of water

bay
part of an ocean or lake extending into the land

island
a body of land surrounded by water

delta
a triangular area formed by deposits at the mouth of a river

oasis
a spot of fertile land in a desert, fed by water from wells or underground springs

desert
a dry area where few plants grow

tributary
a stream or river that flows into a larger river

savanna
a region containing scattered trees and vegetation

sahel
in Africa, a strip of dry grassland between a desert and a savanna

plain
a broad, level area of land

steppe
a wide, treeless plain

glacier
a large ice mass that moves slowly down a mountain or over land

mountain pass
a gap between mountains

valley
low land between hills or mountains

cataract
a large, powerful waterfall

mesa
a wide, flat-topped mountain with steep sides, found mostly in dry areas

canyon
a narrow, deep valley with steep sides

cliff
the steep, almost vertical, edge of a hill, mountain, or plain

plateau
a broad, flat area of land higher than the surrounding land

This Gazetteer will help you locate many of the places discussed in this book. Latitude and longitude given for large areas of land and water refer to the centermost point of the area; latitude and longitude of rivers refer to the river mouth. The page number tells you where to find a map with each place located.

PLACE	LAT.	LONG.	PAGE
A			
Aachen (Charlemagne's capital; Germany)	51°N	6°E	**260**
Aegean Sea (part of Mediterranean)	39°N	25°E	**290**
Agra (early capital of Mughal Empire; India)	27°N	78°E	**179**
Alps (mountain range in S. and central Europe)	46°N	9°E	**296**
Antioch (ancient Syrian capital; Turkey)	36°N	36°E	**10**
Arguin (island trading post of Portuguese off of W. Africa)	21°N	17°W	**374**
Augsburg (city connected with Reformation; Germany)	48°N	11°E	**347**
Avignon (papal city in France)	44°N	5°E	**311**
B			
Baghdad (capital of Abbasid caliphate; Iraq)	33°N	44°E	**85**
Bering Strait (waterway that separates Asia and N. America)	65°N	170°W	**398**
Berlin (capital of Prussia; Germany)	53°N	13°E	**481**
Black Sea (opens onto Aegean Sea through Bosporus)	43°N	32°E	**36**
Bojador, Cape (W. Africa; W. Sahara)	26°N	15°W	**374**
Bombay (city in W. India where English first traded)	19°N	73°E	**522**
Bosporus (waterway connecting Black Sea and Sea of Marmara; Turkey)	41°N	29°E	**290**
Bruges (important trading city in Flanders; Belgium)	51°N	3°E	**330**
Bursa (early capital of Ottoman Empire; Turkey)	40°N	29°E	**171**
C			
Cairo (capital of Fatimid caliphate; Egypt)	30°N	31°E	**171**
Calcutta (English colony in India)	23°N	88°E	**523**
Calicut (city da Gama visited first in India)	11°N	76°E	**374**
Caribbean Sea (W. Indies, Central and S. America)	15°N	76°W	**378**
Caucasus Mts. (mountain range between Black and Caspian seas)	43°N	45°E	**36**
Ceuta (North African port important in the gold trade; Morocco)	36°N	5°W	**96**

PLACE	LAT.	LONG.	PAGE
Chang Jiang (Yangtze R.; major river of China)	32°N	120°E	**193**
Changan (Xi'an; capital of China under Han and Tang dynasties)	34°N	109°E	**205**
Clermont (city where call for crusades originated; France)	46°N	3°E	**296**
Congo Basin (central Africa)	6°N	20°E	**525**
Constantinople (Istanbul; capital of Byzantine and Ottoman empires; Turkey)	41°N	29°E	**67**
Cordoba (capital of Umayyad caliphate; Spain)	38°N	5°W	**96**
Cuzco (capital of Inca Empire; Peru)	14°S	72°W	**430**
D			
Damascus (capital of Umayyad caliphate; Syria)	34°N	36°E	**81**
Dardanelles (waterway connecting Sea of Marmara and the Aegean Sea; Turkey)	40°N	26°E	**290**
Delhi (capital of Mughal Empire; India)	29°N	77°E	**179**
E			
Edessa (Urfa; city held by crusaders; Turkey)	37°N	39°E	**296**
Edo (Tokyo; center of Tokugawa shogunate; Japan)	36°N	140°E	**230**
F			
Fernando Póo (island off W. Africa)	4°N	9°E	**465**
Flanders (region noted for woolen trade; France, Belgium)	51°N	3°E	**330**
Florence (cultural center of Renaissance Italy)	44°N	11°E	**317**
Fustat (Cairo; capital of Fatimid caliphate; Egypt)	30°N	31°E	**80**
G			
Gao (capital of Songhai Empire; Mali)	16°N	0°	**121**
Geneva (center of Calvinism; Switzerland)	46°N	6°E	**352**
Genoa (port on Mediterranean; Italy)	44°N	9°E	**290**

PLACE	LAT.	LONG.	PAGE
Ghent (cloth weaving city in Flanders; Belgium)	51°N	4°E	330
Goa (Portuguese colony in India)	16°N	74°E	142
Good Hope, Cape of (S. Africa)	34°S	18°E	374
Granada (capital of Muslim kingdom; Spain)	37°N	4°W	96
Great Rift Valley (stretches from Jordan to S.E. Africa)	0°N	36°E	525
Great Zimbabwe (capital of ancient Zimbabwe; Zimbabwe)	20°S	31°E	146
Guinea, Gulf of (part of Atlantic; W. Africa)	2°N	1°E	109

H

PLACE	LAT.	LONG.	PAGE
Hangzhou (capital of China during late Song dynasty)	30°N	120°E	166
Hattin (battle where crusaders were defeated; Israel)	33°N	36°E	299
Heian (early name for Kyoto; Japan)	35°N	136°E	230
Himalayas (mountain range in Asia)	30°N	85°E	179
Hindu Kush (mountain range in Afghanistan)	36°N	72°E	522
Horn, Cape (tip of S. America)	56°S	67°W	527
Huang He (Yellow R.; N. central China)	34°N	117°E	193

I

PLACE	LAT.	LONG.	PAGE
Izapa (early Mayan city; Mexico)	15°N	92°W	405

J

PLACE	LAT.	LONG.	PAGE
Jamestown (English settlement in Virginia)	37°N	77°W	470
Jenne-jeno (Djénné; trading city in W. Africa; Mali)	14°N	5°W	109
Jerusalem (holy city of Jews, Christians, and Muslims; Israel)	32°N	35°E	299

K

PLACE	LAT.	LONG.	PAGE
Kaifeng (capital of China under Song dynasty)	35°N	114°E	205
Karakhoto (caravan city; N. China)	42°N	101°E	366
Karakorum (capital of Genghis Khan's empire; Mongolia)	47°N	103°E	166

PLACE	LAT.	LONG.	PAGE
Khanbalik (Beijing; Kublai Khan's capital; China)	40°N	116°E	166
Kilwa (port in E. Africa)	9°S	39°E	142
Koumbi (capital of ancient kingdom of Ghana)	15°N	8°W	121
Kyoto (Heian; city that was early home of Japan's emperors)	35°N	136°E	230

L

PLACE	LAT.	LONG.	PAGE
La Rochelle (port and Huguenot center; W. France)	46°N	1°W	330
Lisbon (capital of Portugal)	39°N	9°W	374
Luoyang (capital of China under Tang and Song dynasties)	35°N	113°E	205

M

PLACE	LAT.	LONG.	PAGE
Machu Picchu (Inca citadel; Peru)	13°S	73°W	430
Madras (city in S. India; fought over by British and French)	13°N	80°E	522
Malacca (trading city; Malaysia)	2°N	102°E	142
Malindi (ancient E. African port; Kenya)	3°S	40°E	142
Marmara, Sea of (separates Europe and Asia; Turkey)	41°N	28°E	290
Mazagan (Al-Jadida; port founded by Portugal; Morocco)	33°N	9°W	465
M'Banza (capital of Kongo Kingdom; central Africa)	5°S	15°E	150
Mecca (holiest city of Islam; Saudi Arabia)	21°N	40°E	67
Medina (holy city of Islam; Saudi Arabia)	24°N	40°E	67
Milan (city-state in N. Italy)	45°N	9°E	317
Moche (site of ancient civilization; N. Peru)	8°S	79°W	412
Mombasa (E. African port)	4°S	40°E	142
Montreal (French settlement; Canada)	46°N	74°W	470
Mpinda (port on Zaire [Congo] R.; Angola)	6°S	12°E	150

N

PLACE	LAT.	LONG.	PAGE
Nanjing (southern capital of Ming emperors; China)	32°N	119°E	193
New Amsterdam (Dutch settlement; New York)	41°N	74°W	470

GAZETTEER

PLACE	LAT.	LONG.	PAGE
New Sarai (later capital of the Mongols; Russia)	49°N	45°E	**166**
Niani (capital of ancient Mali; Guinea)	11°N	9°W	**121**
Nok (center of Iron Age culture; Nigeria)	8°N	9°E	**109**
North Sea (part of Atlantic Ocean)	56°N	3°E	**260**

O

PLACE	LAT.	LONG.	PAGE
Old Sarai (early capital of the Mongols; Russia)	47°N	48°E	**166**

P

PLACE	LAT.	LONG.	PAGE
Panama, Isthmus of (links N. and S. America)	9°N	81°W	**526**
Petra (ancient city cut in rock; Jordan)	30°N	35°E	**53**
Popocatépetl (volcano; central Mexico)	19°N	99°W	**423**

Q

PLACE	LAT.	LONG.	PAGE
Qin Ling (mountain range in N. China)	33°N	108°E	**193**
Quebec (French settlement in Canada)	47°N	71°W	**526**

R

PLACE	LAT.	LONG.	PAGE
Rome (capital of Roman Empire and Papal States; Italy)	42°N	13°E	**317**

S

PLACE	LAT.	LONG.	PAGE
Sagres (town where Henry the Navigator set up a school of navigation; Portugal)	37°N	9°W	**374**
Sahara (great desert; stretches across N. Africa)	24°N	2°W	**121**
Samarkand (Timur's capital; Uzbekistan)	40°N	67°E	**53**
São Tomé (island in Gulf of Guinea; W. Africa)	0°	7°E	**525**
St. Petersburg (Peter the Great's capital of Russia)	60°N	30°E	**481**

T

PLACE	LAT.	LONG.	PAGE
Taklimakan Desert (helped isolate China from W. Asia)	39°N	83°E	**193**
Tenochtitlán (Mexico City; capital of Aztec Empire)	19°N	99°W	**423**

PLACE	LAT.	LONG.	PAGE
Timbuktu (city in Songhai Empire; Mali)	17°N	3°W	**525**
Titicaca, Lake (center of early S. American civilizations; Bolivia, Peru)	16°S	71°W	**412**
Tiwanaku (Tiahuanaco; prehistoric site near Lake Titicaca; Bolivia)	17°S	69°W	**412**
Tokyo (Edo; center of Tokugawa shogunate; Japan)	36°N	140°E	**230**
Tours (battle where Franks stopped Muslims; France)	47°N	1°E	**80**
Trent (city where Counter-Reformation began; Italy)	46°N	11°E	**347**
Tumbes (town where Pizarro landed; Peru)	4°S	80°W	**430**

U

PLACE	LAT.	LONG.	PAGE
Uxmal (capital of later Mayan Empire; Mexico)	20°N	90°W	**405**

V

PLACE	LAT.	LONG.	PAGE
Venice (great port on Adriatic Sea; Italy)	45°N	12°E	**290**
Vézélay (village where Second Crusade was called; France)	47°N	4°E	**296**
Vienna (capital of Hapsburg domains; Austria)	48°N	16°E	**481**

W

PLACE	LAT.	LONG.	PAGE
Wittenberg (city; Germany)	52°N	13°E	**347**
Worms (city; Germany)	50°N	8°E	**347**

X

PLACE	LAT.	LONG.	PAGE
Xi'an (Changan; capital of China under Han and Tang dynasties)	34°N	109°E	**205**

Y

PLACE	LAT.	LONG.	PAGE
Yucatán (peninsula; Mayan lands; S.E. Mexico)	21°N	89°W	**405**

Z

PLACE	LAT.	LONG.	PAGE
Zaire R. (Congo R.; central Africa)	6°S	12°E	**109**
Zürich (city associated with Reformation; Switzerland)	47°N	9°E	**352**

This dictionary lists many of the important people introduced in this book. The page number refers to the main discussion of that person in the book. For more complete references see the Index.

Pronunciation Key

This chart presents the system of phonetic respellings used to indicate pronunciation in the Biographical Dictionary and in the chapters of this book.

Spellings	Symbol	Spellings	Symbol	Spellings	Symbol
pat	a	kick, cat, pique	k	thin, this	th
pay	ay	lid, needle	l	cut	uh
care	air	mum	m	urge, term, firm, word, heard	ur
father	ah	no, sudden	n		
bib	b	thing	ng	valve	v
church	ch	pot, horrid	ah	with	w
deed, milled	d	toe	oh	yes	y
pet	eh	caught, paw, for	aw	zebra, xylem	z
bee	ee	noise	oy	vision, pleasure, garage	zh
life, phase, rough	f	took	u		
gag	g	boot	oo	about, item, edible, gallop, circus	uh
hat	h	out	ow		
which	hw	pop	p	butter	ur
pit	ih	roar	r		
pie, by	eye, y	sauce	s	Capital letters indicate stressed syllables.	
pier	ihr	ship, dish	sh		
judge	j	tight, stopped	t		

A

Abd al Malik *(ahb dul mah LIHK)* c. 646–705, Umayyad caliph, 685–705 (p. 83).

Abd al Rahman I *(ahb al ra MAHN)* 731–788, founder of Umayyad dynasty in Cordoba, 756–788 (p. 95).

Abd al Rahman III 891–961, Umayyad caliph of Cordoba, 929–961 (p. 96).

Abu Bakr 573–634, first caliph after death of Muhammad, 632–634 (p. 65).

Affonso I ?–c. 1550, ruler of the Kongo Kingdom in Africa (p. 152).

Ahuitzotl *(ah WEET soh tl)* ?–1502, Aztec ruler, 1486–1502 (p. 424).

Akbar, Akbar the Great 1542–1605, emperor of Mughal Empire, 1556–1605 (p. 181).

Alcuin 735–804, English monk (p. 259).

Alfonso VI, Alfonso the Valiant ?–1109, king of Castile in Spain, 1072–1109 (p. 100).

Ali c. 600–661, fourth caliph of Muslim Empire, 656–661 (p. 66).

Anna Comnena c. 1083–1148, Byzantine author (p. 297).

Atahualpa *(ah tah WAHL pah)* c. 1500–1533, last ruler of the Inca Empire in Peru, killed by Pizarro's troops (p. 438).

Augustus 63 B.C.–A.D. 14, first Roman emperor, 29 B.C.–A.D. 14 (p. 26).

Aurangzeb *(AWR ung zehb)* 1618–1707, emperor of Mughal Empire, 1658–1707 (p. 185).

B

Babur 1483–1530, founder of Mughal dynasty of India, emperor, 1526–1530 (p. 180).

Bacon, Francis 1561–1626, English philosopher (p. 355).

Balboa, Vasco de 1475–1519, Spanish explorer of Isthmus of Panama and Pacific Ocean (p. 380).

Bayezid II 1447–1513, son of Mehmed II, Ottoman sultan, 1481–1512 (p. 175).

Boniface VIII c. 1235–1303, pope, 1294–1303, had power struggle with Philip IV of France (p. 338).

Brueghel, Pieter, the Elder *(BROY guhl)* c. 1530–1569, Flemish artist (p. 329).

Brunelleschi, Filippo *(broo nuh LEHS kee)* 1377–1446, Italian Renaissance architect (p. 322).

C

Cabot, John 1450–1498, Italian navigator and explorer of North America for English (p. 380).

Calvin, John 1509–1564, French theologian and reformer (p. 349).

Cão, Diego c. 1400s, Portuguese navigator and explorer of Congo River (p. 149).

Cartier, Jacques 1491–1557, French explorer (p. 381).

Catherine II, Catherine the Great 1729–1796, Russian empress, 1762–1796 (p. 480).

Cervantes, Miguel de 1547–1616, great Spanish writer of the Renaissance, wrote *Don Quixote* (p. 322).

Charlemagne, Charles the Great 742–814, king of the

Franks, 768–814, and emperor of the West, 800–814 (p. 258).

Charles I 1600–1649, king of England, 1625–1649, executed by English Parliament (p. 460).

Charles II 1630–1685, king of England, 1660–1685, invited to be king after Cromwell's death (p. 462).

Charles V 1500–1558, Holy Roman Emperor, 1519–1556, king of Spain during conquests (p. 344).

Charles Martel, Charles the Hammer c. 689–741, Frankish ruler, 715–741 (p. 258).

Clement V 1264–1314, pope, 1305–1314, moved papacy from Rome to Avignon, France (p. 339).

Clement VII ?–1394, pope, 1378–1394, pope in Avignon during the Great Schism (p. 339).

Clovis I c. 466–511, king of the Franks, 481–511 (p. 257).

Columbus, Christopher 1451–1506, Italian explorer for Spanish (p. 377).

Conrad III c. 1093–1152, king of Germany, 1138–1152 (p. 299).

Constantine, Constantine the Great c. 280–337, Roman emperor, 306–337 (p. 30).

Copernicus, Nicolaus 1473–1543, Polish physician and astronomer (p. 353).

Cortés, Hernando 1485–1547, Spanish conqueror of Mexico (p. 437).

Cromwell, Oliver 1599–1658, lord protector of England, c. 1649–1658 (p. 461).

D

Dias, Bartholomeu c. 1450–1500, Portuguese navigator, rounded Cape of Good Hope (p. 375).

Díaz, Bernal c. 1492–c. 1581, Spanish soldier and historian (p. 16).

Diderot, Denis *(DEE dih roh)* 1713–1784, French encyclopedist (p. 478).

Diocletian 245–313, Roman emperor, 284–313 (p. 30).

E

Edward VI 1537–1553, king of England, 1547–1553 (p. 351).

Elizabeth I 1533–1603, queen of England, 1558–1603, defeated Spanish Armada (p. 458).

Erasmus, Desiderius *(ih RAZ muhs)* c. 1466–1536, Dutch priest and humanist (p. 332).

Ericson, Leif c. 1000, Norse mariner, explored Newfoundland (p. 380).

F

Faraghani, Ahmad al died c. 861, Muslim astronomer, mathematician, and engineer (pp. 15, 378).

Ferdinand II, Ferdinand the Catholic 1452–1516, king of Spain, 1479–1516 (p. 378).

Francis of Assisi c. 1182–1226, Italian founder of the Franciscans (p. 287).

Francis I 1494–1547, French king, 1515–1547, king during Renaissance in France (p. 381).

Franklin, Benjamin 1706–1790, American statesman, scientist, and philosopher (p. 482).

Frederick I c. 1125–1190, king of Germany, 1152–1190, drowned on Third Crusade (p. 300).

Frederick II, Frederick the Wise 1482–1556, prince of Saxony, 1544–1556 (p. 345).

Frederick II, Frederick the Great 1712–1786, king of Prussia, 1740–1786, student of Voltaire (p. 480).

G

Galileo 1564–1642, Italian astronomer and physicist (p. 354).

Gama, Vasco da c. 1469–1524, Portuguese navigator, sailed to India (p. 364).

Gautama, Siddhartha, "the Buddha" c. 563–483 B.C., Indian philosopher and founder of Buddhism (p. 194).

Genghis Khan, Temujin *(TEHM yoo jihn)* 1162–1227, Mongol conqueror (p. 164).

Gregory III ?–741, pope, 731–741 (p. 293).

Gregory VII, born Hildebrand ?–1085, pope, 1073–1085, quarreled with Henry IV of Germany (p. 284).

Gregory VIII ?–1187, pope, 1187, initiated Third Crusade (p. 300).

Gregory XI 1330–1378, pope, 1370–1378, returned papacy to Rome from Avignon, France (p. 339).

Gutenberg, Johannes *(GOOT en burg)* c. 1397–1468, German inventor of movable type printing (p. 330).

H

Hargreaves, James ?–1778, English inventor of the spinning jenny, 1764 (p. 492).

Henry, Henry the Navigator 1394–1460, prince of Portugal, patron of sea exploration (p. 371).

Henry IV 1050–1106, king of Germany, 1056–1105, quarreled with Pope Gregory VII (p. 285).

Henry IV 1553–1610, king of France, 1589–1610, signed Edict of Nantes (p. 452).

Henry V 1081–1125, king of Germany, 1111–1125, made pact with pope, Concordat of Worms (p. 284).

Henry VIII 1491–1547, king of England, 1509–1547, established Church of England (p. 351).

Heraclius c. 575–641, emperor of the Eastern Roman Empire, 610–641 (p. 45).

Hooke, Robert 1635–1703, English scientist (p. 355).

Huascar *(WAHS kahr)* c. 1495–1533, son of Inca, put to death by his brother Atahualpa (p. 438).

I

Ibn Battuta, Muhammad 1304–1377, greatest Arabian traveler of Middle Ages (p. 13).

Ibn Sina, Avicenna *(av ih SEHN uh)* 980–1037, Abbasid doctor (p. 90).

Ignatius Loyola 1491–1556, Spanish priest, founder of Jesuits (p. 352).

Isabella I, Isabella the Catholic 1451–1504, queen of Aragon and unified Spain, 1479–1504 (p. 378).

J

Jahangir *(juh hahn GEER)*, Conqueror of the World 1569–1627, Mughal emperor, 1605–1627 (p. 182).

James I 1566–1625, king of England, 1603–1625, began colonization of America (p. 460).

James II 1633–1701, king of England, 1685–1688, deposed in Glorious Revolution (p. 462).

Jefferson, Thomas 1743–1826, third president of the United States, 1801–1809 (p. 482).

Joan of Arc 1412–1431, French farm girl who led French against English in 1429 (p. 312).

John 1167–1216, king of England, forced by barons to set his seal to the *Magna Carta* (p. 270).

John II, John the Perfect 1455–1495, king of Portugal, 1481–1495, supported exploration (p. 149).

Joseph II 1741–1790, Austrian king, 1764–1790 (p. 480).

Julius Caesar 100–44 B.C., Roman general and dictator, 49–44 B.C. (p. 26).

Justinian I 483–565, Byzantine emperor, 527–565 (p. 42).

K

Kay, John 1742–1826, English inventor of the flying shuttle, 1733 (p. 492).

Kepler, Johannes 1571–1630, German astronomer (p. 354).

Khwarizmi, al *(al KWAH rihz mee)* c. 780–850, Arab mathematician, developer of algebra (p. 90).

Kublai Khan 1216–1294, Mongol leader, 1260–1294 (p. 167).

L

Labé, Louise c. 1520–1566, French poet and writer, called for women to educate themselves (p. 328).

Laozi 606–530 B.C., Chinese philosopher and founder of Daoism (p. 197).

Las Casas, Bartolomé de 1474–1566, Spanish Dominican missionary and historian (p. 369).

Leo III c. 680–741, Byzantine emperor, 717–741 (p. 293).

Leo III c. 750–816, pope, 795–816, crowned Charlemagne emperor of Holy Roman Empire (p. 258).

Leo IX 1002–1054, pope, 1049–1054, excommunicated patriarch of Constantinople (p. 293).

Leo X 1475–1521, pope, 1513–1521, pope during start of Protestant Reformation (p. 344).

Leonardo da Vinci *(VEEN chih)* 1452–1519, Italian artist and scientific thinker (p. 319).

Li Yuan 565–635, founder and first emperor of Tang Dynasty of China, 618–626 (p. 203).

Locke, John 1632–1704, English philosopher (p. 479).

Louis VI, Louis the Fat, 1081–1137, king of France, 1108–1137, friend of Abbot Suger (p. 284).

Louis VII, Louis the Young c. 1120–1180, king of France, 1137–1180, joined crusade (p. 299).

Louis XIII 1601–1643, French king, 1610–1643, assisted by Cardinal Richelieu (p. 453).

Louis XIV 1638–1715, king of France, 1643–1715, absolute monarch; built Versailles (p. 454).

Louis XVI 1754–1793, French king, 1774–1792, executed during French Revolution (p. 482).

Luther, Martin 1483–1546, German religious reformer (p. 341).

M

Machiavelli, Niccolò 1469–1527, Italian political thinker and writer of *The Prince* (p. 318).

Magellan, Ferdinand c. 1480–1521, Portuguese navigator of the world (p. 380).

Mahmud of Ghazna c. 971–1030, Turkish sultan, 997–1030 (p. 178).

Mansa Musa ?–1332, ruler of Mali, 1307–1332 (p. 119).

Mansur, Abu Jafar al c. 712–775, Abbasid caliph who built Baghdad, 754–775 (p. 86).

Mary I 1516–1558, English queen, 1553–1558, daughter of Henry VIII's first wife (p. 459).

Mary II 1662–1694, English queen, 1689–1694, became queen during Glorious Revolution (p. 462).

Mehmed II, Mehmed the Conqueror 1432–1481, Ottoman Sultan, 1451–1481 (p. 172).

Michelangelo Buonarroti *(BWAN nahr raw tih)* 1475–1564, Italian artist (p. 322).

Moctezuma c. 1480–1520, Aztec emperor (p. 437).

Montesquieu, Charles *(MAHN teh skyoo)* 1689–1755, French lawyer and political philosopher (p. 479).

More, Thomas 1478–1535, English statesman and author (p. 332).

Muawiya *(mu AH wih ya)* ?–680, Umayyad caliph, 661–680 (p. 67).

Muhammad 570–632, prophet of Islam, messenger of Allah (p. 58).

Mwene Mutapa c. 1400s, king of Monomutapa in Africa (p. 148).

N

Newton, Isaac 1642–1727, English scientist, astronomer, and mathematician (p. 356).

O

Oda, Nobunaga 1534–1582, general who unified Japan (p. 238).

Odoacer c. 434–493, barbarian ruler of Italy, 476–493 (p. 256).

Ogodei *(ahg ah DY)* 1185–1241, Mongol leader, 1229–1241 (p. 166).

Osman I 1259–1326, founder of Ottoman Empire (p. 171).

P

Paul III 1468–1549, pope, 1534–1549, (p. 351).

Pepin, Pepin the Short c. 714–768, king of the Franks, 751–768 (p. 258).

Peter ?–c. 64, first bishop of Rome (p. 290).

Petrarch, Francesco 1304–1374 Italian poet, scholar, and humanist (p. 322).

Philip II 1165–1223, king of France, 1180–1223, went on Third Crusade (p. 300).

Philip IV, Philip the Fair 1268–1314, king of France, 1285–1314; moved papacy to Avignon (p. 338).

Pizarro, Francisco c. 1476–1541, Spanish conqueror of Peru (p. 438).

Polo, Marco c. 1254–c. 1324, Italian traveler to China (p. 365).

Ptolemy *(TAHL uh mee)* 90–168, Roman geographer (p. 365).

R

Rabelais, François *(rah BLEH)* c. 1490–1553, French writer and physician (p. 331).

Richard I, Richard Lion Heart 1157–1199, English king, 1189–1199, went on Third Crusade (p. 300).

Richelieu, Armand *(RISH uh loo)* 1585–1642, cardinal and chief minister of Louis XIII (p. 453).

Romulus Augustulus 461–?, last Roman emperor of the West, 475–476 (p. 256).

Rousseau, Jean–Jacques *(roo SOH)* 1712–1778, French philosopher (p. 479).

S

Saladin c. 1137–1193, Muslim leader in crusades (p. 299).

Selim I 1467–1520, son of Bayezid II, dethroned father, Ottoman sultan 1512–1520 (p. 175).

Shah Jahan *(SHAH ju HAHN)* 1592–1666, emperor of Mughal Empire, 1628–1658 (p. 183).

Shakespeare, William 1564–1616, English poet, actor, and playwright (p. 458).

Shotoku, Taishi 573–621, Japanese Soga prince and regent, 593–621 (p. 226).

Sinan c. 1489–1587, Suleiman's architect, designed over 300 buildings including the Selim Mosque (p. 176).

Stephens, John 1805–1852, American traveler and author (p. 404).

Suger *(SOO zhair)* 1081–1151, French abbot of Abbey of St. Denis, 1122–1151 (p. 283).

Suleiman *(SOO lay mahn),* Suleiman the Magnificent 1494–1566, sultan, 1520–1566 (p. 175).

T

Taizu *(ty TSOO)* 1328–1398, founder and emperor of Ming Dynasty of China, 1368–1398 (p. 211).

Timur the Lame, Tamerlane c. 1336–1405, Mongol conqueror, founder of Timurid Dynasty (p. 168).

Theodosius I, Theodosius the Great c. 346–395, Roman general and emperor, 379–395 (p. 31).

Tokugawa Ieyasu 1543–1616, Japanese shogun, 1603–1605, established shogunate (p. 238).

U

Umar c. 581–644, second caliph, 634–644 (p. 66).

Urban II c. 1042–1099, pope, 1088–1099, called for the First Crusade (p. 294).

Urban VI c. 1318–1389, pope, 1378–1389, first pope during Great Schism with France (p. 339).

Uthman ?–656, third caliph, 644–656 (p. 66).

V

Van Eyck, Jan *(van EYEK)* c. 1390–1441, Flemish painter (p. 332).

Verrazano, Giovanni da c. 1485–1528, Italian navigator of North America for French (p. 381).

Vespucci, Amerigo 1454–1512, Italian navigator and explorer of South America; America named for him (p. 379).

Voltaire, *(vohl TAIR),* François Marie Arouet *(a REH)* 1694–1778, French writer (p. 477).

W

William I, William the Conqueror 1027–1087, king of England, 1066–1087, first Norman king (p. 261).

William III, William of Orange 1650–1702, king of England, 1689–1702 (p. 463).

Wycliffe, John c. 1320–1384, English scholar (p. 340).

X

Xian Di *(shehn dee)* ?–220, last Han emperor of China, 189–220 (p. 192).

Xuanzang c. 600–664, Chinese traveler (p. 13).

Y

Yang Jian, Emperor Wen 541–604, founder of Sui dynasty, emperor, 581–604 (p. 195).

Yoritomo 1147–1199, Japanese shogun, 1192–1199 (p. 232).

Z

Zacharias ?–752, pope, 741–752 (p. 258).

Zheng He c. 1371–c. 1433, Chinese admiral and diplomat (p. 213).

Zwingli, Ulrich 1484–1531, Swiss priest (p. 349).

Pronunciation Key

This chart presents the pronunciation key used in this Glossary. For a key to the phonetic respellings used to indicate pronunciation in the text of the chapters, see page 539.

Spellings	Symbol	Spellings	Symbol	Spellings	Symbol
pat	ă	kick, cat, pique	k	thin	th
pay	ā	lid, needle	l	this	*th*
care	âr	mum	m	cut	ŭ
father	ä	no, sudden	n	urge, term, firm,	ûr
bib	b	thing	ng	word, heard	
church	ch	pot, horrid	ŏ	valve	v
deed, milled	d	toe	ō	with	w
pet	ě	caught, paw, for	ô	yes	y
bee	ē	noise	oi	zebra, xylem	z
life, phase, rough	f	took	o͝o	vision, pleasure,	zh
gag	g	boot	o͞o	garage	
hat	h	out	ou	about, item, edible,	ə
which	hw	pop	p	gallop, circus	
pit	ĭ	roar	r	butter	ər
pie, by	ī	sauce	s		
pier	îr	ship, dish	sh	Primary stress ´	
judge	j	tight, stopped	t	Secondary stress ˊ	

A

absolute monarch (ăbˊsə-lo͞otˊ mŏnˊərkˊ) a ruler who has no restrictions of any kind on his or her power (p. 454).

adobe (ə-dōˊbē) bricks formed of mud mixed with straw (p. 415).

Age of Enlightenment (āj ŭv ĕn-lītˊn-mənt) a movement in Europe during the 1700s that critically analyzed ideas and institutions, using human reason (p. 477).

agricultural revolution (ăg-rĭ-kŭlˊchər-əl rĕvˊə-lo͞oˊshən) a series of agricultural developments in Europe during the 1700s that improved both farming methods and the yield of the land (p. 490).

alliance (ə-līˊəns) a pact or union between states in a common cause (p. 424).

altiplano (älˊtĭ-pläˊnō) the land on a high, flat plateau in South America (p. 412).

ancestor worship (ănˊsĕsˊtər wûrˊshĭp) honor and reverence paid to one's deceased relatives, based on the belief that their spirits live on and can influence the gods in one's favor (p. 126).

archaeology (ärˊkē-ŏlˊə-jē) the recovery and study of physical remains from past human life and culture (p. 17).

aristocrat (ə-rĭsˊtə-krătˊ) a member of a privileged class having inherited wealth and high social position (p. 204).

B

balance of trade (bălˊəns ŭv trād) the difference in value between the total imports and total exports of a nation (p. 370).

barbarian (bär-bârˊē-ən) in the ancient Roman Empire, people living along the empire's borders; a person considered by another group to have a primitive culture (p. 29).

Buddhism (bo͞oˊdĭzˊəm) a religion based on the teachings of Siddhartha Gautama; Buddhism stresses that suffering is a basic part of life and that life is a cycle of death and rebirth and that suffering can be overcome (p. 194).

bullion (bo͝olˊyən) gold or silver in the form of bars or ingots of a specific weight (p. 370).

bureaucracy (byo͝o-rŏkˊrə-sē) a type of organization structured like a pyramid, with one person at the top and many at the bottom; workers at each level supervise those below them (p. 82).

bushido (bo͞oshˊĭ-dō) a Japanese code of ethics involving courage, loyalty, and commitment to military life; "the way of the warrior" (p. 273).

C

caliph (kāˊlĭf) the civil and religious ruler of a Muslim state (p. 66).

calligraphy (kə-lĭgˊrə-fē) the art of fine handwriting, such as that practiced in Muslim art and writing (p. 88).

calpulli (kăl-pōō´lē) an Aztec settlement in which families of different social classes lived and shared the land (p. 425).

capital (kăp´ĭ-tl) wealth in the form of money or property used for the production of more wealth (p. 375).

capitalist (kăp´ĭ-tl-ĭst) an investor of money, or capital, in business (p. 493).

caravan (kăr´ə-van´) a single file of pack animals journeying together to transport goods (p. 11).

caravel (kăr´ə-vĕl´) a swift, maneuverable sailing ship used for exploration by the Spanish and the Portuguese in the 1500s and 1600s (p. 373).

charter (chär´tər) a document issued by a monarch or other authority, creating a public or private corporation with special rights (p. 468).

checks and balances (chĕks ənd băl´əns-əz) the system of maintaining a balance of power between various branches of a government (p. 498).

chinampa (chĭ-năm´pə) narrow strips of land about 300 feet long and 30 feet wide built in swampy land and used for farming in Central America, particularly by the Aztec (p. 423).

chivalry (shĭv´əl-rē) qualities such as honor, courtesy, loyalty, and fair treatment of the weak, idealized by knights in the Middle Ages (p. 273).

circumnavigation (sûr´kəm-năv´ĭ-gā´shən) the act of sailing around the world (p. 380).

city-state (sĭtē-stāt´) an independent state made up of a city and the territory that surrounds it (p. 143).

civil war (sìv´əl wôr) a war between factions or regions within a country (p. 438).

clan (klăn) a group of families who claim descent from a common ancestor (p. 163).

classic (klăs´ĭk) a work of art or literature from ancient Greece or Rome; something considered to be of the highest rank or excellence (p. 291).

clergy (klûr´jē) the group of people who have been ordained for religious service (p. 283).

codex (kō´dĕks´) a manuscript volume; record books kept by early Central American peoples such as the Maya and Aztec (p. 409).

colony (kŏl´ə-nē) a settlement in a distant land whose citizens keep close ties to their parent country (p. 375).

commerce (kŏm´ərs) trade, or the buying and selling of goods, on a large scale (p. 45).

commonwealth (kŏm´ən-wĕlth´) a nation governed by the people (p. 461).

Confucianism (kən-fyōō´shən-ĭz´əm) a set of beliefs, based on the teachings of Confucius, that focused on proper conduct, respect for elders, scholarship, and government service (p. 194).

conquistador (kŏng-kē´stə-dôr´) the Spanish term for conqueror used in reference to Spaniards who came to the New World in the 1500s in search of wealth (p. 437).

constitutional monarchy (kŏn´stĭ-tōō´shə-nəl mŏn´ər-kē) a monarchy in which the powers of the ruler are restricted to those granted under the constitution and the laws of the nation (p. 463).

contract (kŏn´trăckt´) an agreement between two or more parties, particularly one that is written and enforceable by law (p. 479).

council (koun´səl) an assembly called to help pick the next Muslim caliph (p. 67); a series of meetings of Roman Catholic Church leaders in the 1400s dealing with issues of church law and faith (p. 340).

Counter Reformation (koun´tər ref´ər-ma´shən) the reform movement within the Roman Catholic Church whose goals were to abolish abuses and reaffirm traditional beliefs (p. 352).

courtier (kôr´tē-ər) a person who takes part in the highly refined social life of a court (p. 228).

crop rotation (krŏp rō-tā´shən) the planting of crops such as turnips, wheat, and clover in alternate years to keep soil fertile (p. 491).

crusade (krōō-sād´) any of the military expeditions undertaken by European Christians from c. 1100 to c. 1400 to win the Holy Land from the Muslims (p. 296).

currency (kûr´ən-sē) any form of money being used as a medium of exchange (p. 150, 206).

D

daimyo (dīm´yō´) the lord of a large agricultural estate in feudal Japan who supported the shogun (p. 232).

Daoism (dou´ĭz´əm) a belief system based on the teachings of Laozi; Daoists emphasis living in harmony with nature and being content with one's life (p. 197).

delta (dĕl´tə) a triangle-shaped landform of mud and silt deposited at a river's mouth (p. 110).

denomination (dĭ-nŏm´ə-nā´shən) a religious body consisting of a group of congregations having the same faith (p. 234).

despot (dĕs´pət) a ruler who holds absolute power and uses it abusively (p. 212).

dissent (dĭ-sĕnt´) to disagree, especially with the accepted doctrine of an established religion (p. 82).

divan (dĭ-văn´) a governing council in a Muslim country, especially the Ottoman Imperial Council (p. 173).

divine right (dĭ-vīn´ rīt) the right of a monarch to rule, based on the belief that this right comes directly from God and that the monarch is responsible only to God (p. 454).

diviner (dĭ-vīn´ər) a person who is believed to communicate with the spirit world and to help other people interact with their gods (p. 126).

dowry (dou´rē) money, land, servants, or any other valuable property given by a bride's family to her husband at marriage (p. 328).

dynasty (dī´nə-stē) a succession of rulers from the same family or line (p. 32).

E

electronic communication (ĭ-lĕk-trŏn´ĭk kə-myōō´ nĭ- kā´shən) communication devices, such as the Internet, fax, telephone, television, and computer that have reduced the time necessary for transmitting information (p. 7).

elite (ĭ-lēt´) a small, privileged group at the top of a society (p. 401).

emir (ĭ-mîr´) a prince, chieftain, or governor, especially in the Middle East (p. 82).

empire (ĕm´pīr´) a political unit often made up of a number of territories, states, or nations, ruled by a single supreme authority (p. 78).

enclosure (ĕn-klō´zhər) the fencing in of common land to form larger estates in England during the 1700s (p. 491).

encomienda system (ĕn-kō´mē-ĕn´də sĭs´təm) a system in which New World inhabitants were granted to Spanish colonists, who were responsible for supervising their work and instructing the inhabitants in the teachings of Roman Catholicism (p. 467).

enlightened despot (ĕn-līt´nd dĕs´pət) a European ruler in the 1700s with absolute power who tried to support Enlightenment ideals such as tolerance and freedom (p. 480).

excommunication (ĕks´kə-myōō´nĭ-kā´shən) the act that deprives someone of membership in the church (p. 285).

extinct (ĭk-stĭngkt´) no longer existing or living (p. 398).

F

faction (făk´shən) a group of persons forming a minority in disagreement with the larger group (p. 91).

feudalism (fyōōd´l-ĭz´əm) a political and economic system in which large landholders or lords gave protection to people in return for their service to the landholder (p. 261).

fief (fēf) a large feudal estate, particularly in medieval Europe (p. 261).

G

ghazi (gä´zē) a Muslim warrior who has fought to expand the frontiers of the Muslim state (p. 171).

grand vizier (grănd vĭ-zîr´) the senior advisor or prime minister who advises the sultan on state matters (p. 172).

griot (grē´ō) a West African storyteller (p. 118).

guild (gĭld) an association of tradespeople made up of merchants, craftspeople, or artisans, particularly in the Middle Ages (p. 269).

H

haiku (hī´kōō) an unrhymed Japanese poem consisting of three lines with five, seven, and five syllables, respectively (p. 241).

harem (hâr´əm) literally, sanctuary or sacred place; the women or the domestic quarters of a Muslim household (p. 173).

heretic (hĕr´ĭ-tĭk) a person who has controversial opinions, especially one who publicly disagrees with the accepted beliefs of the Roman Catholic Church (p. 313).

hierarchy (hī´ə-rär´kē) a group of people organized or classified by rank and authority (p. 261).

hieroglyph (hī´ər-ə-glĭf´) a system of writing that uses picture symbols for concepts, objects, or words (p. 403).

history (hĭs´tə-rē) a record of past human events; the study of the past, including explanations of the events (p. 17).

homage (hom´ĭj) an expression of public honor or respect; in feudalism, the ceremonial recognition of allegiance to a lord shown by a vassal (p. 263).

humanism (hyōō´mə-nĭz´əm) a doctrine or attitude that is concerned primarily with human beings and their values, capacities, and achievements (p. 319).

hunter-gatherer (hŭn´tər găth´ər-ər) early people who obtained their food by hunting wild animals and gathering wild plants, roots, nuts, and berries (p. 397).

hypothesis (hī-pŏth´ĭ-sĭs) an assumption that accounts for a set of facts and that can be tested by investigation (p. 355).

I

icon (ī´kŏn´) a picture or representation of a sacred Christian person, itself regarded as sacred (p. 292).

idol (īd´l) an image used as an object of worship (p. 55).

immigrant (ĭm´ĭ-grənt) a person who leaves one country to settle permanently in another country (p. 500).

individualism (ĭn´də-vĭj´ōō-ə-lĭz´əm) personal independence; the idea that every person should be free to develop and pursue his or her own goals (p. 315).

indulgence (ĭn-dŭl´jəns) certificates, issued by the pope, which were said to reduce or cancel punishment for a person's sins (p. 340).

industrial revolution (ĭn-dŭs´trē-əl rĕv´ə-lōō´shən) major improvements in industry, especially those in Europe during the 18th century (p. 492).

infidel (ĭn´fĭ-dəl) one who is an unbeliever in Christianity (p. 296).

Inquisition (ĭn´kwĭ-zĭsh´ən) a Roman Catholic Church court revived during the Counter Reformation for the purpose of trying, convicting, and punishing heretics (p. 352).

Islam (ĭs-läm´) a religion based on the teachings of the prophet Muhammad that believes in one god, Allah; the laws of Islam are found in the Qur'an and the Sunna (p. 60).

isolation (ī´sə-lā´shən) the condition of being separated from a group (p. 223).

J

janissary (jăn´ĭ-sĕr´ē) an enslaved soldier in the elite Ottoman infantry or government service (p. 173).

K

khan (kän) a Mongol ruler (p. 165).

kinship (kĭn´shĭp´) the relationship among family members (p. 127).

knight (nīt) an armed, mounted soldier of the feudal period who gives military service to a lord (p. 261).

L

lateen sail (lə-tēn´ sāl) a triangular sail (p. 12).

legacy (lĕg´ə-sē) something handed down from an ancestor; something from the past (p. 98).

literacy (lĭt´ər-ə-sē) the ability to read and write (p. 291).

M

magnetic compass (măg-nĕt´ĭk kŭm´pəs) a device used to determine geographical direction, using a magnetic needle that is free to pivot until aligned with the magnetic field of the earth (p. 12).

malaria (mə-lâr´ē-ə) a tropical disease carried by the anopheles mosquito and characterized by chills, fever, and sweating (p. 148).

mandate (măn´dāt´) a command or instruction from an authority; an order to govern (p. 204).

manor (măn´ər) the castle and estate of a feudal lord (p. 266).

matrilineal (măt´rə-lĭn´ē-əl) relating to the system of tracing descent through the females of a family (p. 117).

mercantilism (mûr´kən-tē-lĭz´əm) a European economic system based on establishing colonies as a source of raw materials and as the market for goods from the ruling country (p. 467).

mercenary (mûr´sə-nèr´ē) a professional soldier who is hired by a foreign country (p. 318).

meritocracy (mĕr´ĭ-tŏk´rə-sē) a system in which people are chosen for jobs and promoted on the basis of their performance (p. 204).

migrate (mī´grāt´) to move from one area or country to another and settle there (p. 137).

millet (mĭl´ā) a partially self-governing group of non-Muslims in the Ottoman Empire; the most common millets were Armenian, Greek Orthodox, and Jewish (p. 174).

missionary (mĭsh´ə-nèr´ē) a person sent to a foreign country to do religious or charitable work (p. 152).

monarchy (mŏn´ər-kē) a strong central government ruled by a king or queen (p. 312).

monastery (mŏn´ə-stĕr´ē) a place in which a community of religious people, particularly monks, lives (p. 257).

money economy (mŭn´ē ĭ-kŏn´ə-mē) an economy in which cash is the most common item exchanged for goods (p. 206).

monopoly (mə-nŏp´ə-lē) the total control by one group of the means of producing a service (p. 368).

monotheism (mŏn´ə-thē-ĭz´əm) the belief that there is only one God (p. 59).

monsoon (mŏn-sōōn´) a wind system that switches direction seasonally and brings dry and wet seasons, especially the Asiatic monsoon that brings wet and dry seasons to India and southern Asia (p. 141).

mosaic (mō-zā´ĭk) a picture or design made from small colored pieces of glass or quartz embedded in plaster (p. 43).

mosque (mŏsk) a Muslim house of worship (p. 60).

Muslim (mŭz´ləm) a believer in Islam (p. 60).

N

natural right (năch´ər-əl rīt) one of the rights believed by many to be guaranteed to all people by nature, including life, liberty, and the right to own property (p. 479).

nomad (nō´măd´) a member of a group that moves from place to place following food, water, and grazing land for their herds (p. 53).

O

oasis (ō-ā´sĭs) a small area in the desert watered by springs and wells (p. 53).

oath of fealty (ōth ŭv fē´əl-tē) a feudal oath of loyalty sworn to a lord in exchange for an award of land (p. 261).

oral tradition (ôr´əl trə-dĭsh´ən) the legends, myths, and beliefs that a culture passes from generation to generation by word of mouth (p. 148).

P

pamphlet (păm´flĭt) an unbound published work such as an essay, usually on a current topic (p. 345).

parliament (pär´lə-mənt) a national representative body having the highest lawmaking powers within the state, particularly in England (p. 458).

patriarch (pā´trē-ärk´) the male leader of a family or tribe; in the Byzantine Empire, the bishop of Constantinople (p. 292).

patrician (pə-trĭsh´ən) a member of the highest class of society in Italian city-states during the Renaissance; an aristocrat (p. 327).

patrilineal (păt´rə-lĭn´ē-əl) relating to the system of tracing descent through the males of a family (p. 117).

patron (pā´trən) a person who financially supports scholars or artists (p. 327).

philosophe (fē´lə-zôf´) any of the leading philosophical, political, and social writers of the French Enlightenment of the 1700s from either the aristocracy or the middle class (p. 477).

pilgrimage (pĭl´grə-mĭj) a journey to a sacred place or shrine (p. 57).

plague (plāg) a highly infectious, usually fatal, epidemic disease (p. 310).

plantation (plăn-tā´shən) a large farm where crops are grown (p. 152).

plateau (plă-tō´) a raised and relatively flat area of land (p. 146).

predestination (prē-děs´tə-nā´shən) the belief that God has determined all things in advance, including the salvation of souls (p. 350).

prehistory (prē-hĭs´tə-rē) history that took place before the development of writing (p. 17).

primary source (prī´měr´ē sôrs) a source for historical study that was written by someone who participated in or observed the event being recorded (p. 17).

prime minister (prīm mĭn´ĭ-stər) the chief government official appointed by a ruler (p. 453).

Protestant (prŏt´ĭ-stənt) a reformer who protested against the abuses of the Catholic church in the 1500s; a member of a church descended from those that seceded from the Roman Catholic Church during the 1500s (p. 344).

province (prŏv´ĭns) in the ancient Roman Empire, any of the lands outside Italy conquered and ruled by the Romans (p. 27).

Q

Qur'an (kə-rän´) the sacred book of Islam that is believed to contain the revelations made to Muhammad by Allah (p. 58).

R

realism (rē´ə-lĭz´əm) an artistic style dating from the Renaissance that attempts to visually represent people and objects as they exist naturally (p. 322).

reason (rē´zən) the capacity for logical thought (p. 476).

Reformation (rĕf´ər-mā´shən) the reform movement of the 1500s that resulted in the separation of the Protestant churches from the Roman Catholic Church (p. 344).

regent (rē´jənt) a person who rules for a monarch during periods of illness or absence, or during the monarch's extreme youth (p. 228).

Renaissance (rĕn´ĭ-säns´) the revival of attention to classical Greek and Roman art, literature, and learning that originated in Italy in the 14th century and later spread through Europe (p. 317).

republic (rĭ-pŭb´lĭk) a political order whose head of state is not a monarch and in which supreme power lies in a body of elected citizens (p. 317).

S

Sahel (sə-hāl´) a strip of dry grasslands on the southern border of the Sahara; also known as "the shore of the desert" (p. 109).

salary (săl´ə-rē) a fixed payment for services paid on a regular basis (p. 181).

salvation (săl-vā´shən) the deliverance of the soul from the penalties of sin (p. 285).

samurai (săm´ə-rī´) the feudal military aristocracy of Japan, from the term meaning "those who serve" (p. 232).

satellite (săt´ə-līt´) a relatively small object orbiting a planet or moon; a manufactured object orbiting the earth, often used to transmit information (p. 7).

savanna (sə-văn´ə) a region of grasslands containing scattered trees and vegetation (p. 109).

schism (sĭz´əm) a separation or division into factions, especially a formal separation within a Christian church (p. 293).

scientific method (sī´ən-tĭf´ĭk mèth´əd) a series of logical steps formulated by Francis Bacon and used in scientific research that stressed observation and experimentation (p. 355).

Scientific Revolution (sī´ən-tĭf´ĭk rěv´ə-lōō´shən) the era of scientific thought in Europe during which careful observation of the natural world was made, and accepted beliefs were questioned (p. 354).

secondary source (sěk´ən-děr´ē sôrs) a source for historical study that was written after the event it describes, usually with the aid of a primary source (p. 17).

secular (sěk´yə-lər) worldly, rather than religious, in nature (p. 332).

sedentary (sěd´n-těr´ē) characterized by remaining in one place and not migrating (p. 398).

serf (sûrf) a member of the lowest feudal class, bound to the land and whoever owned the land (p. 264).

Shiite (shē´īt´) a member of the branch of Islam that supports the descendants of Muhammad as his rightful successors (p. 67).

Shinto (shĭn´tō) a Japanese religion whose followers believe that all things in the natural world are filled with divine spirits (p. 225).

shogun (shō´gən) a line of military leaders who ruled Japan under the nominal leadership of the emperor until 1868 (p. 232).

stele (stē´lē) an upright stone column with inscribed hieroglyphs used as a monument, particularly by early peoples of Central America (p. 407).

steppe (stĕp) a vast semiarid grass-covered plain, usually lightly wooded, as found in southeastern Europe and Siberia (p. 162).

sternpost rudder (stûrn´pōst´ rŭd´ər) a paddlelike device under a ship and connected to a handle on deck, for steering sailing ships (p. 12).

stirrup (stûr´əp) a loop or ring hung from either side of a horse's saddle to support the rider's foot in riding and mounting (p. 11).

succession (sək-sĕsh´ən) the sequence in which one person after another succeeds to a title, throne, or estate (p. 238).

sultan (sŭl´tən) the ruler of a Muslim country, especially the former Ottoman Empire (p. 172).

Sunna (soon´ə) traditional Islamic law observed by orthodox Muslims and based on the teaching of Muhammad (p. 61).

Sunni (soon´ē) the branch of Islam that follows orthodox tradition and accepts the validity of the first four caliphs elected as successors to Muhammad (p. 68).

T

terrace farming (tĕr´ĭs fär´mĭng) the building of raised banks of earth on steep land for farming (p. 433).

tithe (tīth) a tenth of one's income contributed voluntarily to a church (p. 285).

tribe (trīb) any system of social organization made up of villages, bands, or other groups with a common ancestry, language, culture, and name (p. 55).

tribute (trĭb´yoot) a kind of tax paid in goods or services to the ruling government (p. 425).

U

university (yoo´nə-vûr´sĭ-tē) an institution of higher learning with teaching and research facilities as well as graduate and professional schools (p. 287).

V

vassal (văs´əl) a person who receives land and protection from a feudal lord in return for loyalty to that lord (p. 261).

vertical economy (vûr´tĭ-kəl ĭ-kŏn´ə-mē) the growing of crops according to the altitude of the land, particularly in South America (p. 433).

Acknowledgments *(continued from page 558)*

442: © Merrell Wood / TIB (l); © Susan Malis / PHOTRI (r). **443**: Biblioteca Nacional, Madrid. **448–49**: The Granger Collection. **450**: Museu Nacional de Arte Antiga, Lisbon, MH (l); Bermuda News Service (r). **451**: Galleria Palatina, Florence / AR (t); Private Collection / NB (bl); The Metropolitan Museum of Art (r). **452**: Victoria & Albert Museum / Bridgeman Art Library. **453**: Bibliotheque Publique et Universitaire, Geneva. **454**: National Gallery, London / AR (t); The Mansell Collection (b). **455**: Comstock, Inc. (t); AR (b). **456**: Gianni Dagli Orti / Corbis. **458**: British Library. **459**: Private Collection / NB (t); Her Majesty's Stationery Office, England (b). **460**: National Maritime Museum, Greenwich, England (t); Victoria & Albert Museum (b). **461**: National Museum of Scotland (t); The Royal Collection (b). **462**: AR (l); Private Collection (lc); The Granger Collection (rc); The National Portrait Gallery, London (r). **463**: The National Portrait Gallery, London (l, rc, r); © Collection of the New-York Historical Society (lc). **464**: New York Public Library, Rare Books Division. **465**: RJB. **467**: The Folger Shakespeare Library (t); RJB (b). **468**: BM / Bridgeman Art Library / AR (l); The Brooklyn Museum (r). **469**: RJB.

471: © Willinger / FPG International. **474**: © Robert Descharnes, Les Delices, Geneva (l); Musee Carnavalet, Paris (r). **475**: © H. Andrew Johnson, Thomas Jefferson Memorial Foundation, Inc. (l); SCALA / AR (r). **476**: BM / Bridgeman Art Library / AR. **477**: Trinity College, Cambridge, England (t); The Granger Collection (b). **478**: Giraudon / AR (t); The Cleveland Museum of Art (b). **479**: Corbis-Bettmann. **480**: Biblioteca Nacional, Madrid. **482**: The Metropolitan Museum of Art, Gift of William H. Huntington, 1883. **483**: Musee Carnavalet, Paris, Giraudon / AR. **485**: Louvre / NB. **490**: AR. **491**: The Newberry Library, Chicago. **492**: Smithsonian Institution. **493**: LPW **494**: The Newberry Library, Chicago (t); © Eddie Hironaka / TIB (b). **495**: © Stephen Wilkes / TIB. **496**: RJB. **497**: © PHOTRI. **498**: © Don Carl Steffan / Photo Researchers, Inc. (tl); © Bill Ross / Westlight (tr); © Craig Aurness / Westlight (c); The National Archives (b). **499**: New York Public Library / NB. **500**: © Pete Turner / TIB. **503**: AR (l); SCALA / AR (r).

Picture Research Assistance by Carousel Research, Inc., Meyers Photo-Art, and Jim Lillie.

Italic numbers refer to pages on which illustrations appear.

A

Abbas, al, 84
Abbasid Empire, 84, 88–91
  and Mongol destruction of Baghdad, 91
Abbasid-Seljuk Empire, 91
Abbesses, 283, 350
Abbots, 283
Abd al Malik, 83
Abd al Rahman I, 84, 91, 95–96, 97
Abd al Rahman III, 96, 99
Abdullah, 84
Abraham, biblical, 57, 62
Absolute monarch, 454
Abu Bakr, 58, 65–66, 69
Abul Fazl, 181, 186
Achebe, Chinua, 125
Acre, siege of, 300
Act of Supremacy, 351
A.D./B.C., 11
Affonso I, 152–153, *154,* 154–155
Africa. *See* Central and southern Africa;
    East Africa; West Africa
Afro-Asiatic languages, 136
*Against the Robbing and Murdering
    Hordes of Peasants* (Luther), 347
Age of Reason, 476
Agricultural revolution, 490–492
Agriculture, developments in,
  in Africa, 112, 125, 138, 146, 205–206, 242
  in Americas, 398–399, 401, 403, 406, 413,
    423, 432–433
  in China, 37, 205–206
  in Europe, 266, 267, 481, 490–492
  in Japan, 225–226
  in Middle East, 54, 87
  in Spain, 99
Ahuitzotl, 424
Ainu people, 224
Aisha, 58
Akbar, 181–182, *182,* 186–187
Akbar-nama, 186, 186–187, *187*
Alberti, Leon Battista, 326–327
Alcuin, 259
Alexander VI, Pope, 379
Alfonso VI, 100
Alfred the Great, 260, 268
Algeria, 177
Ali, 66, 67
Almohads, 99, 117
Almoravids, 117
Altiplano, 412, *413*
American Revolution, 482
Amida Buddha, 234, *234*
Anabaptists, 350
Anatomy, scientific study of, 354, *354*
Ancestor worship, in West Africa, 126
Anda, 163
Andes, 530
Anglo–Saxons, *256,* 260
Ann, Queen, *463*
Apprenticeship, 269
Arabia, 50, 53, 55
  first towns in, 55–56
  trade in, 6, 10–15, 242
Arabic, 53, 74, 83, 87
Arabs
  geographic knowledge of, 15, 366
  invasion of Persia, 33,
  trading by, 142
Aragon, 100
Archaeology, 17, 20–21

Archimedes, 319
Armada, Spanish, 459–460
Armenia, 32, 69
Arouet, François Marie. *See* Voltaire
ar-Razi, 90, *90*
Art
  Byzantine, 43
  history of, 322, 328
  mosaics, 43, 44, *44*
  Muslim, *88,* 88–89, *89*
  realism in, 322
  of the Roman Catholic church, 288, *288*
  understanding, 186–187
Articles of Confederation, 497
Ashanti people, 126
Ashikaga shogunate, 234, 238
Ashkenazic culture, 259
Askia Muhammad, 121
Assumptions, recognizing, 243
Astrolabe, 15, *372,* 373
Astronomy, history of, 12, 15, 90, 99, 208,
    354–355, 365–366, 378
Atahualpa, 439, *440*
Augustus, 10, *26,* 26–27, 33
Aurangzeb, 185, *185*
Avignon, pope's residence, 339, *339*
Awdaghust, 117
Aztec Empire, 16, 18–19, 422–426
  cultural achievements of, 18, 426–427
  fall of, 438–439, 440–442
  primary sources on, 16, 18–19, 422, 427,
    428, 437, 442, 443
  religion of, 427–428

B

Babar-nama (Babur), 181
Babur, 180–181
Bacon, Francis, 355
Baghdad, 72, 74, 76, 85, 87–88
  Mongol invasion of, 91
  Turkish invasion of, 91
Baki, 176
Balance of trade, 370
Balboa, Vasco de, 380
Balkans, Jews of, 43
Ban Zhao, 192, 194
Banking, 88, 314–315
Bantu-speaking people
  in East Africa, 139, 142, 147
  language of, 136
  migration of, 24, 136–139
  society of, 139
Barbarians, 29, 33, 257
Barros, João de, 147
Basho (Matsuo Basho), 241
Bastille, storming of, 483
Bastille Day, 485
Bayeux Tapestry, *272*
Bayezid, 174, 175
B.C./A.D., 11
Bedouins, lifestyle of, 52
Beijing, 210, 212
ben-Isaac, Rabbi Shlomo, 259
ben–Shaprut, Hasdai, 99
Berbers, 79, 112, 113, 117
Bering land bridge, 396–397, *397*
Bessarion, Cardinal, *318*
Bible, the, 62
Bill of Rights, U.S., and *Magna Carta,* 270
Bingen, Hildegard of, 266
Bit (horse), invention of, 11

Black Death, *310,* 310–312, *312,* 315
"Bloody Mary," 459
Boccaccio, Giovanni, 322
Bojador, Cape, 371, 374
Boniface VIII, Pope, 338
Book of the Family (Alberti), 327
Brahmaputra River, 179
Brazil, Portuguese discovery of, 465–466
Brueghel, Pieter, the Elder, 329
Brunei, 241
Brunelleschi, Filippo, 322
Buddha, The, 194–195, *195*
Buddhism
  in China, 36, 192, 194–195
  in Japan, 225–226, 227, 228, 234–236
  in Korea, 69, 225
  in Mongol Empire, 168
  Pure Land, 234
  Shingon form, 228
  in Southeast Asia, 241
  Zen, 235–236
Bullion, 370, *370*
Bureaucracy, 82
Burma, 241
Bursa, Ottoman capture of, 171
Bushido, 273
Byzantine church, 292–293
  schism with Roman church, 293
Byzantine Empire, 31, 33, 42–45, 69, 289,
    290–291
  culture of, 42–43
  daily life in, 291
  religion in, 292–293
  scholarship in, 291
  Turkish invasion of, 294
  war with Persia, 45, 69, 78, 294
  women in, 291
Byzantium, 30, 43

C

Cabot, John 380
Caesar, Julius, 26, 33
Cairo, 91
Cajamarca, 439
Calendar, Mayan, 407, 408, *408,* 409
Calligraphy
  Chinese, 196, *202, 204*
  Japanese, 235, *235*
  Muslim, 88
Calpullis, 425
Calvin, John, *349,* 349–350
Calvinism, 349–350
Cambodia, 69, 241
Camel, physical features of, 11
Canary Islands, 374
Cannons, 313
Canon of Medicine (Avicenna), 90
Cão, Diego, 149
Cape Verde Islands, 375
Capital and capitalists, 375, 493
Caravans, 11, 214
Caravel, 373, *373*
Cartier, Jacques, 381
Cartwright, Edmund, 493
Caste system, 180
Castile, 100
Castles
  in England, 263–265, 272, *274*
  in Japan, 238, 272
Catherine of Siena, 341, *341*
Catherine the Great, 480, 481

Catherwood, Frederick, 404
Central and southern Africa, geography of, 136–137
Cerularius, Patriarch, 293
Cervantes, Miguel de, 322
Ceuta, 371–372
Challenger, space shuttle, 52
Changamire dynasty, 148
Changan, 196, 204
Charlemagne, 88, *258,* 258–260
     as Holy Roman Emperor, 293
Charles I (England), 458, *458,* 460–461, *461*
Charles II (England), 462, *462*
Charles IX (France), 452, 453
Charles Martel, 79, 258, 272
Charles the Bald, 259–260
Charles the Pious, 260
Charles V, 344–345
Charters, 468
Chartres Cathedral, *282,* 282–283
Checks and balances, 498
China
     aristocracy in, 203–204
     and Black Death, 310
     Buddhism in, 194–195, 197
     civil service system in, 203–204
     Confucianism in, 194, 197
     contact with other cultures, 33, 36–37, 209–214
     Daoism in, 197
     economy under Tang, Song dynasties, 204–206
     farming in, 205–206
     geographic knowledge of, 15, 365
     geography of, 193–194
     heritage of, 206–207
     merchant class in, 206, 214
     under Mongol rule, 210–211
     naval power during Ming Dynasty, 212
     poetry of, 200–201
     population growth in Qing Dynasty, 215
     reunification under Sui, 195
     roads and waterways in, 204–205
     role in transfer of learning, 313
     scholarship in, 207–208
     in Southeast Asia, 241
     trade routes, 6, 10–15, 33, 142, 145
     unification under Han, 33, 192–193
     western contact under Ming Dynasty, 214
Chinampas, 423–424
Chivalry, 273, 302
Christianity
     in Arabia, 55, 57
     in Byzantine Empire, 43, 290, 292–293
     in China, 214
     in Japan, 239
     in Mongol Empire, 168
     in Mughal India, 182
     in Muslim Empire, 66, 80, 81
     spread of, 302, 315, 338, 352, 368–369, 465
     ties to Islam, 61–62, 82
Christians
     role in transfer of learning, 15, 34, 98, 302, 313, 322, 323, 365, 372
Church of England, 351, 459, 462
Cicero, 319
City-states
     in East Africa, 142–143

in Italy, 317–318
Civilization, understanding, 35
Civil service system
     in China, 203–204
     in Mughal Empire, 181
Clans
     in Africa, 126, 127, 139
     Mongol, 163
Clement V, Pope, 339
Clement VII, Pope, 339
Climate, world (map), 530
Clovis, 257–258
Codex
     Aztec, 426–427, *427, 428*
     Mayan, 409
Colonialism, understanding, 469
Columbus, Christopher, 15, 377–379, *378, 386,* 466
Commonwealth, 461
Communication, 6–7
     nonverbal, 410–411
Comnena, Anna, 297
Compass
     Chinese invention of, 12, 208
     Henry the Navigator's improvements on, 372–373
     transfer through Muslims, 15
Concordat of Worms, 285
Confucianism, 190, 192, 194
Congo Basin, 137
Congo River, 149, 150
Congo-Kordofanian languages, 136
Conquest, understanding, 167
Conquistadors, 437
Conrad III, 299
Consequences, predicting, 457
Constantine, 30–31, 43, 290
Constantinople, 31, *31,* 42–43, 170, 289, *289,* 290–291, 294, 297, 301. *See also* Istanbul
     Ottoman capture of, 174
     sack of, 301
Constitution, United States, 497–498
Constitutional monarchy, 463, 483, 485
Cook, James, 239
Copan, ruins of, 404, *404*
Copernicus, Nicolaus, 353, 354
Cordoba, 74, 95–99
Correa, Gaspar, 364
Cortés, Hernando, 16, 426, 437, *438,* 438–439
Cotton gin, *492*
Coulomb, Charles, 476
Council of Constance, 340, 341
Courtly love, 302
Crimea, 177
Critical thinking, understanding, 123, 242–243, 357, 443, 457
Cromwell, Oliver, 461–462, *462*
Cromwell, Richard, 462, *462*
Crop rotation, 491
Crusader states, 297
Crusades, 296–297
     effects on Europe, 302, 315
     effects on Jews, 315
     First, 297
     Fourth, 301
     knights of, 296, 298, *298*
     primary sources about, 295, 301
     Second, 299, 300
     Third (Crusade of Kings), 300–301

Cultures, contact between, 32–37, *33*
Cuzco, 529
Cuzco Valley, 523

D

Damascus, 78, 79
Daoism, 168, 190, 197
Dark Ages, 256. *See also* Middle Ages
David, Jacques Louis, 485
Deccan plateau, 179
Declaration of Independence, 482, 509–512
Declaration of the Rights of Man and of the Citizen, 483, 485, 506–508
Declaration of the Rights of Woman, 485
della Casa, Giovanni, 316
Delta, 110
Despot, 212
Dhammapada, The (Buddha), 195
Dhows, *141,* 142
Dialogue Concerning Two Chief World Systems (Galileo), 355
Dias, Bartolomeu, 375
Díaz, Bernal, 16, 18–19
Diderot, Denis, 478
Diocletian, 30
Disease, and Spanish conquest, 380, 441
Dissent, 82
Divan, 173
Divine right, 454
Diviners, 126
Dogon people, 124, *124,* 125, 126–127
Dome of the Rock, *59*
Don Quixote, 322
Doña Marina. *See* La Malinche
Donation of Constantine, 17
Dowry, 328
Dürer, Albrecht, 350
Dutch Protestants, 459
Dynasty, 32

E

Eanes, Gil, 374
East Africa
     city-states in, 142–143
     Portuguese attempts to conquer, 144
     and trade on Indian Ocean, 141–143
Eastern Orthodox church. *See* Byzantine church
East India Company, 468, *468*
East Indies, 465
Education. *See* Literacy and education
Edward the Elder, 260–261
Edward VI, 351
Egypt, 177
     Jews of, 43
Elevation, analyzing, 436
Elizabethan Age, 458–459
Elizabeth I, 458–460, *459*
Emirs, 82
Empire, understanding, 86
Empty Quarter, 52
Encomienda system, 467
Encyclopédie (Denis Diderot), 478–479, 481
England. *See also* Great Britain
     castles in, 263–265, 272
     civil war in, 460–462
     class structure in, 261
     exploration and colonization by, 468–470, 485

feudalism in, 261, 263–270
Jews of, 315
medieval, 260–267
Norman invasion of, 261
religion in, 459
English Bill of Rights, 463, 505
English Civil War, 460–461
Enlightened despot, 480–481
Enlightenment, 477–479
failure of reforms, 481
influences in America, 482
and U.S. Constitution, 500
Epidemics, understanding, 441
Erasmus, Desiderius, 332
Ericson, Leif, 380
Estates General, 482–483
Ethnolinguistics, 136
Europe
geographic knowledge of, 15, 120,
155, 365, 372
growth of trade, 313–314, 345, 365
Jews in, 43, 259, 269, 286, 315, 327,
352
role in transfer of learning, 15, 169,
318–319, 328
Ewe proverbs, 123
Excommunication, 285, 293
Explorers and exploration, 364–370
financing of, 375
and geography, 365
motivations for, 366
and search for new markets, 369–370
Eyck, Jan van, 332, *332*

F

Families
in Africa, 126, 127, 139
nomads, 53, 55
in Reformation Europe, 350
Fang Tazong, 207–208
Faraghani, Ahmad al-, 15, 378
Farming
Aztec, 423
in China, 205–206
and enclosure of land, 491–492
improvements in tools, 491–492
in Inca Empire, 432–433
Mayan, 406, *406*
medieval advances in, 267, *267*
prehistoric, in the Americas, 398–399
revolution in, 490–492
terracing, 433
Fatima, 91
Fatimids, 91, 96
Fax, 7, 416
Fedele, Cassandra, 328
Ferdinand of Aragon, 99, 100, 174, 352,
378, *378*
Feudalism
decline of, 274, 302, 312–313
in Europe, 261, 263–270, 271–274,
296, 302
in Japan, 271–274
and society, 274
Fiefs, 261, 263
Firdausi, 178
Five Pillars of Islam, 63
Florence, 314, 317–318, 325–327, *326*
Florence Cathedral, 322, *322*
Flying shuttle, 492
Forbidden City, *212*

France
exploration and colonization by, 468–470
Jews of, 43, 259, 315
monarchy in, 452–456
Muslim invasion of, 79
peasant life in, 456
religious wars in, 453
Franciscans, 287
Francis I, 331, *332,* 381
Francis of Assisi, St., 287, *287*
Frankincense, 52
Franklin, Benjamin, 482, *482*
Franks, 257–258
Frederick I, 300
Frederick II (the Great), 480, *480,* 481
Frederick the Wise, 345
French and Indian Wars, 470. *See also*
Seven Years' War
French Revolution, 482–485
Fujian, 211
Fujiwara clan, 228
Fulcher of Chartres, 297

G

Gabriel (angel), 58, 59, 62
Galileo, 354–355, 356
Gama, Vasco da, 144, 364, *364,* 375,
382–383
Gambia River, 113
Ganges River, 179
Gao, 120, 122
Gautama, Siddhartha, 194. *See also*
Buddha
GDP, 240
Gedi, 144
Genghis Khan, *165,* 165–166, 209, 210
Genoa, dominance of trade by, 302, 368
Gentileschi, Artemisia, 328
Geography, history of, 10–15, 365, 378
George I, *463*
Germany, 256–257, 347
Jews of, 43, 259, 315
Ghana, 112–117
fall of, 117
religion in, 115–117
as trade center, 113, 115
Ghazan Khan, 168
Ghazis, 171
Ghettos, 327
Glass, history of, 302
Gleaning, 490, *490,* 491
Glorious Revolution, 462–463
GMT. *See* Greenwich mean time
Gold, 112, 113, 114, 117, 146, 147, 370, 380
Good Hope, Cape of, 364, *364–365*
Gothic cathedrals, 288, *288*
Gouges, Olympe de, 485
Government. *See also* individual countries
as a contract, 479
new ideas about, 479
United States, 498
Grand Canal, 196
Grand vizier, 172
Gravity, experiments with, 354–355, 356
Great Domesday Book, The, 263
Great Lakes region (Africa), 137
Great Mosque, 95, *95,* 96, 97, *97*
Great Plague, *310,* 310–312, *312,* 315
Great Rift Valley, 137
Great Schism, 339
Great Wall, 196, *196,* 198–199, *198,* 211

Great Zimbabwe, *145,* 146
Greece, 177
Greek and Roman learning, 34, 89–90,
98, 257, 287, 291, 313, 318, 319,
322, 323, 328, 332, 365, 477
Greenwich mean time, 8
Gregory III, Pope, 293
Gregory VII, Pope, 284–285, 300
Gregory XI, Pope, 339
Griot, 118
Gross Domestic Product, 240
Group decisions, understanding, 275
Guangzhou, 211, 215, *215*
Guide for the Perplexed, The, 99
Guilds, 264, 269, 275, 314
Gunpowder, 208, *208,* 310, 313
Guns, introduction in Europe, 310, 313
Guo Xi, 202
Gupta dynasty, *33,* 35–36
Gutenberg, Johannes, 330

H

Hadith, 61
Hagia Sophia, 42, 43, *45, 174,* 289, *289,*
291, *291*
Haiku, 241
Hajj, 63
Han Dynasty, *33,* 190, 192–195, 225
Harem, in Ottoman Empire, 173
Hargreaves, James, 492
Harold, 261
Harun al Rashid, 88
Hastings, Battle of, 261
Henry (Germany), 284
Henry II (France), 452
Henry III (France), 452
Henry IV (France), 453
Henry IV (Germany, Italy), 285, *285*
Henry of Navarre, 452
Henry the Navigator, *371,* 371–374, 464
Henry VIII (England), 351, 459
Heraclius, 45
Heraldry, 513, *513*
Hideyoshi, Toyotomi, 238
Hierarchy, 261
understanding, 264
Hijrah, 60, 69
Hildebrand, 284. *See also* Gregory VII
Himalayas, 179, *180–181*
Hindus
in Mughal Empire, 181–182
and Muslims, 180, 181, 182
in Southeast Asia, 241
Hira, Cave of, 58, 59
Hiragana, 229, *229*
History, 17–19
Hokkaido, 223
Holy Land, 295–301. *See also* Crusades
Honshu, 223
Hooke, Robert, 355–356
Horns of Hattin, 299–300
Horseshoes, invention of, 11
House of Commons, 460, 461
House of Lords, 460
House of Wisdom, 89
Huang He River, 196
Huguenots, 452–456
Humanism, 319, 331, 332
Humanists, 477
Human sacrifice, 427
Hundred Years' War, 312–313

Huns, 29
  invasion of China, 33, 37
  invasion of India, 33, 36
  invasion of Persia, 33
  invasion of Roman Empire, 29
Hunter-gatherers, 397–398
Hus, John, 341
Hypothesis, and scientific method, 355,
  357

I

Ibn Battuta, 13, 114, 119, 143, 169, 365
Ibn Firnas, Abbas, 99
Ibn Sina, 90
Icons, 292, *293*
Ieyasu, Tokugawa, 238, *238*
Imam, 68
Imperial City, 212
Inca Empire, 429–435
  fall of, 439–440, *440*, 442
  weakening of, 438
Incense trade, 52
Index of Prohibited Books, 352, 355, 478
India
  British colonization of, 185
  contact with other cultures, 35–36
  geographic knowledge in, 15, 365
  geography of, 179–180
  Gupta dynasty, 33, 35–36, 69
  invasion of Mahmud of Ghazna, 178,
    179–180
  Muslim states in, 180
  role in transfer of learning, 36, 178, 310
  trading, 6, 10–15, 214
Indian Ocean, trade network on, 36–37,
  55, 85, 141–142, 145, 211, 214, 241
Indonesia, 241
  trading, 142, 242
Indulgences, selling of, 340, 342–344, *343,*
  351
Indus River, 179
Industrial revolution, 492–493
  decisions about growth, 494–495
Infidels, 296
Innocent III, Pope, 301
Inquisition, 352
International Date Line, 8–9
Internet, 7, 101, 416
Irrigation, 54
Isabella of Castile, 99, 100, 352, 378, *378*
Isidore of Charax, 10
Islam, 60–64. *See also* Muslims, Muslim
    Empire
  caliphs of, 66–67
  Mandinke converts to, 116
  in Ottoman Empire, 173
  spread of, 61, 65–67, 78–84, 115–116, 117,
    120–122, 143, 171, 242
  and women, 64
Isolation, understanding, 239
Istanbul, *174,* 174–175. *See also*
    Constantinople
Italy
  city-states in, 317–318
  Jews of, 43
  trade in, 314–315, 368

J

Jade, *402,* 403, *403*
Jahangir, 182–183
Jahiz, al, 74

James I, 460, 469
James II, 462–463, *463*
Jamestown, 469
Janissary Corps, 173, *173,* 177
Japan
  castles in, 272
  Chinese influence in, 225–226
  class structure in, 240
  court life in, 227–228
  creation legend of, 222–223
  cultural development in, 227–230,
    234–236, 240–241
  early people of, 224–225
  emperor of, 223, 225
  geography of, 223
  isolation of, 223, 239
  literature of, 228–229, 241
  merchant class in, 240
  Mongol invasion of, 167, 232, 234
  provincial life in, 230
  religion in, 225–226, 234–235
  Tokugawa shogunate, 238–240
  unification under Oda Nobunaga, 237,
    238
  warrior government in, 232–234
  warrior monks in, 231, *231*
  writing systems in, 229, *229*
Jefferson, Thomas, 482
Jenne-Jeno (Jenne), 110–111, *111*
Jenny, 492
Jerusalem, 295, *300*
  Crusaders' first conquest of, 297
  conquest by Muslims under Saladin, 300
  treaty regarding, 301
Jesuits (Society of Jesus), 352, 369
Jesus, 290
Jews
  of Arabia, 55, 60
  of Byzantine Empire, 43, 81
  of Constantinople, 174
  effect of crusades on, 302, 315
  of Enlightenment Europe, 481, 485
  intolerance in Prussia, 481
  of medieval Europe, 259, 269, 286, 315
  of Mesopotamia, 43, 81
  of Mongol Empire, 168
  of Mughal India, 182
  of Muslim Empire, 66, 80, 81
  of Ottoman Empire, 174
  of Palestine (Judaea), 43, 81, 297
  persecution of, 43, 81, 174, 269, 286, 315,
    327, 352
  of Persia, 43, 81
  of Portugal, 174, 352
  of Renaissance Europe, 327
  role in transfer of learning, 15, 98, 99
  of Spain, 98, 99, 352
Jihad, 63
Joachim, Georg, 353
Joan of Arc, *312,* 312–313
João II, Dom, 375
John, King (England), 270
John II, King (Portugal), 149, 152, 153,
    154, *154*
Jomon people, 224–225
Joseph II, 480, 481
Judaism
  development of, 81, 99, 259, 327
  ties to Islam, 61–62, 82
Judgments, understanding, 303
Jundishapur, university at, 34

Junks (sailing ships), 206, *206*
Justification by faith, 344, 349
Justinian, 34, 42–45, *43,* 69, 291, *291,* 294
Justinian Code, 43

K

Ka'bah, 57, 60–61
Kabuki theater, 241
Kalahari desert, 137
Kalidasa, 33, 35
Kamakura shogunate, 232, 234
Kami, 225
Kamikaze, 234
Kay, John, 492
Kempe, Margery, 341
Kepler, Johannes, 354
Khans, 165–167
Khoikhoi, 137, 138
Khoisan languages, 136
Khoisan, 137
Khusru Anusharvan, 34
Khwarizmi, al, 89
Khyber Pass, 179
Kikuyu, 136, 139
Kilimanjaro, 138
Kilwa, 143–144
Kinship
  as basis for government, 127
  understanding, 126
Kirina, Battle of, 117, 118
Knights, 169, 261, *271*
  and codes of honor, 273
  of the Crusades, 296, 298, *298,* 313
  and samurai, compared, 271–274
Kongo kingdom, 149–155
Kongo people, 139, 149–150
Korea
  Chinese influence, 225–226
  history of, 225–226
Koryo kingdom, 225
Koumbi, 115, 117
Kritovoulos, 175
Kublai Khan, 167, *209,* 209–210, 232
Kyoto, 227–228
Kyushu, 223

L

Labé, Louise, 328
Ladino language, 99
La Malinche, 439
Lancelot, 273
Land use, world (map), 216–217, 531
Langland, William, 262, 266
Languages
  African, 136–137, 138
  word history, 302
  world (map), 529
Laos, 241
Laozi, 197
Laplace, Pierre, 476
Las Casas, Bartolomé de, 369
Lavoisier, Antoine, 476
Law
  Justinian Code, 43
  in Ottoman Empire, 176
  Roman, 43
Leo III, Pope, 258–259
Leo IX, Pope, 293
Leo X, Pope, 344
Leonardo da Vinci, 319–321, *320–321,* 324,
    324, 331

Li Bo, 202–203
Linear perspective, 322, *323*
Linguistics, 136
Literacy and education, 64, 89, 168, 207–208, 241, 274, 276–277, 291, 327, 328, 330–331, 332, 350, 354, 365
Li Yuan, 203
Location, understanding, 8–9
  decisions about, 216–217
Locke, John, 479, 482
London Company, 469
Lothair, 259–260
Lotus Sutra, 235
Louis the German, 259–260
Louis VI, 284
Louis VII, 299
Louis XIII, 453
Louis XIV, *454,* 454–456
Louis XVI, 482–485
Luoyang, 192
Luther, Martin, 342–347, *343, 344, 345,* 349
  excommunication of, 344
  and printing press, 345, 346

M

Macao, 214
Machiavelli, Niccolò, 318
Magellan, Ferdinand, 380, *380*
Maghreb, 117
Maghribi, Ibn Sa'id al, 76
Magna Carta, 270, 504
Magyars, 259
Mahal, Mumtaz, 184, *184*
Mahmud of Ghazna, 178
Maimonides, Moses, 99
Main ideas, identifying, 94
Malacca, 242, 376
Malaria, 148
Malaysia, 241
Mali Empire, 117–120
Mammoths, 396, *396,* 397
Ma'mun, al, 89
Manchu people, 214
Manco Inca, 440
Mandinke, 116, 117
Mani-Kongo, 150, *151,* 152. *See also* Affonso I
Mansur, Abu Jafar al, 85, 86
Mansur, Abul Kasim, 178
Mantua, 327
Man'yoshu, 226
Manzikert, Battle of, 294
Maps and mapmaking, 14, *372*
  advances in, 365–366
  early, 15
  land-use, 216–217, 531
  latitude and longitude on, 366
  portolans, 365
  relief, 140
  symbols on, 382–383
  T-O maps, 3, 15, 365–366
  topographic, 216–217
  wind and current, 382–383
Map symbols, understanding, 382–383
Marathas, 185
Marguerite of Navarre, 333
Marie Antoinette, 485, *485*
Mary I, 459
Mary II, 462, 463, *463*
Mathematical Principles of Natural Philosophy (Isaac Newton), 356

Mathematics, history of, 15, 36, 90, 366
Matrilineal succession, 117
Matsuo Basho. *See* Basho
Mauritania, 112
Maya, 404–409
Mayors of the Palace, 258
Mazarin, Jules, Cardinal, 454
Mbanza, 150
Mecca, 56–57, *57,* 60, *62*
  Muhammad's arrival in, 60–61
  pilgrimage to, 63
Medici family, 318, *318*
Medici, Catherine de, 452, *452*
Medici, Lorenzo di, *326*
Medicine, history of, 15, 34, 90, 99, 287, 354, 358–359
Medieval Period, 256. *See also* Middle Ages
Medina, 60, 61, 79
Mehmed the Conqueror, 172, 174, 175
Mehmed VI, 177, *177*
Mehrunissa, 183
Mendelssohn, Moses, 485
Mendes Nasi, Doña Gracia, 174
Mercantilism, 467
Meritocracy, 204
Mexico, Valley of, 403, 422,
Michelangelo Buonarroti, 322
Micrographia (Hooke), 355
Microscope, *355*
Middle Ages, 256
  England in, 260–261, 268
  famine in Europe, 311
  farming in, 267, *267*
  peasants in, 266, 312
  and the plague, 310–312
  religion in England in, 268
  rise of central governments in, 312–313
  serfs in, 266
  and social classes, 314
  towns in, 269
  trade and commerce in, 314–315
  warfare methods in, 313, *313*
  women in, 265–266
Milan, 314, 317
Ming Dynasty, 211–214
Missionaries, 152
Moche culture, 412–415
Moctezuma, 16, 424, 437, 438–439, 440
Mombasa, 143
Mona Lisa, 319
Monarchies, 312
  absolute, 454
  constitutional, 463, 485
  and divine right, 454
  growth of, 302, 312, 338–339, 452–456, 458–463
Monasteries, 257, 268, 286–287
Money, history of, 88, 113, 206
Money economy, 206
Mongol Dynasty, 169, 210–211
Mongol Empire, 164–168
Mongols
  clan life of, 162–164
  impact of, 168–169
  leadership among, 164–166
  and religion, 168
  social system of, 163–164
Monks, 283
Monomutapa, 148
Monopoly, 368

Monotheism, 59
Monsoons, 141–142
Montaigne, Michel de, 333
Montesquieu, Charles Louis, Baron, 479, 481, 498
More, Sir Thomas, 332–333
Morelli, Giovanni, 328
Morocco, 100, 122
Mosaics, 43, 44, *44*
Moses, 308, 322
Mosque, 60, *61*
  at Cordoba, 95, *95,* 96, 97, *97*
  Selim Mosque, *172*
Movable type, invention of
  by Gutenberg, 330–331, *331*
  by Pi Sheng, 207
Muawiya, 67, 78–79, 82
Mughal Empire, 180–182
  art of, 186–187
  Hindu rebellion in, 185
Muhammad, 58–61, 65, 69
Murasaki Shikibu, 227, 229
Musa, Mansa, 119–120
Music, 98, 302
Muslim Empire
  under Abbasids, 86–87
  architecture of, 83, *116*
  culture of, 83
  diversity of peoples in, 80–81
  expansion under Umayyad rule, 78–79
  government of, 82
  Umayyad unity in, 83
Muslims, 60. *See also* Islam; Seljuk Turks
  in Arabia, 58–66
  in Europe, 259
  geographic knowledge of, 15, 365, 378
  in Ghana, 115
  and Hindus, 180, 181, 182
  literature of, 74–77, 89
  in North Africa, 67, 79, 83
  and Ottoman Empire, 171
  in Persia, 33, 66–67, 85–91
  political division of, 67–68
  role in transfer of learning, 15, 34, 89–90, 98, 287, 313, 366
  in Spain, 79, 84, 95–100
  Spanish and Portuguese wars against, 368–369
  in Syria, 66, 67, 78–79, 82
  territorial expansion of, 66–67
  tolerance for non-Muslims, 66, 80–82, 181–182
  Umayyad, 81
Mutapa, Mwene, 148, *148*
Mystics, 341

N

Nanjing, 193, 194
Nantes, Edict of, 453, 456
Napoleon Bonaparte, 485
Nara, 226, 227
National Assembly, 483, 485
Natural rights, 479
  and women, 498
Netherlands, 468–469
New Netherland, 469
Newton, Isaac, 356, *356*
Niani, 118, 119
Nicaea, 294, 297
Nichiren, 234–235
Nicomedia, 30

Niger River, 110–111, *111,* 112, 119
Nilo-Saharan languages, 136
Ninety-Five Theses (Luther), 342, *342,* 344
Noh drama, 235–236, *236,* 241
Nok people, 110, 136–137
Nomads, 53, 55
Nonverbal communication, 409, 410–411
Noria, 54
North Africa, Muslim conquest of, 83
North America
  colonization of, 381
  exploration of, 380–381
  first migration to, 396–397
Northwest Passage, search for, 381
Note taking, understanding, 416–417
Novum Organum (Bacon), 355
Nuns, 283, 350
Nzinga, Queen, *153*

O

Oases, 53
Oath of fealty, 261, 263
Octavian, 26. *See also* Augustus
Oda Nobunaga, 237, 238
Odoacer, 256
Ogodei, 166
Olmec civilization, 400–403
On the Revolution of the Celestial Spheres
  (Copernicus), 353
Oral tradition, 148, 431
Orientus, 256
Osman, 171
Ottoman Empire, 171–177

P

Pacal, King, 409
Pachacuti, 530
Palio, 325, 325
Paper, development of, 76, 89, 99
Paper money, development of, 206, *206*
Paracelsus, 333
Parchment, 76
Paré, Ambroise, 333
Parliament, 458, 460–461
Parthian Stations (Isidore of Charax), 10
Pasha, Judar, 122
Patricians, 327
Patrilineal succession, 117
Patterns, identifying, 348
Paul III, Pope, 351
Peace of Augsburg, 347
Peasants
  in agricultural revolution, 492
  in France, 456
  in medieval England, 262, 266, 269
  in Middle Ages, 266, 312
Peasants' War, 345, 347
  in Renaissance Italy, 326–327
Pepin, 258
Pericles, 319
Persia, 32, *33,* 34, 45, 69, 78
  geographic knowledge of, 15, 366
  Muslim era, 33,
  role in transfer of learning, 34
  Sassanid era, 32–35
  trading in, 142, 145, 242
Peter, St., 290
Petition of Right, 460–461
Petra, *55,* 55–56
Petrarch, Francesco, 322
Philip II, 300, 459

Philip IV, 338
Philippines, 241
Philosophes, 477, 498
Piers the Plowman (Langland), 262, 266
Pilgrims
  to Mecca, 57, 63, 119–120
  travel by, 13
  to Jerusalem, 295, 300, 301
Pi Sheng, 207
Pizarro, Francisco, 439–440, *440*
Plagues, 310. *See also* Great Plague
  in the Americas, 380, 439, 440, 441, 466,
    467
Plateau, 146
Poetry, 89, 98, 176, 203, 228, 241, 302
  texts, 18, 35, 89, 144, 176, 200–201, 202,
    226, 228, 241, 262, 266, 287, 333, 428,
    442
Polo, Marco, 169, 209, 210, 365, *367*
Polynesia
  geographic knowledge of, 15, 365
Popes, 338
Population, world (map), 531
Portolans, 365
Portugal
  attempted conquest of East Africa, 144
  colonies of, 375–376
  contact with China, 214
  contact with Japan, 239
  explorations of, 374–375
  geographic knowledge of, 155
  Jews of, 174, 352
  rivalry with Spain, 379–380
  and search for sea route to the East, 370
  slave trade by, 150–153, 464
  trade with Kongo, 154–155
  trade with West Africa, 374
  undermining of Monomutapa, 148
Portuguese Empire, growth of, 465–466
Power loom, *493*
Predestination, 350
Prehistory, 17
Prester John, 368, 372
Primary Sources, 10, 13, 16, 17, 18, 19, 26,
    35, 42, 58, 65, 74–77, 78, 82, 83, 85, 89,
    90, 95, 115, 118, 141, 144, 153, 154,
    172, 175, 176, 178, 192, 195, 200–210,
    202, 203, 206, 208, 209, 226, 227, 228,
    229, 231, 232, 237, 241, 256, 270, 273,
    287, 295, 297, 301, 311, 313, 316, 328,
    331, 333, 338, 341, 342, 345, 358, 364,
    369, 371, 374, 379, 400, 404, 428, 435,
    437, 442, 453, 454, 466, 478, 479, 480,
    493, 497
Prime meridian, 8
Prime minister, 453
Prince, The (Machiavelli), 318
Printing
  Chinese, 206–207
  European, 345, *345,* 346, *346*
Progress, understanding, 499
Protectorate, 461
Protestantism and Protestants, 344–347
  Dutch, 459
  and the Reformation, 344
  spread of, 345–347, 349–351
Proto-Bantu language, 136–138
Proverbs, interpreting, 123
Prussia, 480–481
Ptolemy, 15, 353, 354, 365, 366
Pure Land Buddhism, 234

Puritans, and English Civil War, 461

Q

Qanat, 54
Qing Dynasty, 214–215
Qin Ling Mountains, 193
Quadrant, 15
Quechua language, 431, 442
Quetzalcoatl, 438
Quipu, 431
Qur'an, 58, 61–62, 65, 69, 83, *83,* 95
Quraysh tribe, 56, 57, 59, 61

R

Racism, 467
Radar, 52
Ramadan, and fasting, 63
Rashi, 259
Readers' Guide to Periodical Literature,
  101
Reconquest, 99–100
Reference sources, understanding, 101
Reformation, 344–347
  Calvin and, 349–350
  Catholic church response to, 351–352
  and the Scientific Revolution, 356
  and social changes, 350
Reign of Terror, 485
Relationships, understanding, 471
Relief maps, understanding, 140
Religion
  in Africa, 125
  and art, 288, *288*
  Aztec, 427–428
  Buddhism, 194–195, 197, 225–226
  in Byzantine Empire, 292–293
  Calvinism, 349–350
  in China, 194–195, 197
  Confucianism, 194, 197
  Daoism, 197
  in England, 459
  Hindus, 179–180
  Huguenots, 452–456
  idols and, 55
  in Inca Empire, 431
  indigenous, 125, 426
  Islam, 57, 58–64
  in Japan, 225
  Judaism, 43, 99, 259, 266
  of Mayan civilization, 407
  and Mecca, 57
  in medieval England, 268
  and Mongols, 168
  of Olmec civilization, 402
  in Ottoman Empire, 173
  and predestination, 350
  Protestantism, 344–347, 349–351
  and Renaissance, 318–319, 332
  Roman Catholicism, 283–284, 285–288,
    338–341
  in Roman Empire, 290–291
  Shinto, 225, 226
  in West Africa, 125–127
  world (map), 529
Religious persecution, 43, 99, 182, 239,
    269, 286, 297, 315, 327, 341, 352, 369,
    452, 453, 456, 459, 460, 481
Renaissance, 477
  architecture of, 322, *322*
  and the arts, 319–323, *323,* 332–333
  and biblical scholarship, 332

birthplace of, 317–318
and city life, 325–326
and families, 327–328
literature of, 322, 332–333
and manners, 316
in Northern Europe, 329–333
and religion, 318–319, 332
role of men, 328
role of women, 328
scholarship during, 319
and social classes, 326–327
spread of, 330–332
and wealth, 323
and world view, 318–319
Reports, understanding, 496
Restoration, 462
Rhumb lines, 14
Richard (lion heart), 300–301
Richelieu, Armand Jean du Plessis,
      Cardinal, 453–454, *454*
Rift Valley, 137
Rights
   and responsibilities, 126
   and religion
         in Aztec Empire, 426
         in Byzantine Empire, 43
         in Enlightenment Europe, 478, 481,
            485
         in medieval Europe, 259, 269, 286,
            315
         in Mongol Empire, 168
         in Mughal India, 181–182
         in Muslim Empire, 66, 78, 80, 99
         in Portugal, 174
         in Reformation Europe, 352,
            452–453, 456, 459, 460
         in Renaissance Europe, 327
         in Spanish Americas, 440
   and slavery, 127, 264, 380, 427, 500
   and women, 64, 83, 255, 269, 287, 291,
      314, 315, 328, 350, 351, 485
Robert the Monk of Rheims, 295
Roman Catholic church
   and Charlemagne, 258
   conflict with monarchs, 284–285,
      338–340
   corruption within, 339–340, 342
   Counter Reformation of, 351–352
   daily life of believers, 285–286
   and Galileo, 355
   hierarchy of, 283
   power in Europe, 283–284
   reformers and, 340–341
   religious orders in, 286–287
   schism with Eastern Orthodox, 293
   schism within, 339
   and spiritual movements, 341
Roman Empire
   barbarian invasions, 28–29, 33
   Christianity in, 290
   communication in, 6–7
   contact with Persia, 32, 34
   expansion of, 27
   fall of, 26, 31, 33, 69, 290
   internal problems in, 29–30
   prosperity of, 26–28
   provinces of, 27–28
   and silk trade with China, 194
   transitional years, 30–31
   travel in, 5–6
   world view of, 4

Roman learning. *See* Greek and Roman
      learning
Romulus, Augustulus, 256
Rousseau, Jean–Jacques, 479, *479, 482*
Russia, 177

S

Sahara, 108, *108,* 112, 113
   climates of, 108–110
Sahel, 109, 112, 113, 125
St. Bartholomew's Day Massacre, 452
Saladin, *299,* 299–301
Salt, 113, *113, 114*
Samarkand, 168
Samurai, 232–233, *233, 271*
   and codes of honor, 273
   and knight, compared, 271–274
   and Zen, 235
San, 137, 138
Sanhaja, 117
San Salvador, 379
São Tomé, 152–153, 375, 376
Sassanid dynasty, 32, 34
Savanna, 109–110
Scandinavia, 259
Scapegoat, 315
Schoeni, 10
Schools
   and culture, 276–277
   Muslim, 287
   universities, 287
Science
   decisions about discoveries, 358–359
   Muslim contributions to, 90
Scientific method, 355–356
Scientific Revolution, 354–356
Secondary sources, 17
Selim, 175
Selim Mosque, *172,* 176
Seljuk, 91
Seljuk Turks, 91, 294, *294,* 297
Senegal River, 112, 113
Sephardic culture, 99
Sequence, understanding, 69
Serfs, 264, 266, 269, 425, 481
Seven Years' War, 470, 482
Sextant, 363
Shah Jahan, 183, 184, *184*
Shahrukh, 168
Shakespeare, William, 333, *333,* 458–459
Shihuangdi, 198–199
Shiites, 67–68
Shikoku, 223
Shinto, 225, 226
Shogun, 232, 240
Shona people, 143, 145–147
Shotoku, Prince, 226
Shogun, 232, 240
Silk Road, 36–37, 168–169, *169,* 195, 198,
      211, 214
Silk trade, 33, 36, 69, 214, 241–242, 302, 368
Silla kingdom, 69, 225
Silver, 380
Sinan, 176
Singapore, 241
Sipan, Lords of, 415
Slavery
   in Africa, 127, 464–466, 467
   in Americas, 380, 425, 466, 467
   in Byzantine Empire, 43
   in medieval Europe, 264
   in Ottoman Empire, 173

by Portuguese, 150, 152–153, 376, 464
   by Spanish, 467, *467*
Slave trade, 127, 168, 264, 374, 376, 464,
      465, 467
Sleeping sickness, 137
Smith, Adam, 492, 493
Sobieski, John, 177
Social Contract, The (Rousseau), 479
Sofala, 143
Soga clan, 225–226
Song Dynasty, 203–208
   Mongol attacks on, 210
Songhai empire, 107, 120–122
Soninke, 112, 113
Southeast Asia. *See also specific countries
      and regions*
   trade, 214
   history of, 241
   geographic knowledge of, 365
Spain
   Jews in, 43, 99, 315, 352
   Muslims in, 79, 84, 95–100, 368
   rivalry with Portugal, 379–380
   slave trade by, 467, *467*
   Umayyad rule of, 84, 95–100
Spanish Empire, expansion of, 380,
      466–467
Spice trade, 367, 369, 376. *See also* Silk
      Trade
Spinning jenny, 492
Spirit of the Laws (Montesquieu), 479
Sports and games, origins of, 93
Statue of Liberty, *499*
Steles, 407
Stephens, John Lloyd, 404
Steppes, 162
Stereotypes, identifying, 471
Sternpost rudder, 12, *12*
Stirrups, invention of, 11
Strozzi, Palla, 365
Sugar, 152, 376, 381
Suger, Abbot, 283–284, 288
Sui Dynasty, 190, 195–197, 203–204
Suleiman, 175–177, *176*
Sultan, 172
Sultanate of Delhi, 180
Sumanguru, 117, 118
Sundiata, 118
Sunna, 61, 63, 68
Sunni Ali, 121
Sunnis, 68
Superstition, 315
Swahili people, 142, 143

T

Tacitus, 29
Tactics, 165, 169, 302
Taghaza, 119, 122
Taika Reforms, 226
Taizu, 211–212
Taj Mahal, 183, 184, *184*
Tale of Genji, The (Murasaki Shikibu), 229
Talmud, 81
Tamerlane. *See* Timur the Lame
Tang Dynasty, 69, 203–208
Taureg, 117
Taxes
   in Muslim Empire, 81, 82, 84
   in Japan, 230
   in Mughal Empire, 181–182, 185
Tea ceremony, Japanese, 235, *235,* 241

Technology
  military, 78, 166, 169, 208, 238, 271–273,
      302, 313, 321, 437, 440
  water-related, 54
Telescope, Galileo's use of, 355
Temple of the Sun, 403, 427
Temujin, 164–165. *See also* Genghis Khan
Tenochtitlan, 16, 18, 19, 107, 422, 427
Teotihuacan, 69, 403
Terrace farming, 433
Texcoco, Lake, 422
Text organization, understanding, 348
Thailand, 241
Theodora, 42, *43*
Theodosius I, 31, 33, 290
Third Estate, 483
Thirty Years' War, 454
Timbuktu, 121, *122*
Timelines, parallel, 33, 69
Time zones, 8–9
Timur the Lame, 168, *168*
Tithing, 285
Titicaca, Lake, 413, 415
Tiwanakan culture, 412–415
Tokugawa shogunate, 238–239
Toledo, 100
Toltec, 69, 403
T-O maps, 15, 365–366
Topography, understanding, 436
Tordesillas, Treaty of, 379–380
Tours, Battle of, 79
Towns, growth in medieval Europe, 269
Trade
  in Baghdad, 87
  Byzantine Empire and, 290–291
  caravan routes and, 53, 55
  centers in West Africa, 113
  in China, 206
  Ghana and, 113, 115
  gold and salt, 114, *114*
  Italian preeminence in, 368
  in Mayan civilization, 406
  in Mecca, 56
  in medieval Europe, 314–315
  in Mongol Dynasty, 211
  in Olmec civilization, 403
  in Qing Dynasty, 215
  in spices, 366–368, *367*
  and spread of Renaissance, 330
Trade Routes
  Arabian, 55, 57
  Atlantic, 381, 465, 469
  Eurasian, 5, 6, 10, 11, 35, 36–37, 55, 85,
      87, 168–169, 170, 209, 211, 259, 290,
      301, 302, 303, 313, 314, 330, 366, 368,
      376, 468
  Euro-African, 5, 27–28, 55, 154–155, 313,
      314, 330, 464–466
  Euro-Indian, 10, 35, 55, 177, 178, 182,
      185, 313, 314
  Indian Ocean, 36–37, 55, 85, 142, 145,
      211, 214, 241
  trans–Saharan, 112, 113, 115, 117, 120
Traini, Francesco, 310
Travel
  by explorers, 12–13
  and mapmaking, 13
  by merchants, 11
  modern, 5–6
  by pilgrims, 13
  in Roman Empire, 5–6

by soldiers, 11–12
and world view, 10
Trent, Council of, 351
Triangle Trade, 467
Tribes, Mongol, 163
Tsetse fly, 137, *138*
Tull, Jethro, 491
Turkestan, 294
Turkey, 177
  Jews of, 43
Turkish Empire. *See* Ottoman Empire
Tuxtla Mountains, 400–401
Two Treatises on Government (Locke),
      479

U
Ubar, discovery of, 52–53
Umar, 66, 67
Umayyad Empire, 78–79, 83, 84
Unam Sanctam (Boniface VIII), 338
Universe, theories about, *353,* 353–354,
      356
Universities, 98, 287, 365
Urban II, Pope, 294, 295, *295,* 296
Urban IV, Pope, 339
Uthman, 66, 67
Utopia (More), 333

V
Valla, Lorenzo, 17
Values, identifying, 443
Vegetation, world (map), 530
Venice, 301, 317, 327
  monopoly on trade with the East, 302,
      368
Verrazano, Giovanni da, 381
Versailles, 454, 455, *455*
Vertical economy, 433
Vertical profile, 140
Vesalius, Andreas, 354, *354,* 358
Vespucci, Amerigo, 379
Victoria, Lake, 138
Vienna, siege of, 177
Vietnam, 241
Vikings, 259–260
Vindhya Mountains, 179
Vindication of the Rights of Women, A
      (Wollstonecraft), 498
Visigoths, 33, 69, 99
  Muslim defeat of, 79
Voltaire, *477,* 477–478, 480, *480, 482*

W
Waldseemüller, Martin, 379
Wangara, 113, 119
Wang Wei, 203
War, and cultural contact, 32, 34
Warrior monks, 231, *231*
Warwick, Philip, 458
Washington, George, 497, *497*
Water wheel, 54, 77
Wen, Emperor, 195–197, *197*
West Africa, 110–111
  farming in, 124–125
  government in, 127
  ironmaking in, 110
  religion in, 125, 127
  trade with Portugal, 374
  village society in, 124–127
West Indies, 467
William of Orange, 463, *463*

William the Conqueror, 261, 262, 263, *272*
Wollstonecraft, Mary, 485, 498
Women
  in Aztec Empire, 427
  in Byzantine Empire, 291
  in the Enlightenment, 478
  in feudal Japan, 227, 232
  in leadership roles, 164, 173, 183, 194,
      229, 266, 283, 312–313, 314, 328, 341,
      350, 485
  in medieval Christian church, 283
  in medieval Europe, 265–266, 269, 287,
      302
  in Muslim Empire, 64, 83
  and natural rights, 498
  in post-Han China, 192, 194
  in Reformation Europe, 350
  in Renaissance Europe, 314, 315, 328
  in Tiwanakan civilization, 414
World
  countries of 518–519
  history of, 515–517
  languages of, 529
World view, 4
Wright, Joseph, 476
Writing systems. *See also* Calligraphy
  Arab, 115–116
  Aztec, 426–427
  Mayan, 407, 409, *409*
Wycliffe, John, 340–341

X
Xian Di, 192–193
Xuanzang, 13, 69

Y
Yamato plain, 225, 226
Yang Jian, 195. *See also* Wen, Emperor
Yang Wangli, 200
Yayoi people, 225
Yellow River, 196
Yiddish language, 259
Yoritomo, 232
Yoruba, 126
Yuan Dynasty, 169, 210–211
Yurts, 163, *163*

Z
Zacharias, Pope, 258
Zen Buddhism, 234–235
Zheng He, 212, 213, *213*
Zimbabwe Plateau, 146
Zimbabwe state, 143, 145–148
  breakup of, 148
  gold mines of, 147
Zwingli, Ulrich, 349

Text *(continued from page iv)*

ii Excerpt from December 30, 1941, speech by Winston Churchill to the Canadian Senate and the House of Commons. Copyright by The Estate of Sir Winston Churchill. Reprinted by permission of Curtis Brown Ltd. on behalf of The Estate of Sir Winston Churchill. **iv** The material in the Minipedia is reprinted from *The World Book Encyclopedia* with the expressed permission of the publisher. Copyright ©1998 by World Book, Inc. **10** From *Parthian Stations of Isidore of Charax* translated by Wilfred H. Schoff, Philadelphia: Commercial Museum, 1914. **13** From *Journals of Hsuan-Tsang*, in *Chinese Accounts of India* by Samuel Beal, Calcutta, India: S. Gupta, 1958. **13** From *The Adventures of Ibn Battuta* by Ross Dunn, Berkeley: University of California Press, 1986. **19** Aztec poem translated by Miguel Leon-Portilla from *Broken Spears: The Aztec Account of the Conquest of Mexico,* Boston: Beacon Press, 1962. **19** From *The Conquest of New Spain* by Bernal Díaz, translated by J. M. Cohen, Baltimore, Maryland: Penguin Books, 1963. **26** From letter by Cyprian, Bishop of Carthage, in *Barbarian Europe* by Gerald Simons, New York: Time-Life Books, 1968. **38** Excerpt from "The King's Adviser" from *Kalilah and Dimnah* translated and adapted by Hassan Tehranchian. Copyright ©1985 by Hassan Tehranchian. Reprinted by permission of the author. **74–75** "The Cadi and the Fly" by Al-Jahiz, translated by Charles Pellat from *The Life and Works of Al-Jahiz.* Copyright ©1969 by the University of California Press. Reprinted by permission of International Thomson Publishing Services Ltd. **75–76** "The Disadvantages of Parchment" by Al-Jahiz, translated by Charles Pellat from *The Life and Works of Al-Jahiz.* Copyright ©1969 by the University of California Press. Reprinted by permission of International Thomson Publishing Services Ltd. **76–77** "Good Deeds at Random," "The Spinning Waterwheel" and "The Fountain" translated by James A. Bellamy and Patricia Owen Steiner from *Ibn Sa'id Al-Maghribi: Banners of the Champions, An Anthology of Medieval Arabic Poetry from Andalusia and Beyond.* Copyright ©1989 by James A. Bellamy and Patricia Owen Steiner. Reprinted by permission of Hispanic Seminary of Medieval Studies. **84** From *A Source Book in Geography,* edited by George Kish, Cambridge, Massachusetts: Harvard University Press, 1978. **89** "You Departed From My Sight" from *Lyrics from Arabia* edited and translated by Ghazi A. Algosaibi. Copyright ©1983 by Ghazi A. Algosaibi. Reprinted by permission of Three Continents Press. **90** From "Text 3: The Autobiography" in *Avicenna and the Aristotelian Tradition,* Leiden, The Netherlands: E.J. Brill, 1988. **101** From *Readers' Guide to Periodical Literature,* August 1997, Vol. 97, #6, pp. 408 and 526. Copyright ©1997 by the H.W. Wilson Company. Reprinted by permission of the publisher. **115** From *Book of the Roads and Kingdoms,* in *The Story of Africa* by Basil Davidson, London: Mitchell Beazley, 1984. **118** From a tale recorded by D.T. Niane of Mali, in *History of African Civilization* by E. Jefferson Murphy, New York: Thomas Y. Crowell Co., 1972. **125** From *Things Fall Apart* by Chinua Achebe, New York: Ballantine Books, 1959. **128** "The Cow-Tail Switch" from *The Cow-Tail Switch and Other West African Stories* by Harold Courlander and George Herzog. Copyright 1947, ©1975 by Harold Courlander. Reprinted by permission of Henry Holt and Company, Inc. **141** Excerpt from "The Periplus of the Erythraean Sea" from *The East African Coast* by G.S.P. Freeman-Grenville. Copyright ©1962 by Oxford University Press. Reprinted by permission of the author. **144** From a chronicler's observation of the destruction of Mombasa, in *The Story of Africa* by Basil Davidson, London: Mitchell Beazley, 1984. **144** "He Who Wants to String Pearls" from *Four Centuries of Swahili Verse* edited by Jan Knappert. Copyright ©1979 by Jan Knappert. Reprinted by permission of Heinemann Educational Books Ltd. **148** From annals by Joãs de Barros, in I*ntroduction to African Civilizations* by John G. Jackson, New York: University Books, 1970. **153** From letter by Affonso of Congo to King John of Portugal, in *The African Past* by Basil Davidson, Boston: Little, Brown and Co., 1964. **154** From letter by Affonso of Congo to King John of Portugal, in *The Kingdom of Kongo* by Anne Hilton, Oxford: Clarendon Press, 1985. **162** From a history of Ibn al-Athir, in *A Literary History of Persia, Vol. 2* by Edward G. Browne, Cambridge University Press, 1902. **170** From *Histoire des Mongols* by Rashid ad-Din, in *The Empire of the Steppes* by Rene Grousset, translated by Naomi Walford, New Brunswick, New Jersey: Rutgers University Press, 1970. **172** From Mehmed quotation regarding legalization of fratricide (1460), in *A History of the World* by Stanley Chodorow, New York: Harcourt Brace Jovanovich, 1986. **175** From historical annals (1453) by Kritovoulos, in *The Global Experience,* edited by Philip F. Riley, Englewood Cliffs, New Jersey: Prentice-Hall, 1987. **176** From 1538 inscription, in *The World* by Geoffrey Parker, New York: Harper & Row. **176** "Elegy of Suleiman" by Baki from *Istanbul and the Civilization of the Empire* by Bernard Lewis. Copyright ©1963 by the University of Oklahoma Press. Reprinted by permission of the University of Oklahoma Press. **178** From Chronicler of Mahmud, in *A Concise History of India* by Francis Watson, New York: Charles Scribner's Sons, 1975. **178** From *The Book of Kings* by Firdawsi, in *A History of the World* by Stanley Chodorow, New York: Harcourt Brace Jovanovich, 1986. **192** Quote by Ge Hong from *Sex in History,* revised and updated by Reay Tannahill, Chelsea, Michigan: Scarborough House, 1980, 1992. **195** "On Compulsive Urges" and "Twin Verses" from *The Dhammapada* translated by Eknath Easwaran. Copyright ©1986 by the Blue Mountain Center of Meditation. Reprinted by permission of Nilgiri Press, Petaluma, CA. **198** From *The Great Wall of China* by Robert Silverberg, Philadelphia: Chilton Books, 1965. **200** "Written on a Cold Evening," "In the Gorge: We Encounter Wind," "Evening Lake Scenes," "Rain and Cold" and "Night Rain at Kuang-k" by Yang Wan-Li, translated by Jonathan Chaves from *Heaven My Blanket, Earth My Pillow.* Copyright ©1976 by John Weatherhill. Reprinted by permission of Charles Tuttle, Tokyo. **202** "Quiet Night Thoughts" from *China's Imperial Past* by Charles O. Hucker. Copyright ©1975 by the Board of Trustees of the Leland Stanford Junior University. Reprinted with the permission of the publishers, Stanford University Press. **203** From *Introduction to Painting* by Wang Wei, in *Sources of Chinese Tradition* by Wm. Theodore de Bary, New York: Columbia University Press, 1960. **206** From *Continuation of the Comprehensive Mirror for Aiding Government,* in *The Pattern of the Chinese Past* by Mark Elvin, London: Eyre Methuen, 1973. **208** From a Chinese sailor's report (1119), in *The History of Invention* by Trevor I. Williams, New York: Facts on File, 1987. **208** From *The Pattern of the Chinese Past* by Mark Elvin, London: Eyre Methuen, 1973. **208** From the *Tearful Records of the Battle of Qizhou* (1221) in *The History of Invention* by Trevor I. Williams, New York: Facts on File, 1987. **209** "Kubilai Khan" from *The Travels of Marco Polo* translated by Ronald

Latham. Copyright ©1958 by Ronald Latham. Reprinted by permission of Penguin Books Ltd. **226** "Here I Lie on Straw" from *Anthology of Japanese Literature* edited by Donald Keene. Copyright ©1955 by Grove Press. Reprinted by permission of Grove Weidenfeld. **228** "This Perfectly Still" from *Anthology of Japanese Literature* edited by Donald Keene. Copyright ©1955 by Grove Press. Reprinted by permission of Grove Weidenfeld. **227, 229** From *The Diary of Murasaki Shikibu,* in *Anthology of Japanese Literature,* edited by Donald Keene, New York: Grove Press, 1955. **241** "Old Pond" from *Introduction to Haiku* by Harold G. Henderson. Copyright ©1958 by Harold G. Henderson. Used by permission of Doubleday, a division of Bantam, Doubleday, Dell Publishing Group, Inc. **250** "The Story of Roland" from *Charlemagne and His Knights* by Katharine Pyle. Copyright ©1932 by J.B. Lippincott Company. Reprinted by permission of HarperCollins Children's Books. **287** "The Canticle of Brother Sun" from *Saint Francis of Assisi* by Lawrence Cunningham, San Francisco: HarperCollins, 1981. **297** From *Memoirs* by Anna Comnena, in *The Crusades,* edited by Régine Pernoud, New York: G.P. Putnam's Sons, 1962. **311** Quotation from Sienese chronicler Agnolo di Tura Del Grasso, in *The Oxford Illustrated History of Medieval Europe,* edited by George Holmes, New York: Oxford University Press, 1988. **328** Quote by Louise Labé from *Not in God's Image* edited by Julia O'Faolain and Lauro Martines, New York: Harper & Row, 1973. **341** "The Book of Margery Kempe" from *The Medieval Mystics of England* edited by Eric Colledge. Copyright ©1961 by Charles Scribner's Sons, renewed 1989. Reprinted with the permission of Scribner, a division of Simon & Schuster. **369** From *Bartolomé de Las Casas,* translated and edited by George Sanderlin, New York: Knopf, 1971. **384** "The Audience" from *Columbus Sails* by C. Walter Hodges. Copyright 1939 by Coward-McCann, Inc., copyright renewed ©1967 by C. Walter Hodges. Reprinted by permission of Coward-McCann, Inc., a division of Penguin Putnam Inc. **422** From *The Ancient American Civilizations* by Friedrich Katz, translated by K.M. Lois Simpson, New York: Praeger, 1969. **428** From *Pre-Columbian Literatures of Mexico* by Miguel Leon-Portilla. Copyright ©1969 by the University of Oklahoma Press. Reprinted by permission of the University of Oklahoma Press. **437** From *Pre-Columbian Literatures of Mexico* by Miguel Leon-Portilla, Norman, Oklahoma: University of Oklahoma Press, 1969. **442** Excerpt from *Everyday Life of the Aztecs* by Warwick Bray. Copyright ©1968 by Warwick Bray. Reprinted by permission of B.T. Batsford Ltd. **444** "The Legend of the Lake" from *Warriors, Gods and Spirits from Central & Southern American Mythology* by Douglas Gifford. Copyright ©1983 by Eurobook Limited. Reprinted by permission of Eurobook Limited. **486** Excerpt from "To the Assembly for Protection" from *The Journal of Madame Royale* by Elizabeth Powers. Copyright ©1976 by Elizabeth Powers. Reprinted by permission of Walker and Company. **494** From V*ictorian People and Ideas* by Richard D. Altick, New York: Norton, Publisher, 1973. **543** Pronunciation key copyright ©1985 by Houghton Mifflin Company. Adapted and reprinted by permission from *The American Heritage Dictionary,* Second College Edition.

Illustrations

Literature border design by **Peggy Skycraft**. **Ligature** 22, 33, 132, 156, 163, 188, 235, 267 (tr), 348, 357, 360, 390, 418, 472, 492, 501. **Precision Graphics** 12, 30, 68, 70, 84, 153, 205, 206-7, 229, 238-39, 244, 265, 304, 350, 379, 399, 441, 462-63, 465, 498. **Brian Battles** 151, 346. **John T. Burgoyne** 14, 298. **Susan David** 12, 396. **Ebet Dudley** 406, 423. **Simon Galkin** 261, 265. **Dale Glasgow** 163. **Henry Iken** 410. **Phil Jones** 184, **Guy Kingsbery** 6. **Al Lorenz** 455. **Matthew Pippin** 262. **Frederick Porter** 91. **Joseph Scrofani** 331, 373. **Scott Snow** 61,111. **Gary Torissi** 534-35. **Jean & Mou-Sien Tsen** 232. **Richard Waldrep** 233. **Brent Watkinson** 484. **Oliver Yourke** 282-83. **Other: 129** From *The Cow-Tail Switch and Other West African Stories.* Copyright © 1947, 1975 by Harold Courlander. Illustration by Madye Lee Chastian. Reprinted by permission of Henry Holt and Company, Inc. **407** By Michael Goodman, from :Maya Writing" by David Stuart and Stephen D. Houston. Copyright © August 1989 by *Scientific American,* Inc. All rights reserved. **408** From *Atlas of Ancient Americas.* Copyright © Equinox, Oxford (t, r). **409** From *Atlas of Ancient Americas.* Copyright © Equinox, Oxford. (t, r).

Maps

© GeoSystems Global Corporation G15 (tl), 518–533. **GeoSystems Global Corporation** G1, G2, G5, G11, G14. **Mapping Specialists** G3, G8 G9, G12, 5, 8, 9 (b), 13, 27, 36–37, 53, 67, 80–81, 85, 97, 109, 121, 137, 140, 142, 146, 150, 167, 171, 179, 183, 193, 204, 216, 217, 219, 224, 230, 257, 260, 290, 296, 299, 311, 317, 330, 347, 352, 366, 374, 378, 382–893, 397, 398, 401, 405, 412 (b, r), 423, 430, 436, 465, 470, 481. **Precision Graphics** G 6, G 7, 9 (t). **XNR Productions** 87. **Edward Parker** G 10. **Gary Torissi** G15 (r). **Other: 10** Based on Parthian Stations by Isidore of Charax, commentary by Wilfred H. Schoff, Philadelphia Commercial Museum, 1914.

Photographs

AR: Art Resource, New York; **BM:** British Museum; **LPW:** Laurie Platt Winfrey, Inc.; **MH:** Michael Holford; **NB:** Newsweek Books; **RHPL:** Robert Harding Picture Library, London; **RJB:** Ralph J. Brunke; **TIB:** The Image Bank

Front Cover: Peter Bosey. **Back Cover:** Bibliotheque Nationale, Paris. **ii:** The Water Margin, Chen Hongshou (t); LPW (b). **iii:** AR (l); SCALA / AR (r). **v:** The Water Margin, Chen Hongshou. **vi:** Cameramann International, Ltd. (b). **vii:** BM, MH (t); Private Collection / NB (b). **viii:** © Justin Kerr (bl); Accademia, Florence, SCALA / AR (br). **ix:** Zaire, Western Kasai Province, Mweka Zone, Kuba Peoples, Mukenga mask, Laura T. Magnuson Fund Income, X-Hautelet Collection 1982.1504...Photo by Robert Hashimoto, © 1989 The Art Institute of Chicago, All Rights Reserved(t); Ontario Science Museum (b). **x:** Musee de l'Institute d'Afrique Noire, Giraudon / AR (t); **G1:** BP/NRSC/Science Photo Library / Photo Researchers. **xvii–1:** SCALA / AR. **2:** © Michael O'Neil, The New York Public Library, Rare Books Division. **3** Mark Gibson/Corbis (t); Ancient Art & Architecture Collection (b). **4:** RJB. **6:** © Dave Bartruff / FPG International. **7:** © PHOTRI, MGA (t); © Ferdinando Scianna / Magnum Photos (b); © NASA / Westlight (r). **11:** Yann Arthus-Bertrand/Corbis. **13:** Tokyo National Museum, Wan-go H.C. Weng. **15:** The Dean and

Chapter of Hereford Cathedral. **16:** BM / NB. **17:** RJB (tr, br); © Comstock, Inc. (cr); © Heinz Plenge / RHPL (bl). **18** Bodleian Library MS. Arch. Seld.A.1 Fol.47 Recto. **19** The Granger Collection. **20:** © Arthur Tress / Photo Researchers, Inc. **20–21:** RJB. **21:** Center of American Archaeology (t); Museum of the American Indian (r). **24:** AR (tl); © Ronald Sheridan / AR (cl); SuperStock (bl); SCALA / AR (r). **25:** Louvre / NB (t); SCALA / AR (b). **26:** AR. **27:** AR. **28:** © George Gersten. **29:** Landesmuseum, Trier, Germany (t); Rheinisches Landesmuseum, Bonn (c). **31:** © Werner Forman Archive (b). **31:** Bibliotheque Nationale, Paris. **32:** The Metropolitan Museum of Art. **33:** SEF, Turin / AR (t); AR (c); Isabella Stewart Gardner Museum, Boston / AR (b). **34:** Bibliotheque Nationale, Giraudon / AR. **36:** Royal Ontario Museum, Toronto / Wan-go H. C. Weng (l, r). **37:** Royal Ontario Museum, Toronto / Wan-go H. C. Weng. **42:** Byzantium, Time-Life Books, © Time Inc. **43:** SCALA / AR (tl); AR (tr); Dumbarton Oaks, Washington, D.C. (br). **44:** SCALA / AR (t); RJB (tr, cr, bl, br); J. Claire Deane, J. Paul Getty Museum (cl, bc). **45:** © Werner Dieterich / TIB (t); Bibliotheque Nationale, Paris (b). **48–49:** © Roger Wood. **50:** RJB (t); Trip/Trip Photo Library (r). **51:** The Metropolitan Museum of Art (l); © Steve Northrup/Black Star/PNI (tr); Ancient Art & Architecture Collection (br). **52:** © Wolfgang Kaehler. **54:** Michael Nicholson/Corbis (t); Peter Fraenkel (b). **55:** RHPL. **56:** © John Donat (t); RJB (b). **57:** AR. **58:** © Trip/Trip Photo Library. **59:** © Ilene Perlman / Stock Boston. **60:** The Metropolitan Museum of Art / NB. **61:** © Roger Wood. **62:** © Camerapix. **63:** © Mehmet Biber / Photo Researchers, Inc. **64:** Jalil Bounhar/AP Photo. **65:** © Fred M. Donner. **66:** The Chester Beatty Library, Dublin. **68:** © Roger Wood. **72:** Ancient Art & Architecture Collection (l); © Roger Wood (r). **73:** SCALA/AR, NY (t); © Marc Romanelli / TIB (c); Museo del Ejeroito Espada de Boabdil (r). **76–77:** RJB. **79:** © G. Champlong / TIB. **83:** American Numismatic Society. **86:** SuperStock. **88:** Bibliotheque Nationale, Paris (t); © P. Breidenbach (b). **89** RJB. **90:** Princeton University (t); RJB (tr, cr); Topkapi Museum, Istanbul / AR, NY (b). **92:** Freer Gallery of Art. **93:** Private Collection, MH (t). **95:** © Marc Romanelli / TIB. **96:** © Joachim Messerschmidt / Westlight. **97:** RJB (tr, bl, br); Stuart Cohen / Comstock, Inc. (cl); SuperStock (cr). **98:** Reunion des Musees Nationaux, Paris. **100:** Royal Chapel, Granada. **104–05:** © Huet, Hoa-Qui. **106:** Gift of Mr. and Mrs. Raymond J. Weilgus by exchange, 1988.22...profile. Photograph by Alan Newman © 1989 The Art Institute of Chicago, All Rights Reserved (l); © Victor Engelbert (r). **107:** Comstock, Inc. (t); African and Oceanic Catalogue / AR (c); RJB (bl). **108:** © T. Hopker / Woodfin Camp & Associates (l); Michael Kirtley (r). **110:** Nigerian Museum, Lagos. **111:** © M. & A. Kirtley, ANA. **112:** © Victor Engelbert. **113:** Arthur Tress. **114:** RJB (tl, br); Musee de l'Institute d'Afrique Noire, Giraudon / AR (t); © Cyril Isy-Schwart / TIB (c); © Giorgio Gualco / Bruce Coleman, Inc. (bl). **115:** © P. Breidenbach (l, r); Smithsonian Institution, Museum of African Art / AR (b). **116:** M. & A. Kirtley, ANA (l); Eugene Gordon / Photo Researchers, Inc. (r). **118:** Michael Kirtley. **119:** RJB (t); Bibliotheque Nationale, Paris (b). **120:** Bibliotheque Nationale, Paris. **121:** Bibliotheque Nationale, Paris. **122:** SuperStock. **123:** Mike Dye, *The White Men*, Julia Blackburn, Orbis Publishing, London, © 1979, RJB (t); Nelson Gallery-Atkins Museum (Nelson Fund), Kansas City (b). **124:** Jason Laure / Woodfin Camp & Associates. **125:** © Marc & Evelyne Bernheim / Woodfin Camp & Associates (tr); Garfield Park Conservatory, Chicago, RJB (tl); AR (b). **126:** P. Breidenbach. **127:** Charles & Josette Lenars/Corbis. **134:** BM, Bridgeman Art Library (t); © Leonard Lee Rue III / Bruce Coleman, Inc. (r). **135:** © Rod Allin / Tom Stack & Associates (l); © Don Carl Steffen / Photo Researchers, Inc. (r). **136:** © Bruce Coleman, Inc. **141:** © Owen Franken / Stock Boston. **142:** Werner Forman Archive. **143:** Werner Forman Archive. **144:** Hutchison Library. **145:** © Sue Dorfman / Stock Boston (t); © Norman Meyers / Bruce Coleman, Inc. (b). **147:** © Jason Laure. **148:** Centers for Disease Control (t); National Archives of Zimbabwe (b). **149:** © Eric Axelson. **150:** Zaire, Kasai Provine, Mweka, Kuba People, Mask of a Mythic Royal Ancestor (Ngaang A Cyeem), late 19th-early 20th Century, Restricted Gift of the American Hospital Supply Corp., The Evanston Associates of the Women's Board in honor of Mr. Wilbur Tuggle, et al., and the A.O.A. Purchase Fund, 1982.1505. © 1989 The Art Institute of Chicago, All Rights Reserved (l); American Museum of Natural History (r). **152:** BM, MH. **153:** BM. **154:** © The Pierpont Morgan Library, 1990 (l); The Newberry Library, Chicago (r). **155:** New York Public Library, Map Division (t); Zaire, Western Kasai Province, Mweka Zone, Kuba Peoples, Mukenga mask, Laura T. Magnuson Fund Income, X-Hautelet Collection 1982.1504...Photo by Robert Hashimoto, © 1989 The Art Institute of Chicago, All Rights Reserved (b). **158–59:** Wan-go H. C. Weng. **160:** The Metropolitan Museum of Art (l); Bibliotheque Nationale, Paris (r). **160–61:** Topkapi Museum, Istanbul. **161:** Topkapi Museum, Istanbul, NB (t); Victoria & Albert Museum, London (b). **162:** Topkapi Museum, Istanbul. **163:** PHOTRI, MGA. **164–65:** Topkapi Museum, Istanbul. **165:** Topkapi Museum, Istanbul. **168:** John Massey Stewart (l); © P. Breidenbach (r). **169:** Bham Museum of Art (l); Collection of the National Palace Museum, Taiwan, Republic of China. **170:** e.t. archive. **172:** © Ara Guler / Magnum Photos (l); FPG International (r). **173:** AR (t). **174:** University Library, Instanbul (b); The Jewish National and University Library (tl). **175:** Topkapi Museum, Istanbul. **176:** Topkapi Museum, Istanbul (l, c); Topkapi Palace, Istanbul, Giraudon / AR (r). **178:** © Roger Wood. **180:** Victoria & Albert Museum, London (l); BM, MH (r). **180–81:** © Roger Wood. **181:** Victoria & Albert Museum, London, NB. **182:** © Helen Marcus / Photo Researchers, Inc. (l); Victoria & Albert Museum, London (r). **184:** Kenneth Crossman (tl); RJB (tr, bl); Archaeological Survey of India, Government of India, RJB (c, cr). **185:** Prince of Wales Museum / AR. **187:** © Pramod Chandra. **190:** Seattle Museum, LPW (l); National palace Museum, Taiwan, Republic of China (r); © Charles Liu, Westmont, Illinois (t). **191:** AR (t); © Guido Alberto Rossi / TIB (b). **192:** Asian Art & Archaeology, Inc./Corbis. **193:** RJB. **194:** BM. **195:** © Private Collection, LPW. **196:** SuperStock. **197:** Wan-go H. C. Weng. **198:** © Harald Sund / TIB (t); National Numismatic Society, Smithsonian Institution (bl, bc). **199:** Xi'an Visual Art Company, China (t); © Photo R. M. N., Paris (r). **202:** Wan-go H. C. Weng; National Palace Museum, Taipei. **203:** Wan-go H.C. Weng (t); RJB (b). **206:** National Maritime Museum, Greenwich, London (bl); Freer Gallery of Art (br); National Numismatic Society, Smithsonian Institution (t). **207:** Ontario Science Museum (t); Bibliotheque Nationale, Paris (b). **208:** RJB (t); Wan-go H. C. Weng (cr). **209:** Biblioteca Nacional, Madrid. **210** Private Collection. **211:** AR. **212:** © George Holton / Photo Researchers, Inc. **213:** © Edward Bower / TIB (r); From *The Western Sea Cruises of Eunuch San Pao*, by L. O. Mou-teng, 1597 (tr); RJB (c); AR (cr); © K. Wothe / TIB (bl); Chait Galleries, New York (br). **214:** Wan-go H.C. Weng. **215:** Wan-go H. C. Weng. **217:** SuperStock. **220** © P. & G. Bowater / TIB (l); RJB (r). **221:** LPW (t); Shashinka Photo (b); © Martha Cooper Guthrie / AR (r). **222:** The Museum of Fine Arts, Boston. **233:** © PHOTRI, MGA. **224:** Shashinka Photo Library. **225:** © Norma Morrison / PHOTRI (t); Shashinka Photo Library (b). **226:** © Paul Hurd/Tony Stone Images (t); Cameramann International, Ltd. (b). **227:** Shashinka Photo Library. **228:** LPW **229:** AR. **231:** Shashinka Photo Library. **234:** Shashinka Photo Library (t); Japanese, Panel from Amida Triad, hanging scroll, Kamakura period, 13th century, Gift of Katte S. Buckingham, 1929.856...,©1989 The Art Institute of Chicago, All Rights Reserved (b). **235:** © Urasenke Tea Ceremony Society (l, cl); © Thomas Haar / Shashinka Photo Library (cr); © Norma Morrison / PHOTRI (r). **236:** © Mike Yamashita / Westlight (t); Werner Forman Archive (r); SuperStock (b). **237:** BM, MH. **238:** © P. Breidenbach (c); © Michael J. Howell / Stock Boston (b). **238–39:** Asian Art Museum of San Francisco. **240:** Shashinka Photo. **241:** © Bernard G. Silberstein / SuperStock (t); LPW (b). **243:** AR. **246–47:** Bibliotheque Nationale, Paris / NB. **248:** History Museum, Stockholm, Giraudon / AR (t); © F.H.C. Birch / Sonia Halliday Photographs (r). **249:** Victoria & Albert Museum / MH (l); Private Collection, MH (c); Werner Forman Archive (r). **254:** Cathedral Treasury, Aachen. **256:** Trustees of the BM. **257:** Walters Art Gallery. **258:** Cathedral Treasury, Aachen / AR. **259:** AKG London. **263:** BM, MH. **264:** Musee Conde, Chantilly, France / AR. **265:** AR. **266:** Musee Conde, Chantilly, France, NB. **267:** RJB (b); AR (c). **268:** AR (t); Hotel Lunaret, Montpellier, France, Giraudon / AR (b). **269:** Ecole des Beaux Arts, Paris, Giraudon / AR (t); © Ronald Sheridan / AR (b). **270:** AR. **271:** Trustees of the BM (t); The Granger Collection (b). **272:** City of Bayeux / AR. **273:** LPW **274:** © Alain Choisnet / TIB. **275:** RJB. **276:** Joel Sackett / Michael O'Mara Books, Ltd. (c); RJB (b). **276–77:** RJB. **277:** RJB. **280:** British Library, Bridgeman Art Library (l); Art History Museum, Vienna / NB (b). **280–81:** © N. DeVore III / Bruce Coleman, Inc. **281:** St. Mark's Venice / AR. **282:** BM. **283:** SuperStock. **284:** Treasury, Manza / AR (b); Gianni Dagli Orti/Corbis (t). **285:** AR (t); Her Majesty's Stationery Office, England (b). **286:** Goya Museum, Castres, France, Giraudon / AR (tl); Bibliotheque Arsenal, Paris, Giraudon / AR (c); Musee Condee, Chantilly, France, Giraudon / AR (b, tr). **287:** SCALA / AR. **288:** Musee des Beaux-Arts, Angers, France, Giraudon / AR (l); © Raphael Gailarde / Gamma-Liaison (r). **289:** © Michael Yamashita / Westlight (l); St. Mark's Treasury, Venice, Giraudon / AR (r). **291:** © Ara Juler / NB. **292:** © Nathan Benn / Stock Boston. **293:** RJB. **294:** The Metropolitan Museum of Art. **295:** Bibliotheque Nationale, Paris. **297:** La Reunion des Musees Nationaux, Cluny, France (t); Gian Berto Vanni, AR (b). **299:** BM / Bridgeman Art Library. **300:** Bibliotheque Nationale, Paris. **301:** Staatliche Museen zu Berlin, Preussischer Kulturbesitz, Museum fur Islamische Kunst. **302:** LPW **306–07:** SCALA / AR. **308:** National Museum, Florence / AR (l); SCALA / AR (r). **309:** SCALA / AR (t); RJB (b); AR (r). **310:** Campo Santo, Pisa / AR. **311:** RJB. **312:** AR (t, c); SCALA / AR; © R. Kord, H. Armstrong Roberts, Inc. (b). **313:** Giraudon / AR. **314:** Louvre / AR. **316:** Victoria & Albert Museum / Bridgeman Art Library (l, r); AR (b). **317:** SCALA / AR. **318:** © S. Georgio Schiavoni, Venice, SCALA / AR (b); Corbis / Bettmann (t). **319:** SCALA / AR. **320:** RJB (t); AR (bl, bc). **320–321:** IBM. **321:** IBM (tl, c); RJB (tr); Leonardo da Vinci (bl); AR (br); Leonardo da Vinci (bl). **322:** © Hubatka, Mauritius / Westlight. **323:** SCALA / AR. **324:** Northwestern University Library, RJB (l); IBM (r). **325:** The Cleveland Museum of Art. **326:** Musee de Cluny, Paris (t); National Gallery of Art, Index of the Americas (c); SuperStock (b). **327:** AR. **328:** The Royal Collection © 1998 Her Majesty Queen Elizabeth II. **329:** AR. **332:** Musee Conde, Chantilly, France / AR (t); SCALA / AR (b). **333:** The Folger Shakespeare Library. **335:** RJB. **336:** Isabella Stewart Gardner Museum, Boston / AR. **336–37:** Tribuna de Galileo, Museum of Physics and Natural History, Florence. **337:** Burndy Library (l); Galleria Palatina, Florence, AR (r). **338:** SEF, Turin / AR. **339:** © Peter Menzel / Stock Boston. **340:** The Folger Shakespeare Library. **341:** SCALA / AR. **342:** AR. **343:** AR (t); Lutherhalle, Wittenberg (b). **344:** Library of Congress. **345:** Worms, Museum der Stadt Andreasstift (t); Rhode Island Historical Society (b). **349:** Bibliotheque Nationale, Paris. **350:** Corbis/Bettmann. **353:** BM. **354:** Northwestern University Library, RJB. **355:** Northwestern University Library, RJB (l); RJB (c); BM, MH (b). **356:** Northwestern University Library, RJB (t); New College, Oxford (r). **358:** Northwestern University Library, RJB. **359:** © Lou Jones / TIB (tl); © Gregory Heisler / TIB (tc); © Jay Freis / TIB (tr); © Melchior DiGiacomo / TIB (cr). **362:** RJB (l); Bibliotheque Nationale, Paris (c). **363:** National Maritime Museum, MH (tr); Uffizi, Florence / RHPL (tl). **364:** New York Public Library. **364–65:** © Ernst A. Jahn / TIB. **365:** New York Public Library, Map Division. **367:** RJB (tr, bl, br); Bibliotheque Nationale, Paris (cl); © Roger Wood (cr). **368:** Navale Museum, Pegli, Italy / AR. **369:** AR. **370:** © Scott H. Zieske / Homestake Mining Company. **371:** The Granger Collection. **372:** © Ronald Sheridan (t); New York Public Library, Prints Division (c). **373:** RJB. **375:** BM, MH. **376:** RJB. **377:** © Allan Eaton / Sheridan Photo Library. **378:** Tor Eigeland © Victor Englebert. **379:** American Numismatic Society. **380:** AR. **381:** LPW **383:** Bibliotheque Nationale, Paris. **386:** Giraudon / AR. **392–93:** The Textile Museum, Washington,. **394:** © Robert W. Parvin (l); LPW (r). **395:** © M. Martin / TIB (t); LPW (c); Museum of the American Indian, Heye Foundation (bl, br). **397:** © Jeff Foott / Tom Stack & Associates (t); © Gilcrease Institute (cr, br); LPW (bl, blc, brc). **399:** RJB. **400:** © Justin Kerr. **401:** © Mike Mazzaschi / Stock Boston. **402:** © Lee Boltin. **403:** © Justin Kerr. **404:** LPW (t); F. Catherwood (b). **405:** © Andrew Holbrooke. **406:** © Antoinette Jongen (c); © G. Gallant / TIB (t); © Lee Boltin. **408:** BM, MH (l); © Lee Boltin (r). **410:** © Justin Kerr. **411:** © Joseph Devenney / TIB (t); RJB (b). **412:** David L. Brill, © National Geographic Society. **413:** Victoria & Albert Museum. **414:** © Lee Boltin (t); © Julian Brown / International Film Foundation (b). **415:** Museum of the American Indian, Heye Foundation (t); © Nick Saunders (b). **416:** RJB. **417:** RJB. **420:** MH, Private Collection (l); BM (r); Werner Forman Archive (tl); © George Holton / Photo Researchers, Inc. (tr); LPW (b). **422:** LPW **423:** © Justin Kerr. **424:** © George D. Dodge, Dale R. Thompson / Bruce Coleman, Inc. (t); © Lee Boltin (b). **425:** SuperStock (t); © LPW (b). **427:** LPW (t); National Museum of Copenhagen / NB (b). **428:** LPW **429:** RHPL. **431:** American Museum of Natural History (t); BM, MH (b). **432:** © Hans W. Silvester / Photo Researchers, Inc. (t); RJB (br, bl); American Museum of Natural History (bc). **433:** Comstock, Inc. (t); RHPL (r). **434:** © Francisco Hidalgo / TIB (l); NB (tr, cr, br). **435:** Museo de America, Madrid (t); © Delacorte Gallery, New York / Lee Boltin (b). **437:** Biblioteca Nacional, Madrid. **438:** Museo de America, Madrid / NB (t). **439:** Biblioteca Nacional, Madrid / NB (t); LPW (b). **440:** © Loren McIntyre / Woodfin Camp & Associates (l); Gilcrease Institute / NB (r); AR (b).

—*Continued on page 548.*